MONTGOMERY COLLEGE LIBRARY
GERMANTOWN CAMPUS

NATIONALISM
AND INTERNATIONALISM

Nationalism and Internationalism

Essays Inscribed to Carlton J. H. Hayes

EDITED BY
EDWARD MEAD EARLE

OCTAGON BOOKS
A DIVISION OF FARRAR, STRAUS AND GIROUX
New York   1974

Copyright 1950 by Columbia University Press

Reprinted 1974
by special arrangement with Columbia University Press

OCTAGON BOOKS
A DIVISION OF FARRAR, STRAUS & GIROUX, INC.
19 Union Square West
New York, N. Y. 10003

Library of Congress Cataloging in Publication Data

Earle, Edward Mead, 1894-1945, ed.
    Nationalism and internationalism.

    Reprint of the ed. published by the Columbia University Press, New York.
    CONTENTS: Barzun, J. Cultural nationalism and the making of fame.—Childs, F. S. A secret agent's advice on America, 1797.—Clarkson, J. D. "Big Jim" Larkin: a footnote to nationalism. [etc.]

    1. Nationalism—Addresses, essays, lectures. 2. Hayes, Carlton Joseph Huntley, 1882-1964. I. Hayes, Carlton Joseph Huntley, 1882-1964. II. Title.

JC311.E3   1974   320.5'4   74-4429
ISBN 0-374-92447-3

Printed in USA by
Thomson-Shore, Inc.
Dexter, Michigan

ACKNOWLEDGMENTS

THE EDITOR is indebted to *Foreign Affairs* for permission to republish the article by Geroid Tanquary Robinson, "American Thought and the Communist Challenge," which appeared in the issue of July 1949 under the title "The Ideological Combat."

The article "H. G. Wells, a British Patriot in Search of a World State" by Edward Mead Earle appeared in an abridged form in the January 1950 issue of *World Politics*. Frequent reference has been made throughout the article to a number of Wells's many books and pamphlets. The author wishes to make special acknowledgment to the executors of the estate of H. G. Wells and the following publishers for permission to use sizable passages from Wells's work or to quote passages concerning Wells:

- The Atlantic Monthly Press, Boston: *The Idea of a League of Nations* (1919).

- Cassell and Co., Ltd., London: *An Englishman Looks at the World* (1914).

- Doubleday and Co., Garden City, N.Y.: *The Way the World Is Going* (1929); *The World of William Clissold* (1926).

- E. P. Dutton and Co., New York: *The World Set Free* (1914).

- Faber and Faber, Ltd., London: Sir Arthur Salter, *Personality in Politics* (1947).

- Harper and Brothers, New York: *Anticipations* (1902).

- The Macmillan Co., New York and London: *The Anatomy of Frustration: A Modern Synthesis* (1936); *The Bulpington of Blup* (1933); *Experiment in Autobiography* (1934); *Joan and Peter: The Story of an Education* (1918); *The Outline of History* (1920); *What Is Coming?: A European Forecast* (1916).

- Penguin Books, London and New York: *The New Machiavelli* (1946).

- L. and Virginia Woolf, London: *The Common Sense of World Peace* (1929).

CONTENTS

Introduction	ix
Cultural Nationalism and the Makings of Fame	3
JACQUES BARZUN, *Columbia University*	
A Secret Agent's Advice on America, 1797	18
FRANCES S. CHILDS, *Brooklyn College*	
"Big Jim" Larkin: A Footnote to Nationalism	45
JESSE D. CLARKSON, *Brooklyn College*	
The Heavy Hand of Hegel	64
CHARLES W. COLE, *Amherst College*	
H. G. Wells, British Patriot in Search of a World State	79
EDWARD MEAD EARLE, *The Institute for Advanced Study*	
National Sentiment in Klopstock's Odes and *Bardiete*	122
ROBERT ERGANG	
Arthur Young, British Patriot	144
JOHN G. GAZLEY, *Dartmouth College*	
French Jacobin Nationalism and Spain	190
BEATRICE F. HYSLOP, *Hunter College*	
Nationalism and History in the Prussian Elementary Schools under William II	241
WALTER CONSUELO LANGSAM, *Wagner College*	
The Swiss Pattern for a Federated Europe	261
CHARLOTTE MURET, *Barnard College*	

Sir John Seeley, Pragmatic Historian in a
   Nationalistic Age 285
   THOMAS P. PEARDON, *Barnard College*

The Habsburgs and Public Opinion in Lombardy-
   Venetia, 1814–1815 303
   R. JOHN RATH, *University of Colorado*

American Thought and the Communist Challenge . . 336
   GEROID TANQUARY ROBINSON, *Columbia University*

Friedrich Naumann: A German View of Power and
   Nationalism 352
   WILLIAM O. SHANAHAN, *University of Notre Dame*

Hitler and the Revival of German Colonialism . . . 399
   MARY EVELYN TOWNSEND, *Teachers College, Columbia
   University*

The Nationalism of Horace Greeley 431
   GLYNDON G. VAN DEUSEN, *University of Rochester*

Scandinavia and the Rise of Modern National
   Consciousness 455
   JOHN H. WUORINEN, *Columbia University*

Index 481

The Contributors 509

INTRODUCTION

FIFTY YEARS AGO, as a new century began, Carlton J. H. Hayes entered Columbia College as a freshman. The succeeding half-century, in which he has studied and taught on Morningside Heights, has been momentous in the history of mankind. It has witnessed, among other things, the decline of Western Europe from the undisputed place it had held for half a millennium or more as the center of world power and of Western civilization. It has seen the coincidental rise of the United States to dazzling and somewhat unwelcome heights of influence in world affairs. In 1900 the United States was the western frontier of Europe; today Western Europe is, in a sense, the eastern frontier of the United States. It now appears to be true, as Canning said more than a hundred years ago, that the New World was called into being to redress the balance of the Old.

Americans have been amazed by this turn of events, which none could have foreseen and few would have wished. But they are less bewildered than they would have been had Carlton Hayes never lived or had he not chosen the career of historian. For his devoted and prodigious labors in European history will not be memorialized exclusively in the files of the professional journals. They will, rather, be perpetuated in the careers, the teachings, the writings of generations of Columbia students who were fortunate enough to sit at his feet and to work at his side. Perhaps even more, his work will have left its mark on all those who studied modern history on any college or university campus in the United States. Professor Hayes has been concerned with teaching European history and winning for it a proper place in the academic curriculum. But in a larger sense he has been a public servant—a minister without portfolio concerned with educating the American people, through successive generations of American youth, to a sympathetic understanding of their European heritage and an intelligent appreciation of their responsibilities to European civilization, of which they are an integral part. If as a nation we now know more and comprehend more than we formerly did of the broad basis of our relations with the European world, a considerable measure of the credit should be ascribed to Carlton Hayes. Through his lectures, his seminars, and his enormously successful textbooks he has reached tens of thousands, perhaps hundreds of thousands, of American university students—bringing to them something of his own wide knowledge of Europe and its peoples, its geography, its traditions, its problems, its hopes, and its tragedies.

When Hayes began his teaching career in 1907, Europe seemed remote from America and American concerns. To be sure, Theodore Roosevelt was in the White House breathing fire and brimstone, asserting with characteristic flamboyance that the United States was a world power. But the first Roosevelt's policies were cannier than his pronouncements, and his administration brought no real change in the traditional American policy of nonintervention in European affairs. George Marshall—that noble soldier and public servant whose name has become a symbol of the American stake in Europe—was then a lieutenant of infantry, just beginning his professional career. Neither he nor any other American of his time could have foreseen the impact upon the United States of the thirty-five years of war, revolution, depression, and dictatorship, which, starting in 1914, were to bring Europe to the verge of destruction. Not even the best informed observer of the European scene forty years or so ago could have dreamed that twice in a generation American armies would leave their dead in such unlikely places as Château Thierry, Soissons, St. Mihiel, Oran, Medjez-el-Bab, Salerno, Cassino, St. Lô, Argentan, Bastogne, Aachen, Cologne, Remagen, to mention only a few.

But Carlton Hayes understood and did something about the fact that Americans—for the good of their own souls and in the interest of their country—should know more, much more, about Europe than they knew or apparently cared to know. When, rich with honors, Hayes delivered his Presidential Address to the American Historical Association in 1945,[1] he pleaded for even wider perspectives in historical teaching and writing, for even keener understanding of the debt which Americans owe to Europe; on this occasion he was merely preaching to a different audience the faith which he had been expounding for almost four decades to Columbia undergraduates and, through his printed works, to innumerable teachers and students of history elsewhere than on Morningside Heights.

[1] "The American Frontier—Frontier of What?" *American Historical Review*, LI (January 1946), 199–216.

Introduction

xi

Teaching European history in the early days of Hayes's career was not the relatively simple matter it now is. Interest had to be aroused, not merely stimulated and developed. Libraries were, on the whole, poor in their resources for the teaching of modern European affairs; monographs, biographies, source materials, and maps were hard to come by except in the largest and richest of the universities. Despite the pioneer efforts of James Harvey Robinson, Charles A. Beard, James T. Shotwell, and William R. Shepherd—colleagues with whom Hayes worked loyally and well—there were few satisfactory college textbooks by which teachers could be guided and by which they could guide their students through the four centuries of European history since the Great Discoveries. When one is blazing new trails, as Hayes was doing in the decade before 1917, there is probably no substitute for a basic text. And when the facilities of libraries are inadequate, a text is indispensable. It is no exaggeration to say that the publication in 1916 of the two volumes of Hayes's *Political and Social History of Modern Europe* made it possible for the first time for the smallest college, as well as the largest university, to give modern European history the place which it so richly deserves in the undergraduate curriculum. It put at the disposal of teachers and students an enlightened, objective, and brilliantly written account of the four hundred years of Europe which preceded the Great War of 1914. And it enabled thousands of Americans to acquire a better knowledge than they otherwise would have had of the issues of the war and the problems of the peace.

Some years later, the text of 1916 was "radically revised" to give more scope to intellectual and cultural history, which Professor Hayes considered indispensable to an understanding of history as "past politics."[2] Hayes was one of the Columbia School of historians who, during the decade before the first World War, were concerned with expanding the horizons and extending the frontiers of historical scholarship and historical teaching.[3] For them the New History,

---

[2] *A Political and Cultural History of Modern Europe*. Vol. I, "Three Centuries of Predominantly Agricultural Society, 1500–1830" (New York, 1932); Vol. II, "A Century of Predominantly Industrial Society, 1830–1935" (New York, 1936).

[3] Although "Columbia School" is a term in general usage, it must be accepted with some reservations. These men had a number of interests in common—including a more catholic view of history—but there were other respects in which their views sharply diverged.

as James Harvey Robinson called it, encompassed almost all social activities of mankind, not merely those which concerned politics and war. Indeed, the Columbia group believed that politics could be understood only with reference to the economic, cultural, and intellectual forces which condition political beliefs and behavior. Robinson's course in the history of the intellectual class in Europe, Dunning's extensive work on the Civil War and Reconstruction, Beard's economic interpretation of Hamiltonian and Jeffersonian philosophies, Shepherd's remarkable articles on the expansion of Europe, and Schuyler's notable studies of British imperialism all worked together to create a new, fresh, crisp climate of opinion among American historians. These men and others—for the above is far from a complete roll call—were Carlton Hayes's teachers and colleagues for a decade or more. He was one of their most distinguished pupils and, as a colleague, one of the most co-operative and imaginative and daring; perhaps the ultimate judgment will be that he was *primus inter pares*.

Carlton Hayes was a great teacher of undergraduates at a time when Columbia College was enjoying a Golden Age under Dean Frederick P. Keppel. Beard, Dunning, Schuyler, Erskine, Steeves, Carl Van Doren, Odell, Crampton—these were all exciting teachers who, among other things, led many a Columbia undergraduate to choose teaching as a career. Hayes was far from the least of these. His lecture room was a theater in which was acted out, day after day, the absorbing drama of the Western World since 1500. Across the stage marched some of the great figures of the historical pageant —Henry VIII and Elizabeth, Richelieu and Colbert, Charles V and Philip II, John Hampden and Oliver Cromwell, Mirabeau and Danton and Robespierre, Frontenac and Wolfe and Montcalm, Napoleon and Alexander and Wellington. Who will ever forget the manner in which the impresario, with his own considerable histrionic gifts, rang up the curtain on Louis Philippe, "the man with the green umbrella"; the beautiful Hortense Beauharnais, injecting iron into a spineless Louis Napoleon; Bismarck, tamer of the Prussian parliament; the tragic Maximilian, "emperor" of Mexico; Karl Marx and his friend Friedrich Engels; Marx's devoted wife Jenny von Westphalen and Bismarck's devout wife Johanna von Puttkamer? Throwing the spotlight on individuals was to Hayes no mere dramatic device, since he believed in the biographical approach to history. One learned of conservatism by learning about Metternich, Wellington, Bismarck, Disraeli; one studied liberalism by concerning himself with Mill, Bright, Cobden, and Gladstone. And as will be observed, Hayes's graduate students have found the method valid for themselves—more than half the chapters of this present volume arrive at generalized conclusions through the study of typical historical figures.

In his teaching and in his supervision of graduate research, Hayes had an uncanny gift for foreseeing what was going to be important as well as what had been important to an understanding of human affairs. Long before there was any general discussion of the "welfare state," Hayes had grasped the significance to modern politics of the Lloyd George liberals; his *British Social Politics* (1913) was a pioneer study in "state action for the solution of social problems." Even before the first World War he directed some of his best students into the field of diplomatic history and international relations. He clearly foresaw the portent for Europe and the larger world of a unified, militarized Germany; hence, although he had hoped that the United States might be able, by armed neutrality or otherwise, to remain out of the Great War of 1914, his sympathies from the very outset were with the cause of the Allies.[4] To Hayes the underlying causes of the war were nationalism, imperialism, and militarism; the immediate causes grew principally out of German policy. Because nationalism lies at the root of imperialism, militarism, and war, Hayes has devoted the better part of his life to a study of the phenomenon of nationalism in modern times. The penetrating analyses in his *Essays on Nationalism* (1926) and *The Historical Evolution of Modern Nationalism* (1931) have served as a touchstone for several of the contributions to the present volume. Hayes's graduate seminars at Columbia have produced a notable series of studies, his own and those of his doctoral candidates, which constitute an important contribution to American historiography in our time.

Hayes's studies of nationalism—important as they are—should not altogether overshadow some of his other major contributions to the

[4] See his article "Armed Neutrality or War" in *Survey*, XXXVII (February 10, 1917), 535–38. For comment regarding Wilson's consideration of a Hayes proposal for armed neutrality, see Ray Stannard Baker, *Woodrow Wilson, Life and Letters*, VI (Garden City, N. Y., 1937), 472.

study and teaching of history in the United States. He played an almost unique role during the decade 1910–1920 in the development of international relations as an academic subject in American universities. He was one of the first, too, to encourage more extensive research in the history of modern Germany—a field in which American scholarship may now be considered outstanding. The catholicity of his interests and the breadth of his imagination in themselves would justify high rank for Carlton Hayes among the historians of his time. One of his more recent students has said of him: "Hayes did much to establish the objectivity of intellectual history and to relate it to politics without prejudice in the form of a party viewpoint or a class interest. In this work he deserves comparison with only one man whose stature and whose interests are comparable to his—Friedrich Meinecke. Hayes is the Meinecke of American historiography; this is the most profound compliment that I can pay him. The interest of one in historicism and *Staats raison* is paralleled in the other by an interest in nationalism and social politics. None of these interests falls into the conventional notion of an historical subject; it was the merit of these two historians that they helped to establish the identity of intellectual and social processes with the content of history. This outlook now prevails so generally that their initial insight may easily be forgotten."

Carlton J. H. Hayes was born in Afton, N. Y., in 1882. This beautiful little town, nestled in the rolling countryside of the Susquehanna Valley, has been one of his dearest loves; he has returned to it summer after summer throughout his life, and to it he will retire when his active service at Columbia is over. His roots are in rural America, even though he has lived the greater number of his years in metropolitan New York; and although he is critical of nationalism, he is a patriot deeply devoted to his own, his native land. His father, Dr. Philetus A. Hayes, was Afton's most distinguished citizen during Carlton Hayes's boyhood. This gracious, tolerant, democratic physician and servant of the community left his mark on his professor son. For Carlton Hayes has always had a basic kindliness toward his fellow-men which has endeared him to his thousands of students; his sympathetic and patient understanding of their problems, personal and academic, has made him an even greater teacher than he otherwise would have been. With the exception of intervals of public service in two World Wars, Carlton Hayes has devoted his whole life to the Department of History at Columbia, and his name will be inscribed among her most honored sons "'til the lordly Hudson seaward cease to roll her heaving tide."

In May 1942, at great personal sacrifice, Professor Hayes accepted a commission from President Roosevelt to be ambassador of the United States to Spain. He served in that capacity for three critical years, conducting diplomatic negotiations of grave moment to the winning of the war. He was charged with carrying out the policy of his government, whose principal concern was that Spain be kept from active military co-operation with the Axis powers, particularly during the Allied invasion of North Africa. The Spanish mission, in the nature of things, was both delicate and explosive, and it is doubtful that any American ambassador at Madrid could have discharged the duties of his office to the satisfaction of all sections of American opinion. It is not surprising, therefore, that Carlton Hayes was subjected to criticism—some of it honest; some of it uninformed or vindictive—during his tour of duty as ambassador in Madrid. It is neither necessary nor appropriate to deal with these criticisms at this time. It should be pointed out, however, that an ambassador carries out, does not make, his government's policy vis-à-vis another nation. Whether the policy of the United States toward Franco Spain during the war years was wise or unwise raises a set of questions which are largely irrelevant to Hayes's record in fulfilling the onerous duties with which he was charged. And the inescapable truth is that the objectives of the American government were attained: Spain did not join the Axis, and she did not interfere with Anglo-American military operations in North Africa. Had it been otherwise—in other words, had Hayes failed—the Allied landings at Casablanca and elsewhere probably could not have taken place. As General Eisenhower wrote General Marshall at the time, hostile military action by Spain would have frustrated the entire operation, since the resources then available to us were inadequate to deal with Spain as well as with Germany and Italy.[5]

Carlton Hayes's public services have not been confined to the

[5] *Crusade in Europe* (New York, 1948), pp. 92–93. For other details of Hayes's embassy to Madrid see his own account, *Wartime Mission in Spain, 1942–1945* (New York, 1945), and a sympathetic and well-informed article by Ernest K. Lindley, "How We Dealt with Spain," in *Harper's Magazine*, CXC (December 1944), 23–33.

official sphere. He was from its very inception active in the Foreign Policy Association and was for some years a member of its board of directors. A cause very close to his heart, too, was the Conference of Christians and Jews, of which he was co-chairman for twenty years. A devout Catholic, Hayes has always been a believer in religious toleration and has worked assiduously for better understanding and more effective co-operation among religious groups in the United States.

This is the man to whom his former students proudly and affectionately dedicate these several essays. Some of the men and women who took the doctor's degree at Columbia under his guidance have, for one reason or another, been unable to participate in the enterprise. Only two of these need be specially mentioned here: Parker Thomas Moon, senior among Hayes's advanced students, eminent authority on imperialism, first professor of international relations at Columbia—who died in 1936, while still at the height of his career; and Mildred Wertheimer, a graduate of Vassar in the class of 1917, who wrote a doctoral dissertation on the Pan-German League and who subsequently brought her intimate knowledge of German affairs to the research department of the Foreign Policy Association —who died in 1937, just past forty, heartbroken at the Nazi successes but still hopeful that the worst for Germany and for Europe might somehow be averted.

Several persons who were not students of Carlton Hayes, or who studied with him only incidentally, likewise have contributed to the success of this book, notably Dr. John A. Krout, Dean of the Graduate Faculties of Columbia, and Mr. Charles G. Proffitt, Director of the Columbia University Press. Miss Jean MacLachlan, research assistant at the Institute for Advanced Study, has rendered invaluable editorial services; hers, too, was the exacting task of preparing the manuscript for the printer and seeing the volume through the press.

The editor wishes to thank the contributors, individually and severally, for their generous co-operation. Special mention should be made, however, of Professor William O. Shanahan who did indispensable pioneer work in connection with the enterprise. Directly or indirectly, too, the members of the Department of History at Columbia have done much to assure completion and publication of the book. Various friends of Professor Hayes have made other contributions to the success of the undertaking.

All who have participated in this labor of love hope that Carlton Hayes will find in it some small measure of appreciation for his devoted services to history, to Columbia, and to the nation for half a century.

EDWARD MEAD EARLE

Princeton, New Jersey
November 1949

NATIONALISM AND INTERNATIONALISM

CULTURAL NATIONALISM AND THE MAKINGS OF FAME

JACQUES BARZUN

> Almost invariably it was from the ranks of the bourgeoisie that the professional nationalists were drawn. . . . They patronized societies for the preservation or revival of the national language. They founded museums for the collection of national relics. . . . They gave prizes for the best rendition of national songs and national dances. —CARLTON J. H. HAYES, *Essays on Nationalism*

I

THE HISTORY OF CULTURE considered as a form of national self-expression presents a curious paradox. It shows us great figures which common opinion regards as embodying the soul or spirit of a given people. These famous names—Shakespeare, Dante, Goethe, Cervantes—are symbols of national prestige, objects of national cults, even occasions for the venting of national animus.[1] Yet inquiry shows that most often these idols by no means appeared as true incarnations to their contemporaries, nor to their descendants until a long time after their own death. Rather, these culture heroes attain their special eminence because of secondary virtues long unsuspected in their work and sometimes extraneous to it. They rearise because they serve later passions grounded in faith or politics. Thus Dante did not become the national poet of Italy until the second half of the eighteenth century, and then only after a long controversy: he was thoroughly damned and repudiated as late as 1758.[2] Obviously the hope of Italian unification and the desire for cultural prestige had to be widely shared before the national poet could emerge from the semi-obscurity he enjoyed as a learned author (his sixteenth-century reputation) or an indifferent poet (the seventeenth-century view).

This last opinion was largely due to the cultural hegemony of

---

[1] As a wit put it:
   The people of Spain think Cervantes
   Equal to half-a-dozen Dantes;
   An opinion resented most bitterly
   By the people of Italy.   —E. C. Bentley
                  Biography for Beginners
                  (London [1905], 1930, n.p.)

[2] Croce, *La poesia di Dante* (2nd ed., Bari, 1922), pp. 177 ff.

France throughout Europe. National in one sense, French taste was antinational in another, and as one traces the consequences of its despotism during the next three centuries one finds the answer to a good many riddles. It is not farfetched to suggest, for example, that one strong influence in the rehabilitation of the neglected Shakespeare in the minds of the English was his value as a name with which to oppose the intolerable pretensions of the French. The French having imposed their classic tragedy as an inescapable pattern of right reason, the English chose a native champion and found themselves saying *"Unser Shakespeare"* long before the Germans did—and long before they themselves truly liked their chief dramatic poet.[3]

The German use of Shakespeare in the cultural war against French neo-classicism was precisely similar. Beginning with Lessing,[4] it helped to produce a literary renaissance on native grounds and led to the work of more truly national poets. Finally it raised Goethe to the rank of "national world poet" in a Europe no longer dominated by French models. By the turn of the new century there flourished in England, Germany, and Italy a new type of literature, based in part on the popular national tradition, though showing similarities of purpose across boundaries, and designated generally as Romanticism. The movement was paralleled in the several arts and throve even in the outlying countries of Europe. But France, being the home of the old regime in culture, and being also held back by twenty-five years of war and dictatorship, was the last to slough off the dead classicism and to search its past for neglected traditions capable of revivifying art. So that when by the 1820's gifted young Frenchmen felt the stirrings of a new inspiration, they were met and encouraged by the vivid presence of the "new" poets —Dante, Shakespeare, and Goethe.[5]

[3] L. Wylie, *The Evolution of English Criticism* (Boston, 1894), pp. 32 ff., 76, 85, 142 ff. The *Shakespeare Allusion Book*, ed. by John Munro (Rev. ed., 2 vols., London, 1932), gives a good many instances of "our Shakespeare," especially after 1690 (II, 345, 386, 390, 391, 392, 399, 404, 412, 424, 428). This cultural habit is corroborated by what Voltaire reports in the first quarter of the eighteenth century. As for the English halfheartedness about their poet, it is shown by the polemical work that Hazlitt and Coleridge had to do in the early nineteenth century.

[4] In his *Hamburgische Dramaturgie* (1767-69).

[5] This may be shown quite simply by scanning the works of Victor Hugo, Delacroix, Berlioz, and Stendhal. The evidence of their letters, journals, as well as other direct testimony, is amply corroborative.

Cultural Nationalism

Under the cultural, nonaggressive nationalism of the period, the fact that these representative men incarnated other national "souls" than the French did not matter. Communication was still held possible—indeed it was so much taken for granted that the one living "national poet," Goethe, was known to be an antinationalist in the most literal sense. For this he incurred unpopularity in German-speaking lands, having refused to write songs of hate against the French in the War of Liberation,[6] and for some time after his death he was much more the national poet of Germany in the eyes of foreigners than in those of his own countrymen.

This further paradox adds an important feature to our description of the way in which representative men come to occupy their positions. Clearly, Goethe was "chosen" less for himself as an incarnation of the German spirit than for his undeniable power and his reputation abroad. He himself felt that his works would never be wholly congenial to the Germans, and that the more *gemütlich* and idealistically vaporous Schiller was the true favorite. Still, Goethe's mastery of the national language and the fact that in *Faust* he had given Europe the fullest expression of Romanticist thought made him a better article of export. From which we may infer that Romanticism could keep a balance between the claims of national tradition and those of European culture. It is further evident that in order to be chosen as a people's Representative Man, an artist must be by good luck "available" in these secondary ways which the temper of the times will dictate.

This *Zeitgeist* being almost as changeable as the weather, we find that the very properties which established Goethe as the greatest of Germans during the first half of the nineteenth century proved disqualifications during the more aggressive period that followed the creation of the Empire. He was not removed but overshadowed, by Bismarck first, then by Wagner. Among artists, Wagner was the perfect symbolic figure: acknowledged as a great genius, yet something of a swashbuckler and known to be anti-French[7]; a publicist, moreover, who had echoed every timely doctrine—revolution and pessimism, racism and religiosity; a dramatist who depicted both

---

[6] *Gespräche mit Eckermann*, March 14, 1830.

[7] In his writings from Paris as early as 1839–1842; then in his *Opera and Drama* with its anti-Berlioz campaign; and lastly in his skit on the siege of Paris, *Eine Capitulation*, which parodies Victor Hugo and other French notables.

the recognizable German *Volk* (in *Meistersinger*) and the ancient heroic myths of the tribe (in the *Ring*); finally, a musician.

This last qualification was of the utmost importance, for in modern times it is taken for granted that of all the arts music speaks most directly and naturally the intimations of a people's soul. Requiring as it does little or no explicitness of idea, musical nationalism is the stoutest thread in the close bonds of nationalism at large. It brings together upper and lower classes, excites pride and soothes unspent aggression, speaks out of an immemorial past and gives evidence of vital force in the present.[8]

As if this were not enough to make Wagner "available" in the 1880's, the world at that time was convinced, quite without historical justification, that the art of music was an ancestral monopoly of the Germans: they were born musicians, sixty million strong, who sang four-part chorales from the cradle. Here was the gifted, intuitive, and philosophically profound *Volk* whom Wagner had made the true hero of *Die Meistersinger*. And now, by virtue of prowess in other realms—science, technology, and war—this people had won a place in the forefront of European nations. Wagner deemed himself the counterpart of Bismarck, and though like Bismarck he had unrelenting opponents at home, many of his countrymen supported his claims. After his death, Bayreuth became an industry as well as a Delphic shrine, and by the mutual hypnotizing of home and foreign worshipers Wagner grew willy-nilly into *the* German Artist.[9] His

---

[8] For example, the small mill town of Maynard, Mass., which has a largely Finnish population, lives and breathes by the greatness of Jan Sibelius, whom the local band plays regularly to the assembled inhabitants. When the Finnish conductor Hennukainan came to lead the Boston Symphony, he also accepted an invitation to direct the Maynard players. Sibelius himself has not only exploited national themes and legends, like his colleagues to the east, west, north, and south of him, but his biography—as seems proper—is entitled *Finlandia* (E. Arnold, New York, 1941).

For English manifestations of the same spirit, see the writings of folk song collectors or adapters such as Cecil Sharp and Vaughan Williams. Typical quotations are given in Arnold M. Walter's "Music as a Means to Unify Mankind," *Approaches to World Peace,* ed. by Lyman Bryson, *et al.* (New York, 1944), pp. 511 ff.

[9] Contemporary indications of the purposive creation of national idols may be found in Moritz Wirth, *Bismarck, Wagner, Rodbertus; drei deutsche Meister. Betrachtungen über ihr Wirken und die Zukunft ihrer Werke: Monarchisch, national, social* (Leipzig, 1883). The author speaks of the death of Wagner as that of the greatest artist the world has ever seen. The survivors' goal must be the creation of a *deutsches Musikwesen* in every German city through the production of truly Wagnerian "German stage music" and the avoidance of false foreign tendencies such as those of Gluck and Mozart (pp. 380, 387).

English admirers (to name only one European group) shed all sense of humor and celebrated his fame in a periodical called *The Meister;* the French, as we shall see, adopted him in the same abandoned way and against all *raison d'état.*

The uses which Wagner served in the more recent history of Germany are well known and add nothing to the principle which concerns us here. Visibly, these national champions drawn from the ranks of art were, as time went on, products of a more and more intense feeling of pride and power, of separateness and superiority. Whereas in the period of Romanticism and Resorgimento, the rising nation sought to contribute a poet to the world, in the period of Realism and Unification the nation tried by the same means to dominate the field. Evidence of this shift will be found in the manner of presenting to the home public the achievements of the national idol who has turned national champion. As the need of mass propaganda under authoritarian rule developed, the government took incessant cognizance of art, and pursued its cultural policy precisely as in the realm of trade a manufacturer advertises his products —by showing that they sell widely and enhance the customer's ego.

If we abstract these factors from Wagner's history while keeping in mind similar elements in the rise of Dante, Shakespeare, and Goethe, we find that in order to be "available," the representative man has to fulfill precise prerequisites. He must be a great artist, acknowledged as such for both quality and scope; he must fit the nation's present view of itself—that is to say, he must embody what the nation considers the dominant strain in its national tradition; and he must be able to achieve instant identification in the eyes of foreigners. This last requirement depends on adventitious circumstances, which modern artistic habits happen to facilitate: Sibelius' *Finlandia,* Bartok's *Hungarian Dances,* Grieg's *Peer Gynt* suite by their names alone supply the tag, the indispensable trade-mark. It need be no more than that,[10] even though at times the foreign public does respond to substance itself. Thus to Europeans, Walt Whitman

---

[10] Shaw's discussion of various brands of National Music in the second volume of *Music in London: 1890–1894* (3 vols., London, 1932), pp. 305–7; and particularly of Grieg in *London Music: 1888–1889* (London, 1937), pp. 79–80, should suffice to quash the pretense forever: "Grieg ... is a 'national' composer," says Shaw, "and I am not to be imposed on by that sort of thing. ... All good folk music is as international as the story of Jack the Giant Killer" (p. 79).

is more "naturally" the great American writer than Melville—in just the proportion that Manhattan is more obviously American than Moby Dick.

The facts of history, biography, and art itself will of course suggest other agencies at work in the growth of world reputations. Nothing in the present essay is to be taken as implying that great names are built up wholly by indirect, artificial, or irrelevant forces —much less by fraud or self-delusion on a national scale. But the cultural historian who studies the fame of a man or movement apart from nationalism has to deal in exactly the same way with extrinsic social factors. He must for example explain why a book skyrockets into greatness a quarter-century after its first publication[11]; or why one artist becomes known only after his death whereas another achieves fame early and dies in obscurity. These questions cannot all be answered by reference to artistic technique or business ability. The historian is compelled to point out that criticism is an imperfect mirror of the contemporary output; that individuals and groups choose their heroes from mixed and sometimes unconscious motives; and that once a selection which answers a broad, vague need has been made, every kind of fit or unfit reason justifies and adds to its permanence. This is of course the situation of the national idol, and it makes of nationalism in art but a subhead under criticism at large. This being so, the discovery of recurrences, of a design reproduced under similar conditions, is a matter of more than speculative interest: it leads straight into the thorniest problems of biography and intellectual history by enabling us to answer questions of the general form: "Why did this happen then and not earlier?—Why did it happen to this man and not that other?"

Returning to the domain of national opinion, we have one more step to take in order to verify the conclusions reached earlier. We should study one or more instances in which the crystallization of national fame has not yet taken place even though the ingredients are present. If a really satisfactory example offers itself we will then have isolated the role of national propaganda in the making of Greatness and measured the distance between modern collective

---

[11] E.g., Joseph de Maistre's *Considérations sur la France,* published in 1790 and quite unregarded until the return of the Bourbons in 1814.

cults and the work of art in itself.¹² It so happens that the nineteenth century provides an admirable case history—in the person of the French composer Hector Berlioz.

II

From the nationalist point of view, nineteenth-century Frenchmen needed a great musician and they had him. But circumstances, which can be best unraveled by studying Berlioz' life and afterfame, stood in the way of his glorification. The result is that in spite of a desire at least as great as any other nation's for some "towering figure" in the arts, France had to do without—accepting her neighbors' instead and falling back on military heroes as substitutes: Napoleon was ready to hand, and Joan of Arc was raised to the highest pinnacle.¹³

What permits one to say that Berlioz was cut out to be the great ecumenical representative of French culture in his century is the mass of sober appraisals uttered by competent judges of every nationality during and since his time. Berlioz, they affirm, is the greatest musician France has ever produced.¹⁴ Born in 1803 and dying in 1869, he spans the period of the most abundant artistic output in France since the sixteenth century. In his own lifetime, he was internationally known as composer, conductor, and theorist on his art. His tremendous energy carried him and his ideas from Paris to Prague and from London to Moscow, so that under his leadership musical practice and musical thought were revolutionized to an extent seldom equaled in history. Only in France did a stubborn resistance neutralize his efforts and make him, despite the usual aca-

---

[12] Bernard Shaw and Arthur Machen are not the only critics to assert that the knowledge of Shakespeare in England is not real but conventional and perfunctory. See Shaw, *passim*, and Machen, *Far Off Things* (London [1922], 1931). It may or may not be relevant that the Stratford Theatre usually shows a deficit.

[13] The nineteenth-century historians, especially Michelet, repudiated Voltaire's "debunking" view and interpreted the Maid as a folk heroine. Schiller had made the first attempt characteristic of the liberal-Romantic tradition. Compare *William Tell, Masaniello, Rienzi*, and other subjects of drama and music drama between 1790 and 1840.

[14] See Franz Liszt, Saint-Saëns, Romain Rolland, Cecil Gray, W. J. Turner, Bernard Van Dieren, Ferruccio Busoni, Richard Strauss, Modeste Moussorgsky, F. Bonavia, and R. Wagner himself.

demic honors, a neglected figure, closing his days as the Second Empire was about to topple.

On the first anniversary of his death, that is, in March 1870, Berlioz' Paris disciples and friends managed after grave difficulties to give a memorial concert at the Opera; it did not clear expenses. The regime and its spokesmen might want prestige but not from Berlioz, whose work was held, in common with Wagner's, as a blot upon the century of light.[15] It might be thought that after the disastrous war and peace Berlioz' reputation might take an upward turn. But the situation was not so simple. In 1875, Bizet's *Carmen*, which was felt to be in the Berlioz tradition, failed miserably. A still closer disciple of the master, Ernest Reyer, was told by the critics that he had talent, "though a Frenchman."[16] The incident and the man's very name are indicative, for he was born Ernest Rey, of Bordeaux, and added the Germanic ending to facilitate his musical career. Berlioz' first obstacle was therefore the national belief that music is not a centrally French tradition. To be a musician, which made Wagner so eligible across the Rhine, was a handicap on the "French" side of the river. In the minds of many in France and elsewhere, music comes in two brands; one from Italy, the other from Germany[17]; the Italian is agreeable and the German profound.[18]

These opinions extinguished the one quick flash of chauvinism about Berlioz which followed the dark days of 1870. In 1877, for instance, a new musical society founded in Paris by Edouard Colonne made its reputation as well as a great deal of money by presenting Berlioz' *Damnation of Faust* to a public which had not heard the work for thirty years. From that time forward this secular oratorio has been extremely popular in France, both in the concert room and in adaptations for the stage.[19] But the leading orchestras of Paris in the seventies were pushing Wagner—presumably a recent enemy—

---

[15] Edmond About, *Le Progrès* (Paris, 1867), pp. 324–25.

[16] E. Reyer, *Quarante ans de musique* (Paris, 1909), p. 221.

[17] See the vagaries of Sir Hubert Parry on the national incapacity of the French to produce music: Grove's *Dictionary of Music and Musicians* (6 vols., New York, 1935), V, 232; and *Style in Musical Art* (London, 1924), pp. 162–63.

[18] For example, in 1854 it seemed a commonplace for a Frenchman to write: "The French are too active to be perfect musicians: they want lively and 'busy' music. . . . The English are too thick to be moved by the poetry of tunes: they go to the Opera to be fashionable. The Germans are the true musicians of the world." E. Loudun, *L'Influence des idées anglaises et allemandes* (Paris, 1854), p. 88.

[19] By 1908, it had reached its 156th performance in the Colonne repertory alone.

much harder than Berlioz, and for quite understandable reasons. After the long and deadly isolation of the Second Empire, the French capital was eager for novelty and readily fanatical about foreign artists: in quick succession Wagner, Ibsen, Schopenhauer, Nietzsche, and Dostoevsky became—if not acclimated—at least objects of fads and cults. Anglomania and Japanese prints, Wagnerism and Baudelaire's adaptations of Poe, expressed for the elite their disowning of French Romanticism and their rejection of the immediate past, too long associated with Napoleon III.

There was, it is true, a good deal of nationalist sentiment against Wagner's growing popularity, but it was insufficient to resist the tide.[20] It seemed as if his being German added an opportunity for showing off one's broad-mindedness in admiring him. This was specially true of the artists, poets, and critics who made his reputation by going on a Bayreuth pilgrimage and writing in the *Revue Wagnérienne*.[21] In that extraordinary periodical two notions stand out: one is that Wagner represents not so much the new political Germany as the artistic mind of ancestral Germany, which in his person has conquered the state (King Ludwig of Bavaria). The second is that far from being a Romantic, Wagner is a Realist and Classicist. His works are said to recapture the "realism of Racine,"[22] and Berlioz is specifically mentioned with Hugo and Delacroix as out of date.[23]

Simultaneously, the works of this same Berlioz were enjoying in Germany a fresh vogue, beginning with Hans von Bülow's revival of the opera *Benvenuto Cellini* at Hanover in 1879. Other performances and publications in Germany finally spurred the French to compete and to produce three other neglected dramatic works in the nineties. The Berlioz party was growing. Although in 1885 no ranking member of the French government was present at the unveiling of Berlioz' statue in Paris, by 1900 there was more frequent acknowledgment of what he had done for France. A flourishing

---

[20] Of 25 Wagner caricatures in the Paris press from 1870 to 1890, only nine show any anti-German feeling. See J. Grand-Carteret, *Wagner en caricatures* (Paris, 1891), pp. 299–304.

[21] Edited by the novelist Edouard Dujardin, it numbered among its contributors Mallarmé, V. de l'Isle Adam, Mendès, Péladan, Wyzewa, Alfred Ernst, Verlaine, Huysmans, and Hennequin.

[22] *Revue Wagnérienne*, II (1886), 98.

[23] *Ibid.*, II, 113.

school of composers beginning with César Franck and Bizet and ending with Saint-Saëns, Lalo, Massenet, Ravel, and Debussy, was seen to owe its awakening to Berlioz' single-handed efforts.[24]

But he was no more *popular* than he had been in his own day or in the seventies. Some of the men who admired him in private, dissociated themselves from him in public.[25] And officialdom, which shapes such a large part of French public opinion, continued to treat his memory (for reasons shortly to be explained) with extreme diffidence. The centenary celebrations of 1903 at Grenoble were made memorable chiefly by the presence and the words of Englishmen, Russians, and Germans[26]; and it was the ancient German firm of Breitkopf und Härtel that issued Berlioz' scores in twenty volumes during the years 1900 to 1907.

The First World War gave rise to a good deal of Germanophobia, with no perceptible advantages to Berlioz' reputation. But in 1919 something new was added to this complex critico-national situation. An uncommon state of mind and a public occasion brought forth Berlioz' monumental *Requiem,* which had not been heard under a French conductor since the nineties.[27] It was now performed again in a manner reminiscent of its original purpose, to honor the memory of the French generals killed in battle. Within the next year, the Paris Opera put on *Les Troyens,* the "unique opera in which epic has been successfully dramatized."[28] The work had been denied that official recognition in Berlioz' lifetime; and although this production was in many ways inadequate,[29] it aroused enough public enthusiasm to have it place fourth in a poll of subscribers. But once

[24] "He made us symphonic composers," etc., in the special number of *Musica* devoted to Berlioz (March 1908).

[25] E.g., Debussy: compare his letters in Edward Lockspeiser, *Debussy* (London, 1936), pp. 30, 44, and his published criticism collected in *M. Croche, Anti-Dilettante* (Paris, 1926).

[26] See *Le Livre d'or du centenaire d'Hector Berlioz* (Grenoble, 1906); and Balakirev, letter to Charles Malherbe, in *Rivista Musicale Italiana* (1930), pp. 17–19.

[27] Felix Weingartner had played it in the Trocadéro in 1912, but the critical opinion of that decade may be seen in Romain Rolland's dismissal of the work: *Musiciens d'aujourd'hui* (Paris, 1908), pp. 27, 53.

[28] Donald J. Grout, *History of Opera* (2 vols., New York, 1947), I, 320; and Donald F. Tovey, *Essays in Musical Analysis* (London, 1936), IV, 89 n.: "One of the most gigantic and convincing masterpieces of music drama."

[29] See André Gide's *Journal,* English trans. by Justin O'Brien (New York, 1949), II, 267–68.

again the perfectly sincere *critical* acclaim of Berlioz' works did not ignite that other wider fervor which leads to national adoption. *Les Troyens* was dropped and the *Damnation of Faust* restaged.

The *Damnation of Faust* is by no means an inferior work among the rest, but it has been reduced to the status of a mere opera (which it is not) as if to permit the French public conveniently to pay its debt to the composer. By the mid-1930's a conservative French critic could say that Berlioz was understood and well played only by visiting conductors—Furtwaengler, Toscanini, Kleiber, or Sir Hamilton Harty.[30] At this very time, when Berlioz was enjoying a great boom in England and incurring neglect at the Nazis' hands,[31] the writer of a biography in French complained that Berlioz was being deliberately boycotted at home[32]; and just before the outbreak of the Second World War still another critic prefaced his study of *Berlioz et l'Europe romantique* with the remark that in order to put himself in the mood of writing, he would go and hear performances of Berlioz' music, "so rarely and so shabbily given in France, but which I had formerly studied very closely in Germany."[33]

The cycle, however, does not repeat itself exactly: it is an ascending spiral: for a second time the heightened tension of war drove the French to seek out Berlioz as their musical spokesman. During the German occupation they produced two large recordings—of the *Requiem* and the *Damnation of Faust*.[34] Soon after, Montreal played the great *Te Deum* to celebrate the allied victory, and Paris commemorated the Revolution of 1848 by playing the *Funeral and Triumphal Symphony* and the *Hymne à la France*. The implied association of ideas is of course legitimate. One part of Berlioz' work is intended for just such occasions, and it is this part which should long ago have singled out the composer to his compatriots as the

---

[30] Henry Prunières, Paris Letter on Music, *New York Times*, May 15, 1932.

[31] Several German scholars tried to rescue him from his nationality by showing that his blond hair and blue eyes made him a true Nordic, while his scores showed his full possession of the German *Geist*. (E.g., Fr. Baser, *Die Musik*, January 1934, pp. 259 ff.)

[32] Léon Constantin, *Berlioz* (Paris, 1933), pp. 15 ff.

[33] Guy de Pourtalès, *Berlioz et l'Europe romantique* (Paris, 1939), pp. 1–2. Four years earlier, after great difficulties, Berlioz' birthplace at La Côte St. André was repurchased and officially declared a national museum.

[34] Columbia sets No. MM769 and (French) LFX 614–28. They are now available in the United States, but neither is quite complete or *intégral* as the mendacious French label pretends.

only one in touch with their popular feelings and in scale with their needs.[35] In his "festival" music—a term Wagner borrowed from him for his *Festspiele*—Berlioz serves public occasions in a spirit at once religious and popular. As Wagner said of the *Funeral and Triumphal Symphony:* "No one can deny Berlioz the power to compose works that are truly popular: I say 'popular' in the best sense of the word. When I heard the symphony that he wrote for the commemoration of the victims of the July Revolution, I felt most vividly that every urchin in a blue blouse and a red cap could understand it—a kind of understanding which for my part I should call 'national' rather than 'popular.' . . . The work is noble and grave from the first note to the last . . . and will live as long as there is a nation called France."[36]

III

Wagner's prophecy of a century ago may be on the way to fulfillment. If evidence of the present temper in France is reliable, each solemn performance under stress of recent tragedy enlarges Berlioz' circle of devotees. He is not yet for France what an English poet envisioned—the redeemer of national honor[37]—but he has not slid back into the position of an embarrassing, unclassifiable figure.[38] What we may be seeing at work, then, is the very process which has formed the subject of this inquiry—the creation of a national myth, of a "Napoleonic legend" around an eligible artist. Sometimes—as we saw in Goethe and Wagner—the thing happens quickly, there are no obvious competitors; at other times—as it turned out for Dante and Shakespeare—progress is slow, reluctance and opposition great. Or to put it another way, the collective force of national feeling has to overcome other, dividing forces within the nation. We are familiar enough with this phenomenon in politics: before Lincoln could become the property of all Americans, he had to be dissociated

---

[35] He orchestrated the *Marseillaise* and, in addition to the works cited above, composed half a dozen others that belong to the same genre.

[36] From an article published in Dresden in May 1841 and reprinted in Wagner's *Prose Works*, ed. by W. A. Ellis (London, 1892–1902), VIII, 131–37.

[37] "Berlioz: an Ode" by E. H. W. Meyerstein, in *Music Review* (Cambridge, Eng., November 1943).

[38] As a slight index of change, Berlioz' name appears for the first time in the title of a serial work on the history of French music to mark a date: P. Landormy, *La Musique française de la Marseillaise à la mort de Berlioz* (Paris, 1944).

from one branch of the Republican Party, then from that party itself, then from only a fraction of the whole people, the North.

Since it is a commonplace to say that there are two Frances, whose antagonism interferes with culture no less than politics, we should be prepared for the fact that admission to the country's hall of fame is not to be achieved by tacit majority rule. On this point we can squeeze a last drop of instruction from Berlioz' biography. Its striking feature is that neither in his opinions, writings, or musical subjects does Berlioz ally himself with either Right or Left. He loathed politics, seeing through its shams and crudities. He was a cosmopolitan mind who in castigating nationalistic judgments of art, exclaimed: "Patriotism, fetishism, moronism!"[39] And as a Romanticist he was so alert to a vast body of traditions—native and foreign—that his style, like his subjects, transcends political and social divisions. To particularize: he was reared on the liturgy and southern French folk songs, and therefore wrote a great deal of sacred music whose melodic idiom reflects both these sources. Indeed, he included religious and pastoral themes and scenes in almost all his works. This was enough to make an anticlerical government, such as that of the Third Republic, consider him a man of the Right and boycott him as such. But the Right, thinking of Berlioz' lifelong willingness to compose "music for the masses," to celebrate the July Revolution or the Napoleonic ideal,[40] must necessarily class him with the Left. Besides, his originality and anti-academicism, visible in all he wrote, hardly recommended him to the would-be upholders of conventional order.[41]

The clinching argument was Berlioz' association with Romanticism. His apotheosis as a Frenchman, had it been untrammeled by religion and politics, should have come in the last decade of the nineteenth century and the beginning of the twentieth. But this was a period of militant anti-Romanticism.[42] Conservatives and cler-

[39] *Mémoires* (2 vols., Paris, 1878), II, 261.
[40] Berlioz was very far from having received favors at the hands of Napoleon III; but not having gone into exile with the republicans, he could be lumped with the regime and thus distrusted by both the parties that followed the Empire.
[41] They could moreover gather from his Memoirs that his father, though a country gentleman married to a devout Catholic and royalist, was a physician bred on the Enlightenment who had made his son an unbeliever.
[42] The best proof consists in the major French biography of Berlioz to date—a monument of denigration by Adolphe Boschot: *Histoire d'un romantique* (3 vols., Paris, 1906–13).

icals were especially passionate, but liberals and socialists shared (in their capacity as positivists) the strong antiromantic bias. All joined in an effortless and frequently irresponsible condemnation of a period and an art which they found too exuberant, vivid, and dramatic. They were repeating in louder chorus what the esthetes of the *Revue Wagnérienne* had said in the eighties, adding only the fantastic charge that, in France, Romanticism was a temporary fad of foreign origin.[43]

In seeking for truly native work, criticism went back to the seventeenth century, just as creative artists of the Symbolist and Impressionist schools expressed a preference for Rameau, Couperin, Watteau, and Racine.[44] The perfect master for those concerned about music was obviously Debussy, who had reacted so strongly against both Romanticism and Wagnerism, and he was accordingly canonized by one section of the public as *Notre Claude de France*.[45]

And yet it was apparent that the great Impressionist's slight output and exclusive concentration upon delicate nuance could hardly represent a people as varied—and as split—as the French. It was even a question whether in comparison with the whole French tradition, medieval as well as modern, the work of the *fin de siècle* was not ending in a pin point. If they seek real size and strength to represent them, the French may still find it necessary to make the best of Berlioz, his disadvantages as a nonpartisan becoming in the long run the desirable proof of his power to encompass. His aloofness combined with simplicity, his Romantic variety and clear dramatic structure, his balance between religious and secular tendencies provide without eclecticism a kind of "representation" for diverse national interests. Certainly, the traditions that preceded him find their analogues in his work. The Gothic cathedrals, the festivals of the Revolution, the tragic grandeur of the antique, the comic force of Molière and Beaumarchais, and the special lyricism of his own period inform his varied output.

If French national pride discovers these things which three gen-

---

[43] See Charles Maurras or Pierre Lasserre, *passim*, or in university circles, Louis Reynaud, *Le Romantisme: ses origines anglo-germaniques* (Paris, 1926).

[44] Besides the critical work of the Goncourt brothers, take note of Ravel's *Tombeau de Couperin* and Debussy's *Hommage à Rameau*.

[45] Emile Vuillermoz, *Excelsior*, Oct. 8, 1933; and, subsequently, H. B. Harvey's *Claude of France: The Story of Debussy* (New York, 1948).

erations of scholars have pointed out, the cultural ripening discussed in these pages will have been completed. Berlioz' body will be moved to the Pantheon and the machinery of state will begin to indoctrinate the world, including the young in its own schools. The pageant of nations will have gained another posed and costumed participant, but his distinct voice and look and thought will be dimmed: the living, militant artist will be hidden by the smoke of a nation's tribute of incense, and he will then reveal himself only to those who seek the man behind the flag.

A SECRET AGENT'S ADVICE ON AMERICA, 1797

FRANCES S. CHILDS

AN INFORMAL LETTER addressed to *"cher Alexandre"* and signed *"Je vous embrasse, Maurice"* is a surprise in a volume of French diplomatic correspondence, dealing with Franco-American relations in the late eighteenth century. And five such letters in rapid succession[1]—letters in which considerable detailed information and forthright opinion on contemporary conditions in the United States are interspersed with complaints about nagging ill-health and insufferable boredom—are enough of a surprise to make one wonder whether one may not have unearthed a nugget of gold in this veritable mountain of serious, long-winded, and extremely polite documents. Who is Alexander? Who is Maurice? What is all this about? As one moves backward and forward in the records, their identities emerge and their correspondence can very gradually be put together. The nugget is the correspondence of a French secret agent in the United States during the summer of 1797.

Alexander was Pierre Auguste Adet (1783–1832)[2] who, in June 1795, had succeeded Fauchet and the Commissioners, who in their turn had succeeded Citizen Charles Edmond Genêt as Minister Plenipotentiary of the French Republic, one and indivisible, to the United States of America. Originally educated as a scientist, Adet had served in Santo Domingo and as head of the colonial administration before being assigned to the United States. A somewhat milder man than his predecessors, he was concerned with building up good will for France as well as realizing French aims; but Genêt's dynamic and undiplomatic revolutionary spirit had sown the wind, Fauchet had failed to deflect it, and Adet was left to reap the whirlwind of anti-French sentiment in the United States at the end of the

---

[1] *France, Affaires Étrangères, Paris, Correspondance Politique, États-Unis* (hereafter referred to as *Aff. Étr., Cor. Pol. É.-U.*), vol. 47, folios 393–96; vol. 48, fols. 3–4, 13–16, 66–67 vo., 141 vo.-142.

[2] "Correspondence of the French Ministers in the United States," *American Historical Association Annual Report, 1903* (Washington, 1904), II, Introduction, pp. 12, 728, note a. See also *Nouvelle biographie générale* (Paris, 1858), I, 278–79.

century. Following the election of John Adams as president in 1796, things went from bad to worse, with the result that Adet returned to France in the summer of 1797 leaving French affairs in the hands of the Consul General Létombe. In the course of the instructions Adet left Létombe, he spoke of the increasing difficulty he was having in keeping in touch with the members of the Congress. They were actually avoiding him—some he saw secretly and they had told him to go home. Consequently he had looked around for a man "without public character" who would maintain contacts for him, "a sure, zealous and informed man . . . fit to fill the role of intermediary agent," and found Maurice, i.e. Citizen Hauterive, "whose gifts equal the attachment he has for the Republic."[3]

Citizen Hauterive, actually Alexandre Maurice Blanc de Lanautte, Comte d'Hauterive[4]—who in subsequent years was to become one of Talleyrand's chief diplomatic agents, to draft the Concordat of 1801, to share in the Amiens and Tilsit negotiations—had come to the United States in the spring of 1793 to serve as French Consul in New York. That a man with as obvious an aristocratic background got such an appointment in 1793 is most surprising. Actually it went through over the opposition of Brissot and Genêt. There is, however, no evidence in Hauterive's career in the United States that he was not well qualified to hold office, and the *Journal* he kept in New York in the fall of 1793 reveals him as a sincere supporter of the revolutionary cause.[5] It is true though that when he was succeeded by the Vice-Consul Arcambal in March 1794 and got word that the French agents were pressing the United States government for his

[3] *Ibid.*, pp. 1013–14.

[4] For biographical data on Hauterive, see Michaud, *Biographie universelle* (Paris, 1857), XVIII, 557–71; also A. F. Artaud de Montor, *Vie et travaux politiques du Comte d'Hauterive* . . . (2nd ed., Paris, 1839). Both the Michaud article and the biography are somewhat royalist in tone. Chapter IV in the latter deals with Hauterive in the United States and includes extracts from his letters in defense of his career as Consul.

[5] Hauterive's *Journal* for the autumn of 1793, which is extant in the Library of the New-York Historical Society, contains vivid details on his daily work, his impressions of the United States, and much social theorizing. An article about this *Journal* by the present author appeared in the *New-York Historical Quarterly*, April 1949. J. P. Brissot was one of the few contemporary French leaders who knew the United States at first hand. Author of *Nouveau voyage aux États-Unis* (Paris, 1791), and founder of the *Société Gallo-Américaine* in the interest of accord between France and the United States, he represented, as did Genêt, the point of view of the Gironde. For further information, see E. Ellery, *Brissot de Warville* (New York, Boston, 1915).

extradition, Hauterive became alarmed lest this happen, and sought aid from James Nicholson and Albert Gallatin,[6] determined to go live with the Indians if he could not find "peace, security and an asylum" in this "first homeland of liberty." Nicholson did suggest that he go to the "western country," but Gallatin apparently brought him to his senses concerning the reasonableness of the American authorities. Hauterive probably was unduly alarmed, for the Commissioners reported that "the accounts of the incriminated Consul were accurate and regular and gave evidence of the patience, zeal, integrity and patriotism of a good citizen," and gave ill-health as the reason for Hauterive's remaining in the United States.[7] Critical of French excesses in the United States, Hauterive was also critical, after Genêt's fall, of the policy of the French Executive Council of disgracing its agents, and he wrote the Abbé Barthélemy about his own recall: "The Executive Council was mistaken about me in including me in Genêt's disgrace. I was not known in this country as an aid but as an obstacle to the man whose conduct they wished to censor so noisily." To Fauchet he wrote that patriotism must give place to probity.[8] Subsequently Hauterive retired to private life—poor enough to try to run a truck garden but not too poor to renew his acquaintance with Talleyrand when the latter joined him in exile in the United States.[9] Three years later he was still here—still harping on ill-health—but ready to pick up Adet's assignment. Moreover, in more than three years of civilian life Hauterive had had the time, which most French agents lacked, to modify general French theories on the United States—based in part on romantic visions of a new Eden, in part on emotional concepts of what the American Republic owed to France, and finally on a doctrinaire, revolutionary nationalism which could brook no reverses—with considerable practical experience. He knew America and Americans. And if to some extent Hauterive shared their lot and life, he was not just another disgruntled French refugee carrying on the

[6] *Gallatin Papers*, IV, 90–92, in New-York Historical Society Library. Hauterive to Albert Gallatin, New York, April 12 and 18, 1794. James Nicholson to Albert Gallatin, New York, April 14, 1794. (James Nicholson was Albert Gallatin's father-in-law.)

[7] *American Historical Association Annual Report, 1903*, II, 384–85; Artaud de Montor, *op. cit.*, p. 70.

[8] *Ibid.*, pp. 74, 71–72.

[9] *Ibid.*, p. 74.

ideological quarrels of the Revolution on American soil. All in all, then, Adet's choice was a reasonable one; in the light of Hauterive's subsequent career it seems almost prophetic. Moreover, there is evidence that Hauterive enjoyed his job as secret agent; very probably he saw in it a way back into public life. In any case, he wrote frequently and fully, he kept duplicate records, he at no time revealed his sources, and he got his material through to its destination effectively, as the extant records bear witness.

The setting for this correspondence between Hauterive and Adet is so well known as to need little elaboration. With the outbreak of war between England and France in 1792 the newly formed United States was really neither able nor willing to fulfill the obligations of the Treaty of Amity with France, made in 1778 during the American Revolution, without being drawn into the conflict. As both the country and Washington's Cabinet were divided in sentiment, a neutral policy was the only wise course to pursue. If this for the moment did prevent open hostilities, it did not stop the ideological battle between France and England on American soil. To the French, emotionally whetted by the revolutionary spirit, our policy was a betrayal of our common revolutionary origin and of the Treaty of 1778, and was attributed to British intrigue rather than to the will of the American people. Successive French agents worked, therefore, to counteract British influences and upset this policy; individual ministers appealed over the head of the American government to the people and these tactics were carried so far as to alienate pro-French sentiment in the United States. The Jay treaty with England was an additional blow to French interests. The French, who had not expected this treaty to be ratified, gradually threw all caution to the wind. Depredations on American shipping continued. When Monroe was replaced by C. C. Pinckney, Barras,[10] then President of the Directory, in a farewell address distinguished between Monroe as a representative of the American Republic and as a citizen, and reminded Americans that they owed their liberty to France. Subsequently the Directory refused to recognize Pinckney's credentials as minister pending the adjustment of French grievances. President Adams' further efforts at negotiations resulted in

---

[10] Barras' speech, available in standard French sources, is quoted in *Abridgment of the Debates of Congress, 1789–1856* (New York, 1857), II, 115, in connection with Adams' address of May 16, 1797.

the XYZ affair. All this led finally to an actual but undeclared war with France, which continued until various pressures led the French government to assure the United States that new delegates would be fittingly received.

If this setting has been frequently, extensively, and ably analyzed from diplomatic and political angles, it has perhaps been less common to see in it what it basically was, a conflict of nationalisms. On one side of this conflict stood the new nationalism of the French revolutionary era, militant and dynamic; oblivious of any criteria but its own; weighing non-nationals as nationals by their loyalty to the French Republic, one and indivisible, by their noisy and arrogant *civisme;* convinced that the United States should as a matter of course and regardless of cost act with France, and that all other nations were actuated by base and venal motives. On the other side was the steady, stubborn, and unspectacular strength of the British tradition; the years of commercial intercourse and the mighty web of common institutional and cultural ties with England. Between these two forces a new nationalism, a nationalism defying the French revolutionary concept of the nation as a people with a common past, common customs and traditions, a common tongue and a contiguous geographical area—actually more radically revolutionary in its determination to achieve a common future out of a multiplicity of pasts, *e pluribus unum*—was struggling to maintain its existence, and its precariously uncertain unity was, paradoxically enough, being hammered into shape by these opposing forces.

If this aspect of the setting has not always been stressed in our own time, the French ministers[11] of that day would be the last people to understand it. Undistinguished men in general, they struggled over contemporary issues, supplies for the West Indies, French refugees in distress and acute shortage of funds . . . and were one after another removed from office by a government which had given them inadequate support and information. Their correspondence has long been known as an invaluable source for this period. Scholars have also emphasized the significance of some of the less prominent French officials in relation to policy in the United States—Louis Guillaume Otto, for example, who had been Secretary of the French

---

[11] See F. J. Turner, "Introduction," *American Historical Association Annual Report, 1903,* II, *passim,* for an evaluation of these men.

Legation here and Chargé d'Affaires. Otto's memoir *Considérations sur la conduite du gouvernement des États-Unis envers la France, 1789–1797* criticized French agents, ignorant of English and elementary diplomatic principles, and denied any rift between the American government and people. Victor du Pont, who had served as French Consul in Charleston as well as Secretary of the Legation, also denounced French policy bluntly in answer to a request of Talleyrand's for "facts."[12]

Into this latter category the Hauterive-Adet correspondence fits. Hauterive's assignment was an immediate and practical one; his chief concern was with the current situation. Adams' election was a blow to the French cause. What will that election mean for French interests here? What stand will the new President take? Who will go to France to negotiate? What sort of men will they be? Will positive measures be taken against France? Can English pressure lead the United States into open war? On all of these questions Hauterive reported dutifully, but he didn't stop there. Well educated, well read, sensitive to the philosophic and physiocratic trends of the day, a thinker as well as a man of action, with four long years in this country to his credit, he went further and at times escaped from the finicky details of a situation "delicate in the extreme" and the trammels of revolutionary ideology. Then he initiated themes of his own, dug into causes, and glimpsed the future in a way more characteristic of a statesman and diplomat than of an intermediary agent. Moreover, Hauterive wrote fluently and well—at times with humor and sarcasm as well as maturity of insight. His letters therefore make good reading and are worthy of note.

Coming back to the correspondence, Hauterive it was who, fearing that communication would become increasingly difficult after Adet's return to France under a flag of truce, arranged for a secret if not very subtle means of communication.[13] Letters addressed to "Alexander Felix, signed M. Felix" would arrive "by indirect and

---

[12] See *Aff. Étr., Cor. Pol. É.-U.*, vol. 50, fols. 99–106, for Du Pont's memoir; *ibid.*, vol. 47, 401 ff., for Otto's *Considérations...*, the draft of which was published by Gilbert Chinard, *Bulletin de l'Institut Français de Washington*, No. XVI, December 1943. See also J. A. James, "French Opinion as a Factor in Preventing War Between France and the United States, 1795–1800," *American Historical Review*, XXX, 44–55, and F. S. Childs, "French Opinion of Anglo-American Relations, 1795–1805," *French American Review*, March 1948.

[13] *Aff. Étr., Cor. Pol. É.-U.*, vol. 47, fol. 340.

obscure means." They would be written "in familiar and frivolous forms" to hide the seriousness of their purpose and escape "English vigilance," or "at least not compromise anyone"[14] if they were intercepted. Adet was to "pay attention to the facts only" and draw from them the information of use to the government. This letter, dated Philadelphia, 17 Prairial V (June 5, 1797), bears the number VIII and refers to a "new method" of communication—indicating that there was more to this correspondence than the letters which follow. Perhaps Adet destroyed the originals of Nos. I–VII, for they do not appear in the files in question. However, copies of Nos. I–VI have survived in a document written in Hauterive's own hand and entitled *Situation politique des États-Unis en Floréal et en Prairial An V dans une suite de lettres du C^{en} Hauterive au C^{en} Adet.*[15] This document opens with a *lettre d'envoi de cette correspondance au Ministre des Relations Extérieures,* dated New York, 19 Floréal V (May 8, 1797), in which Hauterive explained his delay in returning to France and apologized for the "precipitation and imperfection of this work."[16] Copies of letters I to VI follow *seriatim*. This was evidently a duplicate file which could be taken or sent to France *in toto* when and if the time came. Two attestations at the end of the file indicate that Hauterive, before leaving for France, deposited it in the care of A. V. Rozier, the French Consul in New York, that Rozier brought it with him when he returned a little later, and gave it back to Hauterive in Paris, 13 Brumaire VI (October 29), on which day Hauterive deposited it with one Lenoir Laroche who kept it until 15 Frimaire VI (November 30). Subsequently it was "received at the division on the 12th Nivôse, VI" (December 27). Very likely it got there through Talleyrand, for Hauterive on his return to France wrote him three separate letters in each of which he referred to his correspondence with Adet. Two of these letters written from Bor-

---

[14] Hauterive refers here to Fauchet's intercepted letter and the anti-French capital made of it, with no reference to its effect on Randolph, then Secretary of State, whose public career it brought to an end. For a brief summary of this episode, see J. S. Bassett, *The Federalist System* (New York, London, 1907), pp. 31–33.

[15] *Aff. Étr., Cor. Pol. É.-U., Supplément,* vol. 2, fols. 155–67 vo. These are labeled *Duplicata.*

[16] In this letter Hauterive explained that he would write Adet in care of the Minister of Exterior Relations. Should Adet be delayed or away, the Minister would then have the information. In letter I, Hauterive explained all this to Adet, thus keeping both channels open and making sure that his reports would not be unnoticed.

deaux,[17] Vendémiaire 1 and 18, VI (September 17, October 4), where Hauterive had landed and was detained by the police, asked Talleyrand to expedite matters for him so that he might get on to Paris and complete the task "he had consented to assume" with a final report on the situation in the United States. This, he suggested, had best be done on a question and answer basis so as not to waste the time of a busy man. Hauterive also congratulated Talleyrand on his appointment to succeed Delacroix, and then referred him to the correspondence with Adet, particularly the six *lettres pseudonymes* in which "he was freed from the trammels of official gravity" and wrote with "sincerity and frankness."

In a third letter from Paris,[18] 29 Brumaire VI (November 14), Hauterive sent copies of five of the letters written under a pseudonym[19] and the explanatory letter No. VIII; another letter about party alignment in the United States was missing but Hauterive planned to assemble the information from his notes and send it to Talleyrand later. Putting all this together, we have first six direct letters, then No. VIII, then five from Maurice to Alexander. There is actually another letter extant from C^{en} Hauterive to C^{en} Adet written in the summer of 1797 and clearly a part of this series.[20] Labeled "copy," it lacks any salutation but is signed Hauterive; dated Prairial 19 (June 7), one day later than No. VI, it is presumably the missing VII. In any case, it fits in between the direct letters, to which it seems closest in context, and the pseudonymous series. Before evaluating this correspondence as a whole, these letters—which are too extensive to quote *in toto* (Hauterive himself referred to his "voluminous correspondence" and he was a master of circum-

---

[17] *Aff. Étr., Cor. Pol. É.-U.*, vol. 48, fols. 265–66, 291 ff. Artaud de Montor said (*Op. cit.*, pp. 78–79) that Hauterive took a chance in returning to France as his name was still on the list of *émigrés*. Nevertheless, within a year of his return he was, thanks in all probability to Talleyrand, a divisional chief in the Department of Exterior Relations "in charge of correspondence with England, Holland, the courts of Vienna and Berlin, the Empire, the German States, Denmark, Sweden, Russia, and the United States," and on his way to a successful career.

[18] *Aff. Étr., Cor. Pol. É.-U.*, vol. 48, fols. 369–70 vo.

[19] *Ibid., Supplément*, vol. 5, fols. 142–53 vo. This duplicate file of five pseudonymous letters is presumably the one sent to Talleyrand. It bears the heading *Correspondance du Cit. Hauterive en mission aux États-Unis faisant suite à celle adressée au citoyen Avret* (sic) *et datée du 1 Messidor au 14 Thermidor an 5 ou du 19 Juin au 1er Aoust 1797*. This file is referred to in *American Historical Association Annual Report, 1903*, II, 1014, note a.

[20] *Aff. Étr., Cor. Pol. É.-U.*, vol. 47, fols. 344–44 vo.

locution)—must at least be summarized and checked with the events they report.[21]

Hauterive's first letter,[22] 19 Floréal V (May 8), opened with an analysis of his job. He was to capitalize on the acquaintances he had made, thanks to "a long and fairly intimate liaison with certain influential people," and he was to be a good reporter. Next followed compliments to Adet who, he inferred, was going home to avoid any suspicion of implication or interference on the part of the Directory in the affairs of the Congress, about to decide on the momentous issue of relations with France (!). Hauterive then got down to business and questioned whether the Directory had made up their minds on what the exact and final character of French relations with the United States was to be. Had they done so, they would certainly have left Adet here to influence discussion and maintain contacts. How could good results be obtained by the pro-French party (the anti-Federalists) if they did not know how to proceed? "Alternately helped or neglected, stirred up or disowned," they were "hesitant and weak," while the Federalists were a well-organized and well-directed bloc. Hauterive concluded with the suggestion that the Directory might be deferring a settlement with the United States until it could be fitted into "the great continental and maritime system which . . . will consummate the glory of the French Revolution by allowing all the peoples of the universe to share in its fruits and bless its benefits."

The theme of the second letter,[23] written a fortnight later, was the address Adams made to Congress on May 16, 1797, after the news of the nonreception of Pinckney reached the United States. Adams' well-known speech explained his sending C. C. Pinckney to France to replace Monroe, praised Pinckney's character and ability,

[21] The following year Hauterive wrote two memoirs on the United States. One bears the title *Du Gouvernement des États-Unis en 1798 par M.* (no longer *Citoyen*) *d'Hauterive,* the other *Des partis qui divisent les États-Unis, 1798.* Both deal with some of the ideas in the 1798 correspondence, but they are lengthy historical and philosophical analyses rather than diplomatic reports. It is not clear that they were written for anyone in particular, but their existence in the French archives and Hauterive's friendly relations with Talleyrand being well established, they were very likely done at his request, if not on Hauterive's own initiative. Be that as it may, the memoirs, bearing the date 1798 only, cannot be related to any specific events; they are therefore, except for certain references, omitted from the above discussion. See *France, Aff. Étr., Mémoires et Documents, É.-U.,* vol. 10, fols. 152–70 vo.

[22] *Aff. Étr., Cor. Pol. É.-U., Supplément,* vol. 2, fols. 155–56 vo.

[23] *Ibid.,* vol. 5, fols. 157–58 vo.

quoted his instructions "to remove jealousies and obviate complaints ... to restore ... mutual confidence," and characterized his nonreception as a violation of "the right of embassy" by which nations dealt with one another. Refusal to hear Pinckney was equivalent to treating the United States "neither as allies nor as friends nor as a sovereign State." However, as "neither the honor nor the interest of the United States absolutely forbid the repetition of advances . . ," Adams planned to "institute a fresh attempt at negotiation." In the meantime, he recommended to Congress the consideration of laws on a Naval Establishment and a militia to meet the French challenge, told them of the French efforts to alienate the American people from their government and the need for manifesting solidarity, and concluded with his conviction that the "conduct of the government has been just and impartial to foreign nations. . . ."[24] Hauterive's letter to Adet was, as he said, not an explanation but a letter of opinion on Adams' discourse. A lengthy tirade against Adams followed; Adams was outdoing Washington; "Washington declaimed against enemy factions . . . Adams associates domestic and foreign factions, and presents them to the Americans as conspiring together against the independence of their government. The pretended appeal to the people of 1793 [i.e. Genêt's] was under Washington only the personal desire of an indiscreet minister; Adams makes it the public and fundamental maxim of the French government. . . ." True, said Hauterive, tensions existed in America but the President was exaggerating them, and an actual split—Hauterive used the term *sission* and came back to the theme repeatedly —might ensue in the newly formed United States.

In the third letter[25] Hauterive began by philosophizing and led gradually up to his point. Here, as in other lands "governed by free institutions and customs less good than their laws," outside events significant to the country as a whole were seen only in relation to "their influence on the relative position of [domestic] parties disputing the control of public opinion and a share in government." In Europe the French Revolution had frightened the parties in power, but these parties had not consequently made war on the ideas of the

---

[24] *Abridgment of the Debates of Congress, 1789–1856*, II, 114–16. Hauterive's remarks have been checked, wherever relevant, with the actual debates in Congress rather than with the general histories of the period.

[25] *Aff. Étr., Cor. Pol. É.-U., Supplément*, vol. 5, fols. 158–60 vo.

Revolution but on their own minorities, whom these ideas might inflame. In the United States the European situation was being used to strengthen the party in power but, granted the vast size of the country, the small population, and the absence of "ships, soldiers, arms, and money," war was, practically speaking, impossible. It was quite possible, however, that a part of the nation might be drawn closer to the evil British system of mercantilism and *fiscalité* as it spread out beyond Britain in accordance with Adam Smith's prediction; and, if so, might not another section of the country prefer a more agricultural type of society? Unaided, this would be impossible; but if a neighboring country or Louisiana were governed by France, the commercial forces might be held in check. These considerations, which "a very near future may realize," Hauterive left for Adet to take up with the Directory.

A few days later Hauterive wrote again,[26] enclosing a series of "observations" he had made and which he was sending on unexpanded because of the pressure of time. These dealt largely with current events—the President's speech of May 16, the negotiators going to France—and followed fairly closely the day-by-day developments in the United States.

In the first "observation," 3 Prairial (May 22), Hauterive reported no formal answer as yet to the President's address, but that both houses were debating their answers, and that a Mr. Nicholas had proposed an amendment which would save the House from as unconciliatory an attitude as the President's and had supported it with an able speech defending the French position. The debate on this amendment actually did bring out all aspects of the problem—French depredations, Pinckney's position, the implications of the Jay Treaty, Barras' speech, support for the President—and indicated both the cleavage in American opinion and the seriousness of the issue. Nicholas himself considered the present crisis "the most important which the country has known since its independence."[27]

By the time Hauterive drafted a second "observation," the Sen-

[26] *Ibid.*, fols. 161–64.
[27] *Abridgment of the Debates of Congress, 1789–1856,* II, 123 ff. 127. John Nicholas, a Representative from Virginia, was not on the committee to draft the answer to the President's speech. As Albert Gallatin, who had been friendly with Hauterive for some years (see above, Note 6), was in the House at this moment, he may well have been one of Hauterive's sources of information.

ate's answer was out. Actually this speech gave the President generous support, favored further negotiation with France, and agreed to consider Adams' measures for defense. It said we would be just to France and all nations, expecting the same in return, but that if injured we would sustain the rights of the government. However, Hauterive considered this distinctly sympathetic to reconciliation with France and negative support only for Adams. Hauterive noted correctly that the first draft was defeated and that two more committee members were added, both anti-Federalists, before the final draft appeared.[28]

The third "observation" dealt with the classic case of Jefferson's letter to Mazzei.[29] As is well known, Jefferson wrote his friend Mazzei a personal letter in which he criticized the growth of aristocratic sentiment in the United States and Washington's pro-English sentiment. This letter appeared in Italian in the press in Italy, in French in the press of France, then was retranslated into English and published in the United States. The various translations left its original meaning in doubt and Jefferson preferred to ignore it rather than to release the correct text. Hauterive felt that had Jefferson acknowledged it frankly Adams could not have been so annoyed with the Directory's attitude towards Monroe. Hauterive recorded here the first criticism that he had heard of Jefferson as the anti-Federalist leader. However, he did not feel that all was lost. An acknowledgment now might have even more effect. Prudence may avoid an attack, courage is necessary to meet one and "courage is the virtue, duty, need, and force of a minority party."

Observations 4 and 5 dealt with the plans for sending commissioners to France. According to Hauterive, Adams had first planned to send a Minister Extraordinary who would be *persona grata* there. Madison, Burr, and Chancellor Livingston had all been mentioned; subsequently opinion had it that a mixed commission representing both Federalist and anti-Federalist points of view should go. Here Hauterive noted astutely that as the approval of the Senate was nec-

[28] *The Debates and Proceedings in the Congress of the United States* (Washington, 1851), 5th Congress, I, 10–14.
[29] Hauterive refers to the *Moniteur,* January 12, *vieux style.* For a recent discussion of the Mazzei letter, see Charles O. Lerche, Jr., "Jefferson and the Election of 1800: A Case Study in the Political Smear," *William and Mary Quarterly,* 3rd series, V (October 1948), 477–79.

essary for the ratification of treaties, it would be foolish to think that they would ratify an agreement in which their point of view was not represented. But, said Hauterive, these plans had now vanished and current opinion had it that the envoys would be "mediocre and undecided," that matters would be aggravated and the French cause weakened. Another scheme then favored was to give Pinckney new powers and let him wait for a colleague and instructions. This Hauterive characterized as "favoring irresolution, timidity, and laziness," but he nevertheless felt it was the most likely course at the moment. Actually, of course, Adams struggled over the issue of the French delegation from the opening of his administration, and the actual negotiators sent—Pinckney, Marshall, and Gerry—were of a distinctly higher caliber than Hauterive had predicted.[30] In Observation 6 Hauterive characterized the publication of documents relevant to the French crisis as "calculated to increase party bitterness" and uphold Adams' position. Actually the eighteen items published did put France in a bad light and Hauterive's reaction was a typically nationalistic one.[31]

In the seventh "observation," 8 Prairial (May 27), Hauterive criticized as foolish Americans who resented foreign influences here. With as extended a trade as the United States possessed, Americans could not be indifferent to the good will of more powerful areas. "Two European nations dispute *l'empire et le commerce de la mer*"; and as American commerce had gone one way, American politics and affections should, according to Hauterive, go the other.[32]

Observation 8 returned to President Adams' address, noting the defeat of Mr. Nicholas' amendment by four votes, which indicated a very narrow Federalist margin. (Actually the vote on Monday,

---

[30] (Charles C. Pinckney of South Carolina, John Marshall of Virginia, and Elbridge Gerry of Massachusetts.) It is interesting to compare Hauterive's repeated denunciation of Adams' bias and incompetence with the more balanced interpretations of the present day. See, for example, G. Chinard, *Honest John Adams,* Bk. III, Chap. II, *passim.* Mr. Chinard says (p. 264), "Although he [Adams] has received very little credit for it and was damned equally by Gallomaniacs and Anglomaniacs, he nevertheless succeeded in keeping the only course the United States could possibly follow."

[31] Congress authorized the publication of 500 copies of these documents. See *Abridgment of the Debates of Congress, 1789–1856,* II, 123.

[32] Cf. Talleyrand, *Memoir Concerning the Commercial Relations of the United States with England* (Boston, 1809). In this speech delivered at the *Institut* in 1797, Talleyrand was well aware of the institutional and cultural ties binding the United States to England and skeptical of separating American affections from American business interests.

May 29, was 46 to 52.) Public opinion, said Hauterive, while deeply hurt by the Pinckney episode, was "decidedly and strongly" against war with France, and the President had been told that war would make him president of the North only.

In Observation 9 Hauterive started philosophizing again. The "real situation of affairs" was not what it appeared, "the less numerous party has all the confidence and force of a well-organized majority" and that majority was acting like "a vanquished minority." If American parties were divided on the Pinckney issue they were both willing "to put France on an equal footing with England" and this amounted to "a disapproval of the preceding [Washington's] administration." Things pointed now to the necessity of the President negotiating with France on terms the anti-Federalists would at least not oppose. These conjectures, said Hauterive, presupposed a willingness to end the discord with France. Hauterive then proceeded to develop another more involved hypothesis to the following effect: If the United States government was, in calling Congress, really seeking an opportunity to stir up indignation against France and thus to justify retaliatory measures which would in turn lead to such a favored plan as the "English alliance"— *l'alliance angloise de grand démembrement* (italics Hautrive's) —then it would be necessary to "see in Mr. Adams a man who wanted to change his own position in changing that of his country." In such circumstances, the PREDICTION (capitals Hauterive's) in Observation 8, i.e. *sission*, would not be a menace but a desideratum. "The nomination of the negotiators may perhaps throw light on this hypothesis."

Hauterive's fifth letter,[33] 18 Prairial (June 6), picked up with the nominations, which he stated categorically were the worst possible in the United States and proved Adams' insincerity. Pinckney, a well-known Federalist from the South, was able, but was so embittered since his return from France that he was ill equipped for a mission of reconciliation. Marshall, if honest and capable and trusted by the Federalists, had never disguised his pro-English sentiment. As for Dana, he had grown up in a Tory ménage, had gone abroad and come back as a Whig, but was distrusted. *"Timeo Danaos et dona ferentes."* A loyal friend of Adams, "his views are

---

[33] *Aff. Étr., Cor. Pol. É.-U., Supplément*, vol. 5, fols. 164 vo.–166 vo.

limited, his character passionate, and his mind narrow." The debate on ratification was on in the Senate, but these nominations would not be defeated unless news of the victory of the French army in Italy influenced votes and converted three more Senators. Then, as in the first letter, Hauterive let loose and urged the Directory to pay some attention to the United States. The sincere good will towards France here was distressed by the current discord. Moreover, whatever the present difficulties, the United States had an immense future and England alone believed in it. After losing the American colonies politically she had reconquered them commercially. She was now using her agents to counteract any cleavage along agricultural lines, and thus assure at least an alliance "guaranteeing resources whose successive development reaches out so far that the perspective is frightening." To Hauterive, foreseeing these dangers was a way to prevent them and, if *sission* was inevitable, "Canada and Louisiana are French. . . . New York and New Jersey belong neither to the North nor to the South and are probably destined to form an intermediary federation, and these states united with Canada form an enclave" connected via the lakes with Louisiana. In a postscript Hauterive reported top-secret information that the English were planning an invasion of Louisiana. This was the first news of the so-called "Blount conspiracy" in which Senator Blount, formerly territorial Governor of Tennessee, was involved in a scheme to attack Spanish Florida and Louisiana with troops raised on American soil, and transfer these areas to English control.[34]

Hauterive's sixth letter,[35] written the same day, concerned the scandalous reply of the House of Representatives to Adams' address, and contrasted the spectacle of the first Congress of the United States ending "its noble career with the solemn expression of its gratitude to the nation which had helped them to free themselves" with this recent act of "political apostasy . . . of a passionate and furious assembly" which accused France of "forgetting . . . the respect owed to the United States." If the Directory intended to treat the United States with increasing severity, here was reason enough to assume that Franco-American friendship was at an end. If the

---

[34] *Dictionary of American Biography,* II, 390–91. Blount was expelled from the Senate but impeachment proceedings against him were dismissed in 1789.
[35] *Aff. Étr., Cor. Pol. É.-U., Supplément,* vol. 5, fols. 166 vo.–167.

A Secret Agent's Advice on America

Directory, however, wanted a reconciliation on the basis of the public will in the United States, they should note the efforts of the opposition and remember that a faction was in control. If the Directory had no desire to bring the United States into a long-range plan, they should view the situation with pity, not hatred, and the only delay on reconciliation would be to find the means to make this appear as a gracious favor, not as an answer to "arrogant pretensions." This ends the series of letters in the "Duplicata" kept by Hauterive.

Actually the House answer, which Hauterive said wore the scars of a two-weeks war, gave Adams somewhat more unqualified support than had the Senate answer. The House desired peace with France and with the world but felt keenly the "indignity" offered the United States in the rejection of Pinckney. "We are not a degraded people ... we can never submit to the demands of a foreign power without examination and without discussion ... an attempt to separate the American people from their government is an attempt to separate them from themselves...." Yet they also were glad that new negotiations would be undertaken and they supported Adams' claim that "the conduct of the government has been just and impartial to all foreign nations."[36]

A day later Hauterive wrote again to Adet[37] (presumably No. VII) in a still harsher tone, ascribing to party spirit the pleasure elicited by Adams' brief answer thanking the House for their support. According to Hauterive a plan for war did exist but was beyond Adams' ability; the negotiators would carry instructions to go no further than putting France on a par with England and would demand compensation for violations of neutrality. Adams probably wanted this negotiation to succeed. Should it fail, it was to be hoped that the reports would hurt the French cause and so advance the work of *l'alliance angloise du démembrement*. . . . While trusting to the wisdom of the Directory, Hauterive repeated that if the Directory was dissatisfied, the negotiations could be "either broken off or neglected or deferred without danger, provided American public opinion is considered." A postscript noted the confirmation of Pinckney, Marshall, and Dana by the Senate.

At this point the direct letters end and those written under a

---

[36] *Abridgment of the Debates of Congress, 1789–1856*, II, 143–44.
[37] *Aff. Étr., Cor. Pol. É.-U.*, vol. 47, fol. 344.

pseudonym begin. Evidently Hauterive enjoyed writing these; he wrote informally, he groaned about his boredom and his ill health, but he nevertheless managed to say a good deal. The first of these letters,[38] 1 Messidor V (June 19, 1797), sets the pattern and can therefore be quoted extensively as illustrative of the group. Maurice apparently did not want to write, but was being hounded to do so by his good friend Alexis, a naturalist who was soon returning to France with "a voluminous research collection on the physical and geographical condition of this country," but who had an "incurable antipathy for political discussion." Therefore "I yield to the demands of Alexis: but I yield with regret: I am sick, long suffering has led me to a state, so to speak habitual, of impatience, ill humor, and almost of misanthropy. . . . I am excessively bored observing the uncertain and false course of an ineffective government which, through gross incompetence, weakness, and perhaps yielding to perverse passions, lets itself be led into the tortuosities of a foreign policy with aims beyond its reach."

The American national character, the letter continued, is as yet unformed. The foreigner who studies Americans is misled by their neutrality of expression. *"La Politique allaite encore ce peuple enfant des premiers sucs de ses principes élémentaires. . . .* I have therefore nothing to say to you about the moral character of the American people because I can say nothing which is consistent, general, and certain. But I am thereby telling you enough to make you understand that what one means by the word *character* can have only a passive influence" on the governing group here. This makes them especially subject to the influences of that European state "which knows so well how to influence the influences in this country." If by any chance an actual war breaks out, it will be waged "in manifestoes, newspapers, deliberative chambers, pamphlets, and proclamations only. There will be neither invasion of territory nor taking of cities . . . troops will be raised which will not march before the day peace is signed, taxes will be levied that no one will pay, generals will be named who will have no soldiers to command, and com-

---

[38] *Ibid.,* vol. 47, fols. 393–96 vo. Hauterive refers in this and subsequent pseudonymous letters to his friend Alexis, whom he describes as a naturalist, but there is no evidence in these letters as to whether Alexis was a real or fictitious person and, if real, who he was. The naturalist André Michaux who had worked with Genêt at an earlier date was already back in France.

modores will go from north to south and from harbor to harbor, ascertaining the absence of building materials and funds. There, certainly, is what one will see in this far from warlike country." In the meantime, factional discord will increase in both France and America, so that both countries will lose sight of the "consideration which two peoples who are friends and two governments which should be [friendly] owe each other." Nor is this all. The disillusioned French, alarmed by the reports of American progress, will then decide "it is high time to enchain young Hercules in his cradle." Spain will help in this; perhaps Canada and Louisiana will be freed . . . and with the assistance of the Indian tribes a barrier formed against the "ever-progressive and invasive cupidity of the Anglo-Americans." Internal strife might, if left alone, actually lead to the break-up of the Union which a few years before had seemed so promising but which is now so "vitiated" as to cause fear that a new England is appearing, pushing out over "unknown lands and rivers" with an avid eye on the eastern coast of Asia. Furthermore, says Hauterive, embargoes and unfavorable laws might handicap American shipping, and special levies on salt fish alone punish Connecticut and Massachusetts, "those two homes of anglomania and hostility towards France," and make them listen to reason. All this relates really to an undeclared war; an open war would "rivet for good the chains with which the mercantile and fiscal spirit of Great Britain now strangles the American government," and transfer millions of American dollars to British credit.

When all this is boiled down, the letter says only that the United States government is ineffectual and may be drawn into commitments beyond its power; that the American national character is as yet unformed, and that British influence is correspondingly strong; that any war with the United States would be absolute madness, as far as France is concerned. None of this was really news for the French authorities, but in this case, thanks to Hauterive's disguise, it is stated with brutal frankness and well enough padded with irrelevant materials to discourage the casual reader.

The second letter written under an assumed name,[39] 13 Messidor V (July 1), was briefer. Alexis had sailed and Hauterive, though sick, would follow shortly, preferring a grave beneath the waves to

[39] *Ibid.*, vol. 48, fols. 3–4 vo.

any further delay. Pending either of these alternatives, he reported the American war activities as those of a pygmy compared with Europe's vast projects, and stressed the "perseverance of the patriot party." Hauterive also noted that Dana had at the last moment been replaced by Elbridge Gerry, a "cold, circumspect, and silent" man. Though claimed by the anti-Federalists, Gerry had voted for Mr. Adams, having agreed to do so when chosen as an elector. "These sorts of agreements are not rare in this country."

This brief political notice was succeeded three days later, 16 Messidor V (July 4), by a grandiloquent geographical treatise[40] which Alexander was asked to follow on a map of the new world. Hauterive began with the Andes in South America, traced this mountain range up north under the Caribbean and into North America, where it split into two branches, thus dividing the continent into three different sections. The eastern section, actually the United States, a narrow band east of the Alleghenies, is drained by thirty-six rivers which, says Hauterive, determine the destiny of the men who people this country and condemn them to all the jealousies and discords of the mercantile and commercial world. The western section, New Mexico and California, he will not discuss, though "if ever this land is involved in European ambitions it will be as a base for the voyages to the coast of Asia and the archipelagoes in between." Over the middle section Hauterive then waxes eloquent. It is a land of milk and honey, in a frame of mountains and lakes. "There innumerable rivers, after having watered innumerable valleys, go to spill their waters into one vast flood . . . which reigns . . . over the most fertile soil of the universe" and will some day rule over a happy agricultural people preserved "forever from the vices and mercantile avidity of the other nations of the world. There a virgin soil produces spontaneously the most life-sustaining vegetables, . . fruits, grains which owe nothing to cultivation. The animal kingdom offers all sorts of species to help mankind. . . ." In the middle of this charming description, reminiscent of "exotic dreams" about the New World and the more visionary prospectuses of the land com-

[40] *Ibid.*, vol. 48, fols. 13–16. In 1798 Hauterive drafted a series of questions on the United States for Citizen Du Pont de Nemours, *voyageur de l'Institut en Amérique*, and proposed a series of maps based on these questions. Hauterive used the *Rivière du Nord*, i.e. the Hudson, for illustration here, but certain points call to mind this earlier letter to Adet. See *Aff. Étr., Cor. Pol. É.-U.*, vol. 49, fols. 330–32 vo.

panies, Hauterive pauses: "I stop, astonished myself by this volley of geography which almost made me lose sight of the end I had in mind in beginning.... A Mr. Blount, a Senator of the United States and Governor of the State of Tennessee, a state of only six months' standing," has been arrested on a charge of planning an Anglo-American "invasion of Louisiana by troops clandestinely enlisted in the United States." The government is keeping it all very quiet, which indicates, first, that they are able to do so, though certain individuals among them "are suspected of complicity"; second, that "the enterprise has failed" and that publicity alone will prevent its renewal. The cause of all this is, of course, according to Hauterive, English greed penetrating into the new states of Tennessee and Kentucky with "agents, conspirators, chiefs, factors, and assassins," causing French travelers "labeled as spies by England" to be tracked down and "massacred by savages." This will go on and, if "we do not decide to take serious measures," end in the loss of Louisiana and all Spanish interests to England. "I do not speak of the nearness of Mexico or of the fur trade. It has been proven that the latter will not cost the inhabitants of Louisiana a third of the price that the English and Canadian companies have paid for their treaty; and the connection via the Missouri with the Spanish possessions of the Southwest, as well as the ease of linking up St. Louis with these possessions by a reliable agent, appears to be ignored only by those interested in preventing them: but these subjects and dangers belong directly to Spain and it seems to me that she is beginning to do something about them."

The Blount affair appeared again in the next letter[41] about a fortnight later, 28 Messidor V (July 16), dealt with this time in more detail and with reference to the information in the hands of the Spanish Minister. Hauterive then returned to the negotiators going to France and said, "I hope very much to be able to arrive [in France] before the opening of the negotiations: for having been a witness here of all the details of the diplomatic drama, the last act of which will take place in France, I admit that my curiosity will be mortified if the first movements of this interesting act open before my arrival." All eyes here are fixed on France, said Hauterive, but opinions and desires differ. "It is hard to know what the head of the government

[41] *Ibid.*, vol. 48, fols. 66–66 vo.

desires"—probably reconciliation; his most important and influential partisans want "a brusque rupture and the nonreception of the American ministers." The "friends of France and of liberty" are not now in favor of a final and immediate accommodation; "wisdom and patriotism seem to unite to counsel the way of a prorogation until a time when the maritime destinies of the European states will be more settled."

Maurice's fifth and last letter to Alexander,[42] 4 Thermidor V (August 1), opened with a discussion of the composition of the American people reminiscent of the accounts of the more disillusioned French travelers or settlers. Hauterive was glad to be leaving "this strange country where so many emigrants from the old world have brought with them from Europe everything but a love of work, a taste for pleasure, and a feeling for the arts; this mixed population of Dutchmen, Germans, Englishmen, Scotsmen, Irishmen, Frenchmen, who have nothing in common to bind them except a sort of spirit I would call the spirit of colonization, which is a shade between the spirit of civilization and the instincts of a savage state: for to settle in the woods, fell trees, build huts of bark, live on *bouillie* ... and salt meat ... finally to trade without money, is for men from Europe to retrogress towards a state of nature."

Returning to the political scene, Hauterive noted that Marshall and Gerry had just left for Europe and continued, "I imagine that one of the three will reach Paris first and if it is Marshall, the one who has ... the highest opinion of himself, he will ... want to begin the negotiations. I do not think that the government of the Republic will share his impatience for, in truth, I see nothing pressing to be finished. The Carthaginians must be led back to Carthage. London is the Carthage of the Americans .. , the three Commissioners will be very much at sea in Paris, far from their customary direction. ... I am sure that nothing will disconcert or try them more than a cold and polite reception, rare, vague, and private discussions, and a far-distant prospect of results." According to Hauterive, this quarrel was not really worth a great deal of government time, for it was basically a commercial issue clothed in diplomatic form. Commercial interests were being served; "the American nation, the French

---

[42] *Aff. Étr., Cor. Pol. É.-U.*, vol. 48, fols. 141–43 vo.

nation, and the government of the Republic" really had little stake in it.

With this letter the correspondence under an assumed name ends. The three letters to Talleyrand follow, containing little American news except for the last letter, in which Hauterive actually told Talleyrand that in the United States *particularly,* "reasons of state are not always honest reasons," and "Gerry, you know, is not an apprentice in this sort of political morality." The "patriots," according to Hauterive, felt unrepresented by the Commissioners and he would not be surprised if some influential anti-Federalist went over on his own initiative to survey the scene. Burr had had it in mind and others were talked of, but whoever came would not be "unknown" like Adams' agents and would prove "that there exists in the United States a party of men sincerely devoted to the Gallo-American cause."[43]

On this note, the key to all French activity in the United States, Hauterive's advice on America ends. What of its value? Before attempting any evaluation it is necessary to remember Hauterive's definite biases, for he was not immune to the nationalist thinking of the day. To read him, as to read contemporary French diplomats, is to see public life in the United States largely in terms of party tensions and to see in these tensions, and in the struggle of American leaders to preserve the integrity of a new people, no nascent American nationalism, but only a bitter battle between British and French influences. Nor for that matter was he immune to revolutionary modes of expression. He reveled in invective, talked of lies, hypocrisy, ignorance, and stupidity, and characterized at least one Federalist opponent as out of his senses. Granted all this, Hauterive's reports on events—on the speeches, the negotiators, the debates, the tension, on Blount's conspiracy—were with minor exceptions valid. He told the authorities what was happening. But comparing, for example, the congressional debates with his reports of them, it becomes clear that his nationalist slant exaggerated the evil and dis-

---

[43] *Aff. Étr., Cor. Pol. É.-U.,* vol. 48, fols. 369–70 vo. This hint reminds the reader of Dr. George Logan, a Quaker who went to France in 1798 armed with a letter of introduction from Jefferson in the interest of Franco-American accord, and the consequent Logan Act passed by Congress forbidding private citizens from taking part in unauthorized diplomatic negotiations. See *Dictionary of American Biography,* XI, 359–60.

torted the picture, thus making a worse case in France for the United States than the facts warranted. Moreover, the disguise Hauterive used for part of his correspondence was on the whole a rather naïve one. His own name was Alexandre Maurice and if a casual reader might be misled by elaborate geographical treatises, personal miseries, or abstract philosophical digressions, the trained observer would probably see through these veils to the form beneath. Yet, if it was a thin disguise, it served its purpose well in allowing him to state his case more dramatically, illustrate more bluntly, and thus drive home what he had to say more effectively than could the average diplomatic agent. The disguise may well have been in his own interest as well as in any one else's.

If Hauterive's advice, as news, suffers from his nationalist slant, so does his advice as counsel, when related to the current scene. His recommendations on how to handle the American negotiators, men whose significance he had undervalued though he had given the Directory pertinent hints on Gerry, were bad. He told the Directory to delay, prorogue, defer, take time. "The sincere and ardent wish of all those who know the general spirit of the country and believe that there really is a mutual interest in the union of the two peoples is that the Ministers Plenipotentiary of the United States be not refused, be not sent back, that they be received without éclat, without manifestation of affection or bitterness, but honorably, with that phlegmatic and almost mute politeness which announces the suspension of a friendship too long ignored."[44]

Moreover, the degree of consistency between this sort of advice and the actual reception the delegates were given is such as to make it seem that Hauterive's opinions may at least have coincided with what Talleyrand felt it was safe to do, if they did not definitely influence his procedure. Hauterive actually wrote Talleyrand: "I have reason to believe that in . . . your communications with the American Commissioners the opinions and information these last [letters] contain will not have been without utility."[45] In the light of American developments this counsel was faulty and may again be laid at the door of Hauterive's French bias, which unconsciously weighted the pro-French forces in the United States. But if Haute-

[44] *Aff. Étr., Cor. Pol. É.-U.*, vol. 48, fol. 66 vo.
[45] *Ibid.*, vol. 48, fol. 291.

rive's advice was here followed in part, it was not *in toto,* for he warned repeatedly that American public opinion must be considered and that it was, even when sincerely pro-French, hurt by the Pinckney affair. Had this admonition been obeyed, the "bribe" issue would not have arisen, and French interests in the United States would surely have been better served.

On the issue of war Hauterive's counsel seems somewhat divided. While he thought that war would be most deleterious to the French cause, he also thought the issue of actual war was, granted American resources, so unlikely as to weaken his warning against its dangers. This was especially so as the war he foresaw would be the fruit not of outraged American nationalism but of British pressures on the commercial interests in power in the United States. It would be a war of manifestoes, accusations, and apologies.[46] As regards a potential war it is interesting to note that the French ministers, Fauchet and Adet, seem in the preceding years less concerned with its likelihood than were the relatively less prominent French agents, and that it is such men as Victor du Pont and Louis Guillaume Otto, noted above, who apparently drove home the seriousness of the situation to Talleyrand in the autumn and winter of 1797–1798. Hauterive's advice, falling between these two groups, was chronologically consistent. One can only speculate as to where he would have stood had he remained longer in the United States. If Hauterive was right on the evils that would result in the event of war, he does seem to have minimized its possibility more than the facts warranted. In counsel as well as in news Hauterive's national bias was a liability.

This bias, a liability on immediate issues, was much less noticeable when he moved into broader themes. There his advice, viewed both as news and as counsel, was more profound, more realistic, and ultimately of more value than that of many of his contemporaries. In a sense, the disguise of an intermediary agent subject to the militant contemporary nationalism is discarded and another more philosophic, more statesmanlike Hauterive emerges. So marked is this contrast that one may well wonder whether the passionate language he so often used on immediate issues was deliberately assumed. Some of the broader themes he picked up were common to the day. He was, for example, as obsessed as were most French agents with the

---

[46] *Aff. Étr., Cor. Pol. É.-U., Supplément,* vol. 5, fol. 160.

Canada and Louisiana mirages. Skeptical in his early days in the United States of Genêt's mad schemes, he was doing more than hinting at long-range plans in his letter on geography and his references to the amenability of the Spanish minister here.

What Hauterive had to say about *sission* was original and unusual. His French contemporaries in the United States made little if anything of it.[47] Hauterive's awareness of a potential cleavage in the United States along economic lines was probably due very largely to his strong physiocratic tendencies, his passion for *la vie agricole*, and his correspondingly bitter antipathy to mercantile and fiscal activity, which he denounced as repeatedly and vehemently as a fellow-traveler of our day would denounce capitalism. This antipathy to business activity in turn supported his anti-British bias.

On the question of American character and an evaluation of American life both Hauterive's information and his counsel were really significant and can be compared with the more outstanding commentators on the American scene. For years French eighteenth-century thinking had seen the United States as a Utopia where the philosophers' dreams would be realized. Early reports had confirmed their optimism, an optimism which, in a sense, flowered in the 1780's in Crèvecoeur's *American Farmer*, "this new man."[48] If the acrimonious reports of disillusioned settlers and travelers and the more balanced accounts of such people as La Rochefoucauld-Liancourt[49] did not destroy this vision for the majority of Frenchmen, for some the bubble was pricked and they swung to the other

---

[47] Hauterive's remarks about *sission* call to mind other contemporary references to such a possibility, and the debates on the Kentucky and Virginia Resolutions. See, for example, G. Chinard, *Thomas Jefferson* (2nd rev. ed., Boston, 1939), pp. 345 ff., and J. T. Adams, *New England in the Republic* (Boston, 1926), pp. 210, 225.

[48] For summaries of this mirage of America, see G. Chinard, *Les Réfugiés Huguenots en Amérique* (Paris, 1925), Introduction, pp. x–xxvii, and *L'Amérique et le rêve exotique* (Paris, 1913), Introduction, pp. vi–vii. See also F. S. Childs, *French Refugee Life in the United States, 1790–1800* (Baltimore, 1940), pp. 1–7. Hauterive's memoir on the United States government in 1797 (see note 21) stresses this contrast between a patriarchal and pastoral existence and utterly unscrupulous commercialism. *Aff. Étr., Mémoires et documents, É.-U.*, vol. 10, fols. 152–53.

[49] F. A. F. La Rochefoucauld-Liancourt, *Voyage dans les États-Unis* (8 vols., Paris, 1799). It is interesting to compare this with La Rochefoucauld's recently published personal diary, *Journal de voyage en Amérique et d'un séjour à Philadelphie . . .*, J. Marchand, ed. (Paris, Baltimore, 1940), and with Moreau de St. Méry, *Voyage aux États-Unis, 1793–1798*, S. Nims, ed. (New Haven, 1913), neither of which were available to eighteenth-century Frenchmen.

A Secret Agent's Advice on America 43

extreme, seeing in the contemporary American only the merchant avid for gain, and the undisciplined, antisocial frontiersman.

According to Hauterive, neither of these points of view was true; "the Americans are, I assure you, neither admirable nor detestable men." Merchants—and he hated merchants—were merchants in America as well as elsewhere. Frontiersmen were frontiersmen; they "work diligently to acquire what is necessary, till the soil carelessly because it is superabundant, are ignorant because isolated." The limitations of this type of life inevitably narrowed or destroyed the life of the intellect and made impossible "the development of what the French call *sensibilité,* a word more unknown in this country than is the quality, for there is no expression for it in the language."[50] It was too soon, according to Hauterive, for a national pattern to have emerged. This view, neither starry-eyed nor cynical, which Hauterive urged the French officials to use as a yardstick, was both valid and valuable.

Nor was this Hauterive's only appeal for facts and a balanced approach. In congratulating Talleyrand on his appointment as Minister of Exterior Relations, Hauterive was happy that "the discussion of our interests in the United States will finally be really understood and that we will see an end to this indifference and inconsistency which lack of knowledge of actual conditions here more than anything else has brought into the policy of the . . . Republic towards the New World." Talleyrand, he trusts, will have facts, and will not succumb to the "passionate judgment" or "frivolous dissertations" circulating in Europe.[51]

Finally, Hauterive sensed the future grandeur of the New World, our incredible, our frightening resources, the majesty of the Mississippi valley, and the coming power of the United States, for "whatever the precocious vices of its rapid colonization" it is striding forward, and "its progressive growth" will "before a century has elapsed have changed the . . . colonial system of the universe and the relative position of all civilized society."[52]

In his appeal for facts and information, not dreams; for reason,

---

[50] *Aff. Étr., Cor. Pol. É.-U.,* vol. 48, fols. 141 vo.–142. Hauterive says elsewhere: "It is time . . . to observe with care, to study without prejudice . . . to appeal to reason, not to the imagination." *Aff. Étr., Mém. et Doc. É.-U.,* vol. 10, fol. 153 vo.

[51] *Aff. Étr., Cor. Pol. É.-U.,* vol. 48, fol. 265 vo.

[52] *Ibid., Supplément,* vol. 5, fol. 166.

not emotion; for experience and understanding; in his occasional glimpses of what lies ahead, Hauterive goes beyond the self-centered nationalism of the day into the larger concepts on which any mature and valid diplomacy, any sound internationalism, must ultimately rest. Because of this it is possible to conclude by quoting the signature of his direct letters, *Salut et respect, Hauterive.*

"BIG JIM" LARKIN:
A FOOTNOTE TO NATIONALISM*

JESSE D. CLARKSON

NATIONALISM, like sin, is a phenomenon so familiar as to defy definition or even precise characterization. For humans to cope with sin, the limits of which can be judged only by God, is infinitely more difficult than to deal with crime; for historians to treat of nationalism, the pervasiveness of which is so clear to all, is far more taxing than to recount the rise and fall of states. In both cases the criteria of evaluation fluctuate too widely on the basis of concepts linked with personal beliefs. Their very ubiquity hampers objective analysis. In particular, what nationalism has meant to divers men in various times and places has varied so widely that it has been extraordinarily difficult to find a satisfactory common denominator. Among other tasks Carlton Hayes essayed to trace a basic common pattern running through all its protean manifestations.

In a work first published eighteen years ago, Professor Hayes made a genetic approach to the problem, distinguishing five principal successive stages in *The Historical Evolution of Modern Nationalism:* "humanitarian," "Jacobin," "traditional," "liberal," and "integral" nationalism. Although it would be a work of supererogation to define each of these, it is of some interest to apply these categories, as a test of their validity, to the history of a country which he left out of direct account in his generalized discussion. The test will be, perhaps, the more rigorous because the very word "Irish" has, in the Anglo-Saxon world, so long been virtually synonymous with "aberrant."

At first blush, indeed, Ireland seems to contradict one of the most usual criteria of nationalism, the role of the national language. An Irish language does indeed exist, and with vigorous official support, but mainly as a grievous nuisance to Irishmen, who would prefer to cherish it as a museum piece, playing at most the role enjoyed by Latin in American colleges of a generation ago. Etiquette requires

---

* ED. NOTE: A fuller development of the theme of Irish nationalism has been made by Jesse Clarkson in *Labour and Nationalism in Ireland* (New York, 1925), and "The Irish Question," *Social Science Encyclopedia* (New York, 1932), IV, 285-95.

that government offices reply to inquiries with brief formal acknowledgments in Irish, but common sense dictates that they follow up with a serious answer in English. Labels such as *"Mna"* and *"Fir"* may suffice to prevent embarrassment to ladies and gentlemen, but more vitally peremptory messages, such as "No Smoking" or "Emergency Exit," are conveyed in the most readily understandable language. One of the most frequently voiced complaints against the long De Valera regime was the widespread use of Irish as the language of instruction in primary schools. Since at home and at play (at least outside the ever-shrinking *Gaeltacht*) the children hear only their native English, the results of such instruction promise to be somewhat bizarre. There seems some justice in the idea that the utmost that can be hoped for in reviving the use of Gadhelic would be the creation of a bilingual bureaucratic upper class, ruling over an English-speaking mass—a paradoxical reversal of the Conquest, for the school and the street sign cannot hope to compete with the home and the market place—or with the Church. Much as Irish nationalists have dreamed of its restoration, the ancient language has certainly not been an actively contributing force to the Irish nationalist urge.

Like modern nationalism in general, Irish nationalism has a long antecedent history. Over a period of centuries—perhaps since Gog and Magog brought to Erin the "stone of Scone," the stone on which Jacob dreamed his dream—the inhabitants of a peculiarly well-defined and isolated territory (or the ruling portion of them) have resented and resisted the encroachments of people from across the waters. Unsupported waves of invaders, whether Danes or Anglo-Normans, were readily enough absorbed; only in the small and fluctuating "Pale" did alien ways establish themselves. Not until England, under the Tudors, began to gather her own strength as a nation was it possible, by the "plantation" of Ulster, for the larger island to make serious impress on the smaller. Not until Cromwell was thoroughgoing conquest effected.

It was this conquest, and the ever-swelling tide of diverse alien immigration to the rising Irish towns, that ultimately made Irish nationalism possible. Throughout these earlier centuries the mass of the population were Celtic, Catholic peasants. Resistance to England had been not their affair, but the concern of the landed aristocrats, few of whom were of Celtic lineage, or deeply concerned about religion. Nor did the nationalism that rose with the growth of an Irish middle class have its roots in the Irish people. Rather it reflected the cosmopolitan stirrings of the Enlightenment, the sometimes peevish criticism of the traditionally existing state of affairs, so characteristic of eighteenth-century intellectuals throughout Europe. The dignified protests of the physician Molyneux,[1] the biting irony of Dean Swift,[2] and the fiery pamphlets of the apothecary Lucas[3] perfectly exemplify what has been described as "humanitarian nationalism." Swift, indeed, was the client of Bolingbroke, imposed by his influence on a reluctant Dublin. Their writings amused and delighted the intellectuals, but no one, either in 1715 or in 1745, thought of converting England's difficulty into Ireland's opportunity. It remained for their greater successors, Henry Flood (1732–1791) and Henry Grattan (1746–1820), to found the first Irish nationalist movement. Using the Irish Volunteers and non-importation agreements as weapons during the American struggle for independence, they achieved the legislative independence of the Irish Parliament and the lifting of restrictions on Irish trade. Significantly, both "the rival Harry's" were sons of English officials in Ireland; both depended on exclusively Protestant voters. Flood served for years in an appointive post under the British crown, and Grattan, after the Union, sat loyally and uncomplainingly in the Parliament at Westminster. Their greatest and most lasting achievements—repeal of the penal laws against the Catholic majority and admission of Catholics to the Irish franchise (though not to the Irish Parliament)—were distinctly humanitarian.

Much weaker in tangible accomplishments, but more powerfully inspiring to later generations, were Ireland's "Jacobin nationalists." Paradoxically, the first fighting Irish nationalists reflected alien, rather than native, influences. The Society of United Irishmen was formed among the Presbyterians of Belfast and shared the internationalist dreams of the early stage of the French Revolution.

---

[1] William Molyneux (1656–1698), *The Case of Ireland's Being Bound by Acts of Parliament in England Stated* (1698).

[2] Jonathan Swift (1667–1745), *Proposal for the Universal Use of Irish Manufactures* (1720); the "Drapier" letters (1724); *Modest Proposal for Preventing the Children of Poor People in Ireland from Being a Burden to their Parents* (1729).

[3] Charles Lucas (1713–1771), *Addresses to the Lord Mayor* (1748–1749).

The support of the Defenders, the organized Catholic peasantry of the North, brought division, not strength, to the movement. Wolfe Tone's[4] ringing appeal to the "men of no property" and his martyr's death obscured the fact that his inspiration and his fighting force were drawn almost wholly from France, not from Ireland. The Society of United Irishmen left few traces; Napper Tandy (1740–1803) was almost the sole survivor of the "wearing of the green" in 1798, while the beloved Robert Emmet (1778–1803) paid on the gallows for his attempt in 1803 to storm Dublin Castle with a band of eighty men.

For conservative "traditional nationalism" there could be no place in Ireland, a subject nation, where nationalism must spell revolt, if not revolution. Burke, though Irish born and Irish educated, though ever eloquent and always "agin the government," was impervious to Irish nationalism. Only personal idiosyncrasy could turn an Irish landlord, whose title rested on English law and whose security in the enjoyment of his property rested on English power, into a champion of Ireland's claims as a nation. The rare exceptions, such as Lord Edward Fitzgerald (1763–1798), who could contemplate the Whiteboys with equanimity, of necessity sympathized with the principles of the French Revolution. Nor could the spokesmen of the Roman Catholic Church, however antipathetic to Jacobinism, find comfort in the preservation of Irish traditional institutions. Despite the improvement in the status of Irish Catholics effected by Grattan's Parliament, the established church continued to be a foreign imposition, and the overwhelming majority of the Irish population still lived under political disabilities which obviously could not be wholly removed without resorting to at least the threat of the use of revolutionary force.

In the first half of the nineteenth century, therefore, the only possible Irish nationalism was "liberal nationalism," in a period when liberalism was still a revolutionary force. Its greatest champion was Daniel O'Connell (1775–1847), whose career so perfectly exemplifies the truths that "the movement attracted the allegiance of the middle classes,"[5] that "each liberal national state in serving its true

---

[4] Theobald Wolfe Tone (1763–1798).

[5] Carlton J. H. Hayes, *The Historical Evolution of Modern Nationalism* (New York, 1948), p. 158.

interests and those of its own citizens would be serving the true interests of humanity at large,"⁶ that "government should be of property-owners inasmuch as the rest of the people do not know their own interests,"⁷ and that "liberal nationalists were high-minded, optimistic, and devoted to the cause of peace."⁸ A Celt descended from ancient chieftains, a Catholic educated in revolutionary France, and an advocate of outstanding ability, O'Connell never strayed from the path of legality. In '98 he kept his skirts clear of the United Irish contamination; in 1803 he did duty against the Emmet rising. Outstanding among his characteristics—and a main factor in winning him the highest place amongst Irish leaders—was his whole-souled attachment to the cause of his religion in Ireland. O'Connell was too practical to be an ultramontane; he himself maintained he would as soon take his politics from Constantinople as from Rome. For him, under Irish conditions, it was a question not of elevating papal authority above the civil power, but of securing the fullest freedom for the Catholic Church under the inescapable aegis of a British Protestant government. Hence O'Connell came to be one of the foremost champions of the "liberal Catholicism" that was later to give so much anguish to Pius IX.

O'Connell's Catholic Association was built by the devoted work of the Irish priesthood, and the Clare election of 1828, though to Wellington it held the menace of revolution, was entirely within the law. For the ensuing enactment of Catholic Emancipation he willingly paid with legal disfranchisement of four-fifths of the Irish peasantry. Although forced by political considerations to lend support to the "tithe war," he stoutly refused to condone any tendency to refuse payment of rent. Neither Irish "Ribandism"⁹ nor English Chartism received any sympathy from the Liberator. His reliance was ever on the urban middle class, for close to his heart lay the advancement of Irish trade and industry: he "would to God, children of 13 years old in Ireland could earn the money which the English

---

⁶ *Ibid.*, p. 159.
⁷ *Ibid.*
⁸ *Ibid.*, p. 160.
⁹ The Ribbonmen, successors of the Defenders of the 1790's, were the nineteenth-century expression of agrarian discontent. Specifically Catholic, in contrast to the earlier Whiteboys, their chief significance was as the forerunners of Michael Davitt's Land League.

factory children might have earned"[10]; his remedy for "the misfortune of Ireland" was "only to be created by tempting capitalists to the country, in order that having cheap labour they might have profits from it."[11] Even in his agitation for repeal of the Union he did not envisage dissolution of a "British connexion." Although the fall of his Liberal friends and the formation of a Tory ministry under Peel (1841) impelled him to launch a vigorous campaign for Repeal, he never regarded it as "worth the price of one drop of blood." In the face of Peel's determined opposition and notwithstanding the undoubted ardent support of the overwhelming bulk of Irish Catholics, O'Connell canceled his plans for a monster demonstration on Clontarf sands (1843). After his death his followers, less willing than King Dan to risk the wrath of Rome, became the tools, rather than the leaders, of the priestly organization O'Connell had effected; known as the "Pope's Brass Band," they were maintained at Westminster by the votes of Irish townsmen and were content to ignore the misery of the famine-stricken Irish peasantry.

The Young Irelanders represented a radically divergent type of "liberal nationalists." Free from religious prejudice and largely "Anglo-Saxon" in their personal antecedents, they yet burned with an ingrained hatred of all things English. Consequently, they could not consciously accept Benthamite teachings. The doctrines of the "Manchester School" they explicitly and emphatically rejected. "Oh, no! Oh, no! ask us not to copy English vice, and darkness, and misery and impiety; give us the worst wigwam in Ireland and a dry potato rather than Anglicise us."[12] Their inspiration came rather from the Continent, as the very name of their movement suggests. As incurably romantic—and as ineffective—as Mazzini, Thomas Osborne Davis (1814–1845) could not refrain from hoping for good even from "the filthy mass of national treason that forms the man's

---

[10] Speech at the General Association, Oct. 31, 1837, in *Life and Times of Daniel O'Connell with Sketches of His Contemporaries Compiled from the Works of W. J. O'N. Daunt, Mr. Fegan, R. L. Sheil, etc., etc.* (2 vols., Dublin, 1867), II, 599; cf. also W. Fagan, *The Life and Times of Daniel O'Connell* (2 vols., Cork, 1847), II, 575–76.

[11] Speech in the House of Commons, Feb. 13, 1838; in Hansard's *Parliamentary Debates*, 3rd series, XL, 1084–97.

[12] Thomas Davis, "Udalism and Feudalism," in *Essays of Thomas Davis* (Dundalk, 1914), p. 75.

part of many an Irish lord."[13] Social revolution formed no part of the creed of John Mitchel (1815-1875): despite his delight that "Louis Blanc and the insurgent of Lyons, Albert, Ouvrier"[14] had in February 1848 discarded "the English or famine system," he had no regret that in the June Days the "communist" workmen "were swept from the streets with grape and canister—the only way of dealing with such unhappy creatures."[15] Far more inspired than O'Connell, but far less in tune with Irish sentiment, and lacking the friendship of the Catholic clergy, Young Ireland failed in the great years of revolution to produce any result more tangible than the easily squelched rising of Smith O'Brien at Ballingarry in Tipperary (October 1848).

One among the Young Irelanders, James Fintan Lalor (1807-1849), whose physical disabilities prevented his active participation in the movement, formulated the true gospel of Irish discontent. "The principle I state and mean to stand upon, is this, that the entire ownership of Ireland, moral and material, up to the sun and down to the centre, is vested of right in the people of Ireland; that they, and none but they, are the land-owners and law-makers of this island; that all laws are null and void not made by them; and all titles to land invalid not conferred and confirmed by them; and that this full right of ownership may and ought to be asserted and enforced by any and all means which God has put in the power of man. . . . Let laws and institutions say what they will, this fact will be stronger than all laws, and prevail against them—the fact that those who own your land will make your laws, and command your liberties, and your lives. . . . Against them [the rights of property] I assert the true and indefeasible right of property—the right of our people to live in this land, and possess it—to live in it in security, comfort, and independence, and to live in it by their own labour, on their own land, as God and nature intended them to do."[16]

The spiritual successors of Young Ireland, the Fenians, organized as the "Irish Republican Brotherhood," reflected a belated throw-

---

[13] "Ireland's People," *ibid.*, p. 174.
[14] Cited in James Connolly, *Labour in Ireland* (Dublin and London, 1920), p. 181.
[15] John Mitchel, *Jail Journal* (New York, 1854), p. 98; entry of Nov. 22, 1848.
[16] Letter to *The Irish Felon*, in L. Fogarty, *James Fintan Lalor, Patriot and Political Essayist (1807-1849)* (Dublin and London, 1918), pp. 60-66 *passim*.

back to the principles of Jacobinism. Democratic as the Young Irelanders were not, the Fenians were persuaded that "It is a waste of time and labour, or worse, to endeavour to arouse the upper and middle classes to a sense of the duty they owe their country. Whatever is not thoroughly rotten in these classes will follow the people. ... It is the *people* who have kept the national faith alive; and whatever of that faith exists among the 'higher orders' is derived from the people. ... In the darkest hour of her dark history the people were true to Ireland. Whoever was false, they never were. Whoever denied her they never did. When she was betrayed and scourged, and spat upon, the hands that lovingly supported her fainting form were the blistered hands of labour. Oh! brave toilers, surely it is reserved for you alone to lift her to her place among the nations."[17] Handicapped by the irresponsibility of American leadership, bitterly opposed by the clergy, and lacking support among the peasantry, the Fenians in 1867 proved as impotent as had the Young Irelanders. Yet their spirit lingered on in Ireland, and the survivors of the "I.R.B." were one of the contributing elements in the Easter Rising of 1916. It was a former Fenian, Michael Davitt, whose organization of the Land League was to give deep meaning to the Home Rule movement under Parnell.

The founders of the Home Rule movement, Isaac Butt (1813–1879) and Charles Stewart Parnell (1846–1891), were concerned not with the realization of an ideal nationalism, but with carrying forward the political work of Grattan and O'Connell. Though both leaders were themselves Protestants and as such objects of suspicion to the clergy, they succeeded in instilling, under lay leadership, a vigor that Irish politics had lacked since the Famine. It was given to them, though not in their lifetime, to achieve a larger measure of success in the realization of Ireland's political independence than had any of their more ambitious predecessors. Their achievement, however, was made possible less by the disciplined parliamentary obstruction of Parnell, than by the acceptance of the argument of Michael Davitt (1846–1906) that "It is exhibiting a callous indifference to the state of social degradation to which the power of the landlords of Ireland has sunk our peasantry to ask them to plod on in sluggish misery from sire to son, from age to age, until we by force

[17] *Irish People*, Jan. 23, 1864.

of party power may free the country."[18] Davitt brought organized leadership to "Whiteboyism," and successfully challenged clerical influence, calling on the aroused peasantry to "convert Peter's pence into Parnell pounds." The Land League and the policy of boycott did for Parnell's Nationalists what the Catholic Association had done for O'Connell. If the English Liberals, outmatched at Westminster, proved incompetent to deliver Home Rule, the Conservative advocates of maintaining the Union were moved to find in land purchase a solution for the agrarian problem of Ireland. Fintan Lalor's ideal was realized, though not by his methods, and England's Unionists ultimately were faced to their cost with realization of the truth of his principle that "those who own your land will make your laws"; the "English interest" in Ireland did not long survive the removal of landlordism.

During the troubled years that followed the "Parnell split," the allegiance of Irish nationalists was divided. In the midst of the confusion a new voice made itself heard, that of the newspaper *Sinn Fein* (at first called *The United Irishman*). Its editor, Arthur Griffith (1872–1922), was a Dublin printer of Welsh antecedents, who had spent a couple of years in South Africa. A devoted Parnellite and something of a Gaelic Leaguer, he had belonged for a time to the I.R.B. The pages of his paper were open to unpaid but distinguished contributors of varied shades, but Griffith's own policy was unwavering—to establish the independence of Ireland (at least to the extent that Hungary possessed independence) and to secure it, not from Westminster, nor yet by physical force, but by passive resistance and self-help of Irish men and women alone. His bitterness against the English and all their works ("Whether the English call themselves Liberals or Tories, Imperialists or Socialists—they are always the English"[19]) was matched only by his hatred of those Irish whose doings did not correspond to his concept of an "Irish Ireland." Savagely he denounced the new school of Irish literati and personally led in the breaking-up of a performance of Synge's *Playboy of the Western World* at the Abbey Theatre. In Griffith there survived no trace of the "humanitarian nationalism" of the eighteenth

---

[18] Speech reported in *Boston Pilot*, Dec. 21, 1878, in Michael Davitt, *The Fall of Feudalism in Ireland* (London and New York, 1904), p. 132.

[19] *United Irishman*, Nov. 19, 1904.

century; he had only the fiercest scorn for "the contemplation of English Friendship, Solidarity of Labour, Co-operative Commonwealth, Universal Brotherhood, and all other Brummagem wares in Cheap Jack's Budget."[20] He was scandalized because "It has been recently discovered that the Irish workingman is not an Irish workingman at all. He is a unit of humanity, a human label of internationalism, a Brother of the men over the water who rule his country. ... Race, tradition, nationality, are non-entities, and history and its formative influences on character and outlook a figment. He is exalted from the meaningless title of Irishman to the noble one of Brother."[21]

Griffith's nationalism may, in limited measure, be taken as the first Irish manifestation of the onset of "integral nationalism." He went far beyond the Fenian principle, "Oughtn't it to be enough for a man to be for Ireland?",[22] enunciated by James Stephens. "As we have spoken to the capitalist," wrote Griffith, "we shall speak to the workman in Ireland, and tell him that his duty to his class can never transcend his duty to his country—that the interests of Ireland are above the special interest of any of its classes, as they are above the special interest of any of its sects, and of any of its parties. The name of Irishman shall never be secondary to the name of aristocrat or democrat, capitalist or labourer, Catholic or Protestant, Unionist or Home Ruler, whilst we live with a hand to write or a tongue to speak."[23] Had Griffith possessed a personality comparable to his integrity, had his moral fervor not been combined with an aversion to the use of physical force (save in incidents such as the horse-whipping of an editor), Griffith might have emerged as the leader of a co-ordinated nation. "Ireland lives today because not men of one class but men of all classes spent their lives in her service, and the man who tells the Irish people that Ireland must use all her energies to combat any foe other than the people of England who stand between Ireland and self-government, tells them the lie that maintains foreign rule in this country and keeps poverty enthroned in the

---

[20] "Re Nationalists and Labour," *Sinn Fein,* Dec. 6, 1913.
[21] "The Economics of the Food-Ship," *Sinn Fein,* Oct. 4, 1913.
[22] *Irish People,* Sept. 2, 1865.
[23] "The Crisis in Wexford," *Sinn Fein,* Sept. 16, 1911.

most fertile island that the hand of God planted in the bosom of the Atlantic."[24]

A wing of the Sinn Feiners, more alert to social evils than Griffith, was at least willing to debate the merits of the labor war then being waged in Ireland by "St. Larkin." To this group of ardently mystical nationalists, so reminiscent in their hatred of all "English importations"[25] of the Young Irelanders of the 1840's, belonged Patrick Pearse (Padraic M'Piarais), who joined hands with Tom Clarke, an old-time Fenian, and with the doggedly socialist nationalist, James Connolly, to lead the hopeless but sacrificial Easter Rising of 1916. As things went, however, it was not the old Sinn Fein, in any of its phases, but the accidental De Valera that drew profit from the Rising and from the later guerilla war, to both of which Griffith was unsympathetic.

The work of Griffith went for naught; the Irish nation of today, despite its severance of all formal links with England, would scarcely have been pleasing to him. For to the "man in the street," the "educated" man in the street today, the distinctive fact about Ireland is simply that it is Catholic. His Catholicism sums up his nationalism. He cannot conceive of a true Irishman who is not a Catholic; to him the long list of Protestant fighters for Ireland's cause are mere "perverts," accidental people not to be taken seriously. It is the Church that rules Ireland today, and no politician, however anxious to differentiate himself from his fellows, would dream of challenging that basic fact. Although the issue of "partition" leads Eire to refuse to promise use of naval bases, few would question that, in the event of war with Russia, Catholic hatred of Bolshevism would drive her to offer her services on any terms.

One aspect of Irish nationalism has been scanted in this brief survey of its evolution. It is the contribution of Irish labor, led by Jim Larkin (1876–1947) and his chief lieutenant, James Connolly (1870–1916). The latter, though ever a convinced socialist and one

---

[24] "The English-made Strike," *Sinn Fein,* Sept. 30, 1911.

[25] "If foreign Socialistic doctrines are being imported, it is as the antidote to the poison of the Capitalist theory, which we also imported. The primary evil is the English occupation, . . and the cleansing of Ireland from the foreigner will involve the abolition of his inhuman and degrading social system." "Spiritual and Material Development," *Irish Freedom,* December 1913.

of the major leaders in the Easter Rising, became reconciled to the Church before his execution and died a devout Catholic. Larkin, a religious sceptic, a man who repeatedly visited Russia in a sympathetic spirit, who was ever ready to challenge any opponent of the cause of the workers, chose to die in the odor of sanctity, clasping in his hands a rosary given him by the Catholic archbishop of Dublin. All the other exemplars of Irish nationalism reviewed in these pages may be tidily fitted into one or another of the categories defined by Professor Hayes; even the systematically Marxist Connolly might find a place in this classification. Larkin, however, presents special problems. Belonging under none of the rubrics, violating all the canons, he seems to require a special footnote.[26]

Larkin's nationalism, one is tempted to suggest, was transmitted through his genes. His family came from the county of Armagh, seat of St. Patrick's episcopate, in Ulster, where his grandfather was a relatively well-to-do farmer and father of fifteen children. The boys were infected with Fenianism, which was anathema to most of the peasantry, obedient as they were to the Roman clergy: the oldest, Barney, taught "hedge-school" and ultimately fled for his life and disappeared; the others drifted away to Liverpool, the youngest arriving there on the day of the execution of the "Manchester Martyrs."[27] There he married a girl from a farming family near Newry and, constantly plagued by ill-health, worked for twenty years as a fitter for an engineering firm, while eagerly following the work of Parnell and Davitt. At his early death in 1887, he left five children and no resources, save the good will of his employers, who accepted the two older sons as apprentices without the usual £50 fee.[28]

Liverpool could scarcely be regarded as a place of exile for an Irish family, and the indomitable widow remained strong in her

---

[26] A thorough study of the life of Jim Larkin would be a fascinating and rewarding task. The varied scene of his activities—England, Ireland, America, and Russia—the manifold facets of his interests, and the profound impression his personality made on all who met him, whether as friend or as foe, would provide very rich material. It is earnestly to be hoped that his biography will be written while his associates, relatives, and enemies are still able to provide assistance.

[27] Allen, Larkin, and O'Brien, hanged on Nov. 23, 1867, for the shooting of a police officer during the rescue of two fellow Fenians from a prison van.

[28] The facts of Larkin's personal life rest mainly on material supplied by his sister Delia (Mrs. Patrick Colgan).

nationalist and Catholic faith. It offered, however, wider horizons than were available across the Irish Sea. Young Jim, the tall and husky second son, born in 1876, who had avoided school as much as practicable, developed a strong resistance to learning the engineering trade. Shifting jobs frequently, at seventeen he shipped as a stowaway on a vessel bound for America; his experiences in irons in the hold gave him good cause ever after to put full meaning into one of his favorite epithets—"rat." Returned to Liverpool, he sought work on the docks and was very soon advanced to be a "boss." During this period Jim Larkin was able to earn better wages than his father had ever made. His personality and industry made him a favorite with employers and men alike, and he became the mainstay of the family. Notwithstanding the strenuous character of his work, he regularly spent his evenings in reading for hours in the attic. Thus, building on the groundwork laid at home by his father, he acquired the store of knowledge that was to stand him in good stead as an impromptu orator, for Larkin was ever able at a moment's notice to mingle blistering epithets with literary and classical allusions, knit together with a thoroughly Irish native humor.

His outstanding characteristics throughout his life were his quick sympathy for all the downtrodden and his flaming resentment for all forms of injustice. In his years as a docker his employers valued him highly, not only for his ability and energy but also for his crusade against drunkenness, and were willing to overlook the vigor with which he threw himself into a strike, from which he, as a "boss" for the Harrison Line, had nothing personally to gain. Larkin, however, who had while still in his teens become a charter-member of the Independent Labour Party, declined to return to his job and accepted the less lucrative post of organizer of the National Union of Dock Labourers. Soon shunted to Belfast by the jealous General Secretary, Jimmy Sexton, Jim Larkin, at thirty, found himself proclaimed throughout the Irish press as the "English strike organiser" in Ireland. Repudiated by his union for causing too great a drain on its funds, he launched at the beginning of 1909 the Irish Transport and General Workers Union.

The story of his achievements in the labor world is not here of primary concern. The magnetism and courage that poured from him and the independent life and vigor that surged up among the apparently hopeless casual laborers of Dublin, Belfast, Cork, and other Irish towns are well-known phenomena. From its meager beginnings (its original assets were a table, a couple of chairs, two empty bottles, and a candle; the Larkin family furniture on occasion was sold to eke out strike pay), the I.T. & G.W.U. rose swiftly to dominate the Irish Trades Union Congress and become the backbone of the nascent Irish Labour Party. Though the Union fell into more cautious hands after Larkin's departure for America in a vain attempt to raise funds and after Connolly's willing martyrdom in 1916, and although the breach caused by his attempt to resume direction after his return in 1923 has not yet been wholly healed, the essence of his work remained. The Dublin slums are no longer the nauseous scene of fetid despair they were before his coming.

Larkin has sometimes been characterized as a revolutionary syndicalist. Certainly he brought to Ireland the "new unionism" with all its syndicalist implications. Certainly his methods and his intent were revolutionary, both in Ireland and in America. Yet he regarded himself not as a syndicalist, but as a socialist. Naturally his hopes went out to the Soviet Union, the self-proclaimed land of socialism; if his experience in Russia was too limited thoroughly to disillusion him, his visits there were marked by violent quarrels over methods and near objectives. He was widely read in socialist literature, but he had an instinctive distrust of any nicely worked-out philosophy. His own activities were ever concerned with trade-unionism, though not in the old bowler-hatted sense. No mere apostle of divine discontent, he had ever in mind practical existing conditions—and the desire to remedy them in the here and now.

If Larkin as a social revolutionary does not fit readily into the usual pigeonholes, the definition of his nationalism is no more simple. If twentieth-century nationalism is dominated by the concepts of "integral nationalism," Jim Larkin was distinctly old-fashioned. The *Führer-Prinzip* was to him wholly unacceptable. Himself an almost unparalleled leader of men, he constantly urged: "Put your trust in no man, you will therefore never be confounded."[29] To the Dublin bakers and confectioners, when they appealed to him for guidance in reorganizing their union, he replied: "It was the duty of every man to see to it that self-respect and self-reliance was the key

---

[29] "Our Anniversary," *Irish Worker*, I, 52, May 11, 1912.

note of their organization."[30] With Griffith's *Sinn Fein* he had no point of contact. Though De Valera shared none of Larkin's social views, it was Larkin who in 1927 was most insistent that the leader of Fianna Fail abandon his doctrinaire views and enter the Dail as the alternative to the all-powerful Cosgrove government.

Larkin's nationalism was innate and intense; it found expression constantly hand in hand with his labor agitation. *The Irish Worker and People's Advocate,* "edited by Jim Larkin," which first appeared in May 1911, always carried on its masthead the words of James Fintan Lalor, "The principle I state and mean to stand upon is:—that the entire ownership of Ireland, moral and material, up to the sun and down to the centre, is vested of right in the people of Ireland." In the first issues a reprint of Lalor's *The Rights of Ireland* occupied the place of honor on the first page. A note proudly proclaimed: "This Journal is exclusively set up by hand labour. Printed on Irish paper, with Irish ink." Denunciations of prominent personages or leading firms ordering goods across the Channel were frequent. "Irish Ireland Notes" were a regular feature.[31] In an interview reprinted from the Edinburgh *Catholic Herald* Larkin replied to the question, "What is your great need at the present time?", by saying, "Men versed in the history and literature of their own land."[32] Classes in the Irish language were regularly announced in *The Irish Worker,* and Larkin's own sons were sent to Scoil Ite, though Big Jim himself could find no leisure to learn the language.

St. Patrick's Day was regularly celebrated with an appropriate editorial.[33] The one hundred and fiftieth anniversary of the birth of Wolfe Tone was commemorated by an editorial in which Larkin readily acknowledged, "There may have been greater men on our country's roll, more lovable, more original, greater in their conceptions, men whose ideals were beyond Tone's imagination." Yet, asserted Larkin, "It was that love, that intense desire to serve Ireland, that was the reason for the man, Tone's, success in life, and his

---

[30] *Ibid.,* I, 53, May 18, 1912.
[31] Under the subheading "Arthur's Anglicised Irish," the quality of the Irish in a play published in *Sinn Fein* was severely attacked. "We would advise all students of the Irish language to shun the Irish of Arthur's sheet if they want to acquire a knowledge of Irish-Irish." *Irish Worker,* I, 44, March 16, 1912.
[32] *Ibid.,* I, 53, May 18, 1912.
[33] "St. Patrick's Day in the Morning," *ibid.,* I, 44, March 16, 1912, and II, 43, March 15, 1913.

triumph in death.... Tone was a Republican, a nationalist, an internationalist, a man who sought liberty not for himself but for his fellows—liberty of thought, liberty of action, liberty to live.... Liberty has reason to be proud of her son, Tone...."[34] That year's pilgrimage to Bodenstown was reported in full,[35] including the remarks of Tom Clarke ("who does not seem much the worse for his sixteen years' imprisonment") and the address of Pat Pearse, the young schoolteacher whom the Easter Rising of 1916 was to make briefly the first president of the Irish Republic. Another editorial, reporting Larkin's attendance at an "Anniversary Celebration of the Birth of Robert Emmet," reflected bitter disappointment that the learned speaker had failed to do Emmet justice: "Of the millions who were faithful—of the millions who proved their worth in their daily lives on the field or the scaffold—none can claim pre-eminence before our glorious young martyr, Robert Emmet; ... Whatever he attempted he excelled in.... Let the life of the beautiful one be an inspiration to us; ... Let us then rejoice that it was vouchsafed to this nation that such a man was given unto us as an example for us to imitate, and, as an inspiration, to uplift us, that his ideal shall be our ideal; that the city beautiful, that was so plain and dear to him, shall also be the city beautiful, for us to strive for and enjoy...."[36]

For professional nationalists Larkin had no respect. Even the Gaelic League did not escape his strictures. When its treasurer protested because he was not allowed to vote when he gave the election officials his name in Irish, *The Irish Worker* commented: "We wonder does he use Irish when he collects his rents?"[37] At a suggestion that the Gaelic League, as an economy measure, dismiss some of its clerks, Larkin inquired: "Fancy the amount that will be saved when a clerk earning £39 a year is dismissed. Why not reduce the salary of the higher officials? ... Or what about the Organiser who bought a farm in the South of Ireland for £1000 some years ago? Couldn't his yearly salary be reduced by £39 and keep on the chap who luxuriates on that sum?"[38] For the politicians, of whatever desig-

[34] "Tone's Resurgam," *ibid.*, III, 5, June 21, 1913.
[35] "At the Grave of Wolfe Tone," *ibid.*, III, 6, June 28, 1913.
[36] "Emmet," *ibid.*, II, 42, March 8, 1913.
[37] "The Modern Gael," *ibid.*, II, 35, Jan. 18, 1913.
[38] "Economy in the Gaelic League," *ibid.*, II, 36, Jan. 25, 1913.

nation, he had scarcely any printable words; at best, they were "common-sense nationalists," interested only in jobs and contracts. Over the Home Rule Bill itself he refused to become excited: "We will be gratified at seeing it become Law immediately for we of the working class have postponed many urgent questions pending the passage of this Bill; and we want to get to work again.... Home Rule —shades of Mitchel, Davitt, Lalor, Emmet, and Tone...."[39]

It was not that Home Rule was of no account to him: "We are demanding it because of whom we are; because it is in our very marrow; because of the men who died that we might live; because, in a word, we want Home Rule that WE MAY RULE OUR OWN HOME."[40] His criticism was rather that Redmond's acceptance of the Bill as a "final settlement" of Ireland's claims to nationhood seemed to give the lie to Parnell's words, inscribed on his monument in O'Connell Street: "No man has a right to fix the Boundary to the March of a Nation; No man has a right to say to his Country thus far shall thou go and no further. We have never attempted to fix the Ne-Plus-Ultra to the progress of Ireland's Nationhood, and We never shall."[41]

A subsidiary, but by no means unimportant, virtue that Larkin saw in Home Rule was the consequences he hoped it would have on sectarianism in the North of Ireland: "My friends, there is no question but that Religion is dragged into this struggle in the North for economic reasons. The employers know that given Home Rule the working class would coalesce, and they are determined to keep them divided."[42] His first headquarters as a labor organizer in Ireland had been in Belfast, and he had come to know well and to understand the techniques by which Orange workers were whipped up to brutal frenzy against their Catholic fellows by bold-faced incitement and free drinks. July 12, accepted as the anniversary of the Battle of the Boyne, was traditionally a day of rioting and head-breaking. In 1907, in the midst of Larkin's first great struggle, it had threatened to destroy the unity of the strikers. Instead, "Big Jim," arm-in-arm with Orange leaders, had led his 11,000 followers through the streets in a fraternal demonstration. "The Protestants," he is reported to

---

[39] "Shall the Bill be a Final Settlement?", *ibid.*, I, 48, April 13, 1912.
[40] "The Right Way to Read History (After Hilaire Belloc)," *ibid.*, I, 51, May 4, 1912.
[41] *Ibid.*, I, 48, April 13, 1912.
[42] "Belfast Bigots' Brutality," *ibid.*, II, 10, July 27, 1912.

have said, "can follow the banners of William of Orange and the Catholics can follow them, too, for they are the colors which the Pope blessed."[43]

In the supercharged atmosphere of 1912, Larkin's lieutenant, Connolly, of much less potency as a charmer, was unable to avert the "Castledawson pogrom." From Dublin Larkin's appeals fell on deaf ears, but their burden was characteristic of his attitude: "This is what sectarianism is doing in Ireland.... Workers of Belfast, stop your damned nonsense.... Let not what masquerades as religion in this country divide you.... Be men! Be Irishmen, and don't disgrace yourselves."[44] In his later years, he was as much irked by Partition as any other. Yet it was not to him a cause for fighting; all that was needed was to convince the Irishmen in the North that, whatever their religious addiction, they were still Irish and, as such, belonged in community with Eire.

Tinglingly conscious as he was of Ireland's national heritage, and earnestly devoted to its preservation and restoration, Larkin never argued nor assumed the superiority of the Irish over people of other nations. Burning hatred of the English was never part of his stock in trade. During the great Dublin labor war of 1913–1914 he had no qualms about accepting assistance from across the Channel. *Sinn Fein's* blindly bitter invective against the Saxon ("The function of the English Brother is to 'stand behind him.' In the recent Boer War the English Brother discharged this function with such ability that he only got hit once in twenty times to the Irishman"[45]) seemed silly absurdity. Nor could Larkin see merit in the opposition of Archbishop Walsh to the proposal that Dublin slum children be cared for in England during the dispute. *The Irish Worker* could sentimentally exclaim, on the death of Bernard Shaw's mother, "What a pity her bones were not brought home to rest in her own land,"[46] but there was scant justice to the complaint of an old-line ex-president of the Irish Trades Union Congress that "Mr. Larkin wanted to build a wall round Ireland."[47]

---

[43] "Not as Catholics or Protestants, as Nationalists or Unionists, but as Belfast men and workers stand together and don't be misled by the employers' game of dividing Catholic and Protestant." Handbills posted in Belfast, *Northern Whig*, Aug. 14, 1907.
[44] "Belfast Barbarians," *Irish Worker*, II, 7, July 6, 1912.
[45] "The Economics of the Food-Ship," *Sinn Fein*, Oct. 4, 1913.
[46] *Irish Worker*, II, 42, March 8, 1913.
[47] Report of the Irish Trades Union Congress, *ibid.*, II, 32, May 17, 1913.

Larkin was voicing his inmost sentiments when, in glorifying the memory of Robert Emmet, he wrote: "Whenever or wherever a rebel is born, breaks a chain, or glorifies her cause by his death, all lovers and worshippers of liberty rejoice at the birth, tug at the chain, or mourn at the loss of a valiant comrade, irrespective of [to] what family or nation the particular rebel belongs. The fight for liberty is not a parochial or national affair. It is a universal struggle, and all nations, all free men and women rejoice when the devotee of liberty shatters another link of ignorance and slavery. The very sound of the word 'Freedom' seems to nerve one for struggle and expansion of body and soul. Go stand in the mart, on the hill, on the seashore, utter aloud the word 'Freedom,' let it be to many or to yourself, you will enjoy a thrill that but few enjoy, but what a satisfaction and awakening of the soul it must be to have struck one blow for the cause...."[48] His was a cosmopolitanism that by no means excluded consciousness of his ancestral nationalism. No less sincere than his tribute to Emmet was his criticism of a performance of Lennox Robinson's *The Patriot* at the Abbey Theatre: "Though we regret we cannot understand his pessimistic view of things we still believe patriotism is the most beautiful thing on earth, ay, or in heaven."[49]

Big Jim's nationalism was not assumed nor yet cultivated. That he was a member of the Irish nation was for him a simple fact, like the fact that he was a member of the Larkin family, like the fact of the nose on his face or of the long arms he used so effectively in his speech-making. It was not something that conferred special privileges or gave him a special mission. It was merely part of him, not an external ideal to guide his destiny. "Be men! Be Irishmen, and don't disgrace yourselves." Big Jim rose above all "ism's." He was simply an outstanding human being—a man of unusual stature, physically and spiritually—who acted in accord with no jelled body of doctrines, who acted intuitively, sometimes blunderingly, but always honestly and fearlessly, in tune with the warmth and breadth of his own nature.

[48] *Irish Worker*, II, 42, March 8, 1913.
[49] "The Abbey Patriots," *ibid.*, I, 48, April 13, 1912.

THE HEAVY HAND OF HEGEL

CHARLES W. COLE

IT IS PERHAPS UNFAIR to blame G. W. F. Hegel for all the sins of the romantic, idealist German philosophers of the early nineteenth century. Fichte, Schlegel, and possibly Kant, not to mention a number of lesser luminaries, should also be held responsible for some of the unfortunate trends in later German thought. But this essay is concerned with historians and historical writings. In this field, Hegel's influence was clearly more important and enduring than that of his fellow idealists.

Hegel's contribution to historical thinking can be most clearly isolated in the *Lectures on the Philosophy of History*. The lectures as we now have them are only in part in Hegel's own words, for the editors who published them (Edward Gans, Charles Hegel), while they had some of Hegel's own manuscript available, were forced to depend for part of the material on lecture notes taken by students in the years 1822–1831. The lectures as edited, printed, and translated[1] are a synthesis of the five deliveries of the course, rather than a report of Hegel's views as presented in any one year.

In his lectures, Hegel dealt not with a single nation or people, much less with individuals, but with what he called "Universal History." To him this meant all history so far as it was historical. He eased his task somewhat by dealing only with what he termed "world-historical peoples"—peoples who have played a role in the process of development which was to him the essence of history. Thus he excluded from consideration great segments of time and wide geographical areas—all Africa (save only Egypt), the Slavic and the early American civilizations, for example. Even the United States was omitted, since Hegel felt that while it might some day become a true historical state, it had not developed into one by his time. China and India were barely admitted, for to Hegel the first truly historical people were the Persians. In connection with them he discussed the Babylonians, Assyrians, Syrians, Phoenicians, Jews, and Egyptians. Thereafter he devoted his attention to the Greeks,

---

[1] G. W. F. Hegel, *Lectures on the Philosophy of History*, trans. by J. Sibree. The edition used for this essay is that published by G. Bell and Sons, London, 1914.

Romans, and Germans. But by the Germans he meant all North Europeans. In Hegel's scheme history commenced only when "rationality" began to manifest itself not as mere undeveloped potentiality but as actuality, or in other words when true states were organized, for they are the chief historic manifestation of rationality.

Thus even the "world-historical peoples" were historical only part of the time. For Hegel declares:

A Nation is moral—virtuous—vigorous—while it is engaged in realizing its grand objects, and defends its work against external violence during the process of giving its purposes an objective existence. The contradiction between its potential, subjective being—its inner aim and life—and its actual being is removed; it has attained full reality, has itself objectively present to it. But this having been attained, the activity displayed by the Spirit of the people in question is no longer needed; it has attained its desire. The Nation can still accomplish much in war and peace, at home and abroad; but the living substantial soul itself may be said to have ceased its activity. The essential, supreme interest has consequently vanished from its life, for interest is present only where there is opposition. The Nation lives the same kind of life as the individual when passing from maturity to old age in the enjoyment of itself—in the satisfaction of being exactly what it was able to attain.[2]

History then was the story of the development of historical peoples after they attained to the formation of a state and before they became static or began to decay. History was conditioned by geography but not dependent on it. On the one hand, no historical peoples have appeared or could appear, according to Hegel, in the frigid or torrid zones. But, on the other hand: "The mild Ionic sky certainly contributed much to the charm of Homeric poems, yet this alone can produce no Homers. Nor in fact does it continue to produce them; under Turkish government no bards have arisen."[3]

The historical development of the world was, to Hegel, a rational process. History was presided over by reason, infused with reason. It was indeed reason in action. History was "the rational necessary course of the World-Spirit."[4] *"Divine Providence* is Wisdom en-

---

[2] *Ibid.*, pp. 77–78.

[3] *Ibid.*, p. 83. It is worth noting that in speaking of North America, Hegel states much of the "frontier" and "safety valve" theories of American development (pp. 89–90), and then adds the provocative comment, "Had the woods of Germany been in existence the French Revolution would not have occurred."

[4] *Ibid.*, p. 11.

dowed with an infinite Power, which realizes its aim, viz., the absolute rational design of the World."[5]

But to Hegel the workings of Reason or Divine Providence were not such as Augustine, or Bede, or Bossuet saw. They were not so much in men or events as in the course, the process, of history taken as a whole. Man's entire life on earth was a manifestation of the development of Spirit, and "the essence of Spirit is Freedom." "It may be said of Universal History that it is the exhibition of Spirit in the process of working out the knowledge of that which it is potentially."[6]

Man was not by nature free, nor was he so in early times, but only when he had formed a state. In fact, Hegel declared, "The *State* . . . is that form of reality in which the individual has and enjoys freedom."[7] Without law, morality, and government there could be no complete, no real, freedom. And the state was law, morality, and government realized and existent. There could be no state without some consciousness of freedom, though there could be various stages in this consciousness. In fact, "The History of the world is none other than the progress of the consciousness of freedom."[8] All history was the unfolding of the Idea of Freedom, the increasing consciousness of men that they were free:

The Orientals have not attained the knowledge that Spirit—Man *as such*—is free; and because they do not know this, they are not free. They know only that *one is free*. But on this very account the freedom of that one is only caprice; ferocity—brutal recklessness of passion, or a mildness and tameness of desires, which is in itself only an accident of Nature—mere caprice like the former. The *one* is therefore only a Despot; not a *free man*. The consciousness of Freedom first arose among the Greeks, and therefore they were free; but they and the Romans likewise knew only that *some* are free—not man as such. Even Plato and Aristotle did not know this. The Greeks, therefore, had slaves; and their whole life and the maintenance of their splendid liberty, was implicated with the institution of slavery: a fact moreover which made that liberty on the one hand only an accidental, transient and limited growth; on the other hand, constituted it a rigorous thraldom of our common nature—of the Human. The German nations, under the influence of Christianity, were

[5] *Ibid.*, p. 13.
[6] *Ibid.*, p. 18.
[7] *Ibid.*, p. 40.
[8] *Ibid.*, pp. 19–20.

the first to attain the consciousness that man, as man, is free: that it is the *freedom* of Spirit which constitutes its essence.[9]

These stages in the development of the consciousness of freedom were reflected in forms of government. Thus the oriental world was one characterized by despotism, the classical world by democracy or autocracy, and the modern, German world by monarchy. The four phases of history were childhood in the East, boyhood in Greece, manhood in Rome, and old age in the German world. But it must be remembered that "The Old Age of *Nature* is weakness; but that of *Spirit* is its perfect maturity and *strength,* in which it returns to unity with itself, but in its fully developed character as *Spirit.*" Thus, "The History of the World travels from East to West, for Europe is absolutely the end of History, Asia the beginning."[10]

In each phase of history the National Spirit, representing a stage of the development of the World Spirit, expressed itself in the art, law, religion, science, and government of the people. All were consonant with each other, for all were manifestations of the same thing. Each institution was thus interlocked with all the others. Greek oracles, for example, served to focus the popular will and thus made democracy workable. Even men, and particularly great men ("historical men," "World-Historical Individuals") were molded by the national spirit, by the phase of development of world spirit in which they lived. They were great simply because their words and deeds were in line with the inner thrust of national or world development.[11]

To Hegel world development culminated in the Prussian monarchy of his day. German monarchy set up a "moral medium" between subjects and sovereign and cemented it with the constitution and organization of the state. Lutheran Christianity, with its emphasis on freedom, made a complete and perfect fusion with monarchy. The Enlightenment produced a revolution in France, where freedom had been shackled and thwarted by Catholicism, but not in Germany, for there the Reformation had already brought a perfect harmony between men and their social and spiritual environ-

[9] *Ibid.,* pp. 18–19.
[10] *Ibid.,* pp. 109–16, cf. p. 48.
[11] *Ibid.,* pp. 30 ff., 50 ff.

ment. This was the end of the road for Hegel. He saw no further.[12] It is said that Hegel concluded his lectures with the remark, *"Bis hierher ist das Bewusstsein gekommen."* But whether he said it in arrogance or humility is not entirely clear.

The philosophical implications of Hegel's theories can best be left to the philosophers. It is likewise not improper to omit all consideration of his dialectical method (more fully developed in works other than his *Lectures on the Philosophy of History*), for of late years it seems to have been taken seriously only by the Marxians.[13] There remain, however, two Hegelian tendencies which profoundly affected later historians of the German and related schools. They were no less influential because they were implicit rather than explicit, and no less pernicious because they seem natural and harmless. The first of these tendencies is the improper personification of abstractions which after having been personified are often made into operative entities. The second is what might be called *a priori* historiography, the technique of deriving an historical notion from rumination, speculation, and some general acquaintance with the historical data in question, and then "proving" its validity by a selection of instances or illustrations.

Neither of these tendencies was originated by Hegel. Neither of them has been confined to German historians; recent and striking instances of the use of the latter technique, for example, are to be found in the work of Arnold Toynbee. But both are so clearly evident in post-Hegelian German historians that it is at least tempting to attribute their persuasive presence in German historiography to Hegel's influence.

As examples of Hegel's personification of abstractions there can be cited his use of "Freedom," "Spirit," "National Spirit," "Reason," "Nature," "State," "Will," "Religion," "German Spirit," "World-Spirit," "People," "Culture," "Nation," "National Genius," "Art," "Science," and a dozen others. It is characteristic of these personifications in Hegel that they are defined vaguely or not at all. Nonetheless they are elevated into operating forces on the one hand and become the basis of dogmatic generalizations on the

[12] *Ibid.*, pp. 428 ff.
[13] It is interesting to speculate on what would have been the result if Hegel (or Marx) had been born late enough to adopt the more appropriate and effective evolutionary theories of development instead of the awkward and artificial dialectic notions.

other. The result is often something that sounds important or significant; yet when it is subjected to analysis it becomes more and more misty and intangible. Take for example the following statements:

> History in general is therefore the development of Spirit in *Time,* as Nature is the development of the Idea in *Space.*[14]

> This is the character of the Chinese people in its various aspects. Its distinguishing feature is that everything which belongs to the Spirit—unconstrained morality, in practice and theory, Heart, inward Religion, Science and Art properly so called, is alien to it.[15]

> But the definite *substance* that receives the form of universality and exists in that concrete reality which is the State is the Spirit of the People itself.[16]

The other tendency, that of *a priori* historiography, is illustrated by the whole of Hegel's *Lectures on the Philosophy of History* discussed above. The ideas contained in them clearly came from Hegel's own speculations, not from a close acquaintance with the materials for the history of the periods he is discussing. History is used by him to illustrate, to enforce, to bear out, to "prove" an elaborate theory of world development, a theory peopled and operated by abstract entities. It is not history that Hegel is writing, but philosophical poetry with historical overtones:

> The Greek life is truly youthful achievement. Achilles, the ideal youth of *poetry,* commenced it: Alexander the Great, the ideal youth of *reality,* concluded it. Both appear in contest with Asia.[17]

> This is the *elementary character* of the Spirit of the Greeks, implying the origination of their culture from independent individualities; a condition in which individuals take their own ground, and are not, from the very beginning, patriarchally united by a bond of *Nature,* but realize a union through some other medium—through Law and Custom having the sanction of Spirit.[18]

> The interests of the community may, therefore, continue to be entrusted to the will and resolve of the citizens, and this must be the basis of the Greek constitution; for no principle has as yet manifested itself which

---

[14] Hegel, *op. cit.*, p. 75.
[15] *Ibid.*, p. 144.
[16] *Ibid.*, p. 52.
[17] *Ibid.*, p. 233.
[18] *Ibid.*, p. 235.

can contravene such Choice conditioned by Custom and hinder its realizing itself in action. The Democratic Constitution is here the only possible one: the citizens are still unconscious of particular interests, and therefore of a corrupting element: the Objective Will is in their case not disintegrated.[19]

In a search for the persistent influence of the Hegelian tendencies toward the personification of abstractions and *a priori* historiography, the nineteenth century would be a happy hunting ground. But it seems even more useful to choose as examples more recent writers of continuing present-day importance. For this purpose there will be selected two Germans, Spengler and Sombart, and one Swede, Heckscher, who, while influenced by English economics, seems as an historian to belong rather with the Germans.

In his major work, *The Decline of the West*,[20] Spengler almost outpersonifies the old master Hegel himself. There is a little less of Spirit and Will, but that lack is more than compensated by personifications that stand for generalizations about cultures and civilizations. In fact, Spengler goes further, and to mere personifications adds all sorts of elaborate symbolic abstractions. The Doric column stands for the "pure Present"; the Brahman Nirvana for "the perfectly ahistoric soul" of the Indian culture; "the near, strictly limited self-contained Body" for the "Classical World view"; "infinitely wide and infinitely profound three-dimensional space" for the Western World view; a path or way for the Egyptian view of life; the color "bluish-green" for Roman Catholic Christianity, and so on.[21]

But of personifications which are more than generalizations or symbols or metaphors, of personifications which act and shape cultures and history there are also a plenty. Though he discusses the difficulty of defining "Will" and "Soul," Spengler goes on to use them. "To call the Faustian-Culture [modern European civilization] a Will-Culture," he says, "is only another way of expressing the eminently historical disposition of its soul." One sentence in a footnote fairly teems with personified forces: "When, therefore, in the present work also, precedence is consistently given to Time,

---

[19] *Ibid.*, p. 262.
[20] Oswald Spengler, *The Decline of the West*, trans. by C. F. Atkinson (2 vols., New York, 1928).
[21] *Ibid.*, I, 9, 11, 174, 188, 247.

The Heavy Hand of Hegel

Direction and Destiny over Space and Causality, this must not be supposed to be the result of reasoned proofs. It is the outcome of (quite unconscious) tendencies of life-feeling—the only mode of origin of philosophic ideas."[22]

"Mass-souls" crop up, too, and "These souls have their special psychology. A single soul is the mark of every genuine order or class. . . ." "It is the hall-mark of the statesman that he has a sure and penetrating eye for these mass-souls. . . ." "Totem" and "Taboo," "Race," and even "Landscape" become operative forces in history, like "mass-souls." "Of all the expressions of Race," says Spengler, "the purest is the House." The "race" is indeed something mystical rather than a matter of bone structure or head shape. It can be detected in "the sound of speech, song and, above all, laughter," as well as in the shape of the houses. It is in the "voice of the blood" which "leads to innumerable procreations that in utter unconsciousness fulfil the *will of the race.*"[23]

The "State" too is a living, moving force in history. "Estate and State, contend for supremacy. . . ." Like Hegel, Spengler feels that *"World-history is and always will be State-history,"* and he feels it strongly, for he italicizes that sentence. He goes on to say, "The more fully matured the State, the higher the standing, the historical capacity and therefore the Destiny of the Nation."[24]

Indeed, all Spengler is a luridly lighted and deeply shadowed theater where personified forces wrestle grimly with abstractions. Space, Time, Destiny struggle with Civilizations, Races, Nations, States, and the wills and souls of peoples, cultures, and institutions play the major roles. That no one of these things discussed can be defined only adds to the rather mysterious, evocative, and poetic power of the work.

Spengler displays, too, the *a priori* quality noted in Hegel. His whole book is written really to "prove" one major thesis, which itself may have been derived from Hegel with Darwinian infusions added. The thesis stated in Spengler's own words is this, *"Cultures are organisms,* and world history is their collective biography." Because they are organisms cultures are born, have a youth, maturity,

---

[22] *Ibid.*, I, 299 ff., 308–9, 308, note 1.
[23] *Ibid.*, II, 18–19, 116–18, 119–20, 126–27.
[24] *Ibid.*, II, 366, 367, 369.

and old age, and die. Even more, the life histories and spans of cultures are always similar. *"Every Culture, every adolescence and maturity and decay of a Culture, every one of its intrinsically necessary stages and periods, has a definite duration, always the same, always recurring with the emphasis of a symbol."* So sure is Spengler of his thesis that he believes the future of modern civilization to be fixed by "the unalterable necessity of destiny" and predictable by comparison with cultures that have died.[25]

All Spengler's erudition, his vast wealth of historical examples, his curious lore, are devoted to "proving" his one idea. He makes the daring attempt to cram all history into this one pattern. It is an interesting, even an exciting venture. But it is not history. It is, as in the case of Hegel, poetry, or poetic-philosophic speculation adorned with, even composed of, historical materials.

In the works of Werner Sombart,[26] we find more history (specifically economic history) and less poetry. Most of Sombart's works are devoted to a study of capitalism, yet it is peculiarly difficult to derive a satisfactory definition of capitalism from his writing. He describes it, he lists its characteristics, he traces its origins. But when he attempts a definition, it is an unsatisfactory Marxian one,[27] clearly insufficient to embrace what he is talking about. Nonetheless, capitalism is in Sombart an entity, even a being: "And so capitalism grew and grew and grew. Today it is like a mighty giant striding through the land treading down all that stands in its path."[28]

[25] *Ibid.*, I, 39, 104, 109–10.

[26] Those referred to here are: W. Sombart, *The Quintessence of Capitalism,* trans. and ed. by M. Epstein (New York, 1915), hereafter cited as Sombart, *Quintessence,* and W. Sombart, *The Jews and Modern Capitalism,* trans. by M. Epstein (London, 1913), hereafter cited as Sombart, *Jews.* See also the article, "Capitalism," in the *Encyclopedia of the Social Sciences.*

[27] "Capitalism is the name given to the economic organization wherein regularly two distinct social groups co-operate—the owners of the means of production who at the same time do the work of managing and directing, and the great body of workers who possess nothing but their labour." Sombart, *Jews,* p. 160. It has perhaps not been sufficiently noted that the materialist Marxian teachings stress a rather mystical idea—"ownership"—as the basic differentiation between economic systems. Recent decades have taught us that who owns the means of production is much less important than who manages them and who enjoys their fruits. In Soviet Russia, the people as a whole own the means of production, but the Communist bureaucracy manages them and directs the enjoyment of their product. In capitalist America millions of individual stockholders "own" the great corporations, but they have little or no voice in the management or in the determination of who gets what share of the profits. These questions are left to much smaller groups of managers.

[28] Sombart, *Quintessence,* p. 357.

The Heavy Hand of Hegel

This giant Capitalism had a multiple parentage (science, technical progress; the Jews), it had an obscure (and prolonged) birth. It passed through stages of development until it reached its full and awesome maturity in the twentieth century. But it is always the same old capitalism. Its traits can be illustrated equally well by examples from Renaissance Italy, seventeenth-century Holland, eighteenth-century France, or nineteenth-century England. In fact, capitalism is so definite and so unique that it can be isolated from its background and discussed through the ages with little reference to the historical context of its various stages.

Capitalism moreover has, for Sombart, a soul—the "capitalist spirit"—and this soul, though it develops and grows and is fed from a dozen different sources, is likewise the same through the centuries. Yet the soul is in some senses distinct from the body and had to develop before the body could come into existence. "It goes without saying that at some time in the distant past the capitalist spirit must have been in existence—in embryo, if you like—before any capitalist undertaking could become a reality."[29]

The Hegelian influence is not very clear or direct in Sombart, but it would seem likely that the tendency to erect a description of how men do business into an operative entity endowed with a soul owed something to the Hegelian tradition. Moreover Sombart, like Hegel, has his work peopled with abstractions or quasi-abstractions. In it we meet not only the Jew, but the Conqueror, the Trader, the Freebooter, the Landlord, the Bourgeois, the Speculator, the Peasant, the Craftsman, the Modern Business Man, not to mention the State and the Church. All of them are more or less abstracted from any real historical setting. All of them are illustrated by prototypes drawn from the most varied areas and periods. All of them work together, one way or another, to help capitalism grow.

Nor do we find a lack of spirits and souls. The Modern Business Man's Soul Sombart explains at length. He likewise investigates the "spirit of undertaking," the "Jewish Genius," the "Jewish soul," the "nomadic spirit," and so on. He analyzes similarly the bourgeois temperament, the middle class nature, national traits, "blood" and races, though he feels that "race" is environmental and cultural as well as biological. Sombart finds that "all European peoples have

---

[29] *Ibid.*, pp. 344, 342 ff.

the qualities necessary for capitalism," but that "each nation has these qualities in a varying degree." In the French, "it is the Celtic blood that explains the strongly marked tendency to live on investments." "The Florentines became traders, became the foremost and greatest trading community in the Middle Ages, because of their Etruscan and Greek (i.e. Oriental) blood."[30]

Sombart likewise displays the Hegelian trait of the *a priori* thesis supported by historical data, illustrations, and reasoning. One of his theses is that the Jews are in large part responsible for the development of the somewhat misty entity "modern capitalism" and the rise of the "capitalist spirit." Some might doubt that the Jews of Old Testament days in Palestine and those in Europe in the Middle Ages or modern times were sufficiently similar to discuss in the same breath. But Sombart answers this doubt to his own satisfaction: "Religion and inbreeding were the two iron hoops that bound the Jewish people and kept them as one body through the centuries."[31]

To "prove" his thesis, Sombart ascribes certain characteristics to the Jews. They are mobile, adaptable, flexible, active, purposeful, intellectual, thrifty. Through the ages they have been moneylenders. They have a gift for figures. Their religion taught them to seek worldly success and to take a rational view of life. These social characteristics and religious teachings, together with the special position of the Jews in Europe, brought it about, according to Sombart, that they were the prime movers in the creation of capitalism. In illustrating his points, the author ranges from "a Jewish student from the far East of Siberia who came to me one day" back to Moses. He draws his examples from dozens of places and periods. He builds up his case by wrenching the Jewish people out of three thousand years of historical context and examining them through the ages from a synoptic view. That the idea of the Jewish contribution to the rise of capitalism came first and Sombart's efforts to prove it second can scarcely be doubted by an impartial reader.[32]

In the case of Heckscher we are dealing with a more careful scholar and a more thoughtful historian, who has made immense

---

[30] *Ibid.*, pp. 213, 215, and *passim*.
[31] Sombart, *Jews*, p. 351.
[32] *Ibid.*, Chapters X, XI, XII, and XIII.

contributions to our understanding of modern economic history. But even on him the heavy hand of Hegel has been laid. Heckscher's major work is his two-volume treatise on mercantilism.[33] In it he makes mercantilism a real entity that brooded immanent over Europe for four or five centuries and manifested itself from time to time in one country or another, particularly in the period from 1500 to 1800. As a matter of fact, mercantilism was never an entity, never a system, never a co-ordinated or coherent body of policy or practice. It varied drastically in different periods and different countries. Those who practiced and preached it never thought of themselves as a school. The very name "mercantilism" was invented by its opponents when the old ideas were already on the wane.

That Heckscher is aware of the danger of lumping disparate things together under a common name and then treating that collection as something real, existent, and even operative is indicated when he remarks, ". . . The method of treating all sorts of disconnected tendencies paving the way to modern economic conditions under the common name of 'modern capitalism' appears to me confusing and a thing to be shunned. . . ."[34] Yet he falls into the same sort of error as regards mercantilism. He regards his work as "a contribution to the history of economic policy as a common European problem," and warns the reader not to expect "a description of mercantilist policy in each country separately, except in so far as has been found necessary for the understanding of common European developments."[35] He carefully states that "Mercantilism never existed in the sense that Colbert or Cromwell existed. It is only an instrumental concept. . . ." Or again he says that for him "mercantilism" stands for "a phase in the history of economic policy."[36] With these remarks there can be no quarrel and Hegel would have thought them impossibly cautious. But even after such caveats, Heckscher goes on to treat mercantilism as if such a thing had really been and was more than a name or an "instrumental concept." He makes of it a definite historical phenomenon that affected all Europe and can be understood as a whole by examining its manifestations in one country or another.

[33] E. F. Heckscher, *Mercantilism*, trans. by M. Shapiro (2 vols., London, 1935).
[34] *Ibid.*, I, 14.
[35] *Ibid.*, I, 13.
[36] *Ibid.*, I, 19.

It is easier for him to do so because he limits his attention very largely to Germany, England, and France, with special emphasis on the latter two. Had he given equal thought to Italy, Spain, Portugal, and Holland, it would have been much more difficult to make mercantilism seem a unified whole or even a closely related series of parallel tendencies. If the mind were cleared of *a priori* notions and of every Hegelian tendency to erect abstractions into entities, it would be clear that: (1) an exact definition of "mercantilism" is very difficult; (2) that the best definition possible applies only very roughly and crudely to the developments in different countries or to the developments in the same country at different periods; (3) that "mercantilism" can be made to have form, shape, unity, and coherence only by implicitly or explicitly contrasting it artificially with the much more clearly and consciously worked-out doctrines of the laissez-faire school.

Indeed, such an examination would almost certainly bring out the vital differences in the "mercantilism" of the various countries. It would show that Portuguese mercantilism in the sixteenth century was focused on the spice trade, while Spanish mercantilism from 1550 to 1650 centered in American bullion; and Dutch mercantilism in the seventeenth century was built around the carrying trade, while English mercantilism after 1660 was based on colonial commerce. If "mercantilism" were then defined as European national economic policies and practices after 1500 and before the advent of developed laissez-faire ideas (say, 1776), it would be possible and profitable to discuss Spanish mercantilism in the sixteenth century, or French mercantilism in the eighteenth century. But it would be a very doubtful procedure to write about "Mercantilism" or "European Mercantilism."

Apart from his hypostasization of "mercantilism," there are other Hegelian traces in Heckscher. In treating mercantilism as a "Unifying System," a "System of Power," and a "System of Protection," he not only makes it artificially systematic but much more teleological than would seem justified by the facts. Similarly, he tends to erect such concepts as a "fear of goods," "staple policy," "policy of protection," and "policy of provision" into operative entities which make people do things rather than treating them as mere descriptive terms applied to what people did. There are not many "spirits" or

The Heavy Hand of Hegel

"souls" in Heckscher. But the "gild spirit" does infuse and shape the early chartered companies.[37]

The *a priori* qualities in Heckscher are to a degree concealed by his thoughtful and careful scholarship. But they are there nevertheless. Basically Heckscher believes in laissez faire, a fact which he recognizes, for he says in his preface that Marshall's *Principles* "were not only the starting point of my theoretical studies, but have also profoundly influenced my approach to economic history."[38]

As one who believes in laissez faire, Heckscher cannot help regarding many of the mercantilist practices as mistaken, unfortunate, and harmful. He points out that the "trade of all countries certainly suffered enormously from the blockading measures brought on by commercial warfare."[39] But he does not adequately examine the possibility that these same measures increased national productivity. It might be, for example, that the foundations of England's nineteenth century industrial greatness were laid by these same "blockading measures."

Heckscher's laissez-faire preconceptions are particularly clear when he comes to discuss such matters as the regulation of industry. He sees clearly that it cramped and hampered change and growth. But he does not adequately assess its importance, in the maintenance of quality, the spreading of technical knowledge, the protection of the consumer, and the winning of markets. Similarly, to him the mercantilist financial measures seem ill-conceived and deleterious. He is, therefore, not prone to examine their possible role in developing industrial and commercial strength. Thus Heckscher is a sort of faint scholarly echo of the diatribes of the early economic liberals. He devoted years of study to something of which he disapproved. And his disapproval inevitably shaped his study.

Even more subtly, *a priorism* is detectable in Heckscher's whole approach. Because mercantilism is an entity, something which manifested itself through the centuries in various countries, he feels perfectly free to illustrate this thing with examples from different contexts in time and place. He tends also (like Hegel or Spengler) to leave out of consideration the material which would run counter

---
[37] *Ibid.*, I, 379 ff., and II, 60 ff., 80 ff., 112 ff.
[38] *Ibid.*, I, 13.
[39] *Ibid.*, II, 317.

to his conception. To him mercantilism was something that arose out of a congeries of medieval trends, blossomed and bore fruit in the three centuries after 1500, and withered after 1800. He himself recognizes that the last century has seen the recreation of almost every one of the mercantilist practices; he attributes this development "to the conservative or historical spirit" which "had its specific home in Germany."[40] It might be more profitable to seek for the origins of neo-mercantilism as of the older mercantilism in the fields of war and nationalism. Perhaps what we have been calling mercantilism is merely economic nationalism.

To note the persistence of Hegel-like tendencies in Spengler and Sombart or their faint shadow on an important work like that of Heckscher should be a warning to historians. They should be careful when they employ a descriptive term like "liberalism" to confine it to the role of a descriptive term and not let it become an operating agent or an historical entity. They should be careful, moreover, to distinguish in its use as a descriptive term between what it is describing in one area at one period and what it is used to describe in another place and time.[41]

Similarly, an awareness of the blatant *a priorism* of Hegel or Spengler should not prevent a historian from approaching his material with ideas or theories. He could not help doing so if he would. But it should make him careful to weigh his theory in the light of the evidence which comes forth from the material. It should prevent him from ignoring the opposing evidence and suppressing the cases which do not fit in with an attempt to "prove" his theory. Most of all, it should make him extremely cautious in illustrating a general notion with examples gathered from varying areas and centuries and ripped from their historical contexts. In short, a study of the vagaries of Hegel (who was not an historian) and of those he influenced directly or indirectly should serve to make the historian of the mid-twentieth century a more sophisticated practitioner of his craft.

[40] *Ibid.*, II, 334.
[41] As, for example, C. J. H. Hayes distinguished the different types, schools, and periods of nationalism in *Historical Evolution of Modern Nationalism* (1931).

H. G. WELLS, BRITISH PATRIOT IN SEARCH OF A WORLD STATE[1]

EDWARD MEAD EARLE

H. G. WELLS exercised an almost unique influence on my generation—the generation which reached maturity during the decade 1910–1920. Only Bernard Shaw among men of letters and Woodrow Wilson among men in public life approached him in capturing our imagination and winning us to a point of view.[2] There was a flippancy and irresponsibility about Shaw, however, which debased his great abilities; to some of us he was a cleverer Oscar Wilde, a court jester for the Fabians and other intellectuals as Wilde previously had been for salon and café society.[3] Wilson, almost a Messiah during the years 1917–1918, was a tragic casualty of the post-war era of disillusion and cynicism. But Wells continued throughout the twenties to command our attention and respect.

Wells and Wilson had this in common—that they were idealists and crusaders. Each visualized a better social order—Wells's New Republic and Wilson's New Freedom. Each believed, too, in the possibility of an ordered international society—perhaps a warless world—to be brought about through a league of free nations or some similar instrumentality. Wells regarded the World War of 1914–1918 as "a war to end war"; Wilson saw it as a war to "make the world safe for democracy." Both were cruelly disappointed that their high

---

[1] This title is suggested by one of Wells's lesser works, *Travels of a Republican Radical in Search of Hot Water* (London, 1939).

[2] Of course we read Kipling, too, but the intellectual climate of the United States was less congenial to Kipling's imperialism than it was in Great Britain. Among academic personalities, the Webbs occupied an especially conspicuous place in our scheme-of-things but a lesser place than they held among our British contemporaries. Sinclair Lewis, a disciple of Wells, has recalled vividly how much Wells "meant to us from 1910 to 1930 in Greenwich Village or Pekin or Sauk Centre or Twitterton-on-Twit"—he should have added Morningside Heights! "A Generation Nourished on H. G. Wells," in the *New York Herald Tribune Weekly Book Review Section*, Oct. 20, 1946. See also four articles in *The Saturday Review of Literature* for Aug. 31, 1946: Clifton Fadiman, "The Passing of a Prophet"; Elmer Davis, "Notes on the Failure of a Mission"; Waldemar Kaempffert, "Evangelist of Utopia"; H. S. Canby, "The Superjournalist."

[3] Concerning Shaw, see also footnote 14 *infra*.

hopes of 1918 failed of realization. Wilson was tumbled from his exalted place because, it was unjustly adjudged, he had betrayed his cause or compromised it away. But Wells, having no political responsibility and no power other than his pen, lived to fight another day. He advanced far beyond advocacy of the League of Nations and became a fervid, uncompromising evangelist of a world state.

I

It is not my purpose to appraise Wells's achievements as a man of letters. As a technician Arnold Bennett was smoother. As an artist Shaw was superior. But Wells was more than a man of letters, certainly more than a successful novelist. Like Dickens, he was a critic of his day and age, and he viewed the novel principally as a weapon in the struggle for social reform. Although in his early career he was profoundly influenced by Henry James, he held in low esteem James's devotion to art for art's sake. He made it plain to James and others that he was not much concerned with literary form and artistry; to him fiction was a means of conveying ideas and inciting to action.[4] As time passed, his novels were more and more the work of the advocate, less and less those of the storyteller. Wells intended them to be so. He had committed himself to the cause of public education, broadly conceived, and in this field "it is the novel that must attempt most and achieve most." Hence, the novelist should write about the whole of human life, not merely about its subjective phases. "We [novelists] are going to write about business and finance and politics and precedence and pretentiousness and decorum and indecorum, until a thousand pretences and ten thousand impostures shrivel in the cold, clear air of our elucidations. . . . We are going to appeal to the young and the hopeful and the curious, against the established, the dignified, and defensive."[5]

Ignorance, stupidity, injustice, prejudice, superstition, conven-

[4] Percy Lubbock, ed., *The Letters of Henry James* (New York, 1920), II, 485–90, for an exchange of letters between Wells and James, July 1915.

[5] "The Contemporary Novel," a lecture delivered to the Times Book Club, London, 1912; subsequently published in *Social Forces in England and America* (New York, 1914), pp. 173–98. See also *Experiment in Autobiography*—hereafter cited as *Autobiography*—(New York, 1934), pp. 410–20; "The Future of the Novel," in *The Way the World Is Going* (Garden City, N. Y., 1929), Chap. XXVI.

tion, inefficiency, and vested interests—these, said Wells, could most effectively be exposed and combated by personification and dramatization. Bumble, in *Oliver Twist,* for example, "lit up and still lights up the whole problem of Poor Law administration for the English reading community." He was "worth a hundred Royal Commissions." Just as Bumble was "a magnificent figure of the follies and cruelties of ignorance in office," so other fictional characters could be created to embody and vivify the inadequacies and frustrations of our time, on the one hand, and its great potentialities and hopes, on the other.[6] But Wells resented having his novels called propaganda novels, because it seemed to him that the word propaganda "should be confined to the definite service of some organized party, church or doctrine. It implies direction from outside. If at times I have been inclined to thrust my views upon my readers, they were at any rate my own views."[7]

Much of Wells's fiction was autobiographical.[8] But more than personal, it was intellectual history—the intellectual history of Wells and his times. It was also, in some instances, the story of the English lower middle class, from which Wells came and which he understood so well. While in *Kipps* and *The History of Mr. Polly* Wells gave graphic and poignant pictures of his own youth, these delightful novels also contain unforgettable portraits of the "little man"[9] who plays an inconspicuous part in British affairs but provides, none the less, so much of the heroism and endurance which carried Britain through two world wars in our generation.[10] *Mr. Britling Sees It Through* was "boldly photographic" of another segment of British society: what might be called, for want of a better name, the intellectual class. Although Wells sometimes denied "putting people

---

[6] "The Contemporary Novel," *loc. cit.,* pp. 192–93.

[7] *Autobiography,* p. 417.

[8] On this point, see the *Autobiography, passim,* and Geoffrey West, *H. G. Wells, A Sketch for a Portrait* (London, 1930), *passim.*

[9] One of the best of Wells's characters in this category is Tom Smallways, "a greengrocer by trade and a gardener by disposition" in *The War in the Air* (New York, 1908).

[10] Of *Kipps,* Henry James wrote Wells, "You have for the very first time treated the English 'lower middle' class, etc., without the picturesque, the grotesque, the fantastic and romantic interference of which Dickens . . . is so misleadingly full. You have handled its vulgarity in so scientific and historic a spirit . . . . And then the book has throughout such extraordinary life. . . . every piece and part of it is so vivid and sharp and *raw.*" *Letters of Henry James,* II, 40–41.

[including himself] in books,"[11] he conceded that *Mr. Britling* was in most respects autobiographical. Mr. Britling is H. G. Wells, and Mr. Britling's views on the War of 1914 are indistinguishable from those which Wells held and which he expounded from other platforms.[12] But the story of Mr. Britling is more than the story of H. G. Wells in wartime. It is the dramatic history of the intelligent, middle class British patriot and his reactions to the catastrophe of August 1914. As such, it could "be repeated with ten thousand variations," if always with one central theme: "the astonishment and the sense of tragic disillusionment in a civilized mind as the cruel facts of war rose steadily to dominate everything else in life." Along with disillusionment went "the passionate desire to find some immediate reassurance amidst the whirlwind of disaster."[13] *Mr. Britling* is an indispensable part of the history of Britain during the First World War. And when I re-read it during the grim days of 1940, I found it still eloquently descriptive of the faith and the stubborn courage with which the British people met an even more exacting ordeal. It is, indeed, a deeply moving account of the response of decent people everywhere to the terrible imperatives of modern war.[14]

Although Wells was a great figure in his day, and although his books remain an invaluable source for British social history in the twentieth century,[15] he is being largely neglected or ignored by the

[11] "A Note before the Title Page" in *The World of William Clissold* (2 vols., New York, 1926)—hereafter cited as *William Clissold*. After saying that Clissold is a fictitious character, Wells goes on: "He is a specimen of modern liberalism, using liberalism in its broadest sense.... Naturally, his point of view is like Mr. Wells'. That was to be expected.... Every author must write of the reactions he knows; he must be near enough to them to *feel* them sympathetically. It is unreasonable to expect the author of this book to write of the inner life of such people as the devout Mr. Belloc, for example, or the aristocratic Duke of Northumberland, or the political Mr. Ramsay MacDonald" (pp. i–ii). In his *Autobiography*, pp. 633–36, Wells admits nevertheless that William Clissold is heavily autobiographical.

[12] West, *op. cit.*, pp. 213–14.

[13] *Autobiography*, p. 573.

[14] Much, although not quite, the same might be said of the sections dealing with the War in *Joan and Peter* (1918) and *The Bulpington of Blup* (1933). Shaw, on the other hand, comes off less well on similar reappraisal. His "Common Sense about the War"—a special supplement of *The New Statesman*, Nov. 14, 1914—explains the war largely in doctrinaire Marxist terms which reveal little of anything about its true nature. See also William Irvine, "Shaw, War and Peace," in *Foreign Affairs*, XXV (1947), 314–27.

[15] Here again Wells resembles Dickens. It is surprising that historians generally have neglected fiction as a historical source. Professor William Aydelotte, of the University of Iowa, is at work on a study of Dickens as a guide to the social historian. As an *ad interim* report, see his "The England of Marx and Mill as Reflected in Fiction," in Supplement VIII to the *Journal of Economic History* for 1948.

present generation. A few of his romantic tales [16] and two or three of his novels [17] remain a permanent part of our better literature, but for every person who reads Wells today there must be fifty, a hundred, or perhaps a thousand who read Shaw. However, there is so much that is worth while in Wells, particularly in his earlier work, that he must surely have a revival.[18] The historian, in particular, must cull out of the profligacy of his work—millions of words, dispersed over dozens of volumes—significant parts of the intellectual and cultural history of our times. Wells cannot long remain a prophet without honor in the Anglo-American world.

II

Wells himself was not much concerned with winning a place among the immortals. He had short-term objectives which seemed to him of greater moment. At various times he considered himself—or was considered by others—a scientist, a popularizer of science, a builder of Utopias, a sociologist, a political essayist, a historian, a novelist.[19] One of his more sympathetic and discriminating critics said that, in the latter books at least, "Wells the reformer, Wells the novelist, and Wells the journalist form an indivisible trinity."[20] Wells himself thought "journalist" and "journalism" would best describe him and his work.[21] But the shrewdest and most nearly apt judgment of Wells is to be found on the editorial page of the *New*

---

[16] For example, shall we say, *The Time Machine* and *The War in the Air*?

[17] *Kipps, The Story of Mr. Polly,* and *Tono Bungay.* Perhaps *The New Machiavelli* and *Mr. Britling Sees It Through* likewise belong in this category.

[18] This revival may, in fact, be under way. *Ann Veronica,* one of the most topical of his novels, was done into a charming play which had a considerable success on the London stage in 1949, with Miss Wendy Hiller in the leading role.

[19] European writers have dealt more seriously and more ponderously with Wells than have Americans or his fellow-countrymen. See, for example, Ullrich Sonnemann, *Der soziale Gedanke im Werk von H. G. Wells* (Berlin, 1935); Wolfgang Simon, *Die englische Utopie im Lichte der Entwicklungslehre* (Breslau, 1937); H. W. G. Halfmann, "H. G. Wells' Vereinigung von Pazifismus und Imperialismus," in *Englische Studien,* LIX (Leipzig, 1921), 193–259; H. Matlick, *H. G. Wells als Sozialreformer* (Leipzig, 1935); Georges Connes, *Étude sur la pensée de Wells* (Paris, 1926). A discriminating American study is Van Wyck Brooks, *The World of H. G. Wells* (New York, 1915). Interesting, too, are E. E. Slosson's *Six Major Prophets* (New York, 1917), Chap. II, and Lewis Mumford, *The Story of Utopias* (New York, 1922), Chap. IX.

[20] J. D. Beresford quoted by West, *op. cit.,* pp. 280–81. See also Beresford's *H. G. Wells* (New York, 1915).

[21] "Democracy under Revision," a lecture delivered at the Sorbonne, March 15, 1927; printed in *The Way the World Is Going,* pp. 51–77. The quotation is on pp. 51–52.

York Times, on the occasion of his death at the age of 80: "From an underling in a small private school Wells rose to the position of the greatest public teacher of our time."[22] This is a satisfactory epitaph. For Wells wrote primarily to elucidate and persuade, not to entertain or to create. If he was less objective than the good teacher is expected to be, it was because he always was driven by a sense of urgency—a feeling that the world was headed for disaster, from which it could be diverted only by the most heroic measures, taken at the earliest possible moment. In former times "ideas trickled; in our times they jet." "Modern civilisation is like an aeroplane in mid-air, an aeroplane with one sole, imperfect engine which is popping and showing many signs of distress. It may win to an aerodrome and repairs and replacements. Or it may make a very unpleasant forced landing presently with little hope of immediate recovery."[23] Wells felt disaster breathing down his neck. Time was running out. The world must find answers and find them soon; hence he was less concerned than he should have been with balanced and reasonable discussion. As he grew older his tone became increasingly strident, hortatory, impatient. These are not the qualities of a good pedagogue. Nevertheless Wells was a teacher and, above all, a teacher and leader of youth. "He was our standard bearer and fought for us so bravely that when he failed we failed with him."[24]

To Wells the most urgent, the most inescapable, problem of our civilization was the problem of war. But the problem of war was only part of a larger problem. It grew out of the fact that science and technology had brought about a state of affairs no longer consonant with the political and social institutions devised for an earlier age. It was imperative, therefore, that every preconception of politics—above all, belief in the national state—must be subjected to exacting scrutiny and, where necessary, must be modified or replaced. Failing this, our civilization must surely perish. No one can hope to understand Wells who does not understand and sympathize with the "dominant and enduring passion" of his life. In his youth

he became obsessed with the thought that scientific invention was putting into the hands of mankind the power which, with suitable direction,

---
[22] Aug. 14, 1946.
[23] *William Clissold,* I, 59, 212.
[24] J. Middleton Murry, *Evolution of an Intellectual* (London, 1916), quoted by West, *op. cit.,* p. 189.

could make an ordered society with a life of happiness and varied richness of activity for all—or without that direction bring universal ruin. The need of the time was to adapt government and organized society to the new power and means of communication, to the new economic and political needs of the scientific age. The framework of society, within and beyond the range of political government, was still that of the horse-and-buggy stage of transport, the pre-invention stage of industry. Adaptation was hopelessly outpaced by modern scientific discovery; and it was retarded by obsolete ideas, loyalties and prejudices which only education, at every stage from school to adult politics, could remove and replace. He therefore devoted himself to the task of educating the public, and to this task he subordinated every other purpose in life, with unrelaxing energy, for half a century.[25]

On the other hand, there is much that is paradoxical and volatile in Wells. For example, although he hated war and distrusted the military profession, he became a keen and discriminating student of war and confessed that it held an absorbing fascination for him. He believed that violence must ultimately be banished from human affairs, but he had little sympathy or patience with pacifism or pacifists. He was a Socialist, but he was an acid critic of Socialism and lampooned all varieties of Socialists from the "proletariat" (he doubted that there was any such thing) to Fabians and other left-wing intellectuals. He was a liberal—in the broadest sense of the word—but he was skeptical of democracy and parliamentary government. He had a passionate, perhaps naïve, faith in education as a way of salvation, but he held the teaching profession in contempt and regarded most educational institutions as citadels of medieval superstition.[26] He believed in progress and in the capacity of mankind to achieve a higher destiny, but he railed at the stupidity of the human race; toward the end of his life, ill and disillusioned, he considered the world a vast asylum inhabited by men mistakenly sup-

---

[25] Sir Arthur Salter, *Personality in Politics* (London, 1947), pp. 121–22. The chapter on "H. G. Wells, Apostle of a World Society" in this altogether delightful volume is the best essay I know on Wells. I had started this present paper long before Sir Arthur's book came my way, but I have nevertheless profited enormously from having read his sympathetic and discriminating critique of Wells's political views and attitudes.

[26] Wells said of himself that "he was indeed so much of an educator that quite early he found it imperative to abandon schoolmastering." If the Empire is lost, it will be lost, "if not precisely on the playing fields of Eton, in the mental and moral quality of the men who staff its public schools." "A time must come when Oxford and Cambridge will signify no more in the current intellectual life of the world than the monastery of Mount Athos or the lamaseries of Tibet do now." *William Clissold*, II, 627–60; quotations from pp. 627, 633, 660.

posed sane. He was unremittingly critical of things British and, more especially, of the casual, smug British way in politics; but he loved England and affirmed that he had always been "intensely, affectionately, and profoundly English."[27] He distrusted imperialism as such, as well as as a manifestation of jingoism and militarism, but he believed that the British Empire was something "to be rescued, not destroyed."[28] He regarded nationalism as a dangerous form of megalomania which held the peace of the world in constant jeopardy, but he was proud to call himself an "undisguisedly patriotic Englishman," conscious of the fact that his people, the English, "have created mighty nations, lived valiantly for freedom and fair play through many sturdy generations, and fertilized the whole world with their adventurous dead."[29]

Some of these contradictions are more dialectical than real. Wells was a brilliant conversationalist, and the art of lively conversation is not always constricted by consistency. He used the Socratic dialogue and similar rhetorical devices for explanation and argument. He frequently stated a point of view more effectively than its own proponents, even though he concluded by demolishing it.[30] His prejudices[31] frequently did violence to his better judgment, and his adolescent desire to shock—less pronounced than that of Shaw—was unworthy of his basic tolerance. But when all this is said, and even deplored, it remains that Wells was no irresponsible jester or intellectual nihilist. On behalf of the things he believed he fought intelligently and valiantly for half a century. Even during the cynical post-war era, he was not ashamed of having a cause or of nailing his colors to the mast.

Is there a clue to the beliefs of this versatile and mercurial genius? There are more than one. But if we were to pick a single clue more revealing than others it would be this: Wells believed passionately that "reason"—with its corollary "order"—was the guid-

[27] *The Way the World Is Going*, p. 78.
[28] "What Is the Empire Worth to Mankind?", *ibid.*, Chap. x.
[29] *What Is Coming?: A European Forecast* (New York, 1916), p. 225; *The Way the World Is Going*, pp. 78–79.
[30] "One of the least satisfactory features of the intellectual atmosphere of the present time is the absence of good controversy," wrote Wells at the beginning of the century. "We no longer fight obnoxious views but assassinate them." *Anticipations* (New York, 1902), p. 295.
[31] Some of these prejudices seem petty, such as those which concerned professionals of the Foreign Office, the Armed Forces, the schools, and the universities.

ing principle for the building of a better world. Perhaps more than anything in life he cherished his scientific training,[32] not only for itself, but because he saw in the scientific method a way of shaping the future of mankind.[33] Conversely, the irrational, the chaotic, the sham, the shoddy were the implacable enemies of a good society (the New Republic) and a warless world (the inevitable world community). Injustice, he believed, grows more out of stupidity than of malice; hence the superstitious, the indifferent, the merely conventional are a threat to the good and the true. "Muddle is the enemy," he wrote in 1911. "Clearness and order, light and foresight, these things I know for Good. It was muddle [which has] just given us all the still freshly painful disasters of the [Boer] war, muddle that gives us the visibly sprawling disorder of our cities and industrial countryside, muddle that gives us the waste of life, the limitations, wretchedness and unemployment of the poor. Muddle! I remember myself quoting Kipling—

> 'All along o' dirtiness, all along o' mess,
> All along o' doin' things rather-more-or-less.' "

He was a Socialist, he said, because Individualism meant muddle, "undisciplined people all obstinately and ignorantly doing things jarringly, each one in his own way." Devotion and order were the very essence of socialism; its goal was "an organized state as confident and powerful as modern science, as balanced and beautiful as a body, as beneficent as sunshine, the organized state that should end muddle for ever."[34]

---

[32] Wells studied biology and zoology for two years under the great Huxley and others at the Normal School (now the Royal College) of Science at Kensington. In *Love and Mr. Lewisham* (1900) he left a vivid record of the life of a young scientist. See also West, *op. cit.,* Chap. III, and *Autobiography,* Chap. v.

[33] Wells believed that science and the scientific method could not only diagnose the present but foretell the future. See his memorable address, "The Discovery of the Future," to the Royal Society in London, Jan. 24, 1902, first published in *Nature* and in the *Report of the Smithsonian Institution* (Washington) for 1902. Also "Forecasting the Future," which is Chap. I of *What Is Coming?*

[34] *The New Machiavelli,* Chap. IV, sections 9–10; quotation is from the Penguin edition (London, 1946), pp. 107–9. Wells was one of the earliest advocates of social planning, and he never lost his faith in its possibilities. "We live in a planning world," he wrote in 1939. "Everything we do is becoming preparatory and anticipatory. Today has vanished almost completely in our enormous preoccupation with tomorrow. I suppose I have responded as much as anyone in my generation to this mental rotation." *The Fate of Man* (New York, 1939), p. 67.

III

It was his faith in reason and order that made nationalism anathema to Wells. Even the most sympathetic critic of nationalism will concede that it is a heady wine compounded partly of irrationality. Wells said he "loathed" it for its parochialism, its egocentricity, its intolerance. It "trumpets and waves its flags, obtrudes its tawdry loyalties, exaggerates the splendours of its past, and fights to sustain the ancient hallucinations."[35] Nationalism tends to subvert the school, the press, the pulpit, and other organs of opinion and propaganda, with the result that issues (domestic as well as foreign) become difficult, if not impossible, of rational judgment or settlement.[36] Nationalism became an exacerbating factor in politics only in relatively recent times. However, it is atavistic since it raises nations to the status of tribal gods.

All men are by nature partisans and patriots, but the natural tribalism of men in the nineteenth century was unnaturally exaggerated, it was fretted and over-stimulated and inflamed and forced into the nationalist mould. . . . Men were brought to feel that they were as improper without a nationality as without their clothes in a crowded assembly. Oriental peoples who had never heard of nationality before, took to it as they took to the cigarettes and bowler hats of the west. India, a galaxy of contrasted races, religions, and cultures . . . became a "nation."[37]

It is necessary, too, in considering Wells's attitudes toward nationalism, to remember what Sir Arthur Salter called "the dominant

---

[35] *William Clissold*, II, 572; *The Way the World Is Going*, Chap. vi, "The Absurdity of British Politics." Wells was that rare phenomenon, a British republican. One of his reasons for distrusting and opposing the Crown was his conviction that it lent authority and respectability to "a sort of false England that veils the realities of jingoism." "While [the King] remains, the old army system remains, Society remains, the militant tradition remains. They are all bound up together, inseparably. The people cannot apprehend themselves in relation to the world while, at every turn and crisis of the collective life, the national king, the national uniforms, the national flags and bands, thrust blare and bunting across the realities. . . . How else can a monarchy work considering how monarchs are made and trained and flattered?" *William Clissold*, I, 282–83.

[36] Wells made this fundamental point as early as 1901. See the eloquent statement in *Anticipations*, pp. 182–83.

[37] *The Outline of History* (New York, 1920), II, 433. Wells, like so many others, was not too sharp in drawing distinctions as among nationalism, patriotism, chauvinism, jingoism, and related phenomena. He was descending to frivolity when he defined a nation as "any assembly, mixture, or confusion of people which is either afflicted by or wishes to be afflicted by a foreign office of its own." *Ibid*. To Wells the most crushing indictment of anything was to call it a bore. The following is not very helpful, even if true: "Patriots are bores; nationalists are bores; kings and princes are *ex-officio* terrible bores." *William Clissold*, II, 573.

and enduring passion" of his life[38]—the desire to have political and social institutions conform to the scientific and technological realities of the modern world. There was a time in the history of Europe when nationalism may have been a progressive, unifying force giving vitality to our civilization. But latter-day nationalism was separatist, disruptive, centrifugal, dividing mankind at the very time that powerful forces of science and technology were working in the opposite direction. These latter non-political forces were not as noisy as nationalism; they worked "mutely, because the world of thought was unprepared for them." Nevertheless, "unprecedented advances in technical and scientific knowledge were occurring, and human cooperation . . . was being made enormously more effective than it had ever been before." On the one hand these advances "render possible such a reasoned coordination of human affairs as has never hitherto been conceivable" and, on the other, "they so enlarge and intensify the scope and evil of war and of international hostility as to give what was formerly a generous aspiration [toward world unification and a world community] more and more the aspect of an imperative necessity."[39] New methods of communication by land, sea, and air; new methods of education, journalism, and propaganda; new and more terrible weapons of war; the rise of the heavy industries and, more especially, of the chemical industries —all these things and more put at the disposal of nationalism greater powers of destruction than ever before, while, at the same time, they put at the disposal of mankind unprecedented opportunities for banishing misery, poverty, and war from the face of the earth. Colossal increases in production—resulting from the industrial revolution and the advance of science and technology—have brought into being a new world economy. Industry is said to be national and trade inter-national. But in truth industry, trade, and finance are cosmo-

---

[38] See *supra*, pp. 84–85.

[39] *The Idea of a League of Nations* (Boston, 1919), pp. 6–7. Although Wells was writing twenty-five years before the development of atomic weapons, one is struck by the similarity of much of his argument to that of the Federation of Atomic Scientists and others since Hiroshima. But Wells was not unmindful of the fact that there would be still more terrible weapons than those used during the War of 1914–1918. He was a close student of physics and had foreseen the development of the atomic bomb. In *The World Set Free* (published in May 1914) he made some truly remarkable prophecies concerning atomic weapons and their impact upon international politics. See *infra*, pp. 116–18.

politan and can be effectively carried on only in virtual disregard of political boundaries and organizations.[40]

Imperialism and protectionism, like the nationalism which gave them birth, likewise are to Wells irrational and anachronistic. In its earlier phases European imperialism may have been a cohesive, civilizing factor in human affairs. Even now—provided the obligation of trusteeship takes precedence over the urge to exploit—imperalism may be in accord with the broad interests of mankind.[41] But the British Empire cannot be regarded as a preserve, to be run on mercenary, acquisitive, selfish, nationalistic lines. Tariff reform, imperial preference, and similar restrictive practices advocated by Joseph Chamberlain and others would bring Britain "into conflict with every other people under the sun."[42] This new Imperialism, said Wells, was born in Germany; the best that could be said for it is that it was based on the Zollverein. "It was invented by professors of Weltpolitik. Milner has grafted it upon us at Balliol."[43] But Britain is not Germany. "Germany is a fist—by geographical necessity. The British Empire is like an open hand. We are an open people—or we are nothing. We are a liberalizing power or we are the most pretentious sham in history."[44] Tariffs—whether in the guise of imperial preference or other monopolistic practices—are "foolish barriers that cut up the comity of mankind." In fact, they are a form of war: "White War, the chronic as distinguished from

[40] These ideas are so fundamental to Wells's thinking that it is probably unwise to document them in detail. They appear, of course, in *Anticipations* and, in much greater detail, in *The Work, Wealth and Happiness of Mankind* (London, 1932). They are dealt with at length in *The New Machiavelli* and *William Clissold*. As we shall presently see, they gave Wells the idea of a world state which, in its early phases at least, might bypass political methods and build its foundations on international economic activities.

[41] For eloquent statements to this general effect, see *An Englishman Looks at the World* (London, 1914), especially pp. 37-38; *Joan and Peter*, especially pp. 222-24, 242-43; *What Is Coming?*, Chap. XI; *In the Fourth Year* (New York, 1918), Chap. v. For a favorable view of certain of the British imperialists—Cromer, Milner, and others—see *The New Machiavelli*, pp. 268, 342, circa; *Autobiography*, pp. 650-55; *The Way the World Is Going*, p. 123.

[42] *Joan and Peter*, pp. 223-24. Chamberlain is here referred to as a "demagogue ironmonger" and "nail trust organizer."

[43] On the curious and unfounded legend that Milner had established an imperialist cult at Balliol College, Oxford, see J. A. Spender and Cyril Asquith, *Life of Herbert Henry Asquith* (London, 1932), I, 146-48.

[44] The quotation is from *Joan and Peter*, pp. 223-24; the tenses have been changed from past to present to conform to my text. The idea of the Open Hand was a favorite of Wells and appears in *The New Machiavelli* and *Autobiography*, as well as elsewhere.

H. G. Wells

the acute form." Unless the civilized peoples of the world stop quarreling over colonies and colonial trade, there presently won't be anything left for them to quarrel over.[45]

As might be expected, Wells rejected *in toto* all the pseudo-science which went along with nationalism and racialism. "People who believe in this sort of thing," he wrote, "are not the sort of people that one attempts to convert by a set argument. One need only say that the thing is not so; there is no Teutonic race, and there never has been.... This nonsense about Keltic and Teutonic is no more science than Lombroso's extraordinary assertions about criminals, or palmistry, or the development of religion from a solar myth."[46] But this belief in nationalistic or racial superiorities is not mere nonsense; it is dangerous and pernicious nonsense. Nationalism and patriotism rarely function in and of themselves; they require active suspicion and hatred of foreigners or minorities if they are to thrive. The vilest form of nationalistic and racial prejudice is anti-Semitism. The Jew, said Wells, is not merely a rightful member of the community, but "he gives the lie to all our yapping 'nationalism,' and sketches in his dispersed sympathies the coming of the world-state."[47]

Wells was convinced that there was no "insurmountable barrier" to a "common citizenship" of all peoples, races, and nationalities in "a world republic." The negro is, perhaps,

> the hardest case. But the negro has hardly ever had a dog's chance of getting civilised in considerable numbers, and yet his race has produced brilliant musicians, writers, and men of scientific distinction. In the eighteenth century he was the backbone of the British navy. I refuse to consider even the black patches of the world as a gangrene in the body of mankind.... I do not propose to write any formal reply to the many preposterous volumes of incitement to race jealousy and conflict that have been published in the last few years, books about the Yellow Peril, the Rising Tide of Colour, the Passing of the Great Race, and so forth. Even the titles are banners and aggressions.... There has never been any Great Race, but a continual integration, dispersal, and even reintegration of active peoples drawn from the most diverse sources, and there is

---

[45] *William Clissold*, II, 582; *Work, Wealth and Happiness of Mankind*, p. 607; *What Is Coming?*, Chap. XI.

[46] *Anticipations*, pp. 237–38. See also Chap. x of *A Modern Utopia* (London, 1905), an exceedingly effective answer to the aberrations of racial and nationalistic "superiority" prevalent in our time.

[47] *Anticipations*, pp. 340–42; *William Clissold*, II, 613–15.

hardly a people which has not contributed some important release or achievement to the common progress.[48]

Wells considered himself a liberal, and he was aware that one of the postulates of liberalism was an acceptance of the principle of nationality and national self-determination. Nevertheless, he believed that application of the principle would fragmentize the political structure of the world. Nationalism meant, almost by definition, an increasing number of inter-national rivalries, exasperations, and suspicions. Advocacy of freedom for insurgent peoples made British liberalism "a champion of nationalities and the instigator of pseudo-liberal nationalism in Germany and Italy. That pseudo-liberal nationalism has brought forward thorns of swords and bayonets and bitterly unattractive fruits."[49] How could it have been otherwise? "The essential idea of nineteenth-century nationalism was the 'legitimate claim' of every nation to complete sovereignty, the claim of every nation to manage all its affairs within its own territory, regardless of any other nation." But, since "the affairs and interests of every modern community extend to the uttermost parts of the earth" it follows that "a world of independent sovereign

---

[48] *William Clissold*, II, 614–15. A German comment on Wells is W. Simon, *Die englische Utopie* (cited in footnote 19 above), Part II, sec. 10, "Wells gegen dem Rassenstandpunkt." But Wells didn't like Jewish nationalism, either. He regarded the Old Testament as one of the most shocking instances of nationalistic history and tribal incitation. In this sense the "German National Socialist movement is essentially Jewish in spirit and origin, it is Bible-born, an imitation of Old Testament nationalism," with all "its barbaric cunning and barbaric racialism." "Only a Bible-saturated people ... could take so easily to national egotism, to systematic xenophobia, to self-righteous ideas of conquest and extermination. The German mind, never a very subtle or critical one, the copious abounding German mind, was poisoned in the Lutheran schools," where the Bible was regarded "as a book sacred beyond criticism." *The Anatomy of Frustration* (New York, 1936), pp. 135–43; quotation from p. 141.

[49] *William Clissold*, II, 662. Wells thought liberals frequently were confused by universal application of dogma. "You will find a Labour paper like the *Daily Herald* scolding vigorously at the private ownership of land and minerals in one column and insisting in the next upon the 'right' of some little barbaric nationality to hold its territories and its natural resources, however vast they may happen to be, against the needs of all mankind. It would wrench the northern coalfields from the Duke of Northumberland and leave all the mines of the Riff to Abd-el-Krim." *Ibid.*, I, 183. Again, "One of the most human and interesting things to watch at the present time is the struggle of the Labour parties in the European democracies against their ingrained nationalist feelings and their belligerent patriotism. And still more edifying are the fluctuations of the Labour movement in such countries as Australia and South Africa with regard to yellow and brown immigration and the black vote." *The Way the World Is Going*, p. 63.

states means a world of perpetual injuries, a world of states constantly preparing for or waging war."[50]

The idea that the sovereign state "is essentially and incurably a war-making state"[51] lay at the foundation of all Wells's thinking on world affairs. As early as 1901 he had become convinced that nationalism would set in motion forces which a democratic state might find it impossible to control. "Consequently, the final development of the democratic system, so far as intrinsic forces go, will be, not the rule of the boss, nor the rule of the trust, nor the rule of the newspaper; no rule, indeed, but international rivalry, international competition, international exasperation and hostility, and at last—irresistible and overwhelming—the definite establishment of the rule of that most stern and educational of all masters—War."[52]

In short, Wells regarded nationalism as perhaps the basic cause of war. He blamed it in part for the war of 1914, for the bitterness with which that war was waged, and for the failure of the subsequent peace. He was skeptical of national self-determination as a war aim or as a peace program, unless the newly-created national states could be linked in an effective form of federalism or federal union on the model of the United States or Switzerland.[53] He castigated Wilson for "his obsession by the idea of the sovereignty of 'nationalities' and his incapacity to think out what he meant by a nationality." "He thought only of nations struggling to be free. He never thought of man struggling to be free of nationality."[54]

In a brilliant and deeply moving address to the Reichstag, April 15, 1929, Wells made it clear that problems of nationalism, and of the political, economic, and psychological aspects of nationalism were the heart of all proposals looking toward the limitation of war.

I am suggesting [he said], that something very fundamental, something very difficult, important and formidable, is being shirked and evaded in

---

[50] *The Outline of History*, II, 435.

[51] *Autobiography*, p. 570.

[52] *Anticipations*, p. 183.

[53] *What Is Coming?* (1916), Chap. IX, "The New Map of Europe"; *In the Fourth Year* (1918).

[54] *The Way the World Is Going*, p. 82; *The Common Sense of World Peace* (London, 1929), p. 32. An earlier judgment of Wilson had been more charitable, although still captious. *The Outline of History*, II, 543–55. For other vignettes of Wilson, see *William Clissold*, I, 294, 325–26; *Autobiography*, p. 604. Wells's views on Wilson were colored by J. M. Keynes' *Economic Consequences of the Peace* (New York, 1920).

all this peace discussion and all these permanent peace proposals [such as the Kellogg Pact]. This difficulty is the *sovereign independence of states*. That is the cardinal difficulty before us, and until we tackle it instead of walking round it, we shall not make much further progress towards the organized peace of the world. We shall go on wasting our virtuous emotions on Peace Pacts and our substance upon war preparation, just as we are doing at the present time.[55]

IV

Wells knew, of course, that nationalism was a formidable force in the world, not to be lightly brushed aside or easily conjured away. But men have not always been nationalistic; even now they might not be, had they not been educated to the "monstrous obsessions" which modern nationalism involves. To be sure, "there is something very fundamental in man's response to patriotism"; man is a gregarious animal, "an adhesive beast." He likes to "belong" to a group. The intellect may be cosmopolitan, but pride and instincts are patriotic.[56]

We have all been so taught and trained to patriotic attitudes, they have been drummed into us from our earliest childhood, they have so impressed themselves upon us at home, at school, in book, in drama, in the common idioms of thought, they have been so built into the substance of our minds, that it is only by a considerable intellectual effort that any of us can liberate ourselves from these forms of thought to which we have been moulded. But we *have* been moulded to them; they are not essential things. It is possible to struggle away from them and out of them .... What man has made man can remake, and if the real way to world peace is to be opened out, if we are indeed to go on towards human federation, this vast complexity of patriotic teaching, emotional appeal, social and police pressure, cultivated hostility and distrust, flag waving, flag saluting and everlastingly reiterated patriotic sentiment which now divides man so implacably throughout the world has to be faced and fought and overcome.[57]

[55] *The Common Sense of World Peace,* pp. 11–12. An address delivered in the Reichstag, Berlin, Monday, April 15, 1929. International law was not one of the subjects in which Wells claimed competence. But on this question of national sovereignty he finds support among the experts. See, for example, P. C. Jessup, *A Modern Law of Nations* (New York, 1946), especially introductory chapter and pp. 40–42. "Sovereignty," says Professor Jessup, "in its meaning of an absolute, uncontrolled state will, ultimately free to resort to the final arbitrament of war, is the quicksand upon which the foundations of traditional international law are built" (p. 40).

[56] *William Clissold,* II, 612.

[57] *The Common Sense of World Peace,* pp. 27–31.

It is not feasible within the limits of this paper to discuss Wells's views on education in general; nor is it necessary to do so, since one cannot read any of his books without being instructed on the shortcomings of education and the ways it should be reformed and redirected.[58] Wells had unlimited faith in education—perhaps more faith than reasonable expectations would warrant. He believed that one of the roads to world peace lay through the gateways of school and university. Mankind needs to be educated to a new concept of duty, honor, responsibility, and loyalties. He was convinced that education in most countries was badly conceived and badly executed. But in Britain especially, as he saw it, the entire system was "a muddle of impulses and antagonisms, commercialism, utilitarianism, obstinate conservatism, humanitarian enthusiasm"; it was hoary with age and precedent.[59] The schools were "meanly equipped and pretentiously conducted"; the universities mere "dens of cramming," places where one could not learn and criticize but merely recite.[60] The teaching profession in Britain was loaded down with "refugees from the novelties and strains and adventures of life"—second class nobodies, residues after the cream of youth had chosen other walks of life. As a result of poor schools, inadequate universities, and wretched teachers

the prevalent Englishman abroad and in public affairs had become [over the generations] a type noticeably different from any other nationality. He had become stiff, arrogant, profoundly ignorant, technically honourable, and utterly incomprehensible to the uninitiated rest of mankind. He was no longer the Englishman of the Elizabethan or Cromwellian model, half Kelt, half Viking; he was no longer any sort of man; he was a public-school boy, the finished product.[61]

That this estimate of British education suffers from hyperbole goes without saying.

Among other things, said Wells, education in our time had a strongly nationalistic bias which, consciously and otherwise, contributed to the political instability of the world. He had profound

---

[58] *Joan and Peter* is subtitled "The Story of an Education"; there are long sections on education in *The New Machiavelli, William Clissold, The Bulpington of Blup, Mr. Britling,* to mention only a few. See also *Autobiography,* especially pp. 264 *et seq.,* 552 *et seq.*

[59] *The New Machiavelli,* p. 21.

[60] *Anticipations,* pp. 289–92.

[61] *William Clissold,* II, 631–33 *et seq.*

admiration for German education because of the emphasis it put upon science and scientific training; on the other hand, he thought, the "puerile militarism" of Germany was in part due to the fact that the Germans, thanks to their schools and universities, were "more thoroughly misinformed" about politics than any other people in Western Europe. The German state waged a constant Kulturkampf to control the education, and hence the minds, of its youth. Germany was worse than other nations in degree, but not necessarily in the essence of things. For in all nations history has been a form of propaganda

taught to larger and larger masses of the people of the world in an intensely nationalistic form. Few of us have escaped some mental distortion in consequence. The results of that prolonged subjection to an intensive misrepresentation of human history have to be washed out of the minds of men. That can only be done by the teaching of a different history, the history of social evolution, the story of the great human society of today, and by the education of the imagination through a realization of man's steady conquest of power and freedom. We need a history teaching that, instead of training us to dwell upon and carry on the conflicts and resentments of yesterday and today, points and leads us on to the great possibilities of the collective human future. We need an education that will turn mankind from tradition to hope. That is the difficult and necessary foundation for any world peace. There is no way to world peace except through these preliminary battles of the mind.[62]

Historians were the last persons in the world, according to Wells, who should be charged with the writing and the teaching of the new history. To professional historians history is "a cave of the winds in which documents whirl about."[63] Teachers of history are pedants, insistent that their pupils continue to "learn the more significant

---

[62] The quotation is from *The Common Sense of World Peace*, pp. 38–39. But the same general idea is continuously recurrent in Wells's writings. It is set forth at length in *Anticipations*, especially the three final chapters, *Joan and Peter*, *William Clissold*, the *Autobiography*, *A Modern Utopia*, and in "The Discovery of the Future." (The last-named, an address to the Royal Society in 1902, cited *supra* footnote 33, drew a distinction between the legal, past-regarding, and the creative, future-regarding, mind.)

[63] *William Clissold*, I, 165. Wells had a curious antipathy to all professionals. Professional army and navy officers were possessed of intelligence below the seventh form and of a moral stature inferior to that of "a Constantinople tourist's dragoman." Professionals of the Foreign Office had minds hopelessly molded by governesses into immutable prejudice and convention.

facts about Queen Elizabeth's doubtful virginity, memorize such legal documents as the Constitutions of Clarendon and the Bill of Rights, and discuss those marvelous world policies invented for examination purposes by dons addicted to self-identification with Julius Caesar or Napoleon Bonaparte or Charles the Fifth or Disraeli or some other of the many exaggerated and inflammatory figures about which history has festered." What we need in our time is to abandon "the clotted masses of un-digested and ill-digested fact," as well as "the time-worn gossip and stale and falsified politics" which now "encumber academic history" and to concentrate instead upon analysis and synthesis of the broad historical process. The field of history must be invaded by the scientific spirit. The newer historians "would be related to the old school of historians much as vegetable physiologists, ecologists, and morphologists are related to the old plant-flattening, specimen-hunting, stamen-counting botanists." "Periods, nations, and races" should be studied only to the extent that they are essential to a broader synthesis of human affairs.[64]

In a sense history is a form of the higher politics, and "historians must stand to the questions a politician can evade."[65] Historians need not lend uncritical obedience and support to such outworn institutions as monarchism, nationalism, and imperialism. They have it largely in their hands to direct the future away from the national state and to point it in the way of the world state. Since historians do not have this larger view of their professional responsibilities, and since they hold no monopoly upon the teaching and writing of history, laymen are justified in redressing their shortcomings. Holding that history was no occult art, Wells himself took it in hand and, after three years of "fantastic toil," published in 1920 a two-volume *Outline of History,* which became one of the most successful books of our times. Its sale of more than two million copies must surely have set a record for any work of history published before or since. Wells has given a fascinating account of how the book came about, what its objectives were, and what he esti

---

[64] *Autobiography,* pp. 552–53. In this passage Wells is summarizing and amplifying views originally expressed in 1901 in *Anticipations.*

[65] *The Outline of History,* II, 432.

mated its achievements to be.⁶⁶ Suffice it to say here that he intended his book to be a departure from "King and Country stuff" and a pioneer effort "to tell, truly and clearly, in one continuous narrative, the whole story of life and mankind so far as it is known today."

The Outline of History was not only history with a Purpose but history with a Mission. It was concerned not merely with a more cosmic analysis and a more cosmopolitan synthesis, but with developing a climate of opinion favorable to an ordered international society. "There can be no peace now [at the close of a devastating war], we realize, but a common peace in all the world; no prosperity but a general prosperity. But *there can be no common peace and prosperity without common historical ideas.* Without such ideas to hold them together in harmonious co-operation, with nothing but narrow, selfish, and conflicting nationalist traditions, races and peoples are bound to drift towards conflict and destruction." Furthermore, "our internal policies and our economic and social ideas are profoundly vitiated by wrong and fantastic ideas of the origin and historical relationship of social classes. A sense of history as the common adventure of all mankind is as necessary for peace within as it is for peace between nations."⁶⁷ The world to which this message was addressed was avid for a knowledge of history as a means of understanding the complicated present. The same world looked to history, too, to point a way of salvation from a recurrence of the ordeal of death and destruction which it had recently survived. As Wells said, the world of 1918–1919 had barely ceased being a battlefield before it became a riddle.⁶⁸ Anyone who could offer a clue, any clue, to the riddle was assured a large and attentive audience.

As might be expected, Well's account of universal history is biased and misinformed. To cite a single instance, his treatment of Na-

⁶⁶ *Autobiography*, pp. 612–16. Wells thought he was writing a tract designed to influence the teaching of history in schools and universities. He found, instead, that he was influencing a much wider audience. "One went to bed," he said, "an educational reformer and woke up a best seller." Wells was amply rewarded by the *History*, which made him a rich man beyond any previous dream. *A Short History of the World*, published in 1922, was a digest of the longer work and likewise had a large sale. *Ibid.*, and West, *op. cit.*, pp. 225–30.

⁶⁷ *The Outline of History*, I, v–vi. This is as good a time as any to point out that Wells was an implacable foe of the economic interpretation of history and the cult of economic determinism. His criticisms of Marx, Marxian socialism, and Communism are devastating. He regarded Marxism as a political system founded upon envy and vindictiveness and believed that the world would be a better place had Karl Marx never been born.

⁶⁸ *William Clissold*, II, 487.

poleon is grotesque. But viewed as a two-volume, 1400-page pamphlet it is a superb *tour de force,* and it is undoubtedly what Wells would most have wished it to be—a tremendously effective piece of public "education." Nor did the professional historians promptly rule it out of court. They said, to be sure, that it was not history. But they conceded that it had rendered history a service. To take the comment of a single American historian, who himself had made noteworthy contributions to the "new history":

> ... [Wells] has rushed in where few "historians" have dared to tread. He has caught a vision denied to most "specialists." He has grasped the unity and continuity of world history, the indivisible and unfolding human epic. Moreover, he has availed himself of scholarly researches in the newer sciences that are allied to history . . . and has sought to make of them an appropriate and strictly up-to-date stage-setting for his play, "Man in the Universe." Further, not content with sketching merely the conventional European background of our present civilization, he has reached out and told us something of [other and less well-known cultures]; and finally, in harmony with a large and influential school of historians in the United States, he has endeavoured to approach history as a utilitarian, dwelling on such facts and events in the past as appear to augment our understanding of the present and to point our path to the future.
>
> A goodly number of "professional historians" have had one or another of these general aims in mind, but the whole synthesis of Mr. Wells is novel and illuminating. It is his synthesis which particularly appeals to the lay reader. . . . Despite hundreds of faults, the "Outline of History" is truly important, because its general synthetic aim is excellent, because it is timely, and because its author has a voice that "carries." Mr. Wells is preparing the way for scholars and making the world safe for historians. Henceforth professors will not fear to walk where Mr. Wells has leaped, and eventually one of them or a group of them will produce a history of man in the universe that will be as sound and reliable as the "Outline" before us is inaccurate and impressionistic.[69]

Whether, as Wells believed, there is a pattern of the past which, properly delineated, will enable us to divine and to influence the future is something on which historians do not agree. One distin-

---

[69] Carlton J. H. Hayes, "The Other Worldly Mr. Wells" (a review of *The Outline of History*), in *The Freeman,* III (New York, 1921), 18–21. For an aciduous 240-page review by a layman, see Hilaire Belloc, *A Companion to Mr. Wells's Outline of History* (London, 1926), examining in minute detail Wells's treatment of religion and, in particular, the Catholic Church. "We are reading in this *Outline of History,*" wrote Mr. Belloc, "the work of a mind closely confined to a particular place and moment—the late Victorian London suburbs. Such a mind has an apparatus quite inferior to the task of historical writing." No professional historian was as derogatory to Wells as this.

guished British historian has said that "history, while it should be scientific in method, should pursue a practical object. That is, it should not merely gratify the reader's curiosity about the past, but modify his view of the present and his forecast of the future. Now if this maxim be sound, the history of England ought to end with a moral; it ought to exhibit the general tendency of English affairs in such a way as to set us thinking about the future and divining the destiny which is reserved for us."[70] To this view Wells would have subscribed, for he believed that the scientific method—when applied to history, as elsewhere—enables us to prophesy for the future as well as to recount the past and describe the present. On the other hand, it has been contended, history pretends to do much less: "Men wiser and more learned than I," writes another British historian, "have discerned in history a plot, a rhythm, a predetermined pattern. These harmonies are concealed from me. I can see only one emergency following upon another as wave follows upon wave, only one great fact concerning which, since it is unique, there can be no generalizations, only one safe rule for the historian: that he should recognize in the development of human destinies the play of the contingent and the unforeseen."[71]

Few would deny, however, that it is possible to take texts from history, as from the Scriptures. And since Wells was more preacher, teacher, and journalist than historian, he may be allowed a license not vouchsafed to those who are dedicated to documentation and footnotes. And if history is to be interpreted—perhaps distorted—to promote a cause, to what cause could it be better dedicated than to the cause of a community of mankind, a world state, and a warless society?

v

Despite his deprecation of nationalism, Wells himself was a nationalist and a patriot. He was not only intensely and proudly Eng-

---

[70] Sir John Seeley, *The Expansion of England* (London, 1883), p. 3. This same view appears in many other places in Seeley's works. See the article by Thomas P. Peardon in the present volume for a study of Seeley as an historian.

[71] H. A. L. Fisher, *A History of Europe* (London, 1935), I, vii. The question at issue has recently been debated by Professor Pieter Geyl, of the University of Utrecht, and Professor Arnold J. Toynbee. See *The Pattern of the Past: Can We Determine It?* (Boston, 1949).

lish, but he was cockney English.⁷² To be sure, he was perennially engaged in "that favourite topic of all intelligent Englishmen, the adverse criticism [and even the abuse] of things British." He tended in his more tolerant moments to regard England as "the amiable summation of a grotesque assembly of faults."⁷³ He detested the drabness, the poverty, and (as he saw it) the planlessness and chaos of British industrial society; he hated such excrescences of industrialism as the London slums—the "vast dirtiness" of London—and the tragedy which is British coal-mining.⁷⁴ He was ashamed of British provincialism and he painted some devastating portraits of the "average" Englishman.⁷⁵ He detested the "clumsy, crawling, snobbish, comfort-loving caterpillar" which was Victorian England, as well as the smug, inert, undisciplined England of Edwardian and Georgian days. "In England everybody talks of changes, but nothing ever changes. Unless something tumbles down here, we never think of altering it. And even then we just shore it up."⁷⁶ Nevertheless, Wells had visions of another England—"England as our country might be, with no wretched poor, no wretched rich, a nation armed and ordered, trained and purposeful amidst its vales and rivers." When he contemplated this England, he was resolved, above all else, "to leave England and the empire better ordered than I found it, to organize and discipline, to build up a constructive and controlling state ... to suffuse education with public intention ... to link now chaotic activities in every human affair ... to bring [industry and finance] back to the service of the general good."⁷⁷

Above all Wells despised and savagely attacked the slackness and smugness, the inefficiency and muddle, of British political behavior.

⁷² Salter, *op. cit.*, p. 134.
⁷³ *Mr. Britling*, pp. 15–16, 35.
⁷⁴ E.g., *Autobiography*, pp. 224–25; *William Clissold*, II, 456–58.
⁷⁵ See, for example, *The New Machiavelli*, pp. 130–31, for a description of a smug, self-satisfied business man who "knew no language but Staffordshire, hated all foreigners because he was English, and all foreign ways because they were not his ways. Also he hated particularly, and in this order, Londoners, Yorkshiremen, Scotch, Welsh and Irish because they were not 'reet Staffordshire,' and he hated all other Staffordshire men as insufficiently 'reet.'" Also the *Autobiography*, p. 582, for an upperclass Englishman who "was a curious mixture of sixth-form Anglican sentimentality (about dear old horses, dearer old doggies, brave women, real gentlemen, the old school, the old country and sound stock: Galsworthyissimus in fact) with an adventurous intelligence." All British professional army officers, *ipso facto*, become Colonel Blimps at a very early age.
⁷⁶ *Mr. Britling*, pp. 53–54, 120.
⁷⁷ *The New Machiavelli*, pp. 111, 149.

The national bungling in the Boer War he considered disgraceful. It had

> laid bare an amazing and terrifying amount of national incompetence. The Empire was not only hustled into a war for which there was no occasion, but that war was planned with a lack of intelligent foresight and conducted with a lack of soundness that dismayed every thoughtful Englishman. After a monstrous wasteful struggle the national resources dragged it at last to a not very decisive victory . . . . Behind the rejoicings that hailed the belated peace was a real and unprecedented national humiliation. For the first time the educated British were enquiring whether all was well with the national system if so small a conquest seemed so great a task.
>
> Simultaneously, the nation became aware that the vitality and the tremendous economic expansion of the United States and Germany boded ill for an older nation which was set in its industrial and commercial ways.[78]

The muddle of the South African War was not, however, exceptional; it was typical, Wells thought, of an easy-going, indolent, unduly optimistic quality in the British character. "The British mind hates crisis; it abhors the word 'Now.' It believes that you can cool water for ever and that it will never freeze, that you can saw at a tree for ever and that it will never fall, that there is always some sand left in the hour glass."[79] British politics, at home and abroad, is "a sort of dignified dexterity of evasion." "The prevailing spirit in English life . . . is one of underbred aggression in prosperity and diplomatic compromise in moments of danger; we bully haughtily where we can and assimilate where we must."[80] Compared with Germany, Great Britain is lacking in education and training, in discipline and efficiency, in comprehension of the value of science to the national welfare and security, and in unity of purpose.[81] If there is a single word which best describes the slackness, inertia, the indolence, and parochialism of British political behavior, said Wells, it is Muddle. And muddle is repugnant to all those who believe in reason and order.

[78] The quotation is from *Joan and Peter*, pp. 215–16, but the same theme appears in *Anticipations* and in *The New Machiavelli*.
[79] *Joan and Peter*, p. 401.
[80] *The New Machiavelli*, p. 258.
[81] *Ibid.*, 256–58; also *Anticipations*, pp. 274–80; *An Englishman Looks at the World*. pp. 36–37.

But after all this was said—and much more—Wells still preferred the British way. He foresaw—long before most of his fellow-countrymen—that the very discipline and order which had carried Germany so far and so fast in the years 1870–1900 might prove to be the means, in the long run, of bringing the Germans to defeat and disaster.[82] He believed that Britain's easy-going, insouciant political behavior might be "one of the essential secrets" of her national and imperial endurance.[83] Britain's failures and dangers lie not so much in the things she has done which should not have been done, as in the things she has left undone which should have been done. Muddle is not something to admire, but at least it is not a direct threat to the peace of the world.[84] The persistence and severity of Wells's attacks on things English were, perhaps, a measure of his love for England. "Whom the Lord loveth he chasteneth."

Wells could be lyrically patriotic, even when he was disillusioned about the state of the world as a whole. In a chapter—called, curiously, "The Absurdity of British Politics"—of *The Way the World Is Going,* published in 1929, Wells gives a deeply moving statement of the reasons for his British patriotism. "I loathe nationalism," he says in this notable passage, "but this does not prevent my being intensely, affectionately, and profoundly English. . . . I am a scion, however unworthy, of a very great race, and heir to an unapproachable tradition of candid speech and generous act." The English have created other mighty nations, including the United States. They are "a people necessary to mankind." There are occasions

when either "God's Englishman"—as our Milton had it—must play his part, or the occasion fail. It is our boast that we say what we think without fear or favor and that we are not easily driven in flocks or cowed by difficulties or defeated—even by defeat. . . . Never have we been a theatrical people; there are few heroic gestures in our story and little rhetoric; we have never pretended to be a race of supermen, and our drama, fiction, and common speech abound in self-derision. . . . Our dearest boast was the prestige of "the word of an Englishman," and it is our claim that we would rather be trusted than exalted among the peoples of the earth. Whatever the diplomatic situation might have been, the great mass of the English folk in the New World, as in the Old, believed that

[82] *Anticipations,* pp. 277 *et seq.;* see also *infra,* pp. 110–11.
[83] *The New Machiavelli,* p. 285.
[84] This is my own summary of Wells's views and cannot readily be documented in a single reference; it is, I believe, essentially accurate.

they were fighting aggressive monarchist militarism in the Great War and preparing the way for a peace without uniforms. They hated Germany more for her goose step than for her fleet.

The League of Nations was a "product of the English mind on both sides of the Atlantic, and could never have existed but for the faith of the English in reasonable dealing."[85] No poet laureate of the patriotic theme could have done better than this.

Wells could speak favorably and admiringly not only of British patriotism but also of British imperialism. Essentially, he said, the Empire was in its origins

> an adventure of the British spirit, sanguine, discursive, and beyond comparison insubordinate, adaptable, and originating. It has been made by odd and irregular means, by trading companies, pioneers, explorers, unauthorized seamen, adventurers like Clive, eccentrics like Gordon, invalids like Rhodes. It has been made, in spite of authority and officialdom, as no other empire has been made. The nominal rulers of Britain never planned it; it happened almost in spite of them. Their chief contribution to its history has been the loss of the United States. It is a living thing that has arisen, not a dead thing put together. Beneath the thin legal and administrative ties that hold it together lies the far more vital bond of a free spontaneous activity. It has a common medium of expression in the English tongue, a unity of liberal and tolerant purpose amidst its enormous variety of localized life and color. And it is in the development and strengthening, the enrichment, the rendering more conscious and more purposeful, of the broad creative spirit of the British that the true cement and continuance of our Empire is to be found. The Empire must live by the forces that begot it . . . . If it is to survive, it must give all its constituent parts such a civilization as none of them could achieve alone, a civilization, a wealth and fulness of life increasing and developing with the years.[86]

This may seem a somewhat idyllic picture of the Empire, and it would be rejected *in toto* by most anti-imperialists. But it has its large elements of truth. The alternative to the Empire seemed to be its disintegration or partial disintegration into smaller political units, including self-conscious national states like Ireland. Wells, it must be remembered, was opposed to any proposal or program which would lead to the further Balkanization of the world. It

---

[85] Pp. 78–82, of which the foregoing is only a brief summary. There is a similar passage in *Joan and Peter,* deeply moving and convincing, but written in the emotion of wartime.

[86] *An Englishman Looks at the World,* pp. 37–38.

seemed to him, during the years 1895–1915 or thereabouts, that the Empire had better be preserved than broken up by Indian, South African, and other nationalisms which he considered just as intolerant, just as irrational, just as petty and narrow-minded as the nationalisms of Europe. "I have never found Nationalism even a plausible excuse for the sterilization of some great area of potential wealth because a backward people happened to live upon it. The whole earth is for the whole earth." Wells visualized the Empire as "the pacific precursor of a practical world-state," its raw materials and other resources "as part of the common estate of the human race, our share in a trusteeship."[87] Furthermore, he could see no "competent receiver" which could take over the constituent parts of the Empire in the event of its dissolution.[88]

During the years before the First World War Wells could be fairly described as a liberal imperialist. As such he was a serious student of imperial affairs. He was a member for several years, for example, of the Co-efficients, a non-partisan discussion group concerned with national and imperial problems on the level of high policy.[89] He never became an emotionalist about the Empire,[90] and he fought to see that it was an empire of the "open hand" rather than the "closed fist." For two decades or more he continued to hope that it might play "a dominating part in the establishment of a world peace and a world civilization." It was with the greatest reluctance that he finally came to the conclusion that the Empire could not survive, that it was being destroyed by centrifugal forces and official stupidities. Even then his hopes went down with colors

[87] *The Way the World Is Going,* Chap. x; *Autobiography,* pp. 650 *et seq.*
[88] On the idea of the "competent receiver," see *Autobiography,* pp. 206 *circa.*
[89] This very remarkable group was first described by Wells in *The New Machiavelli* as the "Pentagram Circle." He discusses it in greater detail in his *Autobiography,* pp. 650 *et seq.,* and in *The Way the World Is Going,* Chap. x. Mr. L. S. Amery has been good enough to give me additional information about the club, of which he was a member throughout its existence, from about 1902 to about 1910. Among the other members were Sidney Webb, Grey, Haldane, H. J. Mackinder, Milner, Bertrand Russell, W. Pember Reeves, W. A. S. Hewins (Mackinder, Reeves, and Hewins were all, at one time or another, directors of the London School of Economics), and Carlyon Bellairs. The club broke up eventually, according to Mr. Amery, because two of its later members, G. B. Shaw and J. L. Garvin, talked it to death.
[90] Wells never knew exactly where he stood on Kipling and Kiplingism. See *The New Machiavelli,* pp. 97–99, and *Autobiography,* p. 650. But Wells had great respect for the actual "colonizers"—Milner, Cromer, Hugh Clifford, Lord Olivier, and Sir Harry Johnston. *The Way the World Is Going,* Chap. x; *Autobiography,* pp. 650, 655; *The New Machiavelli,* pp. 268, 342.

still flying: "It would be all too easy to fly into an attitude of anti-Imperialism, and say with the Communists, 'These imperialisms are evil things; let us destroy them.' But they are not inherently evil things. To destroy imperial systems with nothing to replace them is simply to leap backward because one is not going forward fast enough."[91]

VI

Wells's patriotism reached its apogee in 1914. "In those first days of August," wrote Mr. Philip Guedalla, "when the War swept across Europe like the wind out of Africa, there was an ugly rush of innumerable pilots to weather the storm. Mr. Wells hurried into his oilskins, Mr. Arnold Bennett jumped into his sea-boots, and the Poet Laureate heaved a melodious but archaic lead. . . . The mast was almost invisible under the mass of colours that had been nailed to it."[92] Bernard Shaw said that in the first febrile excitement of war the average British patriot not only lost his head but insisted on kicking it around the streets as well. It is easy, of course, to be wise, calm, and collected long after the event. It is easy to forget how surprised, how profoundly shocked, we were by the mere fact of the war. It is perhaps natural that we should forget, too, how ominous German power appeared to be when it had crossed the Marne and was thundering at the very gates of Paris. (In this respect, at least, the experience of 1940 repeated that of 1914!)

Long after the War, Wells was quite willing to admit that his emotions swept away his judgment in the terrible days of August and September 1914.

As I reassemble all that I can of my hasty, discursive and copious writings during the early stages of the war, and do my utmost to recover my actual states of mind, it becomes plain to me that for a time—in spite of my intellectual previsions—the world disaster, now that it had come, so overwhelmed my mind that I was obliged to thrust a false interpretation upon it, and assert, in spite of my deep and at first unformulated misgivings, that here and now, the new world order was in conflict with the old . . . that the old traditional system [was] falling to pieces, and the world state coming into being.

He identified Germany with the evil of the sovereign state, above any law other than its will, prepared to back that will with ruthless

---

[91] *The Way the World Is Going*, pp. 130–31.
[92] Cited by West, *op. cit.*, pp. 203–4.

militarized might. He saw the Allies as the emerging World State, seeking to sweep away "not simply the Hohenzollerns but the whole of the current political system, the militant state and its symbols."[93] To put it another way, he hoped that "the culminating explosion of the age of armament had arrived, that the essential futility of the prevailing ideas of militant nationalism was to be demonstrated beyond dispute."[94]

Although Wells said and did some foolish things during the first six months of 1914, he did not altogether lose his head. He had a better comprehension than most other journalists, and even most statesmen, of the basic causes of the war. He had long foreseen the possibility, even the probability, that a general European war would be the inevitable consequence of the existing rival nationalisms, competitive armaments, and dynamic imperialisms of the years after 1890. As early as 1901 he had put his finger on German imperial policy as the explosive element in the international situation. But as of the spring of 1914 he doubted that the war, which he had so long foreseen and so often prophesied, would actually occur. The political temperature, which had been above normal since the Agadir Crisis of 1911, seemed to fall in mid-June 1914. Perhaps, after all, the threat of war was like the proverbial cry of "wolf, wolf," and the war, like the wolf, would not come just now.[95] Finally, it seemed impossible to an optimist like Wells that in this kind of world—a civilized world, committed to ideals of liberalism and progress—the monstrosity of a war, however threatening and even imminent, could actually materialize. Wells could have accepted without substantial change the views of an American historian, surveying the international scene in the autumn of 1914 with amazement and incredulity: "To most of us it had seemed a fine civilization, too noble and too beneficent, too charged with the spirit of 'self-improvement' and of 'progress,' to have admitted of any war. Yet out of this very civilization—out of its very elements on which

---

[93] *Autobiography*, pp. 569–71.

[94] *The Common Sense of World Peace*, p. 6.

[95] In the spring of 1914 Wells had said, indeed, that war with Germany was not imminent and that, if it could be avoided for, say, twenty years, it would never occur. *An Englishman Looks at the World*, pp. 143–44. On the other hand, in a futuristic tale published early in 1914, Wells foretold the collapse of the social structure in a war which ended with the use of atomic bombs. The war began, prophetically enough, with a German attack on France by way of Belgium. *The World Set Free*.

chief emphasis had been put—proceeds war of a magnitude without parallel in the world's recorded history."[96]

Amazement and incredulity—these were the first reactions of Britain and the British people during the terrible last week of July 1914 and the fateful first week of August. Wells, more than almost any other contemporary writer, caught the spirit of shocked surprise which the war caused in Britain. From the beginning the threat of war had seemed unreal. The Serajevo plot was "like something out of the *Prisoner of Zenda.*"[97] England was thinking of Ireland, not of Austria and Germany, during the summer of 1914. Not until the first shots were fired between France and Germany did war seem an inescapable fact.[98] The mood of surprise then gave way to an outburst of anger against Germany—"all England was furiously indignant against the Germans."[99] "The armament of Germany, the hostility of Germany, the consistent assertion of Germany, the world-wide clash of British and German interests, had been facts in the consciousness of Englishmen for more than a quarter of a century. A whole generation had been born and brought up in the threat of this German war." But no one believed it would come—except, perhaps, the Navy and Colonel Rendezvous (Wells's equivalent of Colonel Blimp). The threat of war was a bore, a nuisance, a stupidity, a gigantic waste. But it wasn't real. And now war had come![100] And the Germans were responsible for it. And there must be no peace until the militarism which they represented had been banished from the earth. "War and the preparation for war, the taxes, the drilling, the interference with every free activity, the arrest and stiffening up of life, the obedience to third-rate people in uniform, of which Berlin-struck Germans have been the implacable exponents, have become an intolerable nuisance to all humanity." And now on the battlefields of Europe the Germans are "spending and making the world spend the comfort, the luxury and the prog-

---

[96] C. J. H. Hayes, "The War of the Nations," in *Political Science Quarterly,* XXIX (1914), 687.

[97] *Mr. Britling,* p. 91.

[98] Most of this paragraph and the immediately succeeding paragraphs are based upon *Mr. Britling, Joan and Peter, The Bulpington of Blup,* and *William Clissold.* These novels, especially the first two, tell more about wartime Britain than most histories.

[99] *William Clissold,* I, 99.

[100] *Mr. Britling,* pp. 125–26.

ress of the next quarter-century." This must be the last war, the war to end war.[101]

Wells was a superb reporter of the British scene during the War years.[102] If he was a patriot, so were forty-five million other residents of the United Kingdom. If he was inclined to hold the Germans principally or even solely responsible for the war, so were almost all other Englishmen. If he understood something of the complicated character of the circumstances which brought the war about, he was perhaps better informed than most of his fellow countrymen. If he came, in time, to feel that the Great War was not very different in purpose from many earlier wars, he was merely reflecting the growing disillusionment of all ranks and classes of British society as the blood flowed more freely and the list of dead grew longer. And if, finally, he came to put his faith in a league of nations as a way out of future catastrophe, he was here again reflecting the best opinion of the English-speaking peoples the world over. No one can read *Mr. Britling* and Wells's other war novels without feeling that here was a highly sensitive and civilized human being, trying to work his way through doubt and confusion to some sort of rational philosophy for the future. If Wells said some very bitter things about the Germans,[103] they were not altogether unjustified. On the

---

[101] *The War That Will End War*, p. 99; *What Is Coming?*, p. 7.

[102] Take, for example, his keen appreciation of the cruel dilemma in which the war placed British youth. "These youngsters had grown up with an almost unchallenged assumption of their right to self-development. They had come into what had seemed a world of happy opportunity. They had met with little discipline and less punishment. People had asked them, with intimations of unlimited choice: 'What would you like to do?' 'What would you like to be?' Suddenly they were confronted with an immense, a universal compulsion. The picture of human happiness and world amplitude was withdrawn and the real situation revealed. Abandon whatever you are doing, it said, cease to be whatever you had proposed to be, and come into the war. Come into the war. The war is everything and you are nothing, nothing whatever, except what you are in relation to the war." *The Bulpington of Blup*, p. 216; see also *Joan and Peter*, pp. 443–44.

[103] See, as an extreme example, the following bitter passage which constitutes the final paragraph of *What Is Coming?* (1916): "My reason insists on the inevitableness and necessity of this ultimate reconciliation [between the Allied and the German peoples]. I will do no more than I must to injure Germany further, and I will do all that I can to restore the unity of mankind. None the less is it true that for me for all the rest of my life the Germans I shall meet, the German things I shall see, will be smeared with the blood of my people and my friends that the wilfulness of Germany has spilt" (p. 294). This seems less extreme after World War II than it may have seemed during World War I.

other hand, some of his judgments of the Germans were fairer and more sympathetic than those of most other wartime writers.[104]

In a sense, Wells's patriotism could be measured in terms of his attitudes toward the German people, in whom he had been continuously interested for twenty years before the Great War. He saw in them, on the one hand, models of efficiency, discipline, and order, as well as of superior education, science, and technology. In most of these respects the Germans were what he would have liked his fellow countrymen to be. But he saw in them, on the other hand also, exemplars of exaggerated nationalism, truculent militarism, reactionary monarchism, and "preposterous ambitions"—all of which, he was convinced, were anachronistic and dangerous to the peace of the world. He thought that the Germans, more than any other Western people, stood in the way of establishing a genuine community of interest in Europe, despite the fact that they had the greatest stake in an orderly Europe. They were achieving a peaceful conquest of the world before 1914. It seemed impossible, had the war not supervened, that they should have been other than the greatest industrial and commercial power of Europe, rivaled elsewhere in the world only by the United States. For Germany to become involved in a war, therefore, seemed to Wells colossally stupid as well as vicious.[105]

No other popular writer before 1914 had been so shrewd and so far-sighted as Wells in interpreting the meaning to Europe of German history and politics under William II. Writing in 1901, at a time when British opinion viewed France and Russia, rather than Germany, as the potential enemy, Wells saw clearly that conditions existed in Imperial Germany which were ominous for the future. Here were the Germans, said Wells, with the most efficient middle class in the world; with a record of economic progress which was a triumph of intelligence and organization; which possessed military

---

[104] Herr Heinrich, the German tutor in *Mr. Britling*, is portrayed sympathetically and affectionately (see e.g., pp. 50–52, 64–66, 67–69, 167–68). And the final chapter of *Mr. Britling*, consisting of Mr. Britling's letter to Herr Heinrich's parents, is certainly not the work of an unbalanced Germanophobe.

[105] *An Englishman Looks at the World*, pp. 36–37, 143–45; *Anticipations*, pp. 274–81; *Mr. Britling*, p. 436; *Joan and Peter*, pp. 216, 390–94; *What Is Coming?*, pp. 64–66, 97–100, 274–81.

services unparalleled elsewhere; an efficient people, educated and disciplined.

But the very efficiency of the German as a German today, and the habits and traditions of victory he has accumulated for nearly forty years, may prove a very doubtful blessing to Europe as a whole, or even to his grandchildren. . . . The Germanic idea is deeply interwoven with the traditional empire and with the martinet methods of the Prussian monarchy. The intellectual development of the Germans is defined to a very large extent by a court-directed officialdom.

All these things undoubtedly create a formidable efficiency. But energetic and capable people are likely to be intolerant and, "on the under side of their egotism, to be jealous, assertive, and aggressive." The system represented by the Kaiser and the Prussian aristocracy meant that freedom and self-criticism were "steadily fading in the heat and blaze of the imperial sunshine. Discipline and education have carried Germany far; they are essential things, but an equally essential need for the coming time is a free play for men of initiative and imagination." Wells thought that freedom in Germany was being stifled by autocratic institutions. Even at that early date he was convinced that sooner or later German ambitions would precipitate a general European war in which the English-speaking peoples would be found on the side of France.[106] This was either clairvoyance or political analysis of a very high order. It hardly, at that time, could have been the result of nationalistic prejudice alone.

VII

From the very onset of the war of 1914 Wells hoped and believed that it would lead to a better political organization of all mankind, that it would be the first necessary step toward a world state. Otherwise the war would be the "most tragic and dreadful thing that has ever happened."[107] He was aware, of course, that the new order of things would not come of its own accord, and beginning in 1916 he devoted himself in large part to propaganda for a league of na-

[106] *Anticipations,* pp. 274–80. As will be noted, Wells anticipated much of the argument in Thorstein Veblen's *Imperial Germany and the Industrial Revolution* (New York, 1915).

[107] *Mr. Britling,* pp. 427–29. Much later, Wells said that "the war did no more for mankind than the Black Death or a forest fire." *William Clissold,* I, 293.

tions. Wells was not first in the field, as he was only too glad to admit,[108] but he brought to the support of the league idea his great energy, the mighty power of his pen, and his considerable personal prestige. Along with Lord Grey, Lord Bryce, Gilbert Murray, Lionel Curtis, and others he formed the League of Free Nations Association, which late in 1918 produced a memorable booklet *The Idea of a League of Nations.* This statement of the case for a league of free nations is unsurpassed, perhaps, by anything else of its kind. And it bore the Wellsian imprint in its final paragraph, which made it plain that the proposed league would be merely preliminary to a much more ambitious, truly world state. "The League of Nations cannot be a little thing: it is either to be a great thing in the world, an overriding idea of a greater state, or nothing. . . . it is an idle and a wasteful diplomacy, a pandering to timidities and shams, to pretend that the World-League of Nations is not ultimately a state aiming at that ennobled individual whose city is the world."[109] But as the framers of the Covenant at the Paris peace conference had no intention of making the League anything even remotely resembling a world state, Wells was destined to be bitterly disappointed. By 1920 he began to speak disparagingly of the League, which compromised with the twin devils nationalism and national sovereignty. It seemed to him, in the words of his biographer, "a diplomat's device for shelving every constructive proposal."[110]

In rejecting the League of Nations, Wells was conforming to everything he had thought, taught, and believed for twenty years before the League was founded. In 1899, in *What I Believe* he had given the first indications of his belief in a genuine world community. Two years later, in *Anticipations,* he committed himself firmly and irrevocably to the idea of a world state. Thereafter, he was tenacious and uncompromising in his determination to have a world state, an untrammeled world state, and nothing but a world

[108] *Autobiography,* pp. 592–94. For some earlier British and American propaganda on behalf of a league of nations, see a review-article by C. J. H. Hayes, "The Peace of the Nations," in the *Columbia University Quarterly,* XIX (1916), 163–82.

[109] *The Idea of a League of Nations* (Boston, 1919), p. 44. This little volume was almost entirely from Wells's pen. For earlier writings on the League, see *In the Fourth Year* (New York, 1918).

[110] West, *op. cit.,* p. 231.

state. He had accepted the League of Nations—reluctantly for a time—because of a faint hope that it might be a first step toward his ultimate objective. When he found it wasn't moving in his direction—or at least was not moving fast enough—he abandoned his support of the League, became one of its most severe critics, and resumed his original course. He knew what he wanted, says his biographer, and like the baby in the advertisement couldn't be satisfied until he got it. In supporting the League in the first instance he was like a passenger who gets aboard a bus marked, say, Bromley. When he finds the bus isn't going to Bromley, or is going there only by a circuitous route, he gets off. "Unhappily the omnibus service to the World State is as limited as that to Mandalay." But Wells was prepared to start walking rather than to stay on a bus which was going in a different direction.[111]

The argument which Wells made for a World State in 1901 was, in essence, the same argument which he continued to make for it throughout the rest of his life. The world state is inevitable, he said; indeed, in some respects it already is here.

Out of the growth of science and mechanism, and more particularly out of the still developing new facilities of locomotion and communication [which] science has afforded, is the deliquescence of the social organizations of the past, and the synthesis of ampler and still ampler and more complicated and still more complicated social unities. The suggestion is powerful, the conclusion is hard to resist, that, through whatever disorders of danger and conflict, whatever centuries of misunderstanding and bloodshed, men may still have to pass, this process nevertheless aims finally, and will attain to the establishment of one world-state at peace within itself.

National lines and national barriers already show signs of becoming obsolete. "We have ignored the boundaries of language that are flung athwart the great lines of modern communication." Whatever we may say to the contrary, trade is cosmopolitan and largely defies customs barriers; investment leaps across frontiers— "in the economic sense, indeed, a world-state already is established." In the political and cultural spheres, Anglo-Saxonism, Pan-Germanism, Pan-Slavism, Latin-Americanism—despite their irrelevancies

---

[111] *Ibid.*, p. 243.

and excrescences—are moving in the direction of larger regionalisms and away from the exclusiveness of the national state.

"The nations and boundaries of today do no more than mark claims to exemptions, privileges, and corners in the market—claims valid enough to those whose minds and souls are turned towards the past, but absurdities to those who look to the future.... Against all these old isolations, these obsolescent particularisms, the forces of mechanical and scientific development fight, and fight irresistibly." The process which leads to a world state is now going on,

at times almost imperceptibly, as some huge secular movement in Nature, the raising of a continent, the crumbling of a mountain-chain, goes on to its appointed culmination. Or one may compare the process to a net that has surrounded, and that is drawn continually closer and closer upon, a great and varied multitude of men. We may cherish animosities, we may declare imperishable distances, we may plot and counter-plot, make war and "fight to a finish"; the net tightens for all that.

Democracy and representative government tend to impede our progress toward the inevitable because democracy, from the days of the French Revolution, has been committed to nationalism and national sovereignty. Government by the people may impede, but it cannot frustrate, the formation of a single world community, since "a really functional social body of engineering, managing men, scientifically trained and having common ideals and interests, is likely to segregate and disentangle itself from our present confusion of aimless and ill-directed lives."[112] These were the elite, the Samurai—composed of technicians, creative-minded industrialists and financiers, scientists, journalists and other writers, a specially educated group of intellectuals, and the like—who would by-pass the national state and bring the world state into being without regard to political obstacles.[113] These were the groups who would engage in an Open Conspiracy—"a sort of outspoken secret society ...

---

[112] The foregoing summary and quotations are from *Anticipations,* pp. 267 *et seq.* (dealing with "The Larger Synthesis"), and pp. 157-64 (principally concerning democracy).

[113] Concerning the Samurai, see *A Modern Utopia,* Chap. IX; on an intellectual and technical aristocracy in general, see *The New Machiavelli,* especially pp. 243-45; *Autobiography,* pp. 196-97; *The New World Order* (New York, 1939), Chaps. III, X; *William Clissold,* II, 547-77.

an informal and open freemasonry"—a revolutionary force designed not "to overthrow existing governments but to supersede them by disregard."[114] In the modern world politics is obsolete.[115]

"The chief problem before the progressive revolutionary [working for the world state] . . . is to bend, break, evade, minimize, get around or over or through the political institutions of the present time." Above all, he must circumvent the national state, since "each sovereignty is an implicit repudiation of his purpose." The legal, political way is "a way of highly improbable issue. In the end it might, under the most hopeful conditions, give the world a sort of super-Washington, a Supreme Court of international law and a confederated world government with a limited liability to call upon national armies and navies to enforce its decisions." But this would not be an effective political instrumentality able to "perform the chief functions of an adequate world control." All such compromises are not only useless, they are vicious, since they frustrate the desirable and postpone the inevitable. The League of Nations was "a complete recognition of the unalienable sovereignty of states," which permitted the continuance of all the "nonsense" of foreign offices and embassies. Since the League was "a repudiation of the idea of an over-riding commonweal of mankind," it was worse than no league at all; hence the best thing about the Covenant was the

---

[114] *Anticipations*, pp. 298–300; *The Open Conspiracy* (London, 1928); *William Clissold*, II, 557 et seq. It is perhaps interesting to note that Wells rejected the international socialist and labor movements as participants in the Open Conspiracy. The [Second] International is without real influence or significance in the forces of the world. "It is so of necessity because of the limited outlook of the common worker," who is "ill-informed and easily misled" and "has feelings in the place of ideas. His International is a mere community of resentful sentiment directed against the general order of the world and against employers," who, in reality, are more internationally-minded than the workers. The labor leader of today is "vacuously emotional and unsound" and is a transitory type in human affairs. The real revolutionary will "keep to the right now and not try the left." He will travel by the Blue Train to the end of his journey; he will come from America rather than from Moscow. *William Clissold*, II, 555–59. As to Soviet Communism, "it is as intellectually bankrupt as any 'capitalist' government." *Ibid.*, p. 447.

[115] *William Clissold*, II, 447–48. "You could steal and hide Washington away for weeks and, if the newspapers made no fuss, the average citizen of the United States would be unaware of his loss." *Ibid.*, p. 578. Wells's contempt for democracy—perhaps contempt is too strong a word—is disturbing, but cannot be overlooked. It recurs often in his writings but can be summarized in the sentence: "Muddle isn't ended by transferring power from the muddle-headed few to the muddle-headed many." *The New Machiavelli*, p. 255.

fact that it was unworkable.[116] The Kellogg Pact "was contrived by men who either do not realize at all, or who find it advisable at present not to admit that they realize, the possibility of the world being arranged in any way other than as a sort of patchwork quilt of independent sovereign states with their boundaries fixed forever. ... We may sign Kellogg Pacts and Kelloggesque Pacts in Europe until there is a shortage of parchment and gold pens, and we shall have done nothing real for the peace of the world." Indeed, by their very innocuousness such pacts may "destroy the general belief in the honesty and good intentions of the governments that make them."[117] Peace pledges and pacifism are completely ineffective politically and are dangerous forms of self-deception. European federalism, "Union Now," and similar half-way measures are, at best, other forms of the League of Nations; at the worst they are puerile.[118]

Wells cared desperately about the World State.[119] It was an obsession with him. He regarded it as imperatively, critically urgent that the World State be brought about now, before our civilization had wrought its own destruction. In two remarkably prophetic books—*The War in the Air* (1908), published before Bleriot's flight across the Channel, and *The World Set Free* (1914), published more than thirty years before the Bomb was dropped on Hiroshima—Wells foretold that the advancing techniques of war threatened social disintegration, as well as appalling destruction of life and property. As early as 1901, in *Anticipations,* Wells had forecast the mechanization of war and had prophesied that military aviation, in particular, would revolutionize war and revolutionize the social consequences of war. Thereafter a constant theme with him was the argument that the political institutions which were adequate to the seventies —the era of *Around the World in Eighty Days*—were totally and

---

[116] *The Outline of History,* II, 558–59. Wells, reluctant to give up all hope for the League, made several trips to Geneva, the last in the mid-twenties. He came away with all his prejudices confirmed; he disliked the official, bureaucratic atmosphere, on the one hand, and the dilettanteism of the League hangers-on and evangelists, on the other. Cf. *William Clissold,* II, 511–15; Salter, *op. cit.,* pp. 132–33.

[117] *The Common Sense of World Peace,* pp. 12, 15, 21.

[118] "Federation," being Chap. VII of *The New World Order;* "The Puerility of Current Federal Union Schemes," Chap. IX of *The Common Sense of War and Peace: World Revolution or War Unending* (London, 1940); *The Anatomy of Frustration* (New York, 1936), Chap XII.

[119] See an eloquent passage in *William Clissold,* II, 668–72, in which Wells asks and answers the question, "Why should I care? ... Why should I become almost miserly with my days and hours in order to work for ends I can never live to see?"

tragically inadequate to the twentieth century, when every important capital and every industrial city in Europe lay at the mercy of bombing planes operating from bases only hours, or even minutes, away from their targets. Air war, he said, was perforce a "universal guerrilla war, a war inextricably involving civilians and homes and all the apparatus of social life." It would be prepared in secret and launched without warning. It would be incalculably destructive; hence it alters "not only the methods of war but the consequences of war." War, with such winged weapons at its disposal, makes a mockery of civilization.[120]

But air war is raised to the ultimate power by atomic bombs. In *The World Set Free* Wells recounted the story of the bomb long before its development was even thought of in military circles. He discussed atomic problems which are now commonplace: the fission of uranium; the effects of blast, fire, residual radio activity—each destroyed city "a flaming center of radiant destruction that only time could quench"—the towering column of flame and smoke arising from the first flash; the possibilities of underwater explosions. He foresaw, also, the potentialities of atomic energy for peaceful purposes and the necessity for placing it under international controls. In the face of such weapons and such obliteration of life and property, "war manifestly has to stop." If crowns and flags are in the way, "manifestly they must go, too." If outworn political and legal institutions constitute obstacles to a new world order, they must be ignored, reformed, circumvented, or replaced. "Necessities bury rights. And create them."[121]

... The old tendencies of human nature, suspicion, jealousy, particularism and belligerency, were incompatible with the monstrous destructive power of the new appliances the inhuman logic of science has produced. The equilibrium could be restored only by civilization destroying itself down to a level at which modern apparatus could no longer be produced, or by human nature adapting itself in its institutions to the new condi-

---

[120] On this phase of Wells, see *The War in the Air*, especially pp. 249–57, and E. M. Earle, "The Influence of Air Power upon History" in the *Yale Review*, XXXV (1946), 577–93. Wells had been clairvoyant, too, as regards both trench warfare and tanks as the means of breaking the deadlock of trench warfare. An article "The Land Ironclads" in the *Strand Magazine* for January 1904 (XXVI, 661–74) makes extraordinary reading in the light of events thirteen years and, again, thirty-six years later. I hope before very long to write a study of Wells as a student of war.

[121] *The World Set Free* (Copyright 1914, 1942, by H. G. Wells, N.Y., E. P. Dutton & Co., Inc.), pp. 152, 154.

tions. . . . Sooner or later this choice would have confronted mankind. The sudden development of atomic science did but precipitate and render rapid and dramatic a clash between the new and the customary that had been gathering since ever the first flint was chipped or the first fire built together.[122]

Two world wars only confirmed Wells's opinions concerning the necessity, the urgency, and the inevitability of a world state. He was impatient with all those who said it was impracticable. He asserted, on the contrary, that it was the only practicable and "the only sane objective for a reasonable man; it towers high over the times, challenging indeed but rationally accessible; the way is indicated and the urgency to take that way gathers force."[123] No one can place limits to the possible political achievements of even a small body of really determined, devoted, and inspired men. Just think of what already has been done for civilization by a "little straggling, incidental, undisciplined, and uncoordinated minority of inventors, experimenters, educators, writers and organizers!"[124] We can take hope, too, from the story of flying. For two thousand years or more men dreamed of flying and sought to fly.

But for a wearisome sequence of centuries they got nowhere . . . the general wisdom remained quite sure that flying was forever denied to man. There is a long list of names of solitary men, who announced that they were discovering or had discovered flying. They achieved nothing; they left nothing to their successors but broken bodies, broken wings and discouragement. Only when a convergence of tendencies stimulated the general imagination to believe in the possibility of flying was there a sufficient and interlocking continuity and multitudinousness of effort for a real advance. Then in scarcely a dozen years the problem of flying was solved. By whom? You do not know, for the simple reason that it was done by a multitude of men working in correlation.[125]

Is it too much, said Wells, to hope that similar miracles can be worked in the field of politics?

[122] *Ibid.*, pp. 192–93. These words, it must be remembered, were in print before the first shots were fired in 1914 and three decades before the test at Alamogordo!

[123] *Autobiography*, pp. 642–43; *The Common Sense of World Peace*, pp. 22–24. "My reply to anyone who charges me with visionary Utopianism in my demand for the world federation of the common interests of mankind is that it is he who dreams. He is sleeping in a cramped position called patriotism, which can produce nothing for him but a series of . . . nightmares."

[124] *The New Machiavelli*, p. 11.

[125] *The Anatomy of Frustration*, p. 116.

"Thirty-four years ago," wrote Wells in 1934, "the world state loomed mistily across a gulf in dreamland. My arch of work has bridged the gulf for me and my swinging bridge of ropes and planks and all the other ropes and wires that are being flung across, are plainly only the precursors of a viaduct and a common highway."[126] It was not much more than a decade later that Wells died, a bitterly disillusioned man, the viaduct and highway to Utopia still in the realm of fantasy. One of the very last things he wrote was almost a surrender of his ideals and hopes: "Our universe is not merely bankrupt; there remains no dividend at all; it has not simply liquidated; it is going clean out of existence, leaving not a wrack behind. The attempt to trace a pattern of any sort is absolutely futile." No longer did it seem possible to him "that Man could pull out of his entanglements and start a new creative phase of living.... That optimism has given place to a stoic cynicism.... Ordinary man is at the end of his tether."[127]

VIII

"If mankind does after all achieve an ordered world society, there must for ever be high in the list of its prophets and pioneers the man who, in the Gethsemane of his last moments, cried bitterly that he—and mankind—had failed."[128] But in a larger sense Wells did not fail. For he aroused a whole generation to an understanding of one of the fundamental facts upon which the structure of modern politics must be built—that the advance of science and technology has created a new world, in which the old truths may still be true, but only relatively true. Science can create a new world. It can create weapons which threaten the destruction of the world of its creation. But science cannot contribute much to the problem of adjusting political and social institutions to the new order of things. This is a problem for the guile and art of the student and practitioner of politics.

And this is the point at which Wells—who liked to think of himself as a scientist—went wrong. He thought it possible to by-pass,

---

[126] *Autobiography*, pp. 642–43.

[127] *Mind at the End of Its Tether* (London, 1945), pp. 17, 30. This is a depressing book, black with pessimism. It is a mitigating circumstance that at the time he wrote it Wells was not only old but mortally ill.

[128] Salter, *op. cit.*, p. 137.

even to ignore, political institutions and political processes. He was under the illusion that an elite of scientists, intellectuals, and others could build a world independent of politics, in which the national state and other political forms would be immaterial and irrelevant. If democracy stood in the way, democracy, too, must be circumvented and perhaps discarded. This is the approach of the technician, as, during the past few years, it has been the approach of some American and British scientists, shocked into political consciousness by the awful consequences and the foreboding potentialities of the weapons they have brought into being. But the problem of military weapons is a political problem, which must be solved by political methods and in the political arena. Impatience with politics will only produce a second state of affairs worse than the first. "The Dictatorships and wars of our time, and the demonstration they have afforded of the State's power for evil, should be sufficient comment upon these dangerous fallacies [of the non-political mind]. The imperfections of political government can be cured only by reform, and not by replacement. The dangers of national sovereignty may be overcome by its expansion into a true system of world government. There is no short cut."[129] Meanwhile, one must admit that progress is discouragingly small, almost imperceptible.

In 1914, when the First World War burst upon an incredulous Europe, the American people thought they were safe behind the barriers of the broad Atlantic. They agreed, in the large, with Woodrow Wilson that the causes and objectives of the war were of no concern to them. Although *Mr. Britling* had a tremendous reading public in the United States, and although it won wide sympathy for the British cause in American hearts, it is doubtful if it changed in any marked degree the desire of the American nation to remain aloof from the conflict in Europe. It was rather the

---

[129] Salter, *op. cit.*, p. 129. Wells was on debatable ground, too, in proposing to ignore or by-pass the national state. "Whatever academic reflections may be indulged on the relative merits of cosmopolitanism and internationalism, it is the latter, and not the former, which will appeal to the practical realist of the present generation as the possible and desirable antidote to the poison of nationalism. To go from nationalism to cosmopolitanism is to hurdle from a familiar path and start off in an opposite direction along a path that is strange and choked with underbrush. To go from nationalism to internationalism is merely to take a well-marked turn on the very highway on which the modern world is travelling." C. J. H. Hayes, *Essays on Nationalism* (New York, 1926), p. 271.

submarine, a new weapon of war born of the new science and technology, that sent two million young Americans to Europe to participate in the "war to end war," the war to "make the world safe for democracy." Less than a quarter-century later, the thud of bombs on Pearl Harbor gave the people of the United States their second unforgettable lesson in world politics. Now, it seems, they are quite prepared to subscribe to a principal enunciated by H. G. Wells in 1916:

"This is one world and bayonets are a crop that spreads. Let them gather and seed, it matters not how far from you, and a time will come when they will be sticking up under your nose. There is no real peace but the peace of the whole world, and that is only to be kept by the whole world resisting and suppressing aggression wherever it arises."[130]

[130] *What Is Coming?*, p. 217.

NATIONAL SENTIMENT IN KLOPSTOCK'S ODES AND *BARDIETE*

ROBERT ERGANG

IMPORTANT as the role of Johann Gottfried Herder was in the rise of German nationalism in the eighteenth and early nineteenth centuries, his was, of course, not the sole influence. The main stream of nineteenth-century German nationalism was composed of many rivulets springing from various sources. One of these sources was Friedrich Gottlieb Klopstock (1724–1803), styled by his contemporaries "the poet of religion and the fatherland." Klopstock did not, like Herder, develop a philosophy of nationalism; nor does the quality or versatility of his mind rank with those of Herder, Schiller, or Goethe. While Herder, for example, wrote on science, philosophy, ecclesiastical and secular history, art, poetry, religion, criticism, ethnology, esthetic theory, education, literature, and language, Klopstock centered his attention on poetry. His influence was, therefore, not as profound nor as widespread as Herder's; nevertheless, he was an important factor in the development of national feeling, national pride, and national ambitions in Germany. At a time when, as Herder put it, Germany was but "a thing of the imagination," Klopstock gave evidence of a national feeling such as few writers of eighteenth-century Germany exhibited. Moreover, he aided, both by example and by urging his fellow countrymen to follow that example, in stimulating the rise of a national German literature.

Klopstock, born twenty years before Herder, was not the first writer to be conscious of the lack of a national German literature. A number of German authors and critics had previously endeavored to raise German literature to the level of those of England and France. They did not believe, however, that German writers were capable of producing original works; hence they prescribed imitation of foreign literatures as the best means of achieving the goal. For example, Gottsched, the outstanding literary critic of the first half of the eighteenth century, advocated imitation of the French. "What the Greeks," he said, "were for the Romans, the French are for us. They have given us the best models in all kinds of poetry."[1] Consequently the German literature of the period from the sixteenth century to Klopstock's time was largely a poor imitation of French, Italian, and English models. As Herder described the situation: "We came too late, and as we came too late, we imitated others. We imitated the French, the Spanish, the Italians, the English; we hardly know why. Our venerable Opitz was more imitator than poet, and in Weckherlin almost everything is borrowed from abroad."[2]

Klopstock's method was not that of Opitz and Gottsched; in fact, he vigorously denounced the imitation of other nationalities. On the other hand, he did not reach the point at which, like Herder, he believed that each nationality has "the measure of its own perfection within itself." He stood midway between the two. His admiration for Greek art was so great that he regarded it as the absolute standard for all time. This caused him to adhere to Greek forms, but he insisted that the content of the new literature must be German. He agreed with Goethe that "what German poetry lacked was content, substance, and in particular a national substance."[3] A truly national literature, he believed, must depict German life and give expression to German feelings. It is this conviction that made Klopstock an important figure in German literature and in the history of German nationalism. Not only did he preach to his countrymen with religious fervor the doctrine that literature must be the reflection of the national milieu; he also wrote poetry which, in a sense, demonstrated his ideas. His poems were, so to speak, the harbingers of the new national spirit in German literature.

Klopstock's feeling for his fatherland was not limited to a certain part of the country, as was the patriotism of the Prussian school of writers. Inspired by the deeds of Frederick the Great, the members of this school produced a literature which, though German, was specifically Prussian. Their leader was Johann Wilhelm (Father) Gleim (1719–1803), who became popular through his *Prussian War Songs* in which he glorified the Prussian king. Klopstock was ani-

---

[1] Gottsched, *Versuch einer critischen Dichtkunst* (Leipzig, 1751), p. 159. See the article by Jacques Barzun in the present volume for a discussion of French nineteenth-century adulation of German music.
[2] Herder, *Werke* (Berlin, 1877), II, 95.
[3] Goethe, *Sämmtliche Werke* (Weimar, 1889), XXVII, 104.

mated by a national feeling which rose above the provincialism of the time. In an age when the word *Vaterland* signified to the average citizen only the particular German state in which he lived —other German states being regarded as foreign—Klopstock's fervid patriotism embraced the whole of Germany and all Germans. He was, in fact, the first great German poet of the eighteenth century who addressed himself to the entire nationality. Political and economic division notwithstanding, he saw a spiritual unity in Germany. If Germany had no body, it at least had a soul. Thus he proclaimed the spiritual oneness of the German people. "The aim of all his works," Madame de Staël wrote, "is either to awaken patriotism in his country or to celebrate religion."[4]

National feeling manifested itself early in Klopstock's life. While he was a student in his teens at the Gymnasium of Schulpforta, his national pride was hurt deeply by a Frenchman residing in Germany who asserted that the poverty of modern German literature proved that the Germans were devoid of poetic talent. "Name for me," said Eléazar Mauvillon, "a creative mind in your Parnassus; name, I defy you, a German poet who from native sources has produced a work of some reputation."[5] Young Klopstock had to confess that Mauvillon's criticism was not wholly unjust. But instead of sitting idly by he decided that something must be done to improve the status of German literature. In his valedictory at the time of his graduation from Schulpforta (1745) he called for action. "Righteous indignation stirs my soul," he said, "when I see the deep lethargy into which our nationality has sunk. By dawdling with wretched trifles we endeavor to acquire the reputation of being geniuses; with poems which exist only for the purpose of being forgotten we seek, in a manner wholly unworthy of the German name, to achieve sacred immortality."[6] He had a remedy for the poor condition of German literature. "By deeds," he stated, "by producing a great immortal work we must demonstrate what we can do." He closed his speech with an ardent prayer that a great poet might soon appear: "If among our present poets there may be one who is des-

[4] De Staël, *De l'Allemagne* (Paris, 1810), II, 22. Madame de Staël overlooked the odes in which he extolled friendship and love.

[5] Mauvillon, *Lettres françoises et germaniques; ou, Réflexions militaires, littéraires, et critiques sur les françois et les allemans* (London, 1740), p. 362.

[6] C. F. Cramer, *Klopstock: Er und über Ihn* (Hamburg, 1780), I, 54–98.

tined to bestow this honor upon his German fatherland; then hasten to dawn, O glorious day, which shall bring such a poet to light! Hasten to approach, O sun, which shall first behold him and greet him with its friendly beams! May Virtue and Wisdom, together with the heavenly Muse, nurse him with the tenderest care."

In sounding the call for a truly national poet Klopstock had himself in mind. He himself would be the first German singer who would bring great glory to the fatherland. By writing a great national epic he would show other nationalities that the Germans had the gift of poetry in an equal, nay, in a superior, measure. He appears to have conceived the idea of writing such an epic while he was studying Virgil. His epic would be to German what Virgil's *Aeneid* is to Roman literature. In his farewell address he said of his Alma Mater: "Oft will I tenderly cherish thy name and gratefully honor thee as the mother of that work which I began to develop in your arms."[7] He began at once to search for a German theme and a German hero, but had considerable difficulty in finding what he regarded a suitable subject. At one time he fixed on the Saxon emperor, Henry I, surnamed the Fowler, who recommended himself to the poet as having driven the Hungarians out of Germany and as being the founder of the freedom of his native Quedlinburg. "Has Germany no legends?" he asked. "No times of historical interest? No heroes? Does not my native town supply me with such? What better theme could I desire than the deeds of Henry the Fowler?" Later in the ode, "My Fatherland" (1768) he tells of his choice:

> Early did I devote myself to thee,
> Soon as my heart first with ambition throbbed,
>   I chose among the lances and the corslets,
>   To sing of Henry thy deliverer.[8]

But young Klopstock soon relinquished the idea of making Henry the Fowler the hero of a German epic in favor of writing *The Messiah*, his great religious work, which an early nineteenth-century critic styled "the earliest and most notable epic in modern German literature." *The Messiah* comprises the Biblical narrative from Christ's ascent of the Mount of Olives until His Ascension. In ex-

---

[7] *Ibid.*, I, 89.

[8] Klopstock, *Sämmtliche Werke* (10 vols., Leipzig, 1854–55), IV, 214. Further references to this edition will be cited simply by volume and page.

plaining his choice of subject Klopstock wrote: "I searched for a hero and sank exhausted. Then suddenly, as a poet, with one swift triumphant glance I saw Him whom as a Christian I loved." Despite statements to the contrary by a number of German critics, Klopstock was undoubtedly inspired by Milton to write a religious epic; in fact, in a letter to Bodmer, who translated *Paradise Lost* into German, Klopstock himself confesses as much.[9] Klopstock wrote the first three cantos in 1745 while attending the University of Jena and in the next year they were published in the *Bremer Beiträge*. Not until 1751 were the three cantos together with two additional ones published in book form.[10] Before many years passed *The Messiah* was translated into Latin, French, Italian, Dutch, Swedish, and English. Many critics were amazed over the fact that the poem was written in hexameters, a meter which up to that time had been regarded as unattainable in the German language.

As the first outstanding creation of modern German literature *The Messiah* helped to stimulate national pride and national feeling. In the words of a German writer: "Germany imagined that she too possessed a *Paradise Lost* and welcomed in the bard of *The Messiah* the interpreter of its innermost thought. At last Germany had a German poem."[11] The taste of the average German for poetry was not sufficiently developed to appreciate the flight of Klopstock's genius, but in literary circles the poem was widely acclaimed. While some were fulsome in their praise, others did not hesitate to point out weaknesses. All were at one, however, in regarding it as a great literary work. Lessing stated that the "eternal poem" proved beyond a doubt that German minds could produce great works, and Herder styled it "next to Luther's Bible, the first classic work of the German language."[12] The poet Bodmer wrote in 1748:

> Ten, and to a greater extent twenty, years ago it was not necessary to exercise such great care in the choice of material and in developing a subject, for the competition was very poor. Now our younger men write in

---

[9] See K. Biedermann, *Deutschland in achtzehnten Jahrhundert* (Leipzig, 1867), II, Part 2, 111.

[10] Other cantos were added later until the number reached twenty.

[11] K. Hillebrand, *German Thought from the Seven Years' War to Goethe's Death* (New York, 1880), pp. 81-82.

[12] Lessing, "Das Neueste aus dem Reiche des Witzes (1751)" in *Sonntagsbeilage der Vossischen Zeitung* (Berlin, 1904), p. x; F. H. Adler, *Herder und Klopstock* (New York, 1914), p. 23; Herder's *Sämmtliche Werke*, I, 284.

a superior manner, and it is discouraging to be outdone by youngsters. We are on the threshold of the golden age. I have already heard Klopstock sing the praises of the God Messiah in a spirit akin to Milton's; and I have seen Kleist pursue spring through garden and field on zephyrs' wings. I have lived on the isthmus which leads from the iron to the golden age.[13]

Elizabeth Smith, who translated some of Klopstock's writings into English, said: "His *Messiah* has raised the fame of his native country in the highest department of epic poetry to a level with that of every other nation. Such at least is the opinion of many excellent critics."[14]

But while he was writing *The Messiah,* the idea of a German literature that would be national in content was ever in Klopstock's mind. His search for a German hero and a German theme was resumed. At one time it seemed as if he had found his protagonist in Frederick the Great. Like many of his contemporaries he was dazzled by the military exploits of the Prussian ruler. At the conclusion of the second Silesian campaign the young poet gave vent to his enthusiasm and admiration in a "War Song" which depicted Frederick as a conquering hero. It reads in part:

> He rides upon the snorting steed
> Which bears him in the van.
>   Hail, Frederick, hail! in iron mail
>   A hero and a man.
>
> Thou who stridest heaven with thundering step,
> Of battles God and Lord,
>   Still your thunder! as Frederick smites
>   The foe as ne'er before.[15]

Klopstock did not, however, remain under the spell of the Prussian king very long. Just when it appeared as if he might join the group of poets who were trying to immortalize in poetry the deeds of Frederick, Klopstock turned against him. He had hoped that the Prussian monarch, after emerging victorious from the war, would do all in his power to promote the development of German literature, even to the point of providing funds for indigent poets. When he discovered that Frederick had but little interest in and a low opinion of German literature it shocked him greatly. In general,

---

[13] W. Koerte, ed., *Briefe deutscher Gelehrten* (Zurich, 1805), I, 84. Reference is to Kleist's poem "Der Frühling."

[14] *Memoirs of Frederic and Margaret Klopstock* (Boston, 1810), p. 38.

[15] Cramer, *op. cit.,* II, 345.

Frederick's selfish ambition, his absolutism, love of war, disdain for German culture, and devotion to French art and literature evoked a feeling of hostility in Klopstock, a feeling which was intensified by the Prussian ruler's indifference to *The Messiah*. For a time the poet cherished the hope that the monarch might change his mind if he read part of *The Messiah*. He, therefore, had excerpts from it translated into French and sought to bring them to Frederick's attention through the mediation of Voltaire. It was all to no avail. Frederick gave no evidence of being conscious of the existence of either Klopstock or his poetry. Regarding the king's attitude as an insult to German literature generally and to himself in particular, Klopstock deleted all reference to Frederick from the poem and rededicated it to Henry the Fowler. Later he denied that he had ever intended to honor the Prussian king.

For the rest of his life Klopstock continued to heap invective on Frederick. The Prussian monarch was no longer the "best man in the entire fatherland," but a heartless conqueror, an unchristian freethinker and, above all, a despiser of German culture. In the ode "To Gleim" he chided the venerable poet for using his talents to celebrate the deeds of Frederick. He told Gleim that if he did not desist, "I will seize thy lyre, and tear its strings, and regard thee with abhorrence." Frederick, he stated, might have done more for German than Louis XIV did for French literature. "Tell not posterity that he did not esteem to be what he could have been! But since it cannot be concealed, tell it in sad tones and ask your sons to sit in judgment."[16] During the succeeding years he wrote ode after ode in which he castigated Frederick's lack of national feeling, his predilection for French culture, and his contempt for the German language. Thus in the ode "Die Verkennung" he wrote:

> Thou sawest not how German art rose high,
> From a firm root a lasting stem, and threw
>   Deep shadows round. E'en then thou didst deny
>   To its fair growth the freshening dew.
>
> Where then, O Frederick, was thine eagle glance
> When rose the spirit's might, will, power and all
>   That fostering kings can recompense perchance
>   But cannot into being call?[17]

Time and again he raised his hand to point out that Frederick's

---

[16] IV, 95.
[17] IV, 250. Translation by W. Nind.

disdain for German culture would be avenged. In the foregoing ode, for example, he tells the Prussian king that his deeds will not save him from oblivion, "but it is the poet's meed that time touches not the master's work." In "Kaiser Heinrich" he presents a picture of Frederick the Great and the rest of the German princes who did not promote the development of German culture sleeping forgotten and unsung in their marble sarcophagi:

> Let sleep our princes on their velvet thrones,
> Mid fumes of courtier's incense unrenowned!
> Then in their cold and narrow bed of stone
>   Sink to oblivion more profound!
>
> So let them slumber on! And e'en such fate
> On him attends, who where the battle bled
> Won his victorious way; but too elate
>   If he the Gallic Pindus tread.
>
> By him unheard the oak-woods spread aloft,
> And swell sonorous o'er the German fount,
> And waft to heaven their song. An alien scoff'd,
>   He climbs not e'en the Gallic mount.[18]

Klopstock did not stop at attacking Frederick in his odes. Even when he dedicated his drama *Hermannsschlacht* (1764) to Joseph II, he could not refrain from using the opportunity to hurl barbs at the Prussian monarch. In the dedicatory preface he wrote: "The emperor loves his fatherland—but Frederick does not! And Germany is also his fatherland." The reference was, however, deleted from the manuscript at the request of Joseph II.[19] In the *Gelehrtenrepublik* he repeatedly declaimed against those who write in foreign languages and steep themselves in foreign culture. He brands as traitors those who teach the German people to regard German culture as inferior.[20] Klopstock certainly had Frederick in mind when he wrote: "He who writes in a modern foreign language should be exiled until he writes in our language."[21] Klopstock was so deeply hurt by Frederick's disparagement of German art and

---

[18] IV, 146. Translation by W. Nind. In translating Klopstock's odes the present writer in a number of instances has leaned heavily upon a translation of some of the early odes made by Nind in 1848.

[19] Julian Schmidt, *Geschichte des geistigen Lebens in Deutschland von Leibnitz bis auf Lessing's Tod* (Leipzig, 1863), II, 371.

[20] VIII, 59, 69, 78, 80, 81, 90, 121, 203.

[21] VIII, 29.

literature in *De la littérature allemande* (1780) that he even regarded the Prussian's political achievements as of doubtful value. In a series of odes which include "An Freund und Feind," "Der Traum," and "Der Nachruhm," he assailed the ruler who represented to him only *"la nation prussienne."*[22] Especially acid is the ode "Die Rache" in which he said: "Long did we hope that you would shelter Germany's muse, thereby crown yourself with glory and with a more beautiful laurel conceal the blood you shed. You humiliated yourself in stammering foreign tones and have earned only scorn. Even after your song was laundered by Arouet [Voltaire] it was still *'tudesk'* [German]" in French eyes.[23]

His early hopes of making Frederick the Great the hero of his poems shattered, Klopstock sought nourishment for his imagination in the remote Germanic past, which he regarded as the golden age of Germanic life. In his patriotic odes, written in antique unrhymed strophes, he replaced the Greek and Roman gods with references to Germanic and Scandinavian mythology. He speaks of oak groves, temples of Walhalla, and Wingolf, instead of the Elysian Fields. All are used to indicate the abodes of warriors who fall in battle. Frequent reference is also made to Tuisco and his son Mannus, the mythological ancestors of the Germans. In place of the Greek and Roman deities Klopstock substituted Odin or Woden, the father of the Norse gods, and his wife Frigga, also known as Hertha. Instead of Parnassus, he refers to the sacred oak groves and to Mimer's spring which is the source of poetic inspiration. There are also frequent allusions to the oak as the symbol of German poetry. In his ode "To Braga" he summons the god of poetry to inspire the German poets.[24] In the ode "Wingolf" he welcomes his fellow poets at Leipzig into the bardic Elysium and praises each in an appropriate manner. Thus he says to Ebert:

> So be thou welcome! ever welcome still,
> But dearer when thou breathest of the hills
> Of Fatherland, from where the bardic throng
> With Braga sings, and where the telyn thrills
> To touches of Germanic song.[25]

[22] IV, 258, 269, 274.
[23] IV, 276.
[24] IV, 166.
[25] IV, 5.

One of his best-known odes on the early Germanic period is "Hermann and Thusnelda" in which he sang the praises of Hermann or Arminius, the chieftain of the Cheruscans who defeated and heavily slaughtered the Roman legions under Varus in the battle of Teutoburg Forest (9 A.D.). The ode describes how Hermann, returning from the bloody struggle, is greeted by his wife.

> Ha! There he comes, covered with sweat,
> Stained with Roman blood and with battle-dust bedecked!
>   Never was Hermann so fair,
>   Never flashed his eye so brightly.
>
> Come! With desire I tremble! Hand me the eagle
> And thy blood-dripping sword! Come, breathe freely,
>   Rest in my embrace
>   From the terrible fight.
>
> Rest here, that I may dry the sweat from thy brow
> And wipe the blood from thy cheek, a cheek so glowing!
>   Hermann! Hermann! Thusnelda
>   Never loved thee as now.
>
> Not even when first in the shade of the oaks
> Thou seized me wildly with sun-browned arm.
>   Desiring to flee, I stayed
>   And saw undying fame in thee
>
> Which now is thine. Announce it in every grove,
> That Augustus now timidly drinks nectar
>   With his gods, that Hermann
>   Is now immortal Hermann.
>
> Why twinest thou my locks? Lies not the father
> Still and dead before us? Oh, had Augustus
>   Led his hosts to battle,
>   Gorier he would lie there!
>
> Hermann! Let me raise thy drooping hair
> So that it threateningly drops in curls!
>   Siegmar is with the gods!
>   Follow and weep not for him![26]

[26] IV, 82–83.

In another ode dedicated to Henry the Fowler he lauded his early hero for delivering his country from the Hungarian invaders:

> Behold the foe! the fight begins,
>   Come on to victory!
>   The bravest hero leads us on
>   In all our fatherland.
>
> There bear they him along,
>   No illness does he feel.
>   Hail, Henry, hero brave and good
>   In fields of flashing steel.[27]

In the same ode he also points out the glory of dying for the fatherland:

> Welcome, O death for fatherland,
>   Whene'er our weary head
>   Is blood bedecked, then will we die
>   With fame for fatherland.
>
> When we before us see a plain
>   And but the dead behold,
>   Around us conquer then we will
>   With fame for fatherland.
>
> The fame we've won shall long remain,
>   Yea, e'en when we are dead,
>   When we have for our fatherland
>   The death of honor died.

Klopstock's patriotic odes in general strike a note of national feeling unequaled in intensity since Walter von der Vogelweide. Abrupt and unornamented, they are written with a fiery and inspired energy. Thus he opened the ode "Wir und Sie" with the lines:

> What hast thou 'gainst thy fatherland?
> If at its name unmoved thou stand,
>   I scorn thee and disdain.

The closing lines read:

> What hast thou 'gainst thy fatherland?
> If at its name unmoved thou stand,
>   I scorn thee, craven fool![28]

[27] IV, 55.
[28] IV, 179–81.

In the ode "My Fatherland" he wrote:

> Thy brow is wreathed with great renown,
> Immortal dost thou stand,
> And walkest high 'bove many lands.
> How well I love thee, fatherland![29]

The recurring theme of many of his odes is: "A German must be German. He has every right to be proud of his nationality. Even though the Germans are not unified politically, they have many virtues which more than compensate them for their political backwardness." In a series of odes he listed these virtues. An outstanding example is "Vaterlandslied" (1770), one of his most widely known and the most imitated of his odes:

> I am a German maiden!
> My eye is blue and soft my smile,
> I have a heart
> Noble and proud, and free of guile.
>
> I am a German maiden!
> My eye of blue regards him with scorn,
> Him my heart hates
> Who spurns the land where he was born.
>
> I am a German maiden!
> No other land I'd choose by voice
> As fatherland
> If I were free to make a choice.
>
> I am a German maiden!
> My lofty look does him deride,
> Throws scorn on him
> Who hesitates ere he does decide!
>
> Thou art no German youth!
> Not worthy thou to live and die
> For fatherland
> Who lov'st it not as well as I.
>
> Thou art no German youth!
> I do disdain thee heart and soul
> Who fatherland
> Dishonorest, thou alien and fool!

---

[29] IV, 214.

> I am a German maiden!
> My proud warm heart beneath my hand
> Leaps nobly up
> At the sweet name of fatherland!
>
> So leaps it only at the name
> Of that good, noble, German youth
> Who loves his fatherland
> As I with noble pride and truth.[30]

Klopstock impressed on his countrymen that since they possess such superior virtues they must not hesitate to enter into competition with other nations. If they would learn to express their feelings unhampered by the spirit of imitation, he told them, Thuiskon (Tuisco), the father of the race, would be happy when he came down from heaven to see his people.[31] Moreover, the Germans would quickly surpass the other nations and produce a literature second only to that of Greece:

> If other strain affright thee than the lay
>   Of Greece, O Teuton, not to thee belong
> Hermann, and Luther, Leibniz and all they
>   Who listen in the grove of Braga's song.[32]

Besides pointing out what he thought were the outstanding German virtues, Klopstock also extolled other things characteristically German. Thus in the ode "Die deutsche Sprache" he proudly stated: "Let no living tongue venture to enter the lists with the German! As it was in the oldest times, when Tacitus wrote of us, so it still remains—solitary, undefiled and incomparable."[33] He even saw characteristic German virtues in Rhinewine:

> By noblest proof, O Rhinewine, thou canst show
> A worthy son thou art of German ground;
> Glowing, but not inebriating, thou,
> Free from light froth, and strong, and sound.[34]

In the ode "Wir und Sie" he told his compatriots that they must even compete with the English, whose literature he regarded as the best of the contemporary nations:

> Genius is theirs of lofty powers;
> Such lofty genius too is ours.
> That gives us equal worth.

---

[30] IV, 216–17.
[31] IV, 157.
[32] IV, 153.
[33] IV, 297.
[34] IV, 97.

> The subtle science of the wise
> They to the marrow scrutinize;
> We, too—and long have done.
>
> Whom have they, that with soaring flight
> Like Handel can the soul delight?
> There we at least have won.[35]

In "Die beiden Musen" he actually places the Germans and the English in competition:

> I saw—oh, tell me, saw I what now is,
>   Or what shall be?—with Britain's Muse I saw
> The German in the race compete,
>   Fly ardent for the crowning goal.

The English muse goes confidently into the contest saying:

> But the fame reached me, that thou wert no more!
>   O muse, who livest while the ages roll,
> Forgive me that I learnt it not before:
>   Now will I learn it at the goal.[36]

Klopstock is gracious in not pointing out the victor, but he does indicate that the German muse will make the contest an interesting one:

> I love thee, quick Teutona did return;
>   I love thee, Briton, and admire;
> But yet not more than immortality,
>   And those fair palms! Reach if thy genius lead,
> Reach them before me! but when thou dost,
>   I will snatch with thee the garland meed.

In general, Klopstock was not pessimistic about the future of German literature. As early as 1752 he proudly told Gleim that Germany had already produced poetic works equal in worth to those written by the French and English poets. Moreover, he was confident that the Germans would in the future surpass their two rivals. To the French he said:

> You proud Gauls, be silent and ask for mercy
> Or we will pronounce judgment upon you
>   And peremptorily deny you all genius.[37]

---

[35] IV, 179.
[36] IV, 86–88.
[37] X, 407.

In the ode "Unsere Fürsten" he told his fellow German poets that it was their duty to produce superior works:

> Of us, O bards, our fatherland
> Demands a patriotic hymn.
>
> Race of Tuisco, wear the joyous crown,
> The sacred wreath that Braga loves to bring;
>   He brings it from the mountain down,
>   All dripping bright from Mimer's spring.
>
> The tones, ye bards, of exultation swell
> From Braga's harp; ye are his proud delight!
>   With him ye drank at Mimer's well
>   High wisdom and poetic might.
>
> Why do you pause? You triumphed over time
> When felt the princes of our fatherland
>   No pride to cherish song sublime,
>   And ye—whoever might withstand—
>
> Soared a bold flight alone with eagle eye.
> So shall your fame unnumbered ages fill,
>   When names of princes fade and die,
>   Like Echo, when the voice is still.[38]

Whereas *The Messiah* was soon consigned to the limbo of unread works, Klopstock's odes not only evoked widespread enthusiasm when they appeared but also continued to be popular for some decades. An English student of German literature goes so far as to say: "Klopstock's *Odes* ... became the fountainhead of all that is best in the German poetry of the century."[39] In referring to the patriotic odes the German historian Biedermann wrote: "Klopstock's odes had a stimulating effect not only on his contemporaries but also on later generations."[40] Gleim, who had previously read Klopstock's odes, wrote ecstatically to a poet friend upon receiving the collected edition: "Today is holiday Klopstock! The odes have arrived. Klopstock, thou art not Horace, not Pindar, thou art Eloah!"[41] Further evidence of the esteem in which his contempo-

---

[38] IV, 182.
[39] *Cambridge Modern History* (Cambridge, England, 1934), X, 385.
[40] Biedermann, *op. cit.*, II, Part 2, 158.
[41] Klopstock's *Briefwechsel* (Hildburghausen, 1848), II, 151. Eloah is the singular of Elohim (God).

raries held Klopstock is given by Herder when he stated that a single ode of Klopstock outweighs the whole lyric literature of Britain.[42] The poet Boie wrote to Knebel in 1771: "I will whisper it in your ear; I look on Klopstock as the first, perhaps the only poet of our German nation."[43] Ernst Moritz Arndt tells of an occasion during the War of Liberation against Napoleon on which Klopstock's "Hermann and Thusnelda" was read before a group as a means of exciting patriotic feeling.[44]

Some idea of the extraordinary sway Klopstock exercised over his contemporaries may also be gained from *The Sorrows of Werther*, in which Goethe has Werther say of Lotte: "I saw her eyes full of tears; she laid her hand on mine and said—Klopstock!—I recollected the glorious ode which was in her thoughts, and sank in the stream of emotion which she by this watchword had caused to gush over me. I could restrain myself no longer, but, bending towards her hand, I kissed, I kissed it amid a flow of the most ecstatic tears, and looked up again to her eye. Noble bard! Would that in this moment thou hadst seen thy own apotheosis!"[45]

Besides stirring enthusiasm Klopstock's odes also called forth imitations. In 1772 a group of young poets at Goettingen, among them Gottfried August Bürger (1748–1794) and Johann Heinrich Voss (1751–1826), organized the so-called *Goettinger Hainbund*. On a moonlight night they assembled in a grove of oak-trees (regarded as typically Germanic) and, joining hands, solemnly pledged themselves to promote the writing of poetry and to take Klopstock as their model. They concluded the ceremony by crowning themselves with wreaths of oak leaves after the manner of the early Germans. The group succeeded in obtaining control of the *Goettinger Musenalmanach* and for some years published in it, in addition to their own work, the contributions from the young poets of the *Sturm und Drang* movement which Goethe hailed in its first stages as "emerging Germany." The poetic league soon dissolved, but its influence continued in the work of its individual members. During the War of Liberation against Napoleon Klopstock's odes became the inspiration for many patriotic poems. The ode "Ich bin ein deutsches

---

[42] Herder, *op. cit.*, XVIII, 118.
[43] Knebel's *Literarischer Nachlass und Briefwechsel* (Leipzig, 1835), II, 12.
[44] *Germanisch-romanische Monatsschrift*, XIX (1931), 225.
[45] Goethe, *Werke* (Weimar, 1899), Abteilung I, XIX, 36.

Mädchen," for example, inspired Matthias Claudius to write "Ich bin ein deutscher Jüngling" and Ida von Auerswald to compose the poem "Ich bin eine deutsche Frau."

Klopstock's national aspirations found even more complete expression in his poetic dramas or dramatic poems, which he called *Bardiete*. His purpose in writing them was to awaken in his German contemporaries an interest in early Germanic history which he regarded as a period of German greatness. He hoped that such an interest would revive the primitive German virtues which he thought were characteristic of that period. He further wished to interest German poets in the period as one that would furnish materials for truly German poetry. The word *Bardiet* was suggested to Klopstock by the term *barditus* which Tacitus used to describe a Celtic war song. Having not yet learned to distinguish between Celt and Teuton, he identified the Celtic bards with the Germanic tribes. He imagined these bards as dwelling in sacred groves and singing patriotic songs to the accompaniment of the lyre. The poet Kretschmann, a disciple of Klopstock, wrote: "In such songs the bards praised the ancestors and forefathers of their nationality, their first deified heroes. They fired the courage of warriors; they praised the brave man and derided the cowardly and contemptible."[46] The bardic songs interspersed in his drama were imitations of what he thought the songs of the bards might have been. In other words, he believed them to be typically German.

The model for Klopstock's bardic songs was Macpherson's *Ossian* (1760–1763), one of the most remarkable literary impostures of modern times.[47] When the poems appeared in a German translation in 1764 they kindled afresh Klopstock's enthusiasm for the native and the national; in fact, this forgery excited in Germany a more abiding enthusiasm for the primitive than it did in England. The idea that the poems were a forgery was to Klopstock sacrilegious. He regarded them as the genuine expression of the early Germanic soul. With Gleim he believed that "Ossian was a Caledonian, and therefore of German origin."

As the hero of his dramas Klopstock chose the same Hermann he

---

[46] *Deutsche National-Literatur* (Berlin, 1890), XLVIII, ix.

[47] Macpherson had used fragments of Gaelic originals, but had taken such liberties with them that the poems he published were really his work.

had earlier glorified in his odes. He was, of course, not the first to write about Hermann. For two centuries the Cheruscan chieftain had been periodically honored as a great German hero. Among others, Ulrich von Hutten had written his *Arminius-Dialog* (1520), Daniel Casper von Lohenstein had produced a voluminous novel entitled *Grossmütiger Feldherr Arminius und dessen erleuchtigste Gemahlin Thusnelda* (1689), and Klopstock's contemporary Justus Möser had written a tragedy around Hermann. Since Hermann was the outstanding national hero, Klopstock made him the central figure of what he regarded as truly German dramas. In preparation for the composition of these dramas he familiarized himself with everything that was written on the early period. He carefully read all that Tacitus and his contemporaries had set down about Hermann and his people, as well as all the old Nordic literature, which he identified with the ancient Germans.

The first of the *Bardiete* was *Hermannsschlacht* (1769). In writing it Klopstock did not stay within the limits of historical facts. Hermann is depicted as an idealistic figure representing the sum of German virtues. Thus, for example, Klopstock's hero symbolizes the spirit of sacrifice, devotion to duty, discipline, modesty, and chastity. But if the author idealized his hero, he did not overlook what he regarded as the weaknesses of his countrymen. His purpose was to excite national sentiment. Hermann was to him, above all, the symbol of the German national idea, an idea he wished all Germans to accept. To teach his countrymen that there is strength in unity Klopstock pointed out what Hermann might have achieved if the various Germanic tribes had united to support him. *Hermannsschlacht* impressed the composer Gluck so forcefully that he planned to compose music for it, but the plan did not materialize. Lessing, who regarded it as "a superb work," believed that *Hermannsschlacht* would have been an outstanding patriotic musical drama if Gluck had carried out his plans.[48]

Klopstock dedicated his dramatic poem to Emperor Joseph II. "I present this patriotic poem, which is warm from my heart, to our exalted emperor," he wrote. "Only Hermann could fight his battle with warmer feelings. For no one but the emperor could I write a poem on a subject that is so near to our hearts. . . . The emperor

[48] *Preussische Jahrbücher*, XCVII (1899), 477.

loves his fatherland and will demonstrate his love by furthering the development of polite literature. Never have I been more proud of my fatherland than in making this presentation. Even now I seem to hear the applause of all men of judgment because the rededicated lyre of poetry sounds again; I also see the muse of history take up the golden pencil to write your fame in marble."[49] Klopstock had hoped that the dedication would move Joseph II to found a German Academy for the purpose of giving encouragement and support to rising German poets and of turning literature into national channels. Rumor even had it that Klopstock would be president of the new academy. Thus Gleim wrote to Lessing (March 9, 1769): "The emperor intends to found a German Academy of belles-lettres; Klopstock is to be its president. Membership will be open to Catholics, Protestants, Prussians, and Saxons."[50] The idea of the academy remained only a hope. Joseph II did nothing beyond sending Klopstock a letter of thanks and awarding him a medal.

After writing his *Hermannsschlacht* Klopstock sponsored a project to build a *Nationaltheater* in the Harz Mountains. This theater was to be devoted exclusively to the presentation of national dramas, that is, dramas based on materials taken from German life and history. "If I were the heir to the reigning Prince of Brunswick," he wrote Ebert in 1770, "I would stage the *Hermannsschlacht* in the open air in the Harz Mountains on a rocky slope at the edge of a valley in accordance with the scene of the battle. In addition to a few connoisseurs I should also invite several Prussian battalions that distinguished themselves in the last war."[51] Nothing came of Klopstock's project at the time. More than a century later, in 1903, his hopes became a reality when a *Nationaltheater* devoted to national drama was founded on the so-called Hexentanzplatz.

Fifteen years after the publication of the *Hermannsschlacht* the second of Klopstock's *Bardiete* made its appearance under the title *Hermann und die Fürsten* (1784). In it he developed the theme that Hermann had hoped to lead the Germans to further victories over the Romans, but was unable to do so because division, which was even then the great German weakness, triumphed over the

---

[49] VI, 39.
[50] Schmidt, *op. cit.*, II, 370.
[51] *Deutsches Volkstum*, XIX (1917), 61.

spirit of unity and co-operation. Three years later Klopstock finished the last of his *Bardiete*, *Hermanns Tod* (1787), in which the hero confesses that it is the great purpose of his life to unite the Germanic tribes and to lead them across the Alps against Rome, but the Germanic chieftains refuse to join him. Even his friends turn against him and his best friend leads an army to depose him. He is taken captive, tried on the charge of having attacked the "innocent" Romans at Teutoburg, and condemned to death. Thus Hermann becomes a martyr for the cause of German unity. Soon after the publication of this *Bardiet* Klopstock's interests were drawn to contemporary history by the outbreak of the French Revolution. An ardent advocate of freedom, he welcomed the Revolution as an important step in man's progress toward greater freedom, much as he had hailed the American War of Independence. But the bloody scenes of 1793 sickened him and chilled his sympathy.

Klopstock's *bardieten* style was taken up by many imitators, with the result that admiration of the seeming glory and spiritual achievements of the forefathers became a veritable cult in some circles. Among the poets who associated themselves with the so-called bardic movement was H. W. von Gerstenberg (1737–1823) who had previously written *Gedicht eines Skalden* (1766), which is replete with Nordic mythology. Another outstanding member was Karl F. Kretschmann (1738–1809), who just a few months before the appearance of Klopstock's *Hermannsschlacht* published his *Song of Rhingulf the Bard* (1768). Later he became an avowed imitator of Klopstock's *Bardiete*. His *Lament of Rhingulf the Bard over Hermann's Death* was written as a continuation of the *Hermannsschlacht*. The third important member of the movement was Michael Denis (1729–1800), a Jesuit and an ardent admirer of Klopstock, who made his reputation as the translator of *Ossian* and in 1772 published a collection of his own poems under the title *Songs of Sined the Bard*. All believed that the bardic movement held out the promise of producing a truly national literature. "If the poetry of the bards became more general," Kretschmann wrote, "it would strengthen the hope that more patriotic and national subjects will appear on the stage. Should these not make a greater impression on our countrymen than the threadbare Greek and Roman gods and demi-gods who ... are so greatly admired as to make it appear as if our national history has no figure which is worthy of being held up as an example for posterity?"[52]

The hopes of the members of the bardic group were not realized, for the *Bardiete* soon fell into disfavor. Nevertheless, the movement, which was basically a revolt against the prevailing imitation of other nationalities, did contribute to the awakening of interest in the German past and to the rise of a national consciousness. The "bards" brought back from their flights into German antiquity figures which were later more fully developed in the writings of the *Sturm und Drang* period and by the Romanticists in the early nineteenth century. In other circles the attempts to write *Bardiete* gave way to a more serious study of German antiquity; more particularly, of the early Germanic languages and literatures. Such studies gave nourishment to the nascent German nationalism which reached its full growth in the nineteenth century.

In general, Klopstock's doctrine that "true poetry, if it would grow to a mighty tree, must ever strike its roots in the soil of the fatherland" soon found wide acceptance. A literary critic said early in the nineteenth century: "Klopstock, though in form a Greek, was always in spirit a German. It was he who infused into our literature the spirit of patriotic enthusiasm and the reverence for everything German which, in spite of the many new fashions, has never been extinguished.... This was the beginning of that healthy boldness of German poetry which, at length, ventured to cast off the chains of foreign servitude, and to renounce forever that humiliating air of submission which had marked it since the ill-omened peace of Westphalia. It was, indeed, high time for a man to appear who could freely strike his breast and say 'I am a German.'"[53] Another early nineteenth-century critic wrote: "A powerful yet mild spirit was necessary to lead the Germans back to the real German origins and thus to real German poetry. It required the most vigorous prodding and shaking to awaken them from the comfortable dreams which had so long absorbed their thoughts."[54] Among others Herder, Goethe, and Schiller were all influenced to a greater or lesser extent by the national spirit in Klopstock's writings. Goethe

[52] *Deutsche National-Literatur, op. cit.*, XLVIII, ix–x.
[53] Wolfgang Menzel, *Deutsche Literatur* (Stuttgart, 1828), III, 246.
[54] Franz Horn, *Poesie und Beredsamkeit der Deutschen* (Berlin, 1824), III, 39.

himself, as reported by Eckermann, said: "Without Klopstock and Herder, these mighty forerunners, our literature would not have become what it now is. They were far ahead of their time and, so to speak, carried the age along with them."[55] Finally, there is the statement of Madame de Staël who said: "It was with him [Klopstock] that the real German school began."[56]

[55] *Gespräche mit Goethe* (Leipzig, 1884), I, 124.
[56] De Staël, *op. cit.*, II, 20.

ARTHUR YOUNG, BRITISH PATRIOT

JOHN G. GAZLEY

DURING Arthur Young's lifetime, 1741–1820, British nationalism was greatly intensified. As a boy he experienced the stirring days of the Seven Years' War, when the national ego was inflated by the flamboyant patriotism of William Pitt the Elder and the magnificent exploits of Wolfe and Clive. His later life coincided with the titanic struggle between Britain and a France which had become intoxicated with the heady wine of revolutionary nationalism. To meet the very real menace of what Carlton Hayes has called "Jacobin nationalism" of the First French Republic and Napoleon, Britain responded with "traditional nationalism" which was first expounded by Edmund Burke.[1] In the hearts of patriotic Englishmen no names are more beloved and respected than the great trio—Pitt the Younger, Nelson, and Wellington—who played such an important role in the final defeat of Napoleon and the forces of the French Revolution.

The purpose of this essay is to examine the writings of Arthur Young to determine the extent to which he reflected or contributed to the growing nationalism of his age. He cannot be considered without taking into account the fact that he was a member of the gentry and always regarded himself as the spokesman of the agrarian interests. Although his intellectual distinction gave him connections far beyond his own class, most of his friends and neighbors had backgrounds similar to his. Closely attached to king, country, and church, the gentry were as a class intensely patriotic. Almost inevitably, as the self-appointed spokesman of the agrarian upper classes, Young must have reflected their views. A spokesman lacking in patriotism would hardly have been acceptable.

The extent of Young's influence is difficult to measure, but it must have been considerable. As a country gentleman of good family he possessed a social entrée wherever he wished, and he knew most of his important contemporaries. He was a man of national

---

[1] Carlton J. H. Hayes, *The Historical Evolution of Modern Nationalism* (New York, 1931), Chapters III and IV.

and even international reputation, a Fellow of the Royal Society, and an honorary member of numerous English agricultural societies and foreign learned societies. He was an active member for about fifteen years of the Society for the Encouragement of Arts, Manufactures and Commerce.[2] From 1794 until his death he served as Secretary to the Board of Agriculture. His pen was hardly idle from the time he was seventeen years old until his death. His works comprise eighteen books (which amount to twenty-nine volumes), twenty-six pamphlets, and several hundred articles in the forty-six volumes of the *Annals of Agriculture,* of which he was editor.[3] Eighteen of his works went through more than one English edition, while seven were translated into foreign languages, and in 1800–1801 a collected edition of his writings appeared in France in eighteen volumes. Although Young's primary interest was agriculture, he always treated that subject broadly so as to include corn laws, taxation, prices and money, tithes, and poor laws, all of which impinge on national policy.

Arthur Young was primarily a publicist, not a systematic thinker in either economics or politics. One must not expect to find in his writings, then, any clearly defined, consistent statement of nationalist theory. Much of his nationalism was based upon a deep, emotional feeling, a profound love for his country and a pride in her institutions. His writings abound with such phrases as "blest isle,"[4] "this most happy among the nations of the earth,"[5] "the GLORIOUS CONSTITUTION of this kingdom."[6] In this instinctive sense Young was always consistent in his patriotism. Never did he express himself in any way so that a shadow of doubt could be cast upon his essential loyalty. On the other hand, he had a great contempt for theory and prided himself on his devotion to facts and changing circumstances. It is not surprising, therefore, to find him inconsistent on such questions as war and peace, imperialism, and the gov-

---

[2] Cf. John G. Gazley, "Arthur Young and the Society of Arts," *Journal of Economic History,* I, 129–52.

[3] The most complete bibliography of Young's writings is to be found in G. D. Amery, "The Writings of Arthur Young," *Journal of the Royal Agricultural Society of England,* LXXXV, 175–205.

[4] Arthur Young, *Annals of Agriculture,* XXXV, 256.

[5] *Ibid.,* XXXVII, 617.

[6] *Ibid.,* XXXI, 115.

ernment's role in economic affairs. Indeed, he almost gloried in his contradictions. When accused of inconsistency in regard to the French Revolution, he replied:

> I have been reproached in some of these letters with changing my politics, my "principles".... My principles I certainly have not changed, because if there is one principle more predominant than another in my politics, it is the *principle of change*. I have been too long a farmer to be governed by any thing but events; I have a constitutional abhorrence of theory, and of all trust in abstract reasoning; consequently I can rely on nothing but experience; in other words, on events. This is the only principle that is worthy of an experimenter.[7]

In general it can be said that Young's attitude towards nationalism went through three stages. As a very young man he was a rabid patriot of the Chatham school and a complete believer in mercantilism. From the late 1770's until after 1789 he gradually rejected most mercantilist ideas and adopted those of laissez faire. In this whole period he was anti-imperialist, antiwar, pro-French, and very liberal in his politics. The impact of the radicalism of the French Revolution introduced the third stage in which Young became again a very strong nationalist, militaristic, anti-French, and reactionary. The remainder of this paper will be devoted to tracing these changes in some detail.

Arthur Young's first publications were two nationalistic pamphlets[8] which appeared in 1758 and 1759 during the Seven Years' War when their author was in his teens. Although the younger son of a gentleman, Young had been apprenticed to a wine merchant at Lynn. Fond of society and of reading, he did not have sufficient means to purchase both clothes and books, and therefore made a bargain with a bookseller by which his pamphlets were to be paid for in books. The pamphlets were of course hastily thrown together and were nothing but potboilers. Their interest lies in the light which they throw upon the patriotic views of an intelligent youngster. Obviously they could only be reflections of a point of view commonly held during the war.

Young blamed French plots for the outbreak of the war, censured

---

[7] *Ibid.*, XVIII, 582.

[8] *The Theatre of the Present War in North America: with Candid Reflections on the Great Importance of the War in That Part of the World* (London, 1758); *Reflections on the Present State of Affairs at Home and Abroad* (London, 1759).

Maria Theresa for faithlessness in not observing her treaties regarding Silesia, and justified Frederick the Great's invasion of Saxony to prevent the war from being fought on Prussian soil. He described France as Britain's "irreconcilable and enterprizing enemy"[9] and stated that the increase of French power in North America menaced Britain's naval power, upon which "our very being, as an independent nation, depends...."[10] A lasting peace could be made only if France were deprived of her North American colonies and if French power were reduced to such a state "as may leave us nothing to fear from their competition."[11]

Young devoted much space in the two pamphlets to the relations of Britain with her American colonies, and exhibited himself as a thoroughgoing mercantilist. The colonies should be developed economically so as to provide maximum benefits to the mother country. Their competing manufactures should be discouraged, but their production of raw materials, naval stores, and certain foodstuffs should be encouraged. Young also discussed a possible revolt of the colonies, and one of the benefits which he saw in his economic proposals was that they would tend to increase "the dependence of the colonies"[12] on Britain. To strengthen British control over her colonies, they should be united, a viceroy be appointed over them with absolute military power and a small regular army sent over, "as in Ireland."[13] A single parliament should also be established for the united colonies. He concluded, "Some will object, that the colonies would not submit to part with their charters; but every method ought to be taken to force a due obedience."[14] Obviously he was thinking more of British power than of colonial rights.

The number of books and pamphlets which Arthur Young wrote from 1767 to 1774 is almost unbelievable—nine volumes of English tours, eight other books, and four pamphlets. All through the period he was also conducting a farm, and during the last two years was parliamentary reporter for the *Morning Post*. As he wrote later in the *Autobiography* for the year 1770: "What a year of incessant activity,

---

[9] *Theatre*, p. 10.
[10] *Ibid.*, p. 46.
[11] *Reflections*, p. 21.
[12] *Ibid.*, p. 28.
[13] *Ibid.*, p. 42.
[14] *Ibid.*, p. 44.

composition, anxiety and wretchedness was this! No carthorse ever laboured as I did at this period, spending like an idiot, always in debt, in spite of what I earned with the sweat of my brow and almost my heart's blood, such was my anxiety...."[15] Books produced under such conditions and with such incentives are not usually masterpieces, yet some of them were among Young's most popular and influential works. Four of them are important for this study: *The Farmer's Letters to the People of England* (1767); *Letters Concerning the Present State of the French Nation* (1769); *Political Essays Concerning the Present State of the British Empire* (1772); *Political Arithmetic* (1774). The first and last of these works are the most substantial as far as intrinsic merit is concerned, but the second and third, which are mere hack work, are more revealing of Young's opinions as a nationalist.

Throughout this period Young remained essentially a mercantilist, that is, an economic nationalist. He still adhered to the balance of trade theory, and naturally rejected free trade. In this connection he opposed the ideas of the French physiocrats. As he wrote in the *Political Arithmetic:*

A great domestic circulation—a flourishing husbandry—and abundance of national wealth, without a favourable balance of trade, is a chimerical idea—of which an instance cannot be produced in the whole globe.... A general free trade, as there has been no example of it in history, so is it contrary to reason.[16]

He likewise defended the Navigation Acts as measures "calculated with the utmost wisdom."[17] But Young reserved his highest praises for the corn bounty. Indeed he never abandoned mercantilist conceptions in regard to the corn trade, even when in every other respect he had accepted laissez-faire doctrine. The corn bounty was not merely one of the bulwarks of the prosperity of English agriculture; it was also a means of preventing recurring famines, for *"they who grow not a surplus, cannot grow a sufficiency."*[18] The contrary policy of prohibiting export and permitting import would so reduce prices

---

[15] *The Autobiography of Arthur Young* ..., ed. by M. Betham-Edwards (London, 1898), pp. 52, 53.
[16] *Political Arithmetic* ... (London, 1774), pp. 261–62.
[17] *Ibid.*, p. 234.
[18] *The Farmer's Letters to the People of England* ... (3rd ed., Dublin, 1768), p. 75.

as to discourage production, and then famine would almost surely result.

The most complete and extreme statement of Young's mercantilism, particularly from the point of view of colonial imperialism, is to be found in the *Political Essays Concerning the Present State of the British Empire*. One of the essays furnishes the only complete statement of Young's political views at this time. He was obviously a Whig. He urged a very considerable extension of the franchise to the farmers and copyholders, expressed fear of the growing power of the crown, and completely justified the English revolutions of the seventeenth century. The English Civil Wars did result in stripping certain "great men, of prodigious property," of most of their possessions, "but when we speak of a *nation,* such are but of little consequence."[19] The attitudes here expressed would indicate that Young was almost a "radical" in the early 1770's. Certainly his views differed entirely from those which he held in the middle 1790's.

In his essay on manufactures Young supported the classical mercantilist idea that manufactures from native raw materials were more valuable than those from imported raw materials. He advocated vigorous steps to prevent the export of raw wool or its smuggling into France, a position diametrically opposite to his stand in the late 1780's. He proposed the appointment of inspectors of manufactures, reminiscent of those of Colbert. His most extreme proposal was for the justices of the peace to regulate agricultural and industrial wages, so as to maintain a proper balance between wages and prices. "Were proportions between labour and prices of necessaries thus fixed, the poor would always be secure of a proper maintenance, as their pay would ever rise with a necessary rise of their expences. . . ."[20] Such ideas are far removed from those of laissez faire and the conception of the state as a passive policeman.

Certainly the longest and probably the most interesting essay is that devoted to colonies. Young began by stating that colonies are advantageous to the mother country in so far as they produce staple commodities not produced at home, and receive in return the

---

[19] *Political Essays Concerning the Present State of the British Empire* . . . (London, 1772), pp. 68–69.
[20] *Ibid.*, p. 222.

manufactures of the mother country. It followed naturally that he considered the sugar islands the most valuable of British colonies, and the middle and northern colonies on the mainland the least. Indeed, the economy of the latter must be drastically altered, he felt, or Britain would very likely lose them. The middle and northern colonies should be encouraged to produce iron, naval stores, and lumber by means of bounties and a regular market, while on the other hand their manufactures should be ruined by dumping English manufactures in their ports. In addition, these colonies should not be permitted any merchant marine or share in the fisheries. A revolt in the near future could probably be suppressed, for Britain was powerful enough "not only to extirpate their trade, their manufactures, their agriculture, but even the very people themselves."[21] If his proposals were adopted vigorously, Britain might well be able to hold her American colonies for "several ages,"[22] but in the long run they were bound to become independent. Young predicted that eventually the King would move to America, which seemed "almost peculiarly formed for universal dominion," and that North America would ultimately become the greatest state in the world, possessing advantages enjoyed by no previous world empire.[23] But, in the immediate future, he not only hoped that the American colonies could be held, but that Britain could expand her colonial empire by seizing the islands from the Falklands to the Philippines as stepping-stones for control of the Pacific. Such a development was well nigh inevitable, for "Britain does, and will perpetually, colonize."[24] It is interesting that Young recognized the role of the missionary in civilizing the natives, "and extending their wants; consequently their demand for manufactures of all kinds would greatly increase. . . ."[25] The only sign of any laissez-faire tendencies in the *Political Essays* appears in his vigorous attack upon the monopoly of the East India Company, that "most pernicious charter, which never had ten words of sound reasoning urged in its defence."[26]

It is almost a truism that nationalism feeds upon the fear and

[21] *Ibid.*, p. 422.
[22] *Ibid.*, p. 429.
[23] *Ibid.*, pp. 430–31.
[24] *Ibid.*, p. 443.
[25] *Ibid.*, pp. 461–62.
[26] *Ibid.*, p. 525.

hatred of a national enemy. During Young's lifetime Britain's national enemy was France, and therefore his changing attitudes towards that nation are important. His early pamphlets during the Seven Years' War have already been noted. In 1769, when Young was but twenty-eight years old, he published his *Letters Concerning the French Nation*. None of his works had less intrinsic merit, but few are more valuable for the present study. The fact that he had not visited France did not bother Young, but at least he had read widely. Throughout, he assumed that France was Britain's national enemy. France should never have been given back her sugar colonies in the West Indies or any share in the Newfoundland fisheries. He feared a revival of French naval power, and even proposed a preventive war whenever French naval preparations should appear menacing. England "ought *on the political plan,* to take occasion to quarrel with France, whenever the French marine begins to wear a formidable appearance, or threatens in a distant manner to rival her own; by such, and only such means, she can secure to herself the empire of the sea."[27] He devoted much attention to the relative power of the two rivals. He thought France possessed a superior geographic position, a larger population, a more fertile soil, greater total wealth, a superior army, and an arbitrary form of government which made for unity. On the other hand, Britain had the advantages of a more progressive agriculture, more extensive commerce, a better system of taxation, naval superiority, and a free government under which her people would fight better in the long run. In one passage Young summarized, "The *last* age was beyond all doubt that of France, and the *present* of England."[28] In another he wrote, "In the aggregate of the whole, considered as a kingdom, France is superior. As a nation, England."[29]

Young devoted considerable space in the *Letters Concerning the Present State of the French Nation* to such subjects as architecture, painting, music, and literature. On the whole he showed himself remarkably free from national prejudice. He greatly admired many features of French culture, and felt that France was definitely superior in painting, sculpture, engraving, drama, and in writings on

[27] *Letters Concerning the Present State of the French Nation* . . . (London, 1769), p. 434.
[28] *Ibid.,* p. 384.
[29] *Ibid.,* p. 459.

agriculture and natural history. On the other hand England excelled in architecture, music, and in most fields of writing—politics, moral philosophy, novels, and poetry. In the realm of culture he appeared impartial, even cosmopolitan.

Until the late 1770's Arthur Young seems to have been pretty thoroughly a mercantilist and very anti-French. Beginning about 1780 one can note a marked change. For the most part laissez-faire beliefs replaced mercantilist doctrines. Young became an advocate of free trade except where the vested interests of the farmers were concerned, as in the Corn Laws. He reacted very strongly against colonial imperialism and blamed most of the wars of the eighteenth century on the spirit of commercial monopoly. Likewise he tended to become more friendly to France, even to the point of urging an alliance between the hereditary enemies. These laissez-faire, anti-imperialist, and pro-French attitudes continued dominant in Young's writings until the early 1790's and pervade his *Travels in France*. Of course he was not always consistent in his new views. He certainly never overcame his national prejudices, and during the latter part of the War of the American Revolution exhibited as uncompromising a hostility towards France as he had shown during the Seven Years' War, or as he was to show later, beginning in 1792.

There is no contemporary evidence to indicate how Young reacted to the early phases of the American Revolution or to the issues between the colonies and the mother country. As noted above, he manifested very little sympathy for the colonial point of view in the period before the Revolution. In 1776, however, he went to Ireland, first as a traveler and later as the estate agent for Lord Kingsborough.[30] He published nothing from the *Political Arithmetic* in 1774 until a *Tour in Ireland* appeared in 1780. In a lengthy preface to the latter work Young blamed the American Revolution squarely upon "that baleful monopolizing spirit of commerce that wished to govern great nations, on the maxims of the counter."[31] He claimed that if the colonies had been given free trade with the mother country a complete union might have been possible. He went on to state that the War of 1740 had been fought to protect English smug-

---

[30] Robert King, 1759-1799, Lord Kingsborough and later second Earl of Kingston.
[31] *A Tour in Ireland* . . . (Dublin, 1780), I, xiv.

glers, the Seven Years' War to exclude the French from the American markets, and the American Revolution to preserve the markets gained in 1763. He also took the astonishing position that although England and France were at present at war, the two rivals might well have to unite in the future to preserve the independence of Europe from "new devils" arising in the east of Europe,[32] a reference apparently to the first partition of Poland. There is no evidence in this work of any bitterness towards the French.

In *A Tour in Ireland* Young also showed himself sympathetic to Irish grievances. He was indignant over the discriminations against Irish wool manufactures and Irish meat products, and castigated the English government for the penal laws directed against the Irish Catholics. He contended that English woolen manufactures would be invigorated by Irish competition. Since Ireland was an important consumer of English goods, it was to the interests of England to have a rich rather than a poor Ireland. Free trade between England and Ireland was essential to the welfare of both, but could probably be attained only as the result of union between the two kingdoms. Interestingly enough, Young showed himself to be a nationalist even when attacking the abuses of economic nationalism in Ireland. He urged that, while free trade might hurt certain English manufactures, the issues were larger than those of the individual or of a group: ". . . it is THE EMPIRE that is concerned; the general interest demands the measure. . . ."[33] Moreover, he seemed completely blind to the strength of Irish nationalism.

There is no conclusive evidence to explain why Young changed his point of view so drastically between 1774, the date of the *Political Arithmetic,* and 1780, the date of *A Tour in Ireland.* Nearly all of the characteristic tenets of laissez-faire doctrine had been current in the generation before the publication of *The Wealth of Nations,* although it was only in that work that they were all brought together in a great synthesis.[34] Young was certainly familiar with the

---

[32] *Ibid.,* I, xi.

[33] *Ibid.,* II, part ii, 180.

[34] For a discussion of laissez-faire ideas before Smith, cf. L. H. Haney, *History of Economic Thought* (3rd ed., New York, 1936), pp. 207–11; J. K. Ingram, *A History of Political Economy* (London, 1915), pp. 81–85; E. Roll, *A History of Economic Thought* (New York, 1942), pp. 114–24; J. Viner, *Studies in the Theory of International Trade* (New York, 1937), pp. 74–110; E. A. J. Johnson, *Predecessors of Adam Smith* (New York, 1937), *passim.*

work of several of Smith's predecessors, notably with that of Dean Josiah Tucker.[35] There is a close similarity between Tucker's and Young's views on war, imperialism, and monopolistic trade companies, and Young nearly always referred to Tucker with deep respect.[36] It is hard to say how much Young was influenced by Adam Smith. He never once mentioned Smith in *A Tour in Ireland*. Moreover, the first reference to Smith in any of Young's writings, in the *Annals of Agriculture* in 1784, is unfavorable, for Smith was opposed to the export bounty on corn. Young remarked, "I hardly know an abler work than Dr. Smith's, or one . . . that is fuller of more pernicious errors; he never touches on any branch of rural economy, but to start [*sic*] positions that arise from mis-stated facts, or that lead to false conclusions."[37] Later references in the *Annals,* however, were much more respectful to Smith's ideas.[38] Probably Smith re-enforced Young's antimercantilist beliefs, but it seems likely that Tucker was more responsible than Smith for the alteration of Young's views. It is also possible that Young's ideas were changed by personal contacts. Young knew Burke and may have been influenced by him. Certainly he was close to Lord Shelburne at this period, for it was Shelburne who had urged him to undertake the Irish tour and had furnished him with introductions. And Shelburne had been strongly influenced by Smith.[39]

A further important factor in changing Young's views was the impact of firsthand contact with Irish conditions and grievances. There is no doubt that he was shocked at many things which he found in Ireland. It is important that, in *A Tour in Ireland,* Young for the first time showed any real sympathy with the lower classes. His earlier writings had been very harsh towards the poor, whom he had been inclined to blame for all their miseries. Conditions in Ire-

---

[35] Young was of course familiar with the ideas of the French physiocrats, but there is little evidence that they influenced him, except that he reacted violently against their proposals for a single tax on land. Cf. *Political Arithmetic,* pp. 209–66.

[36] *A Tour in Ireland,* II, part ii, 185; *Annals of Agriculture,* III, 267, 417–21. For Dean Tucker's ideas, cf. R. L. Schuyler, *Josiah Tucker* (New York, 1931); W. E. Clark, *Josiah Tucker* (New York, 1903).

[37] *Annals of Agriculture,* I, 380, note.

[38] *Ibid.,* II, 406; V, 404; VII, 421.

[39] *Autobiography,* p. 67. For Shelburne's conversion to ideas of Smith, cf. J. Rae, *Life of Adam Smith* (London, 1895), pp. 144, 153.

land so opened his eyes that he remarked in one place, concerning the poor,

> ... it is they that feed, cloath, enrich, and fight the battles of all the other ranks of a community; it is their being able to support these various burthens without oppression, which constitutes the general felicity; in proportion to their ease is the strength and wealth of nations, as public debility will be the certain attendant on their misery.[40]

It seems only reasonable to conclude that the evils of mercantilism which he witnessed in Ireland helped very materially to convert Young to laissez-faire doctrines.

As already noted, Young displayed no hostility to France in *A Tour in Ireland*, in spite of the fact that Britain and France were at war when it was published. Two years later, however, in 1782, he wrote a series of public letters for the press in which he exhibited an extreme form of nationalism and considerable bitterness against France. The occasion was a proposal of his neighbor and friend, Frederick Hervey,[41] Earl of Bristol and Bishop of Derry, the infamous Earl-Bishop, to raise a large public subscription in Suffolk for the purchase of a seventy-four-gun ship to be presented to the government. It was hoped that other counties would emulate Suffolk. Lord Shelburne gave his support to the scheme. A total of more than £21,000 was raised, with Lord Bristol contributing £1000, and Arthur Young twenty guineas.[42] While the subscription was being raised Young engaged in a newspaper controversy in the *Bury Post and Universal Advertiser* with Capel Lofft,[43] another neighbor who was a thoroughgoing radical and who opposed the scheme. Three letters were written by Young, four by Lofft. The series of letters was also collected and published as a separate pamphlet.

Lofft in his first letter attacked the whole scheme as unconstitutional because it invaded the sphere of parliamentary action and

---

[40] *A Tour in Ireland*, II, part ii, 25.

[41] Frederick Hervey, 1730–1803. In the early 1780's Young was on very intimate terms with the Earl-Bishop.

[42] *An Inquiry into the Legality and Expediency of Increasing the Royal Navy by Subscriptions for Building County Ships* ... (Bury St. Edmunds, 1783); *Autobiography*, pp. 101–2; *The Bury Post and County Advertiser*, Aug. 22, 1782–Nov. 1, 1782.

[43] Capel Lofft, 1751–1824. Young and Lofft were friendly on a personal basis, but they always clashed on politics, and Young was deeply suspicious of Lofft's good faith, apparently without much justification.

might increase the power of a despotic ministry. To him the important thing was parliamentary reform, which might be sidetracked by the subscription. To Young, on the other hand, the defeat of France and the security of Britain were more important than parliamentary reform. Indeed, in his desire to refute Lofft, Young defended the constitution as it was and declared, "I think we are now the freest people on the globe."[44] He feared that agitation for parliamentary reform might lead to civil war, which would eventuate "either in a military despot or a republic.... Far as the poles asunder be this country from either. That bosom which feels not freedom under our constitution, was not born for liberty, but for Bedlam."[45]

Young felt that France had attacked England because her navy was weak, and therefore the important thing was to increase the navy. France was the aggressor and hence England's cause was just. "A restless ambition, and not the love of liberty, sent the French to America."[46] Young granted that one ship would not be much help, but he had hoped that Suffolk's example would inspire other counties to follow suit. What he really desired was a great surge of patriotism throughout England that would unite the country and defeat the French. Repeatedly he said that it was not the size of the contribution that was important, but rather the number of contributors. His appeals were impassioned, even turgid. In his first letter he urged that the contributions would convince the French "that one noble spirit animates every British bosom," and referred to "our determined spirit to resist their boundless ambition."[47] In the same letter he appealed for "an electric spark of patriotism, that darts the hidden fire, in a moment, from one extremity of the country to the other."[48] And in his second letter he described patriotic feelings as "the noblest emotions that can dignify the bosoms of free men."[49] Again in 1782, as in 1758 and 1759, Young expressed, without any inhibitions, an emotional patriotism which was far more deep-seated than his rational adherence to laissez faire in *A Tour in*

[44] *Bury Post,* Oct. 17, 1782, p. 4.
[45] *Ibid.,* Sept. 26, 1782, p. 4.
[46] *Ibid.,* Oct. 17, 1782, p. 4.
[47] *Ibid.,* Sept. 12, 1782, p. 4.
[48] *Ibid.*
[49] *Ibid.,* Sept. 26, 1782, p. 4.

Ireland. When England was in danger, Young was always first and foremost a patriot.

When the danger passed with the war, Young reverted to his liberal, anti-imperialist, laissez-faire, and pro-French position, and continued fairly consistent in such opinions until 1792. In 1784 he began the publication of the *Annals of Agriculture,* one of his real claims to lasting fame. On an average Young wrote from one quarter to one third of the *Annals* himself. In numerous articles he elaborated his opinions on national and international affairs. In general it can be said that he accepted laissez-faire ideas except where they ran counter to agrarian interests, which, of course, were his principal concern.

In the early volumes of the *Annals* Young appears pretty consistently as an anti-imperialist. He was prone to claim that most modern wars originated in the selfish interests of merchants and manufacturers, and in colonial rivalries. Colonies were not worth while, and would probably seek independence as soon as they became prosperous. Colonial wars led to increased taxation, which fell more heavily upon the landed than upon the mercantile and manufacturing interests. Moreover, capital invested in colonies might be spent more advantageously to national interests in improving waste lands—a perennial hobby of Young's.

Most of the above points were vigorously stated in the first number of the *Annals,* which was an essay by Young entitled "An enquiry into the situation of the Kingdom on the conclusion to the late Treaty,"[50] referring, of course, to Britain's situation after the War of the American Revolution. The old colonial system was bankrupt, and Young predicted that probably Britain would in time lose her remaining colonies. He was especially bitter about India:

It is impossible to hold countries that we treat as we have done our Indian dominions. A people plundered without shame or restraint . . . the loss of India! That day *must* come.—It OUGHT to come.—If there is a ruling Providence that oversees the conduct of nations, and that ever yet punished them for their iniquities, we MUST be driven out of India with abhorrence and contempt, and all the peoples of the globe would rejoice at the event.[51]

[50] *Annals of Agriculture,* I, 9–87.
[51] *Ibid.,* I, 17.

He was also worried about Ireland, which was already half independent and which he prophesied might ally herself with France in the next war. An independent Ireland, however, he thought would be "a monster in politics,"[52] and he insisted that a union with Britain was absolutely necessary for the latter's security.

Young also vented anti-imperialist sentiments in an article attacking the window tax, which would fall most heavily upon the small landed gentleman and farmer, and which was made necessary by wars fought for colonial issues. "Cannot our merchants and our mercantile leaders in Parliament," he wrote indignantly, "find some vile rock—some Falklands isle, or Pierre, or Miquelon—some cursed perwannah on the Ganges, or blackened isle that bleeds for sugar—on which to erect their pretentions to future wars?"[53] In the same article he went on to blame Britain for holding Gibraltar after the War of the American Revolution and continued:

> While this nation gives itself such airs of haughty superiority; so humiliating and offensive to the pride and feelings of its neighbours; . . . while it admits the sovereignty and possession of certain isles to be in foreign monarchs, yet prohibits fortifications to be erected, . . . peace can never be permanent, because our neighbours can never cease to be jealous.[54]

In another article, Young burst out: "I confess that wars, especially for commerce, are objects of my detestation: I abhor their principle."[55] Later he even attacked wars for the balance of power, and stated, ". . . we have as often, by our intermeddling and turbulent conduct, endeavoured to overturn that balance, as to establish it. . . ."[56]

In general, Young during these years also advocated free trade. He opposed all restrictions and impediments upon the free movement of goods from one country to another, and believed that government should keep hands off and allow the laws of supply and demand to operate freely. He refuted the mercantilist argument that trade favors one country alone and pointed out that the advantage is reciprocal. No industry which could not meet international competition deserved to survive, for capital invested in such

---

[52] *Ibid.*, I, 22.
[53] *Ibid.*, II, 307.
[54] *Ibid.*, II, 309–10.
[55] *Ibid.*, IV, 520–21.
[56] *Ibid.*, VIII, 421.

an industry might better be put into one which needed no protection. He pointed out that free trade always benefited the consumer. He also rejected the argument that protection was needed against countries with low wages, for it was the productivity of labor, not the money wages paid to labor, which determined the ability of an industry to compete successfully in international trade. The following quotation shows how completely Young had adopted free-trade arguments:

> But till that simple proposition is understood and admitted, *that there is an advantage in our own fabrics being undersold by foreigners;* till that day comes, all our commercial conduct will be blind.... if a frenchman, at Bury, will sell me a shirt better and cheaper than ... a scotchman, or a Devonshire man, it is certainly my interest to buy it of him. By that cheapness, I am enabled to consume so much the more of other commodities; and the capital and industry misemployed in making *dear* shirts, may be turned to making *cheap* hardware and woollen.[57]

In 1785 he strongly supported the relaxation of trade restrictions with Ireland and declared, "... two neighbouring, great, populous, industrious, and wealthy nations are formed to be reciprocal markets to each other...."[58] He welcomed the negotiations which led to the Eden Treaty in 1786, and ridiculed the fears of its British opponents, pointing out that France had no such men as Darby, Wedgwood, Boulton, Wilkinson, or Arkwright. Free trade might also prevent future wars with France, which in itself would overbalance any possible objections.

As champion of the agrarian classes, Young felt specially aggrieved against one particular trade restriction. For more than a century it had been illegal to export raw wool from England, and in his *Political Essays* of 1772 he had supported such prohibitions. In 1786, however, a measure was introduced into Parliament which provided much more minute restrictions and very drastic penalties against smuggling. Young immediately attacked the measure with every possible argument. He filled five volumes of the *Annals* with material against the wool bill, and published two pamphlets opposing it. In the spring of 1787 he was actively engaged in organizing resistance in Suffolk through petitions and public meetings, and was

---
[57] *Ibid.*, IV, 120.
[58] *Ibid.*, III, 261.

repeatedly given thanks for his exertions in behalf of the landed interests. In the spring of 1788 he spent nine weeks in London, giving evidence in both houses of Parliament against the measure. To such an extent was he regarded as the leader in the opposition to the bill that he was burnt in effigy by the woolen manufacturing interests. In spite of all his work, the measure was passed in 1788.[59]

At the very beginning of the controversy Young accused the woolen manufacturers of exhibiting "that vile spirit of monopoly which has so long been the disgrace and curse of this country."[60] In the course of his various writings on this issue Young at several points gave expression to extreme laissez-faire ideas. In his first article he had written, "Regulation may destroy, but it can never make commerce; and this kingdom has grown great, not *by* her numerous restrictions, but *in spite* of them."[61] And again at the very end of the controversy he wrote: "Government never interferes in trade but to do mischief. When are our legislators to be instructed in the true principles of national policy, which, in one word, is to leave every branch of industry to itself. No law—no regulation—no prohibitions."[62]

When laissez-faire arguments supported the interests of the agrarian classes, Young used them, but when the interests of those classes conflicted with laissez-faire principles, he disavowed laissez faire. Shortly after the American Revolution, the West Indies wished to purchase some of their food from the United States. Young insisted, however, that Britain alone should be permitted to provide the colonies with food: "To supply the West Indies with grain, flour, bread, and all sorts of provisions, ought immediately to be secured exclusively to Great Britain. . . ."[63] Similarly, he refused to accept laissez faire when it applied to the Corn Laws. Here he willingly admitted that an absolute free trade was desirable in principle, but he quickly went on to declare that free trade was really im-

---

[59] Cf. *Annals*, VI, 506–28; VII, 94–96, 150–75, 405–28; VIII, 467–90; IX, 73–82, 266–376, 458–65, 657; X, 1–126, 139–86, 235–82, 402–18, 440–57; *Autobiography*, pp. 163–67, 172–74; *Bury Post*, Jan. 24–April 4, 1787, Nov. 7, 1787–July 2, 1788; *The Question of Wool Truly Stated* . . . (London, 1788); *A Speech on the Wool Bill* . . . (London, 1788).
[60] *Annals*, VI, 515.
[61] *Ibid.*, VI, 521.
[62] *Ibid.*, X, 453, note.
[63] *Ibid.*, I, 376.

possible in corn, for once a scarcity appeared, an outcry would arise for the prohibition of export. In 1785 he clearly stated his position on this matter as follows:

I have not touched upon the question of an *absolutely* free trade in corn, because it is a subject that can never come fairly into debate . . . . Could it be positively ensured in all cases whatever, it would be of all others the best regulation. But when prices arose high, petitions would flow in to stop exportation, and such a system would end in this—a free importation, a regulated exportation, and the loss of the bounty to the landed interest. Such a measure, therefore, should be rejected at the first blush, for it never will be brought forward but as a trick.[64]

From 1787 until 1815 Arthur Young's nationalism is to be evaluated almost entirely by his attitudes towards Anglo-French relations, and towards the French Revolution and its results. In general it can be said that he was fairly favorable to France and her revolution until 1792, but very unfavorable after that date. Before 1792 his attitudes were much as they had been since 1780—antimercantilist and anti-imperialist, favorable to laissez faire, quite pro-French, and on the whole liberal. He went to France during three successive years, 1787, 1788, and 1789, and the last trip continued until early in 1790. He traveled over most of the country, keeping a careful daily diary of his journeys. His greatest work, commonly known as the *Travels in France*,[65] was first published in 1792. About half of it consists of the diary, and the other half of an analytical survey of the conditions which he had found. At the end is a very important chapter devoted to the Revolution.

On the whole Young's temper in the *Travels in France* is remarkably impartial and judicious. He was definitely not a cold man, and was given to enthusiasms, was blunt, and inclined to overstate his case. He had often been attacked for being too "warm" in his criticisms of things and people. Moreover, it must be remembered that he had a very deep affection for England and for things English, that

---

[64] *Ibid.*, III, 467–68. Cf. also *ibid.*, III, 419–20.

[65] The full title is *Travels during the years 1787, 1788 and 1789, Undertaken more particularly with a View of ascertaining the Cultivation, Wealth, Resources, and National Prosperity of the Kingdom of France*. The first edition was printed at Bury St. Edmunds in one volume in 1792. It was reprinted in two volumes in Dublin in 1793. A second edition appeared in 1794, the first volume at London, the second volume at Bury St. Edmunds. The edition used for this paper is the Dublin one of 1793.

at times he inclined to provincialism, and had at least the normal Englishman's prejudices. Several years earlier he had been taken to task by one of his closest friends, Maximilien Lazowski, for his tendency to show prejudice against France in the *Annals*. Lazowski pointed out that Young had been too prone to dismiss a French publication with a contemptuous phrase, such as "nonsense" or "execrable stuff,"[66] and warned him that Frenchmen who read the *Annals* "will never believe that you have much love for them."[67]

At times Young was guilty of such impatience, or provincialism, in the *Travels in France*. He was quite naturally piqued when ridiculed at Versailles in 1787 for not knowing that the Dauphin received the *cordon bleu* at birth, but he showed bad taste when he burst forth in the diary: "So unpardonable was it for a foreigner to be ignorant of such an important part of French history, as that of giving a babe a blue slobbering bib instead of a white one!"[68] He was so irked when the French showed ignorance of England that he informed one Frenchman that he himself was a Chinese, and another that England had no rivers. He compared French inns and traveling facilities very unfavorably with those of England. He found Frenchmen at the inns and *table d'hôtes* taciturn, dull, and uninteresting, and at one point exclaimed: "Take the mass of mankind and you have more good sense in half an hour in England, than in half a year in France."[69] But nearly all patriotic travelers, of whatever nation, would probably agree with the sentiment expressed in one of his letters home: his own land was "a country from which none will travel but to love it the better."[70]

On the other hand, Young acknowledged that the French were superior to the English in certain respects. Repeatedly he bore witness to the politeness of the French to him as an Englishman, and at one point exclaimed: "If an Englishman receives attentions in France, *because he is an Englishman,* what return ought to be made to a Frenchman in England, is sufficiently obvious."[71] He was especially struck with the French "invariable sweetness of disposition,

[66] *Annals*, V, 86, 87.
[67] *Ibid.*, V, 87.
[68] *Travels in France*, I, 19–20.
[69] *Ibid.*, I, 283.
[70] British Museum *Add. Mss.* 35, 126, fol. 397.
[71] *Travels in France*, I, 13.

mildness of character and what in English we emphatically call *good temper*."[72]

Throughout the *Travels in France* Young showed himself consistently friendly to the continuance of peace between England and France. He still favored the Eden Treaty, partly at least because it tended to make Anglo-French peace more permanent. He still opposed colonial rivalries and expressed the wish that all nations would abandon all their colonies. He was worried in 1790 about a possible Anglo-French war over their rivalry in Holland at the time of the Dutch internal troubles.[73] Several times he urged an Anglo-French alliance as the best way to preserve the European balance of power against the expansionist policies of the three eastern powers. Although he could not forbear to take digs once or twice at the French for their intervention during the American war, he willingly admitted that past English policy had also been provocative. When he reached Dunkirk he remarked, "Dunkirk, so famous in history for an imperiousness in England, which she must have paid dearly for. Dunkirk, Gibraltar, and the statue of Louis XIV in the *Place de Victoire,* I place in the same political class of national arrogance."[74] Perhaps the most extreme anti-imperialistic, even anti-nationalistic, statement which Young ever made appears in the *Travels in France* in an attack upon the Navigation Acts:

The monopoly of navigation is valuable no farther than as it implies the manufacture of shipbuilding and fitting out; the possession of many sailors, as instruments of future wars, ought to be esteemed in the same light as great Russian or Prussian armies; that is to say, as the pests of human societies; as the tools of ambition; and as the instruments of wide extended misery.[75]

Young's impartiality in the *Travels in France* is best shown, however, in his attitude towards the French Revolution. He was in France during the stirring days of 1789, he attended meetings of the Estates General and talked with many of the leaders, he witnessed the uprisings in the provinces in the summer, and at times was subject to considerable inconvenience, if not physical danger, from the revolutionaries. And yet on the whole his attitude was definitely

[72] *Ibid.*, I, 54.
[73] *Ibid.*, I, 673–81.
[74] *Ibid.*, I, 152.
[75] *Ibid.*, II, 428.

friendly to the Revolution, although there were many things with which he did not sympathize. His diary for 1789 is full of impressions which the Revolution made upon him at the moment. In these the favorable and unfavorable crowd upon each other, as might be expected. His generally liberal position and favorable predisposition is best shown by his comment when he first attended the Estates General on June 15:

The spectacle of the representatives of twenty-five millions of people, just emerging from the evils of 200 years of arbitrary power, and rising to the blessings of a freer constitution, assembled with open doors under the eye of the public, was framed to call into animated feelings every latent spark, every emotion of a liberal bosom. To banish whatever ideas might intrude of their being a people too often hostile to my own country,—and to dwell with pleasure on the glorious idea of happiness to a great nation—of felicity to millions yet unborn.[76]

Nevertheless, Young thought the offer of Louis XVI on June 23 a generous one which should have been accepted. He was certainly disturbed by the violence which he witnessed in the summer in the provinces, and worried over the predominance of Paris and the lack of an informed public opinion outside the capital. His provincialism was all too apparent in his amazement that the French did not adopt essentially the British form of government. He had little sympathy with the idea of a written constitution, "as if a constitution was a pudding to be made by a receipt."[77] He would have solved the problem of the organization of the Estates by copying the English two-house system. Advocating that they take the English constitution as a basis, he did admit the constitution might conceivably be improved, "but improve it cautiously; for surely that ought to be touched with caution, which has given from the moment of its establishment, felicity to a great nation; which has given greatness to a people designed by nature to be little...."[78]

Young's more reasoned evaluation of the French Revolution is to be found in the seventy-page essay which constitutes the last chapter of his *Travels in France*. Presumably the main body of the chapter was composed some time in 1791, for there are two addenda, the first entitled "1792," and the second dated April 26, 1792. Again there

[76] *Ibid.*, I, 231.
[77] *Ibid.*, I, 260.
[78] *Ibid.*, I, 266.

can be no doubt that Young's balance sheet of the Revolution at this time was favorable. The chapter begins with a careful analysis of the background of the Revolution and of the grievances which the French had suffered, based upon his intensive study of the *cahiers,* an analysis which still has much merit. The conclusion which Young reached was that the grievances justified the Revolution. He regretted the violence of the lower classes, but claimed that the government and the aristocracy were basically to blame. In one place he declared:

He who chooses to be served by slaves, and by ill-treated slaves, must know that he holds both his property and life by a tenure far different from those who prefer the service of well treated freemen; and he who dines to the music of groaning sufferers, must not, in the moment of insurrection, complain that his daughters are ravished, and then destroyed; and that his sons [sic] throats are cut. When such evils happen, they surely are more imputable to the tyranny of the master, then [sic] to the cruelty of the servant.[79]

His final statement on this part of his argument demonstrates conclusively Young's sympathy with the Revolution:

The true judgment to be formed of the French revolution, must surely be gained, from an attentive consideration of the evils of the old government: when these are well understood—and when the extent and universality of the oppression under which the people groaned—oppression which bore upon them from every quarter, it will scarcely be attempted to be urged, that a revolution was not absolutely necessary to the welfare of the kingdom.[80]

From a discussion of causes, Young passed on to an analysis of the effects of the Revolution. He readily admitted that the nobility and clergy had been ruined, but he did not seem very much concerned over their sufferings. Strangely enough, he manifested more sympathy for the French clergy than for the French nobility, and for a curious reason—that the French clergy were more respectable than their English brethren, who presumably deserved even more severe treatment than the French. He did feel that the Revolution had hurt the manufacturing classes unnecessarily, he was worried that rents in France were not being paid, he opposed the new system of

[79] *Ibid.,* II, 515.
[80] *Ibid.,* II, 517.

land taxes, and he saw no evidence that much was being done to make agriculture more prosperous and more technically advanced. Young thought the great beneficiaries of the Revolution would be the small landed proprietors and he was inclined to rejoice in their improved position. Again, one of his summaries shows clearly where his sympathies lay: "Go to the aristocratical politician at Paris, or at London, and you hear only of the ruin of France—go to the cottage of the *metayer,* or the house of the farmer, and demand of him what the result has been—there will be but one voice from Calais to Bayonne."[81]

As for the new government of France, Young was inclined to reserve judgment. He thought more power should have been left to the king, there should have been more checks upon the Assembly, and he was especially critical of the fact that representation was not based more definitely on property. On the other hand, he also showed himself very critical of certain evils in the British government. In analyzing the French government he had declared that it was still in an experimental state, and continued:

What can we know, experimentally, of a government which has not stood the brunt of unsuccessful and of successful wars? The English constitution has stood this test, and has been found deficient; or rather as far as this test can decide any thing, has been proved worthless; since in a single century, it has involved the nation in a debt of so vast a magnitude, that every blessing which might otherwise have been perpetuated is put to the stake; so that if the nation do not make some change in its constitution, it is much to be dreaded that the constitution will ruin the nation.[82]

Such a statement was hardly that of a stand-pat conservative.

Young also predicted that the French Revolution would surely affect all other countries, to a greater or lesser degree. In free countries, such as England, reforms must be made. At one point he remarked, "Can such ignorance of the human heart, and such blindness to the natural course of events be found, as the plan of rejecting *all* innovations lest they should lead to greater?"[83] Then he went on to list the reforms which were necessary in England— reduction of taxes, abolition of the national debt, tithes, and re-

[81] *Ibid.,* II, 530.
[82] *Ibid.,* II, 535.
[83] *Ibid.,* II, 537.

ligious tests, a widening of the franchise, destruction of all monopolies, and the thorough reform of the civil and criminal law.[84] Such a program would surely class Young at this time as a Radical. He also brought forward a scheme which he later elaborated in great detail during the wars, the need for a militia of property-owners, to prevent reform from getting out of hand and leading to anarchy. In the course of his discussion Young specifically criticized Burke twice,[85] and almost certainly he was referring to Burke when he remarked, after reviewing the accomplishments of the Revolution: "The men who deny the benefits of such events, must have something sinister in their views, or *muddy in their understandings.*"[86]

The last three pages of the *Travels in France* are devoted to the news of the war between France and Austria. He warned against the prevalent opinion that France would be easily defeated. Her system of defensive fortresses was not to be taken lightly. He also discounted the financial difficulties and prophesied that the Assembly in time of war would make no attempt to maintain public credit. Furthermore, he predicted that talk of a civil war would vanish once France was engaged in a great foreign war, for such talk would become treason. However, if he was mistaken, and if France were in danger of being overrun, it would be to the advantage of England to support her against the powers of eastern Europe. The concluding sentences of the *Travels in France* are interesting in the light of Young's future opinions:

Should real danger arise to France, . . it is the business, and direct interest of her neighbours, to support her.

The revolution, and anti-revolution parties of England, have exhausted themselves on the French question; but there can be none, if that people should be in danger—WE hold at present the balance of the world; and have but to speak, and it is secure.[87]

All of our knowledge of Young's activities and writings in 1791 and the early part of 1792 reveals nothing inconsistent with his attitude towards the French Revolution as expressed in the *Travels in France*. During a month's tour to the central counties of England in the summer of 1791 he saw the ruins of the home and laboratory

---

[84] *Ibid.*, II, 539.
[85] *Ibid.*, II, 534, note, 547–48.
[86] *Ibid.*, II, 549.
[87] *Ibid.*, II, 571.

of Joseph Priestley who had been the victim of a reactionary mob which had resented his liberalism in religion and politics. Young expressed his indignation at an act of vandalism which would only spread "the scandal of the British name," and went on, "These are the principles that instigated a mob of miscreants—I beg pardon;—of FRIENDS *and Fellow Churchmen,* attached to Church and King—to act so well for the reputation of this country."[88] Late in 1791 a serious hydrophobia epidemic appeared in Suffolk, and Young took the lead in arousing county sentiment in favor of a petition to Parliament to introduce a dog tax.[89] In justifying his position Young again took a very radical position. He declared that such a tax should have been imposed long ago, but *"it is not the opinion of* THE PEOPLE *that has authority in this kingdom.* . . . Ministers, and a majority in parliament, govern this country for purposes not entirely public. . . ."[90] It had been claimed that it would be embarrassing for the minister to introduce such a tax, upon which Young indignantly burst out:

Are we to view our children expiring in the tortures of the hydrophobia, and then listen with patience to those who insult us with a minister's convenience, his delicacy, or his objections! Let those who offer such arguments to their fellow subjects, reflect on the conclusion to be drawn from such reasoning. That the minister's private motives are more likely to weigh with the House of Commons, than the interest and direct demands of the people of England: this throws the business on its right issue, and we come at once to the source the nation has to complain of, the representation of the people being such, that that house cannot *feel* for the people. It is a senate that feels for itself. To this cause we may look for tythes, tests, poor rates, game laws, charters, corporations, immense and ruinous taxes, wars, national debts, monopolies, prohibitions, restrictions, and all the mischiefs of the commercial system.[91]

He continued by urging petitions, "conceived in a firm and manly stile, such as becomes the NATURAL legislature of the country speaking to their servants. . . ."[92]

Thus, as late as the spring of 1792, Young was still on the liberal side in the great cleavage in British public opinion that had its

[88] *Annals*, XVI, 531.
[89] *Ibid.*, XVII, 479–86, 533–64. Cf. also *Bury and Norwich Post*, Feb. 22–March 28, 1792.
[90] *Annals*, XVII, 480.
[91] *Ibid.*, XVII, 482–83.
[92] *Ibid.*, XVII, 484.

origin in the French Revolution. Then suddenly, and with no real warning, Young changed his views and became violently opposed to the Revolution in France and to all those Englishmen who were pro-French. The change took place in the summer of 1792 and was expressed in three brief articles in the *Annals of Agriculture,* the first dated August 20, 1792, the second undated but written apparently early in September, and the third dated October 12.[93] The first article opened with the following arresting clauses, "The fearful events which are at present passing in France, with a celerity of mischief that surpasses equally all that history has to offer, or fancy to conceive. . . ."[94] The basis of his attack was that the Revolution was endangering private property through taxation, requisition of crops, and possibly complete expropriation through the principle of "equality." As he wrote, "The word is absurd if it attaches not to property, for there can be no equality while one man is rich and another poor."[95] And the basis for the attack on property lay in the principle of representation by person instead of by property. He had expressed fears on this point in the *Travels in France,* and now he made it the cornerstone of his new position: "IF PERSONS ARE REPRESENTED, PROPERTY IS DESTROYED."[96] He claimed that the experiment of the French Revolution had been made and that it was a failure, and put his idea into good farming idiom: "*. . . the thing is tried; that method of drilling has been experimented and found good for nothing; the crop did not answer.*"[97] He predicted that the ideas of the Rights of Man and of revolution were bound to spread, and urged that the only safety for British property was the formation of a militia of property-owners. He stated that most standing armies were composed of the dregs of the population among whom egalitarian ideas must be popular, and hence that the armies might become an agent in favor of revolution rather than against it. Hence the necessity for arming the property-owners, to defend their property rights against the masses.

Young's first article had led to pained and angry protests from the pro-French party, and in the second he not only defended his

[93] *Ibid.,* XVIII, 486–95, 582–96; XIX, 36–51.
[94] *Ibid.,* XVIII, 486.
[95] *Ibid.,* XVIII, 487.
[96] *Ibid.,* XVIII, 492.
[97] *Ibid.*

right to change his mind as conditions changed, but he opposed very bitterly the pro-French faction. In the second and third articles he attacked Christie, Sheridan, Wyvil, Mackintosh, Cartwright, and especially Paine, "that prince of incendiaries."[98] He admitted that he had favored the early steps in the Revolution, but as it became more radical, he had become opposed. "My feeling at present is, *that the little finger of a French democracy, established on personal representation, is a more odious tyranny than the heavy arm of Turkish despotism.*"[99] He claimed that the pro-French party were still arguing from theory, favorable to the principles expressed in the Declaration of the Rights of Man. Then he went on to show, often quoting from the *Moniteur*, that those principles had all been violated, and had resulted not in liberty, but in tyranny.

In his first article Young had asserted that he still wished parliamentary reform of a very moderate nature, and in the second he declared that he was not opposed to all innovation, but went on to state that the innovation needed in England was one to make property more secure against the dangers of revolution, namely, his militia of property-owners. The third article was by far the most violent of the three. At one point he declared, "... the abominations of democracy are such, that no parallel is to be found in any other species of government."[100] At another he defended the French government under the old regime in terms very different from those used in the *Travels in France*, "... the mildest and most benignant government in Europe, our own only excepted. ..."[101]

Young was seldom content just to express his views publicly, and in this case he followed up his articles in the *Annals* by taking the lead in forming a "Loyal Association" for the Hundreds of Thedwastry and Thingoe. He had a broadside published, in the form of a letter dated from Bradfield, December 18, 1792, calling a meeting at the famous Angel Inn at Bury for December 29. He sent the sheet especially to the clergy with a request to post it on the church door. The purpose of such an association was to bring together those who wished to testify to "their content under the Constitution of this Kingdom as Established at Present" and who desired to take

[98] *Ibid.*, XVIII, 588.
[99] *Ibid.*, XVIII, 583.
[100] *Ibid.*, XIX, 44.
[101] *Ibid.*, XIX, 45.

such measures as would "secure the Blessings we derive from its Influence."[102]

Early in 1793 appeared Young's most famous pamphlet, *The Example of France, a Warning to Britain*, which went rapidly through four editions in England, was translated into French and published in Brussels and Quebec, and also translated into German and Italian.[103] It was a fairly lengthy pamphlet, running to 180 pages. It was definitely based on the three articles in the *Annals,* and nearly every sentence was reproduced verbatim, but the material was completely rearranged. His points were supported by many quotations from the *Moniteur* and other French sources. There is an increased emphasis in *The Example of France* upon the danger to England from the reform party, and he attacked the moderate reformers with even greater vehemence than the more radical ones. He pointed out in considerable detail how the revolutionary principles would be adverse to every interest in England—landed, monied, commercial, and laboring. To halt the progress of revolutionary sentiment in Britain, he urged his landed militia, supported the idea of loyal associations to combat radicalism, and insisted that the government should curb the press and make all prorevolutionary associations illegal. Antirevolutionary sentiment was already being surrounded by a patriotic aura, and Young declared of the loyal associations, "The national spirit is at last roused. . . ."[104]

By the time *The Example of France* appeared, war had broken out between Britain and France. It has been noted that Young had taken an antiwar position, almost a pacifist one, and certainly a pro-French stand pretty consistently ever since 1783, and as late as the spring of 1792. But in *The Example of France,* Young showed himself a complete apologist for the war. He took great pains to prove that the earlier wars of Britain in the eighteenth century against France had been primarily commercial and he still considered them unjust; the present war was entirely different, however. The events of the 10th of August, 1792, and the propagandist decrees of the Convention, made war inevitable sooner or later. Better to make it

---

[102] *An Address Proposing a Loyal Association to the inhabitants of the Hundreds of Thedwastry and Thingoe* (n.p., 1792). The copy in the British Museum is addressed to the "officiating minister" at Hawstead.

[103] The edition used for this paper is the 2nd edition, Bury St. Edmunds, 1793.

[104] *The Example of France,* p. 119.

sooner before the forces of revolutionary France should have become stronger through the conquest of her neighbors. He thus accepted the argument of the preventive war, and stated: "... on the long account, every year of war, at this crisis, will probably secure ten years of peace in its train, and consequently ... the policy of permanent peace is, of all others, that which most clearly calls for temporary war."[105] He put the same argument somewhat differently by asking whether it would not be better to fight in 1793 in St. Domingo and Martinique than in 1796 in Ireland and Sussex. He regarded the war as primarily not against France but against the forces of revolution at home and abroad, and declared, "... in this war with France we have to fight, not thro' ambition or for conquest, but for the preservation of our lives and properties against foreign and domestic foes, combined for our destruction...."[106] Once again he expressed his attitude toward the war in striking phrases:

> He who does not feel his property more secure, and the lives of his family more safe, in consequence of every success gained against that band of cut throat wretches, that usurp the government of France,—has a bosom touched by vibrations in no unison with mine. It is a war of humanity against the ravagers and destroyers of the earth...[107]

The pamphlet appeared at just the right time to create quite a stir. Young received many letters from friends expressing their approval. Burke wrote that he had seen nothing "which stands better bottomed upon practical principle, or is more likely to produce an effect on the popular mind."[108] Lord Sheffield communicated to Young the flattering news that "every Body I have seen approves your Pamphlet very much. Those whose opinion you regard, think it excellent."[109] Young's brother-in-law, Dr. Burney, reported that many of his friends had commented very favorably and quoted from a letter from Mrs. Crewe: "Mr. Arthur Young's pamphlet makes a great noise, and, I think, I never knew any book take more...."[110] When he visited London in the summer of 1793 he was lionized and in one month had invitations from forty "people of the highest rank

---

[105] *Ibid.*, p. 154.
[106] *Ibid.*, p. 161.
[107] *Ibid.*, p. 163.
[108] *Autobiography*, p. 232.
[109] *Add. Mss.* 35, 127, fol. 239.
[110] *Autobiography*, p. 233.

and consequence." The high point of all this adulation came when he was introduced to the great on the terrace at Windsor and was noticed by the King.[111] Formal addresses of thanks were sent to him from the associations of "loyal inhabitants" in Suffolk and from John Reeves in behalf of the more famous Crown and Anchor Society.[112]

Of course, Young's pamphlet was regarded very differently by the Radicals. He admitted himself that he became "exceedingly" unpopular "among the whole race of reformers and Jacobins."[113] Typical of their attitudes was a comment made by Major John Cartwright in a letter: "Of all the books I ever read, this is the most dishonest."[114]

The Example of France had appeared in February 1793. In May of the same year Parliament passed a bill establishing the Board of Agriculture to which Young was appointed secretary at an annual salary of £400. It is not surprising that opponents of the government should have jumped to the conclusion that the appointment was a reward to Young for having changed his opinions regarding the French Revolution. During the debates in the House of Commons Fox and Sheridan had opposed the establishment of the Board of Agriculture on the ground that it would provide patronage for the ministry, and Young's appointment seemed to prove their point.[115] Young was also the object of a vituperative attack by Cartwright in a pamphlet entitled *The Commonwealth in Danger*, published in 1795. Cartwright called Young "the disgraced disseminator of court delusions ... the fabricator of false alarms ... the very personification of political apostasy...."[116] He absolved Young from having accepted a common bribe, but accused him of succumbing to flattery, vanity, and a desire to obtain the Secretaryship. He pointed out in great detail the extent of Young's change of position, and stated that Young "has a *salary, ex officio,* for his pains."[117]

This is the most serious accusation that has ever been leveled against Young's integrity and deserves careful examination. There

[111] *Ibid.*, pp. 223, 224.
[112] *Add. Mss.* 35, 127, fol. 243; *The Example of France*, p. 183.
[113] *Autobiography*, p. 205.
[114] *The Life and Correspondence of Major Cartwright* (London, 1826), I, 211.
[115] *The Parliamentary History of England* ... (London, 1817), XXX, 952.
[116] John Cartwright, *The Commonwealth in Danger* (London, 1795), p. iv.
[117] *Ibid.*, p. clxiii.

is certainly no conclusive proof either way. The suddenness, completeness, and violence of his change in views, together with his perennial need of money, would tend to support the accusation. On the other hand, his impulsive and mercurial temperament had often led him to support vigorously that which he later attacked just as strenuously. In his own words, already quoted, the only principle to which he consistently adhered was the "principle of change."[118]

Moreover, a careful study of the chronology tends to refute the charge of bribery. Although *The Example of France* appeared in February 1793, it was based upon the three articles in the *Annals of Agriculture,* the first of which is dated August 20, 1792, which is therefore the proper date to determine when he changed his views. In all probability, the initiative for the Board of Agriculture came from Sir John Sinclair, its first President. When Sinclair mentioned the project to Young, the latter refused to believe that the Pitt ministry would accept the plan. Accordingly Young and Sinclair made a bet upon the subject, a copy of Young's *Annals* against Sinclair's *Statistical Account of Scotland.* In reply to a letter from Sinclair saying that he was seeing Pitt upon the matter and predicting that Young would lose his bet, Young wrote on January 10, 1793:

You are going TO Mr. Pitt, and I am to lose the wager. When you come FROM Mr. Pitt, I shall win the wager. Pray, don't give Ministers more credit than they deserve. In manufactures and commerce you may bet securely; but they never did, and never will do any thing for the plough. Your Board of Agriculture will be in the moon; if on earth, remember I am to be secretary.[119]

After the Board had been accepted by the Ministry and had passed through the House of Commons, Young wrote again to Sinclair on May 19, congratulating him on his success, and reminding him, "... if you establish a Secretary on a respectable footing, do not forget the farmer at Bradfield."[120] Such statements, and the course of events, show that Young was naturally interested in the position of Sec-

---

[118] Cf. *supra,* p. 146.

[119] *The Correspondence of* . . . *Sir John Sinclair* (London, 1831), I, 407. Cf. also *Communications to the Board of Agriculture* . . . (London, 1797), I, viii, for statement by Sinclair specifically denying charges against Young.

[120] *The Correspondence of* . . . *Sir John Sinclair,* I, 407. The author has searched in vain through the Pitt Papers at the Record Office for letters which might show conclusively that Pitt or his patronage-monger, George Rose, had bribed Young.

retary, but they do not prove that he had sacrificed any principle to obtain it.

There is ample reason for believing, however—and from the lips of Young himself—that the Pitt ministry gave him the Secretaryship as a reward for *The Example of France*. One of his neighbors informed him that "this new board was established with a view of rewarding me for my 'Example of France.'"[121] In talking about the matter, Lord Loughborough remarked to Young, ". . . we all consider ourselves so much obliged to you that you cannot be rewarded in a manner too agreeably."[122] Friction quickly arose between President Sinclair and Secretary Young, and Young wrote retrospectively at a much later date: "I was a capital idiot not to absent myself sufficiently to bring the matter to a question, and leave them to turn me out if they pleased. Mr. Pitt would probably have interfered and effected the object I wanted, and, if not, would have provided for me in a better way."[123]

In conclusion, it appears improbable that Young changed his opinions about the French Revolution in order to secure a government job. Unfortunately, however, it does seem fairly certain that he was given the Secretaryship for services rendered.

If his change in position did not arise from the hope of pecuniary reward, why then did it come about so suddenly? In his pamphlet *The Constitution Safe without Reform*, which was largely an attempt to refute the charges of Major Cartwright, Young attributed his altered attitude to the events of August 10, 1792:

> Because I thought liberty, before the 10th of August, a blessing to France, *therefore* I was to think French liberty, after that period, a blessing also! Because I thought reform in the constitution of England wholesome, before the French revolution, *therefore* I am to think it safe and expedient now![124]

He went on to state that "many of the best and greatest men in the nation"[125] changed their views at the same time and for the same

---

[121] *Autobiography*, p. 219.
[122] *Ibid.*
[123] *Ibid.*, p. 243.
[124] *The Constitution Safe without Reform: Containing some Remarks on a Book entitled The Commonwealth in Danger . . .* (Bury St. Edmunds, 1795). This pamphlet appears in the *Annals*, XXV, 246–93. The quotation is on p. 278.
[125] *Annals*, XXV, 278.

reason. Indeed, if anything, he was understating his case here, for probably most people of his position had shifted their ground earlier than he. After the overthrow of the French monarchy and the September Massacres, only extreme and doctrinaire English Radicals continued to defend the French Revolution. Young also pointed out that the remuneration connected with his Secretaryship was hardly munificent enough to have been an adequate reward for the dishonesty with which his adversaries were charging him, and of course noted that his previous agricultural labors and writings constituted a sufficient explanation for his appointment. It is also more than likely that his reversal of opinion was re-enforced by the presence of French *émigrés* at Bury St. Edmunds. His old friend and benefactor, the Duc de Liancourt, had escaped from France after August 10 and had come to Bury. The harrowing stories which he brought with him, and the tragic death of his cousin, the Duc de Rochefoucauld, whom Young had also known in France, must have had considerable effect upon Young. It is interesting to note, however, that his opinions had altered so completely that he privately blamed Liancourt as one of the moderates largely responsible for opening the floodgates of revolution.[126]

The most novel proposal in *The Example of France* was that for a horse militia of property-owners. Such troops were formed in many parts of the kingdom. Since Young was the father of the scheme it was customary for his toast to be drunk by these corps at their banquets, immediately after that to the King.[127] Although over fifty years old, Young joined the Bury St. Edmunds troop. In preparation he had learned sword exercises at London. In line with his proposal Young, although a gentleman, enlisted as a private. He put great emphasis upon gentlemen serving in the ranks,

... for had gentlemen accepted only the situation of officers, the spirit of entering the corps among yeomen, farmers &c. would have been much cooler; but when they saw their landlords, and men of high considera-

---

[126] Cf. *Diary and Letters of Madame d'Arblay* (Philadelphia, 1842), II, 361–68, for a very interesting account of a visit of Fanny Burney at Bradfield on Oct. 5, 1792, when the Duc de Liancourt was the guest of honor. There is also a letter from Fanny Burney to her father, describing this meeting, dated October 10, in the magnificent collection of Burney papers in the Berg Collection in the New York Public Library.
[127] *Autobiography*, pp. 203–6.

tion in the neighbourhood, in the same situation, their vanity was flattered, and they enrolled themselves with great readiness....[128]

Young continued his crusade against the French Revolution throughout the decade of the 1790's by a succession of articles in the *Annals,* the most noteworthy of which were published separately as pamphlets. Early in 1794 he wrote an important article in the *Annals* which reappeared with some additions as a separate pamphlet in 1795 under the title, *An Idea of the Present State of France.*[129] The pamphlet began by comparing France under the Convention to ancient Sparta, a totalitarian state devoted to war, with a paper currency resting on fiat, and with the peasants sinking to the position of slaves. Young emphasized the tremendous military potential of such a state and demanded extraordinary exertions by Britain and her allies to meet the threat. Peace without victory would only mean the domination of the Continent by France, and the danger of revolution at home from English Jacobins supported by France. The cost of such a victory might be great, but should not be begrudged in comparison with a peace which could only be an uneasy truce. At home Britain must stamp out sedition, create a militia of 500,000 men of property, and build strong fortifications near London. A strictly defensive war should be fought on the eastern front, but a scorched-earth policy should be followed against French offensives in that region. The allied offensive should seize the Channel ports, and invade France through the Seine valley. The Allies should also make it clear that they had no designs on French territory and that their sole objective was to restore a limited monarchy in France. Young admitted that he was no specialist in military strategy, but he pointed out that this was a different sort of war, that the French were using new methods, and that the Allies could never win the war by half-hearted efforts and old-fashioned techniques.

In 1795 his chief writing was the pamphlet, *The Constitution Safe without Reform,* already noted as consisting mainly of an attempt to clear himself from Major Cartwright's charges. On the whole, Young seems to have the better of the argument. He kept his

[128] *Ibid.,* pp. 205–6.
[129] *Annals,* XXIII, 274–311. The pamphlet was published at London.

temper pretty well and refused to descend to the level of personal attacks as Cartwright had done. As for the pamphlet itself, it marks no new development in Young's opinions and merely reiterates the arguments already expressed in his two previous publications.

In 1796 there appeared in the *Annals* a "Sermon on the Scarcity of Corn,"[130] written by the editor, who stated that it had been preached at Bradfield and elsewhere in Suffolk. Young praised highly the Christian resignation of the Suffolk poor in face of scarcity and urged continued patience. The scarcity was an act of God, the effects of which the government of England, "this happy nation, blessed with the best constitution ever yet framed by the weak efforts of mankind,"[131] would do everything within its power to mitigate. Distinctions between rich and poor are inevitable; one need turn only to France to see what happens when attempts are made to abolish them. The English government, with its unique poor laws, guards the rights of the poor against exploitation by the rich: "The sun of diffusive prosperity, that gilds the palace, illumines the humblest cottage."[132] Submissiveness, he pointed out, would also of course induce private charity in greater amounts. On the other hand, riots and public tumults would only aggravate the scarcity, dry up public sympathy and hence private charity, and eventually lead the participants to eternal torments.

In the latter half of 1796 and in the spring of 1797 Young wrote four open letters in the *Annals*,[133] the first addressed to the Yeomanry of Suffolk, and the other three to the Yeomanry of England. All four letters were published in 1797, with considerable supplementary material, as a pamphlet, *National Danger and the Means of Safety*.[134] The national danger sprang from a possible French invasion which might be supported by revolutionary malcontents at home. The means of safety lay in augmenting the yeomanry corps until they should become a mighty militia of property-owners, ready to repel either an invasion of "the new Goths and Vandals,"[135] or an

[130] *Ibid.*, XXVI, 197–208.
[131] *Ibid.*, XXVI, 198.
[132] *Ibid.*, XXVI, 207.
[133] *Ibid.*, XXVI, 516–21; XXVII, 49–54, 528–38; XXVIII, 177–87.
[134] London, 1797. The references from the original letters are from the *Annals*, those from the supplementary material from the pamphlet.
[135] *Annals*, XXVII, 49.

uprising from the dregs of "the cells of the prisons of London."[136] The first article, dated July 1, 1796, was written when invasion seemed unlikely, but Young was fearful of internal riots when the regular troops should be sent to the coast. The later articles, dated August 1 and December 1, 1796, and March 1, 1797, were written under the impetus of the Italian campaign and the fear of imminent invasion. Young was convinced that Italy had fallen because she had relied on a regular army rather than on a militia of property-owners. Traditional methods of waging war no longer sufficed against a nation which had herself adopted revolutionary methods.

> To resort to precedent is idle; the enemy proceed by paths untrodden by human foot . . . . by numbers they vanquish those who have the merit to oppose them in arms, and by sympathy they assimilate with the outcasts of every surrounding nation, to undermine, by treachery and treason, those whom they cannot overcome on the ocean. . . .[137]

His conclusion was: "Such is the alternative: LIVE by new measures or DIE by your old ones."[138]

To meet this menace, Young believed England must arm herself in such numbers that the invader would have no chance for success. His objective was a horse militia of at least 100,000 men. Although numerous companies had been formed in 1793 and 1794, the great majority of farmers and gentry had remained aloof, "sleeping in supine apathy and sloth."[139] Now that the danger was so much greater, would they not respond to the national need? He pointed out that they would lose all their property if the French made good their invasion. Could they not sacrifice a little money to purchase equipment and a little time to drill? If invasion actually came, they would certainly be called to arms, but then it would be too late for them to act effectually. He urged that the clergy should hire men to serve in their places, and even appealed to the ladies to use their influence to ostracize their male friends who were not in yeomanry corps. He depicted luridly what the English upper classes might expect, and attacked the French for seizing Italian art treasures: "The plunderers of the world demand pictures and statues; they seize

---

[136] *National Danger*, p. 53.
[137] *Ibid.*, p. 35.
[138] *Ibid.*, p. 42.
[139] *Annals*, XXVII, 528.

equally the living Venus's and the dead Apollo's [sic]. . . ."[140] He called eloquently to the gentry to leave off their accustomed routine of pleasure:

> Quit a scene, the business of which is nonsense, and its pleasures contemptible, hasten to your estates, forge bayonets for your fowling-pieces, prepare arms of every kind, connect yourself with your neighbours, arm your tenants. . . . Would not this be an employment more worthy of a Briton, who knows how to prize the great inheritance he derives from his forefathers? . . .[141]

By the time he published the pamphlet Young had come to despair of voluntary means to achieve his aims. Indolence, avarice, politics, and apathy had operated to prevent any nation-wide response to his appeals. Not one man in a thousand among the landed interest had joined the voluntary yeomanry corps, and conscription therefore seemed necessary. All men with property to the amount of one hundred pounds should be conscripted, at their own expense. Men of large property should be forced to contribute more than one man. There should be no exemptions and no withdrawals. Drilling should be regular, one hour every Sunday morning, and two hours a month in larger units. As he expressed it, "The defense of the kingdom, in case of invasion or insurrection, is every man's PERSONAL duty."[142] And yet he had confined his scheme to men of property! In a long footnote, Young felt it necessary to explain that men with smaller or no properties had been excluded, not because he doubted their loyalty, but merely because they could not reasonably be expected to bear the expense as the conscripts would have to do.[143] Such an argument seems a bit disingenuous in light of the emphasis which Young put on the corps serving to prevent domestic insurrection as well as to repel foreign invasion.

The problem of financing the yeomanry corps bothered Young. He preferred that each volunteer should pay for his own equipment, but in Suffolk the corps had been financed by public subscription. When these subscriptions lagged in the autumn of 1796 Young called a public meeting for the county to petition Parliament for an increase in the county taxes. He also wrote personally to

---

[140] *Ibid.*, XXVII, 51.
[141] *National Danger*, pp. 45, 46.
[142] *Ibid.*, p. 58.
[143] *Ibid.*, pp. 66–67.

William Pitt, describing the situation and his proposed remedy. At the end of the letter he asked: "I submit to your attention whether there is any way of raising cavalry so cheaply (100,000 costing less a million sterl.) and whether it would not be expedient to adopt some measure that shall increase these corps rather than allow them to diminish?"[144]

The year 1797 was marked by a very serious crisis in Young's personal life. His youngest daughter, his darling "Bobbin," died of tuberculosis in July. No event in his private life ever affected him so deeply, and he turned to religion for consolation. Young had not been irreligious before this time, but he had taken his religion casually. Now he underwent a violent conversion and became an extreme Pietist.[145] He was greatly influenced by William Wilberforce and was closely associated with other leaders of the Evangelical Revival. From this time on, his every opinion, even his politics and his attitudes on international questions, was dominated by religion.

But not even a major emotional crisis could keep Young's pen idle. In 1798 there appeared an open letter to his new friend, Wilberforce, entitled, *An Enquiry into the State of the Public Mind amongst the Lower Classes*,[146] a short but very interesting pamphlet which combined his fear of popular uprising with his new evangelical fervor. At this time Young seemed more fearful of the strength of French revolutionary ideas than of an actual invasion. He was worried that nothing effectual was being done to counteract the revolutionary poison. As he put it, "Blasphemy, sedition, treason, distributed for a penny: their antidotes for a shilling, or half a crown."[147] Of course, he still believed that class distinctions were in the nature of things and equality only "a romantic phantom of the imagination."[148] True, the English working classes were the best-treated in the world and revolution or invasion would certainly worsen, not improve, their condition, but French and revolutionary propaganda were so insidious that it would be dangerous to be complacent about working-class attitudes.

As Young now saw it, the remedy lay in converting the poor to a

---

[144] Public Record Office, Chatham Papers, Young to Pitt, Nov. 2, 1796.
[145] For the death of Bobbin and Young's subsequent conversion, cf. *Autobiography*, pp. 263–311.
[146] London, 1798.
[147] *An Enquiry into the State of the Public Mind*, p. 10.
[148] *Ibid.*, p. 6.

vital religion. Somehow or other they must be imbued with Christian doctrines.

Where are they to learn the doctrines of that truly excellent religion which exhorts to content, and to submission to the higher powers?—Doctrines the most admirably adapted to inspire that content, and to render that submission satisfactory, and even comfortable to the distressed.[149]

One other quotation is worth making: "Genuine christianity is inconsistent with revolt, or with discontent in the midst of plenty. The true christian will never be a leveller; will never listen to French politics, and to French philosophy."[150] Thus in his *Enquiry into the State of the Public Mind amongst the Lower Classes,* Young exhibited a kind of solicitude for the lower classes, based, however, more on fear than love. His care for the welfare of their souls seemed all too closely connected with his worry lest they become revolutionary and thus a menace to the upper classes. Such an attitude was consistent with the neglect or even contempt which many of his earlier writings displayed. He had never been bothered by the effects of enclosures upon the welfare and independence of the poor. Only in *A Tour in Ireland* had he really shown much sympathy for the masses. His religious conversion did open Young's eyes, however, to the sufferings of the poor and made him more sympathetic to their problems. At first his interest was expressed in private charity. As early as 1798 he began the practice of giving dinners to poor children.[151] Later he regularly visited the poor and conducted services for them at Bradfield. There can be no doubt whatever of his genuine interest in the common people in the later part of his life.

In 1800 and 1801 Young published two pamphlets in which he expressed a real solicitude for the physical as well as the spiritual welfare of the lower classes. At last he seems to have recognized that national prosperity must rest upon the well-being of the masses and that Britain could never be safe from revolutionary dangers so long as the real social and economic grievances of the common people were neglected. Thus the whole base of his nationalism was broadened and deepened. The first pamphlet, which appeared in 1800,

[149] *Ibid.,* p. 19.
[150] *Ibid.,* p. 25.
[151] *Autobiography,* pp. 319-20.

was entitled *The Question of Scarcity Plainly Stated, and Remedies Considered*,[152] and was inspired by the miserable harvest of 1799 and the resulting famine prices of the winter of 1799–1800. Among the permanent remedies which he proposed was to give the poor half an acre of land for a potato patch and enough grass land to keep at least one cow.

During the summer of 1800 Young also made an extended tour to examine into the condition of the poor. The trip was suggested by the Board of Agriculture, but his proposals were so radical that the Board refused to sanction them or to print his report. Consequently it appeared in the *Annals*,[153] and subsequently in 1801 as a pamphlet, under the title *An Inquiry into the Propriety of Applying Wastes to the Better Maintenance and Support of the Poor*.[154] At this time there was much agitation in favor of a general enclosure bill to simplify and cheapen the process. Young had been a lifelong enthusiast for enclosures, but now for the first time he urged that the interests of the poor should be more carefully safeguarded than in the past. It was in this pamphlet that his often quoted statement occurs: "... and the fact is, that by nineteen enclosure bills in twenty they are injured, in some greatly injured...."[155] There can be doubt of his complete sincerity when he wrote:

> At a moment when a general enclosure of wastes is before Parliament to allow such a measure to be carried into execution in conformity with the *practice* hitherto, without entering one voice, however feeble, in defense of the interests of the poor, would have been a wound to the feelings of any man, not lost to humanity, who had viewed the scenes which I have visited.[156]

At the same time he took pains to point out the effects of such solicitude for the poor upon public tranquility and national unity. It "would attach the people to their king and country by the closest ties, and give every man such a stake in it's [sic] prosperity as would ensure the last drop of his blood to defend that which was the parental cause of all his comforts."[157]

---

[152] London, 1800.
[153] *Annals*, XXXVI, 497–658.
[154] Bury St. Edmunds, 1801.
[155] *Annals*, XXXVI, 538.
[156] *Ibid.*, XXXVI, 547.
[157] *Ibid.*, XXXVI, 528.

For the years 1801, 1802, and 1803 the sources for Young's political opinions on the negotiations leading to the Peace of Amiens and its breach within a year are very scanty and fragmentary. No pamphlet appeared and even the references in the *Annals* to political issues are very few. In 1802, shortly before the Treaty of Amiens, Young wrote for the *Annals* a "Sermon to a Country Congregation"[158] which is marked by extreme religious obscurantism. England's safety during the late wars, he maintained, was due far more to God's grace than to Nelson's victories, but God's grace "even in temporal benefits" is given to that nation "in whom are found the greatest number of sincere worshippers."[159] Bonaparte has power only through the sin of both the English and French and is to be regarded as an "Assyrian" sent to chastise the British for their sins. To complain of the terms of peace "implies that you doubt of his [God's] power to protect you in peace as he has defended you in war."[160] Only true religion can furnish a bond of union for the English people strong enough to defend them against future French aggression. After peace had been made, Young was doubtful that it could last long, and was very pessimistic early in 1803.[161] He felt that the balance of power was hopelessly broken by French victories and conquests. Revolutionary principles had only been checked and might break forth again, or Bonaparte might take the path of conquest. On the eve of the renewal of war, he reverted to his idea that England had been preserved by God's providence, that she had been ungrateful, that the country was full of "almost universal vice and iniquity." Hence he feared that God's protection might be removed, and concluded, "I must own I tremble at the thought."[162]

Young expressed similar sentiments in a letter to a close friend late in 1803, after the renewal of war:

But what matters enquiry when we are so soon to be swallowed up by ye Corsican? I do not like the aspect of things. I fear that God has a controversy with us in which swaggering will not prove a satisfactory answer in mitigation of ye Divine wrath. He preserved us marvellously before—&

---

[158] *Ibid.*, XXXVII, 613–33.
[159] *Ibid.*, XXXVII, 619.
[160] *Ibid.*, XXXVII, 624.
[161] *Ibid.*, XL, 79–92.
[162] *Autobiography*, p. 388.

I fear ye national heart was far enough from gratitude, and that he will now give us a bit of his mind, as ye farmers say...."[163]

He also expressed himself very vigorously three times in the *Annals* in 1804, and there the patriotic motif overbalanced the religious. One expression took the form of a prayer in which he invoked divine protection against "the bloody band of lawless ruffians who now seek to invade us."[164] In the same issue he referred to the new war as "just and absolutely necessary,"[165] and called for extraordinary exertions both in money and arms. At the same time, however, he strenuously objected to the proposal for new taxes on malt and tea. Both commodities were necessities for the common people; a tax upon malt would mean weaker beer, and hence less effective work on the part of the laborer. Such taxes would tend to make the war unpopular among the masses, while the proper objective should be "to carry on a war which ought to be rendered (if possible) popular among them."[166] At one point he burst out, "If Bonaparte could have dictated a tax for this country, he would have said—*lay it on malt.*"[167] Young might be critical of government policies, but there could be no doubt of his burning patriotism in the national crisis. A brief note *re* hoarding, also of 1804, is worth quoting: "There is but one idea that should animate every bosom: to fight to the last drop of blood in the veins of every man capable of bearing arms: let the French seize the country, and it will be worth no man's living in."[168]

No trace of Young's political opinions during 1805 has survived. The defeat of Austria at Austerlitz, however, spurred him to write one more important article for the *Annals,* primarily patriotic in character. The article appeared in 1806 under the title, "The Example of Europe a Warning to Britain."[169] Curiously enough, Young

---

[163] The author is greatly indebted to Colonel Sir Edward A. Ruggles-Brise, Bart., of Spains Hall, Finchingfield, Essex, for his kind permission to use twelve letters from Arthur Young to Thomas Ruggles. The above quotation is from Letter VI of the collection and is dated Dec. 6, 1803.
[164] *Annals,* XLI, 92.
[165] *Ibid.,* XLI, 40.
[166] *Ibid.,* XLI, 43.
[167] *Ibid.,* XLI, 42.
[168] *Ibid.,* XLI, 239.
[169] *Ibid.,* XLIV, 385–410.

does not seem to have realized the decisive character of Nelson's victory at Trafalgar. What he saw was Austria defeated and overrun, most of western and central Europe "crouching . . . under the foot of a tyrant," and the "people . . . the beasts of burthen to the French."[170] Such developments made Young feel that 1806 constituted "the most fearful moment Europe has seen for many ages."[171] True, such a course of events was doubtless the work of God, "but this does not in the smallest degree lessen the duty of every power resisting, to the uttermost, the attacks that are made upon their liberty and independence."[172] He had high words of praise for the British navy, "glorious and never to be too much commended,"[173] but he still feared invasion.

As in the previous decade, Young still had little confidence in regular armies, which the French seemed able to defeat so easily. Instead he advocated a line of entrenchments at least one hundred miles along the coast opposite Boulogne, backed up by universal military service with the men armed with pikes. He considered volunteers no longer adequate for the emergency. "In the present situation of the kingdom, its defence is the first *business* of every man that can carry arms, and the necessity of exertion is such, that every man should be forced to bear his share in the burthen."[174] No special uniform was necessary and drilling in large numbers in open ground much more important than precision in marching. He admitted that such a plan might sound very wild, but he was anxious to save England from Austria's fate through undue reliance upon regular armies. One fourth of the total population would be called to arms by his plan. Three armies, with adequate reserves, should be ready to meet a French invasion at whatever point it might come. Furthermore, Parliament should pass an act "declaring it to be high treason to receive a flag of truce, or any proposition whatever, from any person amongst the hostile troops."[175] Ringing phrases occur in the article at frequent intervals. England is "the last refuge of liberty, property, and religion."[176] If the moment ever arises when "we

[170] *Ibid.*, XLIV, 386.
[171] *Ibid.*, XLIV, 387.
[172] *Ibid.*
[173] *Ibid.*, XLIV, 391.
[174] *Ibid.*, XLIV, 409.
[175] *Ibid.*, XLIV, 402.
[176] *Ibid.*, XLIV, 387.

must make peace, that moment closes the career of Britain."[177] "Of all the political evils that can befall a nation, that of foreign conquest is, beyond comparison, the worst...."[178] The idea of surrender after losing one or two battles "is the last that is to be admitted for a single moment."[179]

"The Example of Europe a Warning to Britain" was Young's last important writing of a nationalist character. Only fugitive and scattered references exist to indicate his opinions on the stirring events of 1806 to 1820. The last regular volume of the *Annals of Agriculture* appeared in 1808 and hence the chief vehicle for the expression of his views had gone. By the same year his sight was already growing dim and in 1811 he became totally blind. His only important writings after 1806 were in economic or agricultural fields. He became increasingly religious in these last years of his life. Such factors help to explain his relative silence.

A few of his last expressions of opinion pertinent to this paper are worthy of note. Following the inspiration of his friend, Wilberforce, Young had long opposed the slave trade and he called its abolition "The most glorious event in the Annals of Britain," "worth a dozen Trafalgars."[180] In 1808 Young was so aroused by a government proposal to substitute the distilling of sugar for that of barley that he wrote an article in the *Annals*[181] and four letters to *Cobbett's Political Register.*[182] He was worried lest possible economic difficulties might arouse public opinion to demand peace at any price. He felt that England should firmly uphold her blockade of the Continent, although he recognized that in case of a bad crop there might be suffering because Napoleon could cut off grain imports from the Continent. He ended his last letter to Cobbett with a paean of praise for "this happy country" and declared: "Let Britons be true to their God, their king, their country, and themselves, and that unseen, but mighty Hand, which has rendered us the envy

[177] *Ibid.*, XLIV, 408.

[178] *Ibid.*, XLIV, 388.

[179] *Ibid.*, XLIV, 392. This article was also sent to the *Monthly Magazine*, where it was published in June 1806, and from which in turn it was copied in *Cobbett's Political Register* in the issue of June 21, 1806 (IX, 914–25). In the latter publication the article is dated March 1806.

[180] *Annals*, XLV, 211–12.

[181] *Ibid.*, XLV, 513–608.

[182] *Cobbett's Political Register*, XIII, 288–303, 375–78, 568–74, 768–76. There was also a postscript by Young, pp. 818–19.

of the world, will, with infinite wisdom, protect what infinite goodness bestowed."[183]

In 1810 Young was still worried over clamorings for a peace which "must be ruinous if made."[184] In 1812 a friend who was visiting him at Bradfield wrote: "Mr. Young is in despair at the report that Bonaparte has forced the Russians to a peace now he says there will be nothing for him left, but pouring into England."[185] A currency pamphlet which he wrote in the same year, 1812, ended with confidence in the strength of British patriotism and institutions: ". . . not paper, but liberty—not silver, but industry—not gold but national energy, are the foundations of the greatness of Britain."[186]

Young did not regard the efforts of the peacemakers of 1814 and 1815 very highly. He was greatly disturbed over the revival of the Jesuits and even feared Catholic Emancipation because it might mean Jesuits sitting in the English Parliament. Almost the only good thing he ever said of Bonaparte was at this time when he contrasted him—"by far the greatest enemy to Popery that has existed" —with the "imbecilities and bigotry of the wretched Bourbons."[187] He considered the Congress of Vienna "a chapter of human depravity."[188] He also blamed the Allies for protecting Napoleon after his capture "from the vengeance of an enraged people, who were ready to save Europe from future miseries. . . ."[189] He was disgusted at the frivolity of the popular "frolics" with which the return of peace in 1814 was celebrated and declared that he would subscribe nothing for a frolic at Bradfield; the coming of peace should be cele-

---

[183] *Ibid.,* XIII, 776.

[184] *Autobiography,* p. 451.

[185] John Rylands Library, Manchester, *Eng. Mss.* 583, fol. 101. Letter of Marianne Francis to Mrs. Piozzi, Sept. 26, 1812.

[186] *An Enquiry into the Progressive Value of Money in England* . . . (London, 1812), p. 133. This pamphlet may also be found in the rare Vol. XLVI of the *Annals,* pp. vii and 137.

[187] New York Public Library, Berg Collection, Burney Papers, Young to Marianne Francis, Oct. 31, 1815. Cf. also *Autobiography,* p. 461. In the Burney papers in the Henry W. and Albert A. Berg Collection, which the author was permitted to use through the kindness of Dr. Paul North Rice, there are more than one hundred letters by Young, most of them to Marianne Francis, talented Evangelical niece of Fanny Burney, who frequently acted as secretary to Young during the last decade of his life.

[188] Berg Collection, Young to Marianne Francis, Dec. 22, 1814.

[189] *An Enquiry into the Rise of Prices in Europe* . . . (London, 1815). This pamphlet also appeared in the *Annals,* XLVI, 141–219, and was reprinted in the *Pamphleteer,* VI, 166–204. The quotation is from the *Pamphleteer,* VI, 183.

brated as a "day of thanksgiving, a day of religion and not of drunkenness...."[190]

After 1815 the very few comments in his private letters on public affairs have a complaining and very reactionary tone. He felt that the government was "fast asleep"[191] late in 1816, and early in 1817 predicted that no "energetical capital measures"[192] could be expected from the ministry. He was bitter over "the most licentious press that ever disgraced a country" and made special mention of the tremendous circulation of Cobbett's paper, "fifty thousand two penny numbers of rebellion and treason."[193] There may well have been a personal grievance here, for in 1816 Cobbett had dug up the attacks of Major Cartwright on Young, and wrote: "As far as talents go, Mr. Young is an honour to his country; but he has done a great deal of mischief since he has become a stipendiary of the government."[194] Young's bitterly conservative position was shown in a comment in one of his last letters in 1819, "... and I shall be out of patience till I hear that Mr. Hunt is hanged."[195] Only at the time of the Congress of Aix-la-Chapelle in 1818 did Young express himself constructively on international affairs: "... it rarely happens that Kings meet except for mischief, but through the mercy of God I hope that this congress will establish peace on a firm foundation."[196]

As stated above, Arthur Young was not a constructive thinker with a consistent philosophy of nationalism. He was a warm-hearted publicist who could wield a lively pen and often supported his views with heat and even with exaggeration. He had a deep and abiding love for England, her people, and her ways of living. Always the spokesman of agrarian interests, he was apt to identify those interests with those of England as a whole. Thus he was a fairly typical John Bull, calm and detached when times were tranquil, but a flaming patriot whenever his country was in danger.

[190] Berg Collection, Young to Marianne Francis, July 4, 1814. Cf. also *Pamphleteer*, VI, 183.
[191] Berg Collection, Young to Marianne Francis, Dec. 16, 1816.
[192] *Ibid.*, Young to Marianne Francis, Jan. 23, 1817.
[193] *Ibid.*, Young to Marianne Francis, no date, but listed as early 1817.
[194] *Cobbett's Weekly Political Register*, XXXI, 240.
[195] Berg Collection, Young to Marianne Francis, Oct. 12, 1819.
[196] *Ibid.* Young to Marianne Francis, Oct. 19, 1818.

FRENCH JACOBIN NATIONALISM AND SPAIN

BEATRICE F. HYSLOP

IN *The Historical Evolution of Modern Nationalism*, Professor Carlton J. H. Hayes outlined and contrasted the humanitarian nationalism of the early French Revolution and Jacobin nationalism of the period of the Terror.[1] Emphasis upon national unity, upon liberty and equality as natural law, upon democracy in government, and upon cosmopolitanism were characteristics of humanitarian nationalism. The exigencies of civil and foreign war transformed the nationalism of the early Revolution into Jacobin nationalism with four added characteristics: intolerance of dissent, reliance on force and militarism, religious intensity and appeal, and missionary zeal. Professor Hayes used Barère de Vieuzac and Carnot to illustrate Jacobin nationalism, and devoted nearly thirty pages to the propagation of this new Revolutionary nationalism. He described the development of the "nation in arms," national education, the French language, the new journalism, patriotic societies, promotion of national music, art, and literature, nationalism as a religion, and nationalist economics. Not only did Jacobin nationalism spread in France; it was disseminated abroad. In only one paragraph was the role of the new Revolutionary army mentioned by Professor Hayes: "Everywhere they propagated the principles and practices of Jacobin nationalism."[2] The present study will attempt to throw light upon the propagation of Jacobin nationalism outside the boundaries of Revolutionary France.

Inside France, republicanism was a factor differentiating Jacobin from humanitarian nationalism, not sufficiently emphasized by Professor Hayes. Abroad, however, the French Revolution was viewed by the ruling classes as antimonarchical from the beginning. In considering the spread of Revolutionary ideas outside France, therefore, differences between early humanitarian and Jacobin

---

[1] Carlton J. H. Hayes, *The Historical Evolution of Modern Nationalism* (New York, 1931). Chapter II was devoted to humanitarian nationalism, and Chapter III to Jacobin nationalism. Alphonse Aulard published much valuable material on Revolutionary nationalism in his *Le Patriotisme français de la Renaissance à la Révolution* (Paris, 1921), in the *Révolution française*, a review of which he was long editor, and in his *Études et leçons* (9 vols., Paris, 1893–1924).

[2] Hayes, *op. cit.*, pp. 56–57.

French Jacobin Nationalism and Spain 191

nationalism were largely matters of degree of emphasis and of aggressiveness of method. Since France went to war with almost all of Europe, the subject as a whole requires more space than one chapter in the present volume, and the author has chosen to discuss Jacobin nationalism only in its relation to Spain. This topic has received less attention than the relation of the French Revolution to other European countries, and it is one which may be an appropriate chapter in honor of the former American ambassador to Spain.

This topic presents several difficult problems. In the first place, both French and Spanish histories are inadequate. Spanish historians either pass over the period, which was not a glorious one in Spanish history, or devote too much attention to Godoy and court intrigue, or are too strongly nationalist.[3] Standard French histories have gone through all the modifications of interpretation that the history of the Revolution itself has undergone, and such works as those of Sybel, Baumgarten, and Sorel paid slight attention to Spain.[4] Both Spanish and French monographs, in giving details, usually started from a strong bias. In order to facilitate future study and to provide the background of the French Revolution as a whole, a chronological table indicating the general events of the Revolution and Franco-Spanish developments will be found at the end of this chapter.

A second difficulty has been the failure to use Spanish archives with the degree of thoroughness that has characterized the study of French archives. Mlle. Chaumié, of the French National Archives,

---

[3] Altamira scarcely mentioned the period (*Historia de España y de la civilización española*, 4 vols., Barcelona, 1913–14), Lafuente presented an extremely reactionary and nationalist account (*Historia general de España desde los tiempos más remotos hasta nuestros días*, 30 vols., Barcelona, 1850–67), and Ballesteros y Beretta devoted only fifty pages in one of eight volumes (*Historia de España*, 8 vols., Barcelona, 1919–41). The latter gave useful bibliographical references. Antonio Cánoras des Castillon, in his *Historia general de España* (Madrid, 1891), has three volumes on the reign of Charles IV, but gave no significant new material.

[4] On the evolution of the interpretation of the Revolution, see especially Paul Farmer, *France Reviews Its Revolutionary Origins* (New York, 1944), and David Dowd, *Pageant-Master of the Republic* (Lincoln, Neb., 1948), a bibliographical essay. On Sybel's classical volumes, see criticism by Albert Sorel, *Revue historique*, X (1879), 339–49, and XI (1879), 114, and Sybel's reply, *loc. cit.*, XI, 103–14. Baumgarten, using Prussian archives, threw little light on Spanish affairs. The classic by Albert Sorel, *L'Europe et la Révolution française*, also devoted little attention to Spain, and provided no guide to archives or bibliography, but a series of articles by him under the title, "La Diplomatie française et l'Espagne de 1792 à 1796," helps fill this gap: *Revue historique*, XI (1879), 298–330; XII (1880), 279–313; XIII (1880), 41–80 and 241–78.

has been studying papers of French *émigrés* in Spain in the Spanish National Archives and in papers of the Venetian embassy, and the results will be published. The local collections of Barcelona and San Sebastian should be consulted.[5] Both diplomatic correspondence and consular reports, not open in the nineteenth century for consultation at the French Archives des Affaires Étrangères should be investigated more thoroughly than the present author has been able to do, and renewed research in the departmental archives at Perpignan, Pau, and Bayonne undertaken.[6]

Many French documents of the Revolution have been published, and the reader need only be referred to the minutes of Revolutionary assemblies, the great collection on the Committee of Public Safety, and to Pierre Caron's guide to materials on the French Revolution.[7] By contrast, very little has been published from Spanish archives. Among the many volumes of the *Colección de documentos para la historia de España* were only two series of documents useful for the present study, one on the Cortes of Madrid of 1789, and the second on the capitulations of Collioure.[8] The importance of nationalist bias in an attempt to make an impartial study of the topic chosen is revealed by the fact that Ballesteros y Beretta used the *Colección* for documents on the Cortes of Madrid, but never even

---

[5] Mlle. Chaumié and the present author gave papers on this subject before the Société d'Histoire Moderne in Paris, July 3, 1949, and a *compte-rendu* will be published in the *Bulletin* of the Société. Venice served as a center of the activities of the Comte d'Antraigues, who was an active agent in *émigré* activities in Spain. Raymond Guyot cited losses and destruction of Spanish archives in *Le Directoire et la paix de l'Europe* (Paris, 1911), pp. 31-34, and it is probable that further losses occurred during the Spanish Civil War.

[6] French diplomatic documents for the Revolutionary era are divided between the French National Archives and the Archives des Affaires étrangères. The present author has read the four volumes of *Correspondance politique*, covering 1792-95 (Vols. 634-37), and one volume of the Consular correspondence from Barcelona, Vol. 20, 1792-93. The library and archives at Bayonne which should be most revealing suffered extensive losses for the Revolutionary era during the nineteenth century. The author has spent a short time at Pau (Archives départementales des Basses-Pyrénées) and at Perpignan (Archives départementales des Pyrénées-orientales), where the most valuable new material seen was the newspaper, *Echo des Pyrénées*, for 1793. The archives at Perpignan for the Revolutionary period are extensive and a typed inventory provides some guide.

[7] Pierre Caron, *Manuel pratique pour l'étude de la Révolution française* (Paris, 1947), a revision, brought up to date, of his indispensable earlier work.

[8] M. F. Navarrette and others, eds., *Colección* . . . (112 vols., Madrid, 1842-95), Vols. XVII and CIX respectively. For the contents of the *Colección*, see Julian Paz, *Catálogo de la Colección* . . . (2 vols., Madrid, 1930-31).

mentioned the surrender of Collioure and the controversy over the terms—an event that exerted an important influence on Revolutionary attitudes toward Spain.[9]

Newspapers are an invaluable source of public opinion. While French newspapers were accessible, only isolated issues of Spanish papers could be read. Furthermore, censorship suppressed news, so that Spanish newspapers revealed official Spanish attitudes toward nationalism rather than a narrative of the period. In using French newspapers, one should be on guard as to the date of an event and its report, also as to the source of the information, and the relative importance of news about Spain in the whole picture of the Revolutionary era. Both French and Spanish newspapers were revealing as to official nationalism.

A further difficulty in the choice of topic lies in the fact that the Franco-Spanish conflict of the Revolutionary era played only a small part in the national history of both contestants. France devoted far more energy to the propagation of Jacobin nationalism at home and in other European contries than in her relations with Spain. Similarly, internal affairs, the war with Barbary pirates, and relations with her vast colonial empire engaged Spanish attention. By focussing attention only upon the relations between France and Spain, the reader may lose perspective as to the importance of this topic in the Revolutionary era as a whole. This fact may have justified historians of the period in their lack of emphasis upon Franco-Spanish relations, but it also is justification for a chapter that brings together available material from both sides. The exposition that follows should be useful as a background for a comprehensive treatment, and should stimulate research into the many controversial points that it raises.

The period of Jacobin nationalism with respect to Spain extended from August 10, 1792, to August 1796, when a treaty of alliance was signed. The characteristic features of Jacobin nationalism gradually disappeared thereafter from the relations of the two countries. When the Revolution began in 1789, Spain and France were bound by the Family Compact of 1761, formed during the Seven Years War, and further confirming the principle "Il n'y a plus des Pyré-

---

[9] Ballesteros y Beretta, *op. cit.*, V, 241–88. See also later in this essay.

nées," embodied in the Peace of Utrecht. Bourbon monarchs had quite naturally developed mutual relations, especially as regards the common threat to their colonial possessions and commerce exerted by Great Britain. During the reign of Charles III (1759–1788)—generally described as a period of enlightened despotism in Spain—French philosophy spread to some degree among Spanish intellectuals. Societies were formed and masonic lodges organized, providing centers for discussion of the Enlightenment. Churchmen played less part in the Enlightenment in Spain than in France. Although both Catholic countries expelled the Jesuits about the same time, secularism proceeded much further in France than in Spain. Some reform of central administration characterized the enlightened despotism of Charles III, but the privileges of various provinces, the seigniorial economy of rural Spain, and Spanish mercantilism remained unchanged. Enlightened Spaniards manifested the same cosmopolitanism as characterized the Enlightenment elsewhere in Europe. Floridablanca had been prime minister of Charles III, and continued in office under Charles IV, who succeeded to the throne in December 1788. It was Aranda, however, whose name was especially associated with the Spanish aspects of the Enlightenment. The conclusion appears justified that relatively few Spaniards were influenced by the intellectual challenge of eighteenth-century thought.[10]

Despite the Enlightenment, Frenchmen and Spaniards knew little about each other in 1789. Bourgoing, a Frenchman who had been secretary in the French embassy at Madrid, published in 1788 a volume of his travels describing Spain. In his introduction, he asserted that Europe was generally ignorant of Spain, and that most ideas actually held were erroneous. Although Bourgoing had made his visit in 1777, and although eight foreign travelers published descriptions of Spain from visits in the 1780's, Bourgoing was without doubt the best-informed, the most impartial, and probably the

---

[10] In an article of the scope of the present essay, it is not feasible to cite all volumes on Spanish history, or to give footnote references for general information provided by well-known works on the period. Defenders of the Revolution have tended to emphasize the spread of the Enlightenment in Spain, while opponents of the Revolution, whether Catholic or strongly monarchical in viewpoint, have discounted its influence. See, for example, Maurice Legendre, *Nouvelle histoire d'Espagne* (Paris, 1938), pp. 267–68.

most widely read.¹¹ However, it is very doubtful that leaders of the French Revolution had read books on Spain. If Frenchmen thought about Spain, it was in terms of el Cid, Gil Blas, Don Quichotte, or of Beaumarchais' *Le Mariage de Figaro*. There was some disdain for the strength of Spanish Catholicism as contrasted with the religious liberalism and scepticism spread in France during the Enlightenment, and the belief predominated that Spain was politically and economically decadent, but still possessing great commercial riches and a valuable colonial empire. A reading of Bourgoing would have indicated the existence of a renaissance under Charles III, but would have yielded little about the Spanish merchant and peasant.

Few French *cahiers de doléances* of 1789 spoke of foreign affairs, and only a handful mentioned Spain. A few cahiers from the generalities of Auch, Bordeaux, and Perpignan manifested consciousness of the Spanish frontier, but specific reference to Spain was connected with commerce, or with militia service and defense.[12] The cahiers,

---

[11] M. (later Baron) de Bourgoing, *Nouveau voyage en Espagne*, or *Tableau de l'Espagne moderne;* French editions in 1788, 1789, 1797, 1802, 1803, and 1823; in English translation in 1789, 1803 (printed in Paris), 1808, 1809; in German in 1789, 1801, and 1808; and a Danish edition cited by Foulché-Delbosc without date. Editions on the eve of the Peninsular war should be noted. See R. Foulché-Delbosc, "Bibliographie des voyages en Espagne et en Portugal," *Revue hispanique*, III (1896), 1–349. He claimed that the text was probably written or at least polished by the Abbé Girod (p. 143). The only other author cited in this bibliography, published in several languages, was Langlé, based upon travel in 1784, whose work went through eight French and two German editions, as well as one edition each in English, Italian, and Danish. Foulché-Delbosc condemned its bias and stated that it only served to spread misconceptions about Spain. No Spanish editions appeared, but French was widely known among the educated classes. See also J. J. A. Bertrand, *Sur les vieilles routes d'Espagne* (Anvers, 1932).

[12] On general cahiers and frontier consciousness, see Beatrice F. Hyslop, *French Nationalism in 1789* (New York, 1934), p. 30 and note 8. Among preliminary cahiers mentioning Spain were the town of Nîmes and the parishes of Margueritttes, Meyreuis, and Saint Nazaire of the *sénéchaussée* of Nîmes; the joint cahier of the parishes of Pescadoires and Lagardelle of the district of Cahors; the parish of Arguenos of the district of Comminges, and that of Bugard of the district of Bigorre. See volumes in the official series of *Documents inédits*, by E. Bligny-Bondurand for Nîmes, V. Fourastié for Cahors, F. Pasquier and Fr. Galabert for Comminges, and G. Balencie for Bigorre. Possible solidarity between French and Spanish Basques made the cahiers from Ustaritz (Labour) especially interesting. The inventory, *Répertoire critique de cahiers de doléances de 1789* (Paris, 1933), by the present author, gave full information as to where texts of cahiers may be found. See also, by the same author, *A Guide to the General Cahiers of 1789* (New York, 1936), in which the text of the cahier of the third estate of Ustaritz was provided.

by their absence of expressions of hostility to other countries, reflected either the cosmopolitanism of the Enlightenment or mere localism. About half of the electoral assemblies voted to print the general cahiers, and, as we shall see shortly, some of them found their way into Spain.

A study of popular sentiment in Spain on the eve of the Revolution needs to be made. Documents and powers granted to the deputies to the Cortes of Madrid, meeting in the fall of 1789, which may be compared with the French *cahiers de doléances*, throw little light upon conditions, and merely demonstrated the paternalism of the Spanish government.[13] Neither French Revolutionaries nor Napoleon made due allowance for the strength of the monarchical tradition in Spanish nationalism or even for the very existence of a Spanish nationalism.

Between the beginning of the French Revolution and August 1792—the period when humanitarian nationalism was in the ascendant—the Spanish government re-erected the Pyrenees, figuratively speaking, and attempted to bar Revolutionary influences from Spain. After July 14, Charles IV, encouraged by agents of the *émigré* princes, manifested concern for the French royal family, and expressed renewed solicitude for their welfare after the October days, when Louis XVI and the royal family moved to Paris. The learned societies that had served as centers of the Enlightenment were closed. Spanish measures against the propagandism of the early Revolution took three forms: censorship of the press, measures of repression against Frenchmen of suspected Revolutionary sympathies, encouragement to the *émigré* cause.

On November 26, 1789, a measure requiring all foreigners to leave Madrid was issued. It was aimed in particular against Frenchmen, but since the order only required a two-weeks absence from Madrid, it had little permanent effect. In December, fear of French Revolutionary ideas was sufficient to impel the Spanish Inquisition to issue

---

[13] See *Colección de documentos inéditos para la historia de España*, Vol. XVII, ed. by D. Miguel Salvá and D. Pedro S. de Baranda (Madrid, 1850). The powers granted by various Spanish towns merely expressed loyalty to the king, support for the heir to the throne, and rarely mentioned the rural agricultural and town needs. The powers from Cordova were more subservient to the royal will than those of the other towns. The present author is indebted to Miss Elise Fernandez, Spanish major at Hunter College, for aid in translation of these documents.

a list of prohibited pamphlets and newspapers, which by royal decree were to be held up at the frontier. The list of dangerous publications contained forty items: some electoral pamphlets, the *cahiers de doléances* of the nobles and third estate of Perpignan, and of the third estate and town of Lyon, and several French newspapers that started publication soon after the opening of the States-General.[14] Of the three cahiers, only that from Lyon could be called radical, but since the district of Perpignan bordered on Spain, it would naturally be easier to send texts from there into Spain. One may assume from the omission from the list of the more radical cahiers of the generalities of Paris and Orleans that these cahiers did not pass the frontier.[15] The minutes of the sessions of the clergy and nobles in the early days of the States-General, which were on the proscribed list, might have set a dangerous example to the Spanish grandees in the Cortes, but the latter had already closed, and the subservience shown to the king was in marked contrast to the independent action of liberal clergy and nobles in France.[16] Among the newspapers proscribed were the *Courrier de Versailles à Paris et de Paris à Versailles,* edited by Gorgas, which became radical later on; *L'Assemblée nationale* (probably issues of the later *Journal des États-Généraux*), devoted to reporting and discussing the capture of the Bastille; and Prudhomme's *Révolutions de Paris,* the most revolutionary of the three.[17] Two pamphlets, one by Necker

[14] The list was published by the *Moniteur, Réimpression de l'ancien Moniteur* (Paris, 1863), II, 9–11, issue of Jan. 2, 1790, and later by Geoffroy de Grandmaison, *L'Ambassade française en Espagne pendant la Révolution* (Paris, 1892), among the *Pièces justificatives,* pp. 311–13. Time and space do not permit citation of all places where such material can be found. Since the *Moniteur* represented official opinion throughout the period covered by this paper, its use (beginning with the end of November 1789) was valuable. The time-lag in news from Spain was occasionally very significant. Measures against Catholic church property had proceeded further by January 1790 than in early December, when the Spanish list was issued.

[15] See Hyslop, *French Nationalism in 1789,* pp. 286, 209, map, p. 214, and pp. 219–20.

[16] See minutes of the Cortes of Madrid, in the *Colección,* cited note 13 above, and comment by Hans Roger Madol, *Godoy, the First Dictator of Modern Times* (London, 1934), p. 40.

[17] See Eugène Hatin, *Bibliographie historique et critique de la presse périodique française* (Paris, 1866), pp. 116, 132, 157–59. An excellent analysis of the propagandist statements of *Révolutions de Paris* was provided by Arthur G. Terry in a manuscript thesis at the University of Pennsylvania, entitled "The Spirit of Propagandism in the French Revolution, 1789–1793." A digest of the first part was published in Philadelphia in 1906, but is of little use for this paper. Some references to the manuscript will be made. Only about two pages bore directly on Spain.

and one by Rabaut Saint-Étienne, and a deliberation of the town of Nîmes, all three representing Protestant opinion, were forbidden. These proscribed items and several others defended religious toleration. The list included five items in Spanish, all in manuscript: one of them the translation of a sermon by the Abbé Fauchet in commemoration of those killed in capturing the Bastille, and another a translation of a speech by Alexandre Lameth on church property. The list as a whole showed the desire of Spanish authorities to prevent Spaniards from learning of French measures to limit the king's power, of the character of the uprising of July 14, and of anti-Catholic discussions. None of the items included could be called expressions of Jacobin nationalism, but it is significant that the Spanish government took steps so early to prevent the virus of Revolutionary thought from infecting its subjects. The list of prohibited material was to be read in all Spanish churches and then posted—a measure which may have stimulated the curiosity of those already disposed to be influenced. Whether or not French propaganda actually exerted an influence on the Catalan revolt of 1789, the Spanish government believed that it did. Illiteracy, difference of language, and the fact that some material was in manuscript would naturally limit circulation.

Despite measures taken by the Spanish government—limitation on the issuance of passports to Frenchmen, instructions to frontier guards to seize French publications, censorship of mails from France, and prohibition of the reading and discussion of French literature by Spanish officers—French Revolutionary writings appeared in Spain.[18] The statement of the Russian ambassador to Spain, Zinoviev, that Spain was inundated with French pamphlets seems an exaggeration and needs to be checked by Spanish archives.[19] If true, this was proof of the ineffectiveness of the censorship and repressive measures, as well as valid evidence of the effectiveness of propagan-

---

[18] On Spanish measures, see *Moniteur*, II, 313; III, 9, 271, 325; Grandmaison, *op. cit.*, pp. 37–38.

[19] Alexandre Tratchevsky, "L'Espagne à l'époque de la Révolution française," *Revue historique*, XXI (1886), 5–55; the citation from p. 29. Unfortunately, Tratchevsky did not give the dispatches themselves, but a narrative based upon them. Without clarity in chronology, the article should be used with greater reserve than most historians have shown.

dism abroad of humanitarian nationalism and of its spread in Spain despite proscription. Even if an exaggeration, it justified the warnings of the Spanish ambassador in Paris regarding the possibility that French propaganda was crossing the frontier. A dispatch of Nuñez of October 9, 1790, warned his government to watch especially for importations under cover of darkness, for books hidden in furs, sheets hidden in the works of clocks, in trunks with false bottoms, and for the text of the Declaration of the Rights of Man on the cover of a tortoise-shell box and on fans.[20] While ingenious, these methods would not have distributed large quantities of French literature. Opponents of the Revolution complained that there was an influx of propaganda and Revolutionary spokesmen implied it as well. The claim of *Révolutions de Paris* that there was a black market in French publications in Barcelona might be taken either as evidence of scarcity or of quantity.[21] Smuggling had been common in the Pyrenees before the war. It is possible that the goods smuggled now included some French literature, and there is evidence that the strict prohibitions were poorly enforced.[22]

While Spaniards either read Spanish papers giving only an unfavorable view of events in France, or were receiving some clandestine material, what were Frenchmen hearing about Spain? Reports in French newspapers about Spanish censorship, negotiations with *émigrés,* and suspicions that Spain was negotiating with England did not reassure French public opinion. At the theater, the old conception of the decadence of Spain was reinforced by Beaumarchais' *Mariage de Figaro* and *Barbier de Seville* or Molière's *Tartuffe,* all of which were fairly popular in Paris in 1790 and 1791. In addition, newer plays, such as *Nouveau Don Quichotte, Auto da fé, Deux Figaros,* were vehicles for opposition to clericalism and feudalism.[23]

Throughout 1790 and early 1791, relations between the two countries deteriorated. In the first place, difficulties arose over the *émigrés.* The complete story of French *émigrés* in Spain has yet to be

[20] Alfred Mousset, *Un Témoin ignoré de la Révolution, le Comte de Fernan Nuñez* (Paris, 1924), especially pp. 161–62.
[21] Terry, *op. cit.,* p. 118, cited from *Révolutions de Paris,* no. 100.
[22] *Moniteur,* III, 271, and indirectly from IX, 43; Grandmaison, *op. cit.,* p. 9, without citation of source.
[23] Lists of offerings of Parisian theaters given by the *Moniteur* provide some indication of public taste. See also later in this article, note 73.

written.[24] The higher clergy, noblemen, and envoys of the Bourbon princes lived at court and moved among the Spanish upper classes. As many as 20,000 French priests escaped to Spain, where they came into conflict with Spanish priests over Catholic ritual, and were sometimes mistakenly confused with prorevolutionaries. On November 2, 1792, French priests were forbidden to preach, and many lived on the charity of fellow Spanish priests thereafter.[25] In the foreign colony in Madrid, hostility between partisans of the Revolution and *émigrés* caused annoyance and disorder.

The prerevolutionary diplomatic friendship of France and Spain cooled over the attitude of the National Assembly toward the Nootka Sound controversy between England and Spain. When, shortly after the establishment of a diplomatic committee by the National Assembly, on August 1, 1790, with Mirabeau as its most famous member, Spain asked whether France would honor the Family Pact, debate in the National Assembly developed around the idea that wars were made by monarchs, not peoples, and that aid to Spain in connection with Nootka Sound would constitute a violation of the declaration of May 22, 1790. On that date, the Assembly had adopted a renunciation of war: "The French nation will never undertake any war of conquest, and will never use its forces against the liberty of any people." Consequently, the diplomatic committee was instructed to reply that France would increase its defense measures to uphold defensive features of the Family Pact, but promised no direct aid on Nootka Sound. The reply was considered equivocal and a repudiation of the alliance, and Spain

---

[24] The classic on the emigration, F. Baldensperger, *Le Mouvement des idées dans l'émigration pendant la Révolution française* (2 vols., Paris, 1924), devoted attention to other *émigré* centers, and barely mentioned Spain. Grandmaison, *op. cit.*, provides a good deal of information about lay *émigrés*, and he also wrote an article on the clergy in *Le Correspondant*, CLXIV (1891), 938–59. The best work on clerical *émigrés* is by Juan Contrasty, *Le Clergé français exilé en Espagne* (Toulon, 1910), since he used Spanish sources. On the same subject, see also Victor Pierre, "Le Clergé français en Espagne (1792–1802)," *Revue des questions historiques*, XXXI, nouv. sér. (1904), 473–538; Reverend Père Delbrel, "Le Clergé français refugié en Espagne pendant la Révolution," *Études religieuses, historiques...*, LV (September–November, 1891), 5–38, 254–80, 452–79.

[25] Grandmaison, *op. cit.*, pp. v, 107, 87, and article in *Le Correspondant*, *op. cit.*; Contrasty, *op. cit.*, pp. 50–55. On the Spanish decree, see Contrasty, *ibid.*, pp. 58–67, and text in *Mercurio historico y politico*, December 1792. The author wishes to express appreciation to Mrs. R. G. Link, B. A. Hunter College, Ph.D. Columbia University, for aid in translating issues of this Spanish newspaper.

took a more conciliatory tone with England, and eventually, on October 28, 1790, signed the treaty of the Escorial with her.[26]

Between the machinations of the *émigrés* and Charles IV's concern for the Bourbon monarchs, hostility to the French Revolution increased after the flight of the French royal family, and on July 20, 1791, a drastic order was issued, requiring all foreigners in Spain to leave the country or renounce their former citizenship and become Spanish nationals. At the same period, the National Assembly was conferring French citizenship on foreigners favorable to the Revolution. Exceptions, evasions, and indulgence of Spaniards toward individual Frenchmen mitigated this decree, but complaints filled the diplomatic pouches for some time.[27]

Charles IV, like other European monarchs, refused to recognize the Constitution of 1791, even after Louis XVI had taken the oath to uphold it. According to Spanish diplomatic correspondence, as reported by the *Moniteur*, three hundred manuscript copies of the Constitution of 1791 were circulating in Madrid in September, despite the censorship. In token of the new French constitution, the ambassador placed a design representing France embracing genius and liberty over the door of the French embassy in Madrid. Crowds gathered to look at it, and the Spanish government forbade the use of anything but coats of arms, on the grounds that loyalty to the Spanish king was undermined and public order endangered.[28] It would appear that smuggling of French papers and texts in diplomatic pouches and hidden in imported merchandise was being carried on, and a new law with more stringent prohibitions was issued.[29]

A little earlier than the new edict, a report from Perpignan on the Spanish border announced the desertion of two hundred soldiers of a Galician regiment.[30] This may or may not have been true, but it encouraged the French to think that the Spanish people were getting ready to imitate France. Many times in the National Assembly, the idea that France would set an example to the world had been

---

[26] Albert Sorel, *L'Europe et la Révolution française* (11th ed., 6 vols., Paris, 1908), II, 84–95.
[27] *Moniteur*, IX, 250, 277, 394, 435, 442, 503; Grandmaison, *op. cit.*, p. 48.
[28] *Moniteur*, IX, 649, Sept. 14, 1791.
[29] *Ibid.*, X, 134, Oct. 18, 1791; Grandmaison, *op. cit.*, p. 58. Ignorance of the law was no longer allowed as proof of innocence.
[30] *Moniteur*, IX, 790, Sept. 29, 1791.

expressed, and there was an optimistic confidence that peoples everywhere would transform their governments peaceably on the French model. According to Terry, some newspapers and debates in the Jacobin Club showed a more aggressive spirit and greater demand for propaganda than the National Assembly itself.[31]

Between the opening of the Legislative Assembly in October 1791 and the suspension of the monarchy following the insurrection of August 10, 1792, the two topics of the *émigrés* and war on Austria led to many more aggressive statements than those of the first Revolutionary assembly. Pronouncements of the Girondist war party were voiced, however, in terms of mankind or of hostility to Austria and the German princes, rather than toward Spain or England. By February 1792, some improvement in Franco-Spanish relations was observable with the appointment of Aranda as minister in place of Floridablanca, and with the sending of Bourgoing as French ambassador to Spain. His knowledge and understanding of Spain qualified him to smooth over difficulties between the two countries, and to interpret tactfully French actions and declarations. No formal action was taken to end the Family Pact, and in March Spain reassured France that it would not attack its neighbor.[32] Despite the beginning of war on Austria in April, Bourgoing seemed to maintain a better position for French diplomacy than did the hostile *émigrés* in Spain.[33]

The insurrection of August 10, 1792, marked a turning point not only in internal affairs in France, but also in her relations with Spain. Until then, French nationalist propaganda had been an expression of humanitarian nationalism, and the appeal had been to enlightened people everywhere to follow the example of France. French ideas had been disseminated by individuals. After August 10, republicanism triumphed in France, and thereafter it became

---

[31] Terry, *op. cit.*, pp. 8, 12–14.
[32] *Moniteur*, XI, 756, March 30, 1792.
[33] Grandmaison, *op. cit.*, pp. 75–76; *Moniteur*, XII, 241, April 20, 1792; A. Sorel, "La Diplomatie française et l'Espagne, 1792–96," *loc. cit.*, and for this reference, XI, 302. From this point on, these articles by Sorel will be most useful, and provide material not included in his famous *L'Europe et la Révolution française*, which contained relatively little on Spain. Bourgoing's dispatches during his ambassadorship are preserved in manuscript in the Archives des Affaires étrangères, Espagne, *Correspondance politique*, Vols. 634–36. Parts of some letters were in code, with translation written in.

the ideal to work through government-sponsored propaganda and the French armies.

In view of the Spanish attitude toward events and changes of the early Revolution, hostility could be expected toward the imprisonment of the royal family and the suspension of the monarchy. Lebrun, Minister of Foreign Affairs, instructed Bourgoing on the report of the Parisian insurrection of August 10 that he should give in Spain. He was to emphasize the strength of the conspiracy against the French people, and to state that the Swiss Guards fired first, thus placing Parisians on the defensive. Lebrun foresaw Spanish condemnation of any action against Louis XVI and the royal family and feared that Bourgoing might have to leave Spain.[34] The latter prevented a rupture of diplomatic relations, but hostility toward France played a part in the rising opposition to Aranda and in Godoy's machinations at court. Aranda antagonized the Spanish clergy by the decree, already mentioned, forbidding French *émigré* priests to preach. In October, the *Moniteur* reported new and more strenuous decrees to stop French propaganda at the border, and in addition to printed matter, all fans, boxes, ribbons, and merchandise bearing allusions to the French constitution or the principles of the Revolution were to be sent to the Minister of Finance for removal of the Republican symbols before delivery to their destination.[35] Whether or not any unexpurgated examples of such articles have been preserved in Spanish museums, one may guess their nature from those to be found in the collection at the Musée Carnavalet in Paris. A month later Aranda was suddenly dismissed, and the devious, often double-dealing, ministry and diplomacy of Godoy began. An increased anti-French sentiment was soon reflected in an appeal to foreign embassies in Madrid not to allow their diplomatic immunity to be used for the arrival and dispersal of French propaganda.[36] While Spain was technically neutral, Godoy began increasing Spanish defenses along the border. Bourgoing transmitted protests against these measures to Spain, and reported to the French

---

[34] Letter of Lebrun to Bourgoing, Aug. 21, 1792, given in Grandmaison, *op. cit.*, *Pièces justificatives*, pp. 318–19.
[35] *Moniteur*, XIV, 109, Oct. 4, 1792.
[36] *Ibid.*, XIV, 749, Dec. 17, 1792.

government that the Spanish government was frightened by Revolutionary propaganda.[37]

What propaganda was being directed toward Spain? Republicanism had existed among a small minority of Frenchmen before the Constitution of 1791, but had implied, in the use of the term *"république,"* the same meaning Montesquieu gave to the word—a government of good laws. The flight of the royal family and activities of the *émigrés*, real and imagined, weakened support for monarchy. During debates on the problem of the *émigrés* in November and December, 1791, and on war, early in 1792, Girondist oratory became more and more antimonarchical. On November 29, 1791, Isnard stated that if kings made war on the French people, the latter would instigate a war of peoples against kings. The Legislative Assembly voted to print this speech for distribution to the departments, but the proposal of one member that it be sent to foreign countries seems not to have been adopted.[38] Girondists and most Jacobins voted for war on Austria. Republican optimism that the peoples would follow the example of France and themselves overthrow the monarchs, and French confidence in their military strength, received rude blows in the spring of 1792. Fear that enemy troops would actually reach Paris and carry out the threats of the Duke of Brunswick's Manifesto resulted in the insurrection of August 10. Although Louis XVI was not put on trial until December, pronouncements were henceforth increasingly antimonarchical when directed outside of France, and bore the title of the French Republic after the declaration of the National Convention on September 21–22.

The Girondist ministry of foreign affairs, organized after August 10, 1792, was propagandist, but how much of its materials were destined for Spain cannot be ascertained without further research. French historians were concerned with totals, or with propaganda in other areas than Spain, but Masson tells us that 3,000 copies of Condorcet's pamphlet, *Avis aux espagnols*, were ordered.[39] In Oc-

---

[37] A. Sorel, "La Diplomatie française et l'Espagne," *loc. cit.*, XI, 298–330; for this reference, p. 305.

[38] *Moniteur*, X, 503–4; citation from p. 504.

[39] Frédéric Masson, *Le Département des affaires étrangères pendant la Révolution* (Paris, 1877), p. 262. Masson consulted French archives, but additional papers are now open to investigators. Division between the Archives des Affaires étrangères and the Archives nationales, and disorganization of the former during and since the war, have not facilitated research.

tober and November, 1792, Condorcet wrote similar pamphlets addressed to the Germans, the Dutch, and the Swiss. He began his pamphlet for Spain with the statement that Spain was the country in Europe that should feel the greatest benefit from the French Revolution. The welfare of the Spanish people had been sacrificed to satisfy the ambitions of foreign rulers, first the Habsburgs, then the Bourbons. He was aware of the provincial pride of the Catalans, Aragonese, and Castilians. Condorcet asserted that feudalism had virtually disappeared, and that neither nobles nor magistrates were privileged bodies any longer. Furthermore, he said that the Spanish clergy were more concerned with religion than politics, and he hoped that the clergy would lead the revolution in Spain. Condorcet even asserted that the "attachment of the Spanish people to religion is not an obstacle to a revolution."[40] He believed that Spain could change without violence, but he conceded that an attempt to adopt in Spain all the innovations that had been introduced in France might lead to violence. It would be better, he said, for the Spanish to "give themselves the liberty that accords with existing opinions of the Spanish nation."[41] He cautioned that a revolution that went beyond public opinion would lead to reaction, and a revolution that benefited only a part of the citizens would not last long. If the Spaniards would adopt a free constitution, or one that they considered free—for Condorcet recognized that Spain would want to retain the monarchy and the nobility—then Spain would again become a great power in Europe. He asserted that liberal societies had already been preparing a peaceful revolution. The pamphlet ended by presenting alternative courses of action: the Cortes could assemble and carry out reform, or, if the king (a Bourbon) refused to summon the Cortes, the reform movement could be started in individual communes and gradually spread by confederation.

How many of these 3,000 copies of Condorcet's pamphlet actually were smuggled into Spain remains in doubt. Since only the educated Spaniard could read French, it is important to know whether Spanish translations were printed and circulated. The present author has been unable to find any printed example of Condorcet's *Aviso a los españoles*, and on the basis of present research doubts that it ever was printed. Volumes of *Correspondance politique* in

---

[40] Condorcet, *Avis aux espagnols* (Press of the *Moniteur*, s.d., in–8, 23 pp.), pp. 1, 15.
[41] *Ibid.*, p. 13.

the Archives des Affaires Étrangères are full of protests against a translation made, which it was said would do more harm than good; claims to the printing of copies were accompanied by requests for payment, delays in printing reported, economy advised by the Minister of Foreign Affairs (Lebrun), and evidence presented that propagandists were diverted to measures of defense, especially after war against Spain began.[42]

Conflict between ideas expressed in pamphlets written to influence the Spaniards would only have caused confusion. Several Spanish refugees were anxious to propagandize their country, and sent writings to Lebrun for approval. Marchena, a fugitive from the Inquisition, wrote and actually had printed a pamphlet entitled, *A la nación española,* which denounced the Inquisition and was more anti-Catholic than Condorcet, but advocated monarchial federalism. Both Marchena and Condorcet suggested action by local cortes, without waiting for royal decree. No printed texts of the other proposed propaganda have been found. Texts of French laws and famous speeches were sent to be smuggled into Spain, but before his departure from Madrid, Bourgoing himself expressed doubts on their value as propaganda. Evidence from diplomatic correspondence indicates the sending of a dozen or so at a time, not hun-

[42] Standard biographies of Condorcet throw no light on this subject. See the following letters bearing on the printing and circulation of Condorcet's pamphlet, Arch. Aff. ét., *Correspondance politique,* Espagne, Vol. 634, nos. 132, 170; Vol. 635, nos. 3, 11, 47, 51, 78, 81, 86, 124, 134, 142, 152, 170, 181, 194, 200, 217, 225, 239, 261, 276, 290. A letter from Carlès, secretary to the Madrid embassy, indicates that some French texts were sent by diplomatic courier to Bourgoing (Vol. 634, no. 132, p. 317, letter to Minister of Foreign Affairs, Madrid, Dec. 10, 1792), and the same letter claimed a Spanish translation had been sent to Bayonne for the printing of 6,000 copies, since Carlès had been unable to find a printer in Spain who would take the risk of printing it. Carlès was recalled from Spain, and, after activities in the southwest, was appointed to the propagandist committee established at Bayonne. A letter to the Minister from Bayonne, Feb. 13, 1793 (no. 124, p. 244), would indicate that the 6,000 copies had been printed, and speaks of Carlès' having three or four thousand more printed. As of March 5, 1793, the Minister is asking Carlès for a dozen samples (no. 200, p. 387), but a letter from Carlès written March 11, 1793, indicated difficulties and delays in printing (no. 225, p. 440). On March 15, Carlès claimed to send the dozen copies requested by the Minister, but no sample is included in the papers of Vol. 635, whereas samples of printings of Spanish laws, and of translations of some French laws are bound with the manuscript correspondence (no. 239, p. 467). On March 23, the Minister cautions economy in expenditures (no. 276, p. 544). War, rather than propaganda, was increasingly the concern of the Foreign Office. No copy of a Spanish text of Condorcet's pamphlet has been found in French archives, national or departmental, but Spanish local archives along the frontier may contain some, if printed and smuggled into Spain.

dreds or thousands.⁴³ It is doubtful, in view of this evidence and the illiteracy of the mass of Spaniards, that these Girondist propagandists actually succeeded in influencing many Spaniards before war began. When appraising the hostility of the Spanish government, it must be remembered, however, that the French Revolution began with a revolt of enlightened persons.

Following the victory of Valmy in September 1792 and its convocation, the National Convention began promotion of Jacobin nationalism. Carnot and five other commissioners were sent to investigate public spirit in the southwest. Carnot's team reported from Bayonne that in all the departments traversed public opinion supported the Republic and the National Convention. They noted anti-Spanish sentiment, manifested by the tearing-down of the Spanish consul's coat-of-arms, for which apologies were made, and by the demand that the export of meat and animals to Spain be stopped while the French needed these articles. The commissioners allowed a group of nuns to cross into Spain, but stopped their pensions. The report indicated that roads were very poor in this region, reassured the Convention on the state of fortifications at Bayonne and upon the success of the circulation of assignats, but complained of inequalities between departments and urged economic equalization. The commissioners ended the report in a manner typical of Jacobinism: "Order is reborn, entire confidence is re-established, everything is regenerated and purified *(s'épure)*, within the Republic, and we can promise that the neighboring nations will find it infinitely more to their advantage to cultivate our friendship than to make war on us."⁴⁴ The commissioners sent to Perpignan, at the eastern end of the Pyrenees, made a similar appraisal of public

---

⁴³ Hévia, Santivanez, and Revest (a French merchant who had resided in Spain for many years) were among those sending sample writings (Vol. 634, nos. 164, 165; Vol. 635, nos. 128, 255, 310, 311). Regnier advocated a shorter publication than Condorcet's for smuggling (Vol. 635, no. 142, letter of Feb. 19, 1793). Three printed samples of Marchena's pamphlet are bound in Vol. 634, nos. 113, 164, 199, in-8, 4 pp. Marchena was later repudiated. See A. Morel-Fatio, "José Marchena et la propagande révolutionnaire en Espagne en 1792 et 1793," *Revue historique*, XLIV (1890), 72–87; Antonio Richard, "Marchena et les Girondins," *Annales révolutionnaires*, XV (1923), 126–45. Lebrun seems to have temporized on the printing of the various manuscripts submitted (see especially, Vol. 635, nos. 261, 291, 300).

⁴⁴ F. A. Aulard, *Recueil des actes du comité de salut public* (27 vols. and an index volume, Paris, 1889–1933), I, 138, and pp. 150–54, Oct. 16, 1792.

spirit. They reassured the Convention on the attitude toward Catholicism in this area where opposition to the clerical reforms had been strong and many priests had emigrated. Military preparations by the Spanish across the border were reported, and, except for artillery, the French were considered ready to defend the frontier.[45] From this evidence and from the local clubs and societies, we may conclude that French citizens along the Spanish border had become republican even before the trial of Louis XVI, and might have been more antimonarchical than the pamphlets of Condorcet and Marchena.

The confidence of French republicans that other peoples only waited a signal to overturn their "tyrants" or "despots"—in other words, their kings—was expressed in the famous propagandist decree of November 1792. The proclamation from the National Convention, "in the name of the French people, that it will accord fraternity and assistance to all peoples who shall wish to recover their liberty . . ." was to be translated and printed in all languages.[46] The logic of events—absorption of foreign enclaves within French frontiers, espousal of self-determination as in the case of Avignon, petitions of Jacobin minorities for annexation as in the case of Chambéry in Savoy, and victorious war in Belgium—was stronger than the humanitarianism and idealism of the Revolutionary leaders. The December propagandist decree, barely a month after the November decree just quoted, indicated an increased aggressiveness of Revolutionary nationalism. Although French generals were to announce to the peoples of the countries invaded that the French were bringing "peace, assistance, fraternity, liberty, and equality," it was a French brand of revolution that French armies introduced, overriding loyalty to pre-existing institutions. This decree implied intolerance of differences, which Professor Hayes noted as an important feature of Jacobin nationalism, and also prepared the way for the assumption of the cost of the war by the conquered peoples.[47]

---

[45] *Ibid.*, I, 161, report of Oct. 18, 1792, and p. 203, Oct. 28, 1792.

[46] The translation given by Frank M. Anderson in *French Constitutions and Other Select Documents* (Minneapolis, 1904), p. 130, is quoted here. See report in the *Moniteur*, XIV, 517, on the session of November 19, when this decree was voted. See also A. Sorel, *L'Europe et la Révolution française*, III, 164–69. Bourgoing warned the government in November of the strength of Spanish support for Catholicism (Grandmaison, *op. cit.*, p. 84).

[47] Anderson, *op. cit.*, pp. 130–33; *Moniteur*, XIV, 755–56, Dec. 17, 1792; A. Sorel, *L'Europe et la Révolution française*, III, 232–40.

The trial of Louis XVI began four days before this second propagandist decree. The Spanish government had hoped earlier to save Louis XVI by declaring neutrality. It now protested the trial, and offered asylum in Spain for the king and the royal family. This offer only created greater hostility in the National Convention, and confirmed suspicions of treasonable negotiations between the Bourbons. Report of a ceremony in Madrid in honor of Louis XVI after his execution, renewal of measures against French influence, suspension of communication with Bourgoing and his forced departure from Madrid on February 23, 1793, only increased French fears.[48] Debate in the National Convention culminated on March 7, 1793, with declaration of war on France's former ally, Spain.

Barère reported on Spain for the Committee of Defense. It was in this report that he made the famous statement: "One more enemy is only one more triumph for liberty."[49] He accused the Spanish king of "fanaticism"—the Jacobin way of condemning support for Catholicism and clericalism—and the Spanish government of vacillation, insolence, inquisitorial methods, and disloyalty to the French alliance, while he claimed that France had been patient and conciliatory toward Spain. He believed that Spain was weak, and that this was the reason why she had not already declared war. Barère was now against all kings. He concluded with effective oratory: the people of southern France—Barère himself came from Bigorre on the Spanish border—would make the dictum "Il n'y a plus des Pyrénées" a reality, by ending Spanish Bourbon rule and carrying liberty and equality into Spain.

The declaration of war adopted by the National Convention began with a list of grievances against Spain: refusal to recognize the Republic, plotting in behalf of Louis XVI, support for the *émigrés*, hostile action against French nationals in Spain, Spanish naval armament undertaken ostensibly against England but constituting a threat to France, Spanish military preparations, suspension of diplomatic relations, incitement of an insurrection against French authority in Saint Domingue, and alliance with enemies of France. Following this preamble came the actual declaration of war, condemning Spain as the aggressor and authorizing the use of French

---

[48] Grandmaison, *op. cit.*, p. 80; Tratchevsky, *op. cit.*, p. 38; A. Sorel, "La Diplomatie française et l'Espagne," *loc. cit.*, XI, 304–5.

[49] *Moniteur*, XV, 656–59, March 10, 1793. The quotation opened the report.

land and naval forces "to sustain the independence, dignity, and interest of the French Republic." Six representatives were to be sent to the departments along the Pyrenees to stimulate enlistment, provide munitions, and to encourage the French of the border area to "unite to revenge the injuries done to the French nation by a tyrant."[50]

The National Convention voted the declaration of war with enthusiasm and with confidence in the weakness of Spain and hence in the triumph of republican armies fighting under the banner of liberty. News of the declaration of war was received in the Pyrenees region with rejoicing, but local authorities had initiated measures to insure local defense even before the news arrived. The department of the Hautes-Pyrénées forbade import of Spanish food and animals, and that of the Pyrénées Orientales prohibited export to Spain, required deposit of assignats by French merchants who had transacted business with Spain (to prevent circulation of false assignats), and passports to leave Perpignan.[51] Local officials were discovering that Frenchmen coming from Spain did not encourage the war spirit among French civilians near the border. Marchena, already mentioned for his pamphlet on Spain, and Hévia, both Spaniards who claimed that they wanted to help spread Revolutionary ideas in Spain, came to the Pyrenees region, but did not get on well with the local committees. Both were recalled to Paris in April 1793. Carlès and Taschereau from the Madrid embassy came to Bayonne, but all these enthusiasts acted as individuals. Local officials were more concerned with recruitment and munitions than with propaganda, and much confusion prevailed.[52]

All during the trial of Louis XVI, Spanish royalist sentiment

[50] *Moniteur*, XV, 640, March 8, 1793; quotations from Articles II and IV.

[51] Pierre Vidal, *Histoire de la Révolution française dans les Pyrénées orientales* (2 vols., Perpignan, 1855), II, 106–12, March 9 and 12 respectively. Vidal was criticized by Georges Sorel for too great dependence upon Fervel without acknowledgment, and for failure to use Delbrel (*Revue de la Révolution*, XI [1888], 428–29). Vidal provides much local detail, however. Georges Sorel gives his own account of these events in "Les Girondins en Roussillon," *Bulletin de la Société agriculturelle, scientifique et littéraire des Pyrénées orientales*, XXX (1899), 142–224. Sorel used archives not consulted by Vidal.

[52] Antonio Richard, *op. cit.*, 126–45, and "Jean-Pierre Basterrèche (1762–1827)," *Annales historiques de la Révolution française*, I (1924), 427–39; A. Morel-Fatio, *op. cit.*, p. 82, and "Le Révolutionnaire espagnol don Andrés Maria de Guzman," *Revue historique*, CXXII, (1916), 33–64. Minutes for the Jacobin Clubs of Bayonne, Tarbes, and Perpignan are lacking for the end of 1792 and the beginning of the war in 1793.

against France increased. Bourgoing had warned the French government as early as October 1792 that although Spain did not desire war, Spaniards were proud and the fate of Louis XVI touched their honor. The Spanish government had been granting subsidies to the *émigrés*, who continued to agitate and reinforce court solicitude for the French royal family.[53] Bourgoing did his best to prevent a break. In February 1793, the month when Bourgoing withdrew from Spain, the audience of a Madrid theater booed an actress wearing a liberty bonnet, and similar disapproval was shown by Mardi Gras crowds on the street.[54] After the departure of Bourgoing, it was more difficult for either government to be informed of events on the other side of the Pyrenees. The Spanish declaration of war, issued on March 23, 1793, was not reported in the *Gazeta de Madrid* until March 29, in which issue also appeared news of the treason of Dumouriez, and not until May 4 in the *Moniteur*, by which time the Spanish invasion of France had already begun. In the declaration, Spain complained of French impiety, the treatment of Louis XVI, bad faith, seizure of Spanish ships, and of the danger of anarchy and disorder from French license.[55]

Most historians state that the war on France was popular with the Spanish people. Godoy himself seems to have been the chief source of this belief. In his memoirs, published much later, and written in self-defense against his critics and enemies, he claimed overwhelming popular support for the war. Spanish newspapers ran long lists of voluntary gifts to the Spanish treasury, and of volunteers for the army.[56] The *Moniteur*, on the other hand, discounted the sums reported and claimed that the common people did not want the war,

---

[53] A. Sorel, *L'Europe et la Révolution française*, III, 232; Grandmaison, *op. cit.*, pp. 88–89. Grandmaison claimed that Spain aided the *émigrés* more out of charity than politics. See also L. Pingaud, *Un Agent secrèt sous la Révolution et l'Empire* (Paris, 1893), on the Comte d'Antraigues and *émigré* maneuvers. Mlle. Chaumié should throw much new light on this question.

[54] *Moniteur*, XV, 641, March 9, 1793. Since this report coincided with the publication of the French declaration of war on Spain, it would appeal to French patriotism. See correspondence of Bourgoing and the Foreign Office, Arch. Aff. ét., *Correspondance politique*, Espagne, Vols. 634 and 635, *passim*. Taschereau and Carlès complained to Lebrun that Bourgoing was too pro-Spanish, *idem*.

[55] *Gazeta de Madrid* (Bib. Nat. Od. 28), as cited; *Moniteur*, XVI, 285, May 4, 1793.

[56] Don Manuel Godoy, *Mémoires*, trans. by J. G. d'Esménard (4 vols., Paris, 1836–37), I, 194–96 (Esménard's laudatory introduction), and pp. 290–91 (Godoy's text). See *Mercurio de España* and *Gazeta de Madrid* for April and May. Lists in the latter began after news of the execution of Louis XVI, and continued after the declaration of war.

and that they were being aroused by the Spanish clergy, who in turn were urged on by the English court.[57] The two strongest arguments supporting Godoy's claims were the fact that conscription was not used at the beginning of the war, and that the Spanish army, contrary to French expectations, did invade French soil. The early success of Spain was aided, however, by French preoccupation with other theaters of war, French belief that Spain would wage only a defensive war, greater unpreparedness than realized, and internal dissension between Girondists and Jacobins.

In Spain, stern measures were taken against Frenchmen other than *émigrés*. In April 1793, French Revolutionary sympathizers were expelled from Spain, and their property confiscated; in June, an inventory of property was ordered. French *émigrés* now served in Spanish armies, even forming special corps, and as officers on Spanish ships.[58] While Spain was mobilizing for invasion of France, the war was going badly for the French on all fronts. In the critical days following the treason of Dumouriez, the National Convention passed the law of April 13 renouncing intervention in the affairs of other countries, but at the same time warning of resistance to foreign intervention in French affairs. The debate showed that this was not only intended to bolster patriotism at home by reasserting the altruism of the early Revolution, but also to allay fears of Revolutionary aggression abroad. The Convention ordered that the law be printed in French and in foreign languages, including Spanish.[59] Only a few days before, readers of the *Moniteur* had been told that the Spanish people did not want the war. Sorel considered this declaration of April 13, 1793, the end of Revolutionary war and a reversion to the *raison d'état* of the old regime.[60]

Although the declarations of war had taken place in March, the actual fighting got under way slowly, because of winter weather in the Pyrenees. It was Spain who invaded French territory first, and

---

[57] *Moniteur*, XVI, 98–99, April 12, 1793. Taschereau, formerly of the Madrid embassy, reported from Bayonne to Lebrun that recruiting was going badly (Arch. Aff. ét., *Correspondance politique*, Espagne, Vol. 635, nos. 301 and 304), at the end of March 1793. All reports from individuals to Lebrun tended to discount Spanish power and to bolster French confidence (*ibid.*, letters of Cayrol, Carlès, *passim*). See also G. Sorel, "Les Girondins en Roussillon," *loc. cit.*

[58] Grandmaison, *op. cit.*, pp. 88–89, 94.

[59] *Moniteur*, XVI, 143, April 16; Anderson, *op. cit.*, p. 133.

[60] A. Sorel, *L'Europe et la Révolution française*, III, 388.

thereby placed France on the defensive. One more enemy did matter. Although war against Spain never involved the large forces of the Revolutionary wars elsewhere, nor implied the danger to the Revolution that the Austrian advance toward Paris in 1792 had meant, it added one more theater of war, detached from the other fronts.

All historians have accepted the general propagandism of the French Revolutionaries, but few have investigated the propagandism of their enemies. After all, the Duke of Brunswick's Manifesto was a propaganda document. In the case of Spain, secret negotiations had been carried on in behalf of royalty and in support of uprisings against the Revolution, without counting the machinations of *émigrés* centering their activity in Spain.[61] All such activity aimed first to reinforce the old regime, and then to bring it back into full power. In Spain itself, strict censorship of the press resulted in either suppression of news or a strong bias, both implying official efforts to control public opinion. When the Spanish army invaded French soil, Ricardos, the Spanish general, issued a proclamation to the inhabitants that the Spanish came as liberators from "the horrible despotism and tyranny of an illegal, usurping and fanatical assembly."[62] The death of Louis XVI was called an *"atroce parricide,"* and all Frenchmen declaring themselves loyal to the Spanish king were to be protected by Spanish troops. The army would respect persons and property, but those opposed to Spain would be declared rebels against religion, king, and country. Although the proclamation was made in May, it was not announced to the readers of the *Moniteur* until after the fall of the Girondists. The Jacobins must have calculated that announcement of such an appeal to republicans would arouse even greater patriotism in defense of the Republic.

The Basques in both countries shared some common characteristics, and at least one small town succumbed temporarily to Spanish seduction. Two hundred and one inhabitants of the town of Aldules had stronger grievances against the neighboring French town than against the Spanish, and they petitioned Ricardos to take them under Spanish protection, and promised to fight against the French.

---

[61] The correspondence and career of Nuñez, Spanish ambassador in Paris, provide some material on this; see note 20. See also note 53, and Grandmaison, *op. cit., passim.*

[62] *Moniteur*, XVII, 34, July 5, 1793. The proclamation was made in May.

Two months later, the French recaptured Aldules, and feeling ran so high that French officers prevented pillage with difficulty. A plan to use Basques to infiltrate into Spain in order to distribute printed copies of the Constitution of 1793 had to be abandoned, since Basque leaders of the town had left with the retreating Spanish. According to the historian reporting this episode, the Basques were generally local in spirit and lukewarm toward the war, rather than unpatriotic toward France.[63]

The early generosity and promises of the Spanish did not last long, if reports in the *Moniteur* were correct and not themselves propaganda. Before the end of July 1793, the Spanish general issued warning that the army would hang peasants and townsmen shooting at Spanish soldiers.[64] Shortly after this, Ricardos promised the inhabitants of Roussillon and Cerdagne who would declare loyalty to the Spanish king, free entry into Spain for their sheep and cattle —the most lucrative items of prewar trade.[65] Those strongly opposed to the Revolution had emigrated earlier. Spanish invasion and victories and French confusion contributed to local fear and defeatism, and it was not until 1794 that the French armies began to overcome the Spaniards and drive the invading armies back across the border.

Patriotic societies in the southwest received Revolutionary literature as elsewhere; in fact, the same materials were sent everywhere —texts of laws, the Bulletin of the National Convention, famous speeches, single issues of Parisian newspapers, and occasional pamphlets. Evidence available would seem to indicate a desire to bolster local morale rather than to propagandize the Spanish.[66]

[63] Antonio Richard, "Les Basques pendant la guerre franco-espagnole (1793–95)," *Annales révolutionnaires*, XIV (1922), 130–38. See also Pierre Haristoy, *Les Paroisses des pays basques pendant la période révolutionnaire* (2 vols., Pau, 1895–96), who emphasized the strong Catholicism of the Basques.

[64] *Moniteur*, XVII, 170, July 21, 1793.

[65] *Ibid.*, XVII, 273, Aug. 1, 1793.

[66] Crane Brinton indicated that masses of materials were sent to Jacobin Clubs, but that does not prove their use to propagandize Spain (*The Jacobins* [New York, 1930], pp. 76–77). Aside from translations into Spanish, local societies would have to use Marchena or Hévia, or other propagandist agents, to send literature into Spain, and both of these men were recalled to Paris in April 1793. The minutes of the Société des Amis de la Constitution at Perpignan for April–July, 1793, listed literature received which included such items as papers related to the trial and execution of Louis XVI, speeches by Petion, Vergniaud, and Robespierre, an issue of the *Véritable ami du peuple*, etc. No mention of propagandizing Spain appeared (Archives départementales des Pyrénées orientales, I² 23). See also Philippe Toreilles, *Perpignan pendant la Révolution* (Perpignan, 1893); G. Sorel, "Les Girondins en Roussillon," *loc. cit.*

In the spring of 1793, while the war got slowly under way, Lebrun, Girondist Minister of Foreign Affairs, was planning two propagandist committees, one at Bayonne and one at Perpignan, but delays ensued. Authorization to Borel and Comeyras to proceed respectively to these two cities was dated April 27, but Comeyras only arrived in Perpignan July 8, after the fall of the Girondists in the National Convention, and Borel seems to have remained in Toulouse and directed the members of his committee by correspondence. Propaganda material was sent to the committees and payments to the members were made, but aside from an occasional sample included with the French official correspondence, it will be necessary to search Spanish local archives to determine whether any copies actually crossed the Spanish border.[67] The committee members temporized while waiting for their chiefs to arrive, while the correspondence of Borel and Comeyras with the new minister after the fall of Lebrun indicated that the original purpose of the committees—to propagandize Spain—could not be carried out by virtue of the Spanish invasion and the status of the war. Borel and Comeyras were instructed to use the members to facilitate recruiting and provisioning of the armies, and to prosecute the war in general, rather than to propagandize the Spanish.[68] Testimony of representatives on mission corroborated the admission of Borel and Comeyras, and the committees were dissolved.[69] This Girondist effort to spread Revolutionary doctrine in Spain seems to have failed.

After the fall of the Girondists in June 1793, the war was prosecuted with greater vigor, and republicanism received increased emphasis. Colonel Bouchotte, Minister of War after Dumouriez, had reorganized French armies, and was constantly sending republican propaganda to them. His proclamations and instructions empha-

[67] Arch. Aff. ét., *Correspondance politique*, Espagne, Vol. 636. This material includes, first, many letters proposing such committees by Carlès, Bastеrrèche, Taschereau, and others; then, list of members (no. 57), payments to be made (62, 73, 74), instructions to Borel and Comeyras (78), organization and powers of the committees (79), mention of arrival of Comeyras (129), instruction from Borel at Toulouse to committee at Bayonne (157). Among others, items 112 and 132 mention receipt of propaganda to send into Spain.

[68] *Ibid.*, letters from committee members (nos. 111, 117, 122, 129, 130); recognition by the Minister of impossibility of carrying out original instructions (73, 135, 137); admission of Borel and Comeyras of failure to propagandize (157, 158, 167, 188, etc.).

[69] Masson, *op. cit.*, p. 268; Grandmaison, *op. cit.*, p. 95. See also Aulard, *Études et leçons*, Vol. III, "La Diplomatie du premier comité de salut public," and reports of representatives on mission in the great Aulard collection.

sized republican virtues and hatred of the foreigner.[70] New representatives on mission were sent, and purges of popular societies and local administrations ensued. When the representatives to the Basses-Pyrénées claimed that the inhabitants hated federalism (the Girondist point of view) more than Spaniards, the Jacobin Convention might have been reassured of their republicanism, but not of a vigorous prosecution of the war.[71]

The newspaper, *Echo des Pyrénées*, published during 1793 in Perpignan, is an invaluable source of information about conditions in the war area, the problems of waging the war, the state of public opinion, and the intention to propagandize the Spaniards. Each number gave news and communications about other provinces of France, stories of French bravery and public service, description of the fighting, and local news. Several numbers contained articles obviously designed for Spanish readers. The issue of July 13, 1793, attempted to show that Catholicism was still respected and practiced in France, while, after suspension of publication from August 15 to September 7 because of printing troubles, the issue of October 30 and 31 printed in French and Spanish an "Avis au peuple espagnol" ascribed to Revest.[72] How much influence this paper exerted on the victorious Spaniards then occupying French territory is problematical. No similar local newspaper appeared throughout this period at Bayonne.

Parisians were experiencing direct and indirect republican propaganda. After September 1793, the Parisian *sans-culottes* no longer saw Beaumarchais' famous satires on the old regime in Spanish setting. The device of a Spanish locale had probably helped Beaumarchais escape censorship under the old regime, but now would only have incurred the prevalent hostility felt toward Spain. From October 1793 until March 1794, this hostility received stimulation

---

[70] Général Herlaut, *Le Colonel Bouchotte* (2 vols., Paris, 1946), *passim*, and especially the concluding chapter in Vol. II on Bouchotte and republican propaganda.

[71] Henri Wallon, *Les Représentants du peuple en mission et la justice révolutionnaire dans les départements* (2 vols., Paris, 1889), II, 379. Part of the second volume deals with the Pyrenees region.

[72] Issues beginning with May 15, 1793 (no. 15), and with some missing numbers through the end of Dec. 20, 1793, are preserved in the Archives départementales des Pyrénées orientales at Perpignan. The Conseil du département des Pyrénées orientales voted on Aug. 31, 1793, to provide a printing press so that the *Echo* could continue publication, and a subsidy was granted the editor (Arch. dép., L 1128).

from a production of Monnet's *Les Montagnards,* the hero of which was a migrant from Auvergne who had always gone yearly to Spain. His patriotism was contrasted with that of French *émigrés* in Spain, and an unfavorable interpretation was placed on Spanish institutions. The *montagnard* and his family returned to France disillusioned about Spain.[73] Between December 1793 and July 1794, Gamas' play *Michel Cervantes,* with music by Foignet, was given thirty-three times. This was a vehicle for making fun of survivals of Spanish feudalism and medievalism, which Cervantes himself had attacked. While Provost-Montfort's *L'Esprit des prêtres,* with the alternate title *La Persécution des français en Espagne,* must have been strongly anti-Spanish, it was performed only seven times at the Théâtre de la Cité and was not reviewed. Republican virtues and patriotism were constantly represented in the theater in 1793 and 1794.[74]

Newspapers were voicing Jacobin nationalism, especially the *Journal de la Montagne,* and the *Feuille de salut public.* The Ministry of the Interior secretly subsidized the *Feuille de Paris,* ordered 6,000 copies of *La France républicaine,* published by Grand, the same number of a *Catéchisme de la déclaration des droites de l'homme et du citoyen* by J. B. Boucheseiche, and one million copies of the Constitution of 1793.[75] Copies of songs were also ordered. A study of the extensive secret funds received by the Ministry of Foreign Affairs between June 1793 and May 1794, and the exceedingly large ones for July through September 1793, when Jacobins were overcoming Girondist sentiment at home, needs to be made. Neither Caron nor Masson indicates the use of funds for propaganda directed toward Spain.[76] Even the sending of packets of pamphlets to local societies along the Pyrenees does not adequately inform us

[73] On the relative moderation of the Parisian theater during the Terror, see Beatrice F. Hyslop, "The Theater During a Crisis: The Parisian Theater During the Reign of Terror," *Journal of Modern History,* XVII, No. 4 (December 1945). Monnet's play was given twenty times in the period cited. See review in *Journal des spectacles,* no. 107, Sept. 17, 1793.

[74] See *Almanach des spectacles* (1794), II, 9, on Gamas' play. For republican virtues and patriotism, see description of *L'heureuse décade, Au retour,* and others, in Hyslop, "The Theater During a Crisis," *loc. cit.*

[75] Pierre Caron, "Les Publications officieuses du Ministère de l'Intérieur en 1793 et 1794," *Revue d'histoire moderne et contemporaine,* XIV (1910), 5–43.

[76] Masson, *op. cit.,* p. 300, for the table of secret funds. More documents are now available than were open to historians when Caron and Masson made their studies.

of the quantity and identity of the propaganda, or of actual success in transferring it to Spain. One may assume that the order by Dumouriez before his fall for fifty balloons to drop pamphlets on Belgium would not be practical in the Pyrenees![77] Neither Condorcet nor Marchena had advocated overthrow of the Spanish monarchy and substitution of a republic, and hence both pamphlets would no longer be useful.[78] The manner of reporting the rejoinder of De Flers, the French commander, to the threat of reprisals against French guerrillas supported the thesis that the Jacobins were busier developing patriotism at home than in propagandizing the Spanish. De Flers denounced the Spanish proclamation as a violation of international law, and asserted that all Frenchmen were soldiers, their only uniform liberty, equality, and the tricolor cockade. This statement was taken as proof of French strength and defiance.[79]

In July 1793 a new edition of Chantreau's *Lettres écrites de Barcelonne à un zélateur de la liberté* was issued. Chantreau claimed to have been a spy for the French Foreign Office early in 1792, during the period when war with Austria was brewing. If it be true that his use of Spanish and a bribe smoothed all obstacles to crossing the border before war, this was indicative that French propaganda could have been sent into Spain with relative ease despite government prohibitions. This would no longer be the case during wartime, with Spanish armies on French soil. If copies of Chantreau's book reached the Catalans in the summer of 1793, it might have stimulated defeatism by spreading the idea that the war would benefit French *émigrés* rather than Catalans, and by encouraging Catalan separatism.[80] Only Spanish officers understood French, and no Span-

---

[77] *Ibid.*, p. 275.

[78] See pp. 205–6 above. Marchena revised his pamphlet after the execution of Louis XVI, but was convinced that the Spaniards supported the king, and he only redoubled his emphasis upon the Spanish Cortes. See Richard, "José Marchena et la propagande révolutionnaire," *loc. cit.*, pp. 135–43, and Morel-Fatio, "Marchena et les Girondins," *loc. cit.*, pp. 77–82.

[79] *Moniteur*, XVII, 170, July 21, 1793; Vidal, *op. cit.*, p. 239.

[80] The Hispanic Library in New York City possesses a copy of Chantreau's volume. See Foulché-Delbosc, "Bibliographie des voyages en Espagne et en Portugal," *loc. cit.*, and an article in the *Moniteur*, XVII, 230, July 27, 1793. Chantreau asserted that one could buy permission to read prohibited books, and indicated that the list of prohibited writings originally issued in 1789 was kept up to date with added prohibitions (pp. 210, 221–23). Chantreau was describing conditions as of 1792. He provided a vivid description of *émigré* plotting against France.

ish text seems to have been issued. It appears incontestable that French Jacobins wished to propagandize Spain, but whether or not subsidized literature actually reached Spaniards while their armies were on the offensive, it probably helped prevent Spanish propaganda from influencing French citizens of the border areas.

The possibility of divergent interpretation of propaganda may be illustrated by the reports of the celebration of July 14, 1793, at Perpignan. Ardent republicans described the celebration with enthusiasm, and mentioned that Spanish soldiers were camped near enough to hear the singing of the *Marseillaise*. On the other hand, the representatives on mission reported that the texts of the new Constitution of 1793 had not arrived for the 14th and that the celebration showed little éclat. A second fête was held on the 16th when the constitutions had arrived, with enthusiasm for republicanism and for war against Spain manifested.[81]

While these events were transpiring in the war area, the *Mercurio de España* and the *Gazeta de Madrid* were publishing news about France that would make Spanish readers believe that the majority of Frenchmen were in revolt against the Republic. Appeals for Louis XVII were made. The stormier sessions of the National Convention were reported with exaggeration of disorder and violence, and Robespierre was described as a dictator. In the accounts of the war, Spanish losses were minimized and French casualties exaggerated.[82] The accounts resembled closely English denunciations of the French Revolution at the same period, while *émigrés* were undoubtedly coloring their reports.[83] News of Spain itself included little more than items on the royal family, military promotions, texts of *cédules*, and war news.

The conflict in the Pyrenees region was never a main theater of war. Spanish soldiers fought in allied armies on other fronts, and naval warfare was going on continuously. The fighting in the Pyre-

---

[81] J. Calmette and P. Vidal, *Histoire de Roussillon* (Paris, 1931), p. 224; Vidal, *op. cit.*, pp. 253-54; Joseph Calmette, *Histoire d'Espagne* (Paris, 1947), p. 335. Different contemporary accounts were cited. The *Echo des Pyrénées* had propaganda value.

[82] *Mercurio historico y politico de España*, especially the issue of August 1793; *Gazeta de Madrid*, especially Aug. 20, 1793, and May 20, 1794.

[83] See claims of *Moniteur*, XVIII, 521, Nov. 28, 1795. Several issues of the *Gazeta* complained of lack of reliable news, while from August 1793 on, much news about events within France came via Geneva, with considerable time-lag.

nees took place as a threefold campaign—in the west, central, and eastern Pyrenees—most of the time without co-ordination. After the original Spanish success, some minor French victories occurred, but there was a virtual stalemate until the spring of 1794, when French successes began. All through the fall and winter of 1793–1794, the representatives on mission were so busy obtaining provisions and munitions, and supervising the reorganization of the army, that their correspondence throws little light on propaganda.[84] Revolutionary jargon and some of the mounting arrogance of victorious Jacobins were illustrated by the reports of Fabre de l'Hérault, when he declared that it was time to make the slaves (Spaniards) dance the carmagnole, and that "Spain is a cow full of milk, it is high time to milk it."[85] Hailed by Robespierre in December 1793 as the first representative on mission to be a martyr, Fabre was voted the honors of the Pantheon by the Convention. His reports were more aggressive than those of the other deputies on mission and clearly advocated invasion of Spain in order to make the Spaniards pay for the war.

In the early months of 1794, Spain was also having internal difficulties. A government crisis occurred in March, in which Aranda, the former enlightened minister, headed a peace party calling for a meeting of the Spanish Cortes—which, it may be remembered, had been advocated by Marchena and Condorcet—and reform of the Spanish government. Although the stormy meeting of the royal council, during which Aranda and Godoy aired opposing views, was not publicized at the time, Aranda was exiled from the court, and the ascendancy of Godoy and continuance of the war were as-

[84] For details of the campaigns, see Pierre de Marcillac, *Histoire de la guerre entre la France et l'Espagne* (Paris, 1808), and Général de Pelleport, "Campagnes des Pyrénées orientales et centrales (1793–95)," *Revue des Pyrénées*, IV (1892), 237–55, both participants in the campaigns; and J. N. Fervel, *Campagnes de la Révolution française dans les Pyrénées-orientales* (2 vols., Paris, 1851–53). See also Antonio Richard, *Le Gouvernement révolutionnaire dans les Basses-Pyrénées* (Paris, 1923), and criticism of this volume by Jean Annat in *Révolution historique et archéologique du Béarn et du pays basque*, VI (1923), 291–99; E. Lapabe, "Le Rôle des représentants en mission auprès de l'armée des Pyrénées occidentales," *ibid.*, pp. 71–80; J. Adher, "La Défense nationale dans les Pyrénées centrales (1793–95)," *La Révolution française*, LVI (1909), 396–429.

[85] Georges Sorel, "Les Représentants du peuple à l'armée des Pyrénées orientales en 1793," *Revue de la Révolution*, XIII (1888), 68–89, 153–72, and XIV (1889), 40–65; citation from XIV, 46. This same article discounted Jacobin propaganda, and considered Fervel's praise of Fabre as excessive.

sured.⁸⁶ Godoy appears to have promised remission of taxes for six years in order to encourage enlistment. Unrest over the high price of bread and the circulation of pamphlets demanding reform led to special police measures to maintain order in the larger towns.⁸⁷ Although the economic situation continued critical, the leadership of Godoy was now unchallenged.

As one reads of conflicts between military and civilian officials, central and local officials, of local division, together with the difficulties of fighting in the Pyrenees and of providing munitions and food, one is surprised that the Revolutionaries ever achieved victory against Spain, which was only one of its many opponents. In January 1794 the fortunes of the French army changed, when Dugommier, the republican commander who had recaptured Toulon from the English in December 1793, arrived to command the army of the Pyrenees. Disorganization and lack of discipline gave way to discipline, improved military morale, and patriotic fervor. Reports from the representatives on mission abounded with phrases branding the Spanish as slaves, and emphasizing the patriotism of Frenchmen as freemen, implying more concern with civilian and military ardor than with propaganda intended for the Spaniards. The minutes of the popular societies for this period also show the play of local politics and the efforts of the ordinary citizens who were members of the societies to help win the war, but reveal nothing on propaganda directed toward the enemy.⁸⁸

In May 1794 the tide had turned, and the French offensive began

⁸⁶ Godoy, *op. cit.*, I, 302–19; *Moniteur*, XX, 458, May 14, 1794 (news dated April 6; the council met March 14). Reverend Père Delbrel, who used private archives of the descendants of the Spanish general, La Union, provided some details of the royal council not given by Godoy, "L'Espagne et La Révolution française," *Études réligieuses, historiques* . . . , XLVII (August 1889), 644. Delbrel's articles appeared in the issues of June-August, 1889 (XLVII, 235–54, 638–63), and September-November, 1889 (XLVIII, 57–85, 278–98, 428–50). A Jesuit, Delbrel strongly defended Catholicism and La Union.

⁸⁷ Arturo Chuquet, "Négotiation de Dugommier avec l'Espagne en 1794," *Séances et travaux de l'académie des sciences morales et politiques*, LXIV (1905), 443–64; citation from pp. 448–49.

⁸⁸ For a general summary of this period, see Calmette, *op. cit.*, pp. 225–38. On conditions in winter quarters, see Pelleport, "Campagnes des Pyrénées," *loc. cit.*, pp. 248–49, and G. Sorel, "Les Représentants du peuple à l'armée des Pyrénées," *loc. cit.*, p. 63, who claimed widespread desertions from the French army of the Pyrenees. See the register of the popular society at Bayonne, October 1793–May 1794, *passim*, Archives municipales de Bayonne. There is a gap in the register of the society at Perpignan during the winter, but it begins again with April 6.

after the capture of Collioure by Dugommier. He wrote to the central government describing the riches of Catalonia, its love of liberty and equality, and proposing annexation. If this was representative of army opinion, soldiers in the fighting areas developed a more aggressive spirit than the Committees and the Convention. Couthon said that conquests must be for security only, and Carnot stated that annexation of Catalonia was incompatible with French renunciation of conquest. Carnot acknowledged differences of customs and language, and Catalan loyalty to Catholicism, and recommended that a republic be set up under French protection. Couthon advised winning over the Catalans by protecting the poor, crushing the rich, and gradually weaning them from Catholicism. He recommended introducing the French language, building roads, and increasing bonds between France and Catalonia. The French army had not yet invaded Spanish soil.[89]

The French celebrated the surrender of Collioure with patriotic fervor. Following the signing of capitulations, Dugommier released Spanish prisoners, but the Spanish general, La Union, refused to honor the signature of his subordinate, Navarro. The failure to release French prisoners led to a French charge that Spain had violated international law; it intensified French hatred and resulted in more drastic treatment of Spaniards.[90] Acrimonious accusations were exchanged between the opposing commanders.

While negotiations were still going on, the propaganda technique of the conquering French army was demonstrated. When Puycerda was captured, a popular society was organized, and the Spanish *sans-culottes* were encouraged to preach reason (anti-Catholicism) and hatred of tyranny. Printed materials—such as proclamations of French representatives on mission and of French generals, texts of the Declaration of the Rights of Man, and of the Constitution of 1793, famous speeches in the Convention, including those of Robespierre on public fêtes and Barère on help to the poor—were cir-

[89] Chuquet, *op. cit.*, p. 443; A. Sorel, *L'Europe et la Révolution française*, IV, 90.
[90] For the Spanish version, see the *Colección* cited in note 8, and note 9. Godoy stated in his memoirs that a delay of two days by Navarro was used to rescue an *émigré* corps (*op. cit.*, pp. 334–35). One of the main points of difference was as to whether the prisoners returned could fight again. The French stipulated that they should not. Barère reported to the Convention on the capitulation on June 2, while the *Moniteur* printed on August 14 further complaints by Barère on the failure of the Spanish to fulfill the terms of surrender (XX, 641–42, and XXI, 467–68).

culated, posted on trees and even, according to Chuquet, scattered on the roads.⁹¹ Aside from this specific example, both Dugommier and the representatives on mission issued proclamations to Spanish civilians, declaring that French entry on Spain soil was "only a goodneighbor visit for the welfare of the Spanish people."⁹² French soldiers talked with Spanish soldiers about the *"douceur de vivre"* under the new regime, and encouraged desertion. It would appear that French soldiers infiltrated into Spanish-held towns and mingled with soldiers and civilians, telling them that a republic was the best form of government, promising the freeing of the peasants and the rebuilding of houses destroyed in the fighting. Appeal was made to the separatist spirit among the Catalans, and also to peace sentiment and to the commercial interests of Spanish merchants.⁹³

Morale in the Spanish army was low. Spanish soldiers released after the capture of Collioure were reported to have called out, *"Viva la casa!"* (or, "Home, sweet home!"), while the French soldiers replied, *"Vive la République!"*⁹⁴ La Union's private correspondence revealed the poor condition of the Spanish army when he took command, and he initiated measures to raise discipline and to stop the spread of French propaganda. He ordered sentinels to fire on French soldiers approaching Spanish camps, in order to prevent infiltration, and he forbade dealings between Spaniards and Frenchmen, and with Spaniards coming from French territory. He ordered the seizure and burning of pamphlets, and prohibited the employment of French servants by *émigrés* and Catalans. La Union complained that the French waged war with pen and silver rather than with fire and sword.⁹⁵ A devout Catholic himself, he appealed to Catalan religious fervor. He promised that religion (right) would triumph over error and called upon the example of Christian martyrs in urging Spaniards to make sacrifices, and even to die if

---

⁹¹ Chuquet, *op. cit.,* pp. 444–45, based upon a report from Representative Delbrel.
⁹² Wallon, *op. cit.,* p. 390.
⁹³ Chuquet, *op. cit.,* pp. 445–46; also Angel O. Gallardo, "Historia del pensamiento politico catalán durante la guerra de España con la Republica francesa," *Revista arch., bibl. y mus.,* XXIX (1913), 127–33.
⁹⁴ Pelleport, *op. cit.,* pp. 248–49. He also reported anxiety of French soldiers to return home.
⁹⁵ Delbrel defended La Union and gave a graphic account of his difficulties in "L'Espagne et la Révolution française," *loc. cit.,* XLVII, 644–62. See also Chuquet, *op. cit.,* pp. 445–47.

necessary for religion, *patrie,* and royalty.⁹⁶ All his proclamations expressed these same sentiments, and he accused the French armies of destruction of sanctuaries, persons, and property, and of letting their horses trample cemeteries. La Union did make a distinction between Frenchmen in general and this "revolutionary madness."⁹⁷

While negotiations were still going on over the return of French prisoners, and Dugommier began to threaten to take no prisoners, San Sebastian was captured by the French in July 1794. Two quite different accounts of what happened were reported. On August 13, 1794, after the fall of Robespierre, the *Moniteur* printed a report from the Pyrenees that freedom of religion was proclaimed, a tax levied on the clergy and nobles, and tithe and seigniorial dues suppressed. Proclamations denouncing the Spanish king were posted. The report closed with the warning that clergy and nobles would be held as hostages if La Union did not return French prisoners. The Convention voted to print this report.⁹⁸ Nine months later, Tallien, one of the chief enemies of Robespierre, reported atrocities committed at San Sebastian: arrest of the local representative body, imprisonment of priests and nuns, violations of women, mutilation of some of the inhabitants, and pillage and destruction of property.⁹⁹ Two French scholars who have used local papers and records attested less severe treatment of San Sebastian than Tallien, but church ornaments were sent to Paris, a Jacobin policy which, naturally enough, was denounced by Spanish Catholics.¹⁰⁰ Popular belief in French terrorist action, even if exaggerated or unjustified, would explain the passive resistance of the Spaniards, which in turn aggravated the conquerors, who needed food and supplies. Food speculation seems to have been carried on both by French and Spanish at San Sebastian. Godoy claimed in his memoirs that the surrender of San Sebastian was not a defeat of the Spanish army but due to treason of some Biscayans.¹⁰¹

⁹⁶ Delbrel, *loc. cit.,* XLVII, 649–50.
⁹⁷ *Ibid.,* XLVIII, 60–61 (from provincial Spanish archives).
⁹⁸ *Moniteur,* XXI, 458.
⁹⁹ *Ibid.,* XXIV, 230–31, April 18, 1795.
¹⁰⁰ Antonio Richard, *Le Gouvernement révolutionnaire dans les Basses-Pyrénées* (Paris, 1923), especially pp. 225–29; Jean Barada, "Un Épisode de l'invasion française en Espagne, 1794," *Revue historique et archéologique du Béarn et du pays basque,* IX (1908), 299. The latter recounted treatment of a priest and others with him.
¹⁰¹ Godoy, *op. cit.,* I, 337.

French Jacobin Nationalism and Spain 225

The fall of Robespierre in Thermidor (July 27–28, 1794) did not result in a change of policy toward Spain. The new Committee of Public Safety was assured by the representatives on mission of the loyalty of the army of the Pyrenees not alone to Robespierrist Jacobinism, but to the Republic, their *patrie*.[102] In behalf of the new Committee, Carnot issued instructions to the generals and representatives on mission, exhorting officers to maintain discipline (perhaps an admission of excesses) and to destroy arms manufacture in conquered territory, and authorizing the requisition of horses, mules, sheep, cloth, leather, and food for the army. Pillage was denounced, and the inhabitants were to be assured of life, property, and even "their prejudices" (their religion). Only the rich were to be taxed. The aim should be to make the Spanish repent of their violation of the surrender terms of Collioure and return French prisoners. The instructions ended with advice to use young soldiers to harvest crops in the conquered territory, or volunteers from the territory, who would receive a share as reward.[103] Carnot's instructions showed consideration for the conquered Spaniards, but also the policy of making the war pay for itself. These conciliatory instructions were, however, secret. French public opinion and the National Convention were still aroused against Spain because of the failure to return French prisoners, and on August 10 the National Convention voted war *à outrance* and authorized the taking of no Spanish prisoners until French prisoners had been released. It was Barère again who read the reports from the Pyrenees, aroused the Convention with his Jacobin eloquence, and proposed the motion. The next day, he further inflamed the Convention by quoting the Spanish general, La Union, who had referred to France as the "*prétendu république.*"[104] Warnings that no prisoners would be taken were printed in Spanish. Thereafter, as the Spanish retreated, they seem to have adopted a scorched-earth policy.

In August 1794, the situation in Spain was becoming increasingly critical, with the Spanish army in retreat on all fronts. Godoy began highly secret peace feelers, but published a patriotic appeal to the Spaniards. He pled for loyalty to king and religion, and branded

---

[102] *Recueil des actes du comité de salut public,* Vol. V/XV, report of Cavaignac and Garrau, of Aug. 2, 1794.
[103] *Ibid.,* V/XV, 795–96, Aug. 9, 1794.
[104] *Moniteur,* XXI, 464, Aug. 13, 1794, and XXI, 469, Aug. 14, 1794.

as false reports painting France and the Revolutionary regime as desirable. He asserted that Spain was stronger than France, and that the French armies used only terror, death, and the guillotine to force obedience. He called the French "slaves"—a favorite Jacobin term for the Spaniards. By contrast, said Godoy, Spaniards were freemen, and Charles IV headed patriotic Spaniards who were good Catholics. Spaniards should imitate the king's zeal and fight to destroy the "troop of bandits." The proclamation ended with an appeal for prayers for victory. When a small section of this proclamation was printed in the *Moniteur* in October 1794, French forces were advancing on Spanish soil in an aggressive spirit, and Parisians reading the appeal would consider it evidence of Spanish arrogance and blindness.[105] Godoy's words seem to have aroused Spanish patriotism and firmer support for the war, but defeatism in the army itself grew as the French victorious advance continued.[106]

While Spain was taking drastic action to stem the French advance and to combat defeatism, a newspaper published for the army of the Pyrenees was bolstering morale among French soldiers, and developing a belief in the invincibility of republican armies.[107] At the head of the issue of *L'Avant-garde de l'armée des Pyrénées orientales* for August 22, 1794, was the quotation: "Liberty is the mother of all virtues, of order, and of the permanence of a state; slavery, on the

---

[105] On early peace maneuvers, see Chuquet, *op. cit.*, p. 451; A. Sorel, "La Diplomatie française et l'Espagne, " *loc. cit.*, XI, 315–16; Delbrel, "L'Espagne et la Révolution française," *loc. cit.*, XLVIII, 62. On the war in July and August, see Gustav Bord, "Notes du conventionnel Delbrel sur l'armée des Pyrénées orientales," *Revue de la Révolution*, V (1885), 18–30, 49–61, 82–87, 100–13, 132–38; reference from pp. 18–30. For reprint of Godoy's appeal, see De Marcillac, *op. cit.*, pp. 73–78; *Moniteur*, XXII, 261, Oct. 21, 1794.

[106] The Navarrese cortes voted conscription, more *émigrés* volunteered (although they may have been more trouble than help), volunteers from other provinces of Spain came forward, and patriotic gifts once again were offered. The Spanish royal council refused to grant La Union the power to use the death penalty and other drastic measures to restore army discipline. See Delbrel, "L'Espagne et la Révolution française," *loc. cit.*, XLVII, 644–62. Père Delbrel, in defending La Union, claimed that subordinate Spanish officers had succumbed to Revolutionary propaganda (p. 647).

[107] *L'Avant-garde de l'armée des Pyrénées orientales*, appearing Feb. 23, 1794–Sept. 6, 1794, was continued as the *Journal de l'armée des Pyrénées orientales* on into 1795. See Eugène Hatin, *Bibliographie de la presse périodique* (Paris, 1866), pp. 244–45. Aulard cited these newspapers in his article, "La Presse sous la Terreur," in *Études et leçons*, Vol. I. See also Gérard Walter, *Catalogue des journaux révolutionnaires, 1789–1799* (Paris, 1943), item no. 117 on p. 130, and item no. 630 on p. 274. The Harvard Library possesses nos. 37, 39–41 of *L'Avant-garde*, and nos. 16–20 of the *Journal*.

contrary, produces only vices, cowardice and misery."[108] Each issue, in octavo of eight pages, gave an account in Jacobin terms of the fighting, emphasizing the heroism of the French, and reporting victories of small numbers of French soldiers over vastly superior numbers of Spaniards. "History will say to future generations that the courage and patriotism of the French saved, in an instant, the liberty of the world," and, further on, "The terrible volcano of the vengeance of *sans-culottes* will cover lands and destroy the support for despots, and will force them, on their knees, to ask for peace which will be granted only to friends of liberty and defenders of the People." Barère had used similar words in the Convention in the preceding month.[109] Each number of *L'Avant-garde* also reported the activities of the civil administration. The evolution of French militarist spirit could be traced in these army papers. By December 1794, the same number of the *Journal* that explained the need for more French soldiers, necessitated by draft-dodgers and malingerers, stated that there were "still laurels to gather," and "It is not enough to chase Spaniards from the territory of the republic, it is necessary to make them tremble for their own homes."[110] Adverse reports were branded as false rumors spread by aristocrats and enemies of the Republic.[111] These papers circulating in the Pyrenees region are a valuable supplement to reports of representatives and generals published as part of later debates in the National Convention, subsequently in memoirs, or much later in official collections of documents. There was often a striking resemblance between the language of the army papers and Jacobin oratory in the Jacobin Club or the Convention.[112]

Bellegarde, the last portion of French soil held by the Spanish, was recaptured in September 1794, but the French government continued to say that it would not treat with an enemy occupying

---

[108] No. 37 (5 fructidor, an II).

[109] *L'Avant-garde*, no. 40, 20 fructidor, an II (Sept. 6, 1794), pp. 351–52. Barère used the simile of a volcano on August 11 (*Moniteur*, XXI, 460, Aug. 13, 1794). Newspapers for the army received official subsidies and direction.

[110] *Journal de l'armée des Pyrénées orientales*, no. 16, 10 nivôse, an III (Dec. 30, 1794), p. 62.

[111] *Ibid.*, no. 18 (19 nivôse, an III), p. 69, and no. 20 (27 nivôse, an III), p. 77.

[112] Compare especially issues cited with *Moniteur*, XX, 459–60, Aug. 13, 1794. Barère was challenged in the Convention as a Robespierrist in December 1794.

French soil. Since Spain had still refused to carry out the capitulation agreements of Collioure, there were no direct communications between the two armies, and Godoy was forced to use circuitous methods for the successive secret proposals that he began to initiate in the fall of 1794. La Union refused to transmit his suggestion that a French republic be set up in the French West Indies and France itself restored to the monarchy, for the Spanish general recognized that the Revolutionaries would insist on a republic in France. Delays and difficulties arose over the employment of Simonin, the French paymaster for French prisoners, as envoy between the two countries. Strict secrecy was maintained on both sides. In October 1794, Spanish anxiety for the Bourbons was shown in the proposal that a kingdom be created for Louis XVII between France and Spain, and in November a revised plan at last promised recognition of the French Republic, but also stipulated that the royal children be sent to Spain and a frontier province given to Louis XVII. This last proposition was delayed in reaching the Committee of Public Safety until November 16 because of the movements of the representative on mission to whom it was conveyed. The Committee sensed the storm of public protest that the publication of the Spanish proposal would arouse, and only increased its demand for prosecution of the war on Spain. At this time, both the Spanish and the French governments were aware of the increasing difficulty of waging the war and wished to continue negotiations, but the French Committee was in no mood to compromise on the fundamental point of recognition of the Republic. On November 21, the Committee of Public Safety commanded the French army to reply to the Spanish with cannon.[113]

"*Frappez*"—"strike"— was the order of the French government. Although Dugommier lost his life on November 17, and La Union three days later, the French armies continued their advance and, after siege, captured the fortified city of Figuèras on November 28, 1794. Its rich stores were much needed by the French army, which had been hampered by the scorched-earth policy and the difficulties of transport of supplies. Republican virtues claimed by the French were not displayed. Discipline broke down and pillage was rampant

[113] Chuquet, *op. cit.*, pp. 448–64; A. Sorel, "La Diplomatie française et l'Espagne," *loc. cit.*, XI, 317, 320–24; Delbrel, "L'Espagne et la Révolution française," *loc. cit.*, XLVIII, 285–92.

until a soldier caught in the act was summarily executed. Discipline and order were gradually restored.[114] Delbrel, the representative on mission to the army, claimed surprise on the part of French and Spanish alike that so strong a fortress should be captured. The Spanish general attributed French success to the lack of strong fighting spirit among the Spanish soldiers and to the strength of republican zeal in the French army.[115] In his memoirs, Godoy ascribed French victory to the new French technique of undermining the morale of the enemy's army.[116]

In the terms of surrender, priests were to be held as hostages because of the failure to return French prisoners after Collioure, the Spanish were to identify any French *émigrés* captured or found in the city, and Article IX promised protection to civilians and property. Pérignon, who had succeeded to the command after the death of Dugommier, was later reported to have claimed that no clause guaranteeing humanity of treatment to the defeated Spaniards was necessary since the laws of the French Republic enjoined humane conduct.[117] The *Moniteur* printed the glowing account of the capture of Figuèras sent by French officials, and the surrender terms read in the Convention on December 5, 1794, but the subsequent reports of Delbrel, recounting pillage and terror, remained among the files of the Committee of Public Safety to be published later.[118] As far as the Convention and the French public knew, a great French victory had been achieved, and republican patriotism was further stimulated. When, in April 1795, Tallien condemned the treatment of Spaniards at San Sebastian as Robespierrist severity, he barely mentioned Catalonia, for whose bad treatment the Thermidorians were responsible. The French public long remained ignorant of the reprehensible conduct of its army in Spain in December 1794.

The fall of Figuèras contributed further to a belief among the Spanish in the invincibility of French armies. Vittoria in the west

---

[114] Bord, *op. cit.*, pp. 82–102. Delbrel, the representative on mission, did not blame the military authorities, but also claimed for himself credit for restoration of discipline.
[115] *Ibid.*, pp. 85–87.
[116] Godoy, *op. cit.*, I, 350–51: "l'art de frapper le moral de l'ennemi."
[117] De Marcillac, *op. cit.*, pp. 293–98; Bord, *op. cit.*, pp. 82–87. See *ibid.*, pp. 82–84, for the text of the surrender terms.
[118] *Moniteur*, XXII, 679–80, Dec. 8, 1794. One report mentioned the killing of Spanish soldiers (no prisoners were to be taken), but these reports dealt with the victory and not with events after the capture.

was soon captured, but Rosas, which would be useful for transport of provisions by sea into Catalonia, held out until February 1795.[119]

The Thermidorian government did not immediately change Robespierrist foreign policy, and was responsible for the command to strike further into Spain in November 1794, and for events in Catalonia. The Foreign Office was reorganized, however, and Otto, who had had experience in Spanish affairs, was placed in charge of the department dealing with Spain; Simonin, who had insisted in his negotiations on republican directness and *tutoiement,* was repudiated. Although the Committee of Public Safety was keeping channels for peace negotiation open, it was not until early in March 1795 that Goupilleau-Fontenay, a Thermidorian, was sent to replace the former representatives on mission, with secret instructions as to the necessity for peace. Two envoys, of whom Bourgoing was one, were sent to negotiate under his supervision. Albert Sorel has described in detail the intricate negotiations that culminated in the Treaty of Basle, the Spanish phase of the pacification policy of the Thermidorians, and he ascribed to them the same singleness of purpose—*raison d'état*—and diplomatic methods as those of governments of the old regime.[120] It would seem, however, that the Revolutionary government paid more attention to public opinion than had Bourbon monarchs, if indeed a public opinion existed before 1789. Investigators of public spirit in Paris in the spring of 1795 reported strong republicanism, but also a growing demand for peace.[121] In April 1795, the National Convention disavowed the cruel treatment of Spaniards at San Sebastian, and reassured the inhabitants of Biscaya.[122] The Committee of Public Safety and the Foreign Office, in their secret discussions, ceased to talk of annexation of Biscaya, and instead began to evince a desire for Louisiana.

After devious and protracted negotiations, monarchist Spain and Republican France signed the Peace of Basle on June 22, 1795, and

[119] Fervel, *op. cit.,* pp. 226–67; Bord, *op. cit.,* pp. 103–12.
[120] See A. Sorel, "La Diplomatie française et l'Espagne," *loc. cit.,* XII, 279–313, XIII, 41–80, and especially XII, 288–94, on instructions to Goupilleau. See also Sorel's *L'Europe et la Révolution française,* Vol. IV, Book III, Chapters III and IV. The introductory chapters of the latter work, dealing with the diplomacy of the old regime in Europe, have appeared in English translation by Francis Herrick, *Europe under the Old Regime* (Los Angeles, 1947).
[121] Adolphe Schmidt, *Tableaux de la Révolution* (3 vols., Leipzig, 1867–70), especially II, 328, report of 10 floréal, an III (May 2, 1795). See also Pierre Caron, *Paris pendant la Terreur* (3 vols., Paris, 1910–42), Vol. III, *passim.*
[122] See above, pp. 224, 229.

there was rejoicing on both sides of the Pyrenees.¹²³ While Parisians were impatient and anxious over delays in ratification, the National Convention, which had originally declared war on Spain, finally approved the treaty on August 1, after more than a month's delay, and Charles IV ratified it on August 4, 1795.¹²⁴

The *Moniteur* published the seventeen articles of the treaty, but not its three secret articles. Treilhard, who reported the treaty, asked that it be printed and distributed before discussion of its terms, and this was voted, but before the Convention turned to other matters, Tallien, who in April 1795 had sponsored the denunciation of ruthlessness, asked that news of the signing of the treaty be sent to all departments and to the armies in order to counteract operations of speculators and to reassure republican public opinion.¹²⁵ This was done.

According to the published articles of the treaty, fighting was to cease as soon as ratifications had been exchanged. During the delay, the French army had advanced further into Spain. Both sides were so anxious for peace that both agreed to compromises. Spain recognized the French Republic in return for re-cession of Spanish territory occupied by French troops. Spain ceded Spanish Saint Domingue, but the treaty said nothing about Louisiana. Confiscated property and money were to be restored by both governments to the nationals of the other. All merchants were to engage in trade again under the terms of the Family Pact, until a new trade treaty was negotiated. All prisoners of war were to be returned, irrespective of the number held. Neither country was to allow foreign troops to use its territory or enemy ships [tacit] to use its ports. Spain recognized Holland as an ally of France, and France accepted mediation of Spain in respect to peace with Portugal, Naples, Sardinia, Parma, and other Italian states. France also agreed to accept Spain's "good offices" to negotiate a general European peace. The exact boundaries between France and Spain were left for a border commission.

---

¹²³ In addition to A. Sorel, already cited, see reports of the Russian ambassador to Spain, Tratchevsky, *op. cit.*, p. 43 (Godoy was made Prince of the Peace), and also the *Moniteur*, XXVI, 41, Sept. 28, 1795.

¹²⁴ See reports of agents, Schmidt, *op. cit.*, II, 380 (12 thermidor, an III—July 30, 1795), and p. 392 (29 thermidor, an III—Aug. 16, 1795). On ratifications, see *Moniteur*, XXV, 366, 390, 534, 563, 603, and XXVI, 41.

¹²⁵ *Moniteur*, XXVI, 366, meeting of July 29, in issue of Aug. 3, 1795. The Convention approved Tallien's proposal, but rejected the severe punishment of speculators asked by Dubois-Crancé.

The secret articles, which both parties agreed were to have equal force with the public articles, included a special concession for France to import Spanish sheep and horse studs for five years, intervention of Charles IV in Vienna in behalf of the daughter of Louis XVI, and acceptance of Spanish mediation between France and the Papacy.[126] Public opinion might have been critical of the second and third secret clauses.

In the omissions, and the secret clauses, and in the relations of Spain with England and other European countries, were the seeds of further war, but both countries gained time for internal reconstruction by the conclusion of peace. As Treilhard, in introducing the treaty, said, "There was now one enemy less and one more ally."[127] The Directory could start its career with peace instead of a war begun by its predecessors. In objectives and diplomatic methods, however, the Directory pursued Jacobin nationalism. The grandiloquent announcement of the Directory that it would "consolidate the Republic and reawaken patriotism" may have been prompted more by the war on England than by relations with the powers with whom peace had recently been signed, but it expressed aggressive defense and propagation of Jacobin nationalism.[128] Ambassadors were to wear the cockade and, after July 1796, a costume designed by David. They were to be addressed as "citizen" and were expected to set an example of republican virtue.[129] General Pérignon, the victorious commander of the Spanish campaign, was sent as ambassador to Madrid. Although Pérignon himself did not typify Jacobinism, an indiscreet first secretary, Mangourit, did, and his conduct was one of several factors that embroiled the new allies. In March 1796, in one of Mangourit's unofficial letters to the Foreign Office,

---

[126] The full text of the treaty is given by Alexandre J. H. de Clercq and Jules de Clercq, *Recueil des traités de la France depuis 1713 jusqu'à nos jours* (21 vols., Paris, 1864–1905), I, 248–49. On the secret articles, as well as discussion of the treaty, see Raymond Guyot, *Le Directoire et la paix de l'Europe* (Paris, 1911), p. 236. Louis XVII had died in the spring of 1795.

[127] *Moniteur*, XXXVI, 366, Aug. 3, 1795.

[128] Emile Bourgeois, *Manuel historique de politique étrangère* (4 vols., Paris, 1898), II, 139. See also Charles Ballot, "La politique extérieure du Directoire," *Revue d'histoire moderne et contemporaine*, XIX (1914), 117–28. Guyot, already cited, corrected A. Sorel by use of added sources, and treated of propaganda elsewhere, but gave little on Spain. See also A. Dry (Fleury), *Soldats ambassadeurs sous le Directoire* (Paris, 1906), Vol. I.

[129] Masson, *op. cit.*, pp. 378–79, and on costumes, p. 360. See also Guyot, *op. cit.*, p. 92.

French Jacobin Nationalism and Spain 233

he stated that the French were popular in Spain.[130] It was at this time that a pamphlet, *Pan y toros,* written anonymously by Jovanellos, a famous, enlightened Spanish author, which satirized to some degree the Spanish clergy, the government, and economic conditions, and especially condemned bull-fighting, was circulating in Spain.[131]

Pérignon was instructed to seek an alliance with Spain and to urge measures against French *émigrés.* Negotiations were slow, both because the Directory wanted an immediate cession of Louisiana and a declaration of war on England, and because Godoy was simultaneously trying to establish friendly relations with England. Scandals in the French embassy at Madrid and difficulties over the *émigrés* further complicated negotiations. France began to increase her demands, but Pérignon indicated the impossibility of further concession by Spain, and a treaty of alliance was signed at San Ildefonso, on August 19, 1796, and ratifications exchanged on September 12.[132]

The treaty contained nineteen public articles and six secret ones. Among the published articles, Spain agreed to declare war on England within four months, and both parties guaranteed mutual defense of their European and colonial territory. Article XVIII further recognized that the main aim was mutual aid against England by affirming Spanish neutrality as regards other European countries. The military and naval articles were quite specific. Among the secret articles were extension of the alliance to include Holland, and invitation to other powers to sign, the promise of Spain not to use *émigrés* on Spanish ships, and to apply pressure on Portugal to close her ports to England, use of colonial ports in case of war, and the same privilege for France to cut timber as England already enjoyed.[133] The objective of mutual aid against England was

[130] "Extrait d'une dépêche du citoyen Mangourit," from Madrid, 12 ventôse, an IV (March 2, 1796), ms. Arch. Nat. AF III 62, dossier 246, plaque 1. On Mangourit and the ambassadorship of Pérignon, see Grandmaison, *op. cit.,* pp. 117-26. Mangourit was a Freemason.

[131] The pamphlet is available at the New York Public Library in an edition published in Madrid, 1820, in-12, 47 pages. See comment by Russian ambassador in Tratchevsky, *op. cit.,* pp. 48-49. Jovanellos showed no sign of Revolutionary influence, but Frenchmen would have criticized the same conditions in Spain.

[132] Guyot, *op. cit.,* pp. 235-39, 240-43. Guyot warned against Grandmaison as being inaccurate on this treaty of alliance, p. 243, note 3. See also A. Sorel, "La Diplomatie française et l'Espagne," *loc. cit.,* XIII, 241-78.

[133] *Moniteur,* XXVIII, 427-28, Sept. 14, 1796, for published terms; full text, De Clercq, *op. cit.,* I, 287-91.

achieved, but the treaty was silent about Louisiana, a new trade treaty had not yet been negotiated, and the boundary had not yet been drawn.

In 1789, France and Spain had been allies. Now again, in the summer of 1796, they were allies, despite the differences between their internal regimes. Spain ceased to support the *émigrés* and to make efforts in behalf of the Bourbons, and the French government ceased attempts to convert the Spanish to republicanism and other Jacobin ideas. Although there appeared to have been some revival in Spain of Freemasonry and of societies advocating social and economic reform, there was no longer a French government policy to propagandize Spain.[134] The report of the Danish ambassador of February 1799 that the Spanish king had learned the French Constitution by heart, and wore to diplomatic gatherings a white satin vest with the text printed on it, indicated friendship between the two countries, and a very different attitude on the part of Charles IV from his hostility and efforts to prevent the spread of French Revolutionary ideas between 1792 and 1796.[135]

In the summer of 1804, a French citizen from Rouen, Charles Tarbé, who had been deputy to the National Assembly and imprisoned for his support of monarchy during the Terror, journeyed to Spain for the commercial interests of Rouenais merchants. Twenty-two letters written from Spain and from Lisbon have been preserved by his brother's descendants.[136] These letters, written to one of Tarbé's brothers, are as illuminating about Spain as were the travels of Arthur Young about France and the corner of Spain he visited. Tarbé's letters are cited here because, though a keen observer, he gave no evidence of French Revolutionary influence during his journey from Bayonne to Madrid, thence to Cadiz, and overland to the Portuguese border. His remarks on the Spanish peasants foreshadowed their patriotism during the Peninsular War. Spanish

---

[134] Grandmaison, *op. cit.*, pp. 117, 134–42; Guyot, *op. cit.*, p. 551; Tratchevsky, *op. cit.*, p. 4. The *Moniteur* ascribed reforms in Spain to Cabarrus, XXIX, 69, Nov. 24, 1797.

[135] E. Gigas, "Lettres d'un diplomate danois en Espagne (1798–1800)," *Revue hispanique*, XXII (1910), 393–439, and citation from dispatch of Schubart, p. 404. Denmark had helped bring France and Spain together to negotiate the treaty of Basle.

[136] A notebook containing copies of these letters, of which the originals have disappeared, is in the hands of Tarbé-Saint Hardouin of Paris. The author has obtained microfilm and will publish them. The letters were not mentioned by Foulché-Delbosc in his bibliography of travels in Spain.

Catholicism had not changed since the travels of Bourgoing and was ardently supported by the Spanish people. Tarbé noted the independent spirit of the Catalans, and described provincial differences of other areas traversed. There had been many Frenchmen in Spain in 1789, but only once did Tarbé report meeting a compatriot—a French lady married to a Spaniard. His attention to her may have been prompted in part by gallantry, but it also breathed loneliness, and the joy of meeting a countryman in a foreign land. The omission of reference to French merchants during this visit for mercantile affairs would seem to indicate a paucity of Frenchmen in Spain. The absence of French Revolutionary influences reported by Tarbé implies either that Jacobin nationalism did not spread in Spain, or that there was much less Jacobin propaganda than its Spanish opponents and some of its Jacobin sponsors affirmed.

There is little doubt that Jacobin nationalism was propagandist within France and also in some conquered areas.[137] Spanish nationalism and localism formed barriers against French Revolutionary ideas, and the Spanish government itself attempted propaganda in behalf of monarchy and Catholicism, with aid afforded counter-revolutionaries. There is little doubt that Jacobins such as Barère aimed at propagandizing Spain, but evidence is still lacking that much was actually done. The Spanish invasion of France distracted the Jacobins from the propagation of liberty, equality, and secularism, and necessitated military effort. The French seem to have been more concerned to undermine Spanish morale and support for the war than to attack Spanish institutions. During the French invasion of Spain, the policy pursued resembled that of any conquering army, rather than a Revolutionary crusade.

The most outstanding evidences of propaganda in the foregoing narrative were drawn either from the reports of Fabre, Delbrel, or other deputies on mission, or from the Reverend Père Delbrel, the nineteenth-century Jesuit who based his narrative on these reports and the private archives of La Union. Fabre and his associates, who

---

[137] Terry demonstrated the thesis of A. Sorel that the French armies were propagandist only when victorious, and described the techniques used (*op. cit.*, p. 192). These included proclamations to the inhabitants, financial levies on the privileged classes, the formation of pro-French clubs, sending of French civilians to fraternize with the inhabitants, and the introduction of such Revolutionary customs as the planting of liberty trees and the wearing of the liberty cap. Terry used the Austrian Netherlands as his chief illustration, and devoted only two pages to Spain.

had instructions to use propaganda, naturally wished to report their efforts, while Delbrel, the Jesuit, was defending La Union against his Spanish critics and pictured him as a hero of the counterrevolution. This later Delbrel claimed a vast, systematic propaganda,[138] but convincing evidence is still lacking to substantiate these extreme allegations.

At the beginning of this chapter, it was pointed out that the results of the study would be tentative, and that further research along several lines needs to be done. Spanish national and local archives, Spanish newspapers, private archives and memoirs, the records of the Inquisition, the diplomatic correspondence of other nations (such as Austria, Venice, or Denmark before 1798) than those already published, records of the War Office and the army, should reveal information not presented in existing Spanish histories. On the French side, a re-examination of certain material in the archives of the Ministry of Foreign Affairs and of the Archives Nationales, comparison of typical French newspapers, and especially those subsidized by the government, a study of the items that the Convention, the Committee of Public Safety, and the Jacobin Club voted to print in Spanish, a re-examination of archives of the Pyrenees region, local newspapers, and local clubs, should all provide information overlooked or ignored by previous investigators.

The present essay has assembled considerable material attesting Jacobin nationalist propaganda, but also has presented a challenge to the claims of some authorities. It may be said, however, that there are two histories: what actually happened, and what was believed to have happened. There is little doubt that the Spanish government feared French propaganda, and took steps to prevent its spread. There is insufficient evidence that the propaganda was either as extensive or as dangerous as the Spanish government believed. A passage from Sorel's classic volumes is significant here:

They [members of the coalition against France] felt the influence of this Revolution penetrate their countries. The organized propaganda of the Jacobins was only a phantasmagoria, and the police could stop it from entering; but there was another propaganda, unseizable and insinuating,

---

[138] Delbrel, "L'Espagne et la Révolution française," *loc. cit.*, XLVIII, 67–77. At the end of his study, Père Delbrel cited the treatment of Fabre and Louvet as forgotten heroes of the Revolution, and was inspired to write on La Union (*op. cit.*, November 1889, p. 450).

against which there existed neither customs barriers nor sanitary cordons: this was the propaganda of example, that which operated by the sole reverberation of the war. Newspapers, even censored, which preached the struggle against the Revolution, spread among the people the notion of that revolution that declared all men equal and which freed the peasant from seigniorial dues. Nothing more was necessary for the Revolution in France to carry its echo to the extremities of Europe. Everywhere that there was unrest and misery, everywhere that the seigniorial regime was abusive, where taxes were heavy and unjustly apportioned, everywhere that the aristocracy was odious and governments detested, France found adherents and imitators.[139]

Sorel ignored the obstacle of illiteracy, the repercussions of the bad example French soldiers set at San Sebastian and Figuèras, and the fact that any subtle influence by example may have applied less to Spain than to other European countries. The reaction of Spaniards to the French Revolution strengthened their nationalism and bore fruit in their resistance to Napoleonic rule. Once again, there were the Pyrenees, and Spain evolved in the nineteenth century, despite periodic intervention, largely independent of European developments. During this period only a minority of Spaniards ever challenged the monarchy or the Catholic Church, twin pillars of Spanish nationalism.

CHRONOLOGICAL TABLE

Date	General Events	Franco-Spanish Relations
1789		
July 14	Capture of Bastille	
	Beginning of emigration	
November	Confiscation of church property	Two weeks' expulsion of foreigners from Madrid
December		Prohibition of French publications Cortes of Madrid
1790		
May	Discussion of powers of king	Nootka Sound controversy
May 22	Renunciation of war	
August	New diplomatic committee	
October		Nuñez dispatch warning of Revolutionary propaganda
October 28		Treaty of Escorial between Spain and England
November	Civil oath required of clergy	

[139] A. Sorel, *L'Europe et la Révolution française*, IV, 2.

CHRONOLOGICAL TABLE (continued)

Date	General Events	Franco-Spanish Relations
1791		
June	Flight of royal family	
July	Declaration of Pilnitz	Renunciation of French citizenship or leave Spain
September	Louis XVI takes oath of Constitution	Report of French constitutions in Madrid
		Report of Spain from Perpignan
October	Opening of Legislative Assembly Discussion on *émigrés* begins	Censorship tightened
November	Louis XVI vetoes decrees on *émigrés* and non-juring clergy	
December	Ultimatum on *émigrés* in Rhineland	
1792		
January	Isnard denounces kings Fauchet on peace between peoples	
February		Fall of Floridablanca; Aranda minister
March	Roland ministry	Spanish declaration of neutrality
April	War on Austria	
June	Dismissal of Roland ministry	
July	Duke of Brunswick's Manifesto	
August	Insurrection of August 10	Instructions on reporting August 10
September	Opening of National Convention Declaration of Republic Battle of Valmy	
October	Girondist propaganda	Condorcet's *Avis aux espagnols* Mission to Pyrenees region
November		Spain forbids French clergy to preach
	1st Propagandist decree	Aranda falls, Godoy minister Foreign embassies to avoid propaganda
December	2nd Propagandist decree	Enforcement of anti-French measures Movement of troops to frontier by both parties
1793		
January	Execution of Louis XVI	Memorial service in Madrid for Louis XVI
February	French declare war on England and Holland	Spanish hostility to French in Spain
		Perpignan takes local measures of defense
March 7		French declaration of war on Spain
March 21		Spanish declaration of war on France Expulsion of French from Spain

CHRONOLOGICAL TABLE *(continued)*

Date	General Events	Franco-Spanish Relations
1793 (continued)		
April	Decree of April 13 against intervention Treason of Dumouriez Organization of Committee of Public Safety, etc.	Preparations for war
May	Committee of Twelve created	Spanish invasion of French soil Ricardos' declaration to French
June	Overthrow of Girondists Large sums to Ministry of Foreign Affairs for propaganda	Inventory of French property in Spain
July	Constitution of 1793 Assassination of Marat	Threat of Ricardos against guerrilla warfare Perpignan celebration of July 14
August	Robespierre added to C. of P. S. *Levée en masse* English capture Toulon	Ricardos' promise of trade to French Anti-French decrees in Spain
September	Revolutionary legislation	
October	Execution of Marie Antoinette	Ariège plot against Republic
November	Worship of Reason inaugurated	Spanish clergy active to stimulate Spanish patriotism
December	Constitution of Terror decreed French recapture Toulon	Severe censorship of Spanish press Spanish capture Collioure
1794		
January		Dugommier takes command against Spain Spanish celebration of January 21
February	Ventôse decrees	
March	Fall of Hébertists	Crisis in Spanish royal council
April	Fall of Dantonists	
May		French invade Spanish soil Capture of Boulou and Collioure Fete of Reason at Perpignan Proclamation of Dugommier to Spanish
June	Worship of Supreme Being Law of 22nd prairial Battle of Fleurus	Large number of Spaniards surrender Trouble over failure of Spanish to return French prisoners
July	Capture of Antwerp Fall of Robespierrists Thermidorian period begins	Spanish declaration to Catalans Spanish *levée en masse* French capture San Sebastian
August	Thermidorian reaction	Reports to Convention of Republican victories. War *à outrance* Proclamation of Godoy to Spanish

CHRONOLOGICAL TABLE *(continued)*

Date	General Events	Franco-Spanish Relations
1794 (continued)		
September		Fall of Bellegarde to French
October		French pillage; French advance
November	Jacobin Clubs closed	Deaths of Dugommier and La Union French ordered to "strike"
December	Girondists readmitted to Convention	Further French advance in Spain
	Pichegru invades Holland	French capture Figuèras
		Peace moves
1795		
January	Pichegru occupies Amsterdam	Danish mediation
February	Treaty of peace with Tuscany	Fall of Rosas
March	Trial of Barère, Vadier, Billaud, Collot	Sending of Goupilleau-Fontenay
April	Treaty of Basle with Prussia	Tallien condemns ruthlessness at San Sebastian
May	Treaty of peace with Holland	
June	Death of Louis XVII	Treaty of Basle completed (June 22)
July	Treaty with U.S.A.	
August 1 and 4		Treaty of Basle ratified
November	Directory begins	
1796		
March	Napoleon in command in Italy	Pérignon is French ambassador
August 19		Treaty of San Ildefonso
September 12		Treaty of San Ildefonso ratified

NATIONALISM AND HISTORY IN THE PRUSSIAN ELEMENTARY SCHOOLS UNDER WILLIAM II

WALTER CONSUELO LANGSAM

DURING the nineteenth century the rise of national consciousness among the peoples of the Western world and the increasing interest of governments in popular education were closely linked. Astute officials sensed in directed public education an effective stimulus of nationalism. With the advantage of hindsight, it is obvious today that this close relation between the instruction of youth and the development in it of a fervent national spirit may not always react to the benefit of mankind.

Nationalistic indoctrination seems generally to involve the planting and nurturing of pride in the national culture, the national historical background, the record of national achievement in the various fields of human endeavor, and the national destiny. In theory, such pride would seem to be a wholly legitimate and useful emotion. It would seem capable of imbuing its possessors with a virtuous desire to live up to the splendid traditions of the nationality, to cherish the national heritage and emulate worthy ancestors, to carry forward the civilizing influences and the cultural "unfinished business" of the forefathers.

In practice, therefore, it becomes vitally important which exploits and contributions of the past are emphasized to the youth by its teachers, which examples of past action are held up for veneration and imitation. Simultaneously, since no nationality lives by itself but each lives among others, it becomes important that due recognition be given to the parallel developments in other countries. The national story, in other words, should be presented in its appropriate international setting.

When, however, the practice involves the singling-out for praise of war and conquest, when it makes exaggerated claims of national superiority and belittles other peoples, when it glorifies ruthlessness and a disregard for the rights of others, then this practice would seem to bring evil to mankind rather than good. Then it would seem that nationalistic indoctrination, far from being legitimate and wholesome, becomes merely a campaign of militaristic propaganda. Then education for nationalism would appear to be chiefly a device for preparing the youth to be slaves to a political state and to its greed for power over additional slaves of supposedly lesser breed.

A clear example of this unwholesome practice of nationalistic indoctrination was offered by the Nazis who controlled Germany from 1933 to 1945. In Nazi Germany the interrelation between education and nationalism was especially close. But the politicians of the Third Reich in this case had a sturdy foundation upon which to build—a foundation laid during the Second Reich, particularly in the Prussia of William II. The design of this foundation emerges clearly from the history instruction offered the youth of Prussia between 1888–1914, for history instruction is peculiarly suited to the indoctrination of a national spirit. Let us, therefore, briefly review the official aims of history instruction under William II, as well as the courses of study that were used and some of the widely circulated teachers' guides.

History was, for the first time, made a separate subject of instruction in the Prussian elementary schools through an official regulation of October 15, 1872.[1] Sixteen years later, with the accession of William II, the propagandist possibilities of the *Volksschule*, especially of its history curriculum, received royal recognition. William issued an order on May 1, 1889, which read in part: "For some time now I have been occupied with the idea of making the school in its various grades useful in combating the spread of socialistic and communistic [sic] ideas. In the first place, it will fall upon the school to lay the foundation for a healthy conception of political and social relations, through the cultivation of fear of God and love of country."[2]

Soon after receiving this communication, the Ministry of Education drafted an edict which set forth the official purposes and aims of history instruction. The following rules were drawn up for all schools, approved by William, and then issued in 1890:

[1] "Die allgemeine Verfügung, betreffend Einrichtung, Aufgabe und Ziel der preussischen Volksschule vom 15. Oktober 1872," in *Die preussische Volksschule. Gesetze und Verordnungen,* ed. by E. von Bremen (Stuttgart, Berlin, 1905), p. 655.

[2] "Allerhöchste Order vom 1. Mai 1889," *ibid.,* p. 230.

Nationalism and Prussian Schools 243

"1) The national history is, in all circumstances, to be carried up to the time of the accession of His Majesty William II; 2) such instruction is to be given in the middle as well as in the upper grades; 3) in the upper grades the efforts of the Prussian rulers on behalf of the popular welfare are to be given special emphasis; 4) where the particular conditions of a school necessitate some curtailment of instruction, this must not be done at the expense of modern history; rather, a later starting point in history must be chosen."[3]

"These regulations," continued the edict, "do not need special justification. German patriots, and in particular citizens of Prussia, are so fortunate as to have a country and a ruling dynasty of whose history they may well be proud. ... It would be a sin against the coming generation if we were to delay familiarizing it with the blessings which accrue to it by virtue of its connection with the Prussian state. It would be an equally great injustice to the state itself if an unpatriotic generation were reared."

In the same year the Potsdam government reminded its district school inspectors that "one of the most essential purposes of the *Volksschule* is to point out to the children the blessings which come to them through the regained national unity, independence, and culture which were restored by the hard and self-sacrificing struggle of the glorious Hohenzollern rulers." The school must make the children realize that "the national blessings can be retained only as long as the national features are preserved." Finally, the *Volksschule* must rear the children "as active members of German society, as self-denying subjects, and as men who will be glad to pay the supreme sacrifice for king and country."[4]

The implementation of these principles did not satisfy William. In December 1890 he addressed the opening session of a Prussian *Direktoren Konferenz*, saying that *"das Nationale"* needed much more emphasis in the schools than it was receiving. "We must bring up nationalistic young Germans, and not young Greeks or Romans. ... More than ever, the instruction in history must provide an understanding of the present, and especially an understanding of our country's position in the present. For this purpose, German

---

[3] "Staatsministerialbeschluss vom 27. Juli 1889," "Allerhöchste Order vom 30. August 1889," and "Allgemeine Verfügung vom 18. Oktober 1890," *ibid.,* pp. 236, 233, 661.

[4] *Verfügung der königlichen Regierung zu Potsdam vom 3. III. 1890.*

history, particularly that of modern and contemporary times, must be stressed more, whereas ancient and medieval history is to be taught primarily to prepare the pupils for heroic and historic greatness ... and to give them a view of the origins and development of our civilization."[5] Three years later the Minister of Education expressed his satisfaction over the progress which had been made in conformity with these principles.[6]

Obviously the aims of history instruction had to be impressed upon the future teachers—the persons who would share responsibility for the patriotic rearing of coming generations. Hence the following regulations were issued for teachers' training schools and seminaries:

"The aim [of history instruction in normal schools] is to give an accurate knowledge of the national history, an acquaintance with the most important events of ancient history, and a familiarity with the history of the great modern peoples insofar as this may be of consequence to the national history. Thus the students [future teachers] are to be led to impart, in turn, a form of history instruction to elementary school children that will develop in the latter a spirit of patriotism. . . . The future teachers should learn to understand and love the Fatherland, its laws, and its institutions, so that they may be able to awaken and foster a similar love for king and country in the hearts of their pupils."[7]

Finally, from the official point of view, the Minister of Education in 1908 resummarized the aim and content of history instruction, saying: "The time devoted to earlier and medieval German history is to be limited so as to include only a consideration of the more important biographies. . . . The main emphasis will be placed on modern national history, particularly on Prussian history. . . . Not only must the external political development of the state be portrayed, but the internal national development and the extensive social welfare arrangements are to be considered as well. . . . As the aim it must be kept constantly in mind that the children are to

[5] "Bericht der Direktoren Konferenz zu Berlin 1890," in the collection: *Verhandlungen der Direktoren-Versammlungen in den Provinzen des Königreichs Preussen seit dem Jahre 1879* (Berlin, 1879 ff).

[6] "Ministerial Erlass vom 22. August 1893," in Bremen, *op. cit.*, p. 661.

[7] "Lehrpläne für Präparandenanstalten und Lehrerseminare, sowie methodische Anweisungen zu beiden Lehrplänen. Erlass vom 1. Juli 1901," in *Zentralblatt für die gesamte Unterrichts-Verwaltung in Preussen* (Berlin [1859–1934], 1901), pp. 633–34.

leave school with the most important facts of national history fixed firmly in memory."[8]

Government directives were supplemented by the writings of prominent Prussian pedagogues and writers. District School Inspector Max Hübner, for example, in 1898 published one of the first volumes on the teaching of history. In this he declared:

"Instruction in history teaches us to prize and love our nation. Through this instruction the pupil learns of the power and greatness of our people in the past and in the present. It was the Germans who at one time overthrew the mighty Roman Empire and spread their authority over Central, Southern, and Western Europe, indeed, over the northern coast of Africa as well; the German Holy Roman Empire was the most powerful state in Europe during the reigns of Charles the Great, Otto I, and the Hohenstauffens. After the decay of the empire all Europe marvels at Frederick the Great . . . ; through Emperor William I, the powerful new German Empire, which guarantees safety and security to every German citizen no matter in what part of the world he may be, is founded. The teacher is to tell the pupil of these eras in order that the latter may come to feel himself a member of a great and mighty nation.

"History instruction further shows the pupil the great intellectual and economic achievements of our people. Savants, artists, and inventors have been produced by our nation, and their attainments have reached the peak of human knowledge. Kant, Hegel, Schopenhauer have had a great influence on the thought and philosophy of all Europe. Just as Goethe and Schiller in poetry, Mozart, Beethoven, and Wagner in music, are among the greatest artists of all time, so the great domes and city halls of the Middle Ages are among the most marvelous of buildings. The art of printing, gunpowder, which have brought about an entirely new development of Europe, are German inventions. In the Middle Ages German craftsmanship did great things and German trade and commerce ruled supreme in Northern and Eastern Europe. In modern times England is ahead of us as far as trade and industry go, but Germany leads as far as military power is concerned.

"Again, history instruction familiarizes the pupil with our politi-

[8] "Weisungen betreffend die Schulrevisionen. Erlass vom 31. Januar 1908," *ibid.* (1908), p. 383.

cal and social institutions, and teaches him to value them. Love of country does not merely mean attachment to the birthplace of a man; rather, and above all, it means love of one's fellow-countrymen, attachment to the social and political institutions, and the willingness to exercise both the rights and duties of citizenship. . . .

"Finally, history shows how the German and Prussian people, through the course of centuries, have constantly offered blood and possessions against foreign aggression and in defense of their language, their customs, and their social and political institutions.

"Through this instruction and knowledge the pupil should be led a) to appreciate and exercise his rights as a citizen (voting); b) willingly to assume his duties as a citizen (taxes, military service, school attendance, respect for authorities); c) in case of emergency to sacrifice everything for his nation and his country; and d) to preserve his language and his customs even if he migrates to foreign lands, and not, as unfortunately is the case in America, in Hungary, and elsewhere, there substitute for them foreign languages and customs."[9]

Friedrich Nadler, in a book of "helpful hints" for elementary-school teachers, pointed out that "history instruction has a manifold aim. The blessed efforts and accomplishments of our noble rulers and the great deeds of our nation are brought home to the child in lifelike character sketches, so as to implant in its heart love and a sacred enthusiasm for emperor, king, nation, and country. Instruction in history is particularly well suited to the inculcation of patriotism. The latter may also be inculcated by a consideration of the progress of civilization, that is, by showing the child how our people have excelled in the intellectual sphere, and how our princes have supported progress in this direction as well as in national matters. Hence, the newer history instruction must place a greater emphasis than before on the progress of our civilization."[10]

In 1895 a teachers' conference at Altenburg listened to a lecture by Richard Fritzsche on the principles which must underlie the kind of history instruction calculated to awaken patriotism. "To warm the young heart," he said, "towards the leading personages of its nation and the joyful and sorrowful destinies of its people, to carry

[9] M. Hübner, *Der Volksschulunterricht* (4 vols., Breslau, 1898), I: *Der Unterricht in der Geschichte*, 14–15.

[10] F. Nadler, *Ratgeber für Volksschullehrer* (Langensalza, 1900), p. 568.

over to the children the patriotic and loyal attitude of the fathers, to foster the idea that the welfare of the citizens is dependent upon the protection of the state, to awaken and quicken a reverence for existing conditions, ... that is the task which must be accomplished by history instruction in the *Volksschule!*"[11]

Some of the educators stressed the opportunity for history instruction to tie together patriotism and religion, or Germanism and Christianity. Thus, Ernst Kornrumpf held that "history should not merely develop the pupil's mental powers so as to arm him for his struggle for existence. It should, in equal measure, develop in him a noble attitude, a determined will, and a strong character, so as to enable him to carry on this struggle with the proper moral earnestness. The correct spirit is always exemplified by love of God and of one's fellowmen. But since Christianity portrays the Supreme Being more clearly and loftily than does anything else, and since love of one's fellowmen is limited primarily to love of those who stand closest to us, who speak the same language, in short, who belong to our race, it follows that instruction in history, to use the Emperor's words, 'must emphasize more religion and more of that which is national.' Indeed, love of God and love of country, *Christentum und Deutschtum,* must be the twin guiding stars which illuminate the path along which the pupil travels."[12]

One of the foremost German methodologists, Wilhelm Rein, believed that the empire's future greatness depended in part on the history instruction received by its youth. "Contact with national history," he wrote, "should lead the pupil at once to feel himself an active part of the nation. He must know that some day responsibility will be placed upon him and he must want the nation to count on him. History instruction therefore becomes an important factor in the educational process. Indeed, our future depends upon the cultivation in the coming generation of an understanding of con-

---

[11] R. Fritzsche, "Nach welchen Grundsätzen ist der Geschichtsunterricht zu gestalten, wenn er monarchisch-patriotische Gesinnung wecken und historischen Sinn bilden soll?", in *Sammlung pädagogischer Vorträge,* ed. by W. Meyer-Markau (Bielefeld and elsewhere [1888–1908], 1895), VII, *10. Heft,* 2.

[12] E. Kornrumpf, *Methodisches Handbuch für den deutschen Geschichtsunterricht in der Volksschule* (2nd ed., 3 vols., Leipzig, 1906–1907), I, iii-iv. See also the article by P. Zillig on "Geschichtsunterricht in der Erziehungsschule," in *Encyklopädisches Handbuch der Pädagogik,* ed. by W. Rein (2nd ed., 10 vols., Langensalza, 1903–1910), III, 466–81.

temporary problems. Our pupils should be reared in the firm belief that our people are destined to do great things in times to come; they should be so armed that the future may not be met by a puny race."[13]

Almost lyrical in its praise of the German mind and of what history could do for the mind of German youth, was a lecture delivered in 1891 by Rector van Ekeris of Dortmund: "It is one of the most beautiful traits of the German mind that it can become inspired and enthusiastic over everything that is noble and great. But this inspiration, in contrast to that of our westerly neighbor, is not a passing fancy which disappears as suddenly as it arose. It is a state of mind which is based on . . . clear recognition of genuine greatness and which therefore is lasting. Before the German can love or admire anything he must be able to evaluate it; and what he is to evaluate must first have become familiar to him. Hence education for loyalty to the king presupposes first and foremost familiarity with the ideals, goals, and deeds of the Brandenburg-Prussian princes. . . . For the same reason, a careful introduction to Germany's past is the most successful way to give root to a love of country. As the child, in its travels through history, meets the thoughts and deeds, the battles and cares, the fortunes and misfortunes of the forefathers—with whom it feels itself becoming ever more closely united by bonds of blood, language, and common Fatherland—there awakens in it a sympathy for the story of its own people; and thus the germ of love for the great German home and its inhabitants gradually sinks into the receptive young heart."[14]

There were, as might be expected, some educational officials and publicists who were less militantly nationalistic in outlook. One of these, Heinrich Weigand, regarded character-building as the chief function of education. He believed that the aims of national history teaching should be "to help the pupil find out how the life of his nation has coursed hitherto . . . and to discover what can be done to permit the further normal development of this national life. This knowledge should awaken in him a love for his country and

---

[13] W. Rein, A. Pickel, and E. Scheller, eds., *Theorie und Praxis des Volksschulunterrichts nach Herbartischen Grundsätzen* (3rd ed., 8 vols., Leipzig, 1886–1897), V, 35.

[14] Van Ekeris, "Der Geschichtsunterricht in der Volksschule," in *Sammlung pädagogischer Vorträge, op. cit.* (1891), IV, 4. Heft, 6–7.

his people." Similarly, growing acquaintance with the contributions of members of the ruling house and other leaders would arouse in the child a desire for emulation, would "engender in him courage and develop in him a strong character."[15]

Ernst Blümel stressed the value of modern history teaching as a means of leading children to realize "how God has led Germany from division and impotence to unity and strength, from darkness to light." But he also wished the pupils to be informed "that other countries, too, are engaged in the honorable race for supremacy in the intellectual and material fields and there also are foreign rulers and statesmen who deserve high praise and esteem." Thus would be avoided a "blind overestimation of national greatness."[16]

The advocates of *Kulturgeschichte,* while opposed to the purely political and military interpretation of history, nonetheless often displayed strong nationalist feelings in their writings. Karl Biedermann, for example, warned against making the children "accustomed to enjoy only the military events in history." In doing so, however, he added: "Fortunately our German nation as a whole, despite its wars and its resulting dominance, has remained free from that accursed mania (chauvinism) which keeps our westerly neighbor in so restive a state."[17]

Another exponent of *Kulturgeschichte,* and one who was frequently quoted by Prussian writers although his own work was published in Bavaria, was Ferdinand Krieger. It was his view that "not until the history instruction in elementary schools is so arranged that the political developments are given in conjunction with the determining civilizational factors can historical knowledge be made really fruitful for later life." And then he added: "The history of German civilization is truly the most precious pearl in the history of the world, for no nation in Europe has accomplished such intellectual feats as the German nation."[18]

[15] H. Weigand, *Der Geschichts-Unterricht nach den Forderungen der Gegenwart* (2nd ed., 2 pts., Berlin, 1900), pt. 1, p. 36. See also F. Polack, "Über den Helferdienst der Schule bei Heilung sozialer Schäden," in *Sammlung pädagogischer Vorträge, op. cit.* (1890), III, 7. Heft, 15.

[16] E. Blümel, "Die neueste Geschichte in der Volksschule," in *Sammlung pädagogischer Vorträge, op. cit.* (1888), I, 6. Heft, 11.

[17] [F.] K. Biedermann, *Der Geschichtsunterricht auf Schulen nach kulturgeschichtlicher Methode* (Wiesbaden, 1885), p. 17.

[18] F. Krieger, *Methodik des Geschichtsunterrichts in Volksschulen* (Munich, 1887), pp. 27–28.

During the reign of William II, two of the most popular texts dealing with historical method were those by Hermann Rosenburg and Carl Reim. In 1910 Rosenburg's book appeared in its eleventh edition. Succinctly it answered the question, "How does instruction in history lead to the exercise of civic duties?", as follows:

"I. It presents a picture of the origins and development of our culture and thereby teaches reverence for what has developed historically.

"II. It shows that important changes in the life of the state and the people must evolve gradually, if they are to be of any blessing. Violent overthrow of that which exists is wrong, and well thought-out reforms should be the means of change.

"III. It teaches various forms of government, and shows that ours is the best, namely, a strong monarchy, limited in legislation by the representatives of the people, but supreme in administration.

"IV. It shows how the whole nation has offered up blood and possessions for the common causes of independence, liberty, honor, right, and social institutions.

"V. It leads the pupil to emulate individuals who worked and fought for the country: heroes of war, both officers and privates; heroes of peace, inventors and discoverers.

"VI. Thus the majority of children who lack the opportunity for great deeds can show their love for country by a) freely and conscientiously exercising their civic rights and duties; b) closing their ears to revolutionary talk; c) doing their duty in case of war."[19]

Reim's volume was offered to the history teachers in a seventh edition in 1911. Its opening pages were devoted to a bristling chapter entitled "History Instruction as a Means of Developing a Patriotic and Monarchical Spirit." Typical of the contents are these paragraphs:

"A glance at the desolation caused by the Thirty Years' War and recognition of our unfavorable geographic position shows us the necessity for a standing army.... It was only the military reorganization brought about by King William I which led to the victories of 1864, 1866, and 1870–71. The expenditures for a strong fleet, crushing as they may seem to be, are small when compared with our losses in the event of an unsuccessful war. We can advance in all

---

[19] H. Rosenburg, *Methodik des Geschichtsunterrichts* (11th ed., Breslau, 1910), pp. 16–17.

phases of trade and industry only under the protection of a strong army and navy. That is why thousands of patriotic Germans founded the Naval League. Without a powerful army we should soon fall prey to our greedy neighbors.... We have much to protect, much to uphold, much to lose. The greatest guarantee of peace lies in compulsory military service for everyone. A nation in arms is the best protector of peace.

"To defend honor, liberty, and right; to offer up life, health, and property on the altar of the Fatherland, these have always been the joy of German youths. It is an honor to wear the king's coat. The duty of defending the country is an old German heirloom. Arminius forced the impertinent, victory-flushed Romans to leave the German fields, and in 1812 all Prussia rose to shake off the yoke of the Corsican conqueror. Small, crushed, exhausted Prussia, with a population numbering hardly five millions, put 277,000 men in the field—one man in every eighteen people! All classes, of all ages, even women, took up arms at the call of the king. The teacher is to mention Theodore Körner, Jahn Friesen, Elenore Prohaska, Auguste Kruger, Nettelbeck. In the Seven Years' War, the counts of Mark rushed to the colors of Frederick the Great, to serve as volunteers. The Kleist family lost fifty-four members, the Belling family twenty members for their country. On June 26, 1866, twenty-one pupils of the seminary at Oranienburg volunteered service in the army. The teacher must note such instances carefully. And the courageous warriors in China and our African colonies are ample proof that the heroic blood of the fathers still pulsates in the veins of our people.... In order that it may continue thus for all time, we portray these examples of courage, bravery, and endurance to our boys for emulation....

"Love of country is a treasure imbedded in the heart of man by God.... Our Fatherland is a holy land. Our ancestors preserved it with their blood.... This land, fertilized with the blood of heroes, is a holy heirloom, not one foot of which shall be robbed from us. We are worthy of the fathers.... More national consciousness, much more than we now possess! That is the end to which we history teachers must help our youth."[20]

Most of the Prussian cities issued official history courses of study

---

[20] C. Reim, *Methodik des Geschichtsunterrichts* (7th ed., Halle a.d.S., 1911), pp. 7–8, 17.

in line with the principles established by higher authority and discussed in the books on methods. There is not room here to quote the documents at length, but certain observations may be made about them.[21]

A striking common feature of the courses of study is the predominance of national history. The history of other nations was entirely omitted in the lower grades and was to be considered in the middle and upper grades only when there was obvious influence on German development. Out of 195 weeks of instruction devoted to history as a separate subject in the fifth through the first classes, only ten weeks were to be devoted to foreign nations as such. The remaining 95 per cent of history instruction was to be devoted to national history.[22]

Further, there is a marked tendency to hero worship and the glorification of military prowess. Albert the Bear, Henry the Lion, Frederick the Great *("der alte Fritz"),* the heroes of the Wars of Liberation, Frederick III *("unser Fritz, der Kriegsheld")* are listed as the outstanding personalities. The names of a majority of the great and distinguished men whose biographies and deeds were to be studied are connected with war. Indeed, the whole history of Prussia and of Germany, from the earliest times, was to be considered as one continuous struggle on the part of the German people, especially under the leadership of the noble Hohenzollerns, to bring about a free and united Germany despite the greedy and sinister machinations of the surrounding peoples. The numerous wars which this condition brought about must be thoroughly familiar to all pupils, who in turn would be expected to carry on the work of the glorious forefathers. *Kulturgeschichte,* however, or the development of civilization, was not to be neglected, particularly in the upper grades. Here certain heroes of peacetime were to be held up with military heroes as equally worthy of emulation.

[21] See, for example, the "Grundlehrplan der Berliner Gemeindeschulen" and the "Lehrplan für die 7-klassige Volksschule in der Residenzstadt Potsdam" (1903), as quoted in Reim, *op. cit.,* pp. 82–84 and 90–92; also the "Amtliches Schulblatt für den Regierungsbezirk Magdeburg, 3. Jahrgang, Nr. 3. 23. Mai 1891," as quoted in Rosenburg, *op. cit.,* pp. 72–75.

[22] "Ein Beitrag zur Spezialisierung des Grundlehrplans (von Berlin). Herausgegeben vom Berliner Rektoren-Verein," in Reim, *op. cit.,* pp. 84–90.

Nationalism and Prussian Schools 253

The part played by the Hohenzollerns is emphasized and reemphasized. The Magdeburg course of study went so far as specifically to demand the "explanation and application of the '*Hohenzollernworte*,'" these being aphorisms associated with the Hohenzollern rulers from Frederick I (1415–1440) to William II. To illustrate: Frederick I *("Jedem das Seine"*—"To Each His Own"); Frederick the Great *("Für Ruhm und Vaterland"*—"For Glory and Fatherland"); Frederick William IV *("Ich und Mein Haus wollen dem Herrn dienen"*—"I and My House Wish to Serve the Lord"); and William I *("Gott mit uns"*—"God with Us"). By way of visual aids or *Anschauungsmittel,* moreover, the walls of every Prussian schoolroom were required to be adorned with pictures of Hohenzollern rulers or military leaders.

Finally, the courses of study generally established a close relation between religious history and national history. Intensive study was required of Luther and the Protestant Revolt. Lutheranism and Germanism, often specifically Prussianism, were to be presented as signs of divine favor to the subjects of the Hohenzollerns. Verily, the courses of study were well calculated to make patriotic generations out of the children and grandchildren of the "heroes of 1870."

The government regulations and the opinions and directives of the educators found their application in classroom work. Hence it will be interesting to consider some typical lesson plans offered to the teachers of the recitation periods. The following is an example of a lesson planned for the lower grades by an educator who was relatively moderate in his emphasis on the military aspect of history for this lowest age-group:

"Tomorrow is the Emperor's birthday; hence I want to talk to you about him now. Our Emperor was born ―― years ago in a large castle in Berlin. Many people stood around the castle waiting, and at last a man called out to them: 'Folks, an able recruit has just arrived.' The people were delighted and thought: 'Then he'll doubtless also be an able emperor.'

"At first he was only a little prince. He was baptized William. When William grew up he, too, had to learn, just as you are doing. His father had special tutors for him and his brother Henry, for they had much to learn and they could not afford to be held back by other pupils. But when the princes were older, their father sent them to the *Gymnasium* at Kassel and then to the University of Bonn, so that they might also study with other students.

"When Prince William was ten years old he received a soldier's uniform for his birthday gift. Eight years later he actually became a soldier. Now he was an officer and could issue commands! All the soldiers liked him and used to tell everyone about their good captain. Once another prince invited our Prince William to a hunt. There he met a wondrously beautiful princess, Auguste Victoria, whom he liked so well that he wished to marry her. The parents were willing and in a year the young people were married. Now William has been Emperor for —— years and Auguste Victoria has been Empress. They live in a large castle in Berlin and are happy over their six princes and one princess.

"Every year the Emperor travels through the land to see that his soldiers drill well, and to see that everything is going on as it should, for he is the sovereign and must care for law and order. Tomorrow many people will travel to Berlin to congratulate the Emperor, and if it were not so far away we should go there, too, and shake hands with him. But since that is impossible, we at least want to pray for him: '*Gott erhalte unsern Kaiser.*' "[23]

For the middle and upper grades, this same educator placed far more emphasis on military affairs. Thus, he urged the teacher to assign the following homework after a lesson spent on the German army and navy: "Define: Recruiting list, reparation commission, recruit, soldier of the line, reservist, militia, army, army corps, division, brigade, regiment, battalion, infantry, cavalry, artillery, scout, train, squadron, battery, company, cuirassier, uhlan, dragoon, hussar, guard, sentinel, corporal, sergeant, sergeant-major, lieutenant, captain, major, lieutenant-colonel, colonel, general, fleet, naval defense." Throughout the book, about 125 military and naval terms were given, all of which the teacher was to require his elementary-school pupils to learn.[24]

The author of another popular teachers' handbook offered the following as an introductory lesson on the accession of William II:

"All Europe expectantly regarded the young Emperor. France

---

[23] Weigand, *op. cit.*, pt. 1, p. 55.
[24] *Ibid.*, pt. 2, p. 420.

and Russia had been waiting for years for an opportunity to wage war on Germany, and many were of the opinion that the young and active ruler, who was considered to be ambitious and warlike, would begin a great war at the first opportunity in order to make a name for himself. But they were mistaken. Ten days after the death of his father, surrounded by all the German princes, William uttered the following words at the opening of his first Reichstag: 'I am determined to keep peace with everyone, as far as I am concerned.' And he kept his word. In order to guarantee peace he renewed the Triple Alliance with Austria and Italy, whose rulers he visited shortly after his accession. He also visited other courts in order to show his love of peace and thereby to ensure peace....

"Naturally he is of the opinion, as was his grandfather William I, that a strong, well-equipped army is the best guarantee of peace. For he considers the army 'to be the sole pillar on which the Empire rests.' Moreover he considers himself as one with the army as shown by his first military order issued on June 15, 1888. In this he said: 'Thus we belong together—I and the army, thus we were born for one another, thus will we ever cling steadfastly to each other, may there be war or peace, as God wills it.' He was very careful to see that our own army was not outnumbered by the increasing armaments of our neighbors, France and Russia. For this reason all the newer inventions in equipment and armaments were introduced among our troops....

"A strong fleet is essential to protect our coasts, to protect our overseas trade, to protect our colonies, and to protect German citizens in foreign lands. In 1906 the German navy numbered about 250 vessels with a personnel of about 43,000, so that our Emperor's care for the development of our navy already has been crowned with success. But our navy still lags far behind those of France, the United States, and especially England."[25]

Hitler, had he known of its existence, might well have applauded the following lecture proposed by still another educator for use by elementary-school history teachers:

"Who, then, was it, who freed the Germans [from the Roman yoke]? It was the son of Prince Segimer, Arminius, a powerful youth with blonde hair and blue eyes, who vowed to his father to avenge

[25] Kornrumpf, *op. cit.*, III, 489–91.

the shame which had been done to his German brethren, and swore not to rest until the reign of the enemies in Germany was crushed and until the Roman yoke was broken. But why did Arminius go to Rome first, before attempting to accomplish this? Because the enemy was superior to the Germans in military knowledge and power. The Germans could not withstand the Romans in open battle. Hence he wanted to learn the Roman art and method of warfare so as to be able to defeat his enemies with their own weapons.

"What induced Arminius to enter the Roman army? He had seen how his Fatherland lay pining in Roman bonds, how his German brothers, who once had enjoyed golden liberty, sighed beneath the yoke of the conquerors. He then determined to help his distressed people, to give them back their religion, speech, traditions, customs, and liberty. That is why he vowed vengeance to the death against the Romans. His heart was imbued with a genuine love for nation and Fatherland.... And this love impelled him to accept service in the army of the hated enemy, in order to learn how best to annihilate him.

"But might not this step have proved very dangerous for Arminius? Certainly. He might have fared in Rome just as had so many other German youths: in these delightful surroundings he might have forgotten about his German brethren at home; he might have forgotten the vow which he had made to his father; he might have lost his German sympathies and become a Roman, for the temptations were great. But every tempter who approached him was repulsed with great cautiousness. He remained German despite the great honors with which he was overwhelmed, and despite the great future which was promised him. What was it, then, that predestined Arminius to be the savior of his people? His deep and sincere love of the Fatherland, his wisdom and caution, his iron will and courage, his rich experience, and his knowledge of Roman military tactics....

"It is true that Arminius' cunning and deceptive measures are subject to censure, but in no other way was liberation possible. And this cunning and deception were conceived of a noble attitude and feeling: love of people and Fatherland. Hence we must excuse his actions."[26]

[26] R. Fritzsche, *Bausteine für den Geschichtsunterricht in der evangelischen Landschule. I. Kursus. (Mittelstufe.) II. Kursus. (Oberstufe.)* (Altenburg, 1896–1897), *II*, 7–9.

The same pedagogue urged the teachers to explain the medieval victories of Henry I and Otto the Great over the Magyars in such fashion as this:

"How were these victories won? Formerly such victories had been impossible. Since the German tribes still quarreled among themselves and each wanted to go its own way, it would have been impossible to stem the tide of the onrushing Magyars and to drive them back. But now that all German tribes were united once more and all bowed before the same sovereign, they all arose as one man and went forth to battle together in order to overcome the enemy with their combined strength. Without German unity the victory would have been doubtful. And combined with unity was the German military machine, founded and tried by Henry I and strengthened and steeled under Otto the Great, which accomplished wonders of heroism. But another thing which was equally helpful in bringing about victory was the enthusiasm and courage of the German warriors, both of which flowed from the living faith in God that possessed all the German fighters. Thus we see that union creates strength, the military system gives rise to courage, and faith in God braces up this courage. *Hence, German unity, German faith in God, and the German military organization achieved the victory.*"[27]

Finally, it may be interesting to note a typical outline, presented to teachers, of what the elementary-school pupils should know about history at the completion of their school career:

ASSIGNMENTS COVERING THE WHOLE FIELD OF GERMAN HISTORY

1. Germany's great Emperors according to their importance for the German nation.
2. Germany's most important princes in ancient and modern times.
3. Germany's great statesmen.
4. Distinguished German military heroes.
5. Germany's great men in peace activities.
6. German wars of conquest.
7. German defensive wars.
8. German religious wars.
9. German civil wars.
10. The different forms of government which appeared in Germany during the various eras.
11. Settlement and development of German lands by the Germans.

[27] *Ibid.*, p. 57.

12. Development of architecture in Germany.
13. Fundamentals for a story of the German peasantry.
14. The chief epochs in the development of German agricultural life.
15. The chief epochs in the development of German industry.
16. Fundamentals for a story of the German nobility.
17. Development of commercial intercourse in Germany.
18. Development of German education.
19. Fundamentals for a story of the spread of Christianity in Germany.
20. Development of German jurisprudence.
21. Development of the German army.
22. Development of the German system of taxation.
23. Development of the German bureaucracy.
24. The rise and fall of the old German empire.
25. Development of the Brandenburg-Prussian state.
26. Influence of Germany's neighbors in war and peace.
27. Military and peaceful relations between Germans and Romans.
28. The great historical migrations westward and the counter-migrations eastward.
29. The social differences in the German nation during the various periods of German history.[28]

The material presented in books and in the schoolrooms appears to have been much more militaristic in spirit than either the government regulations or the courses of study seemed to demand. Thus, Kornrumpf devoted 68 per cent of his book to purely military history. Fritzsche gave 64 per cent of his volume to a consideration of the military history of Prussia and Germany. Weigand allotted 60 per cent of his work to an outline of wars and military affairs. In general, the remaining 30 or 40 per cent, in each case, was taken up with a eulogy of the efforts and accomplishments of the Hohenzollern dynasty. The more important battles of every war were given in great detail, including the names of the leaders on the opposing sides, the numbers of troops involved, the formations and plans of battle, the reasons for victory or defeat, and so forth. The teacher was constantly urged either to use printed maps, available at moderate prices, or to draw battle maps on the board, and whenever possible to explain the movements and terrain in terms of the local landscape familiar to all pupils. Such procedure, it was pointed out, would make the whole story more real and more vivid, for it

[28] Weigand, *op. cit.*, pt. 2, p. 461.

would enable the children to visualize the actual conditions and circumstances.

The bad traits, characteristics, and deeds of the heroes and rulers were not always omitted, but whenever they were mentioned, there was an accompanying excuse which explained the matter satisfactorily, at least to the German mind. Perhaps these educators and history writers, who were government officials, felt it incumbent upon them to laud their exacting employer.

Furthermore, these books were written expressly for the use of teachers, to guide them and to help them teach history in accordance with the orders of the authorities. The teachers were to make the history lesson a study in the development of nationalism and patriotism, and a stimulus to the awakening of love for king and country. To do this properly they had to have some means of finding out just what phases of German history were best fitted to achieve these ends, and so the guidebooks and handbooks were provided to make the task easier and to ensure its success.

Hatred of France is conspicuous in most lesson plans and history outlines. The Frenchmen were considered the archenemies of Prussia and Germany. They were accused of always trying to keep Germany as weak, disrupted, and small as possible. The war of 1870–1871 was studied in great detail, and its consideration was generally accompanied by a bitter denunciation of France's whole policy, as well as by the recitation of stirring poems written by such ardent nationalist poets as Arndt and Koerner.

This, then, was the type of educational background of the Prussian men and youths who fought in the First World War, and of the Prussian women who tended the home front. Many died and many became disillusioned; many others, however, continued to be imbued with the nationalistic spirit instilled in them during schooldays and, later, army days. Eventually the "inner feelings" of this last group were hurt by the inability or unwillingness of the Weimar Republic to pay due attention to Germany's nationalistic tradition.

There was growing resentment over the official toleration, after 1919, of attempts to drag down the ideals and heroes of Imperial Germany. There was bitterness over the readiness with which the new officials abandoned the imperial flag. There was nostalgia for the colorful old military uniforms that were outlawed. There was hatred for the "politicians" who derided the military and military exploits, who sneered at the old-fashioned concept of *Kultur,* and who limited the bounds of Germany's "mission" of dominance.

The Nazi leaders understood these and other grievances, and with their remarkable propaganda methods capitalized on them. Posters, banners, songs, uniforms, ceremonies, hero-worship, ritual, discipline, historic tradition, theories of race superiority, ultra-nationalism, these things eventually attracted millions of Germans and filled them with a new and yet old national enthusiasm. Psychologically, at least, the Third Reich was firmly founded on the Second. And in both eras, nationalistic indoctrination was practiced in a manner to make the indoctrinated people a menace to their neighbors. The fault lay not with the spirit of nationality, but with the use to which this spirit was put by power-seeking political leaders.

THE SWISS PATTERN FOR A FEDERATED EUROPE

CHARLOTTE MURET

TODAY statesmen and economists on both sides of the Atlantic are working to create a United Europe, in the belief that only by federation can that continent recover strength and prosperity. Many difficulties, however, lie in the way. The nations of Europe are deeply divided and the idea of absolute national sovereignty, so harmful both to the League of Nations and the United Nations, has not yet been abandoned.

Those who are working for a European Union would find the study of Swiss history valuable, for the Swiss Confederation is a small-scale model of what a United States of Europe might become in the future. The Swiss cantons have enjoyed 650 years of independence and self-government. Switzerland lies in the very heart of Europe, exposed to all its cross-currents, yet the Confederation has survived a series of wars and upheavals, some of which, like the Thirty Years' War, the wars of the Revolution and the Empire, and the two World Wars, have involved the whole continent and destroyed entire nations. Moreover, the Swiss have managed better than most of their neighbors to adapt their social and economic structure to the developments of the modern world. They have, in fact, demonstrated that a number of diverse sovereign states can act together and create a strong and durable union.

Arguments based on Swiss history are often rejected on three principal grounds; first, that Switzerland is so small that no valid comparison can be made between its cantons and the larger nations of modern Europe; second, that the cantons were less unlike than are the nations of today; and, third, that nationalism as it has developed in modern times was virtually unknown in the age when the Confederation evolved.

In regard to the first objection it may be advanced that in the thirteenth, fourteenth, and fifteenth centuries, while the Confederation came into being, a great majority of the sovereign states of Europe were no larger than the federated cantons, and the problems faced by the latter were of much the same kind as those faced by the nations of today. Size is relative, and nations which once loomed large on the European scale are today no bigger in proportion to such colossi as the U.S.S.R. or the United States of America than was the Swiss Confederation in comparison with France or Austria, countries against which the Swiss were able to hold their own. It was not mere insignificance that made the Swiss union durable.

As for internal dissimilarities, differences in culture, religion, social and economic structure, and forms of government as great as those which today exist among the European nations existed between the Swiss cantons, and violent antagonisms, even open conflicts, at times divided them. Yet they have managed to maintain their union.

It is true that nationalism as we know it today had not yet developed when the Confederation grew up, but the fierce local patriotism, the narrow particularism of the cantons, was in most respects its equivalent, and those small communities clung at least as tenaciously to their individual sovereignties as do the modern nations. Indeed a distinguished Swiss historian has recently called such local patriotism "cantonal nationalism."[1]

The authority of a well-known writer on international subjects, William Rappard, further justifies the comparisons involved in this discussion. "For those who have carefully followed the international evolution of the last twenty-five years," wrote Mr. Rappard in 1944, "and who have afterwards studied five centuries of Swiss development, the analogies are so striking that one must be wholly devoid of perception not to be moved by them."[2] A number of suggestions significant for a federated Europe can, in fact, be drawn from Swiss history. Only an outline is attempted here, for to study them in detail would require a large volume.

The first of these suggestions, one which in the light of Swiss history may be called a conclusion, is that, contrary to accepted belief, a state can be strong without being highly centralized, and even without possessing an entirely homogeneous population.

The centralized state, organized in the manner of a spider-web, with every thread leading directly to the center, has always been the

---

[1] D. Laserre, "Le 'Miracle' de 1918," *La Suisse Horlogère*, No. 26 (June 24, 1948), 566.
[2] W. S. Rappard, *Cinq siècles de sécurité collective* (Paris, Genève, 1945), p. 592.

The Swiss Pattern of Federation 263

ideal of absolute monarchs. They have usually also tried to create a "monolithic" nation, all of whose inhabitants would think, feel, and act alike, for this is highly convenient to the ruler. It was partly at least to eliminate heterogeneous elements that Ferdinand and Isabella expelled Moors and Jews from their realms, that Louis XIV revoked the Edict of Nantes, that Bismarck inaugurated the *Kulturkampf*. The same idea lay behind the "Russification" policy of Alexander III and the efforts of the Young Turks to "Ottomanize" the populations of their heterogeneous empire. Homogeneity and centralization were aims of the Nazis and motivated their racist theories. Yet the early history of Switzerland clearly demonstrates that a loose confederation, composed of diverse elements, can be exceedingly strong.

During the early years of their union the achievements of the Swiss cantons in proportion to their material resources were remarkable. The original Confederation consisted of three small mountain communities, whose inhabitants were few and poor, yet at Morgarten in 1315 they defeated the highly armed and redoubtable forces of the Habsburg Duke, to the astonishment of Europe. Although the terrain favored them, the Swiss in this battle faced a greatly superior number of knights, who, mounted and clad in steel, were the armored divisions, the tanks, as it were, of that time. The success of the mountaineers was so great that it won for them at one stroke recognition from their Habsburg lords as a sovereign state instead of a band of rebels.[3]

The same success fell to Swiss arms three-quarters of a century later at Sempach (1386). By that time the Confederation had grown and become more complex. To the original Forest Cantons had been added other units, such as Lucerne, Berne, Glaris, Zoug, and Zurich. The city-states were unlike the original cantons in social, economic, and political structure, and they had not, like the signers of the Pact of 1291, sworn to make no separate alliances.[4] Jealousies and conflicts among them were not uncommon, yet the confederates were able to unite against the Habsburg Leopold III and defeat him. The legendary tale of Arnold von Winkelried, who sacrificed himself to open a passage for his fellow confederates among the ser-

---

[3] W. Martin, *Histoire de la Suisse* (Lausanne, 1943), pp. 39-40.
[4] *Ibid.*, p. 50.

ried spears of the knights, while its authenticity is disputed, is symbolically true, since it exemplifies the Swiss motto, "One for all and all for one."[5]

Again in 1477 the Confederation engaged in a struggle with Charles the Bold of Burgundy, one of the richest and most powerful sovereigns of the day, and defeated him three times, at Grandson, Morat, and Nancy, thereby destroying the vast Burgundian power which three generations of able Dukes had erected. Once more in the first years of the sixteenth century the Swiss went to war with France over the Milanese, and in 1513 they defeated the French army overwhelmingly at Novara.

Thus, in two hundred years, this loose union of small and diverse states, which had no common government and whose Diet was scarcely more than an assembly of ambassadors, had vanquished three of the mightiest princes of Europe, the Habsburgs, the Burgundians, and the French. It had actually become the leading military power of the day,[6] yet neither homogeneity nor centralization had been necessary to attain this strength. It may be objected that two hundred and fifty years later, in the period of the Revolution, the Swiss offered little resistance to the armies of Bonaparte, but in this they showed themselves no weaker than larger and more centralized states, such, for instance, as Prussia.

A loosely knit confederacy can, then, be strong, but it should be noted that such a union is much more powerful for defense than for aggression or conquest. Since the essence of the union is mutual support, a foreign threat will bring the allies together, whereas expansions which may benefit some states more than others become sources of discord.

The Swiss quarreled fiercely over the spoils of Burgundy, and here, as in Europe today, arose the question of the privileges to be given to power and responsibility as against the rights of the weaker members of the group. So acute were the differences among the

---

[5] *Ibid.*, p. 51; K. Daendliker, *Histoire du peuple suisse* (Paris, 1879), pp. 70–72; A. Daguet, *Histoire de la confédération suisse* (Genève, 1879), pp. 250–52. On Winkelried, see references in footnote of this latter work, p. 262. Also A. Burkhli, *Das wahre Winkelried* (Zurich, 1886), and R. Rauchenstein, *Winkelreid's That bei Sempach ist keine Fabel* (Aarau, 1861).

[6] Martin, *op. cit.*, p. 87; W. Oeschli, *History of Switzerland, 1499–1914* (Cambridge, 1922), pp. 4, 21–22, 44–46.

The Swiss Pattern of Federation 265

Swiss that when their Diet met at Stans in 1481 it seemed a break-up was inevitable. Strangely enough, it did not take place. On the contrary, there was a genuine reconciliation, and a new pact was sworn, each canton surrendering a part of its demands for the sake of union.[7] This reconciliation was largely due to the influence of the hermit, Nicolas von der Flue. The disinterested wisdom of this remarkable man recalled the leaders of the various cantons to a sense of the value of their old alliance. Some Swiss writers have compared "Brother Nicolas" to Joan of Arc, because of his unifying influence. The Pact of Stans, freely consented, was the product of the Swiss will to remain together, and it is interesting to note that it carefully delimited the share of each canton in any future gains.[8]

Since they held the Alpine passes and depended largely on their traffic for prosperity, it was natural that the Swiss should have tended to reach out across the mountains to the small Italian communities that commanded the entrances to those commercial highways. In the last part of the fifteenth century the cantons did indulge in an imperialistic expansion which led them to become first the allies and then the rivals of the French for the possession of Milan.[9]

After the victory of Novara the Confederation was at the height of its power. Its territories and those of its allies extended from the Rhine to Milan, and it seemed destined to realize under the leadership of an able and far-seeing statesman, Cardinal Schinner,[10] the dream of the Burgundian Dukes, and create in central Europe a strong state, lying between France and Germany, and including the north of Italy. But profound divisions arose among the cantons. Those of the western area saw little advantage to them in wars fought for territory beyond the Alps. Others were unwilling to embrace the cause of the Pope against France, as Schinner desired. As a result of these dissensions a peace was signed with Francis I at Gallarate that has been considered disgraceful by nationalistic

---

[7] Rappard, *op. cit.*, p. 56.

[8] D. Laserre, *Alliances confédérales* (Zurich, 1941), pp. 59–72; Martin, *op. cit.*, pp. 74–76; Daendliker, *op. cit.*, pp. 124–25; Daguet, *op. cit.*, pp. 371–75 and footnotes; Rappard, *op. cit.*, pp. 55–65. On Nicolas von der Flue, see also W. Durrer, *Dokumente über Bruder Klaus* (Luzern, 1947), and H. Felerer, *Niklaus von Flue* (Frauenfeld, 1928).

[9] Martin, *op. cit.*, pp. 84–88; Oeschli, *op. cit.*, pp. 44–47.

[10] Oeschli, *op. cit.*, pp. 48–50; Daguet, *op. cit.*, pp. 406–8; H. Buchi, *Kardinal Matthaus Schinner, Staatsman, und Kirchenfürst* (Zurich, 1937).

Swiss historians. Lack of unity was in part responsible for the defeat of the Swiss at Marignan in 1515. This battle may be called in a sense decisive, for it marked the end of Swiss imperialism in Italy.[11]

Rarely has a country once embarked on imperialism abandoned that policy while it still had strength enough to maintain it, yet it was not military weakness that halted the growth of the Confederation. Marignan was a defeat, but the conduct of the Swiss, who fought for three days, retreating step by step and carrying all their dead and wounded from the field of battle, was so magnificent that their military prestige was not at all diminished. Indeed the Confederation acquired further territories beyond the Alps after the battle, and Francis I was glad to buy off Swiss claims on Milan with much gold.[12] But continued expansion would probably have involved greater centralization, and brought about the leadership, perhaps eventually the domination, of one or two of the stronger cantons over the others. This they would not accept. In spite of their proverbial love of gold the Swiss preferred to keep their individual independence and their local sovereignties. "Discouraged," as a Swiss historian says, "by the impossibility of agreement, they followed more and more the advice of Brother Nicolas: 'Do not meddle with the quarrels of others.' "[13]

With the abandonment of their claims to Milan, the Swiss withdrew into the confines of their old territories and during the following centuries the Confederation grew little in comparison with its neighbors. Local independence had, in fact, been purchased at the price of size and power. The decision was certainly not a conscious one, as the history of the times clearly reveals, yet in the last analysis a choice was made, whatever its motives, and instead of following the prevalent pattern of centralization and absolutism, the individual members of the small Confederation kept their freedom and their self-governing institutions.

A second conclusion to be drawn from the history of Switzerland is that the strength of a confederation springs from the very fact that the member states retain their independence and their own particular institutions. This is what gives them the will to act and remain together. Such a union implies on the one hand a willingness

---

[11] Martin, *op. cit.*, pp. 86–88; Oeschli, *op. cit.*, pp. 55–59; Rappard, *op. cit.*, p. 45.
[12] Oeschli, *op. cit.*, pp. 59–62.
[13] Martin, *op. cit.*, pp. 87–88.

to make sacrifices for the common defense, and, on the other, a wide mutual tolerance, implemented by the use of arbitration to settle disputes or differences of interest among the member states.

These were the conditions that prevailed among the Swiss cantons. A solemn pledge to support each other in times of need was the essence of the original pact and of all those which followed it. "The principle of all the alliances and leagues," wrote Josias Simler in the sixteenth century, "concerns the help which each must give to the others against those who would unjustly attack them. . . . If one canton asks two or more allies to come to its help all the cantons assemble."[14]

The Confederation as a whole had neither legal right nor power to intervene in the internal affairs of its member states, and no machinery for such interference existed. The only federal organ, the Diet, was not a law-making body, nor had it any administrative powers in the cantons.[15] In fact, the Confederation was more like the Holy Roman Empire or even the League of Nations as to structure and function than it was like a modern centralized nation. Yet, unlike these multinational organizations, it had at its disposal a common military force in time of need, even if this force was at first organized on a temporary and more or less feudal basis.

Two principal grounds of dissension repeatedly threatened the reciprocal tolerance on which Swiss union was based. The first was the wide difference in economic and also in social and political structure between the rural peasant cantons, the *"pays,"* as some Swiss historians call them, and the city-states. A large part of the internal history of Switzerland in the earlier centuries is concerned with the struggles which arose in one form or other between these two elements. An echo of them can still be found in differences of interest with regard to such matters as tariffs which exist between agricultural cantons like Vaud and Valais and industrial cantons like Zurich. These differences sometimes give rise to vigorous discussion in the Federal Chambers, but with the spread of industry throughout Switzerland the problem has grown less acute. Without entering into the details of Swiss internal history, it can on the

---

[14] See D. de Rougemont and C. Muret, *The Heart of Europe* (New York, 1940), p. 41.
[15] Oeschli, *op. cit.*, pp. 19–22; A. Heusler, *Histoire des constitutions suisses* (Lausanne, Genève, s. d.), pp. 137–44, 149–62; J. M. Vincent, *Government in Switzerland* (Baltimore, 1891), pp. 18–21.

whole be asserted that it was the existence of the federal system, the fact of cantonal sovereignty, which allowed such disputes to be settled as a rule by arbitration or by negotiations in the Diet. Tension between the cities and the *"pays"* was often sharp, but it seldom resulted in armed conflict, and it did not break up the basic union.

Reciprocal tolerance was even more severely tried in the era of religious upheaval. Nowhere in Europe was religious fervor more intense than in the cantons. Calvinism found its staunchest supporters in the Swiss cities, while Catholicism had no more devout followers than the inhabitants of the Waldstetten, of Lucerne, of Fribourg. Religious passions were as keen in that era as economic and social ones are today, and it seems a miracle that the Confederation survived the age of the Reformation.

Zwingli, who first preached reform in Zurich,[16] wished for a closer and more democratic union among the Swiss, but the actual results of his activity were two wars between the cantons, in the second of which he was himself killed. However, these wars of Capell ended in 1536 in a peace that was called "national," which gave to each canton the right to choose its own form of religion. Moreover, in the lands held in common by two cantons the inhabitants were allowed similar freedom of choice.[17] It was, in fact, a kind of Swiss Edict of Nantes, preceding by almost a century that document which is so often called the first example of religious tolerance in Europe. The principle of noninterference and cantonal sovereignty was its basis.[18]

The internal struggle by no means ended with the Peace of Capell; indeed, as the Reformation spread, there came to be as it were two Switzerlands. Catholics on the one hand and Protestants on the other drew closer together, and the creation in 1586 of a close alliance, known as the League of Gold, or Borromean League, between seven of the Catholic cantons was indicative of the internal dissension. Yet neither of the warring factions was strong enough to eliminate the other and a *de facto* tolerance inevitably resulted.

---

[16] Martin, *op. cit.*, pp. 9, 101–5; Oeschli, *op. cit.*, pp. 72–124.

[17] Martin, *op. cit.*, p. 104; Rappard, *op. cit.*, pp. 186–88; Oeschli, *op. cit.*, pp. 119–26.

[18] Even during these two wars of Capell there was apparently a certain amount of "fraternizing" among the belligerents. An old Swiss chronicle tells how once when some of the men of the Forest Cantons had a huge bowl of milk they called the men of Zurich in the opposite camp to bring the bread they had and eat the soup in common. The burgomaster of Strassbourg is said to have exclaimed: "You Confederates are queer people! You fight, but in spite of your quarrels you are united!" Daendliker, *op. cit.*, p. 147.

Great was the temptation both in the sixteenth century and during the Thirty Years' War for each group to take part actively in the wars waged by their co-religionaries. As early as 1529 five of the Catholic cantons signed a treaty with their old enemy, Austria, now the defender of their common faith, and another was concluded with Spain in 1557. These alliances were renewed in 1587 and 1588, and again in 1604 and 1624, in the middle of the Thirty Years' War. In 1560 these same cantons also entered into an alliance with the Count of Savoy, on whom their fellow confederates of Berne had made war in 1536, and who was the mortal enemy of Berne's ally, the city of Geneva.[19] Similarly, when in 1631 Gustavus Adolphus sent an ambassador to propose to the Swiss Diet an alliance with Sweden, the sympathies of the Protestant cantons were deeply involved.[20]

These leagues and alliances were contrary to the spirit of the Swiss Pact, yet in no case did the Confederation take active part in the European struggle on either side. The Swiss remained neutral, and so managed to survive that stormy era. Switzerland issued from the Thirty Years' War divided as to religion but united politically. Indeed, a new pact, the Defensional of Wil, signed in 1647 just before the end of the war, was a first attempt to create a permanent federal military organization.[21] The cantons had been spared the horrors of a war which so ravaged the Germanies as to alter their whole future, and the settlement of Westphalia recognized their entire independence, and broke the last feeble link that bound them to the Empire.

All these benefits the Swiss owed to their neutrality. This neutrality had been possible partly because of their alliance with France, which, though Catholic, followed under the guidance of Richelieu a purely national policy.[22] More important, however, was the influence of their federal structure and the principle of cantonal sovereignty. Without this, some of the cantons would almost inevitably have drifted into one camp and some into the other.

During this period a curious state of affairs prevailed in the Diet. A majority of the thirteen cantons which then belonged to the Con-

---
[19] Martin, *op. cit.*, pp. 117–18.
[20] *Ibid*, pp. 121–22.
[21] *Ibid.*, p. 124.
[22] *Ibid.*, pp. 120, 121, 132, 135.

federation were Catholic. The proportion is given by some historians as seven to six, by others as seven and a half to five and a half. But though the Catholic cantons had a numerical majority in the Diet, in wealth and in population they were greatly inferior to the Protestant city-states such as Berne and Zurich. For this reason both parties hesitated to carry out their aims. Both valued the old alliance, which would be destroyed by overt action; both respected the basic doctrine of cantonal sovereignty and nonintervention. A kind of equilibrium resulted which led to a neutrality that became the permanent foreign policy of Switzerland.

A further proof of the value of cantonal sovereignty, or at least independence, is to be found in the history of the short-lived Helvetian Republic of 1798. Its Constitution, drawn up by Peter Ochs and inaugurated at the time of the invasion of Switzerland by French troops, was planned according to the French model. The new Republic was declared first of all to be "One and indivisible."[23] It created in place of the old loose alliance of sovereign and independent states a bureaucratic and unitary nation. The cantons, which had always commanded men's loyalties, were to become mere administrative areas, like the recently made French departments. "The numerous cantonal governments were to be replaced by the single Helvetic government; instead of the numerous capital cities and chief towns, there was to be one seat of government; in place of the many legislative bodies, one legislature and one uniform administrative system."[24] The executive power was given to a Directory framed on the French model and acting through six ministries.

Every aspect of this Constitution was directly contrary to Swiss tradition, and the unity it arbitrarily imposed entailed for the Swiss a total loss of their ancient liberties, which were grounded in local independence. All the defects of the overcentralized French system were suddenly imposed on them. "In the political life of a nation," declares a recent Swiss historian, "it is hardly possible to conceive of a greater leap than Switzerland was now expected to make."[25]

[23] See texts of the Proclamation. All public documents of the period bore these words.
[24] Oeschli, *op. cit.*, pp. 319–21.
[25] *Ibid.*, p. 318.

As a result, the Helvetic Republic was never felt to be a national government.[26] It was cordially disliked and struck no roots among the people, in spite of the many worth-while laws that it enacted. At first it met with determined resistance in some cantons, and in 1799 the hatred it inspired led the inhabitants of eastern Switzerland to welcome their old enemies, the Austrians, with enthusiasm. In many places trees of liberty were angrily destroyed.[27]

In the course of its short life, the Helvetic Republic saw four *coups d'état*.[28] In 1800 the dissolution of the Directory was voted and confusion and semi-anarchy followed. The very semblance of legal government almost disappeared among the quarrels of the "unitarians," as the centralizers were called, and the "federalists" or decentralizers. At last an appeal was made to Bonaparte, then First Consul. Napoleon's policy was always to make use of tradition when it could serve his purpose, and the Malmaison Constitution, which he promulgated in 1801, was much more in harmony with Swiss conceptions than that of the Helvetic. The Act of Mediation, promulgated in 1803, gave back, at least in appearance, a large measure of their old freedom and authority to the cantons.

Partly as a result of the bitter experience of the Helvetian Republic and partly because of the complete inability of the Swiss to agree among themselves after sixteen years of artificial unity, the new Constitution, set up in 1815 with the approval of the Great Powers at Vienna, recreated to a large extent the old system of a loose alliance of sovereign cantons. In fact, the experience of a premature and foreign-imposed centralization helped to play into the hands of reaction, and retarded the natural process of amalgamation. It was in part responsible for the postponement for some thirty years of the development of Switzerland from an alliance of small sovereign states into a modern nation.

The settlement of 1815, which returned their independence to the cantons, left the forces of reaction in power in many of them, but liberalism, strong during the era of the Revolution, continued its work underground, and after 1830 took on fresh force. A movement known as the Regeneration developed, and under its influence a

---

[26] Martin, *op. cit.*, pp. 186–87.
[27] Daendliker, *op. cit.*, pp. 195–96.
[28] Oeschli, *op. cit.*, pp. 342–45.

number of cantons revised their constitutions in a democratic direction.[29] This was not always accomplished without violence, and tension arose between the unregenerate cantons and those which were in favor of reform. The first aim of the liberals was a revision of the Pact and the creation of a stronger federal power, necessitated by the development of the industrial revolution and the resultant democratic trend.[30]

During the late eighteenth century there had already been a considerable growth of industry in Switzerland. Textile manufacture, in particular, had developed, and in many cantons cheese-making had taken the place of agriculture. But after 1815, with the lifting of the Continental blockade, the Swiss were obliged to face increased competition, especially that of England. Moreover, all the surrounding countries promptly set up high tariff barriers which injured Swiss trade.[31] A severe economic crisis followed. "Switzerland," says William Martin, "then resembled the Europe of today. The cantons were entire masters of their individual economic policy, and they could not agree among themselves. They made use of all kinds of aggressive measures against each other. Almost all the errors that we have committed recently in Europe had their precedents in the Confederation during the era of the Restoration."[32]

Against this internal disorder, and the tariff wars of foreign Powers, the small individual cantons were unable to act effectively. The existence of tariff barriers at every cantonal frontier, although these were sometimes only a few miles apart, the use of different weights and measures, of different systems of coinage in each region, was intolerable. Moreover, industry continued to develop, thanks to the initiative and energy of the Swiss people, creating an urgent need for the free movement of individuals within the Confederation; labor had to be able to adjust itself to demand and factories required hands to thrive. But under the old regime the people of the different cantons had been even more sharply divided from each other than are the inhabitants of modern Europe; a man from Glaris, for instance, could not settle in Berne or Zurich without special permission. The Constitution of 1815 had restored these re-

---

[29] Martin, *op. cit.*, Chapters IX and X; Oeschli, *op. cit.*, pp. 361–68.
[30] See A. Gassner, *Vom Stattenbund zum Bundesstaat* (Zurich, 1926), pp. 1–20, for a detailed discussion of the Liberal Movement; also Martin, *op. cit.*, Chapter X.
[31] Martin, *op. cit.*, pp. 239–45.
[32] *Ibid.*, p. 241.

strictive rights to the cantons, and some of them had taken advantage of the fact to expell Swiss citizens from other regions who had settled within their borders. The need of a central authority, both to protect Swiss interests abroad and to co-ordinate production within, was more and more evident. This was a prime factor in the demand for a revised constitution.

At the same time, the shifting of population which resulted from growing industry made in itself for better understanding among the Swiss and the development of a sense of national unity. Common interests and occupations tended to break down local particularisms and jealousies. In fact, the industrial revolution had much the same result in Switzerland as in the Germanies at the time of the Zollverein. In studying the period, one is reminded of the poem of Hoffman von Fallersleben in honor of that institution:

> Leather, salmon, eels and matches,
>   Cows and madder, paper, shears,
> Ham and cheese and boots and vetches,
>   Wool and soap and yarns and beers ...
>
> Articles of home consumption,
>   All our thanks are due to you!
> You have wrought without presumption
>   What no intellect could do.
> You have made the ... nation
>   Stand together hand in hand,
> More than the Confederation
>   Ever did for Fatherland.[33]

The building of the railroads also made for unity. Not only did they bring the inhabitants of the various cantons into much closer contact with each other and open the remote mountain regions to outside influences, but it was obviously impossible that in so small a country trains should stop at the borders of every canton and be subjected to a diversity of rules and regulations. With the development of railroads Switzerland became a land of passage, and the necessity of dealing with other countries in regard to international travel made a central authority imperative. In fact, even if no other factors making for unity had existed, the railroads alone would probably have imposed it.[34]

[33] J. G. Legge, *Rhyme and Revolution in Germany* (London, 1918), p. 189.
[34] Martin, *op. cit.*, 273–75.

The growth of the democratic movement itself served to bring the Swiss together. It was in popular assemblies such as the great Federal Schützenverein that the national ideal found expression, that Swiss as distinguished from cantonal patriotism was fostered.[35]

A closer union and a stronger central authority were therefore obviously both needed and desired by a majority of the Swiss, but they were opposed by the older rural cantons, which had long found protection in the principle of total cantonal sovereignty. They held that the agreement of 1815, like the ancient alliances, was a treaty, and so could only be modified by the consent of all the subscribing parties. This was also, on the whole, the opinion of the Great Powers, signatories of the agreements of Vienna, which guaranteed the neutrality of Switzerland.[36]

The question of cantonal sovereignty was closely related to that of religion. The liberals were animated by the anticlerical spirit of their Jacobin predecessors. They were impatient, and the tone of their attacks not only on the Jesuits but on the monastic orders, which played a great part in the life of the Catholic cantons, were extraordinarily violent. The Jesuits were compared by them to ravens, to bats, to devils. They were said to be *"mit nacht bedeckt ... vom Todes Worm gequalt."* "A monk is a creature unfit for the present times," declared Augustin Keller in a speech made before the Council of his canton on January 13, 1841. "Imagine a monk in the greenest corner of paradise—wherever his shadow fell the grass would wither, life would perish." He ended this speech by announcing that the modern version of "Carthago delenda est" was "The cloisters must be destroyed."[37] Small wonder that the Catholic cantons felt their religious freedom threatened; yet they were almost as intransigeant as their opponents, and at last they formed a separate league, the Sonderbund.

Alliances between individual cantons had existed in the past, but they had always been regarded as a threat to the Confederation. With the formation of the Sonderbund which, as its name indicates, represented a definite secessionist movement, the situation became dangerous, for the foreign Powers were looking on, ready to find

---

[35] Gassner, *op. cit.*, pp. 20–30.
[36] Oeschli, *op. cit.*, p. 390; Martin, *op. cit.*, pp. 255, 261.
[37] Gassner, *op. cit.*, pp. 32–39.

The Swiss Pattern of Federation 275

profit in a dissolution of the Bund. Some of them were actually on the point of active interference when the Swiss at last settled their own problems.[38]

A series of incidents such as the arbitrary closing of certain convents in the Canton of Aargau and the recall of the Jesuits to Lucerne in defiance of the decision of the Diet at last brought armed conflict in 1847. The war, however, was short and relatively bloodless, and once it was over the desire for unity reasserted itself. The cantons which formed the Sonderbund had been willing to look beyond the national frontier for support, but secession was a council of anger and despair—perhaps, to some extent, a kind of political blackmail—and they had no real wish to be absorbed by their Catholic neighbors. On the other hand, the victorious Confederation showed itself, on the whole, generous. It imposed no heavy burden on the defeated Secessionists, and in the new Constitution which transformed Switzerland from a *Staatenbund* into a *Bundesstaat*, the rights of the cantons were retained to a remarkable extent. Although this Constitution was consciously modeled on that of the United States it granted the federal government much less power than does our own.[39] Moreover, the religious rights of the communities were carefully safeguarded, and religious freedom was combined with state support of the church of the majority in each canton. Tolerance and the principle of states' rights saved the Confederation.

The value to Switzerland of this principle and of the reciprocal tolerance and respect on which it was founded was again evident during the First World War. Her position at that time was extremely difficult, for her commerce was chiefly with the Allies, from whom she got the food she needed, while the coal for her industries came from Germany, so that she was obliged to steer a careful course. Yet, among her people opinions were sharply divided and passions extremely violent. The German Swiss were, for the most part, strongly wedded to the German cause, while French Switzerland was vehemently pro-Ally. Indeed, the French-Swiss press was fre-

---

[38] Oeschli, *op. cit.*, pp. 391, 394, 395.
[39] *Ibid.*, pp. 396–99; Martin, *op. cit.*, pp. 263–68. See also M. L. Tripp, *The Swiss and United States Federal Constitutional Systems* (Paris, 1940), and W. Rappard, *La Constitution fédérale de la Suisse* (Neuchâtel, 1948). For American influences, see in the latter work pp. 75, 88, 117, etc.

quently so outspoken in its attacks on the Germans as to cause embarrassment to the government at Berne, and bring down on itself angry criticism from other cantons for its lack of patriotism and misconception of neutrality.[40] On the other hand, the mere suspicion that certain officers of the General Staff who were pro-German in sympathy had sometimes passed on information given to them as neutrals to the German representatives in Berne evoked a storm of protest throughout the country.

It seemed that a nation composed of groups so closely related to the peoples engaged in a mortal struggle at their very doors could scarcely hold together, yet Switzerland resolutely maintained her neutrality in the face of every kind of pressure. This was not from a cowardly wish to avoid fighting, but from a deep conviction that only by standing aloof could she hope to keep her integrity at the end of the war. German and French Swiss alike knew that if they were involved in the struggle the Confederation would probably be broken up and its territories partitioned among its neighbors. Much as some might believe the cause of the Allies to be just, much as others might sympathize with Germany, none had the least desire to become a province of the Reich or a department of France. The knowledge that only within the Confederation could they keep their independence and their own way of life united the Swiss, in spite of difference of opinion.

The same tolerance was evident in recent years when several cantons, including the once aristocratic Geneva, elected Communist administrations. Ever since 1917, Switzerland has been consistently anti-Bolshevik, and the Confederation only recognized the Soviet Union officially after the Second World War. Yet interference with the internal affairs of Leftist cantons was not even considered.

Swiss history, then, proves that the strength and durability of a federation depends on voluntary co-operation and the principle of nonintervention in the internal affairs of member states. On the other hand, the development of Switzerland in the nineteenth century also indicates that in the modern world the surrender of absolute sovereignty on the part of each member of a federation is

---

[40] The history of this controversy can be followed in the pages of the Swiss daily press during the war years. The *Gazette de Lausanne* and the *Basler Nachrichten* are particularly typical. The foreign editor of the *Gazette* was always referred to by the German-Swiss press as *"der Perfide M.M."* because of his pro-Ally sympathies.

necessary. Only by modifying it and accepting the democratic principle for states as well as for individuals can a wider unity and a power of common action be secured. The Constitution of 1848 was necessary if the Swiss Confederation was to survive. The history of Switzerland in the nineteenth century, like that of the United States, illustrates the fact that once such a surrender is voluntarily made, science and industry tend to favor a growing unity by making the world smaller and its people increasingly interdependent.

Once the Constitution of 1848 had created a genuine federal government, its powers tended constantly to increase. In 1874, barely twenty-six years after the passage of that seemingly revolutionary document, the need for a greater amount of federal authority led the Swiss to write a new Constitution. By it the organization of the army, the power to legislate in regard to companies, the regulation of marriage laws, and, in certain cases where the public safety was concerned, the care of forests and waterways were all placed in the hands of the federal government.[41] Since then further powers have frequently been conceded to the federal authority; in fact, the trend, as in the United States, has constantly been in the direction of greater centralization.[42] However, because this evolution has been gradual and has taken place only in response to widespread demand, it has roused little active antagonism.

At the same time, a remarkably large amount of power still lies in the hands of the cantons and their councils. For instance, there is no federal income tax in Switzerland and the only revenues of which the Central Government disposes come from tariffs. The civil and criminal codes of law are still cantonal matters. Even the army, although it is entirely under federal control, is organized in some respects along cantonal lines.[43] That these elements of decentralization have not been unduly weakening to Switzerland is evident from the relative prosperity and stability which that small country has enjoyed under the difficult circumstances of modern times. Preservation of local responsibility has helped to make Swiss society at once progressive and stable. It has prevented the anonym-

[41] Oeschli, *op. cit.*, pp. 410–11; Rappard, *La Constitution fédérale de la Suisse*, Chapters XV, XVI.
[42] See Rappard, *Constitution fédérale*, Chapters XVI–XIX, for details.
[43] De Rougemont and Muret, *op. cit.*, Chapter IX. See also Rappard, *Constitution fédérale*, pp. 265 *et seq.*, 419, 420, 434; Oeschli, *op. cit.*, p. 410.

ity that lessens democracy's value in huge, highly centralized countries.

Another suggestion relevant to modern Europe emerges from the history of Switzerland in the era of Napoleon. It is that dissensions within individual states may weaken a confederation far more than interstate disputes.

During the eighteenth century, which was a period of prosperity for Switzerland, the ruling oligarchies in many cantons became very narrow. The patricians who governed the city-states were reluctant to open their doors to citizens from the lower ranks or rural districts, or to allow emigration from other parts of the Confederation.[44] Social and economic inequalities grew, and there were rumblings of discontent. This was fertile soil for revolutionary ideas, but at first the French Revolution had little positive effect in Switzerland. The ruling classes mistrusted it, and the French conception of liberty and equality was very unlike the Swiss tradition of freedom. Moreover, Switzerland had an alliance with the King of France, dating back to the days of Louis XIV, which had been extremely precious to her in maintaining her independence. The violences of the Revolution, the brutal massacre of the Swiss Guard, the execution of the King, alienated many Swiss sympathies. It was only in 1798, when Bonaparte's wish to command the passes into Italy and the greed excited in the penniless Directory by rumors of the treasure of Berne led to an invasion of Swiss territory, that the revolutionary storm broke over the cantons.

However, from the first, many Swiss had been attracted by the ideas of the Revolution and some went to France to take part in the struggle for liberty. A Swiss club was set up in Paris which became the headquarters of these ardent spirits, and they inundated their own country with pamphlets, brochures, and propaganda.[45] In each canton the discontented found in the Revolution a cause to which they could rally. These revolutionary parties within the state were much like the "fifth columns" of our day; won over to the new ideology, they were ready enough to act as agents of France, which proclaimed it.

---

[44] Martin, *op. cit.*, Chapter VII; Oeschli, *op. cit.*, Chapter XXIII. See also Daendiliker, *op. cit.*, pp. 219–26.

[45] Oeschli, *op. cit.*, pp. 290, 292–93, 300–6 *et seq.*; Martin, *op. cit.*, pp. 174–80.

No country was at this time more broken up and divided than Switzerland. As we have seen, all kinds of inequalities and differences existed both between the cantons and between their inhabitants, and a national spirit was not yet born to unite the Confederation. Existing injustices were the best "talking points" of the revolutionary parties, and their propaganda, their gospel of the Rights of Man, were important in breaking down resistance among the Swiss. Men like Peter Ochs and Frederic de la Harpe, sincere idealists though they were, not only prepared but took part in the subjugation of their country.[46]

The complete story of Napoleon's dealings with the Swiss proves how useful to him were these revolutionary groups in the various cantons. They furnished him with information and with creatures favorable to his interest whom he could put in power. In fact, the revolutionary minorities showed themselves far more willing to accept foreign aid in carrying out their ideas than the warring cantons had been in the age of religious wars. The universal aims of the revolutionary doctrines cut across the old patriotic concept, just as the Communist creed of world revolution cuts across the national ideal today.

A final suggestion for our time, arising from recent Swiss history, is that the existence of several lines of cleavage within a federal state is not, as might be supposed, a source of weakness, but rather of strength.

In Switzerland three general and more or less permanent grounds of difference exist among the cantons: cultural, religious, and economic. We have seen that the last two, the religious and economic divergencies between Catholic and Protestant cantons and between peasant and city states, gave rise in every century to conflicts and even wars. The first-named factor, cultural differences, has become important in the last 150 years. Yet in the Confederation as it has developed since 1848 these very divergencies have helped to maintain the union as a whole. They have obliged the various cantons to rely now on one group in the Confederation, now on another, according to the question at stake.

Had the lines of cleavage been everywhere the same, had there existed two "blocs"—one, for instance, Catholic, French-speaking,

---

[46] Oeschli, *op. cit.*, pp. 316–18.

and agricultural, and the other Protestant, German-speaking, and industrial—these monolithic organisms would probably have broken away from each other sooner or later. But, fortunately for the Swiss, the three principal lines of fission do not coincide. "The linguistic frontiers," says André Siegfried in his remarkable book, *La Suisse, démocratie témoin*,[47] "do not coincide with the religious frontiers nor do either correspond to those of the Cantons." "If, for instance," he goes on, "Romance Switzerland had been entirely Protestant and German Switzerland entirely Catholic, their precious equilibrium would probably never have been secured." Had the Protestant Cantons also been entirely industrial and the German wholly agricultural, or vice versa, an equilibrium would have been even harder to maintain. It is the fact that every variety of combination exists—that, for instance, Vaud is Protestant, French-speaking, and rural, while Berne is Protestant, but industrial and German-speaking, and Valais half French and half German culturally, but wholly Catholic and largely rural—that has made co-operation in the Federal Chambers possible. Each group has need of each of the others in some respect. This is the essence of a true federal union.

To recapitulate, the points concerning federation of states that I have drawn from Swiss history are, first, that a confederation, even if it remains largely decentralized, may be strong, although more so for defense than for conquest. Second, the strength and durability of a confederation will depend on observance of the principle of states' rights and of nonintervention in the internal affairs and ways of life of the member states; that, in short, the real basis of federal union is tolerance. The third point is that in spite of the principle of local autonomy some central authority is necessary, and that it can be secured without infringing too much on local freedom if the idea of absolute national sovereignty is modified in favor of a democratic principle among states. Fourth, a too rapid centralization, a premature effort at standardization and uniformity may impede the evolution of co-operation and genuine union. If it is not supported by public opinion in all the member states, centralization may be a dangerous error and delay the growth of a common will

[47] André Siegfried, *La Suisse, démocratie témoin* (Neuchâtel, 1948), pp. 133-36.

and purpose. Fifth, ideological dissensions within a member state are more dangerous to the stability of a federation than divergencies among the states themselves. Lastly, the existence of various differences and lines of cleavage among member states is no barrier to common action, but may, on the contrary, help in the evolution of the federal system.

Where Europe is concerned, the first point, that of the possible strength of a union, even a loose one, is important. Yet the statement must be qualified. Rappard points out that, in addition to their various agreements, two factors contributed to the survival of the Swiss cantons.[48] One was a common will and purpose, that of resistance to foreign tyranny, and the other was the resolute courage and military capacity of the Swiss people. Had the free nations of Europe possessed such a common resolution in the years between the two World Wars, they, too, might have united. It is true that in modern warfare industrial resources count for more than individual courage (although without that even the best of weapons are useless), but Europe had and still has great industrial and military potentials which, if resources were to be pooled, would make her strong for defense. It was, in part at least, the hope of each separate country to avoid war and its sacrifices, the wish to stand, if possible, outside the conflict, whatever became of the rest of the world, that prevented whole-hearted union and effective preparation, and caused the collapse of Europe. Hitler was able to destroy its disunited and unready nations one by one.

Many Europeans, seeing where such selfish policies lead, are now eager to act together and make part of an effective common organization. They are increasingly willing to take the first step and create a federation among themselves. Both fear of danger from without and hope of economic advantage in union tend to bring them together. But whether a real will to fight, to resist aggression at all cost, and, above all, a readiness to fight in the defense of others with the conviction that all must stand together, actually exists, no one can tell.

As to the second point, the value of the principle of states' rights, a divergence of opinion already seems to exist among the members of the future European federation. The French idea of a United

[48] Rappard, *Cinq siècles*, pp. 587–90.

Europe is quite unlike that of the Swiss or the Anglo-Saxons, as a number of speeches by M. Reynaud and other French politicians show. The French have, in fact, never been able clearly to grasp the concept of a true federation and their history shows how foreign it is to them. Not only did her kings early centralize France, but even with the fall of the old regime, the Revolution carried on the process by destroying the ancient provinces. The Jacobins, who triumphed over the decentralizing Girondists, set up a regime even more rigidly centered in the hands of the sovereign than that of the monarchs whom they overthrew, and Napoleon carried the process even further.

The present French conception of a United Europe seems to be a general rallying of all peoples around a central government. This conception would be inacceptable to all the smaller countries of the Continent, who would be obliged by it to abandon their independence without any guarantee of nonintervention in their internal affairs. In this connection, the dark story of the Helvetic Republic, product of French centralizing democracy, should be remembered.

But the threat to Europe springs today as much from revolutionary parties within each nation as from the menace of foreign aggression. A striking resemblance exists here to conditions in the Revolutionary and Napoleonic era. The supernational appeal of Communism to the present generation had its parallel in the universal and humanitarian doctrines of the French Revolution, with their stress on the Rights of Man and their slogan of Liberty, Equality, Fraternity. The same rejection of old loyalties in the name of wider principles, the same determination to destroy the established order is evident in the revolutionaries of 1793 and in present-day Communists, and then, as now, a strong and ruthless foreign Power, proclaiming revolutionary ideas but animated by imperialistic aims, was ready to profit by the breakdown of each state. Napoleon, long before Hitler or Stalin, knew the value of secret allies, of a fifth column in the countries he wished to dominate. The harsh and ruthless exploitation of Switzerland by those who invaded her in the name of Liberty and Equality, the total disappearance of those very principles during the foreign occupation, might well be pointed out to men who are ready today to sacrifice their countries to the cause of World Revolution in the hands of imperialistic Russia.

As to the final point, various lines of cleavage exist among the nations of modern Europe, as they do among the cantons of Switzerland. Some are cultural, some religious, many are economic. But the history of the Swiss Confederation suggests that such lines of cleavage may not be fatal to co-operation, that they may even, on the contrary, be useful in the perpetual series of compromises that is the life of a democratic federation, or indeed of any free state.

Those who hope for European union must not demand that all the nations who adhere to it follow their own model, even if they believe it to be best. A federal Europe, like the old Swiss Confederation, should be open to all nations who want to join it, whether they are socialist, democratic, monarchist, or authoritarian, provided that their ambitions do not endanger the safety of the union or of the world. That such a European union should begin on the economic level is both the best solution and the one that is actually being adopted. With time a progressive amalgamation may take place.

It will be objected that the difficulty of combining into one union states whose economy is collectivist with others still living under a regime of free enterprise is greater than was that of uniting Protestants and Catholics or peasants and city workers. This may be true where Revolutionary Communism as it exists in Russia is concerned. The Marxian doctrine of World Revolution is entirely hostile to any such union. Some modification both of total collectivism and total free enterprise would certainly be necessary for co-operation within a federation. But, on the other hand, a degree of social control exists in every European state today, and relations between such semisocialized countries as Great Britain under the Labour Government and states built on the principle of co-operation, like Denmark, or on relative freedom of enterprise, have not proved impossible. Were a United Europe to be created, the various economic systems might even act upon each other, so that modifications of both would follow, as they did in Switzerland.

It is not desirable that the peoples of the world should be alike. Variety is the source of progress and the chief quality which distinguishes human beings from ants and termites. The most hideous aspect of modern collectivism is that, whatever its declarations, in practice it tries to reduce all men to a single pattern imposed by the state. This is characteristic of tyrants, since it makes their rule easier, but it is the end not only of personal liberty but of progress and civilization. The federal state implies a certain amount of permanent struggle, since it must constantly reconcile varying interests by consent rather than by force, but it has often been said that the price of freedom is perpetual vigilance. The monolithic state as conceived by totalitarians of all kinds can only endure by the use of force, and it entails for the individual a living death of the spirit.

It should, on the one hand, be consoling to impenitent nationalists to find that the Swiss have not given up their cantonal characteristics, nor lost the feeling of local patriotism. If asked what he is, an inhabitant of the Confederation will be more apt to answer, "I am Vaudois" or "I am Bernese," than to say, "I am Swiss." On the other hand, those who fear the weakness of the federal system should realize that although German and French Swiss do not fully admire each other and each is deeply convinced that his own group has contributed most to civilization, this does not prevent loyalty to each other in time of danger. Switzerland, being composite, illustrates in a measure the fruitful conceptions of Harold Laski's early work, *The Pluralistic State,* and it also answers to Ernest Renan's definition of a nation as "peoples who, having accomplished great things in common in the past, wish to accomplish them in the future."[49]

Such an organization, a United Europe might become. In it, as in Switzerland, variety of culture as well as local pride and patriotism would have place, yet a common bond would gradually come to unite the component parts. The thing is not impossible, since it has actually been achieved on a small scale in Switzerland.

---

[49] Ernest Renan, *Qu'est-ce qu'une nation?* See G. P. Gooch, *Nationalism* (London, 1920), p. 7, for a discussion of the term.

SIR JOHN SEELEY, PRAGMATIC HISTORIAN IN A NATIONALISTIC AGE

THOMAS P. PEARDON

THE REPUTATION of Sir John Seeley illustrates the danger of writing an enormously successful book on a subject of great public importance. Apart from the interest that students of intellectual history have in his *Ecce Homo* (1865), he is remembered chiefly as the author of *The Expansion of England* (1883), which is treated as a philosophy of Imperialism, and as the writer of some dubious aphorisms about the study of history. A philosopher of Imperialism he certainly was, but not in the sense that is sometimes alleged; and his views concerning history were broader and more sagacious than is generally agreed. For Seeley had one of the most vigorous and acute minds of his generation. He was not an original thinker, but he was sensitive to the problems and intellectual currents of his time and greatly gifted in the art of lucid and stimulating exposition. He represents one phase of the impact on a liberal mind of science, nationalism, and democracy.

The English have paid little attention to Seeley except to remember *Ecce Homo* and *The Expansion of England*. The French treat him somewhat more extensively, but as a philosopher of British Imperialism.[1] The Germans have taken him more seriously, both as an Imperialist and also as a man of wider significance. Only in German are there books or monographs devoted to Seeley exclusively; of these there are at least three,[2] one a biography and critical study, the others doctoral dissertations dealing with his views on history and politics and his *"Humanismus."* The biography, by Adolf Rein, was published in 1912, seventeen years after Seeley's death. Rein visited Cambridge, talked with the widow and old associates of his subject, and gathered together what he could of the man as well

[1] Jacques Gazeau, *L'Impérialisme anglais: Son évolution: Carlyle-Seeley-Chamberlain* (Paris, 1903).
[2] Adolf Rein, *Sir John Robert Seeley: Eine Studie über den Historiker* (Langensalza, 1912); Erich Rosenblüth, *John Robert Seeley: Sein Historisches und Politisches Weltbild* (Berlin, 1934); Georg Brettschneider, *Der Humanismus John Robert Seeleys: Ein Beitrag zur Geschichte der Ideologie des Britischen Imperialismus* (Borna, Leipzig, 1937).

as the writer. But the fruits of this research are less rich than one would wish. Seeley was not one to pour out his soul in letters and journals, which are the delight of biographers. We know him chiefly from the few books and more numerous articles that he wrote, in a style admirable in force and lucidity, but spare and restrained, a style made wholly subordinate to the task of exposition, seeking to persuade men's minds but scorning to try to influence them through their emotions.

Born in 1834, Seeley was the son of a London publisher, Evangelical in religion and Liberal in politics. From his earliest days he manifested exceptional ability. At school and at Christ's College, Cambridge, his dominant interests were in literature and philosophy rather than politics. As an adolescent he published some poems and later, after becoming Professor of Latin at University College, London, he edited Book I of Livy. In the meantime he had come under the influence of F. D. Maurice and Charles Kingsley. Evangelical Christianity was replaced by a kind of ethical and social religion of which *Ecce Homo* (1865) and *Natural Religion* (1882), the latter planned years before it was published, were the expressions. These characteristically mid-Victorian attempts to resolve the conflict between religion and science may be taken to represent a second stage in the development of Seeley's mind, as the youthful poems represented the first. It was only after he became Regius Professor of Modern History at Cambridge in 1869 that Seeley found his true calling as a writer on politics and history. That appointment coincided more or less closely with the beginning of the era of crisis and adjustment from which British politics, domestic and foreign, have not yet emerged. It may fairly be said to have been his purpose during the remaining twenty-five years of his life to analyze the nature of that era and to prescribe solutions for its problems. He concluded that the foundations of politics had been shifted and he meant to arouse men to the necessities of the new day.

Yet Seeley's views on religion always had strongly historical and political overtones that give continuity to the successive phases of his intellectual life. It has been well said that *Ecce Homo* portrayed Jesus as the Founder of a Society, a kind of statesman. Salvation is pictured as coming to the individual only through the common life of the state. Whatever may have been his early views, in later life Seeley had a very special and somewhat meager understanding of religion. By it, in the words of H. A. L. Fisher, "he understood not a belief in the supernatural, but an habitual and regulated admiration, either for a moral ideal, or for beauty, or else for the unity of nature."[3] The elements of truth in this conception are apt to impress themselves upon a man in proportion to his decline in faith in the supernatural. So it seems to have been with Seeley. His interest in religion came to be noticeably political—or perhaps it would be fairer to say that he developed an increasingly sharp appreciation of the political importance of religion, its role in producing such agreement on basic principles regarding life, destiny, and politics as is essential for social survival. *Natural Religion* has been interpreted in this sense as a search for a religion to correspond to the modern nation state,[4] while the *Introduction to Political Science*, like other writings, stresses its state-building as well as its state-preserving qualities. This is a revealing emphasis in a man's thinking; its development may account for the contrast which Rein[5] correctly draws between the warm, confident, enthusiastic tone of *Ecce Homo* and the cold reasoning of *Natural Religion*. We detect a note of tragedy in the incidental reference, in the *Life of Stein,* to the "desperate despair which overtakes so many in these days in the midst of prosperity, and which makes the slightest visitation of calamity intolerable, the disbelief in life itself and in the whole order of the universe."[6]

More directly relevant than these intellectual concerns were doubts about the trend of government, at home and abroad. For the first time England was to be ruled by organized public opinion and democracy. "Few principles are better settled in the politics of the present day," Seeley wrote, "than the absolute sovereignty of public opinion. If the nation demands a thing, there is no politician or party of politicians that will now undertake to refuse it."[7] First demonstrated in the campaign for Catholic Emancipation, the rule of public opinion had taken on new significance with the extension of the suffrage. The manifestations of democracy in the elections of 1874 and 1880 aroused foreboding in Seeley's mind, and like

---

[3] H. A. L. Fisher, "Sir John Seeley," *Fortnightly Review*, LX, new series (1896), 186.
[4] Brettschneider, *op. cit.*, pp. 24–47.
[5] Rein, *op. cit.*, p. 103.
[6] *Life and Times of Stein* (Cambridge, 1878), III, 546.
[7] "The English Revolution of the Nineteenth Century," *Macmillan's Magazine*, XXII (1870), 348.

many other Liberals he was frightened by the movement for Irish Home Rule. The center of gravity in the state had been shifted to the workers; and thereby had been created a problem of political education whose solution was by no means certain. He was doubtful if the mass of the working class could ever be educated to the point of having sound judgment on complicated questions of national policy, and depressed by the reflection that a little education seemed to dispose to criticism rather than to a following of "wiser" persons. Even among the educated he detected little precise political knowledge.[8] But he was certain that the experiment in education must be made and to it he devoted a great deal of thought.

Equally significant changes were transforming the international system. The triumph of nationality had produced a new type of organic state, far more united and powerful than the dynastic forms of an earlier day. Moreover, the progress of science and invention—especially the application of steam and electricity—were working a revolution in communications and therefore in the world of nations. Like De Tocqueville, Seeley looked eastward to Russia and westward across the seas to America and saw the dawning of a new world of states. Without benefit of high-powered institutes and organized research, he had discovered the "super-powers." He concluded that "a larger type of state than any hitherto known is springing up in the world" with portentous consequences for the state system:

> Russia already presses somewhat heavily on Central Europe; what will she do when with her vast territory and population she equals Germany in intelligence and organisation, when all her railways are made, her people educated, and her government settled on a solid basis?—and let us remember that if we allow her half a century to make so much progress her population will at the end of that time be not eighty but nearly a hundred and sixty millions. At that time which many here present may live to see, Russia and the United States will surpass in power the states now called great as much as the great country-states of the sixteenth century surpassed Florence.[9]

It was such considerations as these, along with the impression made upon him by the success of nationalist uprisings against

---

[8] "Political Somnambulism," *Macmillan's Magazine*, XLIII (1880–1881), 28–44.
[9] *The Expansion of England* (London, 1883), pp. 349–50.

Napoleon, by the rebirth of Germany, and by his sense of the superiority of Continental thought and research over those of England, that lay back of Seeley's later writings. They are reflected even in his early pleas for reorganization of university education and for the teaching of English in schools. They shine through the numerous pages of reflection and moralizing in his three volumes on Stein. They were with him during the twenty-five years of teaching at Cambridge. And they were the direct inspiration of all his books on history and politics. All these works were directed towards two great aims: the political education of the people, and the prescription of national policy for the new era.

As he saw it, the first step toward the realization of these aims was to develop an "inductive science of politics" which could be made the basis for sound political education and successful prescription of political remedies.[10] Such a science must be founded on history, but on history studied in a new spirit. For the ruling schools of historians, Seeley had little respect. They sought literary effect rather than scientific accuracy. They were partisan, reading back contemporary alignments and controversies into a past to which they did not apply. They "lost themselves in mere narrative," collecting miscellaneous facts, arranging them in more or less pleasing order, but lacking all clue to their real meaning or any principle of arrangement other than that involved in presenting a chronological story.[11]

Against this "old school of historians" Seeley set the ideal of a history that would concern itself with general laws, laying the foundations for that "philosophy of universal history" to which a succession of thinkers from Vico and Herder to Comte and Buckle had moved. Never before had the conditions of its search been more favorable, Seeley felt, than in his own day. New methods of investigation had provided a body of tested facts; new scientific attitudes had replaced or could replace the old literary and ethical interests,

---

[10] The most famous of Seeley's pronouncements on "the science of politics" was the inaugural lecture given under the title "The Teaching of Politics" and reprinted in *Lectures and Essays* (London, 1870), pp. 290–317. Some others are: "Political Education of the Working Classes," *Macmillan's Magazine*, XXXVI (1877), 143–45; "History and Politics," *Macmillan's Magazine*, XL (1879), 289–99, 369–78, 449–58, and XLI (1879–1880), 23–32; "Political Somnambulism," *Macmillan's Magazine*, XLIII (1880–1881), 28–44; "Our Insular Ignorance," *Nineteenth Century*, XVIII (1885), 861–72; "The Impartial Study of Politics," *Contemporary Review*, LIV (1888), 52–65.

[11] "History and Politics," *loc. cit.*; *The Expansion of England*, p. 4.

while the state itself had been shown to be a phenomenon with definite laws of growth that could be uncovered.

The last of these points was of vital concern. For if history was to be itself a science, as well as part of a science of politics, its study must observe definite criteria. One of these was that it restrict itself to the study of the state. Seeley did not underestimate the importance of the nonpolitical aspects of society. Above all, he did not make the mistake of equating state and society. "A nation is not merely a state. It is not only a governed community. It is also an industrial community, a church, a tribe or enlarged clan—to mention only some of the many aspects in which it may be considered."[12] But he felt that the historian had always been more successful when dealing with politics than with anything else. He was contemptuous of the inadequate chapters on manners and customs with which historians had often interlarded their narratives. He proposed that these affairs be left to the anthropologist and sociologist who might give them the serious treatment they deserved.

The politics with which the historian was to deal should be mainly modern politics. Here again, Seeley must be protected from false accusations. He did not contemn the study of the distant past. Indeed, some years after he became a Cambridge professor, at a time when the requirements for the Historical Tripos were being changed, he protested against the decision to reduce the amount of ancient history required for the degree.[13] He regarded the Roman Empire as standing "in the very center of human history . . . the foundation of the present civilization of mankind."[14] His own essays on "Roman Imperialism"[15] were among the best things he wrote; and in his *Political Science* he moved freely back and forth, drawing his illustrations from antiquity or the present, from the primitive and the modern. But he saw special pedagogical value in the study of modern history, partly because its lessons bear so directly upon the problems of the student's own day, partly because it is itself full of unsolved problems upon which the beginner can train his judgment, and partly because the materials for the study of modern times are rich and accessible.

[12] *Ibid.*, p. 297.
[13] Jean O. McLachlan, "The Origin and Early Development of the Cambridge Historical Tripos," *The Cambridge Historical Journal*, IX (1947), 78–105.
[14] *The Expansion of England*, p. 277.
[15] *Lectures and Essays*, Essays I–III.

These criteria of a scientific history were mainly concerned with its content or range. Others dictated the spirit in which the historian must work. Thus he must avoid absorption in petty details so as to deal with great themes and large considerations. He must base himself upon a precise political philosophy in which principles are carefully determined and terms defined closely. He must avoid the use of ethical norms so as to attain a purely naturalistic analysis of state behavior. He must eschew narrative in favor of the statement and solution of problems. And in presenting his conclusions, he must elevate scientific accuracy above the meretricious attractions of beautiful style and popular appeal.

So anxious was Seeley about the last point that he sought means to insulate the researcher from corruption through direct contact with the public. He envisaged a sort of scholarly hierarchy. At the top would be a highly trained set of specialists engaged in research according to the most rigorous techniques. Their results would be presented for the use of other specialists and without any reference to the general reader. In addition to these austere investigators, however, there would be another type of specialists consisting of men trained to appreciate technical scholarship, but also skilled in presenting its conclusions in readable form for the public. Thus real scholarship would be kept pure, while the ordinary reader would be given accurate history instead of the romantic stories upon which he had been fed by Macaulay, Carlyle, and others.[16]

Above all, the study of history must be free from parochialism. Europe, said Seeley, is "a complex of states" with a common history and a common membership in the international society, "the modern brotherhood of European nations, the vast whole of civilization."[17] The history of these states must be studied together, as we study that of the ancient Greek cities. To interpret English history by English causes alone is to ignore the impact of foreign policy upon domestic affairs and institutions. In particular, we must avoid explanations in terms of national character. "No explanation is so vague, so cheap, and so difficult to verify. . . . It is the more suspicious, because it gratifies national vanity."[18] Seeley's own interest was in what he called "International History," which would place

---

[16] "History and Politics," *loc. cit.*, pp. 31–32.
[17] *Ibid.*, p. 32.
[18] *Introduction to Political Science* (London, 1896), p. 134.

due emphasis upon the interrelations and mutual influence of states.

There have been two main criticisms of Seeley's school of historical study: (1) that it narrows the field unduly by restricting it to politics; (2) that it falsifies the past by making it subordinate to the solution of today's problems.

It would certainly be difficult to exaggerate the strength of the political bent in Seeley's mind. We have seen its manifestation in his attitude towards religion. It may be significant, too, as a German writer has suggested,[19] that when he wrote two essays on Milton, he considered Milton's political opinions before his poetry. He was too wise, as we have said, to treat the state as if it were the whole of civilization, but he had an exalted conception of the dignity and importance of the state in human affairs as the essential condition of the good life. And so it was in his views of history. If he had had his way, the Historical Tripos at Cambridge would have been called the Political Tripos. Failing to secure this, he sought to include as much political science and political economy as his colleagues would accept. A decade or so later, he resisted strongly the efforts of younger men to lessen the emphasis on theory and to increase the proportion of pure history.[20]

But it is worth noting that Seeley took a pretty broad view of the scope of politics. He had little interest in the recapitulation of political events or the episodes of party warfare. Rather, he sought to explain the genesis and transformations of broad policy or even, as in his *Political Science,* the forces that produce the rise and fall of states themselves. Specifically, he warned his pupils against the danger of writing the history "rather of the Parliament than of the state and nation."[21]

We have already pointed out the importance Seeley attributed to nonpolitical factors in history. Political economy he regarded as important in the making of political scientists,[22] and few men can have shown more appreciation of the state-building power of religion. When, in one of his essays on Milton, he declares politics

---

[19] Brettschneider, *op. cit.,* p. 90, note 9.
[20] McLachlan, *loc. cit.,* p. 84.
[21] *The Expansion of England,* p. 30.
[22] "The Teaching of Politics," *Lectures and Essays,* p. 299; "A Historical Society," *Macmillan's Magazine,* XLV (1881–1882), 45.

to be "the greatest and most important of human pursuits,"[23] it quickly appears that he meant more than is sometimes included under the head of politics. He was drawn to Milton by the breadth of that poet's views of national well-being and of the revolution through which he had lived. "He felt the unity of national life" and the implications of contemporary events for literature, education, and life in all its aspects. Especially, Milton saw the importance of "culture," by which Seeley meant chiefly education. In the same connection, Seeley criticizes Carlyle, rightly or wrongly, for not seeing "how much depends upon culture and what infinite hope lies in it. It is scarcely too much to say that culture is the larger half of politics." With a low opinion of human capacity, pessimistic about the possibility of raising the average of intelligence among men, Carlyle depends for national salvation upon the accidental and intermittent supply of geniuses. He sacrificed liberty to organization and thereby accepted depotism. But Milton believed that by proper education both the values of order and those of liberty could be preserved. In this, Seeley found Milton's message for the nineteenth century. It is a doctrine that reflects Seeley's conception of the state, which was that of Milton and of the ancients: "a community living together in the practice of virtue, in the worship of God, in the pursuit of truth." So broad a conception of state and politics could hardly restrict unduly the scope of history.

Seeley was undoubtedly open to the charge of "present-mindedness." It was not enough merely to enter into the minds of past ages, to share their values and judge events as they did. "The average contemporary view of a great event is almost certain to be shallow and false."[24] It is "the newspaper treatment of affairs," full of superficiality and party passions. The real test of events is their "pregnancy," that is, the scale of their consequence. Of this, we who look back over the past in the light of the present are the best judges.

One might make these contentions the basis for a criticism of Seeley's emphasis on modern history; but it will be enough to point out that in the treatment of past ages his historical practice was better than his preaching. He is really very careful to distinguish between the way an event appears to us in retrospect and the way it

---

[23] "Milton's Political Opinions," *Lectures and Essays,* pp. 89–119.
[24] *The Expansion of England,* pp. 166–67.

must have impressed contemporaries. He shows imagination in recreating historical situations—the condition and prospects of Catholicism after the Restoration is a good example[25]—and is particularly good in analyzing the alternative policies open to statesmen at any given time. His teaching must have been marvelously stimulating to the Cambridge undergraduates as an example of a keen mind lucidly speculating on the stream of politics. And the instruction was made more vivid by the lecturer's fertility in association and analogy.

The fertility in ideas was so great and the stress on interpretation so marked that irreverent undergraduates dubbed Seeley's school of history: "Thought Without Facts."[26] Of course, this was wide of the mark. Seeley's books and lectures were never the product of that brand of research that takes delight in ransacking manuscript stores and spending long hours in dusty libraries. He had neither the depth nor the originality of his younger contemporary, F. W. Maitland. But he was a learned man himself and he enjoyed the respect of learned men like Acton and Creighton.

History written in accordance with the principles thus laid down would be more informative than amusing, more intellectual than inspiring. These were indeed the characteristics of the writing in which Seeley laid down his precepts and illustrated their application. In addition to numerous essays and articles,[27] he produced five important works on politics and history during the twenty-five years of his professorship (including those published after his death in 1895). These books fell into three groups. Two of them dealt with Continental Europe, two with phases of English history; the other was an introductory treatise on political science composed of two courses given at Cambridge. In effect they were all essays on great themes, designed to convey political lessons.

Thus the first of his important historical works *(Life and Times of Stein*[28]*)*, while valuable for its account of Prussian internal reforms and of the work and character of various men such as Arndt, Hardenberg, Dalberg, von Humboldt, Niebuhr, as well as of Stein

---

[25] *The Growth of British Policy* (Cambridge, 1895), II, 182–84.
[26] McLachlan, *loc. cit.*, p. 84.
[27] The only collection published was *Lectures and Essays* (1870), but several of his books were made up of courses given at Cambridge.
[28] Three volumes, 1878.

himself, may be viewed as an essay on nationality. Here was the dynamic force that had overthrown Napoleon, and that was to unite Germany and transform Europe. Seeley saw in the events in Spain a third revolution aiming at the independence of nations as the English Revolution had aimed at liberty and the French Revolution at equality. Napoleon failed in Spain because there, for the first time, he had to deal with a national state. The strength of that form, said Seeley, constituted the "peculiar political lesson of the nineteenth century." In Spain, the government might yield, but the nation rallied in a way that ultimately proved fatal to Napoleon. The Spanish rebellion failed in itself; but

> a new idea took possession of the mind of Europe. That idea was not democracy or liberty; how could Spain have had anything to tell about either of these? it was nationality. It was the idea of the nation as distinguished from the state; the union of blood as distinguished from the union by interest; the idea of the strength and stubborn solidity of that society, which, while it has the form of a state, is a nation also, and of the feebleness of that which is only a state, which can appeal to no inbred instincts, no natural affections, however complete its administrative machinery may be.[29]

Although Seeley attributed so much importance to nationality, he nowhere gives an extended analysis of the factors entering into its formation. In *The Expansion of England,* however, he treats the matter briefly,[30] singling out three main elements: community of race, "or rather the belief in a community of race"; the sense of common interests along with "the habit of forming a single political whole"; and a common religion. Of these, religion seemed to him the strongest and most important element. The omission of language is striking, but it is mentioned in other places; for example, Spanish nationality was found by Seeley to be based especially on language.

Seeley was no eulogist of the national state. He felt that the old concept of European unity for which the Holy Roman Empire stood was superior as pure theory to that of nationality. He saw that the intensification of national feeling had turned Europe into an armed camp of competing states; and he looked forward to the day when it would be united once again. But he saw, too, that this unity must

---

[29] *The Life and Times of Stein,* II, 24.
[30] *The Expansion of England,* pp. 255–62.

take a new form. The old theory of the Empire standing above other states no longer had meaning. The old cosmopolitanism of men like Herder and Goethe had merely weakened their resistance to Napoleon's lure of unity at the cost of slavery. It was better that Europe as a whole should escape this danger by rallying to the cause of nationalism, even though this meant a disunited continent.

For Seeley believed that this disunity could be brought to an end by the formation of a new federal association. The national state would be merely one stage in political evolution. As early as 1870 Seeley delivered a lecture before the Peace Society with the significant title "The United States of Europe."[31] Here he argued for an international federation to be based on the American model rather than on that of the old German Bund. In particular, the federal government alone was to be given the power to levy troops, a provision in which the lecturer found "the indispensable condition of success."

This estimate of the place of nationality is far superior to the eulogies of the Germanic races indulged in by Seeley's predecessor in the Cambridge chair, Charles Kingsley. It is better even than that of his successor, Lord Acton. For Acton's famous essay on "Nationality" is too unbending in its prediction of ruin as following inevitably upon the spread of nationality and nationalism. Seeley saw that nationality had saved Europe from Napoleon. We have seen its part in saving Europe from Hitler, and may yet live to rejoice in the contribution of national sentiment and national loyalty to saving Europe from Stalin.

Seeley's short sketch of the life of Napoleon,[32] a book which developed out of an article contributed to the *Encyclopaedia Britannica,* is hardly more than a supplement to the three large volumes on the life and times of Stein. The work did not pretend to be more than an outline and interpretation. The interpretation is often acute, but the general estimate of Napoleon is too low. Seeley was never an admirer of the men of force.

The two books on English history were meant to fill a gap in previous writings. Seeley felt that historians paid too much attention to internal developments, writing in a spirit dangerously in-

---

[31] "United States of Europe," *Macmillan's Magazine,* XXIII (1870–1871), 436–48.
[32] *A Short History of Napoleon the First* (London, 1886).

sular. In any event, the Constitution had been formed by 1688. Thereafter, the important questions were the rise of the British trade empire and the story of Britain as a member of the European system. To each of these he devoted a main work.

The effect of *The Expansion of England* (1883), Seeley's most famous work, was to justify the British Empire and prescribe means whereby it could be made permanent. But the chief aim professed is merely to impart "a just view of the object and method of historical study" by a series of lectures showing how expansion was the key to understanding the history of the eighteenth century.

> I am concerned always with a single problem only, that of causation. My question always is, How came this enterprise to be undertaken, how came it to suceed? I ask it not in order than we may imitate the actions we read of, but in order that we may discover the laws by which states rise, expand and prosper or fall in this world. In this instance I have also the further object, viz., to throw light on the question whether Greater Britain, now that it exists, may be expected to prosper and endure or to fall.[33]

The tone adopted is one of studied moderation. Specifically avoided is the glorification of size, interpretation in terms of admiration for the energy and heroism of the empire builders, or argument for maintaining the empire as a matter of honor or sentiment. Equally, however, the author rejects interpretation in terms of aggression and rapacity and the pessimistic view that colonial possessions were a useless burden on England, depriving her of the advantages of insularity, exposing her to wars and foreign dangers, and fit only to be abandoned. Rather the colonies are treated as an extension of England overseas which could be made the basis of a new national greatness.

Seeley denied that they could be treated as a manifestation of Imperialism, for by Imperialism—in this book, as in all his writings —he understood a government in which power had been usurped by a standing army. Its first form, according to his analysis, is usually republican, with a small clique of officers in secret control of the highest assembly of the state. But the system usually becomes monarchical with a successful general as the supreme ruler. Of this system of government he found many examples both in ancient and

---

[33] *The Expansion of England*, p. 155.

modern history—Rome under the Triumvirate and then under the emperors, England under Cromwell, France under the Directory and then under Napoleon.[34] Thus he seems to have meant regimes that would be designated a type of dictatorship by students of government in our day.

In the same way, Seeley used the term "empire" in a special way to designate "a congeries of nations held together by force."[35] It must be founded on conquest, consist of peoples of different nationalities, and will generally be found to be of vast size. Only in this last respect did the British Empire resemble the great empires of history, "Persian or Macedonian or Roman or Turkish." Otherwise it was simply an expression of the English state and nation overseas.

It is obviously difficult to fit India into Seeley's conception of the nature of the British Empire. He himself saw that its relationship with Britain was different from that of the colonies of European settlement. But he was careful to show also the differences between the way in which British rule had grown up in India and the way in which the great empires of history had been brought into existence. So far as any conquest had taken place, it had been by a Sepoy army, not an English one. And there had been no conquest of one state by another. What had occurred lay within the area of Indian domestic history rather than of foreign relations. The Mogul Empire fell, and in the competition for power following its fall the East India Company was more successful than its rivals. This success was easy enough to understand, since the English adventurers enjoyed over their Indian rivals the advantages of money, European military techniques, and the backing of English statesmen. The event was "wonderful rather in its consequences than in its causes."[36]

That these consequences were vast could not be doubted, but whether for good or ill was an open question with Seeley. He could not find that England had reaped much benefit from India and was uncertain about her ultimate effects on India. "In the academic study of these vast questions we should take care to avoid the optimistic commonplaces of the newspapers. Our Western civilization is perhaps not absolutely the glorious thing we like to imagine it"[37]

[34] *Napoleon*, pp. 59, 241, 242, 274; *Political Science*, pp. 318–19.
[35] *The Expansion of England*, p. 60.
[36] *Ibid.*, pp. 272–73.
[37] *Ibid.*, p. 354.

—an observation that hardly seems the very stuff and substance of "flamboyant Imperialism." Yet, whatever its outcome, the experiment of British rule must go on to its logical conclusion, whether it be separation or continued unity with Great Britain.

Running throughout *The Expansion of England* is a lesson in policy as well as an analysis of a process of expansion. Science, having abolished distance, had made it unnecessary for England to fall behind Russia and the United States into a second class of states. For the scattered parts of the Empire could now be welded into a powerful political union, less strong perhaps than the United States, but certainly stronger than polyglot Russia.

The Expansion of England, in spite of the absence of jingoism, certainly contributed to the rebirth of interest in the Empire and the rise of British Imperialism in the later nineteenth century. Yet it should be pointed out that not only is Seeley free from jingoism in tone, but that he is always talking about the old trade imperialism rather than the new expansionism that was to add so many square miles of territory to the British flag. His advocacy of a sort of imperial federation is really concerned with the old colonies settled by Europeans. About India, as we have seen, he was by no means easy in mind. In any case, it is clear that his was a defensive Imperialism, the Imperialism of retreat and integration rather than that of advance and aggression.

The Growth of British Policy[38] was a study in "International History or the History of Policy." It dealt with the period, from 1558 to 1688, in which Britain progressed from a dynastic to a national attitude in international affairs. These years were made the vehicle for a skillfully constructed essay in five parts. There is first an extended analysis of Elizabeth's "negative statesmanship," which by its sagacious inaction saved England from foreign invasion and laid the foundations for union of the kingdoms. Her reign sketched in the outlines of a truly national policy. The early Stuart period is treated as one of reaction to dynastic principles; but with Cromwell a truly national policy was for a time definitely pursued. A second reaction, however, came with the Restoration, especially under James II. His policy is attributed to family influence, that is, the relationship of the Stuarts to the Bourbons whom "almost

[38] Two volumes, 1895.

all English parties, the Catholics included" had come to regard with animosity. The English people, both Catholic and Protestant, were determined on resistance to French aggression. In this they were supported by the large part of Europe which needed English aid in the stand against France. "It thus became the interest of half Europe that a change of government should take place in England. . . . The leaders of this second English revolution were not, as of the first, members of Parliament and popular agitators, but foreign statesmen."[39] A revolution in England was "necessary to the cause of Europe."[40]

With the revolution British policy has taken on its settled, modern form. A concluding section sketches briefly the establishment of "the commercial state" in the reign of William III and immediately thereafter. In commercial interests is found the explanation of Scotland's willingness to enter union with England; in similar economic interests are to be found the roots of the War of the Spanish Succession. In Frederick the Great's phrase, England had become the modern Carthage.

Very characteristic is the emphasis placed in these volumes on the impact of foreign events on British policy. England is considered as a part of the European states system, domestic developments being made subordinate to the "interaction of states," including under this head relations not only between Britain and the Continental powers, but also between England, Scotland, and Ireland. Long sections deal with the Spanish Monarchy, the policies of Richelieu, and the growth of the House of Habsburg. Effort is made to avoid sectarian or national bias. Seeley is obviously a Protestant historian, but this does not preclude fair analysis of the forces wherein lay the strength of the Counter-Reformation and of the Catholic revival in the seventeenth century.

The *Introduction to Political Science* (1896) consisted of two sets of lectures delivered at various times during Seeley's incumbency of the chair of modern history at Cambridge. Seeley proposed to work in the manner of the naturalist. Eschewing ethical norms, mere legalism, and an exclusive concern with the state in its modern form, he wished to examine political societies as the botanist

---

[39] *The Growth of British Policy*, II, 271.
[40] *Ibid.*, II, 281.

studies plants—collecting facts, grouping them into appropriate categories, analyzing structure, tracing development, and finally emerging with the laws governing the state. The factual foundation had already been laid and Seeley, therefore, in this book turns mostly to the task of classification. In his hands the performance was not arid as it might have been in the hands of a lesser person. The distinctions drawn between city-state and country-state and between organic and inorganic states marked an advance in political analysis. There were many stimulating reflections on liberty, government interference, the rise of toleration, the relations between executive and legislative in England, the nature of responsible government in general, the relations between religion and the state, and on other matters. The lectures can still be read with profit.

As Rein has pointed out,[41] Seeley was not a practical politician like Macaulay and Grote, nor closely connected with leading political figures of the day as was Acton. But he carried the advocacy of his causes outside of the writing of books. He was an active and prominent worker in the Imperial Federation League. In the field of popular education he lectured and wrote for lay audiences, and was the founder and president of a society for the social and political education of the workers. His efforts for university reform sought to bring the English foundations up to the supposed level of efficiency of the Continent.

Seeley represents a stage in the development of English liberalism. The contours of politics were being sharply altered by the growth of democracy at home and the rise of Germany, Russia, and the United States abroad. He belonged to a generation of liberals whose minds were turning from considerations of liberty to those of unity and power. He felt the necessity of drawing together the resources of country and Empire. He sought to awaken his contemporaries to the urgencies of their time, to induce in them a new seriousness of purpose and to train a new race of statesmen.

In these efforts he met much failure. No science of politics was founded as the result of his teachings, nor was the study of history pursued along the lines he had marked out. A new generation, trained in historical methods from their youth up, demanded less

[41] Rein, *op. cit.*, p. 69.

theory, more research, and less concentration on purely pragmatic values in the study of the past. Still less was he successful in his advocacy of imperial federation; the Commonwealth ideal of an association of autonomous nations soon triumphed decisively over the dreams of closer union.

In other respects, his influence seems to have been considerable. His oral teaching inspired a generation of students; his historical writings fixed attention on some neglected themes; and his *Political Science* is a small landmark in the study of comparative government. Few academic writers have had a greater impact on public opinion than has been attributed to the author of *The Expansion of England*. At the very least, that work was a conspicuous expression of the new interest in the Empire. And the contribution of the Dominions in two world wars showed how right Seeley was in his estimate of the accession of strength that could come to Britain from her overseas settlements. Of him it seems correct to say that he both reflected and helped to shape the political and intellectual trends of late nineteenth-century England.

THE HABSBURGS AND PUBLIC OPINION IN LOMBARDY-VENETIA, 1814–1815[1]

R. JOHN RATH

WHEN Austrian troops first marched into the Kingdom of Italy in October 1813 to begin the "War of Liberation" against Napoleon in that theater of operations, they were greeted everywhere as liberators and friends. Almost to a man the inhabitants looked upon the Habsburg armies as emancipators who would chase their French oppressors from Italy, destroy the Napoleonic administrative and fiscal systems under which they had suffered, and inaugurate in the Apennine peninsula that era of peace, stability, and prosperity which the Italian people so fervently desired.[2] In place after place the arrival of Austrian soldiers gave occasion for triumphal celebrations. In Verona, for instance, the citizens stopped all work, and "people rushed out of the market place to the surrounding regions to be the first to bring the joyful news home."[3] The appearance of the Austrians in the city of Venice was not only acclaimed with loud "hurrahs" but it inspired some of the populace to make threatening demonstrations against the French and their sympathizers.[4] Even in Milan General Neipperg's advance guard was hailed "with universal joy"[5] when it appeared on April 28, and in the evening the city was more extensively and more brilliantly illuminated than at almost any other time in its history.[6]

The strong pro-Austrian feeling of the Italians at the moment when the Habsburg armies first set foot on Italian soil did not long endure. As early as January 3, 1814—less than six weeks after the

---

[1] Much of the material on which this article is based was collected by the writer while he was a pre-doctoral field fellow of the Social Science Research Council.

[2] Adolf von Wiedemann-Warnhelm, *Die Wiederherstellung der österreichischen Vorherrschaft in Italien (1813–1815)* (Vienna, 1912), pp. 34–35.

[3] Report from Florence, Feb. 10, 1814, *Wiener Zeitung*, March 5, 1814.

[4] Cicogna diary, April 20, April 21, May 7, and May 23, 1814, in A. Pilot, "Venezia nel blocco del 1813–14. Da noterelle inedite del Cicogna," *Nuovo archivio veneto*, I (1914), 207–10, 215–16, 220.

[5] Strassoldo to Bellegarde, Milan, April 30, 1814, Haus-, Hof-, und Staatsarchiv (Vienna) MSS (hereafter cited as "St. A."), *Kaiser Franz Akten*, Fasc. 1, Sec. 1, fol. 49.

[6] Entries of April 28 and 29, 1814, Luigi Mantovani, *Diario politico-ecclesiastico di Milano* (MSS in the Ambrosian Library, Milan) (hereafter cited as "Mantovani diary"), V, 258–59.

Austrians had entered Venetian territory—the Austrian police president, Baron von Hager, expressed his concern over the fact that "the good opinion which prevailed at first" no longer existed.[7] A few weeks later the Venetians were so disillusioned with the Austrians that many of them expressed open jubilation over the military reverses which the Habsburg army suffered on the Mincio in February 1814.[8] And in Lombardy such bitter anti-Austrian feeling developed among some groups that a few months after their arrival certain malcontents actually conspired to drive the Austrians from Italy. Why this reversal of public opinion in Lombardy-Venetia? And what was its effect upon the Italian liberal and national movement? To attempt to answer these questions is the aim of this paper.

In Venetia the sudden change in the attitude of the populace towards the Habsburgs can be ascribed largely to the conduct of the Austrian troops and to economic reasons. Embittered and impoverished as the Venetians were by the exactions of the Napoleonic regime, they had expected from the Austrians an immediate alleviation of the military and financial burdens which the French had put upon them. Instead, soldiers (this time Austrian soldiers) continued to insult them and to exact requisitions from them. Furthermore, the burdensome taxes levied by the French were still collected relentlessly.

In spite of the Austrian emperor's insistent orders that discipline be strictly enforced in the army,[9] many Austrian soldiers plundered the countryside and forced the inhabitants to accept at exorbitant rates of exchange the depreciated paper money with which they were paid.[10] Even more vexatious to the Venetians than the conduct of the Austrian troops were the special military requisitions demanded from them. The local population had to provision and

---

[7] St. A., *Kabinets-Akten*, 1814, No. 957.

[8] Hager report, as summarized in the *Staats-Kabinet* report of April 5, 1814, *ibid.*, No. 1371.

[9] Imperial resolution, Jan. 2, 1814, St. A., *Conferenz Akten*, Ser. b, 1814, No. 104; *Staats-Kabinet* report, Jan. 17, 1814, St. A., *Kabinets-Akten*, 1814, No. 957; Imperial resolution, March 27, 1814, *ibid.*, No. 1320.

[10] Sardegna to Emperor Francis, Verona, April 2, 1814, *Kriegsarchiv* (Vienna) MSS (hereafter cited as "Kr. A."), *Feld Akten (Italien)* 1814, Fasc. 4, No. 23 2/4; Hager report, May 17, 1814, St. A., *Conferenz Akten*, Ser. b, 1814, No. 1102; *Staats-Kabinet* report, March 25, 1814, St. A., *Kabinets-Akten*, 1814, No. 1320; Hager report of Jan. 3, 1814, as summarized in the *Staats-Kabinet* report of Jan. 17, 1814, St. A., *Kabinets-Akten*, 1814, No. 957.

The Habsburgs and Lombardy-Venetia 305

quarter the troops stationed among them and to supply them with transport and other equipment. A special loan was levied on landowners and merchants, and numerous extraordinary war taxes were collected from the populace. The Venetians complained loudly and bitterly that, exhausted as they were from the exigencies of warfare, they were too impoverished to pay these new assessments,[11] which were over and above the regular taxes still collected at the exorbitant rates established by the preceding regime.

For over half a year after their arrival in Venetia, the Austrians attempted to collect the high taxes which the French had levied upon landed property, as well as such levies as the poll tax, the taxes on salt and tobacco, and the hated consumption tax.[12] Disillusioned and desperate, many inhabitants, especially in the mountainous districts, took matters in their own hands. In numerous communities there were riots and uprisings against the collection of the odious consumption tax[13] and against the relentless essays of tax collectors to sequester the belongings of persons delinquent in the payment of their taxes.[14]

Eventually, after the military campaign against Napoleon was

[11] See especially Bombardini to Hiller, Bassano, Nov. 11, 1813, *Archivio di Stato* (Venice) MSS (hereafter cited as "A. S., Ven."), *Atti Hiller*, 1813, No. 28; Prefect of Brenta to Thurn, Padua, Nov. 29, 1813, A. S. Ven., *Pubblico politico*, Busta VI–VII, Rub. 3, No. 26,737; Prefect of Bacchiglione to Central Government, Vicenza, March 23, 1814, A. S., Ven., *Imposte*, 1814, Busta XXXII, Fasc. 226, No. 5664; and Hager to *Staats-Conferenz*, April 16, 1814, St. A., *Conferenz Akten*, Ser. b, 1814, No. 917.

[12] Prefectural Council of Passariano to Marenzi, Udine, Nov. 20, 1813, A. S., Ven., *Finanze*, 1813, Busta I–II, Rub. 5, No. 18,714; Report of the Prefect of Bacchiglione, Vicenza, Jan. 10, 1814, A. S., Ven., *Polizia*, 1814, Busta XXXIX, Fasc. 11, No. 451; Porcia to Reuss, Treviso, Jan. 30, 1814, A. S., Ven., *Imposte*, 1814, Busta XXXII, Fasc. 64, No. 1693; Emperor Francis to Zichy, Dijon, April 6, 1814, St. A., *Kabinets-Akten*, 1814, No. 1371; *Staats-Conferenz* report, May 24, 1814, St. A., *Conferenz Akten*, Ser. b, 1814, No. 954.

[13] See especially the letter of the Prefectural Council of Passariano to Marenzi, Udine, Nov. 20, 1813, A. S., Ven., *Finanze*, 1813, Busta I–II, Rub. 5, No. 18,714; Prefectural Council of Udine to Reuss, Dec. 21, 1813, A. S. Ven., *Pubblico politico*, Busta VI–VII, Rub. 4, No. 2038; Prefect of Piave to Reuss, Belluno, Jan. 5, 1814, A. S., Ven., *Dazi consumo*, Busta XIX–XX, Fasc. 1, No. 2126; Report of the Prefect of Bacchiglione, Vicenza, Jan. 10, 1814, A. S., Ven., *Polizia*, 1814, Busta XXXIX, Fasc. 11, No. 451; and Prefect of Bacchiglione to Reuss, Vicenza, Feb. 28, 1814, A. S., Ven., *Imposte*, 1814, Busta XXXII, Fasc. 47, No. 4249.

[14] See especially Prefect of Piave to Reuss, Belluno, Jan. 15, 1814, A. S., Ven., *Polizia*, 1814, Busta XXXIX, Fasc. 55, No. 73/74; Prefect of Bacchiglione to Central Government, Vicenza, Feb. 1, 1814, A. S., Ven., *Imposte*, 1814, Busta XXXII, Fasc. 53, No. 1983; Prefect of Piave to Central Government, Belluno, March 14, 1814, *ibid.*, Fasc. 190, No. 240b; and Hager to *Staats-Conferenz*, June 7, 1814, St. A., *Conferenz Akten*, Ser. b, 1814, No. 1163.

over, the tax burden was substantially reduced. On his own responsibility, Prince Reuss-Plauen, the military governor, postponed the collection of the May quota of the land tax until after the harvest in July.[15] A little later, upon Prince Reuss-Plauen's urgent recommendations for a reduction in the tax burden,[16] the Austrian emperor approved reductions in the salt, poll, and registration taxes.[17] In early July the salt tax was reduced about 20 per cent.[18] A month later the poll tax was lowered from 5.80 L. to 4 L.,[19] the registration tax was cut to one-third of the previous rate,[20] and the consumption tax was substantially decreased.[21] Finally in October the land taxes were reduced to one centesimo, two millesini (Italian money), for every scudo of assessed value,[22] which was the rate then prevailing in Lombardy.[23] Taxes were thus substantially cut in the summer and fall of 1814, but the damage to public opinion had already been done. If the Austrians had been in a position to reduce the most vexatious taxes of the French immediately after their entrance into Venetia, they would have won friends everywhere. Instead, they had to face an irritated and sullen population, convinced that they were merely exchanging one oppressive master for another.

The very bad crop failures in Venetia in 1813 and 1814 made the weight of taxation especially oppressive. By the spring of 1814 the villagers in numerous mountainous districts were actually on the verge of starvation.[24] The situation was desperate. Many breadless left Venetia for Trieste, Hungary, and Germany[25]; others remained home in indescribable misery. To make the matter all the more galling, there were certain instances where tax collectors took

---

[15] Reuss to Hager, Padua, May 27, 1814, as summarized in the *Staats-Conferenz* report of June 21, 1814, St. A., *Conferenz Akten*, Ser. b, 1814, No. 1143; Notice, May 25, 1814, *Collezione di leggi e regolamenti pubblicati dall'imp. regio governo delle province venete*, 1813–14 (Venice, 1814), I, 240–41.

[16] Secret Credit Commission report, June 11, 1814, as summarized in the *Staats-Conferenz* protocol of June 21, 1814, St. A., *Conferenz Akten*, Ser. b, 1814, No. 1146.

[17] Imperial resolutions of June 5 and July 7, 1814, *ibid.*, Nos. 954 and 1146.

[18] Notice, July 1, 1814, *Collezione di leggi venete*, 1813–14, II, 3–4.

[19] Notice, Aug. 4, 1814, *ibid.*, pp. 21–22.

[20] Notice, Aug. 4, 1814, *ibid.*, pp. 19–21; Notice, Oct. 19, 1814, *ibid.*, p. 66; Imperial resolution, Vienna, July 7, 1814, St. A., *Conferenz Akten*, Ser. b, 1814, No. 1146.

[21] Notice, Aug. 4, 1814, *Collezione di leggi venete*, 1813–14, II, 23–24.

[22] Decree, Reuss, Venice, Oct. 8, 1814, *Giornale di Venezia*, Oct. 13, 1814.

[23] Hager report, Nov. 13, 1814, St. A., *Kabinets-Akten*, 1814, No. 850.

[24] See my article on "The Habsburgs and the Great Depression in Lombardy-Venetia, 1814–18," *The Journal of Modern History*, XIII (1941), 308–11.

[25] Hager report, Nov. 13, 1814, St. A., *Kabinets-Akten*, 1814, No. 850.

away from starving peasants grain that had been given to them in way of relief by other officials.[26] Conditions in the city of Venice were little better than they were in the hinterland. Commerce, the mainstay of the city's prosperity, was almost nonexistent.[27] Furthermore, the lot of the pensioners of the former Venetian militia and of the dissolved monasteries and convents was particularly miserable. They had received no pay whatever since September 1813, and nearly all of them were utterly destitute and lived only by the charity of others.[28] In May the disbursement of three months' pay was finally approved, but since there was no money in the treasury this measure was but an empty gesture.[29] With actual famine in the country districts, commerce utterly stagnant, pensioners without means of support, and unemployed soldiers and deserters on the highways, it is no wonder that the Venetian police complained about the increase in theft and robbery and the growing insecurity.[30]

The onerous economic burdens were the main reason for the sudden disillusionment of the Venetian populace with their new Austrian rulers. There were also political grounds for dissatisfaction. The Venetians were at first amazed[31] and then disgruntled and irritated because the French laws and judicial system and nearly all of the administrative machinery of the previous French government were kept intact for months after the entrance of the Austrian army into Italy.[32] Probably even more galling to the Italians was the fact that the old French officials were kept in their posts for a long time after the change in government. Many were the charges

[26] Hager report, Dec. 20, 1814, *ibid.*, 1815, No. 334.
[27] Report of the commercial picture of Venice in May 1814, dated June 4, 1814, *Carte segrete ed atti ufficiali della polizia austriaca in Italia dal 4 giugno 1814 al 22 marzo 1848* (3 vols., Turin, 1851–52), I, 18; Hager report, Nov. 13, 1814, St. A., *Kabinets-Akten*, 1814, No. 850.
[28] Baron von Raab's report, Padua, May 13, 1814, as summarized in the *Staats-Conferenz* protocol of June 15, 1814, St. A., *Conferenz Akten*, Ser. b, 1814, No. 1101.
[29] Baron von Raab's report, June 6, 1814, as summarized in the *Staats-Conferenz* protocol of June 17, 1814, *ibid.*, No. 1346.
[30] Hager report, June 17, 1814, *ibid.*, No. 1174.
[31] Hager report, July 15, 1814, *ibid.*, No. 1393.
[32] See the *Staats-Kabinet* reports of Jan. 17, March 1, March 25, and April 6, 1814, St. A., *Kabinets-Akten*, 1814, Nos. 957, 1193, 1320, and 1385; Hager report, July 8, 1814, St. A., *Conferenz Akten*, Ser. b, 1814, No. 1346; and Reuss to Mulazzani, Padua, July 26, 1814, *Carte segrete della polizia austriaca in Italia*, I, 22. For a detailed account of the provisional government established by the Austrians in Venetia, see my article on "The Austrian Provisional Government in Lombardy-Venetia, 1814–1815," *Journal of Central European Affairs*, II (1942), 249–54.

leveled against them. They were accused of being corrupt and oppressive, of being thoroughly hated and distrusted by the populace, and of being disloyal to Austria, and it was charged that they maltreated the population in order to incite it against the Habsburgs.[33]

The ruinous military requisitions and taxes, the poor crops and economic stagnation, and the retention of French administrative forms and French officials by the Austrians turned many Venetians against their new masters within the course of a few short months. During the period immediately after the arrival of the Austrians in Venetia, the dissatisfaction did not result in the outpouring of a strong feeling of *Italian* nationalism[34]; it did, however, give a strong stimulus to the narrower program of Venetian patriotism. The hopes of a rebirth of the old Republic of San Marco had never been completely extinguished among some of the Venetian aristocrats.[35] Unfortunate Austrian policies, in addition to the fact that as late as May 1814 the Venetians were still completely ignorant of their future fate, served to regenerate the idea of Venetian independence among many of the upper classes.[36] The great masses of people were still indifferent to the program of the republican party, but among the nobility the independence program gained more and more momentum as the summer of 1814 approached.[37]

In Lombardy, where the French government was overthrown by a revolution in Milan on April 20, it was the strong spirit of nationalism and liberalism stirred up among certain classes of the population during the Napoleonic era by nationalist writers, British agents,

---

[33] See especially the *Staats-Conferenz* reports of Jan. 11 and June 14, 1814, St. A., *Conferenz Akten*, Ser. b, 1814, Nos. 38 and 1102; the *Staats-Kabinet* reports of Feb. 6 and March 1, 1814, St. A., *Kabinets-Akten*, 1814, Nos. 1077 and 1193; Baron von Hager's reports of Jan. 3, April 16, and May 23, 1814, St. A., *Kabinets-Akten*, 1814, Nos. 957 and 1583; Baron von Hager's reports of April 16 and June 17, 1814, St. A., *Conferenz Akten*, Ser. b, 1814, Nos. 917 and 1174; and Emperor Francis to Zichy, Basel, Jan. 12, 1814, *ibid.*, No. 131.

[34] All the documents the writer has seen in the Viennese and Venetian archives indicate that there was no noticeable feeling of Italian nationalism in Venetia during the first few months after the arrival of the Austrian army in Italy.

[35] Hager report, June 2, 1814, St. A., *Conferenz Akten*, Ser. b, 1814, No. 1152.

[36] Hager reports of May 17 and July 8, 1814, St. A., *Conferenz Akten*, Ser. b, 1814, Nos. 1102 and 1346.

[37] Josef Alexander Freiherr von Helfert, *Kaiser Franz I. von Österreich und die Stiftung des Lombardo-Venetianischen Königreichs* (Innsbruck, 1901), pp. 109-10; Pietro Peverelli, *Storia di Venezia dal 1798 sino ai nostri tempi* (2 vols., Turin, 1852), I, 251.

The Habsburgs and Lombardy-Venetia 309

and secret societies[38] that made small but highly vocal and influential groups strongly anti-Habsburg within a few weeks after the arrival of the Austrian army. Although the Austrian troops were loudly acclaimed as liberators for a brief moment after they entered Lombardy, various revolutionary factions from the first hastened to clamor for the type of government they desired for their country.[39] The liberals and nationalists were particularly articulate. Numerous were their resolutions and loud were their entreaties for independence, a "good" king, and a constitution based on the principle of a division of powers, providing for some kind of a national representative body to make laws and decide on taxes, and guaranteeing such freedoms as those of speech, assembly, the press, and commerce.[40]

The liberals were divided, however, in regard to the person who should be king of their independent country. Some of the more radical, particularly among the commercial classes,[41] wanted a British prince. Desiring British support for their constitutional projects and favorable commercial relations with England, they requested the appointment of either the Duke of Cambridge or the Duke of Clarence as their sovereign.[42] Others among the partisans of inde-

[38] For a detailed discussion of the stirring up of a liberal and national sentiment in Italy during the Napoleonic period, see Chapter II of my monograph on *The Fall of the Napoleonic Kingdom of Italy (1814)* (New York, 1941). For an account of the Milanese revolution of April 20, see *ibid.*, Chapters VI and VII.

[39] Theresa Confalonieri Casati to Confalonieri, Milan, May 2, 1814, Giuseppe Gallavresi, ed., *Carteggio del conte Federico Confalonieri ed altri documenti spettanti alla sua biografia; con annotazione storiche* (3 vols., Milan, 1910–1913), I, 92.

[40] See especially McFarlane to Bentinck, Milan, April 29, 1814, Francesco Lemmi, *La restaurazione austriaca a Milano nel 1814* (Bologna, 1902), pp. 418–19; Sommariva to Bellegarde, Milan, April 28, 1814, Kr. A., *Feld Akten (Italien)*, 1814, Fasc. 4, No. 226; Alberico Felber to Confalonieri, Milan, May 2, 1814, Gabrio Casati, ed., *Federico Confalonieri, memorie e lettere* (2 vols., Milan, 1889), II, 295; Hager report, May 23, 1814, St. A., *Kabinets-Akten*, 1814, No. 1568; Protocol of the Electoral Colleges, April 23, 1814, *Giornale italiano* (Milan), April 24, 1814; Durini to Bentinck, Milan, April 20, 1814, Giuseppe Gallavresi, "La rivoluzione lombarda del 1814 e la politica inglese secondo nuovi documenti," *Archivio storico lombardo*, Ser. IV, XI (1909), 108–9; McFarlane to Bentinck, Milan, April 29, 1814, *ibid.*, p. 134; and Milanese Provisional Regency to its deputation in Paris, Milan, May 5, 1814, *Carte del Giacomo Beccaria* (MSS in the Milanese *Museo del Risorgimento italiano*) (cited hereafter as "*Carte Beccaria*"), Busta I, Carte 8, Fasc. I, No. 21.

[41] Strassoldo to Bellegarde, Milan, April 30, 1814, St. A., *Kaiser Franz Akten*, Fasc. 27, Sec. 1, fol. 50.

[42] See especially McFarlane to Bentinck, Milan, May 6, 1814, in Gallavresi, "La rivoluzione lombarda e la politica inglese," *loc. cit.*, pp. 153–54; Borda to Battista, Milan, May 3, 1814, Giuseppe Gallavresi, ed., *Il carteggio intimo di Andrea Borda*. Reprinted from the *Archivio storico lombardo*, XLVII (Milan, 1921), 48; Borda to

pendence were resigned to letting the course of events decide who would be their monarch[43] or limited themselves to requesting a prince who "by his origin and qualities, may cause to be effaced the calamities which have been suffered under the government abolished."[44] Still others asked for a prince from the Habsburg house.[45] The largest group of Italian liberals, however, demanded Archduke Francis of Austria-Este as ruler, for not only was Francis an Italian by birth but it was felt that his candidacy might have the backing of the Habsburg monarch.[46]

Then, too, various Lombard liberals in late April and early May, 1814, felt that if Francis of Este were their ruler, Modena would automatically become part of the constitutional kingdom which they hoped to create.[47] Many of them had vague hopes of procuring a large enough territory to assure the economic prosperity of their kingdom and land on both the Mediterranean and Adriatic coasts to facilitate the export of products from their country.[48] A few misty-eyed dreamers thought that their country should be united

---

Battista, Milan, May 10, 1814, *ibid.*, pp. 53–55; Gallavresi, "La rivoluzione lombarda e la politica inglese," *loc. cit.*, p. 110; and Domenico Spadoni, "Federazione e re d'Italia mancati nel 1814–15," *Nuova rivista storica*, X (1931), 418–19.

[43] Provisional Regency to its deputation in Paris, Milan, May 10, 1814, *Carte Beccaria*, Busta I, Carte 8, Fasc. I, No. 28.

[44] Proclamation of the Provisional Regency, April 23, 1814, *The Times* (London), May 9, 1814.

[45] Bellegarde to Emperor Francis, Verona, April 28, 1814, Kr. A., *Feld Akten (Italien)*, 1814, Fasc. 4, ad No. 2291½; Sommariva to Bellegarde, Milan, 11.30 P.M., April 28, 1814, *ibid.*, No. 226.

[46] Giovanni de Castro, "La restaurazione austriaca in Milano (1814–1817). Notizie desunte da diarj e testimonianze contemporanee," *Archivio storico lombardo*, XV (1888), 631; Provisional Regency to its deputation in Paris, April 27 and May 10, 1814, *Carte Beccaria*, Busta I, Carte 8, Fasc. I, Nos. 3 and 28; Provisional Regency, protocol of the sitting of April 29, 1814, *Protocolli originali della reggenza provvisoria del Regno d'Italia nel 1814* (MSS in the Brera Library, Milan) (hereafter cited as "*Protocolli, reggenza provvisoria*"); Spadoni, "Federazione e re d'Italia mancati," *loc. cit.*, pp. 418–20; Borda to Battista, May 10, 1814, Gallavresi, *Carteggio di Borda*, p. 53; McFarlane to Bentinck, Milan, April 29, 1814, Lemmi, *La restaurazione austriaca*, p. 418.

[47] Porro Lambertenghi to Confalonieri, May 13, 1814, Gallavresi, *Carteggio del Confalonieri*, I, 122.

[48] Giovio (President of the Electoral Colleges) to McFarlane, Milan, n.d., Gallavresi, "La rivoluzione lombarda e la politica inglese," *loc. cit.*, p. 146; Memoir of the College of Commerce of Cremona, given to McFarlane by G. P. Cadolino on April 30, 1814, *ibid.*; Protocol of the Provisional Regency, sitting of May 3, 1814, *Protocolli, reggenza provvisoria*.

with Piedmont,[49] while others, for a fleeting moment at least, thought that Parma, Piacenza, and the Estense should be annexed to Lombardy.[50] As soon as it became evident that all these grandiose plans were unrealizable, the champions of independence and constitutional government became much more modest in their requests and began to limit their demands to Lombardy, to the portions of Lombardy west of the Ticino River that had been acquired by Piedmont in 1703, 1738, and 1743, and to the lands of the former Republic of Genoa. These territories, they insisted, would be the least possible compensation for the severance of Venetia[51] from the independent kingdom which they claimed they had a right to create.

The proclamations and resolutions of the Milanese provisional government, which was temporarily left in power by the Austrians when they first entered Lombardy, show that the majority of its members were heartily in favor of the establishment of an independent, constitutional kingdom. The actions of Italian army officers and colleges of commerce of various cities show that a highly vocal group wanted national freedom. Various English agents in Milan in early May 1814, all of whom were staunch liberals by conviction, reported that the overwhelming vote of the Milanese was for independence and that the Austrians were highly unpopular.[52] The accounts of the Austrian generals Strassoldo, Sommariva, and Bellegarde, who were charged by the Allied Powers with the re-

---

[49] Porro Lambertenghi to Confalonieri, May 13, 1814, Gallavresi, *Carteggio del Confalonieri*, I, 122; Renato Soriga, "Bagliori unitari in Lombardia avanti la restaurazione austriaca (1814)," *Bollettino* della società pavese di storia patria, XV (1915), 4.

[50] Protocol of the Provisional Regency, sitting of May 3, 1814, *Protocolli, reggenza provvisoria*.

[51] Bellegarde report, May 31, 1814, St. A., *Conferenz Akten*, Ser. b, 1814, No. 1249; McFarlane to Bentinck, Milan, May 6, 1814, Gallavresi, "La rivoluzione lombarda e la politica inglese," *loc. cit.*, p. 153; McFarlane to Castlereagh, Milan, May 4, 1814, Lemmi, *La restaurazione austriaca*, p. 421; Protocol of the Provisional Regency, sitting of May 3, 1814, *Protocolli, reggenza provvisoria;* Provisional Regency to its deputation in Paris, Milan, May 3, 1814, *Carte Beccaria,* Busta I, Carte 8, Fasc. I, No. 359.

[52] See especially McFarlane to Bentinck, Milan, April 29, 1814, Lemmi, *La restaurazione austriaca*, p. 418; McFarlane to Castlereagh, Milan May 4, 1814, *ibid.,* p. 420; Entries of April 27 and May 7, 1814, Robert Wilson, *Private Diary of Travels, Personal Services, and Public Events, during Mission and Employment with the European Armies in the Campaigns of 1812, 1813, 1814* (2 vols., London, 1861), II, 360, 364–65; and Bentinck to Castlereagh, Genoa, May 1, 1814, Gallavresi, "La rivoluzione lombarda e la politica inglese," *loc. cit.*, p. 140.

sponsibility of preserving the peace and security of Lombardy until the fate of the country was decided, differed decidedly from those of the few British liberals who were on the spot. Although they admitted that a large number of people wanted an independent, constitutional government under an Austrian prince, the Austrian officers maintained that the large mass of population was adamant in its loyalty and devotion to the House of Austria.[53]

Both the English and the Austrian observers, however, may have exaggerated the sentiment for independence and constitutional government that actually existed in Lombardy in late April and early May, 1814. It was only the *politically active* sections of the population who passed resolutions for independence and who came into actual contact with the English and Austrian officials in Milan. Perhaps some of the liberals may have had ulterior motives. According to at least one prominent Milanese observer of the time, many of the Milanese liberals were interested mainly in "exciting new tumults and sowing seeds of dissension in order to be able in some way to assure their existence."[54] Perhaps most Lombards, as Domenico Spadoni, the best recent Italian authority on the subject, has said of the great mass of Italians, were "tired of war and incessant tribute and of the persecution of the clergy and the venerated pope" and "desired only the return of the old, peaceful, and religious regimes."[55] It seems highly probable that the great majority of Lombards desired only peace and were well satisfied to be governed by any regime, provided that it brought them peace, security, and prosperity.

It should also be noted that the great majority of the members of the liberal and national party in the spring of 1814 were "Lombard" rather than "Italian" nationalists. They wanted an independent kingdom with Lombardy as its nucleus and with such additions of territory as they could procure from the Allied Powers. Few of

[53] Strassoldo to Bellegarde, Milan, April 26, 1814, St. A., *Kaiser Franz Akten*, Fasc. 27, Sec. 1, fols. 35–36; Strassoldo to Bellegarde, Milan, April 30, 1814, *ibid.*, fol. 49; Bellegarde to Metternich, Milan, May 9, 1814, Lemmi, *La restaurazione austriaca*, p. 423; Bellegarde to Emperor Francis, Milan, May 9, 1814, Kr. A., *Feld Akten (Italien)*, 1814, Fasc. 5, No. 351½.

[54] Alberico Felber to Confalonieri, Milan, May 2, 1815, Casati, *Confalonieri*, II, 295. Also in Gallavresi, *Carteggio del Confalonieri*, I, 94–96, with the notation that it was Rasini and not Felber who wrote the letter.

[55] In his "Aspirazioni unitarie d'un austriacante nel 1814," *La Lombardia nel Risorgimento italiano*, XVIII (1933), 71.

them seem to have hoped for the creation of a united Kingdom of Italy that would extend over the whole Apennine peninsula.

The state of uncertainty as to the future fate of Lombardy which had existed since the overthrow of the French government on April 20, and which had given the populace ample opportunity to speculate about the future of their country and to petition various Allied Powers to establish the type of regime they wanted, was soon to be cut short. During the last few days in April or the first few days in May[56] the Allied Powers at Paris decided to give Lombardy, as well as Venetia, to the Habsburgs, and on May 14 the Austrian emperor wrote Count Bellegarde, his commander-in-chief in Italy, to take over control of the government of Lombardy in his name.[57] Bellegarde informed the Milanese of his new appointment on May 25,[58] and on June 12 he officially notified them that the Allied Powers had given their country to the Austrians.[59] On July 27 he abolished the various ministries of the former Kingdom of Italy, all of which had been left in existence up to that time.[60]

A few hot-heads, feeling that their fate had been arbitrarily decided in Paris without the rights and aspirations of the Lombard people being taken into consideration,[61] openly expressed their displeasure over the actions of the Allied Powers when they heard the news that Lombardy was to go to Austria. At Brivio, for example, the Austrian coat of arms, which had been raised by pro-Austrian citizens to celebrate the change of government, was torn down by malcontents.[62] On the night of June 14, when the pro-Allied play, *The Battle of Leipzig*, was shown at the Canobbiana Theater in Milan, the spectators hissed so loudly that the production was

[56] See my *Fall of the Kingdom of Italy*, pp. 180–88.

[57] Emperor Francis to Bellegarde, Paris, May 14, 1814, St. A., *Conferenz Akten,* Ser. b, 1814, No. 996.

[58] Proclamation, Bellegarde, Milan, May 25, 1814, *Raccolta degli atti del governo e delle disposizioni generali emanate dalle diverse autorità in oggetti sì amministrativi che giudijiarj* (hereafter cited as *"Atti del governo lombardo"*) (Milan, 1816–19), 1814, pp. 52–53.

[59] Proclamation, Bellegarde, Milan, May 25, 1814, *ibid.,* pp. 60–61.

[60] Bellegarde to Emperor Francis, Milan, Aug. 5, 1814, *Hofkammer Archiv* (Vienna) MSS, *Kredit Akten,* Fasc. 2C/4, ex Oktober 1814, No. 7973. Also see Bellegarde's various decrees in regard to the above on July 27, 29, and 30, Aug. 16, and Oct. 20, 1814, as found in the *Atti del governo lombardo,* 1814, pp. 92–102, 109–12, 118–20, 143–44.

[61] Giovanni de Castro, "I ricordi autobiografici inediti del Marchese Benigno Bossi," *Archivio storico lombardo,* XVII (1890), 911.

[62] Sormani to Provisional Regency, Milan, June 7, 1814, *Archivio di Stato* (Milan) MSS (hereafter cited as "A. S., Mil."), *Atti segreti,* Busta I, Fasc. 24, fol. 7.

stopped and orders were given to clear the theater.[63] But some of the more responsible liberals assumed the attitude that it was now best to make a virtue of necessity and demonstrate the loyalty of the Lombards to their new masters, making every effort to obtain the most satisfactory possible kind of government from them.[64] They hoped to get from their new emperor at least the promise that their country would become a "Lombard" kingdom dependent upon the emperor and governed in his name by an archduke residing in Milan. They also wanted to procure from the Habsburgs a system of administrative, political, and judicial organization, as well as laws, that would be in conformity with the customs and needs of the people. In addition, they expected the Austrians to grant some kind of national representation to Lombardy.[65] If they could obtain concessions like these, many liberals felt that they could look forward to a reasonably satisfactory future.[66]

Thus in the early summer of 1814 the state of Lombard feeling in regard to the Austrians was divided. The nobility, the clergy, and the great mass of country people were strongly pro-Austrian and happy again to become subjects of the Habsburg emperor. The military, the officials of the former Kingdom of Italy, and the middle classes were dissatisfied with the new arrangements made for their country,[67] but even a substantial number of persons in these groups were inclined to co-operate with their new masters, provided that their country was given some degree of self-government.

Unfortunately, certain policies of the Habsburgs constantly irritated the liberal elements in Lombardy and finally served to goad some of them into open opposition. Bellegarde himself was popular enough with most of the populace. Many Italians were pleased with his tolerance and moderation, his patience and fairness, and

---

[63] Castro, "La restaurazione austriaca in Milano," *loc. cit.*, pp. 619–20; Josef Alexander Freiherr von Helfert, *La caduta della dominazione francese nell'alta Italia e la congiura militare bresciano-milanese nel 1814* (Bologna, 1894), p. 147.

[64] Rasini to Confalonieri, Milan, June 18, 1814, Gallavresi, *Carteggio del Confalonieri*, I, 182.

[65] Verri to deputation in Paris, Milan, May 13 and 24, 1814, *Carte Beccaria*, Busta I, Fasc. I, Nos. 36 and 71; Bellegarde to Metternich, Milan, June 4, 1814, Lemmi, *La restaurazione austriaca*, pp. 424–25.

[66] See, for example, Porro Lambertenghi to Confalonieri, May 14, 1814, Gallavresi, *Carteggio del Confalonieri*, I, 124–25.

[67] Bellegarde report, May 31, 1814, St. A., *Conferenz Akten*, Ser. b, 1814, No. 1249.

his willingness to listen to the opinions of all groups of people.[68] Nevertheless, there were complaints that he could take no steps without first consulting Vienna,[69] and his mildness was often mistaken for lack of energy.[70] Some Lombards grumbled because a permanent government suitable to the customs and religious habits of the people had not yet been instituted.[71] Numerous partisans of the Habsburgs, on the one hand, were indignant because the supporters of the previous French government, former republicans, immoral priests, and men without religious principles had not been discharged from their posts, while loyal pro-Austrians were not only excluded from government positions but were despised and subjected to the vengeance of anti-Austrian intriguers.[72] The liberals, on the other hand, complained loudly that too many Germans were being placed in the Lombard administration,[73] and all classes of people muttered against the ruthless and high-handed tactics of Baron Bernard Rossetti,[74] Bellegarde's special adviser in civil and financial matters.[75] Soon anonymous threats were sent not only to Rossetti but also to Bellegarde by various individuals who were incensed at the way governmental affairs were being conducted.[76]

The Italian officials of the former Kingdom of Italy created a special problem for the Austrians. Although nearly all of them were

[68] Borda to Battista, July 6, 1814, Gallavresi, *Carteggio di Borda*, p. 60; Castro, "Bossi," *loc. cit.*, p. 911; Hager report of Aug. 2, 1814, St. A., *Conferenz Akten*, Ser. b, 1814, No. 1506; Hager report, Sept. 5, 1814, St. A., *Kabinets-Akten*, 1814, No. 220; Pietro Dolce report, June 30, 1816, Alessandro Luzio, *La massoneria sotto il regno italico e la restaurazione austriaca*. Reprinted from the *Archivio storico lombardo*, XLIV (Milan, 1918), 73.

[69] Castro, "Bossi," *loc. cit.*, p. 911; Freddi to Hager, Vienna, Dec. 26, 1814, Maurice H. Weil, *Les Dessous du Congrès de Vienne, d'après documents originaux des archives du ministère impérial et royal de l'intérieur à Vienne* (2 vols., Paris, 1917), I, 745.

[70] Entries of June 30 and July 7, 1814, Mantovani diary, V, 286, 288.

[71] Entry of Aug. 1, 1814, *ibid.*, p. 296.

[72] Hager reports of June 25, 29, and July 16, 1814, St. A., *Conferenz Akten*, Ser. b, 1814, Nos. 1262, 1276, and 1407; Castro, "La restaurazione austriaca in Milano," *loc. cit.*, p. 624.

[73] Theresa Confalonieri Casati to Confalonieri, Milan, July 27 and Aug. 6, 1814, Gallavresi, *Carteggio del Confalonieri*, I, 224–25, 229–30.

[74] Castro, "La restaurazione austriaca in Milano," *loc. cit.*, p. 631; Lemmi, *La restaurazione austriaca*, p. 304; Hager report, Sept. 5, 1814, St. A., *Kabinets-Akten*, 1814, No. 220.

[75] Rossetti was appointed to his position as Bellegarde's chief assistant in July 1814.—Emperor Francis to Ugarte, July 8, 1814, St. A., *Staats-Rath Akten*, No. 2224.

[76] Entry of Sept. 10, 1814, Mantovani diary, V, 309; Theresa Confalonieri Casati to Confalonieri, Milan, July 20, 1814, Gallavresi, *Carteggio del Confalonieri*, I, 221.

left in their former positions after the change in government, many of them, including some of the police agents, were still openly attached to Napoleon.[77] Some were violently anti-Austrian and openly insisted that they would never submit to the new government.[78] The Austrian police gave warning that officials and former officials were buying knives and stilettos[79] and were conspiring against loyal Austrians.[80] Bellegarde himself admitted to the Austrian emperor that he could not count on the co-operation and loyalty of most of the officials and police agents in his government.[81] Nevertheless, little was done to dismiss unreliable and suspected employees during 1814. Immediately after the Austrians took control of Lombardy, all officials born outside the territorial limits of Austrian Lombardy were discharged. At the same time Bellegarde expressed the opinion that all criminals and persons who had lost the respect of the people through their immorality, as well as persons whose dislike of the new order was proved, should be ousted from the government,[82] but he proceeded with his customary caution. He always insisted that the conduct of employees during the previous French regime should not in itself make them subject to special investigation or dismissal and that the only test should be their present behavior.[83] As a result, very few Italians were actually discharged.

The retention of disloyal employees in positions of trust might not have been so dangerous had not other Austrian actions constantly served to vex a growing number of Italians. One of these was the continuance of conscription.[84] Like other people under the Na-

[77] Hager report, Aug. 2, 1814, St. A., *Conferenz Akten,* Ser. b, 1814, No. 1506; Maurice Henri Weil, *Joachim Murat, roi de Naples, la dernière année de règne (mai 1814-mai 1815)* (5 vols., Paris, 1909–10), I, 223.
[78] Theresa Confalonieri Casati to Confalonieri, Milan, July 20, 1814, Gallavresi, *Carteggio del Confalonieri,* I, 221.
[79] Police report, Milan, Sept. 10, 1814, Kr. A., *Feld Akten (Italien),* 1814, Fasc. 9, No. 39d.
[80] Note, for instance, the police report from Milan on Sept. 14, 1814, found in *ibid.,* and No. 41.
[81] Letter of Nov. 11, 1814, *ibid.,* Fasc. 11, No. 141½.
[82] Bellegarde report, May 31, 1815, St. A., *Conferenz Akten,* Ser. b, 1814, No. 1249.
[83] Hager to Bellegarde, Vienna, Aug. 8, 1814, in reply to the latter's letter of July 27, A. S., Mil., *Atti segreti,* Busta II, No. 195; Lemmi, *La restaurazione austriaca,* pp. 301–2.
[84] Hager report, June 29, 1814, St. A., *Conferenz Akten,* Ser. b, 1814, No. 1276; Hager to Bellegarde, Vienna, July 17, 1814, A. S., Mil., *Atti segreti,* 1814, Busta II, No. 124; Castro, "Bossi," *loc. cit.,* p. 914.

poleonic yoke, the Lombards had chafed under the ever-increasing conscription lists which the French had imposed upon them. The retention of the same practice by the Habsburgs only served to inflame public opinion against them.

The conduct of the Austrian troops in Lombardy also gave grounds for discontent. In the first place, the very fact that, contrary to the French practice of housing troops in barracks, the Austrian soldiers were quartered in the homes of the inhabitants provided ample reason for constant friction.[85] Then, too, although the troops were supposedly under strict discipline, some of them behaved quite badly and went around provoking the inhabitants through their insults and their misconduct.[86] Before long bad blood developed between the Lombards and the Austrian troops, and quarrels and fighting between them became all too frequent.[87]

There was also some muttering against the rate of taxation in Lombardy, even though after the change of government nearly all of the most oppressive French taxes had been hurriedly reduced. As early as April 20 the tobacco, salt, and consumption taxes had been cut to one-half of their former amount,[88] and within the next week the registration tax and the tax on arts and business were abolished, the tariff on sugar was reduced by two-thirds, and the postal rate was cut to one-half of the previous one.[89] In June the land tax rate for July was lowered from the French rate of 48 denari[90] to one centesimo per scudo of assessed value,[91] and the tax on capital that had been levied by the French was abolished.[92] Although these

---

[85] Police report, Sept. 18, 1814, St. A., *Kabinets-Akten*, 1814, No. 386.

[86] Emperor Francis to Colloredo, Schönbrunn, June 21, 1814, Kr. A., *Hofkriegsrath Akten*, 1814, Fasc. 6, No. 7; Castro, "Bossi," *loc. cit.*, pp. 912, 914.

[87] Hager to Bellegarde, Vienna, July 20, 1814, A. S., Mil., *Atti segreti*, Busta II, No. 120; Wiedemann-Warnhelm, *Die Wiederherstellung der österreichischen Vorherrschaft in Italien*, p. 44.

[88] Notification, Barbò, Milan, April 21, 1814, Kr. A., *Feld Akten (Italien)*, 1814, Fasc. 13, No. 84.

[89] Decree, Provisional Regency, Milan, April 21, 1814, *Atti del governo lombardo*, 1814, p. 5; Decree, Barbò, April 23, 1814, *ibid.*, pp. 10–11; Decree, Provisional Regency, April 26, 1814, Massimo Fabi, *Milano e il ministro Prina. Narrazione storica del Regno d'Italia (aprile 1814). Tratta da documenti editi ed inediti* (Novara, 1860), Appendix XXXIV, b, p. 141.

[90] Bellegarde report, May 31, 1814, St. A., *Conferenz Akten*, Ser. b, 1814, No. 1249.

[91] Decree, Provisional Regency, Milan, June 14, 1814, *Atti del governo lombardo*, 1814, p. 68.

[92] Decree, Provisional Regency, Milan, June 16, 1814, *ibid.*, pp. 71–72.

tax reductions had a salutary effect on some of the population,[93] a number of malcontents still continued to grumble about excessive taxation.[94] Had the people been prosperous, they would no doubt have expressed their appreciation for such substantial tax reductions as had been made for them. But in the summer of 1814 the Lombards, like the Venetians, were suffering from hard times. The vicissitudes of war, the stopping of public works projects that had been started by the French, and the succession of bad crops, in particular,[95] were responsible for a good deal of misery and a great increase in begging and bread riots.[96]

With such sources of irritation always present and with hard times and misery affecting large classes of people, it is hardly to be wondered at that, as the summer went on, there were reports of open demonstrations of hostility against the Austrians. Menacing libels against the Germans and the Habsburg emperor were posted on the streets of Milan,[97] and the Milanese police began sending in reports about an anti-Habsburg paper which was published supposedly in secret in Milan[98] and about the circulation of pamphlets satirizing the Germans.[99] In other places there were reports of open demonstrations. At Rivarolo an anti-Austrian, anti-Semitic demonstration broke out in which various distinguished citizens were insulted.[100] There was a bloody quarrel between aristocrats and "Jacobins" at Faenza,[101] while at Brescia, reputedly the center of anti-Austrian feeling in Lombardy, there were several reports of bloody fighting between the Italians and Austrian soldiers.[102] The Viennese

[93] Report of the Police Prefect of Olona, Milan, June 17, 1814, A. S., Mil., *Atti segreti*, Busta I, No. 9929.
[94] Hager report, Aug. 2, 1814, St. A., *Conferenz Akten*, Ser. b, 1814, No. 1506.
[95] See my "Habsburgs and the Great Depression in Lombardy-Venetia," *loc. cit.*, pp. 307–9.
[96] Lazanzky to Bellegarde, Vienna, Sept. 10, 1814, A. S., Mil., *Commissario plenipotenziario, Polizia*, Busta 26, No. 3112; Decrees of the Provisional Regency, Dec. 13, 1814, and July 2, 1815, *Atti del governo lombardo*, 1814, pp. 163–64, and 1815, I, 130.
[97] Report of the Police Prefect of Olona, Milan, June 18, 1814, A. S., Mil., *Atti segreti*, 1814, Busta I, Fasc. 18, No. 9978.
[98] Police report, Milan, Aug. 7, 1814, Kr. A., *Feld Akten (Italien)*, 1814, Fasc. 8, No. 25.
[99] Hager report, July 18, 1814, St. A., *Conferenz Akten*, Ser. b, No. 1423.
[100] Sormani to Bellegarde, Milan, July 20, 1814, A. S., Mil., *Atti segreti*, 1814, Busta I, No. 61.
[101] Hager report, July 8, 1814, St. A., *Conferenz Akten*, Ser. b, 1814, No. 1335.
[102] Hager report, June 8, 1814, *ibid.*, No. 1153; Weil, *Murat*, I, 235.

The Habsburgs and Lombardy-Venetia 319

authorities had grounds for their concern about the increasing discontent in Lombardy.[103]

In Venetia in the summer of 1814 public opinion was much more favorable to Austria than in Lombardy. It is true, as we have seen, that the serious depression, the continued high taxation, the military requisitions, the bad conduct of Austrian troops, and the retention of the French form of government and unpopular officials of the preceding regime had in the spring of 1814 irritated many people and had helped to revive among the upper classes a desire for the restoration of the old Venetian Republic. By the summer of 1814, however, some of the worst causes for complaint had been removed. Discipline had been restored in the Austrian army and the heavy military requisitions had been done away with, and early in the summer the most vexatious taxes were substantially reduced. There were still numerous complaints over certain Austrian policies and the living conditions of most of the inhabitants remained deplorable, but, in general, the population was more favorably inclined towards the Habsburgs than it had been in the spring. Everywhere the Austrian police commented on how much more pro-Habsburg the Venetians were than the Lombards, how the former privileged classes under the French regime were the only really dissatisfied element among the population, and how the vast majority of the Venetians loyally accepted their new government with resignation if not with joy.[104] There was some discontent in Venetia, but Lombardy was definitely the center of the anti-Austrian movement in northern Italy in the summer of 1814.

Various foreign influences, as well as the secret societies, were at work to fan the discontent of the dissatisfied groups in Lombardy, as well as that of the few faultfinders in Venetia, into a spirit of open rebellion. First of all, Napoleon Bonaparte's very presence on the near-by Island of Elba encouraged the hopes of all nationalist elements, who banked on the possibility of his deserting Elba to make

---

[103] Hegardt to Engsetroem, Vienna, July 30, 1814, Weil, *Les Dessous du Congrès de Vienne*, I, 35–36.

[104] Hager reports of June 17, July 15, and July 16, 1814, St. A., *Conferenz Akten*, Ser. b, 1814, Nos. 1174, 1393, and 1407; Hager report, May 11, 1814, St. A., *Kabinets-Akten*, 1814, No. 1547; Report to Raab, Venice, July 16, 1814, *Carte segrete della polizia austriaca in Italia*, I, 21–22; Giuseppe Solitro, "Maestri e scolari dell' università di Padova nell' ultima dominazione austriaca (1813–1866)," *Archivio veneto-tridentino*, I (1922), 111–12.

a sortie in the Apennine peninsula to give independence to the Italian people.[105] Habsburg officials particularly concerned themselves with the effects of Napoleon's prestige upon Italian malcontents, made lists of the enthusiastic supporters of Napoleon, carefully watched all comings and goings of persons to and from Elba, and investigated the rather extensive correspondence between various Italians and Napoleon or his agents.[106] A sharp watch was also kept on Joachim Murat, the King of Naples, who was strongly suspected of wanting to make himself king of a united Italy. The gradual increase in the size of his army and his correspondence with members of secret societies and with Lombard malcontents were closely scrutinized. The Austrians felt, and in this they were partly right, that all Italian intriguers had their eyes fixed on King Joachim and expected help from him when they undertook to chase the hated Germans from Italy.[107]

It was the influence of England and the partisans of England, however, which gave the Austrians the greatest concern. Habsburg officials in Italy suspected the English of wishing to put the Italian national party under their protection[108] in the hope of becoming master of ports on both the Adriatic and the Mediterranean.[109] They were especially apprehensive over the influence of Lord William Bentinck, the British commander-in-chief in the Mediterranean during the war against the French, upon Italian malcontents.[110] The

[105] See especially Hager report, May 13, 1814, St. A., *Kabinets-Akten*, 1814, No. 1568; Raab to Hager, Padua, Aug. 13, 1814, Lemmi, *La restaurazione austriaca*, p. 436; Police report, Milan, Sept. 24, 1814, Kr. A., *Feld Akten (Italien)*, 1814, Fasc. 9, No. 86; and Helfert, *Kaiser Franz und das Lombardo-Venetianischen Königreichs*, p. 151.

[106] See especially Weil, *Murat*, I, 231–35, 289–308, 385, 449–66; Pagani to Metternich, Milan, Aug. 11, 1814, A. S., Mil., *Atti segreti*, 1814, Busta II, No. 179; Hager to Bellegarde, Vienna, Sept. 16, 1814, *ibid.*, Busta V, No. 628; Metternich to Bellegarde, Baden, Aug. 28, 1814, St. A., *Staatskanzlei, Provinzen, Lombardei-Venedig*, Fasc. 3, Sec. 2, fol. 68; and Lemmi, *La restaurazione austriaca*, p. 323.

[107] See especially Reuss to Hudelist, Padua, July 17, 1814, St. A., *Staatskanzlei, Provinzen, Lombardei-Venedig*, Fasc. 18, Sec. 8, fols. 1–2; Report from Bologna, June 30, 1814, A. S., Mil., *Atti segreti*, 1814, Busta II, No. 118; Hager report, July 8, 1814, St. A., *Conferenz Akten*, Ser. b, 1814, No. 1423; Excerpts from letters between Florence and Bologna, July 28, 1814, Kr. A., *Feld Akten (Italien)*, 1814, Fasc. 8, No. 79b; and Raab to Hager, Padua, Aug. 13, 1814, Lemmi, *La restaurazione austriaca*, p. 436.

[108] Reuss to Hudelist, Padua, July 17, 1814, St. A., *Staatskanzlei, Provinzen, Lombardei-Venedig*, Fasc. 18, Sec. 8, fols. 1–2.

[109] Raab to Hager, Venice, Oct. 6, 1814, Lemmi, *La restaurazione austriaca*, pp. 444–45; Soriga, "Bagliori unitari in Lombardia," *loc. cit.*, p. 5.

[110] Raab to Hager, Venice, Oct. 6, 1814, Lemmi, *La restaurazione austriaca*, pp. 444–45; Bellegarde to Metternich, Milan, Jan. 1, 1815, St. A., *Staatskanzlei, Provinzen, Lombardei-Venedig*, Fasc. 4, Sec. 4, fols. 7–10.

Austrian officials complained that his irresponsible proclamation, contrary to the intentions of the British government, of the restoraion of the Genoese Republic[111] and his remark in Verona to the Italian Countess Marioni that he "did not know why a physically and morally strong nation like the Italian one did not think of its independence"[112] had a very unwholesome effect upon Italian public opinion. Reports also reached Habsburg officials of the existence in London of a society for Italian independence that counted among its members prominent Englishmen like the Duke of Buckingham.[113] This group, along with revolutionary clubs belonging to the parliamentary opposition,[114] was said to be actively at work stirring up a spirit of independence in the Italian peninsula.

With fears like these obsessing various Austrian officials in Lombardy-Venetia, it is no wonder that they kept an eagle eye on all possible relations between English liberals and Italian malcontents. When Confalonieri, Litta, and Somaglia went to London in the summer of 1814 as representatives of the liberal factions in the former Milanese provisional government to try to get the support of the British government for their independence plans, they were ordered to leave London immediately, and after their return to Milan their actions were closely watched.[115] The conduct and conversations of English officers and travelers, and particularly their associations with Italian liberals, were closely supervised.[116] The Austrian police were especially perturbed over the arrival in Italy of the Princess of Wales[117] and Bozzi Granville. Every action of the princess was reported on, while Granville, a former physician in the English

---

[111] Hager report, June 7, 1814, St. A., *Kabinets-Akten*, 1814, No. 1603.

[112] *Ibid.* Also see Hager report, July 5, 1814, St. A., *Conferenz Akten*, Ser. b, 1814, No. 1356.

[113] Bellegarde to Metternich, Milan, Dec. 5, 1814, St. A., *Staatskanzlei, Provinzen, Lombardei-Venedig*, Fasc. 4, Sec. 4, fols. 192–97; Saint Agnan to Metternich, Sempsal, Switzerland, Dec. 4, 1814, *ibid.*, fols. 207–8.

[114] Hager to Rossetti, Vienna, Aug. 16, 1815, A. S., Mil., *Atti segreti*, 1815, Busta IX, No. 114; Rossetti to Strassoldo, Milan, Sept. 4, 1815, *ibid.*

[115] Hager to Bellegarde, Vienna, Aug. 12, 1814, A. S., Mil., *Atti segreti*, 1814, Busta II, No. 216; Bellegarde to Hager, Milan, Sept. 7, 1814, *ibid.*; Hager reports of Sept. 18 and Dec. 11, 1814, St. A., *Kabinets-Akten*, 1814, Nos. 705 and 910.

[116] See especially Hager report, July 5, 1814, St. A., *Conferenz Akten*, Ser. b, 1814, No. 1356; Police reports, Milan, Aug. 6 and 8, 1814, Kr. A., *Feld Akten (Italien)*, 1814, Fasc. 8, Nos. 24 and 26; Metternich to Bellegarde, Vienna, Oct. 12, 1814, St. A., *Staatskanzlei, Provinzen, Lombardei-Venedig*, Fasc. 3, Sec. 2, fols. 84–85; and Pagani report, Milan, July 16, 1814, A. S., Mil., *Atti segreti*, 1814, Busta II, No. 114, Report No. 12,153.

[117] Weil, *Murat*, I, 440.

army and the bearer of dispatches from the British Foreign Office to Italy, to the great relief of a nervous police, was arrested in Bologna after he had gotten into a fight with some citizens of that city.[118]

Without doubt, English agents and travelers did play a role in keeping alive a spirit of independence in Lombardy-Venetia in the summer of 1814. The Austrian police at least emphasized in their reports the critical influence which English proselytizers had upon Italian malcontents and upon the Freemasons and other societies[119] which throve in Italy during the last days of the Napoleonic regime and the beginning of the restoration. Masonic lodges had existed in Italy since the eighteenth century and flourished during the Napoleonic period.[120] Freemasons were also active in the summer of 1814 and were a rallying point for various dissatisfied elements, including even members of the police and other government officials.[121] From the very first they worked to stir up hatred against Austria[122] and to win over the inhabitants to the cause of Italian independence. Soon news was sent to Vienna that the Masons were concocting an uprising in the Trentino for August, to be followed by one in Lombardy,[123] and the Viennese government took immediate steps to order their officials in Lombardy-Venetia to make an accurate list of all members of the Masonic order in Italy[124] and to decree the dissolution of the Freemasons and all similar societies.[125]

---

[118] Metternich to Bellegarde, Vienna, Oct. 12, 1814, St. A., *Staatskanzlei, Provinzen, Lombardei-Venedig*, Fasc. 3, Sec. 2, fols. 84–85; Soriga, "Bagliori unitari in Lombardia," loc. cit., pp. 4–18; Paulina B. Granville, ed., *Autobiography of A. B. Granville, M. D., F. R. S., — being eighty-eight Years of the Life of a Physician who practised his Profession in Italy, Greece, Turkey, Spain, Portugal, the West Indies, Russia, Germany, France, and England* (2nd ed., 2 vols., London, 1874), I, 350–452.

[119] Raab to Hager, June 25, 1814, A. S., Mil., *Atti segreti*, 1814, Busta I, No. 65; Hager report, June 7, 1814, St. A., *Kabinets-Akten*, 1814, No. 1603.

[120] Dolce to Saurau, November 1815, Alessandro Luzio, *La massoneria e il Risorgimento italiano. Saggio storico-critico. Con illustrazioni e molti documenti inediti* (2 vols., Bologna, 1925), I, 117; *Carte segrete della polizia austriaca in Italia*, I, 78.

[121] Excerpts from police reports, Aug. 31–Sept. 3, 1814, Kr. A., *Feld Akten (Italien)*, 1814, Fasc. 9, ad No. 10.

[122] See especially the anonymous memoir enclosed in Hager to Bellegarde, Vienna, July 7, 1814, A. S., Mil., *Atti segreti*, 1814, Busta I, No. 88.

[123] Antonio Zieger, "I primi risultati delle ricerche austriache sui massoni lombardi nel 1814 e 1815," *La Lombardia nel Risorgimento italiano*, XIII (1928), 6–8.

[124] *Ibid.*, pp. 5–11; Hager to Bellegarde, Vienna, Aug. 8, 1814, A. S., Mil., *Atti segreti*, 1814, Busta II, No. 195; Bellegarde to Hager, Milan, July 27, 1814, *ibid.*, Busta I, No. 87.

[125] Hager to Bellegarde, Vienna, July 15, 1814, A. S., Mil., *Atti segreti*, 1814, Busta I, No. 99. Decrees to this effect were published in Milan on August 26 and in Padua on September 9.

The Habsburgs and Lombardy-Venetia 323

Not only the Freemasons, but members of other secret societies busied themselves with championing the cause of Italian independence. The Carbonari, who originated in the Kingdom of Naples as an offshoot of Freemasonry,[126] had spread through all Lombardy by the spring and early summer of 1814. At that time Brescia was the chief center of their activities.[127] As early as June the Austrian police reported that Carbonari emissaries were circulating all through Lombardy, collecting the signatures of persons promising either to take up arms or to give money to support an armed insurrection against Austria.[128]

There were other societies, too, of which the Adelfi, the Guelfs, and the Centri were the most active in Lombardy-Venetia in 1814. The chief centers of the first of these organizations were in Bologna, Milan, and Turin.[129] The Guelf society's headquarters were in Bologna, but its members were diffused throughout northern Italy.[130] The Guelfs were strongly pro-English and worked for the establishment of a united Kingdom of Italy ruled by a prince from the English royal family.[131] The Centri, whose headquarters were in Mantua, became the chief center of opposition and intrigue for the many officers of the Italian army who in the summer of 1814 were obsessed with a bitter spirit of hatred against the Austrians.[132]

The spirit of the Italian army was especially ominous for the Austrians. On May 30 the army of the Kingdom of Italy was dissolved, and it was announced that its officers and enlisted men would be enrolled in special Italian regiments in the regular Habsburg

---

[126] See my *Fall of the Kingdom of Italy*, pp. 40–41.

[127] Pietro Dolce report, June 30, 1816, Luzio, *La massoneria sotto il regno italico e la restaurazione austriaca*, pp. 72–73; Anonymous report enclosed in Goess to Archduke Rainer, Venice, May 25, 1818, St. A., *Kabinets-Akten*, 1818, ad No. 453.

[128] Hager report, July 5, 1814, St. A., *Conferenz Akten*, Ser. b, 1814, No. 1356; Hager to Bellegarde, Vienna, July 5, 1814, A. S., Mil., *Atti segreti*, 1814, Busta I, No. 65; Hager to Bellegarde, Vienna, July 8, 1814, *ibid.*, No. 46.

[129] See especially Arturo Bersano, "Adelfi, Federati e Carbonari. Contributo alla storia delle società segrete," *Atti* della r. accademia delle scienze di Torino, XLV (1909–10), 409–30; and Angelo Ottolini, *La carboneria dalle origini ai primi tentativi insurrezionali (1797–1817)*, in the *Collezione storica del Risorgimento italiano* (Modena, 1936), p. 47.

[130] Secret police report No. 43, n.d., n.p., *Carte segrete della polizia austriaca in Italia*, I, 100.

[131] See Domenico Spadoni, "Gli statuti della Guelfia in possesso della polizia austriaca nel 1816," *Rassegna storica del Risorgimento*, XI (1924), 704–38; and Domenico Spadoni, "Il sogno unitario e wilsoniano d'un patriota nel 1814–15," *ibid.*, XIII (1926), 353.

[132] See especially Ottolini, *La carboneria*, pp. 93–100.

army.[133] Loud were the denunciations of this action by Italian soldiers. Large numbers deserted rather than become part of the Austrian army. Some of them took up service with Murat's forces, while others roamed the countryside as brigands.[134] Those who remained manifested their discontent with their lot at every turn, praised Napoleon openly, and expressed the hope that he would soon come to Italy to free the people.[135] At Como the Italian troops shouted loudly, "Long live Napoleon!" when a German general inspected them.[136] The Italian troops took advantage of every opportunity to insult the Germans, and there were numerous fights between them, especially at Pavia and at Brescia.[137] Discontent was so prevalent among the officers of the former Italian army that on the night of June 26–27 a large number of them openly took an oath that they would never serve the Austrians and then broke out in loud denunciations of everything Austrian.[138]

With a violent anti-Austrian spirit prevailing among the Italian army officers, with the secret societies conspiring to bring about a united kingdom of Italy,[139] and with numerous plotters always hoping to get help from such outside sources as Napoleon, Joachim Murat, and the English, the atmosphere was charged with a spirit of revolution against the Habsburgs. The Austrian police reported the discovery early in August of large quantities of guns and ammunition at a house belonging to a certain Soresi in Milan,[140] and there were notices of guns and powder being found at the home of a merchant at Brescia.[141] There were disturbing missives about the

---

[133] Bellegarde order, Milan, May 30, 1814, *Oesterreichischer Beobachter* (Vienna), June 13, 1814.

[134] Weil, *Murat*, I, 184–85; Lemmi, *La restaurazione austriaca*, pp. 308–9.

[135] Raab to Hager, Padua, Aug. 13, 1814, Lemmi, *La restaurazione austriaca*, p. 436.

[136] Theresa Confalonieri Casati to Confalonieri, Milan, July 6, 1814, Gallavresi, *Carteggio del Confalonieri*, I, 212–13; Borda to Battista, July 6, 1814, Gallavresi, *Carteggio del Borda*, pp. 60–61.

[137] See especially entry of July 15, 1814, Mantovani diary, V, 290–91; Pagani report, Milan, July 19, 1814, A. S., Mil., *Atti segreti*, 1814, Busta II, No. 114, Report No. 12,393; Hager to Bellegarde, Vienna, July 25, 1814, *ibid.*, Busta I, ad No. 67; and Theresa Confalonieri Casati to Confalonieri, Milan, July 20, 1814, Gallavresi, *Carteggio del Confalonieri*, I, 221.

[138] Raab to Hager, Padua, July 2, 1814, Kr. A., *Hofkriegsrath—Präsidial Akten*, 1814, Fasc. 7, No. 22; Hager report, July 13, 1814, *Conferenz Akten*, Ser. b, 1814, No. 1371.

[139] See especially the police report of Feb. 22, 1815, St. A., *Kabinets-Akten*, 1815, ad No. 339.

[140] Police report, Milan, Aug. 9, 1814, Kr. A., *Feld Akten (Italien)*, 1814, Fasc. 8, No. 34.

[141] Weil, *Murat*, I, 308.

The Habsburgs and Lombardy-Venetia 325

dangerous public spirit in such isolated places as Bologna, Brescia, Bergamo, Milan, Pavia, Verona, and Udine[142] and about a plot's being concocted to murder all Germans in Italy on July 10.[143] The Viennese government became alarmed about the possibilities of an uprising and ordered their officials in Italy to be especially alert to the progress of any possible conspiracies.[144]

The progress of events soon proved that the Austrian central police headquarters were justified in their alarm over the reports of conspiracies coming from Italy. It has been revealed that as early as May a group of conspirators met in Genoa and Turin to make plans for a united kingdom of Italy in the form of a renewed Roman Empire with its capital in Rome, and sent emissaries to Elba to offer the crown of this Roman Empire to Napoleon.[145] On July 15, Saint Agnan, a man of letters with an instinct for intrigue, revealed to the Austrian Count Bombelles in Paris the existence of a similarly fantastic plot to recreate a Roman Empire which he alleged had been confided to him the preceding month in London by a certain Count Comelli de Stuckenfeld.[146] The plan was to be executed during the early days of October, when a revolution was to break out in all Italy and a Roman Empire be created under the auspices of three consuls and an emperor, who was to be chosen from one of the ruling families of Europe. A meeting of the conspirators was to be

---

[142] Raab to Hager, Padua, June 25, 1814, A. S., Mil., *Atti segreti*, 1814, Busta I, No. 65; Hager report, July 8, 1814, St. A., *Conferenz Akten*, Ser. b, 1814, No. 1335.

[143] Hager report, July 18, 1814, St. A., *Conferenz Akten*, Ser. b, 1814, No. 1423.

[144] Hager to Bellegarde, Vienna, July 17, 1814, A. S., Mil., *Atti segreti*, 1814, Busta II, No. 120.

[145] This plot was revealed in an anonymous book, which was actually written by a certain De Laugier, first published in 1825 in Brussels under the title, *La Vérité sur les cent jours principalement par rapport à la renaissance projetée de l'empire romain par un citoyen de la Corse*. In 1829 an Italian edition was published under the title, *Delle cause italiane nell'evasione dell'imperatore Napoleone da l'Elba*. Mazziotti believes that this account was a true one. — M. Mazziotti, "L'offerta del trono d'Italia a Napoleone I. esule all'Elba," *Rassegna storica del Risorgimento*, VII (1920), 1–18. Domenico Spadoni is also inclined to believe this account. — See his "Federazione e re d'Italia mancati," *loc. cit.*, p. 423; and his *Milano e la congiura militare nel 1814 per l'indipendenza italiana: Il moto del 20 aprile e l'occupazione austriaca* (Modena, 1936), pp. 287–98. Buccella, however, does not believe that the facts contained in the above volume coincide with what actually happened. — M. R. Buccella, "La congiura e l'offerta dell'impero romano a Napoleone all'isola d'Elba," *Nuova Antologia. Rivista di lettere, scienze ed arti*, LXV (1930), 352–62.

[146] For a good account of Comelli's life and activities, see Domenico Spadoni, "Carlo Comelli de Stuckenfeld e il trono de' Cesare offerto a Casa Savoja nel 1814," *Rassegna storica del Risorgimento*, XIV (1927), 593–656.

held in Milan on August 5, with Comelli present. Saint Agnan promised to attend the meeting as an informant if given adequate police protection.[147]

When Saint Agnan refused, however, to go to Milan without first securing an advance of 8,000 francs from Bombelles[148] and when August 5 passed by without the slightest disturbance, the Austrians became suspicious of Saint Agnan's intentions and would probably have forgotten about the whole matter[149] had not Roschmann, the imperial commissioner in the Tyrol, sent in a further report about new plots in Italy and ordered the ex-mayor of Trent, Cheluzzi, to proceed to Milan to make an investigation.[150]

Roschmann's suspicions that some kind of conspiracy was afoot in Lombardy-Venetia were well founded. For some time various malcontents in the secret societies and in the Italian army had been conjuring up schemes against the Austrians. In the fall of 1814 their activities were intensified. In September Colonels Moretti, Pavoni, and Olini met together in a theater in Brescia, where they decided that the time was right to make thorough preparation for action. Moretti and Pavoni went to Monza to win Inspector Brunetti over to their plans. Other dissatisfied personages also joined the plot. Among them were the young lawyer Lattuada, who brought with him the support of the Centri and who thought he could win over the Carbonari, De Meestre Huyoel, Caprotti, Cavedoni, Gerosa, Theodore Lechi, Bellotti, Marchal, Delfini, Mancini, Gasparinetti, and Rasori, nearly all of them officers of the Italian army. Numerous meetings were held but nothing definite was agreed upon. Soon the conspirators in Brescia began to complain loudly that their ac-

---

[147] Count Bombelles to Metternich, Paris, July 16, 1814, Helfert, *La caduta della dominazione francese*, pp. 235–41. Bombelles' revelations were sent by the Council of War to Bellegarde on August 31, along with instructions to put Saint Agnan under careful surveillance when he arrived in Milan. — St. A., *Staatskanzlei, Provinzen, Lombardei-Venedig*, Fasc. 3, Sec. 2, fols. 70–71.

[148] Bombelles to Metternich, Paris, Sept. 1, 1814, Helfert, *La caduta della dominazione francese*, pp. 242–44.

[149] On Sept. 22, 1814, Bellegarde wrote Metternich to acknowledge receipt of Bombelles' report from Paris, which Metternich sent him on August 31. Then he continued: "I have employed the most exact surveillance to search into and verify the symptoms given by M. de St. Agnan and nothing leads me to believe the existence of the conspiracy which has been the object of his revelation." — St. A., *Staatskanzlei, Provinzen, Lombardei-Venedig*, Fasc. 3, Sec. 4, fols. 105–6.

[150] Hager to Emperor Francis, Vienna, Oct. 21, 1814, Helfert, *La caduta della dominazione francese*, pp. 245–47.

The Habsburgs and Lombardy-Venetia 327

complices in Milan and Monza were doing nothing. They insisted that since the departure of the Italian troops to other parts of the Austrian empire was imminent it was dangerous to temporize any longer. Fully realizing that time was running short, the Milanese and Monza plotters invited their Brescian compatriots to a meeting at Brunetti's house in Monza on November 3 to make definite plans for action. Here it was decided that at a given moment, which was later fixed as the night of November 19–20, the Italian regiments stationed at Cremona, Bergamo, and Brescia were to lead the inhabitants of these cities to revolt. At the same time Italian battalions were to go to Peschiera, Rocca d'Ango, and Verona to seize these fortified places from the feeble Austrian garrisons which held them, while an Italian officer, assisted by the Centri, was to take over the citadel at Mantua. At Milan the population was to be called to revolt by the ringing of the tocsin by all the city clocks. Bellegarde and the other Austrian officers were to be seized, and the plotters would declare the re-establishment of the Italian kingdom with a provisional regency temporarily in control of the government.[151]

Thus far everything seemed to progress smoothly for the conspirators, but in the early days of November they made a false step which resulted in the denunciation of the whole complot to the Austrians. After trying in vain on the 5th and 6th to get Generals Pino and Fontanelli to head the movement, they unfortunately decided to turn to Piedmont to find a chief and assigned this delicate task to the Piedmontese General Gifflenga, who happened to be in Milan at the time. As soon as Gifflenga crossed the frontier, he revealed the plot to the Sardinian authorities, who, in turn, immediately got in touch with Bellegarde.[152] Now having definite de-

---

[151] For the details of the plot see Lemmi, *La restaurazione austriaca*, pp. 345–59; Helfert, *La caduta della dominazione francese*, pp. 193–204; Weil, *Murat*, II, 49–61; Domenico Spadoni, "Il processo per la congiura bresciano-milanese del 1814," *Atti* del XIII congresso nazionale della società nazionale per la storia del Risorgimento italiano, tenutosi in Genova nei giorni 26–28 ottobre 1925, pp. 81–99; and Domenico Spadoni, *Milano e la congiura militare nel 1814 per l'indipendenza italiana: La congiura militare e il suo processo* (Modena, 1937), pp. 1–48.

[152] See especially Domenico Perrero, "Il generale conte Alessandro di Gifflenga e la congiura militare lombarda del 1814," *Rivista storica del Risorgimento italiano*, I (1895), 295–304. Also see Spadoni, "Il processo per la congiura bresciano-milanese," *loc. cit.*, pp. 96–97; and police report, Milan, Nov. 23, 1814, Kr. A., *Feld Akten (Italien)*, 1814, Fasc. 11, No. 46. On Nov. 11, 1814, Bellegarde wrote Emperor Francis to inform him of the need to leave at least three regiments of the Austrian army in Italy. After giving several reasons why he thought this was necessary, he wrote: "In order to give

tails about the conspiracy, Bellegarde moved rapidly to frustrate it. Measures were immediately taken to order the Italian regiments to march from Italy to other parts of the Austrian empire on November 26,[153] while the guard was strengthened in Milan for the night of the 19th–20th and detailed instructions were drawn up for the Milanese garrison on what they were to do in case of an actual uprising.[154]

Conclusive documentary proof, however, was still needed before the conspirators could be arrested. Saint Agnan supplied this. Although Bombelles had a very unfavorable opinion of Saint Agnan, he felt, nevertheless, that Saint Agnan had relations with the Italian intriguers, and early in November he sent him to Milan, preceded by a trusted confidant, the Abbé Altieri, who was to inform Bellegarde about Bombelles' doubts in regard to Saint Agnan.[155] Saint Agnan left Paris on November 2. On the way he won the confidence of Marchal, one of the chief affiliates of the plot, by revealing to him that he was coming to Italy on a secret mission to ascertain whether the state of opinion was such as to permit Louis XVIII to take the lead in forming an independent Italy under the rule of his nephew, the Duke of Berry. Upon their arrival in Milan, Marchal introduced him to the conspirators, and in a meeting on the evening of the 23rd Saint Agnan revealed his alleged mission to the plotters. He insisted that Louis XVIII needed to have written copies of their program and plan of operations and samples of proposed propaganda proclamations before he could decide whether he could help

---

Your Majesty new proof that continuous caution and intelligence are necessary, I am humbly submitting in the enclosures a report which I have received from the Sardinian government." — Kr. A., *Feld Akten (Italien)*, 1814, Fasc. 11, No. 14½. In Hager's report of Nov. 27, 1814, he wrote, among other things: "The concern over such disturbances [when the Italian troops would leave Italy] rests on secret notices which F. M. Count Bellegarde has received and which are supposed to have been confirmed by a ministerial work from Turin." — St. A., *Kabinets-Akten*, 1814, No. 883.

[153] Bellegarde to Emperor Francis, Milan, Nov. 11, 1814, Kr. A., *Feld Akten (Italien)*, 1814, Fasc. 11, No. 14½; Order by Klenau, Milan, Nov. 25, 1814, *ibid.*, No. 53.

[154] Bellegarde to Hager, Milan, Nov. 22, 1814, Lemmi, *La restaurazione austriaca*, pp. 453–55; Bellegarde project No. LXVIII, dated Nov. 23, 1814, Kr. A., *Feld Akten (Italien)*, 1814, Fasc. 11, No. 42.

[155] Bombelles to Metternich, Paris, Nov. 2, 1814, Helfert, *La caduta della dominazione francese*, pp. 247–49; Bombelles to Altieri, Paris, Nov. 1, 1814, Weil, *Murat*, II, 494–96.

The Habsburgs and Lombardy-Venetia 329

them. Lattuada, Rasori, and Gasparinetti promised to draw up such plans and proclamations and to give them to him on the evening of the 26th. At the meeting on the 26th, Saint Agnan read the papers which had been presented to him, put them in his pocket, and when, according to a prearranged plan, Austrian police appeared near the house, he fled from the meeting place, taking all the damaging evidence with him.[156] He gave the papers, which contained conclusive proof that Rasori, Lattuada, Gasparinetti, and others were conspiring to overthrow the Habsburg government in Italy,[157] to Bellegarde. Immediately thereafter he left for Paris, where he wrote Bellegarde asking for a title of nobility and a little territory in Germany as recompense for his services.[158] The Austrians finally gave him 4,000 francs for his work.[159]

With definite proof of a conspiracy in his hands, Bellegarde ordered the arrest of the chief plotters. On the night of December 3–4 Rasori, Gasparinetti, Lattuada, and Marchal were taken into custody.[160] On the night of December 10–11 Theodore Lechi, Bellotti, and De Meestre were arrested.[161] Their detention was followed on the 12th by that of Gerosa,[162] on the night of the 14th–15th by that of Olini, and on the night of the 17th–18th by that of Cavedoni.[163] Early in January further arrests were made. Varese was taken on the night of the 5th–6th, Caprotti on the 7th, Brunetti on the 9th,

---

[156] See especially Domenico Spadoni, "I documenti della congiura milanese carpiti da St. Agnan nel 1814," *Il Risorgimento italiano*, XIX (1926), 299–326; Spadoni, *La congiura militare*, pp. 90–114; Weil, *Murat*, II, 84–89; Lemmi, *La restaurazione austriaca*, pp. 366–70; and Helfert, *La caduta della dominazione francese*, pp. 221–26.

[157] Bellegarde to Hager, Milan, Dec. 14, 1814, A. S., Mil., *Atti segreti*, 1814, Busta III, No. 305; Bellegarde to Metternich, Milan, Dec. 27, 1814, St. A., *Staatskanzlei, Provinzen, Lombardei-Venedig*, Fasc. 3, Sec. 4, fol. 218.

[158] Saint Agnan to Bellegarde, Paris, Dec. 10, 1814, St. A., *Staatskanzlei, Provinzen, Lombardei-Venedig*, Fasc. 3, Sec. 4, fols. 219–20.

[159] Imperial resolution, Dec. 19, 1814, St. A., *Kabinets-Akten*, 1814, No. 916.

[160] Bellegarde to Metternich, Milan, Dec. 5, 1814, St. A., *Staatskanzlei, Provinzen, Lombardei-Venedig*, Fasc. 3, Sec. 4, fol. 193; Cheluzzi to Roschmann, Milan, Dec. 5, 1814, Lemmi, *La restaurazione austriaca*, pp. 460–61; Bellegarde to Hager, Milan, Dec. 6, 1814, *ibid.*, pp. 463–64.

[161] Bellegarde to Metternich, Milan, Dec. 12, 1814, St. A., *Staatskanzlei, Provinzen, Lombardei-Venedig*, Fasc. 3, Sec. 4, fol. 206; Ghislieri to Hager, Milan, Dec. 11, 1814, Weil, *Murat*, II, 519.

[162] Ghislieri to Hager, Milan, Dec. 12, 1814, Weil, *Murat*, II, 520.

[163] Ghislieri to Hager, Milan, Dec. 17, 1814, *ibid.*, pp. 516–17; Hager to Emperor Francis, Vienna, Dec. 27, 1814, *ibid.*, p. 520; Count Munarini to Bellegarde, Modena, Dec. 18, 1814, *ibid.*, pp. 520–21.

and Pavoni somewhat later, to be followed on February 1 by Ragani. The accused were tried by a special commission at Mantua and in 1816 were sentenced to varying terms of imprisonment.[164]

The first plot against Austrian rule in Lombardy-Venetia thus ended in miserable failure. Its leaders—chiefly disgruntled officers of the army of the former Kingdom of Italy and members of secret societies—had demonstrated their daring, but at the same time they had showed an almost childlike naïveté in their belief that they could drive the Austrians out of Italy without first devising effective plans for military operations and ensuring help from outside sources. Nevertheless, the bitter anti-Austrian sentiments of a certain part of the population had made them feel that their efforts might be met with at least some degree of success.

It should not be forgotten, however, that although the Italian national and liberal groups were loud and bitter in their denunciation of the Habsburgs and although they caused Austrian police officials and some foreign observers no little concern for the tranquillity of Italy, they comprised only a minority of the population in Austria's Lombardo-Venetian provinces. Although they were seldom referred to in the Austrian police reports—and peaceful, satisfied elements rarely are—the "property owners, the masses of people, and religious persons"[165] were decidely pro-Austrian. This pro-Austrian spirit of the large majority of the population, plus the fact that the dissatisfied elements were disheartened and cautious after the discovery of the military conspiracy, probably explains why when Joachim Murat, the King of Naples and a former marshal of Napoleon, proclaimed his war of Italian independence[166] against the

---

[164] Helfert, *La caduta della dominazione francese*, pp. 228-31; Weil, *Murat*, II, 93-96; Imperial resolution, Vienna, May 20, 1816, Kr. A., *Hofkriegsrath—Präsidial Akten*, 1816, Fasc. 8, No. 35.

[165] Bellegarde to Metternich, Milan, Sept. 22, 1814, St. A., *Staatskanzlei, Provinzen, Lombardei-Venedig*, Fasc. 3, Sec. 4, fol. 106.

[166] In 1927 at the Congress of the Italian Risorgimento Domenico Spadoni expressed the opinion that Murat's war of 1815 and not the 1848-1849 movement was the first war for Italian independence.—"Quella del 1815 fu veramente la prima guerra per l'indipendenza italiana?" *Atti* del XV congresso nazionale della società nazionale per la storia del Risorgimento italiano, tenutosi in Macerata nei giorni 1-2-3 settembre 1927, pp. 121-34. Antonio Monti, however, has maintained that Spadoni was wrong, for the majority of Italians in 1815 wanted neither unity nor independence but were either content to be under foreign control or accepted it with resignation.—"L'impresa di Gioacchino Murat nel 1815 e la prima guerra di indipendenza," *Rendiconti* del reale istituto lombardo di scienze e lettere, Ser. II, LXIII (1930), 191-200.

The Habsburgs and Lombardy-Venetia 331

Austrians after Napoleon's escape from Elba in late February 1815,[167] the Lombards and Venetians were on the whole indifferent to his appeals and showed actual disrespect to him as a foreigner.[168]

It is true that the ever-suspicious Habsburg police reported that the Centri and Carbonari were active in favor of Napoleon's cause in Piedmont, Lombardy-Venetia, and the Tyrol,[169] that a liberty tree was planted at Soldo while malcontents shouted, "Long live Napoleon, the Saviour of Italy!", that proclamations favorable to Napoleon were being posted in Verona,[170] and that an uprising was to take place in Mantua, Peschiera, Legnago, and Verona,[171] but no actual disturbances occurred. Nevertheless, the Austrian government took energetic measures to forestall possible trouble. In a proclamation on April 5 Bellegarde castigated Murat as a foreigner who tried to plunge Italy into war to realize his own selfish ambitions.[172] Two days later, in order to do away with the dissatisfaction that had arisen because the Italians knew nothing definite about their future fate, he announced to the Lombards that they, along with the Venetians, were to form a special Kingdom of Lombardy-Venetia within the Habsburg monarchy.[173] At the same time, the police were ordered to take energetic measures against all disturbers of the peace[174] and to prevent all meetings that would incite the inhabitants or disturb public order.[175] A special court was established

---

[167] Especially in his proclamation at Rimini on March 30, 1815, Murat made a fervent appeal to the Italians to follow him in his war to create an independent and united kingdom of Italy.—See Grégoire Orloff, *Mémoires historiques, politiques et littéraires sur le Royaume de Naples*, publié, avec des notes et additions, par Amaury Duval (5 vols., Paris, 1819-21), II, 441-43.

[168] See especially Francesco Lemmi, "Gioacchino Murat et le aspirazioni unitarie nel 1815," *Archivio storico per le province napoletane*, XXVI (1901), 169-211.

[169] Hager to Stipsitz, Vienna, June 11, 1815, Kr. A., *Hofkriegsrath—Präsidial Akten*, 1815, Fasc. 6, No. 9.

[170] Hager report, March 31, 1814, St. A., *Kabinets-Akten*, 1815, No. 794.

[171] Marziani to Imperial Military Government, Verona, March 24, 1815, Kr. A., *Feld Akten (Frimont in Italien)*, 1815, Fasc. 3, No. 88a; Hingenau to Hager, Venice, March 25, 1815, Kr. A., *Hofkriegsrath—Präsidial Akten, Italien*, 1815, Fasc. 4, No. 1a; Raab to Hager, Venice, March 26, 1815, *ibid.*, No. 1r.

[172] St. A., *Staatskanzlei, Provinzen, Lombardei-Venedig*, Fasc. 4, Sec. 2, fol. 133. Also in the *Atti del governo lombardo*, 1815, I, 35-38.

[173] *Atti del governo lombardo*, 1815, I, 47-51.

[174] Hager to Saurau, Vienna, June 2, 1815, Helfert, *Kaiser Franz und das Lombardo-Venetianischen Königreichs*, p. 566; Bellegarde to Metternich, Milan, March 17, 1815, St. A., *Staatskanzlei, Provinzen, Lombardei-Venedig*, Fasc. 4, Sec. 2, fol. 65.

[175] Decree, Strassoldo, Milan, April 3, 1814, *Notizie del Mondo* (Venice), April 10, 1815.

in Milan to try all persons charged with having committed crimes against the security of the state,[176] all Lombards and Venetians serving with the Neapolitan army were enjoined to desert their posts and return to their native country on pain of losing their property or the right to inherit it,[177] and orders were issued to transfer to other Austrian provinces all persons whose presence in Italy was considered dangerous to peace and security.[178]

All these measures, if they were necessary, were effective in preventing disturbances in Austria's Italian provinces. Although some malcontents insisted that the proclamation of the creation of a Lombardo-Venetian kingdom was given only to tranquillize the inhabitants,[179] the vast majority of the populace appeared to be satisfied with the announcement. The police reports from Italy throughout the course of Murat's campaign on the whole were full of assurances that Lombard and Venetian public opinion was favorable to the Austrians. The police insisted that the few partisans of independence hardly dared to express themselves openly and that the universal demand in all Lombardy-Venetia was for peace.[180]

It was the same after King Joachim's defeat and overthrow. In his report of November 6, 1815, in which he summarized the police reports from Lombardy in August and September, Baron von Hager expressed the opinion that public opinion was neither bad nor good. Many young people, who accepted revolutionary ideas during the Napoleonic period, and many persons who had had personal advantages under the French regime could not be expected to be wholly satisfied with the new order of things. Many complained because the costly, cumbersome old French system of government was still in existence. The landowners had expected more tax reductions from the Austrians than they had obtained. Householders were displeased because troops were quartered among them.

---

[176] Decree, Bellegarde, Milan, March 31, 1815, *ibid.*, April 4, 1815.

[177] Bellegarde proclamation, Milan, May 3, 1815, *Atti del governo lombardo*, 1815, I, 93–94; Proclamation No. 45, *Collezione di leggi venete*, 1815, I, 164–65.

[178] A. S., Ven., Polizia. Presidio di Governo, 1815–19, Fasc. II, No. 1459.

[179] Bellegarde to Metternich, Milan, April 13, 1815, St. A., *Staatskanzlei, Provinzen, Lombardei-Venedig*, Fasc. 4, Sec. 4, fol. 16.

[180] See especially Torresani to Hager, Venice, March 19, 1815, A. S., Ven., *Polizia. Presidio del Governo*, 1815–19, Fasc. II, No. 5/13–1000; Report to Vienna from Milan, March 24, 1815, as quoted in Helfert, *Kaiser Franz und das Lombardo-Venetianischen Königreichs*, p. 174; Police reports, Vienna, April 14 and 15, 1815, St. A., *Kabinets-Akten*, 1815, Nos. 811 and 821; and the *Allgemeine Zeitung*, July 14, 1815.

The Habsburgs and Lombardy-Venetia   333

The peasants were unhappy over the reintroduction of conscription, and all classes of people were angry over the steadily increasing price of food.[181] Thus many of the same grievances which had vexed the Lombards in 1814 were still present in the summer of 1815.

Similar conditions prevailed in Venetia. In his report on the state of public opinion in the Venetian provinces, dated November 11, 1815, the Venetian police director, Baron von Raab, maintained that some people were still unhappy because many Napoleonic laws and much of the former French administrative system still existed and because so many of the former French officials had been retained in the government. Landowners complained that they had barely enough to eat, although they were generally happy over the tax reductions which had been made. There were angry denunciations of the poll tax, which the peasants still had to pay, and of the harsh methods used by tax collectors in collecting delinquent taxes. The inhabitants of the cities were unhappy over the poor conditions of trade and industry, and all classes were bitter over conscription, over the high postal rates, and over the fact that the famine conditions which had caused so much suffering in 1814 had not been alleviated.[182]

It is evident that by the fall of 1815 the Lombards and Venetians were decidedly less pro-Austrian than they had been late in 1813 and early in 1814, when Austrian troops first entered the Apennine peninsula. The starvation, misery, and poor business conditions resulting from bad crops and the vicissitudes of more than two decades of warfare, the retention of the former French administrative and judicial system along with many officials of the former Kingdom of Italy, the conduct of the Austrian troops, and other vexations which seem to be an almost inevitable concomitant of military occupation, whether in 1814–1815 or in 1945–1950, had irritated large numbers of Italians who had at first received the conquering Habsburg army with open arms.

Nevertheless, dissatisfaction with Austrian rule did not encourage any sizable group of Lombards or Venetians to become nationalists or liberals during the years immediately following the overthrow of the Napoleonic regime. In spite of the agitation of nationalist

[181] St. A., *Kabinets-Akten*, 1815, No. 815.
[182] St. A., *Hofreisen*, Fasc. 43, fols. 536–43.

writers, British agents, and secret societies during the years immediately preceding the demise of the French regime, it was only a handful of conspirators, nearly all of them from the former Italian army or from the ranks of the secret societies, who in the fall of 1814 intrigued to chase the Austrians from Italy as a preliminary to creating a united Italian state, and in the spring of 1815 the Lombards and the Venetians turned a deaf ear to Joachim Murat's spirited appeals to join a war of national liberation. What national feeling existed was nearly all of a strictly local variety. In Venetia there were a few who desired a resurrection of the old Venetian republic, but this group was limited to a small number of nobles. In Lombardy there was an important and vocal group which longed for the establishment of an enlarged and independent kingdom of Lombardy, but the "Lombard nationalists" were confined to officials of the former Kingdom of Italy, army officers, and the middle classes.

The liberals were also relatively few in number. Many among the middle classes, as well as a sprinkling of liberal nobility, wanted self-government, a constitution, and some kind of national representation, but the vast majority of the populace looked upon Austrian rule as the best way of assuring that peace, stability, and prosperity which they so ardently cherished.

As elsewhere in Europe, the national and liberal movement was in 1814–1815 still too undeveloped in Lombardy-Venetia to make an impression upon more than a small part of the population. Still, the seed of nationalism and liberalism had already been planted before 1814 and the unpopular policies of the Austrian military occupation served slowly but surely to germinate them. As early as 1818 and 1819 a small group of Lombard liberals busied themselves with introducing economic, technological, and educational reforms in Italy,[183] and at the same time they actively championed liberal and

---

[183] For a more detailed discussion of the activities of the Lombard liberals in this respect, see especially Domenico Chiattone, "Nuovi documenti su Federico Confalonieri per le sue relazione intime e patriottiche prima del processo," *Archivio storico lombardo*, XXXIII (1906), 89–114; Bernardo Sanvisenti, "Una lettera di Pietro Borsieri ed altra di Federico Confalonieri," *ibid.*, LVIII (1931), 359–63; Giovanni de Castro, "Patriottismo lombardo (1818–1820). Notizie desunte da diari e testimonianze contemporanee," *ibid.*, XVI (1889), 898–909; Pio Ferrieri, *Dalla via del Monte di Pietà allo Spielberg* (Milan, 1889), pp. 24–34; and Rosina Cicchitti, "Federico Confalonieri e la Società Fondatrice delle Scuole Gratuite di Mutuo Insegnamento in Milano (1814–1821), secondo il carteggio inedito dell'Archivio di Stato di Milano," *La rassegna nazionale*, XXXI (1909), 147–67, 335–51.

The Habsburgs and Lombardy-Venetia 335

national ideas in the Milanese biweekly, *Il Conciliatore*.[184] The Austrians, too, gave at least tacit approval to the fostering of a spirit of Italian nationalism, and the government-sponsored literary and scientific journal, the *Biblioteca Italiana*, contained abundant appeals to Italian nationalism.[185]

It was, however, not before the early 1820's, when the arrest and trial of a large number of Lombard and Venetian liberals for conspiring with the Sardinian rebels in 1821 to join forces to drive the Austrian out of Italy alarmed and disgusted a large number of the population,[186] that the seed of liberalism and nationalism really began to grow into the plant which was to reach full bloom in the mass revolts against the Austrians in 1848 and again in 1859. Before 1820 the vast majority of the population, permeated with a universal longing for peace, though by no means happy with all the trappings of Austrian rule, were resigned to the Habsburg regime.

[184] *Il Conciliatore; Foglio Scientifico-Letterario*. The first issue was published on Sept. 3, 1818, and the last on Oct. 14, 1819, after difficulties with the Austrian censorship made it impossible to continue publication. A complete set of this journal can be found in the H. Nelson Gay collection, Widener Library, Harvard University.

[185] Note, for instance, such articles as the following in the issues published in 1816: Madame de Staël's article entitled, "Sulla maniera e la utilità delle traduzione," in the January issue (I, 9–18); the review of the first volume of Domenico Balestrieri's *Collezione delle migliori opere scritte in dialetto milanese* in the February issue (I, 173–79); "Sul Discorso di Madama di Stael—Lettera di un Italiano ai compilatori della Biblioteca," in the April issue (II, 3–14); "Lettera di madama la baronessa de Stael Holstein ai signori compilatori della Biblioteca Italiana," in the June issue (II, 417–22); and the review of Leopoldo Cicognara's *Storia della scultura dal suo risorgimento in Italia fino al secolo di Canova*, in the August issue (III, 235–44).

[186] See especially Baron Sardagna's two letters to Metternich sent from Verona on Oct. 15, 1822, Pietro Pedrotti, "La missione segreta del Consigliere Aulico De Sardagna in Italia durante i processi dei Carbonari," *Il Risorgimento italiano*, XXII (1929), 206–13; Camillo Ugoni to Sismondi, Ile de Saint Pierre, May 20, 1822, Giuseppe Calamari, "Lettere di Camillo e Filippo Ugoni al Sismondi," *Rassegna storica del Risorgimento*, XXV (1938), 649–50; and Cesare Cantù, "Il Conciliatore. Episodio del liberalismo lombardo," *Archivio storico italiano*, Ser. III, XXIV (1876), 109–10.

AMERICAN THOUGHT AND THE COMMUNIST CHALLENGE*

GEROID TANQUARY ROBINSON

I

THE UNITED STATES is facing the crisis of 1949 with the military equipment of 1950 and the ideological equipment of 1775. America was well armed, philosophically, for the early conflicts with the parliamentary monarchism of Britain and the reactionary absolutism of Metternich. In those times we were able to make the Europeans and the Latin Americans understand us clearly, because we understood ourselves. But between the day of the Monroe Doctrine and the day of the Truman Doctrine, vast changes have taken place in American life. Many of these changes are, or have appeared to be, in conflict with the testament of the Founding Fathers. It can be argued that a revised philosophy is implicit in the major developments of the last half-century; but if this is so, the efforts to make this philosophy explicit have had but poor success. American theory has lagged far behind American practice; often it has seemed that without benefit of philosophy, we are backing tail-first into the future. For our own guidance at home and abroad, and for the enlightenment and inspiration of our neighbors overseas in this new age of conflict, we need to know what kind of country this is and where it is going.

As matters stand, the Europeans must have great difficulty in making us out, when they look this way. For example, the French probably understand well enough what kind of Germany the Russians want; but do the French understand what kind of Germany America wants? Are we sure about this ourselves? Until the time comes when we can speak out of a clear philosophy, the voice of America is bound to be muffled and confused.

It is painful, but it is also very salutary, that in this time of transition the Communists are forcing us to take stock of our position. In the latter half of the eighteenth century, the great majority of

---

* ED. NOTE: This article was published in *Foreign Affairs*, XXVII (July 1949), 525–39, under the title, "The Ideological Combat."

our people found themselves in conflict with parliamentary-monarchist theory and with British power. That theory and that power had a strong loyalist following in the American colonies; the crisis here was both domestic and foreign, and out of it came the great burst of creative energy that formulated our early philosophy and established the republic. From that time until the end of World War II, this country did not again experience such a simultaneous domestic and foreign crisis; there was no substantial following within the United States for the power of the Holy Alliance, or of Kaiser William, or of Hitler, or for the philosophies that were represented by these powers. But today we are involved in a crisis both at home and abroad: a rival Power and its official philosophy have expanded threateningly in Europe and Asia, and have gained significant support within the United States. This dual crisis must be met by a re-examination of our position and a renewal of our pattern of thought.

Seldom if ever in history has a social philosophy been at one and the same time so clearly formulated, so generally accepted as an ideal, and so widely realized in practice, as in America in the first half of the nineteenth century. The new state had arisen out of a revolution against too much government (a "tyranny" that was mild indeed, as compared with the full-blown dictatorships of our own time); and in the pursuit of small trade, small crafts, and above all small farming, a very large proportion of the citizens of the new republic could exercise a great measure of control over their own daily activities, and work out for themselves a substantial measure of what they regarded as the good life.

The typical citizen could be, and wanted above all to be, not so much a participant in any collective, as an independent and self-directing individual. This attitude is perfectly reflected in the fact that the first amendments to the Constitution (combining to provide an essentially negative bill of rights, and guaranteeing all citizens against certain forms of interference by the state) were adopted, on popular demand, long before the positive right of participation in the state power was extended to the masses of the (male) citizens through the broadening of the suffrage. Even with this extension of the rights of active citizenship, the increasing popular participation in government was not directed so much toward getting the government to assume new responsibilities as toward checking and restricting the government in its powers and functions. The dominant attitude toward government was essentially negative: decentralization, democracy, and individualism were the controlling elements of faith and action—and individualism was easily the most significant of these, in the daily life of most Americans.

When President Monroe warned the monarchs of Europe, in 1823, against "any attempt on their part to extend their system to any portion of this hemisphere," both European monarchists and Latin American republicans were reasonably clear as to the system that we on our part would foster and promote, by precept and example if not by other means, in the Western world.

As time passed, the clarity of the American position was somewhat obscured by the expansion of slavery; but at a prodigious cost that institution was abolished, and democracy, decentralization, and individualism still remained the essence of American faith and practice. In abolishing slavery, the Civil War prolonged the dominant American tradition; but at the same time the war promoted two other trends that were in conflict with that tradition. For one thing, the necessities of battle required an unwonted concentration of power in the federal government, and the use of that power to accomplish ends desired by the majority of the people certainly did much to diminish the popular suspicion of political power as such. Again, the demands of the armies drove industry forward under forced draft, along a path of quantitative expansion and qualitative change that seems even today to have no end.

Measured in terms of the old American philosophy, by far the most important change that has taken place in American life since the 1860's is not the vast increase in the output of goods (with the accompanying rise in the standard of living), but the shrinkage of individual self-direction in the productive process. This change affected industry first and most profoundly, but more recently it has been extending its effects to agriculture also. Generally, machine industry seems to require that men work in masses and under discipline. For decades now the trend has been to concentrate production in enterprises of increasing size, and to develop and tighten the control of the work-process within each such enterprise: "The technical character of the apparatus itself demands an iron discipline; the movements of the workman must be timed exactly to the movements of the machine."

If large-scale mechanized enterprise is a comparatively recent development in the field of agriculture, it is chiefly the fault of the tilt of the planet: the succession of the seasons requires that each year a number of different types of work shall be done, not simultaneously, but one after another. In nearly all types of manufacture, on the other hand, the work may be split into a number of specialized processes, all of which can operate continuously; and this means, of course, that in industry the various types of specialized machines can be employed steadily throughout the year. The agricultural cycle makes this kind of continuous, parallel operation impossible; generally speaking, the farmer's specialized machines can be used each season for a short time only, and in succession (for example, the gang plow, the seeder, the harvester, the thresher). Thus, much of the fixed capital in mechanized agriculture is bound to be idle for a large part of each year. Yet in spite of all this, the development of large-scale mechanized farms is now proceeding at a rapid rate.

Obviously, only a very limited number of Americans can operate and direct large-scale enterprises in the field of industry and agriculture. Obviously, too, the great and increasing proportion of our people who work in these enterprises are no longer the independent, self-directing Americans of the old philosophy.

These changes that have taken place in recent decades are the source of most of the material power that America now possesses. But they are the source, too, of nearly all of our confusion as to what kind of country this is and ought to be, and as to how its great power ought best to be employed.

II

With the change in character and the expansion in scale of economic enterprise, millions of once independent craftsmen and farmers have become disciplined machine tenders in industry, and have suffered thereby a very fundamental loss. And now a large part of those who continue to work in agriculture may be entering upon a similar change, involving a similar loss.

In a half-century of hasty improvisation, Big Government has developed, as in some sense an offset to Big Enterprise—a new system of national checks and balances. Big Government was to do for the citizen some of the things that he no longer could do for himself. Some think that what the individual has lost to Big Enterprise and Big Government has been made good, or could be, by a rising level of consumption and a shorter working day. Yet it is doubtful whether many thoughtful Americans have come to believe seriously that a man's loss of independence and self-direction as a producer can be compensated by high wages and more free time in which to spend the pay-check. Conscience is still at work here; a deep sense of values is involved—a sense of what it takes to make the full man. The devotional words in the American vocabulary have not yet become "abundance and leisure"; they are still "freedom," "liberty," "independence," "self-confidence," "self-determination," "individual initiative"—all words that are drawn from the old philosophy. These words are not mere forms; they are the expression of a warm and deep conviction. What is lacking is any clear idea as to how, and even whether, these values can be preserved in a machine age. Gone, certainly, is any foundation for the belief that if things are left to take their own course, some sort of law of nature will preserve the values of individualism. The dominant trend of the time, in economy and in government, is undoubtedly in the direction of discipline and dependence for the citizen. But is that trend inevitable; is it destined to be all inclusive; or can it be radically modified by taking thought?

The idea of freedom has a vast appeal. One of the strange and startling evidences of this is the fact that freedom is still presented as the ultimate goal of one of the most authoritarian societies that has ever existed on the planet—the Soviet Union. Marx and Engels saw the society of the future as "a free association of individuals" where production would be organized "on the basis of a free and equal association of producers," and where "the free development of each is the condition for the free development of all." This last phrase appeared in the Communist Manifesto, and the Marxians have therefore had one hundred and one years to work out a convincing plan for the promised transition from the promised revolutionary dictatorship to the promised free society that is said to lie beyond. Yet in the massive Marxian literature, which lays down detailed plans, in advance, for the establishment of dictatorship, there are only the ghostliest suggestions as to how dictatorship is to be disestablished and freedom brought into being.

There has been some tendency to excuse this Communist neglect, on the ground that that which is inevitable does not have to be planned—though this reasoning would seem to make planning for dictatorship quite as superfluous as planning for the free society to come after. If the excuse of inevitability ever had any validity, in terms of the Communist logic, that validity has been destroyed by several decades of Russian Communist revisionism (a word that the Communists detest, but a process in which they have been engaged, nonetheless). In the course of this process, they have arrived at what might be called a theory of selective inevitability: non-Communists are obliged by the laws of social development to do the self-destroying things that the Communists want them to do, while the Communists are held to be comparatively free to do the self-serving things that *they* want to do. Of course this leaves the Communist Utopia about as little inevitable as anything could possibly be; and it is one of the most valid criticisms of Communism that it has still produced so little on the subject of its own goal.

In our own society, there is not a shadow of an excuse for failure to maintain and develop an adequate philosophy of ends and means. Without some such guidance, what are we to do, for example, with the grain combine and the mechanical cotton-picker? What are we to do with the wealth of electric power that our rivers can produce? What are we to do with the vast potentialities that atomic energy may offer for the alteration of American life? It is dangerous in the extreme, simply to extemporize piecemeal answers at the moment when such practical questions happen to come along.

The more we believe in freedom, the more we need to plan for it—even to plan how to avoid overplanning. And broad planning is impossible, except in terms of a philosophy.

III

Our principal weakness today is not economic or military but ideological—not a matter of goods or guns, but of ideas. This is our chief weakness abroad, precisely because it is our chief weakness at home. It is not piecemeal answers that inspire men in "their finest hour"; it is a total conception of the good life—a conception that has some valid connection with their experience and some valid promise of a fuller realization in the future. Such a conception provides guidance, and inspires maximum effort. But it is startling how often (for example, in "orientation courses" for our soldiers, or in broadcasts to countries overseas) we have felt obliged to turn back a hundred and fifty years and more (to such documents as the Mayflower Compact, the Declaration of Independence, the State Bills of Rights, the first amendments to the Federal Constitution, the writings of the Founding Fathers) for quotable and generally accepted formulations of an American philosophy—formulations still sound and valid in many ways, but by themselves inadequate for our time.

In this situation, there is urgent need for philosophic reconstruction and renewal. This undertaking has some resemblance, on the one hand, to that of the *philosophes* of the French Encyclopaedia, and on the other, to that of the authors of the Declaration of Independence, the Virginia Bill of Rights, or the French Declaration of the Rights of Man and the Citizen. All these monumental achievements were products of collaboration, and a somewhat similar collaborative effort would give the best promise of meeting our present need—a task for philosophers, in all the eighteenth-century breadth and richness of that term.

Many of the building materials for a philosophic reconstruction are at hand, though in vast disorder. Time presses for results that can be presented, under the finest auspices, to our people and to people overseas. Is it an idle dream that a group of qualified men might sit down together, for a year, or two years, or whatever time it would take, to produce tentative results on two levels: first, to distill and clarify the philosophy that is now embodied piecemeal in American life—to say what America *now is;* and second (a far more difficult task) to consider the adequacy of this philosophy for the future—to suggest what America *might become?*

It will be said that what is suggested here is an attempt to produce an official American philosophy, even possibly a compulsory one, and that the entire proposal is therefore essentially un-American; but on the contrary, the procedure suggested is entirely unofficial (though if it succeeds, the government will ultimately be affected); and as to uniformity and compulsion, the objective sought is only some such level of voluntary and conscious agreement as the country attained in the early decades of the republic—when sharp and healthy differences were of course abundant. However, the main emphasis in this paper is upon a fundamental need; if that need is once felt, in all its urgency, a way will be found of meeting it.

The proposed discussion might perhaps be made to revolve around one single proposition: that the end and aim of society and the state ought to be the nurture and wide propagation of a certain kind of man—the independent and self-directing individual. This proposition is rich in difficulties and rich in promise, and the chief business of the remaining pages of this article will be to examine, very tentatively, a few of the pertinent debits and credits.

IV

Before the Civil War, American political philosophy and American law were in a considerable measure negative in their emphasis; they were concerned largely with the protection of the individual against interference by other individuals, and particularly against interference by the state. Basic to all this was a fundamental theory which accorded in large measure with the conditions of American life at the time—the theory that if a minimum of negative protection were provided, the individual could and would be able to fend for himself and to stand up on his own feet as an independent and self-directing personality.

For the period since the Civil War, and especially for the years since the great crash of 1929, there is a vast mass of new evidence, on the levels of both fact and theory. In vital and economic statistics, in laws and court decisions, in the programs of organized labor, of organized farmers, and of both political parties, in the declarations of the New Deal and the Fair Deal, in the proposals respecting human rights presented by the United States to the United Nations, evidence will be found of the diminishing importance of small-scale undertakings, of the wholesale development of large private enterprise, of the vast expansion of governmental activity—and of the coexistence of three sets of ideas which correspond in some degree with the three sets of facts just mentioned. The first of these sets of ideas constitutes the old and well-formulated philosophy of individualism, which persists from the early decades of the republic; the second is the doctrine of competitive capitalism, now badly crisscrossed and confused by ideas favorable to large combinations of capital and even to monopoly; the third is a jumble of all sorts of notions centering largely on the achievement of mass objectives through the agency of the state. These three sets of ideas overlap, compete, and conflict, in a bewildering variety of ways, but in recent years the victories have gone most of all to the ideas that are least systematic of all—those of the new stateism. In this growth of a more positive attitude toward government, the United States already shares to a limited degree in a trend that is much farther advanced in Britain and in Western Europe—the trend toward Democratic Socialism—and in this, some basis might be found for a common understanding with these European countries. Indeed, it appears that if the voice of America should speak in terms of the new stateism, the majority of our European neighbors would understand us fairly well. But is this trend toward Democratic Socialism predetermined, here and abroad? If the question lies within the range of conscious and deliberate choice, has that choice been taken by our people? Or is the decision still to be made?

It has been suggested that the chief business of society and the state ought to be the nurture of independent and self-directing individuals. Not only under Communism, but in a lesser degree under Socialism and capitalism as well, the trend of the times would seem to be rather in the opposite direction—but is that trend inevitable?

Something of a case can be made for the idea that the major movements of historical change are not specifically inevitable, but that there exists at any given time a certain variety of possibilities and a certain range of free selection. Most men, when they are faced with specific personal situations, have the feeling of being restricted within certain limits, and at the same time the feeling of being free and self-directed within those limitations; the one feeling appears to have exactly as much validity as the other. It is certainly true that many major historical trends have not been, as such, the subject of conscious choice on the part of the millions of men whose lives are affected by them; and such trends therefore have the appearance of being "inevitable." Yet it is arguable that this appearance is superficial, and that each "inevitable" trend is in part the result of innumerable individual choices in matters of detail—choices made freely, within limits, by men who neither foresee nor desire the major result to which they are thus themselves contributing.

Probably most of our people would agree that there is a great and irreducible difference between a society that attaches primary importance to the independence and self-determination of the individual, and a society that is built essentially on the discipline and dependence of a large majority of its members. If faced with a broad choice between the former society and the latter, most of our people would almost certainly choose the former. Not only that, but they would be prepared to make great sacrifices in support of their choice. Yet the choice hardly presents itself in this form, but rather in the form of innumerable opportunities to make minor decisions which cumulate (in obscurity) to produce the great decision.

One of the minor choices which is offered an innumerable number of times is the choice between a less efficient method of production and a more efficient one (efficiency being measured here exclusively in terms of output). "Technology solves its problems with a beautiful perfection; it offers self-evident and self-demonstrating truth; its contributions have an immediate value that usually wins acceptance without argument." It is essentially the character of the tools, rather than the character of their ownership, that produces mass organization and mass discipline in an industrial society; in both Pittsburgh and Magnitogorsk, the forces of technology operate to this end. Technological advance tends not only to require mass organization and mass discipline within each plant, but to produce an increasingly complex web of connections between plant and plant, region and region; and both by disciplining the worker on the job and by surrounding him with forces and problems with which he feels unable to deal, machine industry seems to prepare the worker to appeal to the state for help, and to accept the discipline of the state. In a society that is to a significant extent industrialized, people who are not themselves subjected to the disciplinary training of machine work are nevertheless faced with the vast complexities of a machine-based culture; and more and more they too tend to turn to the state for help. The line of descent is clear: technology is the father of Great Enterprise and the grandfather of Great Government.

v

Today there is hardly a man in the United States who does not believe that within recent decades it has become necessary for the Government to do much more for the people than it did a hundred years ago. Yet there still persists here, and perhaps much more vigorously here than in any other great country, a lusty individualism and a strong and wholesome fear of all great concentrations of power, whether in private or public hands. If the fundamental objective were agreed upon, and kept steadily in mind—the nurture of a certain kind of man—might there not be hope of at least a partial reconciliation of the old individualism with the new stateism of today? Could not the beginnings of a reconciliation be made by recognizing as fundamental the difference between government action which is designed to build up the independence and self-sufficiency of the individual citizen, and government action which tends to establish permanent discipline and dependence? The government policy that contributes to the desired type of personality may be either negative or positive, depending on the nature of the concrete problem involved in each particular case. The suggested test of policy is the contribution that it makes to the desired end—not some abstract theory that state action as such is either good or bad. In many instances, the test would be exceedingly difficult to apply in practice; but in our time the suggested principle might prove far more valuable as a guide to action than either the pure (and now unattainable) individualism of the horse-and-buggy past, or the indiscriminate stateism that may well be in the making for the future.

If the recent history of American government swarms with conflicting actions that contribute sometimes to individualism and sometimes to a cumulative stateism, it is partly because of a lack of understanding of the effect that given concrete measures will produce, but still more because of obscurity and indecision respecting the major end to be sought. A vast confusion lies hidden within such terms as the New Deal, the Fair Deal, the welfare state, the social-service state.

If the major objective of society and the state were the nurture and propagation of independent and responsible individuals, the method of production that yields the maximum in goods would not necessarily be the method to be preferred. If personality is the end, the maximizing of production is desirable in the degree in which it serves that end, and in that degree only. The interest of the producers, as well as that of the consumers, must be considered: the adoption of a new technique may result in a larger output of goods, but in human terms this advantage may be more than offset by the damaging conditions which the new technique imposes upon the worker. If the producer feels strongly enough about it, he may refuse to accept mechanization and consolidation, or he may insist upon some humane compromise; and in this fight for life, the state may give him invaluable support if the nature of the issue is widely understood and the democratic process is effectively employed.

All this is not simply a set of speculations, afloat in the air; it rests on millions of items of evidence. The chief surviving centers of fundamental self-determination in America today are the individual farm and the individual household. The vigorous persistence of these institutions as centers of production is of course due in part to inertia, and in part to special technical situations; in the case of the household, it is obviously due in some degree also to the ties of the family. But for anyone who wants to consider it, there is a great mass of evidence that this persistence is also due, in part, to the deliberate choice of innumerable human beings who *prefer* to cook their own meals and to sow and harvest their own crops. It is a primary fact that hundreds of millions of people, in this country and in other countries, *want* to make their own decisions, on the land, and that still larger numbers *want* the home to be something much more than a biological bedroom. If this were not the case, large-scale farming and barracks living would have developed far more rapidly than they have to date.

The spirit of independence in these two institutions is so powerful that even the greatest of the dictatorships has had to compromise with it. Soviet Russia never succeeded in developing communal living to any great dimensions. Again, the mass of Soviet agriculture is not organized in the ideal Communist pattern (the great state farm, or "grain factory") but in small peasant collectives which have in a limited degree the aspect of producers' co-operatives, and leave the peasant a little less subject to authority than is the worker in Soviet industry.

Government may act, in America, not to destroy but to save the individual farm and the individual household. Government loans may aid in the purchase or building of homes. Government hydroelectric plants may help to maintain the economic significance of the household by supplying power to thousands of electric ranges, dish washers and washing machines. Government loans may help to establish and maintain individual farms, as may government projects for irrigation and drainage; and in some cases the dams and canals may themselves be transferred in the course of time to the farmers of the community. Government loans on the most liberal terms may be made available to groups of small farmers, for investment in large and complex machines which no one of these farmers could purchase independently or employ economically; and these machines may then be used, up to their capacity, on one farm after another, within the co-operating group. These farms, so operated, may not be quite so efficient as large mechanized farms with hired labor; but through an entirely voluntary association, with state assistance, the participating farmers will have salvaged a large measure of the life that they want, and democratic society will have preserved in active form some of the individualistic spirit that it must have to survive.

There is no reason given in the law of nature why the new mechanical cotton-picker must run wild through the agriculture of the South, converting millions of independent cultivators into day laborers; men made this machine, and men can control it, if they know what it is that they want, and have the will to act. If men ran from the enemy in battle, as they run from "inevitable economic trends," where would bombed London be today?

In industry the path is much more obscure than in agriculture; it is in industry that the advantages of mechanization and consolidation are most apparent, and it is here, of course, that mass organization and mass discipline have advanced at maximum speed. But even here a path might perhaps be found, if it were once recognized that the most important end-product of the industrial system is not a certain quantity of goods but a certain quality of personality. This is a problem that cannot be solved simply in terms of maximizing the output of goods and raising the general level of consumption. In an industrialized society, it requires also that a substantial proportion of those engaged in machine production shall maintain some degree of individuality and self-direction within the work process itself. Perhaps there is no solution for this problem; perhaps the age of robots is upon us. But one may believe that the current trend is in that direction and still refuse to accept the outcome as inevitable.

Consider, for example, the possibilities for the future that may lie hidden in the employment of atomic energy for peaceful purposes. If the output of goods alone is considered, this new source of power may only strengthen the prevailing trend toward concentration, mass organization, and mass discipline—under either private or public direction. But if some thought is given to the making of men, as well as the making of goods, a quite different result is conceivable. "The unique mobility of atomic fuel," the ease of transporting such material, may perhaps make possible the establishment of small and widely scattered prime movers, to generate and distribute cheap electric power to innumerable industrial undertakings of the smallest size. Under such conditions, a share of industrial production could be recaptured by village shops, and even by farmers working with small power machines in the winter season.

However, it goes without saying that under any conceivable condition much of the work of industry cannot possibly be decentralized in this way, but must be carried on in large plants, by large groups of interdependent machines and large forces of operatives. It is here that the problem of maintaining the individuality of the worker arises in its most acute form. The issue cannot be reduced to an immediate conflict over wages and hours, and an ultimate conflict over the ownership of the machines. These are matters of enormous importance, but concentration on them, to the exclusion of the work process itself, is evidence of intellectual poverty on the part of all concerned. Even if nationalization should solve all the problems of maximum output and equitable distribution (it is doubtful indeed that it could), it might still leave the work of production a deforming and deadly routine. There is reason to believe that state management might well tighten this routine. The problem of humanizing the work process in machine industry is one for which no one has yet found an adequate solution; but perhaps the most hopeful prospect lies in the development of labor participation in management, with special emphasis on the smallest functional division of the plant, where the issues are simplest and the worker is best able to deal with them (a Jeffersonian principle in a new setting). Such arrangements, coupled with piece-rate wages and profit-sharing, might do something to give the individual worker a sense of vital participation in the day's work. But no such system as this will develop widely unless the workers press for it earnestly, and unless the managers and owners welcome the compromise and help to bring it into vigorous life.

If in the machine age the philosophy of individualism is to be preached, with full effect, to our people, the practice of individualism must be accessible to them—even in the factory.

VI

The Soviet Union is challenging the United States to renew and develop for our time the magnificent inheritance of Western individualism—an inheritance that has come to us out of the faith and morals of Christianity, the rationalism of the Renaissance and the Enlightenment, the English gift for compromise, the liberty of the democratic revolutions, and the ancestral independence of the farms and shops and homes of America.

If this renewal can be brought about, our people will feel a new strength and a new sense of purpose and direction. This country can have again, in Europe, an even greater moral influence than it had a century and a half ago; perhaps it can even extend that influence to Asia and Africa, where Communism ought not to be the only accessible philosophy of change, in societies that have got to be remade.

If we can first learn it, we can teach the new individualism overseas by precept, and above all by example. We can encourage it by special forms of economic aid and by the temperate use of our influence with foreign governments. But for the advancement of this cause, force is a doubtful and dangerous instrument. No man can be compelled by force to think and live as an individualist; but certainly men can be forced to live as Communists, and the blackest danger of all is that in time (where all the modern armament of indoctrination and suppression is in the hands of the Party) men can probably be forced not only to live but to *think* as Communists.

The individualist is powerfully tempted to try by force to dash these instruments of indoctrination and suppression from the hands of the dictators; but he knows, too, the danger to individualism of war-discipline at home, and the measureless difficulty of bringing his philosophy to life abroad after another great conflict. In this dilemma, he will hardly initiate the use of force, and only as a last resort will he respond with force to such an initiative. Certainly he can have no easy answer to the problem of our relations with the Soviet Union; yet he would feel that we must press consistently one policy or the other: "Live and let live," or "Kill or be killed." On balance, he would say that for years to come we should strive to maintain a predominance of power, while at the same time attempting through a long series of adjustments of current issues to convince the veiled prophets of the Kremlin that compromise and stabilization, not crisis and conflict, can set the norm of our relations. Even against the light of their revelation, we might possibly convert them thus, in the long run, into nonpracticing World Revolutionists.

FRIEDRICH NAUMANN: A GERMAN VIEW OF POWER AND NATIONALISM

WILLIAM O. SHANAHAN

FRIEDRICH NAUMANN'S life and works embodied the hope and the disillusionment experienced by many intellectuals in Wilhelmian Germany. He was a nationalist whose lifetime of public service sought its object in strengthening the German nation. At first Naumann was confident that this could be achieved under William II, but eventually he gave way to despair over the Kaiser's shortcomings. That grave domestic issue of William II's reign, the relation between the working class and the monarchy, long absorbed Naumann's political interest and brought forth a prophetic statement of the means whereby authority and democracy could be combined. An ardent support of the German navy and an unbounded enthusiasm for industrialism and technology marked him as a man of the times. Naumann was clearly aware that urbanization and the dependence of the masses upon factory employment had given rise to new social problems, yet he was confident that there were rational means for banishing the evils of the machine age while harnessing it for the benefit of all men. Naumann's views on nationalism, which were representative of the Wilhelmian intelligentsia, found their final justification in the German cultural mission to the modern world. Like so many of his compatriots, Naumann considered Germany to be one of the first modern states, a pathfinder for the others in science, technology, the power to organize, and especially in the grasp of the intellectual resources which history had placed at mankind's disposal.

I

Naumann's career began with a preparation for the ministry. As a Lutheran pastor's son, born in Saxony in 1860, his youth was conditioned by life in an austere and penurious rectory. Chiefly to please his father he entered theological studies, first at Leipzig and then at Erlangen, where he came under the influence of Franz Frank, the liberal theologian. He taught Naumann to bring personal faith into the middle of religious experience by supplanting the austerities of rational theology with a mystical acknowledgment of God. Another teacher, Gerhard Zezschwitz, who was less interested in making theologians than in awakening young pastors to the practical implications of Christianity, turned his attention to social quesions. Naumann had never had any dogmatic convictions and, even before taking his final examination in 1883, he declared that he would take up charitable work.[1]

Political and social currents, to which the German universities of the seventies and eighties were unusually sensitive, probably bore upon this decision. Industry was beginning to change the lives of the people; religion had been placed on the defensive by the increasing materialism; the *Kulturkampf* had just come to an end, leaving unsolved the relation of the churches to the Bismarckian system; and the close of the liberal era was implicit in Bismarck's protective tariff program and in the announcement from the throne in 1881 that a great system of social legislation was impending. That these events had stirred Naumann was made clear by his participation in founding the German Students' Association, a nationalist and anti-Semitic organization sponsored by Adolf Stoecker. The first meeting between these men in 1881 occurred on this occasion. Anti-Semitism was not at first repugnant to Naumann; in fact, he discussed it with Stoecker during their second meeting at Leipzig in 1885.[2]

Several kinds of Protestant social action were being carried on in Germany when Naumann embarked upon his pastoral duties.[3] The Inner Mission, founded in 1848 by Johann Hinrich Wichern, partly in reaction to the excessively private aspects of Pietism, sought to enliven the community by reasserting the primacy of the church and the family. Wichern was the pioneer of German Protestant concern for the life of religion amid urban and industrial conditions since he was primarily interested in deepening religious conviction

---

[1] The best biographies of Naumann are by his co-workers: Theodor Heuss, *Friedrich Naumann; Der Mann, das Werk, die Zeit* (Stuttgart and Berlin, 1937); and Martin Wenck, *Friedrich Naumann; Ein Lebensbild* (Berlin, 1920). Two articles in English emphasize the liberal phase of his career: Erich Eyck, "A Great German Liberal," *The Contemporary Review*, CLV (1939), 320–27; and Felix E. Hirsch, "Friedrich Naumann," *Forum*, CVI (1946), 105–11.

[2] Heuss, *op. cit.*, p. 57.

[3] There is a convenient survey in Paul Göhre, *Die evangelisch-soziale Bewegung ihre Geschichte und ihre Ziele* (Leipzig, 1896), pp. 3–40. At the time of publication Göhre was a follower of Friedrich Naumann.

among the working classes. But Wichern's activity, although it had great consequences for both Stoecker and Naumann, lacked a program and tended to find expression only along the customary lines of charity and welfare work.[4]

Another direction had been taken in 1877 with the founding by Rudolf Todt of the Central Association for Social Reform, the first organization of Evangelical origin to justify social reforms upon a monarchical basis. Other tendencies were represented by the writings of Victor Amé Huber, to whom both Wichern and Stoecker were indebted, the latter especially for the view that workers' associations could be one of the chief means of solving the social question. And it should be borne in mind that in the work of those economists known as "socialists of the chair," notably in the case of Adolf Wagner, a strong religious influence was often present.[5] Adolf Stoecker was, however, the first to seek an outright political basis for strengthening the Protestant religion by intervening for the betterment of the material issues of the workers' lives. Protestant social action entered the electoral lists with the founding in 1878 of Stoecker's Christian Socialist Party. From among these possibilities Naumann chose to begin what was to be a lifelong absorption with the social, political, and ethical problems of his fellow men by joining the *Rauhes Haus;* this was an establishment of the Inner Mission in the vicinity of Hamburg which cared for orphans and wayward youths.

Several years at the *Rauhes Haus* were followed by appointments to pastorates in small Saxon towns slowly being transformed by industrialism. Here Naumann had ample opportunity to see how religion was being eroded by the new social conditions. He talked endlessly to the poor, who were the principal members of his flock, learning at firsthand about their daily problems. A growing concern for social questions led him to examine the literature of socialism. Both Stoecker and Naumann had sufficient insight to realize that the growth of socialism expressed the drift of the masses away from a Protestant orthodoxy which had failed to develop preaching meth-

---

[4] Paul G. Hübner, *Die sozialethischen Anschauungen Adolf Stöckers in genetischer und systematischer Darstellung* (Wittenberg, 1929), pp. 19–25.

[5] On Wagner's monarchical socialism and his relation to Adolf Stoecker, see Ralph H. Bowen, *German Theories of the Corporative State* (New York, 1947), pp. 119 ff.; and Evalyn A. Clark, "Adolf Wagner: From National Economist to National Socialist," *Political Science Quarterly*, LV (1940), 378–411.

ods and social interests appropriate to an industrial age. Stoecker's attraction for Naumann lay partly in his direct and energetic methods of preaching to urban classes.[6] For Stoecker's orthodox theology Naumann had little sympathy, and although he never became a member of the Christian Socialist Party, Naumann did recognize the significance of a political movement which sought by means of social reforms to bring the masses once more within the monarchical and the religious fold.

Between Stoecker and Naumann there was never any agreement more profound than a friendly understanding. Naumann found much to praise in Stoecker's work with the Berlin City Mission and he did not hesitate to express his views. But not all Evangelical circles looked favorably on Stoecker, and as a result of his praise, Naumann came to be considered a disciple and possibly a protégé. The latter relationship was encouraged by Johannes Wichern, the son of the Inner Mission's founder, and after 1881 the director of *Rauhes Haus*. Nothing came of these overtures, partly because Naumann's father objected to Stoecker, whom he regarded as a wild demagogue, and because Naumann was still chiefly interested in the Inner Mission. An association with Stoecker would have meant the wholehearted pursuit of those political and clerical intrigues to which the court chaplain was addicted. And Stoecker's attachment to the Hohenzollerns tended to make his political ventures little more than a splinter movement of the Conservative Party. In later years Naumann characterized Stoecker as a "child of the fifties," too late for '48 and too early for '71. This expressed with some accuracy Stoecker's view that the Hohenzollern monarchy had dogmatic equivalence with the Evangelical Church, and that the great historical issue was the establishment of their relations while grounding both in the affection of the people.[7]

By 1890 Naumann's journalistic activity and his innovations in the pastoral care of villages had made him well known in the Inner

---

[6] Despite his eventual withdrawal from the ministry, Naumann retained an interest in the problem of bringing Protestantism to the lowest urban classes and he spoke appreciatively of the methods used by General Booth in the Salvation Army. Cf. *Einige Gedanken über die Gründung christlich-sociater Vereine* (Bern, 1896), pp. 13–14.

[7] The historical gifts of Walter Frank were first revealed in his doctoral dissertation, the biography, *Hofprediger Adolf Stoecker und die christlich-soziale Bewegung* (Berlin, 1928). An early supporter of the Nazi movement, Frank did not conceal his sympathy for Stoecker's anti-Semitism. On Stoecker's relation to Naumann, see *ibid.*, pp. 316 ff.

Mission.[8] A following of young theologians and pastors interested in social questions had already gathered around him. He had gained some notice in the academic world, especially that part of it which had religious interests, and among the larger public his extraordinary command of style had begun to attract attention. His writing was remarkably free from the tendency of German prose in the late nineteenth century to be turgid. It was distinguished by clarity, word economy, and the frequent use of pungent phrases which often made the argument more impressive than its logic warranted. Its rhetorical effect depended upon a skillful use of material drawn from the best scholarship and upon an awareness of the prevailing intellectual currents. This synthesis was blown into life by Naumann's originality and his gift for restating complicated matters in terms appropriate to the average intelligence. These gifts and an uncanny ability to discern the tendency of history made Naumann one of the great modern writers on problems of social welfare and politics.

Naumann's prestige among the young pastors was a factor which Stoecker counted upon for the success of his Evangelical Social Congress, founded in 1890.[9] Its full significance for the Protestant social reform movement could not be realized because at the end of the same year Stoecker lost his post as court chaplain and with it much of the prestige of a connection with the monarchy.[10] Yet the Evangelical Social Congress eventually opened up a larger domain for Naumann's work by bringing together pastors, theologians, historians, and economists who shared an interest in social reform. Such academic figures as Max Weber, Rudolf Sohm, Gerhard von Schulze-Gävernitz, and Karl Rathgen were drawn into his circle of acquaintances. Stoecker's fall from grace at court also tended to

---

[8] Interest in Naumann's political views should not be allowed to obscure his continued awareness of moral questions; his address to the third Evangelical Social Congress on *Christenthum und Familie* dealt with the religious and moral rather than the social aspects of family life. *Bericht über die Verhandlungen des Dritten Evangelisch-sozialen Kongresses* (Berlin, 1892), pp. 8–28.

[9] Its establishment expressed the encouragement which the Protestant social reform movement derived from William II's concern for the working class in 1889–1890. The first meeting, occurring on May 27–29, 1890, attracted 800 persons. On the congress, see Göhre, *op. cit.*, pp. 135 ff.

[10] Details of Stoecker's fall in Frank, *op. cit.*, pp. 284–86. Stoecker's resignation was accepted on November 5, although he continued to preach in the Berlin Cathedral until the end of the year.

free the Protestant social reform movement from a long-standing entanglement with the Conservative Party, which continued to pay lip service to reform but in its Tivoli program (1892) became committed to anti-Semitism and the economic interests of agriculture.[11]

During the early nineties Naumann's views on religion, the social question, and the monarchy began to take form. A new environment helped to clarify his views, for in February 1890 he had begun to serve the Inner Mission caritative work in Frankfort on the Main. Its former status as a Free City provided Frankfort with an ecclesiastical autonomy which favored the social reform tendencies among the young clergymen. Frankfort's Jewish population also enabled Naumann to take stock of the anti-Semitic views which he had held since his university days. Under Stoecker's influence he had regarded Jews exclusively as agents of finance capitalism, promoters of social discord, and enemies of religion. In Frankfort he discovered Jews who shared his philosophic and humanitarian views. While traces of anti-Semitic spirit always remained present in his outlook, after his Frankfort days Naumann tended to assess Jews on their merits as individuals.[12]

As Germany embarked upon the "New Course," he became aware of a refreshing draft let into public affairs by the young Kaiser. Both the imperial decrees on labor issued in February 1890 and the Kaiser's exemplary attitude during the miners' strike the year previous made a strong impression.[13] Naumann's response to social questions was still determined by a religious viewpoint but a mystical element began to enter his writing in the form of references to the *Volksleben* and "a new wave of folk feeling."[14] He also showed more sympathy to the Social Democrats than Stoecker's religious predispositions had allowed. Marxism began to take form in Naumann's mind as an historical and secularistic tendency which

---

[11] Cf. Felix Salomon, *Die Deutschen Parteiprogramme vom Erwachen des politischen Lebens in Deutschland bis zur Gegenwart* (3rd ed., Leipzig and Berlin, 1924), II, 64–67, 67–70.

[12] Heuss, *op. cit.*, pp. 112–13, 312.

[13] Cf. Josef Kliersfeld, *Die Haltung Kaiser Wilhelms II. zur Arbeiterbewegung und zur Sozialdemokratie* (Kallmünz, 1933), pp. 23–24, 31–33, and the *Februar Erlasse* in Anlage III, pp. 86–87.

[14] Naumann's tract, *Was heisst Christlich-Sozial?* (Leipzig, 1894), manifested this tendency.

he described, at the Congress of the Inner Mission at Nuremberg in September 1890, as the "first great heresy of the Evangelical Church." By this he meant not only that Marxism should be studied objectively, but that it was a true embodiment of the *Volksleben* with its own historical legitimacy.[15] It had become a factor in the life of the people and was therefore indicative of the nation's temper and of the direction in which history was moving. Attempts to understand Marxism and an active role in the Evangelical trade unions helped Naumann to gain an insight into economic questions. A brief association in 1893 with Maximilian Harden may also have assisted him in clarifying his social and political views.

By 1894 Naumann commanded the affection of a large group of the young reform-minded pastors and even within the Evangelical Social Congress his eminence rivaled that of its founder. This was evident in his popularity with the laity, especially among the academicians who were attracted to the congress. At one of the early meetings the lifelong friendship of Nauman and Weber began, a relationship which bore heavily upon Naumann's eventual view of the nation and its sovereignty. Another professor and close friend who influenced Naumann's outlook was Rudolf Sohm, a profound student of Roman law and church history, who successfully combined scholarship with participation in public affairs. Together with Weber, he oriented Naumann toward the national state by concluding that while there might be a national social politics, there was certainly none based on Christian principles. From his Roman law studies Sohm, although not an unreligious man, had inferred that the state was a sword-bearing heathen whose sole method was compulsion. Sohm and Weber awakened Naumann to the idea of a national social reform which instead of condemning the Social Democrats as anti-Christian materialists would succeed in reconciling them to the German state.[16]

The emphasis upon the national and proletarian aspects of social

---

[15] See Naumann's comments on the orthodox Evangelical view of the Social Democrats in *ibid.*, pp. 70–97. Also see *ibid.*, p. 3, for his declaration that the age of Christian-socialist activity could come only after the Social Democratic period.

[16] Marianne Weber, *Max Weber: Ein Lebensbild* (Tübingen, 1926), p. 143; and Alfred Neumann, *Friedrich Naumanns christlicher Sozialismus* (Leipzig, 1927), pp. 16–17. Sohm expressed these views about the state at the convention of the National Social Association at Leipzig in 1900. Marcus Van Der Voet, *Friedrich Naumann: Een Hoofdstuk uit de sociale Ethiek* (Leyden, 1934), p. 200.

questions gave rise to profound differences between Naumann and Stoecker over the handling of Marxism.[17] The re-emergence of the Social Democrats in 1890 had raised anew the question of their conversion or destruction. Among the Protestant social reformers two parties were aligned on this issue: the "old Christian Socialists" under Stoecker and the "young pastors" recognizing Naumann's leadership.[18] Stoecker's followers saw in the Social Democrats an inexorable danger to throne and altar; Naumann's group regarded Marxism as a tendency of the age, to be moderated by Christian zeal, the advancement of the Evangelical trade unions, additional social welfare legislation, and a positive religious teaching applicable to contemporary problems. Although the last was agreeable to his followers, Naumann began to have serious doubts about it.

At first there was nothing more at stake for Naumann than his personal conviction, whereas Stoecker had political considerations in mind. Control of opinion in the Protestant social reform movement was essential for Stoecker's public prestige. The turn which his career had taken made him look upon the Evangelical Social Congress as a graceful means of withdrawing from politics, yet if he chose to remain a political figure, his significance for the Conservative Party depended upon his ability to command the allegiance of the Protestant reformers. Stoecker could therefore not afford to ignore the larger implications of Naumann's challenge. A compromise was made difficult by Stoecker's continued anti-Semitism and by another difference of opinion over social problems associated with large-scale agricultural holdings. Land questions had won a broad significance for Naumann as a neglected aspect of social politics and as a weak point on which to attack the Social Democratic program. As a politician heading a fraction element of the Con-

---

[17] Stoecker summarized his views at the first meeting of the Evangelical Social Congress. After his preliminary remarks about the justice of some Social Democratic objectives, Stoecker condemned the party for advocating the violent overthrowing of the state, the church, and the family. *Bericht über die Verhandlungen des Ersten Evangelisch-sozialen Kongresses* (Berlin, 1890), pp. 119–40. For additional comments, see Adolf Stoecker, *Christlich-Sozial Reden und Aufsätze* (2nd ed., Berlin, 1890), pp. 6–12, 216–19.

[18] The origins of the "young pastors" and the points on which they disagreed with Stoecker's group are made clear in Göhre, *op. cit.*, pp. 161–62. The former insisted that the materialist interpretation of history was only a means of agitation and not a principle of the Social Democrats, and that there was no basic hostility between this party and Christianity.

servative Party, the organ of the East Elbian Junkers, and as a careerist who constantly deferred to aristocracy, Stoecker could not really come to grips with this issue.[19]

The cleavage within the Evangelical Social Congress and Naumann's inability to turn the Inner Mission from its traditional attachment to charity forced him by degrees into a larger world of politics and journalism.[20] In pursuing this course Naumann was gradually led away from the ministry. For his public life the founding of a weekly magazine of social comment, *Die Hilfe,* in December 1894, was decisive: it made possible that career as a publicist for which his writing talent was so clearly suited. There was more emphasis upon politics in *Die Hilfe* than in Naumann's previous writing, since it was addressed primarily to the lay world toward which he was slowly gravitating.[21] Before he could embark wholeheartedly upon a life in politics his relations to the Christian Socialists had to be clarified, and events of the mid-nineties forced Stoecker to take the initiative in this matter. Stoecker's usefulness to the Conservatives appeared to be at an end; even the anti-Semitism which he had first used as political capital had become an autonomous movement under Ahlwardt's leadership.[22] And Stoecker's own career, whether as a political or a religious figure, had been placed in jeopardy by revelations about the private life of Hammerstein, the *Kreuzzeitung* editor who was his journalistic advocate.[23]

To revitalize the Christian Socialists, whose program had become meaningless since the enactment of Bismarck's social insurance legislation, and win the affection of the group which had turned to Naumann for leadership, Stoecker called a party convention during

---

[19] Frank, *op. cit.,* pp. 309–10, 319–21.

[20] Göhre identified the weakness of all Evangelical-social movements in the polarity of the conservative-patriarchal and proletarian principles; the former he identified with Stoecker, the latter with Naumann. In view of Göhre's subsequent conversion to Marxism his neglect of Naumann's nationalism is understandable. Cf. Göhre, *op. cit.,* pp. 163, 164. Naumann's critical view of charity is made evident in his *Soziale Briefe an reiche Leute* (Göttingen, 1895), p. 53.

[21] Neumann, *op. cit.,* pp. 13–14, which emphasizes Naumann's discouragement with the practical realization of social reforms by the church-inspired programs. In support of this, see Naumann's comments in *Christliche Welt,* XIV (1900), No. 22.

[22] Consult Waldemar Gurian, "Antisemitism in Modern Germany," in *Essays on Antisemitism,* ed. by Koppel Pinson (New York, 1946), pp. 232 and 235, note 51.

[23] Hammerstein, although a violent anti-Semite, was shown to have supported his Jewish mistress in luxurious style with funds obtained fraudulently. Cf. Frank, *op. cit.,* pp. 328–30.

June 1895.[24] It merely brought into relief the divergent views of the chief Protestant social reformers. Naumann had not changed his mind since his declaration in 1893 that anti-Semites had little understanding of the social question. With Max Weber's encouragement Naumann continued to emphasize agrarian problems, while Stoecker could not endorse the view which Weber had expressed before the Evangelical Social Congress that the pastors would have to lead the struggle of the land workers against their masters.[25] There also remained the long-standing difference over the tactics of handling the Social Democrats, so that nothing was concealed by the convention's empty phrase that Naumann's group "marches separately toward the same goal." It was now manifest that Stoecker no longer commanded the corps of pastors, theologians, and academicians who were the moving spirit of the Protestant social reform. And the following year his last tie with the Conservative Party withered under the effect of the *Scheiterhaufen-Brief*.[26]

From the Evangelical *Oberkirchenrath* on December 16, 1895, there came a sharp criticism of the "social-minded pastors" which had more significance for Stoecker than for Naumann, who was beginning to examine his conscience about the nature of religion and his future as a pastor. On welfare questions the outlook of the Evangelical Church reflected the vagaries of the Kaiser's own policy since he had first become interested in issues affecting the working class. The Kaiser had now fallen under the spell of Freiherr von Stumm-Halberg, who with Emil Kirdorf was successfully counter-

[24] Stoecker attempted, according to Frank, to retain his foothold with the Conservative Party and to placate the "young pastors." Frank, *op. cit.*, pp. 324–25. For an analysis of Stoecker's program, see Gertrud Traeder, *Die sozialpolitischen Anschauungen Adolf Stöckers nach dem christlichsozialen Arbeiter-Programm von 1878* (Bonn dissertation, n.d.), pp. 4–9.

[25] Paul Göhre and Max Weber held a symposium at the fifth congress on the social issues of agriculture. *Bericht über die Verhandlungen des Fünften Evangelisch-sozialen Kongresses* (Berlin, 1894), pp. 43–61 (Göhre's address), and pp. 61–96 (Weber's address). Weber's remarks were notable in coupling the names of St. Thomas Aquinas and Friedrich Naumann as representatives of the continuous interest of the Christian churches in social questions. *Ibid.*, p. 72.

[26] The publication of this letter grew out of the revelations about Hammerstein. On Sept. 5, 1896, and again in facsimile on Nov. 3, 1896, the Social Democratic newspaper, *Vorwärts*, published a letter of Aug. 14, 1888, from Stoecker to Hammerstein which suggested that the court chaplain was engaged in sowing discord between the young Kaiser and Bismarck. The national storm of disapproval over this revelation can be understood only in view of the feeling which had set in by 1895–1896 that Bismarck was a German hero and a second Barbarossa. See Frank, *op. cit.*, pp. 333–36.

ing social reform agitation with a crude mixture of paternalism and force. Interest in reform had consequently gone out of fashion for clergymen. This atmosphere bore on Naumann's decision to resign from the ministry, although a more immediate cause arose out of a conflict with the church authorities in Frankfort.[27]

By the end of 1896 Naumann was prepared to sever all connection with Stoecker. This action took on a new significance in view of Naumann's withdrawal from the clergy and his gradually waning belief in the power of religion to sustain ideals for the secular world. Its immediate consequences were felt by the movement to which Stoecker had devoted his life. The Protestant social reformers were left without an effective leader, and Stoecker's program for freeing the church from the state so that German Protestantism might win a new importance by applying its ethic to political and social problems appeared to be doomed. Naumann's politics now ceased to have their anchorage in religion and he abandoned the concept of the church as one of the ruling orders of society.[28] Nationalism and the German Empire usurped the place held by religion and the church during the period when he had admitted his indebtedness to Stoecker. In publicly acknowledging his breach with the Christian Socialist leader, Naumann declared his willingness to reconcile the monarchy and the people by means of democratic Caesarism.[29]

II

To organize his followers in a political party, Naumann issued a call for a congress to be held at Erfurt on November 23–25, 1896.

---

[27] On Jan. 9, 1895, Stumm-Halberg as a Free Conservative member of the Reichstag had attacked Naumann, *Die Hilfe,* and the socialists of the chair. Naumann did not help matters by replying that he regarded the Social Democrats as potential Christian Socialists. There were outbursts also in the Prussian *Landtag* where Stoecker, in his own interest, defended Naumann. The discussion showed that many conservatives thought that the danger lay in Naumann's appeal to dissatisfied elements in the Social Democratic Party. Heuss, *op. cit.,* pp. 125, 127–28. On Freiherr von Stumm-Halberg, also see Erich Eyck, *Das persönliche Regiment Wilhelms II* (Erlenbach-Zurich, 1948), pp. 106, 108.

[28] In 1896 Naumann was able to write that the renewal of Evangelical Christianity had coincided with a social movement in the domain of politics; these were simultaneous movements which had embraced one another without becoming identical. And he denied that recognition of the social reform movement implied a more profound or a more true understanding of Christianity; each tendency could only claim to be a small wave in the vast sea of history. *Einige Gedanken über die Gründung christlich-socialer Vereine,* pp. 6–7.

[29] Frank, *op. cit.,* pp. 373–74. On the development of Naumann's religious outlook between 1896 and 1903, see Van Der Voet, *op. cit.,* pp. 79–93.

He believed that the usefulness of leagues for the unification movement in the fifties might be repeated for the social question. Although Hans Delbrück, the historian and influential editor of the *Preussische Jahrbücher*, had suggested that the party title include both "national" and "democratic," the name National Social Association was chosen instead. Most of its members were pastors or theologians, since Naumann's following was still largely recruited from the Evangelical Social Congress.[30] This clerical element had more sympathy for social reform than for questions of armament and sovereignty. From its beginning two tendencies struggled within the party: one toward welfare legislation and the other toward Germany's mission as a world power. To the latter Naumann became increasingly sympathetic. He had come forward in 1895 as a champion of armaments, especially battleships,[31] and within a few years he was willing to endorse armaments as the first need of the nation. About the Tsar's appeal for international disarmament he could comment that periods of war and disorder were generally the consequence of national weakness. With an equal intensity the National Social Association took up issues affecting labor, such as the Hamburg dock workers' strike of 1897 in which it participated actively. The working class remained in the forefront of Naumann's interest since the strengthening of its nationalism was a task to which he had set himself. To this end Naumann entertained close personal relations with such Social Democratic leaders as August Bebel and Klara Zetkin, discussed Marxist issues with Werner Sombart, and intervened in the rough and tumble of Social Democratic political rallies. Theodor Heuss, his biographer and friend, sums up this period of Naumann's life as the search for the form in which a popular mandate could sustain a power state.[32]

---

[30] This explains Naumann's continued interest in the congress. After the spring of 1896 Stoecker and other orthodox theologians were unable to stem its liberal tendencies both in theology and in social politics. Stoecker withdrew to form in July a new but short-lived center of Protestant social activity: the *Freien Kirchlichsozialen Konferenz*. Frank, *op. cit.*, pp. 365–66. To the Evangelical Social Congress in which liberal theology prevailed, Naumann even as a layman was considered a man of religious principles. At the meeting of 1897 in Leipzig he assisted in the discussion of a paper on the Christian concept of property. Cf. *Die Verhandlungen des achten Evangelisch-sozialen Kongresses* (Göttingen, 1897), pp. 50–56, 63. Although he did not attend the next congress, Naumann did express his best wishes in a telegram to the chairman. Cf. *Die Verhandlungen des Neunten Evangelisch-sozialen Kongresses* (Göttingen, 1898), p. 5.

[31] *Die Hilfe*, I (1895), No. 10.

[32] Heuss, *op. cit.*, pp. 163–65, 167. Theodor Heuss has subsequently become the first president of the Federal German Republic.

The pursuit of such contrary interests as power and welfare was hurtful to both the party's unity and its growth.[33] There can be no doubt that Naumann considered one of its main objectives to be the winning of the Social Democrats to the ideal of the German nation. In many quarters the National Social Association was considered little else than a clerical wing of the Social Democratic Party. But to the working class the party leader's endorsement of the Kaiser seemed out of keeping with his reform proposals. Beside the contradictions of its policy and the tension among its members, the party lacked a territorial base from which to launch itself in national politics. To remedy this, and to win over some of Stoecker's following, a daily paper, *Die Zeit*, was established in Berlin. There was insufficient time to organize effectively for the elections of 1897, and although the party named candidates in eleven districts, none was returned. Little effort was made by Naumann to attract supporters from the Center Party, or to act in combination with it, even though the Catholics had been favorably inclined toward social welfare legislation and the fleet. It was not an anti-Catholic bias which hindered Naumann so much as the feeling that the Center Party was neither German nor national. It puzzled him why the Center, with roots in the rural population rather than the urban masses, could pursue what he called a "National and Germanic" course on basic political issues.[34]

Of more immediate concern was the dilemma his own party faced in supporting the Kaiser on questions of power and armaments, while opposing his interest in legislation which threatened striking workers with jail sentences.[35] By 1899–1900 the ranks of the National Social Association were divided over Naumann's esteem for the Kaiser.[36] Paul Göhre, one of the leading spirits in founding the party, broke with Naumann over the tendency to emphasize

[33] Max Weber, who had advised Naumann during the forming of the National Social Association, was very critical of its confused objectives and the political dilettantism of its membership. Marianne Weber, *op. cit.*, pp. 234–35.

[34] Naumann never ceased to mistrust the Center Party. In 1910 he wrote that its long domination of German politics was making the nation into another Spain. *Die politischen Parteien* (Berlin, 1913), p. 82.

[35] On the *Zuchthausvorlage* of 1899, see Eyck, *op. cit.*, pp. 179–81.

[36] Rudolf Sohm told Lujo Brentano in 1899 that the party was "on its last legs." It is significant that Brentano was not at first attracted to Naumann, whom he considered a follower of Adolf Stoecker. Lujo Brentano, *Mein Leben in Kampf um die soziale Entwicklung Deutschlands* (Jena, 1931), pp. 208–9.

sovereignty at the expense of the workers' well-being. Sovereignty had indeed gained the foreground in Naumann's political perspective, even though he had not finally resolved the question whether politics is a technique of power relationships or an applied ethics.[37]

Demokratie und Kaisertum, which Naumann first published in 1900, sought to answer this question. It was also an attempt to provide the ethos which the National Social Association so badly needed.[38] Large sections of the book dealing with power and authority were intended to convince wavering party members. That it was more than a party tract was soon made evident by the exhaustion of several editions. The circumstances of German political life at the beginning of the new century undoubtedly contributed to the public's interest in Naumann's book. There was no lack in Germany of nationalist movements but each was touched with some measure of special interest, either for the colonies, the fleet, or the colonization of the Polish lands; the championship of national unity as embodied in the *Reichs* government had suffered since that political decline which had set in among the liberal parties between 1878 and 1881. Nationalism had always been a foremost principle among German liberals, whose support of Bismarck had given liberal overtones to the period of unification.[39] A common ground in nationalism was a factor which made possible Naumann's subsequent political career in a liberal party. In *Demokratie und Kaisertum* he attempted to revive that abundance of national enthusiasm and optimism which had once been associated with the founding of the German Empire.

This confidence in the national appropriateness of the Kaiser and empire was in such marked contrast to the cynicism and lassitude which had begun to characterize the handling of public affairs

---

[37] Heuss, *op. cit.*, pp. 169–71; *Die Hilfe*, IV (1898), Nos. 18, 21.

[38] The party platform, while mentioning a number of areas in which reform was necessary and admitting that Christianity was the foundation of the public order and an influence for peace, placed its chief emphasis upon foreign affairs: "Wir stehen auf nationalem Boden, indem Wir die wirtschaftliche und politische Machtentfaltung der deutschen Nation nach aussen für die Voraussetzung aller grossen sozialen Reformen im Innern halten. . . ." Salomon, *op. cit.*, II, 152; see *ibid.*, II, 152–53, for the complete statement of the platform.

[39] Weber's views illustrate the union of liberalism and nationalism. Like Delbrück he believed that the National Social Association had erred seriously in the tone of its original program, since Germany stood in great need of a "National Democratic Party." Marianne Weber, *op. cit.*, p. 235.

that sentiments which had lain dormant for more than a generation seemed about to awaken. Nowhere on the political scene was there a party standing for the nation upon principles which could attract support from every class in every region. German parties had come to be based upon narrow economic, class, or religious viewpoints. By 1900 the liberals, still unable to shake off their doctrinaire economic views, appeared content to look back on their Golden Age; the Center, under a mask of constitutionalism, stood ready to endorse any program or any legislation which was not hurtful to its confessional basis; the Conservatives were well-launched on a policy of expedients intended to link the agrarians of base as well as noble birth with the new aristocrats of industry; the Social Democrats were strait-jacketed in their Erfurt Program and powerless to attract support outside the proletariat. All these political views seemed selfish and decadent by contrast with the vitality of Naumann's proposal that the nation rally behind William II.[40] In industrialism, the self-consciousness of the working class, and in the increasing authority of the Kaiser, Naumann found dynamic ingredients for restoring the idealistic movement of German history.

III

Naumann's interest in developing a new theory of the Hohenzollern monarchy was made evident by the bankruptcy of Stoecker's leadership.[41] In the secular elements upon which Naumann proposed to base his view of the monarchy the tendencies of the Protestant social reform movement were plainly revealed. The religious impulse which had sustained Stoecker and his political movement had now waned. There was no longer a formal connection between the National Social Association and any of the Protestant churches, indeed the Evangelical consistory continued to denounce the social interests of the young pastors. The party leader was a layman of questionable religious views who had close relations with Marxists.[42]

---

[40] The Kaiser for his part regarded Naumann's movement with derision; he was inclined to see in it another phase of the clericalism in politics which he had found so distasteful in Stoecker's case. Eyck, *op. cit.*, pp. 157–58.

[41] The atmosphere of dissatisfaction is fully revealed in Göhre's summation; *op. cit.*, pp. 173–99.

[42] This is not to say that Naumann ceased to be "a man of religion," for despite his lack of orthodoxy he impressed his contemporaries as a man of real piety who embodied the Christian ideals of justice and fortitude. Notwithstanding his personal virtues, Christianity had ceased to provide him with the elements of his politics.

Even though the party enjoyed the support of numerous Protestant clergymen, and though it did not cease to have an attraction for laymen of religious mind, the formal canons of Protestant theology did not underlie its program. What had begun under Stoecker as a movement for Protestant social reform intended for the strengthening of the church and the monarchy had become a nationalistic political movement of wholly secular nature.[43] In its emphasis upon personal freedom and nationalism Naumann's party resembled the liberals, and in seeking mass support by a frank recognition of social issues it resembled the Social Democrats.

The chief difference between Naumann and Stoecker is to be sought in the importance each attached to religion. There was a large element of personal vainglory in Stoecker's career, but insofar as it had objectives the foremost was the strengthening of Protestantism in its Evangelical Lutheran form. Religion for Stoecker was a dogmatic finality upon which a political ethic could be based; his Christian Socialist Party and its theory, however incomplete it may have been, rested upon this conviction.[44] Demagoguery was surely part of his political method, but it would be idle to dismiss Stoecker as a thundering pulpit orator who had ventured into the street. There is ample evidence that Stoecker was a well-informed man who shared the intellectual currents of his time.[45] He was clearly a product of that dogmatic renewal of Lutheranism known as the *Erweckungsbewegung,* which began first among laymen and gained ascendancy among clergymen by the 1830's and 1840's. Its object was to restrain those rational tendencies of the Enlightenment which made Christianity appear to be a simple moral lesson. Closely related to the *Erweckungsbewegung* was its counterpart in politics, "Old Conservatism," which denied the rational view of social relationships peculiar to liberalism and socialism and asserted that

---

[43] W. F. Bruck points out that almost all German religious revivals ultimately become nationalist movements. *Social and Economic History of Germany from William II to Hitler* (Cardiff, 1938), p. 64.

[44] Note this assertion in Stoecker's Reichstag speech of Dec. 14, 1882: "Es ist meine politische Ueberzeugung, dass durch unsre [sic] Zeit hindurch im Grunde ein einziger grossen Konflikt geht: entweder christliche Weltanschauung oder nicht! Und ich glaube, dass unsere politischen wie unsere sozialen Nöte ohne die Wiederbefestigung der christlichen Weltanschauung nicht geheilt werden können." *Christlich-Sozial,* p. 313.

[45] A list of the books and periodicals, including *Das Kapital,* read by Stoecker before 1872 is given by Hübner, *op. cit.,* pp. 34–35.

society was an organism. Its supernatural causation justified both a class order and patriarchal authority.[46]

What had been remarkable in Stoecker's social theory was his abandonment of the "official church" concept which had long dominated the relations of the Prussian monarchy to Lutheran and Reformed Protestantism.[47] In place of church and state relations the core of the state was to be a social viewpoint. This social-minded state would embody Christian ideas of justice but the church organization was to be independent of it. Because religion was a fundament of all life, Stoecker expected that the monarchy would be charged with its spirit, even though the church was free to pursue its own mission which was the care of the "people's soul." There was a large degree of nationalistic mysticism in this concept which might be understood to be a suprapersonal spiritual element summing up all aspects of individual life.[48] To care adequately for the "people's soul" the church had to have a social policy, and in economic questions this meant a specific teaching about wages, housing, hours of work, and so forth. German Protestantism had previously been weakened in this most important aspect of its work by the domination of the state. The arrangement whereby the *summus episcopus* was also the monarch meant that church affairs were usually handled by a department called the Ministry of Cults. Even the work of the *Oberkirchenrath* and the consistories, though these were staffed by clergy, had been compromised, according to Stoecker, by being mixed with the state's point of view. Under these conditions the church could not fulfill its religious and social mission; to be effective the church had to pursue its ends apart from the state.[49]

According to Stoecker, a monarchy afforded the best means of realizing Christian ideals because it was a natural expression of the hierarchy characteristic of a well-ordered society. Some of his ad-

[46] Cf. *ibid.*, pp. 12–19.

[47] This attitude is summed up in Stoecker's statement: "Kein Kirchenstaat, aber auch kein Staatskirchentum! Die Kirche muss frei sein; wenn irgend etwas Recht auf Freiheit hat, so ist es die Religion." *Christlich-Sozial*, p. 269. Naumann was not insensitive to this point and in the championship of church rights he recognized a source of strength for political parties having a religious spirit. *Die politischen Parteien*, p. 68.

[48] This aspect of Stoecker's nationalism is considered in the chapter dealing with him in Louis L. Snyder, *From Bismarck to Hitler: The Background of Modern German Nationalism* (Williamsport, Pa., 1935), pp. 19–20.

[49] Cf. Hübner, *op. cit.*, pp. 83–87.

miration for the Hohenzollerns arose, no doubt, from a sense of obligation to William I for having elevated him to the post of court chaplain. There was always a good deal of awe-struck wonderment of monarchy about Stoecker, whose humble background contrasted sharply with the aristocratic circles to which he eventually gained entrance. Yet he also championed monarchy because it appeared to be the most suitable government for combating secularism among the urban classes. For an elite element in the world of commerce and industry this secular tendency appeared to take the form of liberalism, a doctrine and a world view which Stoecker hated intensely. Liberalism in its assertion of individual self-interest denied the organic unity of a Christian people, and in seeking rational motivations it ruled out divine discipline. Stoecker also sensed the corrosive effect upon religion of that positivistic outlook which accompanied mid-nineteenth-century liberalism. His instinctive dislike for Bismarck was grounded chiefly upon personal factors, but the dalliance with the German liberals between 1867 and 1878 also made him suspect the Chancellor.[50]

As the basis of a political platform these views had serious limitations. Any politician who represented himself as an advocate of monarchy and the Evangelical Church had to be on a secure footing with both. A miscarriage of fortune with either one would make him out to be more royalist than the monarch or more religious than the church. Unfortunately for Stoecker, ecclesiastical officialdom had rarely looked approvingly on his political adventures, and when the course of his intrigues at court began to be unfavorable, he also earned the ill-will of the emperor. Personal shortcomings may have contributed much to Stoecker's failure, yet it was symptomatic of the inability of an orthodox Protestantism to launch and sustain its own political movement. This was not the least among the conclusions which Naumann drew from Stoecker's experience.

When Bismarck had completed his edifice of social insurance legislation, Stoecker had little to offer except a sentimental attach-

[50] See the comments on Stoecker's view of liberalism, the monarchy, and the state in Arnold Poepke, *Der christliche Sozialismus Adolf Stoeckers* (Würzburg, 1938), pp. 70–76. Also Stoecker, *Christlich-Sozial*, pp. 98–99, 250–54, 256–57. On Stoecker's hatred for liberalism, *ibid.*, pp. 127, 220, 223, 266–67, 314–15. On Stoecker's religious conviction and his sympathy for aristocracy, see Frank, *op. cit.*, pp. 21–23, 34–35, 37.

ment to aristocracy, a suspicion of the secular state, an anti-Semitism largely derived from his ethics and religion,[51] and an abiding faith in Lutheran dogma. Stoecker could not resolve the conflict of his religious-traditionalist conviction with the new requirement that politics accept either a nationalist or materialist basis and offer some form of salvation in this world. And by the nineties the force of the conservative teaching about a patriarchal society, even though adapted to the conditions of the times in the form of a "social monarchy," had long been spent. Secularization fed by the increasingly scientific and technical atmosphere of German life had made sufficient inroads in the outlook of the middle and lower classes to doom any political mass movement having a religious foundation. What had been the Protestant social reform movement was now ready for secular leadership and a secular point of view. It was Naumann's task to provide both.

As Naumann's religious perception gradually became obscured by his secular interests there opened to him those political possibilities which had remained closed to Stoecker by his refusal to question Lutheran orthodoxy. A sense of the historical relativeness of truth had already disclosed to Naumann that since Christianity lacked a dogmatic basis, there were no Christian principles upon which a modern government could be founded. It was self-evident to Naumann that the ever-recurring beat of history upon human institutions precluded the existence of a final or perfect form of government, whether conceived along religious or rational lines. All politics were determined by time and circumstance, and if government had any purpose it was to advance the well-being of the nation conceived as an historical and economic collective,[52] and to protect the individual so that the uniqueness of personality could be realized. Between these poles of authority and individuality Naumann's

---

[51] Göhre comments on this with great insight in *op. cit.*, pp. 76–78. Stoecker's anti-Semitism originated in his belief that there could not be a legitimate role for non-Christians in a monarchy and a society which rested upon Christian principles. In *Christlich-Sozial*, p. 409, he added that persecution fulfilled God's will that the Jews be punished. Racial prejudice did not enter into Stoecker's outlook; this is made clear in Gurian, *op. cit.*, pp. 230, 232.

[52] Yet Naumann consistently mistrusted collectivism as a principle of social organization having its own priority; the conjunction of individuality with it forms the substance of his proposals, however. For an expression of this, see *Was heisst Christlich-Sozial?*, p. 84.

political theory constantly fluctuated. Since he was inclined neither toward philosophy nor political science, Naumann had no disposition for systematizing his ideas about government and society. To most natural rights political philosophers, his attempt to combine such opposites as authority and individuality seems preposterous. How absolute authority could be reconciled with political equality was by no means clear even to his contemporaries. Only the experience of history since World War I has revealed Naumann's extraordinary prophecy of authoritarian regimes which rest upon equalitarian democracy. This was only one aspect of his special insight into the forms of politics appropriate for the age of the masses.[53]

A vision of mass man standing amid new values of his own making enabled Naumann to decide whether ethics or power is the basis of politics. One of Stoecker's most profound insights reappeared here in the outlook of his erstwhile disciple, namely that the conditions of an urban-industrial society enable the masses to form and lead their own cultural life apart from the traditional values encouraged by the church and the monarchy. Whereas Stoecker had attempted to change the direction of history by reinforcing orthodox religion and the traditional aristocracy, Naumann embraced the historical tendencies which were weakening the average man's veneration for them. No politics could succeed which ran contrary to this impulse. A deeper immersion in Marxist studies than Stoecker had ventured gave factual meaning to Naumann's secure grasp of the significance of the proletariat for the politics and the culture of a technical world. From Marxism came his idea that man could be remade in the image of his technical industrial society. But Naumann struggled against this frightful capacity of a machine age to technicize man himself. It was his hope and wish that mankind might develop its

[53] The term "masses" as Naumann used it did not have the same meaning that it has acquired under the influence of Ortega y Gasset and other writers. These profess to see in the masses not social nor even economic types which spring from the traditional classes, but a new variety of men who are disinterested in civilization and are prone to revolt against European culture in order to satisfy their crude materialist ambitions. Cf. José Ortega y Gasset, *The Revolt of the Masses* (London, 1932), and the illuminating comment in Arturo Barea, "The Conservative Critics: 1. Ortega and Madariaga," *University Observer*, I (1947), 31–34. On the other hand, Naumann understood by the "masses" merely the working class or the proletariat. It was a class gaining in political power and experience, but which was still forced to compete with the historic classes for national leadership.

intellectual and spiritual resources in order to keep pace with an advancing technology.[54] For Naumann the good man was a pilgrim in search of the truth who might lean upon science and technology not only for aid but guidance; his confidence in the power of the human intellect to create its own ideals enabled him to embrace the consequences of science and technology for the traditional culture and religion. In this sense he founded his politics upon power—upon the practical knowledge which advances secular interests. To win the mass man of the industrial age in order to effect a rebirth of German national life there had to be an energetic handling of the foremost technical apparatus, which was the state itself. Only absolute authority was confident of fulfilling this task. Hence in Naumann's writing and speech the figure, *Dämonie der Macht,* found more frequent use. In compulsion he eventually identified the nature of the state, and found in militarism the only guarantee that social relations might proceed undisturbed.[55]

The development of Nauman's political views quickened under the influence of Max Weber's social teaching. It would be an oversimplification to assume that he alone taught Naumann the idea of the national state whose foundation is power. Sohm's conclusions had also pointed in the same direction. Even before Naumann's first encounter with Weber there were signs that he was ready to embrace this concept. Yet Weber's influence must be considered one of the formative elements in Naumann's life. Their friendship had been encouraged by Helene Weber, who had introduced her son to the potentialities of the Evangelical Social Congress in order to strengthen his religious interests. For the specific religious issues of the congress Weber showed little concern, but to the social questions, especially the critical issue of East Elbian agriculture which dominated the sessions of 1894, he brought that great power of analysis upon which his fame rests. What Weber succeeded in teaching Naumann was the need of approaching social and political phenomena rationally, of making more systematic and detached in-

---

[54] Cf. Friedrich Naumann, *Das Blaue Buch von Vaterland und Freiheit. Auszüge aus seinen Werken* (Königstein im Taunus and Leipzig, 1913), pp. 134–35, 151, 159. This anthology, published by the *Hilfe* press, offers the most convenient survey of Naumann's works.

[55] For an estimate of Naumann's significance as a social prophet, see Van Der Voet, *op. cit.,* pp. 272 ff. Stoecker, unlike Naumann, clung to an ethical basis for his politics: he hoped to win industrial man for Protestant Christianity.

quiries, instead of pouring out bitter criticism with no other basis than a burning sense of injustice.[56] Naumann recognized the advantage of a thorough academic preparation in dealing with contemporary problems, and throughout 1894 he willingly submitted his economic views as expressed in *Christliche Welt* to Weber's merciless criticism.[57] These exchanges deepened their friendship and laid bare the historical views which they held in common.

Both men were enthusiasts of machines and industrialism,[58] not only as portents of a new age, but as indispensable means of sustaining a great power with ambitious policies and an expanding population. They were apprehensive of the danger inherent in the capitalistic development of large estate agriculture, with all its attendant evils of a rootless proletariat and the political strengthening of an aristocratic class whose outlook they considered hopelessly unfit to cope with modern problems. Naumann's inclination toward a politics of power and nationalism was encouraged by Weber's convictions about the advancement of Germany's great power status. It was not a duty imposed by traditional feeling for the Fatherland and its hereditary rulers, but a requirement of an industrial-technical age for the well-being of the state, which was nothing more than "the monopoly of the legitimate use of physical force."[59] Presently both men were to see the goal of political action in the establishment of a national sovereign state, armed with a plenitude of powers, and sustained by a population made aware of its civic responsibilities and made happy in its work by political liberty and the enjoyment of basic rights. While the relation of Weber to Naumann was always

---

[56] Weber even paused in his address on agricultural issues to the Evangelical Social Congress in order to chide Naumann about his "unlimited yearning for mankind's happiness." *Bericht über die Verhandlungen des Fünften Evangelisch-sozialen Kongresses*, p. 80.

[57] *Die Christliche Welt* developed from the *Evangelisch-lutherischen Gemeindeblattes* founded in 1886 by Martin Rade, a young village pastor. Both journals provided Naumann with valuable writing experience. For the former, which was intended for the educated classes having an interest in religious and theological matters, Naumann wrote articles about the Inner Mission activities; in fact, through *Christliche Welt* Naumann tried to strengthen his influence within the Inner Mission. Cf. Joachim Ganger, *Geschichte des "Nationalsozialen Vereins"* (Elberfeld, 1935), pp. 4–13.

[58] Note Naumann's article, "Der Christ in Zeitalter der Maschine," in *Was heisst Christlich-Sozial?*, pp. 30–41, which concludes that technology is not unchristian but a valid means of progress which all Christians must embrace, for "Gott will den technischen Fortschritt, er will die Maschine." *Ibid.*, p. 35.

[59] H. H. Gerth and C. Wright Mills, eds., *From Max Weber: Essays in Sociology* (New York, 1946), p. 78.

that of teacher to pupil, despite Naumann's seniority, each found much to admire in the other's character.[60] Weber sensed Naumann's instinct for politics in the sureness with which he seized issues and interests made apparent to others only by tedious investigation. Naumann admired Weber as a young realist, equipped for quick appraisal of men and ideas, a rebel against conventions who did not hesitate to bring into public notice the issues first raised in the classroom. And Naumann found in Weber a man of deep learning who shared his anxiety about the German future. Where was the class and who was the man to lead Germany in the fulfillment of her historical mission?

In helping Naumann to frame an answer to this question Weber's inaugural lecture at Freiburg in the spring of 1895 was of extraordinary importance.[61] Its subject, *Der Nationalstaat und die Volkswirtschaftspolitik,* was unfolded in Weber's customary style, which combined reconditeness with sweeping observations on current history. At the outset he established the connection of economic development and the national well-being and demanded that economic policy be framed with the nation's power interests in mind. The art of handling economic policy was therefore handmaiden to politics. And by politics he understood not the day to day affairs of bureaucracies and parliaments, but the continuing interests of the national state. Here Weber saw not a mystical entity arising out of history and the natural grouping of mankind, but a technical apparatus whose requirements provided a criterion of all political and economic values. By these terms, measures of welfare and economic assistance were not "helps" conferred upon individuals, but the self-preservation of the state, whose actions had always to be conceived according to its own reason.[62]

From these general considerations Weber proceeded to analyze the political ambition of the several classes in the light of their capacity for leadership, which he judged with reference to their under-

---

[60] Marianne Weber presents a one-sided picture of their relationship in *op. cit.,* p. 143. Her observations are reflected in the handling of this topic in J. P. Mayer, *Max Weber and German Politics* (London, 1943), pp. 35–36.

[61] Martin Wenck and Theodor Heuss who were close to Naumann agree to this. Cf. Heuss, *op. cit.,* p. 137. Marianne Weber also mentions the significance of her husband's address for Naumann's development, *op. cit.,* p. 232.

[62] Max Weber, "Der Nationalstaat und die Volkswirtschaftspolitik," *Gesammelte Politische Schriften* (Munich, 1921), p. 20.

standing of the national aspects of power and economics. This approach was subsequently reflected in Naumann's treatment of the social classes in *Demokratie und Kaisertum,* in which he also corroborated Weber's denial of the Marxist concept that the state and political life embody the predominant class interests. Weber and Naumann were alarmed lest the future of industrial Germany be cut short by an agrarian ruling class. Both men professed to see the social classes struggling for influence within the state, which they conceived with some degree of Hegelian majesty and suprapersonal completeness, but without a foreordained historical course which would permit it to dispense with enlightened guidance.

Weber had little hope that the toiling masses would have true political instincts, since their souls stirred to an awareness of national power only in wartime. Upper levels of the working class were economically mature—more so than the property-owning class believed—yet the proletariat had less political awareness than was pretended by the journalistic clique which spoke for it. These disembodied men of the middle class toyed with phantoms of the past in imagining that they were the latter-day Jacobins. Neither a sense of the energy of deeds, nor a genuine pathos for the national fate, moved them as it had the true revolutionaries of the Convention. Without real instincts for power these self-chosen representatives of the working class could never rise above the petty details of politics.[63] A true candidacy for political leadership would be advanced in the future as it had been in the past by first attaining economic power. National interest would be imperiled if the class exercising authority had declining economic fortunes; more dangerous was an over-rapid economic maturity which advanced a class to power in a state of political unwisdom. Both possibilities threatened Germany, and Weber found here the true key to an understanding of the national plight.[64]

Since the most remote times Prussian rulers had depended upon the Junkers, a class which Weber now believed to be in the throes of a life and death struggle over its economic destiny. Its crisis had

[63] *Ibid.*, pp. 24, 28. Weber's political theory remained consistent with these views; he considered that a goal of political activity, even in a constitutional government, was the development of a leadership qualified to increase the world power and world position of Germany. See the comment on this idea in Albert Salomon, "Max Weber's Political Ideas," *Social Research,* II (1935), 371–72.

[64] Max Weber, *op. cit.*, pp. 24–25. Also see the analysis in Mayer, *op. cit.*, pp. 31 ff.

been manifest in the oversights and omissions of its last great representative, Prince Bismarck.[65] At his hands the nation had acquired political unity without attaining an inner solidarity made necessary by the great economic transformation which had brought industry to the fore of national life. No Junker leader could grasp the importunity of Germany's social and industrial development. If this class were to remain in power Germany would be frozen by an icy wind from the past. Whether the German bourgeoisie were mature enough to guide the nation in the place of the Junkers appeared very dubious to Weber. Politics had long been remote from their interests. They had been saturated with the apparent success of Bismarckian leadership, and in imagining that German history had come to an end, had developed an unpolitical and unhistorical outlook. Middle class philistinism was clearly a sign of decadence.[66]

One of the first requirements of a great political talent was the awakening of the Germans to the enduring importance of power questions. None of the German classes appeared ready to accept this responsibility. Here was the touchstone of national politics. The danger did not consist in the unsatisfactory economic circumstances of the masses, but in the uncertain political enterprise of the existing and the emergent classes. Social politics and questions of economic security derived meaning only from their role in shaping political intelligence. Not worldly satisfactions but the social unity of the nation, temporarily dislocated by economic change and tension, was the first objective of social politics in preparing for "the heavy battles lying in the future."[67] A self-sufficient social political ideal, framed in platitudes and beclouded with fatuous optimism, which was intended only for the philisitinistic indulgence of the impoverished, would substitute at great hazard for true political decisions. Great though the needs of the working class might be, the needs of the nation before history were greater. Every nation could will its destiny, and Weber believed that his generation, standing in the shadows of the Bismarckian triumphs, must resolve to bring forth an even greater era. Years alone did not lay the weight of age upon nations; their youth consisted in the courage to recognize the class with true political instincts. The German future would

---

[65] Weber did not mention Bismarck by name, however.
[66] Max Weber, *op. cit.*, pp. 25–26.
[67] *Ibid.*, p. 29.

be secure when the decisions of politics were shaped in that clear and sober air free of all perceptions save that of national honor.[68]

Echoes of Weber's inaugural address resounded throughout Naumann's writing in the late nineties and eventually entered into the making of *Demokratie und Kaisertum*. At Stoecker's hands Naumann had seen social welfare politics pressed into the service of religion; from Weber he learned its usefulness for sovereignty and nationalism. The most striking consequence of Naumann's association with Weber was his willingness to subordinate social issues to requirements of national power. Evidence of this had been forthcoming in his comments on Weber's address published in *Die Hilfe*, which emphasized the nationalistic overtones and sharpened the remarks about the political fitness of the German classes. As if to make the point clear to the most obtuse readers, Naumann added that all social reforms would be made useless if the Cossacks came. Whoever undertook to carry out a social policy must first safeguard the people, the Fatherland, and the frontiers.[69] First among all issues was the strengthening of armaments, and in failing to perceive this the Social Democrats had fallen into their greatest error. We require, said Naumann, a socialism that is capable of governing, and this means the ability to form and carry out a better total politics than Germany has known heretofore. Naumann found no evidence that such talent was at hand in existing forms of socialism; if one were to appear it would have to be German and national.[70]

Naumann was deeply indebted to Weber, yet he remained independent of him in one important respect, which was their chief point of controversy during the first half of a long friendship. Until 1908 they had no point of agreement about the Kaiser's abilities. An early suspicion of the Kaiser's dilettantism was nourished by Weber into a conviction of his incompetence, and finally into an implacable rage over the maladroitness in foreign affairs which threatened to bring ruin to Bismarck's work. Upon the accession of William II in 1888 Weber had looked askance at his romantic illusions and reactionary tendencies, and as these gathered strength under the guise of a new Caesarism, both the orderliness of administration and the security of the empire appeared to be endangered.

---

[68] *Ibid.*, pp. 29–30.
[69] *Die Hilfe*, I (1895), No. 28.
[70] Cf. Heuss, *op. cit.*, pp. 138–39.

What had first appeared to Weber as a harmless inability to concentrate upon a single goal, was revealed in the Kaiser's conduct of diplomacy to be an irresponsible and reckless use of authority which lacked all talent for discerning true objectives. World politics at the Kaiser's hands had become a sham and an illusion. And Weber was horror-struck in contemplating the catastrophes which might befall the Kaiser's exercise of military command. None of the Hohenzollerns, except Frederick the Great, remarked Weber, had been able to distinguish the substance from the appearance of authority. All that mattered to William II was its corporal aspect: giving commands, standing at attention, and bragging. To be ruled by him was like riding an express train and having doubts whether the next switch was set correctly.[71]

Against these charges Naumann zealously defended the Kaiser.[72] His justification of the German monarch excluded the dynasty loyalty to the Hohenzollerns, and the satisfaction with simple vassalage, which had been characteristic of Stoecker. The Kaiser appealed to Naumann as a modern ruler, a man in sympathy with the times. Evidence of this had been forthcoming when the Kaiser had appeared eager to understand and aid the working class, and when he had shown anxiety about the social discord which arose from Bismarck's handling of the socialists. The short life of these perceptions had not discouraged Naumann, even though the Kaiser veered immediately to the opposite pole by taking his social outlook from the great industrialists and threatening to imprison the workers. Naumann believed that valid sentiments of rulership lay concealed beneath these impulsive alternations of policy. Most striking among these was the Kaiser's sensitivity to industrialism and technical change as elements of modern life. William II was unique among his fellow monarchs for seeming at ease amid modern engineering and technical marvels. That he was a fit ruler for a technically gifted

---

[71] Marianne Weber, *op. cit.*, pp. 129–31; also see the letters from Weber to Naumann found in Max Weber, *op. cit.*, pp. 451–57.

[72] Kliersfeld offers a sympathetic treatment of the Kaiser's viewpoint with respect to social questions which makes Naumann's enthusiasm more understandable. On the basis of the Kaiser's public utterances, his sympathy and interest in industrial conditions could easily be conjectured. The frequent reference in the Kaiser's speeches to the quality and skill of German work would also have impressed Naumann, since apart from his pride in Germanic perfection, he was interested in the quality and the design of industrial products. *Op. cit.*, pp. 8–19.

people was shown by his effort to stimulate engineering and scientific progress, and, so Naumann thought, in equating it not only with the mastery of political problems, but also with the advancement toward that destiny which man's increasing control of nature seemed to hold forth.[73] Germany was fortunate to be ruled by a man who encouraged the launching of faster steamships and the building of more factories, a dynast, the first of his line to feel the pulse of the nation in industry instead of agriculture.[74]

Naumann may have read more depth of understanding into the Kaiser's personality than was actually there. Not all of his followers in the National Social Association shared his view about William II; hence the party's unity, already endangered by the debate over the relative importance of power and welfare, was further weakened. Naumann was prepared, however, to accept the consequences of his devotion. When a German contingent was dispatched to China in 1900 to suppress the Boxers, the Kaiser's bellicose speech of July 27 startled the nation.[75] Conservatives were embarrassed by its excess and liberals combined with socialists to launch a storm of protest. Readers of *Die Hilfe* were surprised to learn that Naumann considered such criticism affected and prudish; it would be justified only if the nation was more moral than the Kaiser. Except for the religious note which the Kaiser had struck, Naumann found nothing objectionable. The idea of a crusade seemed thoroughly outmoded, since he believed that Germany would wage war as a sovereign nation, not because it believed in the Gospel. These remarks set up new tensions within the party and a large number of

[73] Naumann's mystique of machines was capable of reaching lyric heights; machines were the black *Knechte* through whose work all men might one day be made free. These mechanical men would eventually do all the work and give men leisure. Machines at the moment might be enriching some and impoverishing others, and their history might combine happiness and misfortune, yet in the end machines would be man's salvation. *Das Blaue Buch von Vaterland und Freiheit*, pp. 140–41.

[74] For an expression of these views, see Friedrich Naumann, *Demokratie und Kaisertum: Ein Handbuch für innere Politik* (4th ed., Berlin-Schoneberg, 1905), pp. 171–73, 217–19, 224.

[75] There were a number of these speeches throughout July and August, since the Kaiser felt called upon to address each departing transport; that of July 27 aroused the most comment. Cf. Eyck, *op. cit.*, p. 272. The edited version of the speech printed in the *Reichsanzeiger* is given in Christian Gauss, *The German Emperor as Shown in His Public Utterances* (New York, 1915), pp. 164–66. This version gives the impression that the Germans expected no quarter, whereas the Kaiser had urged his troops to give no quarter.

academicians resigned. In the socialist press Naumann now found himself described as the leader of the "Revolver Christians."[76]

IV

Naumann's defense of William II was dictated in part by the need of remaining consistent with the views expressed in *Demokratie und Kaisertum,* the first edition of which had appeared during the spring of 1900, only a few months before the Kaiser's sensational speech. The book represented the full scope of Naumann's political intellect during the period when he sought to combine democracy and Caesarism. That there were contradictions in it beyond the implication of its major theme remains undeniable. Not even Naumann's gift for aphorism could cloak them. *Demokratie und Kaisertum* stands primarily as a literary exercise, the work of a gifted man sensitive to the currents of industrialism and materialism then running strongly in European history, who suspected that parliamentary governments and their morality were inadequate for the new times. By virtue of his stylistic gifts Naumann was able to combine elements of history, political theory, economic moralism, and party polemic in a lucid narrative which balanced novelty with sufficient academic assurance to appeal to the already well-informed, and yet attract first seekers after political knowledge. As a statement of Naumann's political ethos the book was a literary rather than a polemical sensation. It did not convert many Social Democrats to nationalism, and it did not succeed in moderating the strife within Naumann's own party. The factious spirit had not been diminished by the furor over the Kaiser's speech, which at Naumann's prompting now provoked another question, whether the Kaiser was a modern ruler who embodied an understanding of power and social responsibility.

Neither democracy nor kaisership was regarded by Naumann as a form of government made preferable by its inherent virtues. He was not a simple admirer of royalty, and at this stage of his political life, he did not believe that man enjoyed basic natural rights. Democracy and kaisership appeared to be the most effective means of coping with the problems of twentieth-century Germany. Com-

---

[76] Heuss, *op. cit.,* pp. 167–69; *Die Hilfe,* VI (1900), No. 31.

pared to the other elements in the German government, the Reichstag, the bureaucracy, and the member states of the empire, none had more fitness for dealing with industrialism and the military and imperialist issues arising from it. Industrialism was the only course open to Germany if the chief needs of the masses were to be provided. The masses were a factor of modern politics which no government could afford to overlook. Owing to the extraordinary increase in the population during the nineteenth century an historical and political environment quite different from that in any other time had come into being. That an expanding population was one of the chief motors of history was repeatedly asserted by Naumann.[77] By 1925 he foresaw a German nation of eighty millions.[78] This stupendous fact of more people, whose appetites for food, struggle for higher wages, need for housing, demand for education, and yearning for luxuries had come increasingly to the fore as political issues, determined the character of modern government.

The tempo of the age and the stirring of the same forces in other nations required a politics of action.[79] Constitutionalism was too calm, too detached for the swift decisions upon which successful rulership had to be based. Fortunately for Germany, the Kaiser had emerged from the obscurity which had, perhaps with the intent of the Reich's founder, originally surrounded his office. Now the Kaiser was prepared to make policy and execute it. More significantly, by virtue of his dynastic tradition and Hohenzollern instincts, the Kaiser understood the issue of power. Nothing could be of greater consequence for industrialization and the solution of the social question. Upon naval and military power depended the beat of industrial life: winning markets, gaining colonies, and acquiring raw materials. Only within a nation made secure by armaments could social reforms be carried out successfully. All domestic problems were subordinate to foreign relations. Success here would

[77] Naumann was not a Malthusian; he insisted that production rises with the population and pointed to the improved standard of living in Germany and England. Instead of being a menace to progress, the masses were indispensable to it. *Das Blaue Buch von Vaterland und Freiheit,* pp. 119–20, 121–23.

[78] *Demokratie und Kaisertum,* p. 67 (all references are to the 4th ed.).

[79] A concern for humanity was generally remote in Naumann's vision, yet he believed that the stirring of the masses, industry, and technology among the chief nations would eventually bring about a new world order. "Kinderzahl und Maschine sind die schiebenden Mächte für das Kommen der Menschheit." *Das Blaue Buch von Vaterland und Freiheit,* pp. 253–54.

make possible an intensified industrialism and an earnest attack on social problems, both of which would deepen the nationalist ardor of the masses, whose technical skill and military vigor were dissipated because they were crowded into tenements, underfed, and tossed to and fro on the tide of revolutionary appeals, an appalling waste of human energies which rightfully belonged to the nation.

Democracy embodied the life surge of the masses. It was a paradox that the action of millions, a heaving and rolling with the authority of a tidal wave, had its origin in the struggle of individuals to realize themselves. Each individual was endowed with a unique personality, whose development and enrichment was at once the mainspring of social actions and the goal of politics. But liberalism, in seeking to free the personality by protecting it from the state, had given democracy a large content of negative principles. The new democracy must begin to act positively; it must advance industrialism and technology, since without them the masses could not live.[80] This political claim had to be asserted in terms of working class strength, which consisted neither in education, property, nor civic experience, but solely in numbers. Majority was the only principle and justification of the new democracy whose realization was brought nearer with every additional birth. Both the individual and his collective expression, the masses, must recognize the dependence of industrial life upon military power. When wholehearted patriotism descended upon the masses and they became reconciled to the Kaiser and marched with him in a democratic Fatherland, Germany would be invincible.[81]

Both oversimplification and keen insight were present in Naumann's analysis. It had Max Weber's sociological orientation toward politics, and with less profundity though with more journalistic skill, combined social theory with political argument. Beneath an elaborate sociology of the classes, which appeared to be derived entirely from Weber, there was a straightforward appeal for imperialism. This was conceived chiefly in terms of overseas trade and colonies, and was urged even at the risk of war. The importance of the colonial trade for the national economy was exaggerated, while

---

[80] This view is central to all of Naumann's political and economic thinking. For expressions of it, see *ibid.*, pp. 127–28; and *Demokratie und Kaisertum*, pp. 21, 23–24.

[81] For illustrations of these salient elements in Naumann's outlook, see *ibid.*, pp. 20, 28, 33–34, 45–46, 150–51, 177–78, 214–16.

the less dramatic but far more substantial trade among the European nations was virtually ignored. Under the stimulation of the tariff issue, which played a large role in German politics, Naumann may have been inclined to overstress the competitive rather than the collaborative aspects of European economic relations. Like so many of his contemporaries, Naumann believed that trade followed the flag and that cruisers were effective advertising, an outlook that was especially popular in Germany during the nineties when enthusiasm for colonies and a navy was beginning to mount.[82]

V

At the very outset of *Demokratie und Kaisertum* Naumann came to grips with the issue upon which his political construction depended: the unity of the masses and the nation. It had been commonly asserted in Germany since the attempts upon William I's life that the working class seethed with revolutionary spirit; officialdom, the army, and the propertied classes had a proper horror of the rising tide of Marxism. This apprehension was unjustified, said Naumann, because the Social Democrats were revolutionary only on paper. Furthermore, to establish democracy and begin the socialist reconstruction of Germany, a revolution, in the sense of a bloody struggle, was unnecessary. The ground swell of the masses was gradually moving the left-wing parties into power. By pursuing obstructionist tactics and refusing to accept the responsibility for leadership within the government, Social Democracy was beginning to disappoint the workers. Few of them had any interest in the endless debates over Marxist theory. But workingmen were beginning to realize the extent of their political influence and had begun to inquire how this could be brought to bear on the existing state.[83] Winning authority within the state, not its overthrow, was the im-

[82] It should be borne in mind that Naumann drew upon the economic theories of the German historical school, which was not inclined to regard either war or armament expenditures as an unprofitable undertaking. The theories of Roscher, Knies, Schäffle, Lorenz von Stein, and Schmoller are summarized in Edmund Silberner, *The Problem of War in Nineteenth Century Economic Thought* (Princeton, N. J., 1946), pp. 172 ff. On the significance of the tariff for Naumann, see *Die politischen Parteien*, pp. 36, 48, 73.

[83] It has been maintained that the "state" was more in the forefront of Naumann's political outlook than German nationalism, that he recognized his mission in the clarification of the issues and the advancement of the means whereby the life and existence of the German Empire might be assured. Cf. Van Der Voet, *op. cit.*, p. 198.

mediate political goal. What the masses required was a leadership which would allay the suspicion of revolutionary aims and secure legislation to minimize political inequality, especially in the suffrage. To the masses would then fall the task of fulfilling liberal as well as socialist ideals within the German Empire.[84]

To his belief that democracy and socialism could be introduced by electoral means, Naumann added his conviction that an actual uprising of the people was very unlikely. His sociology of revolution first considered the monumentality of the nineteenth-century state and the advantage of rapid communications and standing armies for its defense. Naumann argued that as soon as a few soldiers had been killed the army would become a pitiless machine. Railways and highways would permit the rapid concentration of large military forces, before whose cannon and magazine rifles barricades would be useless. Germany was not Austria of 1848. Whether industrial man with his materialist outlook could make a great revolution appeared doubtful to Naumann, especially since the workers considered themselves part of a vast mechanism[85] and were little inclined to sacrifices in the name of heroism. Some of that spirit which Marx had attributed to the petty bourgeoisie had been caught by the masses, a spirit fearful of risk which preferred not to take a speaking role in the drama of history. Revolution on the grand scale had gone out of fashion; the masses could act decisively merely by inclining their vast numbers, which exerted a pressure equal to the weight of the Alps.[86]

Foremost in the interest of the masses was the question of wages; a steady wage and a higher wage were very often the workingman's only ambition. By identifying itself with this economic issue the Social Democratic Party had become the chief spokesman for the masses. All creative political effort ought to be directed toward enrolling this leadership for a constructive solution of the wage problem, which could mean nothing else than the promotion of industrialism. There was no future for the working class movement unless it realized that industrialization depended upon the activity

---

[84] *Demokratie und Kaisertum*, pp. 1–10.
[85] Naumann had remarked this tendency very early. In 1894 he commented, "Im Zeitalter der Maschine haben sich die Menschen gewöhnt, alles als Maschine anzusehen." *Was heisst Christlich-Sozial?*, p. 35.
[86] *Demokratie und Kaisertum*, pp. 11–15.

of the entrepreneurs. These bourgeoisie had been the heart of that historic German liberal movement which was now scattered in several diverse and contradictory tendencies. What was left of liberalism had to recognize, on its part, that without a democratic majority the deepest hope of the movement could not be realized. This was the belief in the sanctity of personality, the very force which moved the masses.[87] Until the workers and the middle classes set aside their differences and agreed to combine in one party there could not be a democratic government in Germany. The real issue of the moment was the ability of the Social Democrats, who commanded working class affection, to develop so as to embrace the old task of liberalism without prejudicing the middle class.[88] Social Democrats had to realize that they could not hope to govern a nation of sixty millions supported only by the workers. The coming German democracy needed roots in the industrial classes, among workers and employers alike, united in their dependence upon industry and in their devotion to the nation.[89]

A new culture, based on technology and the increase of the population, was another goal of democratic politics. The men of the new age must be modern in every respect, responsive to technology and aware of its importance for progress and personality, the twin words which signified the ends of democratic action. Germans must take the age of the machine as their special province. Before all other nations the Germans, down to the last man, had to become a quality people, educated and made healthy by the rational exploitation of technology.[90] Consciousness of nationality and the fulfillment of individual potentialities through the marshaling of national energy were fundamentally the same thing. Nationalism, industrialism, and the masses marched together on the same goal. No small risk would be involved in remaking the "old" German people into a modern nation of technicists; nonetheless it was a risk which had to be taken. Population pressure and foreign danger prohibited any other course. The new Germans would rejoice in the future and

---

[87] This idea is developed in *Das Blaue Buch von Vaterland und Freiheit*, pp. 169–70.

[88] Naumann's practical suggestions for accomplishing this included the decentralization of industry, worker participation in management, and the further development of unions and co-operatives. Cf. *Demokratie und Kaisertum*, pp. 65–66, 72–75.

[89] *Ibid.*, pp. 15–21, 23–25, 27–30.

[90] See *Das Blaue Buch von Vaterland und Freiheit*, pp. 128, 132, 133–35.

in their working together, because they had served German history and the need of a people whose stature was equal to its suffering and deeds.[91]

Leadership in this movement to transform the nation would be assumed by the natural aristocracy of labor, as it would be opposed by the natural aristocracies among the other classes.[92] By "aristocracy" Naumann had in mind something akin to an elite. In common with other thinkers who have wrestled with the problem of mass social action, he fell back upon the theory of a leadership having extraordinary spiritual or "charismatic" qualities.[93] Naumann distinguished between an elite of leaders, active in the conduct of politics, and those articulate elements adept in forming opinion, such as the skilled trades which had been able to popularize the basic issues of labor. A mass movement depended upon its natural aristocracy for a clear statement of social aims, the management of its electoral and parliamentary battles, and the direction of the immense power inherent in its numbers. The masses could not themselves create the new world; the democratic movement would be determined by the force, will, and energy of its leaders. The most eminent among these were those "people's dukes" who managed the Social Democratic Party and made all its critical decisions; the rank and file of party members counted for nothing. Naumann wished that this proletarian elite would closely observe the other aristocracies in order to learn their political technique. If the masses wanted to make their numbers effective in parliamentary politics, their leaders must first learn its tactics.[94]

Germany's mass movement had to deal with three hostile aristocracies: the agrarian, the industrial, and the clerical. None was a more determined opponent than the land-dwelling Junkers, a class little moved by personal considerations and filled with brutal energies. Its norms were the practical, the natural, and the small-scale. Everything belonging to industry, export, technology, and large cities was alien to its conservative outlook. Only political

---

[91] *Demokratie und Kaisertum*, pp. 26–27, 36–37, 38, 39.

[92] A groping toward this idea is evident in Naumann's demand made in 1896 for an "aristocratic democracy," that is, for the selection and training of leaders who could move the masses. Cf. *Einige Gedanken über die Gründung christlich-sozialer Vereine*, pp. 16–17.

[93] Here his dependence upon Weber should be apparent. Cf. Gerth and Mills, *op. cit.*, pp. 245–52, on Weber's concept of charismatic authority.

[94] *Demokratie und Kaisertum*, pp. 22–23, 80–83, 84, 87–88.

tactics required the squire to be a *Weltpolitiker*. For all their short-sightedness the Junkers clung to one infallible political expedient: in time of crisis they put on the cloak of patriotism. Any political movement could profit from this tactic, Naumann observed, for by advancing patriotism it became identified with the national future. Nothing would be easier for democracy, since the proletariat had a deep and fierce pride in its ancestors who had fought at Leipzig and Königgrätz. On the issue of power and national security the masses and the aristocrats really stood as one. By refusing to admit this, democracy had allowed the most urgent and vital of all political questions to slip into its opponent's hands. There could be no greater mistake, since the nation would not trust itself to a party which was not reliable on the issue of national power.[95]

Second among the great aristocracies Naumann singled out the industrialists of the Ruhr and Westphalia, a class rich in capacity for political development which yearned to take the place of the Junkers. Political consciousness had first begun to stir in this class upon the accession of William II, who had awakened in it the idea that there could be an industrial regimen. Its form had become one of the crucial issues in the struggle between the aristocracies of industry and of democracy. Neither socialism, in the doctrinaire sense of a national economic bureaucracy, nor private ownership with its destructive zeal for profits, appeared suitable to the interest which the nation maintained in its industry.[96] No form of management could be more effective than the existing one, Naumann believed, so that the task of democracy was to win influence within it. This did not appear to be impossible: the great entrepreneurs were nothing more than the thin upper crust of the new industrial masses. Compromise with the conservatives or with democracy was the alternative before the industrial aristocrats: upon their decision hung the fate of Germany.[97]

Naumann suspected that the clerical aristocracy, or the Catholic hierarchy, lacked patriotic motives. He found Protestantism more agreeable to the German nature. Under the Protestant Hohen-

---

[95] *Ibid.*, pp. 88–96.
[96] Naumann had expressed this view earlier in *Soziale Briefe an reiche Leute* (Göttingen, 1895), p. 35, which recognized the role of private capital in creating new industry, and which discounted the possibility that an economic bureaucracy might usurp the role of private management.
[97] *Demokratie und Kaisertum*, pp. 110–18.

zollerns Germany had been united; he believed that commercial and industrial progress had been made chiefly by Protestants; Naumann even detected a Protestant spirit in the machine! Catholicism was tainted with an internationalism which tended to dissociate the German Catholic, often in the most subtle way, from a true connection with the nation. So it was that the Center Party was most concerned with ethical and pedagogical issues rather than economic development or national power. The Center had nothing to say about the life issue for Germany, whether the national development should be under agrarian or industrial leadership. And the Center was hopelessly unfit for the great work of technicizing Germany, without which the masses could not live. Against the Center, Naumann urged democracy to struggle relentlessly, and to gird itself with a world view at once popular, contemporary, and technological, to affirm a religion of freedom against the religion of suppression. Who gave aid in this battle earned God's grace for the German people.[98]

Despite the momentary ascendancy of the agrarians and clericals in the Reichstag, Naumann was confident that in the future all majorities would reflect the forward-looking industrial point of view.[99] The type of conservatism which served landed or religious interests had gone out of fashion in favor of a new political outlook shared by the social strata being brought forward by industrialization. There was nothing unusual about this analysis except Naumann's conclusion: the trend of the times would eventually force democracy to come to terms with the Kaiser. Naumann had correctly read the temper of the nationalism which moved the masses and had penetrated to that mysterious connection which they had established between their own well-being and that of the nation. In the interest of national security, the imperative of all politics, he

[98] *Ibid.*, pp. 122–34. Naumann was aware of the degree to which German politics was permeated with the confessional spirit; only the Social Democrats were free of it, he said. But he saw no reason for the prevalence of religious interests and, speaking as a liberal, he subsequently argued that an individual could be connected directly to the political community without an association in religion. *Das Blaue Buch von Vaterland und Freiheit,* pp. 71–72.

[99] The struggle against the conservative-clerical alliance was one of Naumann's life interests: "Um des Vaterlandes willen bekämpfen wir sie und warten auf den Tag der deutschen Freiheit." *Die politischen Parteien,* p. 115. He feared that under this moribund leadership Germany could not realize its great future, for "Noch hat es grösse für Menschheit zu tun." *Ibid.,* p. 114.

urged democracy to strike an alliance with the Kaiser, his armed forces, and the experience in war and diplomacy which were attributes of his dynasty.[100]

Monarchy and nation were words which the Hohenzollerns had given a common meaning. If industrialism and democracy were to triumph over the old agrarian viewpoint, Germany must strengthen the union of nation and ruler. They had first been brought together by the Bismarckian revolution of blood and iron, which had created not only a new state but the first economic unit to embody the German commercial and industrial striving. Militarism and capitalism had sustained the dynamism of the Reich from its beginning, and they were the only certain guarantee for the future.[101] William II —unlike his grandfather, who still thought like a Prussian king— understood this and was prepared to be a modern prince, a virtuoso of the age of technology. No ruler used modern transport and communications so readily; none understood so well the advantages which they conferred upon the executive. The realities of the technical world were beyond the understanding of the traditional aristocracies; the new aristocracies of labor and industry were not sufficiently mature to exercise authority. There was no other course than to accept the Kaiser's leadership, based on the will of the masses and the army. These conditions of modern Caesarism had first been made clear by Napoleon, whose system recognized popular sovereignty but insisted that it be exercised by a single individual.[102] The same compromise would enable the Kaiser to combine democracy and authority and provide Germany with a dictator embodying the national will for an industrial future; this dictatorship must develop from the Prussian ruling house.[103]

The Kaiser's unlimited authority was also justified by the in-

[100] Cf. *Demokratie und Kaisertum*, pp. 148–49.

[101] Naumann believed that German capitalism had acquired a special character as a result of its long association with Hohenzollern militarism. Much of his economic argument depended upon the assumption that German industry was more highly organized than similar business in other countries. This is denied in Abbott Payson Usher, "Interpretations of Recent Economic Progress in Germany," *American Historical Review*, XXIII (1918), 803.

[102] For his understanding of plebiscitary democracy Naumann was probably indebted to Weber, who subsequently worked out Bismarck's handling of universal manhood suffrage as a technique to bind the masses to the new German state. These elements of Weber's theory are discussed in Mayer, *op. cit.*, pp. 17, 64.

[103] *Demokratie und Kaisertum*, pp. 150–57, 171–73, 175–76, 180–81.

fluence of foreign policy upon industrialization, for Naumann believed that a bold policy brought new markets into being. Parliamentary handling of foreign policy was apt to be ineffective because of party strife, but a consistent diplomacy could be expected from a dynast whose interests were identical with the nation. Foreign policy also needed skilled direction, because all domestic policy hung on its outcome. No social reforms were possible without a foreign economic policy behind which there lay a well-polished sword; all freedom, civil rights, prosperity, and education would collapse from the moment that German military security failed. Military command had some of the monarchical attributes and Germany was fortunate that its history and law made the Kaiser the commander in chief.[104] Political requirements were only one source of the Kaiser's authority; a large share of it derived from industrialism and the steady growth of the population.[105]

The masses brought concentrated authority into being, Naumann asserted, anticipating Weber's comment that the dictatorship of the masses requires a dictator. In their numbers and urgent economic needs Naumann recognized forces which were reshaping the nineteenth-century liberal ideal of an atomistic society under limited government. A mass society dependent upon industry and imbued with a common national ambition determined its own form of politics, which was the sovereignty of one man. On the very threshold of the twentieth century, when limited monarchy and republics seemed everywhere to be established securely, Naumann correctly forecast the strong challenge of dictatorship to liberalism.

Dictatorship's inherent superiority, insofar as the masses were concerned, was expressed by a more effective pursuit of the interdependent objectives: power and well-being. Since the masses brought with them the industry which made possible the fleet, the army, and vast public expenditures, in the last analysis the Kaiser's authority, industrial aristocracy, and the masses were one and the same phenomenon. All proceeded from the transformation of an agrarian into an industrialized Germany. Its political ordering could not be solved under a constitution which limited the dy-

---

[104] *Ibid.*, pp. 177–79.
[105] *Ibid.*, pp. 179–80. Brentano did not think this a very original observation, but he was very critical of *Demokratie und Kaisertum*, especially its hopefulness that the masses would rally to the Kaiser. Brentano, *op. cit.*, pp. 227–28.

namism necessary to modern political life. Politics, which consisted entirely of the struggle for power under conditions determined by history, now pointed toward the dictatorship of industry and the masses by the Kaiser. This necessity Naumann had intended to make clear by the title of his program: *Demokratie und Kaisertum*.[106]

When Naumann turned to the condition of politics, he did not gloss over the basic issues standing between the Kaiser and the party which represented German democracy.[107] None was more important than the military question, about which Naumann believed the Kaiser had sound ideas. To expand the Prussian-German military state to world stature was impossible without a large army and a modern fleet. Nothing about the Kaiser appeared so praiseworthy as his championship of navalism in an age of industry and world communications, nor offered more contrast to the Social Democrats, who remained sunk in the military politics of *Kleinstaaterei*. In failing to see that requirements of power came before social reform the Social Democrats were sacrificing the real interests of the people. Among the workers Naumann found no aversion to war, since they were enthusiastic for the Boers and fearful lest the want of first-class armaments injure their cause. That antimilitaristic front of European proletarians which the socialists spoke about was a myth; all antimilitarism would disappear upon the outbreak of war. The German working class would realize that for its own existence it must wage war and carry it deep into the enemy's territory.[108]

His correct estimate of the hold of nationalism upon the working class gained force by a remarkable prophecy about the nature of future wars.[109] Naumann belonged to that small group of civilians who succeeded before 1914 in foretelling the character of war more accurately than most professional officers. The importance which he attached to industry and population enabled Naumann to depict

---

[106] Cf. *Demokratie und Kaisertum*, pp. 44–46, 180, 181, 229.

[107] Naumann did ignore the single element which deprived his political construction of a pragmatic basis: this was the Kaiser's conviction that the Social Democrats were not a German party but an international revolutionary society. Cf. Kliersfeld, *op. cit.*, pp. 76, 79.

[108] *Demokratie und Kaisertum*, pp. 148–49, 166, 191–92, 198–99. These remarks derived their meaning from Naumann's tendency to regard the "next war" as a clash between Germany and Russia. Such a war would advance progress and European culture by overthrowing Russian autocracy, which to Naumann, as well as most German liberals and socialists, stood for all the reactionary forces in history.

[109] See especially *Das Blaue Buch von Vaterland und Freiheit*, pp. 51–53, 263–64.

war as an armed collision of the masses. Numbers alone when animated by patriotism and equipped with the best weapons would prove to be decisive; conscription, industry, and great populations combined in the army of millions to diminish the importance of heroism and the traditional soldierly virtues. Warfare itself had been industrialized by complicated machines which were better served by factory workers than the best drilled Prussian sergeants. Millions of factory workers were an incalculable military asset, especially in a conflict between Germany and a "Slavic nation." The German army in preferring to conscript peasants acted unwisely, Naumann believed, since the growth of the industrial population would make the proletariat the chief element in the army within a generation.[110] Military security would then depend in large measure upon their loyalty to the state, which for its part must begin to answer questions that common soldiers would ask about the purpose of war. To this end Naumann proposed that military and social policy go hand in hand, and to the Kaiser's role as commander in chief there be added his role as social lawgiver. This would assist the workers to realize that their well-being depended upon national security, for "Nothing, nothing matters in world history, education, culture, or morals, if it is not protected and supported by power."[111]

To reconcile German democracy—that is, the working class and that part of it already enrolled by the Social Democrats—to the Prussian military institutions was a task which Naumann did not attempt to evade. He observed that the Social Democrats, despite their unremitting hostility to the existing military organization, were not hostile to armies; in fact, their proposal to give military training to all able-bodied men was the basis of a genuine militia system.[112] Though he found much to praise in the democratic aspects of militia service, Naumann considered it inadequate; what might be satisfactory for the Swiss in their Alps would be unsuited to

[110] The preference for peasant soldiers was founded partly on the belief that their physique was better adapted to military training, but also on the army's fear of admitting Social Democratic recruits into the barracks. On the warfare of the Social Democrats with the army before 1914, see Erich Otto Volkmann, *Der Marxismus und das deutsche Heer im Weltkriege* (Berlin, 1925), pp. 45–53.

[111] *Demokratie und Kaisertum,* pp. 206–7; also pp. 199–203.

[112] Note the sociological insight in his comment: "Die deutsche Arbeiterbewegung ist der grösste freiwillige Militarismus der Erde. An ihm kann mann sehen, was das Volk von seinen Militärfürsten gelernt hat und nun für sich allein probiert." *Das Blaue Buch von Vaterland und Freiheit,* p. 205.

German military tasks. He preferred a well-trained army and urged that the two-year service be combined with the advances toward universal conscription already suggested by Caprivi.[113] Militarism should not be considered an onerous burden, Naumann believed, because in the hour of national danger Germany would become a unified, weapon-braced, living mass.[114]

On naval policy Naumann agreed completely with the Kaiser. It was self-evident to Naumann that the masses needed the fleet as well as the army for the fulfillment of their future needs.[115] International economic rivalry without a fleet was futile; to renounce naval power would mean abandoning the world's markets to the English. Goods run toward power, Naumann confidently asserted, adding ominously that the Germans must be ready for the day when their ships would sail past Gibraltar and Suez without paying tribute. For the warfare of commerce, Germany was fortunate to have a "Fleet Kaiser." On no other policy did the monarchy and the people stand so close. By misjudging this common sentiment for the fleet, democracy was compromising its own future, unlike the conservative and clerical parties which had not mistaken the compact of the nation with its naval armaments. These parties, though committed to narrow views of trade and industry, were shrewd enough to bargain for their projects with votes for naval bills. Democracy should do the same with full conviction that its project was the national good."[116]

Social politics was the final element binding the Kaiser to the masses. Naumann believed that William II genuinely sympathized with the working class, and that the imperial writ of February 4, 1890, which announced a broadening of the social welfare legislation, was the beginning of a "social Kaisership." This era had been postponed due to the temporary ascendancy of the agrarians and clericals, but its resumption was inevitable because William II realized that social politics must accompany industrialization and the newly won importance of the proletariat. Naumann suspected a

---

[113] Caprivi was one of the chief architects of the pre-1914 German army, but his ideal was far greater than the proposals made to the Reichstag in 1892. Cf. Johannes Werdermann, *Die Heeresreform unter Caprivi* (Greifswald, 1928), pp. 44, 54, 124.

[114] *Demokratie und Kaisertum*, pp. 204–5, 207–8, 212.

[115] This was consistent with the suggestion in *Soziale Briefe an reiche Leute*, pp. 56–57, that in addition to municipal auditoriums, better roads, commons, parks, and libraries, the donation of warships was an appropriate way for the rich to advance social welfare.

[116] *Demokratie und Kaisertum*, pp. 212–18, 220.

certain deceit in Bismarck's social legislation as being intended for the suppression of working class political ambitions.[117] Because the bureaucracy continued to administer it in this spirit, Naumann was convinced that they had ruined the fine opportunity to begin anew in 1890.[118] Social Democrats were also at fault for failing to take the outstretched hand proffered by the Kaiser at that time. Until a majority of the voters on the left rallied behind the idea of Freedom and Fatherland, William II would be obliged to advance Germany's interests with the support of parties committed to decadent views. This could only be temporary, inasmuch as the Kaiser in his chief work of defending the nation needed the support of the masses. Authority and democracy would inevitably be reconciled in Germany because industrialization fed by the increase of the population demanded it. [119]

VI

Despite the extraordinary sale of *Demokratie und Kaisertum*, there was little evidence that it had gained adherents to the National Social Association. The middle class was skeptical of its proposed social reforms, and the workers were not easily detached from a party which had successfully weathered Bismarck's opposition. Indeed, the Social Democrats proved to be a lure for Naumann's own followers. Paul Göhre, one of his most skillful journalistic aides, after breaking with him over the issue of the Kaiser, joined the Social Democrats in 1901. Others followed his course when the association was dissolved two years later. Financial weakness was another serious handicap for Naumann's political venture; upon an annual budget of 5,000 marks an impressive propaganda could not be sustained. *Die Zeit* proved to be a failure, although *Die Hilfe* continued to be popular with its religious and academic subscribers. Naumann's hope that he could reach the religious-minded workers

---

[117] Consult Erich Eyck, *Bismarck: Leben und Werk* (Erlenbach-Zurich, 1944), III, 367–75, which in treating Bismarck's social insurance legislation from a liberal standpoint illuminates Naumann's suspicion.

[118] It is interesting to note that Kliersfeld reaches virtually the same conclusion, for he finds in the unwillingness of Graf Posadowsky to embark after December 1897 on new social legislation a factor which quieted the Kaiser's interest in it. Kliersfeld, *op. cit.*, pp. 59–60.

[119] *Demokratie und Kaisertum*, pp. 221–22, 224–29.

through the Evangelical Unions proved illusory.[120] The failure of the National Social Association as a political movement was made painfully clear by the elections of 1903.[121]

The association entered the campaign hopefully, although it presently faced bitter opposition from the *Freisinnige,* who considered their constituencies endangered. Naumann's own candidature in Oldenburg, made possible by the generosity of Max Weber's mother and aunt, met defeat. Only one of the party's candidates, Hellmuth von Gerlach standing in Marburg, was successful. The disaster convinced Naumann that his ideas were more mature than the nation could accept, so that political agitation except for its educational value was useless. Some voices were raised in favor of joining forces with such groups as the *Bund für Bodenreform,* or the *Gesellschaft für Soziale Reform,* but the association's last convention at Göttingen agreed with Naumann that dissolution was the best course. He was not content to lead a fraction element, since national organization and the swift winning of power with mass support were alone consistent with his political outlook.[122]

Notwithstanding the failure of his first mission in politics the period from 1896 to 1903 was fruitful for the development of Naumann's political and ethical views. He had secularized his politics by accepting the concept of the state as a power complex. All trace of those "old conservative" motives which had sustained Stoecker's brief political career had vanished from Naumann's world view. His religion had lost its doctrinal content and had become a simple moralism. Of social politics he could say that it was neither a matter of religion nor morality but a power issue in the life of the state. For Germany he recognized the foremost problem to be the continued nationalization of the proletarian masses which, despite a superficial attachment to the symbols of international socialism, still retained their loyalty to the Fatherland. History has subsequently offered an abundant proof for his analysis of the

---

[120] From 1895 until 1902 Naumann served on one of the central committees of the Evangelical Unions and his experience made only too clear that the Protestant unions could not be made a sustaining element in a Christian socialist movement. Cf. Neumann, *op. cit.,* pp. 12 and 94, note 41; and Theodor Böhme, *Die christlich-nationale Gewerkschaft, ihr Werden, Wesen und Wollen* (Stuttgart, 1930), pp. 23, 67–69.

[121] Heuss, *op. cit.,* pp. 203–6; Ganger, *op. cit.,* pp. 52–55.

[122] Heuss, *op. cit.,* pp. 221–23; Mayer, *op. cit.,* p. 36. The party's epitaph was written by Martin Wenck, *Die Geschichte der nationalsozialen Bewegung* (Berlin, 1904).

strength of nationalism among the German workers. Under nationalist leadership the German masses have been stirred to great political adventures, even to risk the calamities of war and to suffer the loss of national honor.

VII

Several elements directed Naumann into the liberal movement after the debacle of 1903.[123] There was the personal influence of Theodor Barth, editor of the liberal journal, *Die Nation,* and of Lujo Brentano, who deepened Naumann's understanding of economic questions.[124] Like the liberals Naumann had always believed in the value of personality, in individualism as the source of economic development, in German nationalism, and with them he admired science and technology as agents of progress. But German liberalism, divided into numerous factions under an embittered leadership, clung to Manchesterism and tended to peer into the past, toward the great days of 1871 and the constitutional battles of the sixties. For more than a decade before his decision to join the liberals, Naumann had been aware of the effect of great capital concentrations upon the individual and the ideal conditions of his freedom. While opposed to capital concentrations he had nonetheless continued to champion large-scale industry, both as a means of raising the worker's standard of living and as a necessary stage in the social development of Germany.[125] Into German liberalism Nau-

[123] Writing in 1913 about his approach to liberalism, Naumann commented that the center of his political outlook had been social politics, that he could be numbered among those who had been caught up in the labor movement about which he had found much truth in Karl Marx. If the Social Democrats had shown any understanding of the national issues affecting Germany, he could have embraced their program. Then, since the electoral experience of 1903 showed that there was no opportunity for a party standing between socialism and liberalism, he had embraced the second because its weaknesses appeared to be less threatening to the German future than those of the Social Democrats. From *Freiheitskämpfe* (Berlin, 1913), cited by Van Der Voet, *op. cit.,* p. 151.

[124] Brentano says that he succeeded in convincing Naumann in 1903 that the most important objective was to arouse a social spirit among the German bourgeoisie. Brentano, *op. cit.,* p. 229. Their friendship was seriously affected in 1907 by what Brentano regarded as Naumann's continued Pan-Germanism, and by a disagreement over the values of a liberal world. Cf. *ibid.,* pp. 276–81.

[125] Cf. *Was heisst Christlich-Sozial?,* pp. 22, 26–27; and *Das Blaue Buch von Vaterland und Freiheit,* pp. 198–99, in which Naumann asserts that unless the individual is protected against the demands of large-scale business the Germans will become "industrialized Chinese."

mann now began to infuse his view that the individual needed the state for protection against the tempests of economic fortune. Naumann's historical significance must be judged with respect to this, rather than by his contribution to the theory of democratic Caesarism, for he stands among the theorists who have revalued classic liberalism in terms of twentieth-century economics.[126] Such a compromise between liberalism and socialism was worked out in the second edition of one Naumann's most polished literary works, *Neudeutsche Wirtschaftspolitik*, published in 1906.[127] It retained many overtones from his earlier political experience and conveyed a deep understanding of the new age of industrialism and the masses.

Not until the *Daily Telegraph* interview (October 28, 1908) did Naumann lose faith in William II's talent for governing an expanding nation. Max Weber had long maintained that the Kaiser's character and ability were unequal to his task, and within two days after publication of the interview Naumann confirmed this judgment. Weber's letters to Naumann raged at the Kaiser's incompetence which was suddenly revealed as the chief danger to the German state.[128] The event made Naumann support the parliamentary principle more earnestly, although he was aware of the weakness of the legislature in German government, and had taken alarm at the unwillingness of the Reichstag to assume responsibility after the dreadful revelations of 1908.

Naumann was able to observe the Reichstag at firsthand, since he held a seat after 1907, and he had learned something about parliamentary strategy in attempting to organize that coalition of socialists and left liberals which he called "the bloc from Bebel to Bassermann." Notwithstanding his political career, Naumann found time to deal with problems of art and industrial design, and to write books about travel and popular religion. During the war his pen was at the service of his country, and the book for which he is

---

[126] See Neumann's conclusions on this point, *op. cit.*, pp. 20–23, 88–90. For some of Naumann's statements about the new liberalism, see *Die politischen Parteien*, pp. 91, 93–94, 99–107, 110.

[127] The second edition was virtually a new book, having 431 pp. as against only 113 pp. in the first edition of 1902. This expansion owed partly to the controversy, into which Naumann had entered with Gustav Schmoller at the 1905 meeting of the *Verein für Sozialpolitik*, over the advisability of the public control of cartels. This incident is summarized in Bowen, *op. cit.*, in the note on pp. 189–90.

[128] See particularly the letter of Nov. 12, 1908, Max Weber, *op. cit.*, pp. 455–57.

best known in the English-speaking world, *Mitteleuropa* (1915), described what he regarded as the German future, bound to the Continent as in Bismarck's time, but presiding over the economic and political destinies of the peoples in the heart of Europe. In the National Assembly which met at Weimar in 1919 he took a leading role. It was characteristic of his views of man and politics that he should be concerned with drafting the statement of fundamental rights to be guaranteed by the new constitution. Death robbed him of an opportunity to serve the republic, for hard work, anxiety, and wartime privations brought on a stroke only a few weeks after he had been acclaimed head of the newly formed Democratic Party.

HITLER AND THE REVIVAL OF GERMAN COLONIALISM

MARY EVELYN TOWNSEND

RECENT "REVELATIONS" afforded by the captured German documents and archives confirm the important role played by colonialism in the policy of Hitler's Third Reich. To be sure, these sources are as yet far from complete. They are supplemented, however, by the diaries, correspondence, and memoirs, so far published, of the leading figures of the period; and by the voluminous German colonial literature, especially that published between 1939 and 1945, which has now become accessible. Taken together, these materials all bear testimony to a definite and insistent shaping of Nazi policy towards a revival of the German Colonial Empire, lost at Versailles in 1919.

It is not at all surprising that an active colonial policy formed one of Hitler's objectives, since it coincided so well with his plans for a Greater Germany and also supplied him with another popular support for his regime. The interesting factor, however, is to discover the intensity and completeness of the colonial campaign within Germany, which was organized in so short a time, and the prominent part which colonial objectives played in the foreign policy of the Third Reich beginning with the year 1936.

I

Among the many failures of the ill-fated Weimar Republic, on which Hitler so ably capitalized to establish and strengthen his Third Reich, was its inaction and its timidity in regard to the lost German colonies. Throughout the immediate postwar years, 1919–1933, *"Kolonialraub"* (colonial robbery) and the *"Kolonialschuldlüge"* (colonial-guilt lies) had taken their place alongside *"Kriegschuld"* (war guilt) and *"Reparationsklaverei"* (reparations-slavery) in press, radio, schoolbooks, and in every instrument of propaganda, as burning and grievous resentments against the "infamous" Versailles *Diktat*. The government of the Weimar Republic, however, made no move to assuage the colonial grievance or even to cooperate with the movement in Germany.

Its negative policy was strengthened, furthermore, by adverse criticisms from the parties of the Left and even from some industrialists, merchants, and bankers from the parties of the Right. These critics maintained that colonies were more of a liability than an asset; that they were too costly; and that the government should first set its own house in order before embarking on colonial "ventures."[1] Indeed, in view of its stupendous financial and political difficulties, its internal disunion, its economic disorganization, its lack of respect and prestige abroad, the fact that the German Republic failed to adopt a definite colonial policy is not strange.

The entire responsibility, therefore, for keeping alive the "colonial idea" and for promoting a campaign directed towards the return of the colonies was relegated to the private initiative of the colonial enthusiasts and their organizations. These never ceased to prod the government into taking official action, but their efforts elicited no response.

To be sure, the leaders of the Weimar Republic, as individuals, often voiced their resentment of the colonial settlement of 1919 and joined in the general clamor to "right the colonial wrong."[2] Time and again, also, they stated the German claims and referred to the "colonial injustice" at important international meetings: at Locarno in 1925,[3] at Thoiry, and at the Paris Economic Conference of 1929.[4] But these complaints and abstract demands were not pressed beyond mere statements. The government, however, issued an official memorandum in 1924, demanding that at some future time Germany should be admitted to the mandate system; it protested to the Council of the League of Nations against Belgium's incorporation of her Mandate, Ruanda Urundi, formerly a part of German East Africa, into the Belgian Congo (1926); it appointed Dr. Kastle and later his successor, Dr. Ruppel, on the Mandates Commission

---

[1] W. Moock, *Hochland*, September 1928, pp. 561–71; A. Etscheit, *Deutsche Rundschau*, August 1928, pp. 111–18; A. Mendelssohn-Bartholdy, *Europäische Gespräche*, November-December, 1932, p. 310. See also the report on a questionnaire sent by the *Austwärtiges Institut* in Hamburg to government officials on the advisability of a German colonial policy; one half of the replies were opposed. *Europäische Gespräche*, November-December, 1927.

[2] G. Stresemann, *Essays and Speeches,* trans. by C. R. Turner (London, 1930), p. 69; his *Diaries, Letters and Papers,* ed. and trans. by E. Sutton (London, 1935–1940), II, 268.

[3] *Ibid.*, II, 182, 198.

[4] *Übersee und Kolonial-Zeitung*, April 1931, p. 75.

of the League of Nations, after Germany entered the League, although it failed to direct or support them in a strong policy. But these meager gestures constituted the extent of their activities.

On the other hand, the Weimar government ignored all the urgent demands of the *Kolonialgesellschaft:* that Germany's right to a mandate be included in the discussions at Spa (1920), at Locarno (1925), and as a condition to Germany's entrance into the League in 1926[5]; that the return of the colonies be considered with the whole reparations question, in the revision of the Dawes Plan and in the acceptance of the Young Plan; that the colonial issue be discussed at the Hague Conference in 1929[6]; and that official, decisive action be taken against the rumored plans of England and France to annex their mandates.[7] Likewise it failed to include the colonies in the agenda of the Lausanne Conference in 1932, despite Chancellor Brüning's promise to do so.[8] Finally, the Weimar government neglected to establish any official colonial bureau or agency. In short, its attitude during the years 1919–1933 may be described as one of enforced, albeit unwilling, avoidance of the colonial question and the colonial movement itself, therefore, was entirely unofficial.

The unofficial agencies, however, thrown back upon their own resources, proved to be as active and as enthusiastic regarding colonialism as the government was inactive and cautious. Ably led by the *Kolonialgesellschaft,* the parent colonial association, which embraced some 25,000 members during the 1920's, the movement effectively promoted the "colonial idea." Lectures, school programs, movies, radio, exhibits, and special publications were all devoted to that one end. Schools for the training of settlers, administrators, and other colonial personnel for nonexistent colonies, such as the *Kolonialinstitut* at the University of Hamburg, the *Kolonialschule,* Wilmersdorf, at Witzenhausen, and schools for nurses and teachers, were supported and crowded. Scientific research into all matters pertaining to colonial life, such as native dialects, customs, diseases, soils, plants, and the like, was pursued continually in the *Tropeninstitut* in Hamburg, the Seminary of Oriental Study at the University

---

[5] *Die Arbeiten der Deutschen Kolonialgesellschaft, Jahresbericht* (1932), p. 5.
[6] *Ibid.,* pp. 5–6.
[7] *Übersee und Kolonial-Zeitung,* August 1930.
[8] *Übersee und Kolonial-Zeitung,* July 1932, p. 149.

of Berlin, and elsewhere. Colonial congresses met, "colonial week" was celebrated each year at Berlin or Hamburg, appropriate ceremonies commemorated the birthday of the German colonial empire, April 24, 1884, monuments were erected to colonial pioneers, and tourist parties began to visit the former German colonies when opened to them by the mandatory powers. Literature and propaganda in the shape of colonial histories, treatises, novels, pamphlets replete with statistics, magazine and newspaper articles poured from the press, telling the Germans more about their former colonies than they knew when those lands were German.

Supplementing the *Kolonialgesellschaft* was the work of many smaller colonial organizations such as the *Kolonialkriegerdank* (Colonial Veterans Society), the *Reichsverband der Kolonialdeutschen und Kolonialinteressen* (Society of German Colonials and Friends), the *Frauenbund der Deutschen Kolonialgesellschaft* (Woman's Auxilliary of the Colonial Society), the *Frauenverien vom Rotem Kreutz für Deutsche über See* (Women's Branch of the Overseas Red Cross), and the *Überseeklub Hamburgs*.

Thus, when Hitler assumed control in 1933, he found ready to hand a considerable bloc of public opinion, organized, united, and actively focussed upon a goal, the recovery of the lost colonies; but, like so many similar groups within the Republic, utterly frustrated by governmental inaction. Not insensitive to the unappeased yearnings of such a close-knit and articulate sector of the populace, the *Führer* immediately channeled its emotion and its organization into his own regime's support and assumed official control. Part of the general *Gleichschaltung,* his action was easier for and more welcome to this group than to many others which met the same fate, because its objectives coincided so well with those of the National Socialist Party. The colonialists, moreover, belonged for the most part to the parties of the Right; their opponents were found in the parties of the Left. Both colonialists and Nazis suffered from an intense nostalgia; they writhed under the "loss of territories," the "disgrace of disarmament," the "colonial lies"; and, as a goal of foreign policy, they both strove for "revisionism."

Just as National Socialism won strong support and acceptance in Germany by giving jobs to the jobless, by replacing an inferiority complex by the "master race" psychology, by substituting union for division of parties, so it likewise added considerably to its popularity by giving to an unofficial and frustrated colonial movement the backing and strength of official support and control. In so doing, Hitler cemented the adherence to the Third Reich of a large group of colonial enthusiasts, as well as silenced a considerable number of those who were opposed both to his policies and to further colonial adventures. Among the latter were, of course, the Communists and the Social Democratic party, which, despite the favorable attitude of some of its leaders like Noske, maintained its consistent opposition to colonialism. To crush these hostile elements in the Reich naturally served Hitler's ends only too well.

Having attempted to show in the foregoing survey the part, even though inconsiderable, which the colonial issue played in contributing to the establishment of the Third Reich, the analysis of its fortunes during the years 1933–1942 can proceed forthwith. Two roads of inquiry must be pursued: first, the character of the internal leadership and the technique employed in the revival of colonialism in Germany itself; and, second, the part played by the colonial issue in Hitler's foreign policy and in his relations with other states.

II

To peruse all the many books, pamphlets, theses, and the like on the subject of colonies which poured from the Nazi-controlled press, especially between the years 1936–1944, one would conclude that Hitler had from 1933 onwards been the active and vigorous champion of a colonial policy. For these publications all maintain the same consistent thesis that the Third Reich took over the colonial movement in its unofficial enthusiasm and its official weakness in 1933 and then led it steadily on with ever-increasing fervor and zeal until the recovery of the colonies became one of the objectives of World War II.

The record, however, reveals a different story. When Hitler seized power in 1933, he first made sure, as we have seen, of absolute control of the colonial movement and its activities, as he did of every other element in the country. He achieved this by two decrees: first, the union, on October 6, 1933,[9] of all the many colonial societies (see

[9] H. Nachrodt, *Der Reichskolonialbund* (Berlin, 1933).

above), including even the venerable parent organization, *Kolonialgesellschaft,* whose president was the distinguished Dr. Heinrich Schnee, former governor of German East Africa, into one new organization called the *Reichskolonialbund* (RKB); and, second, the establishment on May 5, 1934, of the *Reichskolonialpolitisches Amt,*[10] a centralized government bureau. This was a Nazi resurrection of the old imperial *Kolonialamt* which had died in 1919. Its province was to direct all political and economic policies of the colonial movement, the press, education, and propaganda activities. It was to work in close co-operation with the *Reichskolonialbund* and to act as a liaison between it and the government. At its head was appointed the colorful Ritter von Epp, a leader in the military circles close to Hitler. His record shows that Hitler could be sure of him: a hero of World War I, he fought the Spartacists in Dortmund in 1919, joined the NSDAP in its early years, represented it in the Reichstag in 1928 and was made leader of the *Kolonialreferat* of the National Socialist party in 1932. At the close of Hitler's first year of control, therefore, the first steps towards the *Gleichschaltung* of the colonial movement had been taken.

Beside assuming command of all the machinery of the colonial movement, the National Socialist government then stretched out its hand to direct its major activities and bring them under governmental direction. This was particularly manifest in its seizing the direction of the Colonial Jubilee organized by the *Kolonialgesellschaft* in 1934 to commemorate the fiftieth anniversary of the founding of the German Colonial Empire on April 24, 1884. The formal invitations to the three major national celebrations held respectively on April 24, June 14, and October 3, were a summons to "a new struggle in the spirit of the new Germany," and closed with *"Heil* Hitler"; the programs stated that they were arranged in consultation with the propaganda minister, Herr Goebbels; and the government issued special postage stamps, bearing the portraits of the four colonial pioneers, Lüdderitz, Peters, Nachtigal, and Wissman.[11] By 1934, therefore, the complete National Socialist control of the colonial movement had been established, as was essential to the totalitarian government and its security. No movement, whatso-

---

[10] *Die Arbeiten der Deutschen Kolonialgeschaft, Jahresbericht* (1934), pp. 14–15.
[11] *Der Koloniale Kampf,* May 15, 1934.

ever, let alone the colonial, with its scores of adherents, could be permitted to function independently. Beyond the setting-up of this machinery for control and direction, however, the record can show nothing active and aggressive undertaken in the colonial field by the Third Reich for at least three years.

It is true that the *Führer* had demonstrated from the very beginning of his party that he was interested in colonialism. In the original program of the NSDAP (1920), point 3 read: "We demand lands and territories [colonies] for the nourishment of our people and for settling of our superfluous population."[12] When this idea was expanded in *Mein Kampf,* on the other hand, the emphasis was placed upon a sound territorial policy inside Europe rather than upon colonies and trade.

> Instead of a sound territorial policy inside Europe, our political leaders have preferred one of colonies and trade.... There can only be sense in our foreign policy if it offers opportunity for extending the space which our people inhabit in Europe. For acquisition of colonies will not solve the question, nothing in fact but acquisition of territories for settlement which extend the area of the mother country itself.... We have finished with the pre-war policy of colonies and trade and are going over to the land policy of the future.[13]

Hitler further confirmed the above point of view in a statement regarding his party's principles (1931),[14] which definitely indicated eastern and middle Europe as the future goal of German expansion, the object being a compact German state in Europe, politically and economically independent. He also stressed the necessity of Germany's recovering her political might in Europe before colonies were thought of.... Dr. Lindquist, then president of the *Kolonialgesellschaft,* commented upon this statement in July 1932 before Hitler assumed power, as follows: "This is doubtless a beautiful objective but one never to be realised.... We must cling to our original goal, .. not political power at the sacrifice of colonies, but political might and colonies."[15]

The apparent contradiction of the *Führer's* attitude towards colonialism gave serious concern to all its advocates in Germany as

---

[12] G. Feder, *Das Program der N.S.D.A.P.* (München, 1932).
[13] A. Hitler, *Mein Kampf* (1930 ed., London, 1930), pp. 741–43.
[14] *Die Arbeiten des Deutschen Kolonialgesellschaft, Jahresbericht* (1931), pp. 9–10.
[15] Interview with Dr. Lindquist, July 9, 1932, and letter to the author, July 29, 1932.

he assumed power. They were able to find some comfort in his encouraging statements to British news correspondents that: "Germany required colonies as much as any other power"[16]; "Germany had by no means abandoned her colonial aspirations"; and, "The colonial problem must be justly solved."[17] Furthermore, their new *Führer* at least did not contradict Dr. Schnee, the prominent colonial leader, who hailed the Nazi government in March 1933 as: "The dawn of a new era, from which we may expect the final attainof our colonial goal."[18]

Yet, on the other hand, contrary to these colonial hopes, there ensued during the first three years of the Third Reich no implementation of any statements favorable to a colonial policy. Quite the contrary was the case. Hitler made no mention of colonies in his speech at Potsdam when he assumed power. His government afforded no support to Hugenberg, Minister of Economics, when he pleaded for the return of the German colonies at the World Economic Congress in June 1933; and, in August 1934, he declared in an interview with Mr. Ward Price of the *London Daily Mail* that: "Germany did not want colonies; the former African colonies were an expensive luxury."[19]

In the light of all this conflicting evidence two major conclusions may be drawn. First, it is obvious that Hitler, exactly like Bismarck in a similar situation in the 1870's, was temporizing with the colonial issue for reasons of policy both foreign and domestic. Evidently he really favored colonies, but, in accordance with the plans so clearly expressed in *Mein Kampf,* he wished to avoid antagonizing Britain, at least until he had reached some understanding on the naval question and perhaps until he had reoccupied the Rhineland as well; and, in Germany, he had first to put his own house in order and establish his absolute supremacy. In short, he was merely waiting until he could secure sufficient power and prestige both abroad and at home to launch a successful colonial policy. As in the case of Bismarck, Hitler's ensuing record in regard to colonies assuredly confirms this hypothesis.

A second explanation of the *Führer's* apparently wavering policy

---

[16] *Daily Mail,* Feb. 11, 1933.
[17] *Sunday Express,* Feb. 12, 1933.
[18] *Der Koloniale Kampf,* April 15, 1933.
[19] *Daily Mail,* August 5, 1934.

lies in the division of opinion among the Nazi leaders themselves. Many of them, such as Rosenberg and Darré, advocated expansion in Europe. They represented the school of so-called *Geopolitik* which taught the necessity of political and economic autarchy within Europe. Later, these *Geopolitikers* reconciled their teachings with the need for colonial expansion, as we shall observe, but during the early years they opposed it. On the other hand, the more militant Nazis, like Goering and von Epp, always advocated colonialism, and their opinion gradually gained ground, but did not gain control until the year 1936. We are led to conclude, therefore, in the light of this record, that the Nazi writers appear to be in error when they claim a consistent colonial policy of steady activity for the Third Reich beginning in 1933. On the contrary, the first three years of Hitler's rule, aside from the assumption of command and direction of the colonial movement, which formed part of the general *Gleichgeschaltung,* record no official promotion of the colonial idea whatsoever.

III

As the year 1936 unrolled, however, the picture of colonial activity within Germany underwent a complete change. An ever-increasing promotion policy, both at home and abroad, replaced the passivity of the earlier years.

The first evidence within the Reich was manifest in the perfecting of governmental machinery controlling the colonial movement. This began to display all those ramifications and elaborations characteristic of every department under totalitarian control, such as labor, education, industry, fine arts, recreation, and all the rest. Already, as we have seen, there existed the *Reichskolonialpolitisches Amt* (1934) under Ritter von Epp, and the *Reichskolonialbund* (1933)—a merger of all the colonial societies under the veteran *Kolonialgesellschaft*—with Dr. Heinrich Schnee at its head. Now, in June 1936, the *Reichskolonialamt* replaced the former as a full-fledged government bureau with Ritter von Epp as Colonial Minister[20]; and a *Reichskolonialbund,* purged of all the organizations hitherto constituting the merger (even the *Kolonialgesellschaft* was dissolved) replaced the latter, also with Ritter von Epp at its head.[21]

[20] *Deutsche Kolonial-Zeitung,* October 1936.
[21] *Ibid.,* July 1936, pp. 167–68.

Symbolic of these changes, the swastika made its appearance upon the colonial flag.

The new *Reichskolonialbund* was described as a *Kolonialvolksbund* and the only valid colonial association in the nation. It was organized into two major organs: the *Kolonialrat* and the *Ausschuss*. The former functioned in an advisory capacity to the *Kolonialamt* (Ritter von Epp), especially on matters of colonial economy, which became an object of special research to its variously designated sections. Twenty-seven members belonging to the old colonial movement and representing the state, the party, the intellectuals, the economy of the Reich, constituted its personnel, and its president was the last imperial Colonial Secretary, Dr. Lindquist. The *Ausschuss*, composed of members of the *Kolonialrat* and the *Gauleiters* of the various branches, made all the important decisions together with the Colonial Minister, met at least once a year, and maintained headquarters in Berlin, Munich, and Hamburg.

By 1939, the *Reichskolonialbund* was reported to number over 1,000,000 members, over 8,000 offices, 39 *Gau* organizations, 750 district and 6,809 local branches. It maintained a publishing center which distributed about 138 papers and pamphlets a month in Germany and to overseas Germans. Its chief publications were the *Kolonial-Zeitung, Kolonie und Heimat, Die Frau und die Kolonien,* a youth magazine, *Jumbo,* and *Deutscher Kolonialdienst,* a teaching manual. Its propaganda bureau was extremely active promoting lectures, exhibits, radio, movies, and every kind of mass media for colonies.[22]

Included in the *Reichskolonialbund* was a Women's Section which continued to support German schools and schoolhouses for German settlers in East Africa and Southwest Africa, the former German colonies. Also, it maintained a school in Germany near Bad Harzburg, where sons and daughters of German planters and farmers in the former colonies were educated and imbued with the "idea of the Greater Germany." Likewise, the *Gau Verband* in Düsseldorf maintained such a *Jugendheim* in Wupperthal. Assuredly, the Nazi government was supporting the colonial movement; the *Gleichschaltung* was complete.

It was the year 1936–1937, moreover, which marked the complete

[22] Nachrodt, *op. cit.*

surrender of the administration to colonialism and the projection of an aggressive campaign at home, and, as we shall later observe, abroad. A "wave of colonial consciousness" seemed to sweep the country and was reflected by the speeches of the government officials, the literature of the period, and by the extent of official propaganda.

Appropriately enough, Goebbels set the wave in motion in January 1936, when, opening the election campaign for the Reichstag, he asserted: "We hope for a solution of the colonial problem in the not too distant future. . . . But the time will come when we must demand colonies from the world."[23] He was followed by Dr. Schacht, Minister of Economics, who led the campaign both by speeches and articles based on Germany's poverty and urgent economic needs. "The possession of colonial raw materials and of raw material territories is essential for an industrial nation." He deprecated the "Open Door" in colonial territories as wholly insufficient for Germany, "which must have her own raw materials within her own currency sphere."[24]

Supplementing Schacht's economic arguments and setting forth their own, Goebbels, Goering, Ribbentrop, von Epp, Schlescher, and other official lights burst into a chorus of speeches during 1936–1937, demanding the return of the colonies on grounds of "justice," "equality," "moral right," "need of raw materials," and the like.[25] Even Hitler himself—who, as we have observed, made singularly few pronouncements on the subject prior to 1935–1936—now gave every evidence that he was thoroughly converted to colonial restoration. In a speech at Munich in January 1936, he asserted: "The white race is destined to rule. . . . By what right do nations possess colonies? By the right of taking them."[26] Throughout the year, he continually referred in his speeches to "Germany's poverty"; to the fact that the country "was bursting with population and ability." In August at the Great *Parteitag* at Nuremberg, he stressed the need of colonies[27]; in September, when launching the Four Year Plan at

[23] Speech reported in the *New York Times,* Jan. 17, 1936.
[24] *New York Times,* Jan. 17, 1936; H. G. Schacht, "Germany's Colonial Demands," *Foreign Affairs,* XV (January 1937), 223–34.
[25] *Germany's Claim to Colonies,* Royal Institute of International Affairs, Information Department Papers, No. 23 (2nd ed., London, 1939), pp. 30 ff.
[26] *Daily Telegraph,* Jan. 26, 1936.
[27] *New York Times,* Aug. 4, 1936.

the Party Congress, he made the reservation: "Nevertheless Germany cannot renounce her colonial claims"[28]; and, in February 1937, he assured the Reichstag: "The demand for colonies for our densely populated country will again and again be raised as a matter of course."

Accompanying the pronouncements of the leaders was an intensive official propaganda drive, reaching into the formal educational system of the Reich. For example, *The Nazi Primer,* after giving a brief history of the former colonies, closes by stating: "The German Reich will at all events never cease to demand the restoration of its colonies."[29] Machinery was set up to prepare all kinds of colonial material for the schools; some 341 lectures on the colonies were scheduled in higher schools and universities during 1936 alone; many doctoral theses selected the colonies as their subject; exhibits, plays, the radio, newspapers, magazines, brochures, and pamphlets all combined to promote "the spontaneous expression of the natural desire for the reacquisition of the colonies."[30]

IV

Turning now to the foreign policy of the Third Reich, we discover that colonial objectives became very apparent beginning with the year 1936, coinciding precisely with the domestic campaign described above.

There were, of course, many reasons why Hitler restrained his colonial demands before 1936 and why he selected that year for their debut. Like Bismarck, who refrained from initiating a colonial policy until 1884 while he was putting his house in order at home during the 1870's, so Hitler was engaged in consolidating the Third Reich throughout the first three years of his rule and in bringing Germany back to a place of quasi-equality with other nations. Furthermore, by and during the year 1936, he had succeeded in repudiating most of the "shames" of the treaty of Versailles: disarmament, reparations, the naval strictures, the Saar, the unoccupied Rhineland; only the restoration of the colonies remained. In German eyes, he was pursuing a brilliant foreign policy, espe-

[28] *Ibid.,* Sept. 11, 1936.
[29] *The Nazi Primer,* trans. by H. Childs (New York, 1938), p. 171.
[30] *New York Times,* Feb. 10, 1936.

cially when that policy was compared with the humiliating and frustrated efforts of the Weimar Republic. His successive triumphs in the Saar, in the Rhineland, in the Anglo-German Naval Treaty, in his repudiation of the Locarno Treaties, in his defiance of the League of Nations by leaving it, and in his formation of the Rome-Berlin Axis and his treaty with Japan during 1936—all gave him the essential prestige abroad. He had succeeded in restoring Germany to an important position among the European nations and now felt that he was in a position to embark upon colonial objectives in his foreign policy in order to eliminate "the last inequality that remained."

Foreshadowing this determined move toward the recovery of the colonies, Hitler injected the subject into his interviews with Sir John Simon and Anthony Eden, who came to Berlin in the spring of 1935 to discuss a "general settlement." At that time he made it plain that Germany had not abandoned her "intention to reopen the colonial question,"[31] which he proceeded to do later in the year in his so-called "peace speech" of May by demanding "full justice" in the colonial issue.[32] Later in the same year, 1935, he bluntly told Sir Eric Phipps, the British Ambassador, that Germany would not consider Britain's proposals for an air agreement until Germany obtained practical recognition of her demand for colonies.[33]

Fortified by these warnings to Britain and by the accompanying intense colonial campaign at home, Hitler assumed a bold stand in his demands during the years 1936–1937. He linked his claim for colonies with his so-called "peace plans," raised the solution of the colonial issue from the economic to the political plane, and made the restitution of the colonial empire a question of equality and of political prestige. In the memorandum handed the signatory powers to the Locarno Treaties in March 1936, he declared that Germany was ready to re-enter the League of Nations, "with the expectation that . . . by friendly negotiation the question of equality of colonial rights be cleared up."[34] Again, at the *Parteitag* in Nuremberg in

[31] *Deutschland-England 1933–1939. Die Dokumente des deutschen Fridenswillens.* Herausgegeben von F. Berber (Essen, 1940), pp. 65–66.
[32] *New York Times,* May 22, 1935.
[33] *New York Times,* Dec. 27, 1935.
[34] *Deutschland-England 1933–1939, op. cit.,* p. 104, clause 18.

September, he served notice on the world by insisting on Germany's "right to colonies."[35]

During these months of 1936, Hitler was also leading Germany out of its isolationism and into a *rapprochement* with Italy which culminated in the Rome-Berlin Axis, established by agreement of October 25, 1936. Based upon Germany's recognition of an Italian Ethiopia, the pact coincided with the new mood of the German government in regard to colonies and reinforced its demand for *Gleichberechtigung* in international circles. Whether or not Hitler was promised concessions in Africa, as was rumored at the time,[36] the colonial boldness of Mussolini inevitably served as a further stimulant to colonial objectives.

Results of Mussolini's example and a consequent growth in confidence are all too evident in the increasing audacity of Hitler's public utterances during 1937. In his speech to the Reichstag, January 30, 1937, he demanded the return of the colonies as a moral right and continued to harp upon the colonial issue in all his subsequent speeches that year, including those at the Nuremberg and other Party festivals.[37] So truculent and insistent were his claims that Anthony Eden took it upon himself to rebuke him from Geneva.[38] Indeed, emphasis upon colonial grievances and upon future German objectives to right them reached a crescendo at the end of 1937, especially after Mussolini's visit to Berlin in September. The visit further cemented the Axis before the world, and upon his return to Rome the *Duce* declared: "Germany must regain her place beneath the African sun. . . . It is necessary that a great people like the German people recover the position which is due it."[39] Hitler, therefore, could well afford to announce at the close of the year 1937: "The colonies are our lost property and the world will be obliged to return them."[40]

Accompanying these declared colonial objectives in foreign policy which, after all, appear somewhat vague in precise aim, were the specific plans drawn up and published during these years by the

---

[35] London *Times*, Oct. 26, 1936.
[36] *Ibid.*, Oct. 27, 1936.
[37] *The Speeches of Adolph Hitler*, ed. by N. H. Baynes (2 vols., London, 1942), II, 1343–44, 1358, 1364.
[38] *New York Times*, Oct. 5, 1937.
[39] *Ibid.*, Oct. 29, Nov. 1, 1937.
[40] *Ibid.*, Nov. 22, 1947.

professors and proponents of *Geopolitik*, who were working, of course, under government direction.

Beginning with the year 1936, significantly enough, the science of *Geopolitik* in Germany departed from its hitherto concentration upon expansion in Europe (which, it will be recalled, provided opposition to the colonialists)[41] and commenced to embrace colonial expansion. This was called, conveniently, an "enlarged" interpretation of *Geopolitik* to include colonies. "The German *Lebensraum* is too small without being supplemented by colonies," it was argued, and with true Teutonic thoroughness a new branch of *Geopolitik* was created, known as *Kolonialpolitik*, whose function was declared to be the "evaluation" of colonial areas.[42]

The results of the "evaluation" were startling, to say the least, but they provide a tangible background to Hitler's speeches and indicate the reality of his colonial aims. Africa was to be their major objective. French North Africa was the first territory in this hypothetical road of German colonial advance; then, apparently, a push down into Central Africa was contemplated; the securing of Dakar as a spearhead pointing towards the New World was to be undertaken; and, ultimately, the control of all of Africa was to be assured, for "only Germany can substitute continental unity for the existing colonial partition."[43] Any reference to a German navy in these projections of the new order in Africa is conspicuously lacking and for a very good reason. These geopolitical writers about *Kolonialpolitik* envisioned German control of the Mediterranean Sea and a Spanish land bridge to Africa. The proposed approach to the African colonies, in their view, lay across Spain, a Spain so strengthened by Germany as to be "a challenge to French imperialism in those waters" (the Mediterranean Sea). "Spain forms the only Bridge between Europe and Africa," they asserted, and they proceeded to speculate upon a tunnel under the Gibraltar Strait which would create an "Euafrican" land route.[44] It was significant that no specific territories were allotted Italy.

Another result of the "evaluation" of colonial territories by these specialists in *Geopolitik* was their concern over the islands in the

---

[41] See *supra*, p. 407.
[42] O. Maul, *Das Wesen der Geopolitik* (Berlin, 1936).
[43] D. Whittlesey, *German Strategy of World Conquest* (New York, 1942), p. 211.
[44] W. Pahl, *Das Politische Anlitz der Erde: Ein Weltpolitischer Atlas* (Leipzig, 1939).

vicinity of Africa. "The islands of the eastern Atlantic fit into the strategic picture to extend Germany's potential power far into the ocean."[45] Plans to gain control of these islands loomed large in their writings and contributed to the decision to enter the Civil War in Spain on the side of Franco; later, as we shall learn, they played an important part in the negotiations with Franco, in 1940, regarding his entrance into World War II on the side of the Axis. Admiral Raeder expressed the situation aptly when he said: "If ever the Vigo-Canaries-Azores triangle should be constituted and placed under a single military authority, the automatic consequences would be a complete reversal in the European situation and the relations with all other continents—a reversal in favor of the power which occupies the points of the triangle."[46]

The writings of the proponents of *Geopolitik* in its "enlarged" interpretation reached an unprecedented output in 1939. Besides many books and articles, magazines and newspapers published special sections and issues devoted to the subject.[47] The majority of this literature dealt with Africa so far as territorial acquisitions were envisioned. Territory in the Near and Middle East was apparently not desired for actual colonies, although a wholesale infiltration into these regions by German merchants, industrialists, technicians, and agriculturalists was contemplated. As for the Far East and the Pacific, where many of Germany's former colonies were located, it seemed to be generally recognized that they would fall into Japan's orbit. Help to Japan in her drive against the European colonial powers was, however, advised.

Another important factor in Hitler's foreign policy which indicated the reality of his colonial objectives may be found in the very material assistance the Third Reich extended to Germans in the former colonies. As we have observed, the colonial societies and ex-colonial officials had always kept in touch with and aided those Germans of the lost colonies who became stranded in the mandates of France and Great Britain in Africa. When Hitler's government

---

[45] Whittlesey, *op. cit.*, p. 216. See also E. Banse, *Unserer grossen Afrikaner* (Berlin, 1943); K. Haushofer, articles in *Zeitschrift für Geopolitik*, XII (1935), 443; XVI (1939), 781; XVII (1940), 395; XVIII (1941), 369.
[46] W. H. Carter, "Spain and the Axis," *Foreign Affairs*, XX (October 1941), 176.
[47] E. Obst, K. Sapper, *und andere*, "Spezialheft über die Kolonialfrage," *Zeitschrift für Politik* (1939), Heft 1, 2.

took over all the colonial societies in 1936, it began at once to accelerate these overseas activities. The colonial press in these areas received government subsidies; all the organizations of Germans therein, such as the *Bund* in East Africa and in Southwest Africa, were closely tied into the National Socialist Party groups which had been rapidly formed. The coalescence of Nazis and German colonists had the effect of activating and stimulating the aims of the latter towards ultimate recovery of the colonies. More money, also, was forthcoming for German economic projects, such as the government aid afforded the West African Plantation Company in former Togoland.

It was in Southwest Africa that the direct interference of Hitler's government on the side of the German nationals against the government of the South African Union became most apparent. In 1924–1925, the South African Parliament had extended naturalization to the 3,489 eligible Germans then making their home in Southwest Africa, all but 262 of whom had accepted it. For a time, these Germans co-operated with the South African members of the legislature, although they opposed the desire of the South Africans to incorporate Southwest Africa as a province into its own territory. This cleavage between Germans and South Africans became accentuated in 1934, after Hitler's rise to power, because of Nazi propaganda and organization: the German members resigned from the Legislative Assembly; the Nazi party was banned; and the Assembly passed a resolution for the incorporation of Southwest Africa into the Union, to be administered under the League as a fifth province of the Union but subject to the provisions of a League mandate. This resolution was never carried out, but created unrest among the German inhabitants, whose numbers had greatly increased, and stiffened their desire to recover the territory for Germany.

Further aroused by the German colonial propaganda of 1937, the Union of South Africa issued a proclamation prohibiting all aliens, including non-naturalized Germans, from belonging to any political organization and making it illegal for British subjects to take an oath of allegiance to any foreign political organization. The German government protested against these measures, while the Germans in Southwest Africa addressed a memorandum to the Mandate Commission at Geneva. In March 1938, notes were exchanged between Germany and the Union of South Africa: Germany maintained her claim to all her former colonies and disputed South Africa's contention that the legal status of Southwest Africa had been settled in 1923.[48]

V

Probably the most convincing proof of the reality of colonial objectives in Hitler's foreign policy is the reaction of Great Britain to his colonial drive both at home and abroad. During 1936–1937, the subject was debated constantly in the House of Commons and various propositions to meet Germany's demands for colonies were advanced with no success.

Action in England was precipitated by von Ribbentrop, Germany's ambassador to the Court of St. James, who introduced German colonial demands into his first speech to a British audience at a dinner for Anglo-German fellowship in December 1936. He seized the occasion to thunder against Germany's loss of colonies and to defend Germany's right to colonies. "The Führer sees now that the possession of colonies for the supply of raw materials on the one hand and for world trade on the other are the two most essential means of improving the standard of living of his people from the present subsistence level."[49]

Already alarmed by the German campaign for colonies and also by the German sympathizers in England, such as Lord Rennell, the Marquess of Lothian, Lord Mount Temple, and the Marquess of Londonderry, a group of Tories, headed by L. S. Amery, former Minister of Colonies in the Baldwin government (1924–1929), formed a committee to combat the transfer of any British mandates or cession of any British territory to Germany. Again and again the Baldwin government was questioned as to its "intentions" regarding the former German colonies under its control; these questions became more persistent as the colonial campaign in Germany grew louder and louder and the speeches of its leaders more and more demanding. Both Mr. Baldwin and J. H. Thomas, Colonial Minister, replied that the government contemplated no cession of man-

---

[48] *Germany's Claim to Colonies, op. cit.,* pp. 85–86; E. Noel-Buxton, *Monatsheft für Auswärtige Politik* (1938), Heft 5, 263.
[49] *New York Times,* Dec. 16, 1936.

dates, but they hedged their statements about with such cautious reservations as that: "They would not commit themselves to any settlement without giving the fullest opportunity for discussion with the House."[50] The critics remained unsatisfied, however, deplored the lack of firmness in the government, and demanded a pledge covering the future, which they failed to secure.

One reason (besides the general trend towards appeasement) for the British lack of firmness may be found in the voluminous and lively discussions of the colonial issue during 1936–1937. Official, semi-official, and lay circles of all kinds earnestly debated Germany's right to colonies as well as the measures which might be adopted to satisfy her. Parliamentary debates, editorials, magazine articles reveal that a considerable section of British opinion favored some kind of colonial adjustment to Germany's advantage.[51] Eminent Britishers, such as Viscount Cecil, Lord Snell, Sir Evelyn Wrench of the English Speaking Union, Lord Noel-Buxton, Lloyd George, Lord Plymouth, and others, all expressed their belief in a serious consideration of the problem in connection with a "general settlement." Viscount Samuel urged in the House of Lords the return of Germany's colonies along with the elimination of the "war guilt" clause[52]; Lord Crewe asserted: "I have never concealed my view . . . that the complete taking over of Germany's colonies by this country, and to some extent by others, was a radical error of judgment."[53]

On the other hand, accompanying almost all these expressions of sympathy with Germany's "moral" and sometimes "economic" right to colonies went a certain hesitation, a kind of disapproval of any practical solution. These hesitations included fear of Germany's "aggressive nationalism"; opposition to the "pooling of colonial possessions"; dislike of transferring "masses of Negroes back under German rule"; apprehension of the "military and naval uses to which Germany might devote" her returned colonies; fear for the "safety of the empire." In short, British opinion seemed to say: England wants to settle the colonial problem provided she loses

[50] *Ibid.*, April 24, 1936, Sept. 11, 1936, Feb. 14, 1937.
[51] *International Affairs* (January–February, 1938), p. 45; H. Nicolson, "Germany and the Colonies," *Fortnightly Review* (December 1937), p. 641; E. Noel-Buxton, "England and Germany," *Contemporary Review* (January 1938), p. 9.
[52] *New York Times*, Nov. 16, 17, 18, 1937.
[53] Lord Crewe in the House of Lords, Hansard, Feb. 16, 1938, col. 728.

nothing by it and, above everything, any concession must be part of a "general settlement."[54]

Besides discussing Germany's right to colonies, measures to be taken to satisfy or appease Germany were actively debated also. Foreshadowing some such compensation, Sir Samuel Hoare had set the ball rolling in his speech at Geneva, in September 1935, which offered a proposal for an international discussion of the redistribution of raw materials,[55] assuming the position that Germany's discontent was economic rather than political or territorial. Both Mr. Baldwin and Mr. Eden, the Foreign Minister, agreed with Mr. Hoare's proposals and, largely due to Britain's initiative, a Committee for the Study of Raw Materials was appointed by the League Council early in 1937. Its Report, published September 7, 1937, pointed out, first, that: "The total present production of all commercially important raw materials in all colonial territories is no more than 3 per cent of world production"; and, second: "The only general and permanent solution to the problem of commercial access [to raw materials] is to be found in a restoration of international exchanges on the widest basis."[56] The Report precipitated a widespread debate upon extending the "Open Door" to those colonies not covered by the Congo Basin Convention and the A and B Mandates. The British government took the position, however, that while it was ready to discuss with any country any proposals which such country thought likely to be of mutual benefit, it doubted that any modification of British or any other preferential system could provide an adequate remedy for "the difficulties of those countries which by maintaining exchange control find themselves at a disadvantage in obtaining imports of raw materials."[57] In other words, German autarchy was found to be incompatible with any "Open Door" policy.

It might be pointed out at this juncture that the colonial rivalry reflected in this Anglo-German debate, as well as the efforts of the British to effect some kind of colonial compromise, are reminiscent of the situation existing in 1911–1914 between Germany and Great

[54] *Germany's Claim to Colonies, op. cit.*, pp. 41–50.
[55] *New York Times*, Sept. 12, 1935.
[56] League Document, A27, 1937, IIB. Summary in London *Times*, Sept. 8, 1937.
[57] Statement of Anthony Eden in League Assembly, Sept. 20, 1937; *New York Times*, Sept. 21, 1937.

Hitler and German Colonialism 419

Britain. Then, as in 1936–1939, Germany was insisting that she was deprived of her just share of colonies and was bending every effort to increase that share. Then also, Great Britain, realizing to some extent the justice of Germany's claim and yet fearing intrusion upon her own preserves, had recourse to such conciliatory expedients as the Anglo-Portuguese treaty of 1913, the Anglo-German agreements over the Bagdad Railway of 1914, and even the sending of Lord Haldane to Berlin.

Other proposals to solve Germany's colonial demands for equality of status were to extend the mandate system to all colonies, and the very radical proposals to transfer all colonies as well as the present mandates to the administration of an international colonial service acting for the League of Nations, and to transfer actual territory to Germany either as a mandate or as sovereign territory. Needless to say, these last suggestions met with violent opposition, and the government turned them down.

Meanwhile the government was considerably embarrassed by the statements made by Mr. Pirow, Minister for Defense in South Africa, who claimed to have discussed the colonial question with members of the government in a visit to London and was reported to have stated: "Influential quarters in England feel there will be no permanent settlement of the colonial question unless Germany is given adequate territorial compensation in Africa."[58] Pirow then developed his own idea that while the possibility of Great Britain returning Tanganyika or Southwest Africa was not feasible, Germany might be appeased by giving her the Belgian or Portuguese possessions or parts of them. All these rumors in regard to Mr. Pirow were later categorically repudiated by Mr. Eden,[59] who also sought to discourage further parliamentary discussions of the colonial issue.

Despite official efforts, however, it was impossible to stifle discussion, especially in view of the intensification of German propaganda during 1936–1937 and the acerbity and virulence of the reaction to British propositions for colonial adjustment. The German leaders would have nothing of mandates, of the "Open Door," of any economic arrangements for international trade, nor any redistribution of raw materials. "The colonial problem cannot be solved

---

[58] London *Times*, July 15, 1936.
[59] *New York Times*, Dec. 22, 1937.

by arguments that a sufficient supply of raw materials can be assured to her by the policy of the 'Open Door.' "[60]

As the battle of words, charges, and counter-charges waxed stronger, the British government, or that part of it led by Neville Chamberlain and the "appeasement" group, made a conciliatory move: it sent Lord Halifax to Berchstesgaden to interview Hitler. Ostensibly, the object of his visit was to hunt with Goering at Karinhalle, but this proved a rather unsuccessful camouflage. On the eve of his departure both the *Manchester Guardian* and the *Evening Standard*,[61] published what claimed to be Germany's bases for negotiations as forwarded from Berlin through unofficial intermediaries. Among them appeared the proposed bargain: Germany to postpone colonial claims for six years; Great Britain to give her a free hand in Central Europe. The German official press furiously denied a deal.[62]

Lord Halifax's interview with Hitler undoubtedly included a discussion of the colonial issue and *der Führer* was asked to define his wishes.[63] His reply, repeated in his speech in Augsburg soon afterwards, demanded the restitution of the German colonies but suggested that the restitution could wait, could be postponed, in fact, "for five or six years."[64] There appears to exist no doubt that some conditions were stated, despite violent German denials. But not even the *Manchester Guardian* claimed that a deal was consummated.

The Halifax visit precipitated many questions and a sharp debate in Parliament. Chamberlain vigorously denied all the rumors concerning the visit; Lord Halifax discoursed upon the aspect of Anglo-German fellowship and upon the pleasures of his hunt with Goering[65]; while Anthony Eden categorically rejected in the House of Commons any intention of His Majesty's Government "to reach a settlement in the colonial field with Germany on the basis of a deal at the expense of other colonial powers."[66] Moreover, Britain

[60] Count von Krosigk, Minister of Finance, London *Times*, Sept. 13, 1937.
[61] *Manchester Guardian, Evening Standard*, Nov. 13, 1937.
[62] *Deutschland-England 1933–1939, op. cit.*, pp. 133–34.
[63] A. C. Johnson, *Viscount Halifax: A Biography* (London, 1941), pp. 432 ff.
[64] *Speeches of Adolph Hitler, op. cit.*, II, 1371. Cf. Sir Neville Henderson, *Failure of a Mission, 1937–1939* (London, 1940): "When I spoke to Hitler about colonies in March, 1938, his attitude was they might wait four, six or ten years" (pp. 64, 118).
[65] *Deutschland-England 1933–1939, op. cit.*, pp. 134–35.
[66] *New York Times*, Dec. 22, 1937.

and France agreed at a subsequent conference, held in London in November 1937, upon two major points in regard to Germany's increasingly persistent demands: first, that the issue was one which "could not be considered in isolation and would involve a number of countries"; and, second, that "Germany must be asked to give a *quid pro quo* if she is to receive any colonies,"[67] which would preferably entail her support of a "general settlement" providing security —a theme continually harped upon by Anthony Eden.

To these pronouncements and to the visible stiffening of the British mood, not unaffected by the Reich's attack on the Jews, Hitler replied: "The German colonies are not to be made the subject of bargaining," and also: "Germany is not interested in a general settlement, but in direct bilateral agreements."[68] Thus, during the opening months of 1938, the colonial issue became part of the struggle between the principles of collective security and unilateral or bilateral action. And when the latter triumphed with the split in the British cabinet and the resignation of Anthony Eden, the demand for the unconditional return of the colonies became stronger. Sweeping aside all proposed economic adjustments, Hitler declared in his famous speech of February 20, 1938:

The claim for Germany's colonial possessions will be voiced from time to time with increasing vigor .... Such claims cannot be averted by granting credits .... We do not want credits but a foundation to live .... I cannot allow that our natural claims shall be coupled with political business .... We do not want naïve assurances that we shall be permitted to buy what we need .... Such declarations are felt in our country to be only a mockery.[69]

Hitler further coupled his expression of contempt for Anthony Eden with his colonial demands, indicating his repudiation of Eden's many suggestions that a colonial settlement be part of a "general settlement," and also reflecting how Eden's disappearance from the political scene had strengthened his colonial policy. It was to be expected, therefore, that when von Ribbentrop presented the German conditions of Anglo-German *rapprochement* on the eve of the Austrian *coup*, "a recognition of Germany's colonial de-

---

[67] *Ibid.*, Dec. 1, 2, 1937.
[68] *Ibid.*, Dec. 6, 1937. See also *The New Statesman*, Nov. 27, 1937.
[69] London *Times*, Feb. 21, 1938; *Speeches of Adolph Hitler, op. cit.*, II, 1409–10.

mands"[70] should appear second in the list. With the success of the "cold *Anschluss*," Hitler's method of unilateral action overwhelmingly triumphed; the unconditional return of the colonies remained to be realized by the same principle.

The startling events of the year 1938 in Austria and Czechoslovakia pushed the colonial issue aside temporarily. It was briefly referred to by Hitler in the Godesberg conversations, September 22–23, and again in his speech at Munich, November 8, 1938. On both occasions Hitler appeared to have been so exalted by his triumph that he expected the colonies would soon fall in his lap, as Czechoslovakia was in the process of doing. For at Godesberg he remarked, *apropos* of his wish for British friendship: "There is one awkward question—the colonies—but that is not a matter for war . . . . there will be no mobilization about that."[71] And, feeling even stronger at Munich, he said: "The word understanding is somewhat incomprehensible to us, because we do not want anything from these men, except perhaps our colonies which were taken from us under false pretense. This, however, is not a matter to go to war about, but a question of justice."[72]

After Munich, however, the question emerged again in the field of international relations outside Germany, which had its inevitable impact upon the Reich's foreign policy. The effect of Munich, of course, was to alarm all the colonial powers, as they feared that further appeasement of the Third Reich very likely would be expressed in colonial concessions. This is made more than clear by the chorus from the colonial powers that they "intend to keep what they have." Every one of them, including the mandatory powers, were heard from[73]: Great Britain, France, Belgium, Portugal, Australia, New Zealand, the Union of South Africa. Until this date, any statement on colonies had been rare in France, but now resolutions opposing any curtailment of the French Empire were passed by the party congresses of the Radical Socialists, the *Alliance Démocratique,* the *Démocrates Populaires,* and the *Fédération Républicaine.* On November 15, 1938, M. Bonnet, after a conversation with MM. Deladier and Reynaud, stated: "France is not prepared to

---

[70] London *Times*, Feb. 21, 1938.
[71] Hansard, Sept. 28, 1938, col. 22.
[72] London *Times,* Nov. 9, 1938.
[73] Italy, Japan, and Spain, of course, excepted.

cede any of her colonies"; while on November 17 M. Deladier issued a communiqué:

The Government did not await the campaign about colonial questions now in progress to make known their attitude towards this problem. Some weeks have now passed since they made it known that France will oppose any inroads upon her Colonial Empire and that she will resolutely maintain the integrity of her possessions as constituted at the end of the world war.[74]

Matching the French statement, Colonial Minister McDonald climaxed the many speeches made in England inside and outside Parliament by finally rejecting any idea of returning the German colonies.[75]

Throughout this period from Munich to the outbreak of war in 1939, colonial objectives became more and more persistent in German foreign policy and were announced with an audacity never hitherto manifested. Attention has already been called to the fantastic plans of the writers in *Geopolitik,* and references in the German press to Germany's claims were frequent and full of confidence. Ritter von Epp declared that: "The German colonies must be handed back or compensation secured elsewhere." Hitler threatened that: "Germany wishes to negotiate, but if others decline to grant our rights, we shall secure them in a different way."[76]

Confidence in the eventual recovery of the colonies was likewise expressed in the undiminished propaganda at home, in the revival of the Colonial Institute at Hamburg, the establishment on October 30, 1938, of a new School of Colonial Politics at Ladeburg to provide a training center for colonial administrators "against the day of justice," and in the report that Dr. Schacht had established a special department of the *Reichsbank* to study the preparation of new colonial currencies; as well as in the outpouring from the Nazi press of all kinds of colonial atlases, handbooks, picture books, and tables of statistics.[77]

---

[74] London *Times,* Nov. 17, 1938.
[75] *Deutschland England 1933–1939, op. cit.,* pp. 177–78.
[76] London *Times,* Nov. 9, 1938.
[77] This outpouring of colonial literature continued into the War. The apparently certain expectation that the African colonies would be won back led the German press to foster the "colonial idea" by all kinds of Special Colonial Sections. See the *Muenchner Neuesten Nachrichten,* the *Bremer Zeitung,* the Berlin monthly *Volk und Reich, Deutscher Lebensraum,* and many others.

Another disturbing factor in colonial affairs, responsible at once for more frequent enunciation of German claims and the universal counterclaims of the colonial powers, was the second appearance in Europe of Mr. Pirow, Defense Minister from South Africa. At the end of the year 1938, he made a tour including Berlin, Lisbon, Brussels, Rome, London. Ostensibly, his object was to discuss inter-African trade, air services, and defense with those countries having colonies, mandates, or colonials in Africa. His visits, however, led to considerable speculation and anxiety as to the likelihood of his purpose being to discuss the possibility of "colonial bargains" whereby Germany might be compensated with territories in Africa other than the return to her of Tanganyika and Southwest Africa, which the Union of South Africa vigorously opposed.[78]

There exists no proof of such conversations but, nevertheless, Pirow's visits were accompanied by more declarations from the colonial powers in their former tone of "what we have we keep." Even Portugal in the person of Salazar, the Prime Minister, announced: "Great Britain under the treaties of alliance undertook to defend them [our claims]. France does not want them and Herr Hitler has declared that he wants only the former German colonies. . . . No discussion of Portuguese colonial sovereignty is admissible."[79] Also, from the other side—the "Have Nots"—came the following comments, *apropos* of Pirow's visits: "This problem is vital and actual. . . . It is not only one of raw materials, but of positions, of moral and political prestige; in short, of genuine equality of rights between the Powers. It is a problem of order and justice. As such, it appears legitimately for Germany. It is also live and actual for Italy."[80] Germany, of course, also was heard from, as we have already seen, and even the London *Times* pointed out that whatever Pirow had to present to Germany as a substitute for Southwest Africa, it "could not be harmonised with the German colonial claims set forth in Herr Hitler's speeches."[81]

VI

The final and most convincing proof of Hitler's colonial objectives can now be found in his diplomatic dealings with allies and

[78] London *Times*, Oct. 17, 26, Nov. 28, 1938.
[79] London *Times*, Oct. 17, 1938.
[80] Signor Gayda in the *Giornale d'Italia*, Nov. 29, 1938.
[81] London *Times*, Nov. 28, 1938.

enemies in the preliminaries to and during the course of World War II. The pattern of these colonial objectives, which may now be assumed to constitute one minor contributory cause of World War II, was carefully and precisely defined as early as 1937. In November of that year when, it will be recalled, the Anglo-German debates on colonies were at their height, Hitler summoned his six chiefs of staffs, Blomberg and Fritsch of the Army, Raeder of the Navy, Goering of the Air Force, and Foreign Minister Neurath, to a secret meeting in the Berlin *Reichs* Chancellery. Here among other plans they discussed the chances of recovering the former German colonies, and Hossbach, Hitler's *aide-de-camp,* took it all down in what have now become known as the Hossbach *Minutes.*[82] Hitler, addressing his chiefs, declared: "Britain is in no position to cede any of her colonial possessions now, owing to the resistance [to such cession] which she has been receiving from the Dominions[83] and also because she has lost prestige in Africa because of Mussolini's conquest of Ethiopia. . . . A return of East Africa cannot now be expected." He then continued to point out that Britain, being so hard pressed, could, at best, only be able to meet the German demand for colonies by ceding to Germany colonies not now in British hands, such as Portuguese Angola. *Der Führer,* as well as his companions, appeared to be not at all disturbed at this prospect. Apparently, it seemed quite correct to them that England would rob Portugal or any other small power to pay her "colonial debt" to Germany. Finally, Hitler concluded by saying:

A serious discussion regarding the return of the colonies could only be considered at a time when Britain is in a state of emergency and the German Reich is strong and well-armed. The *Führer* does not share the opinion that the British Empire is unshakeable. It is held together by power politics . . . . The German question can be solved only by force.[84]

Consistently pursuing this objective, Hitler even introduced the colonial theme into those hectic last-minute conversations with Neville Henderson, the British Ambassador in Berlin, when Britain was seeking to prevent Germany from attacking Poland. On August 25, 1939, summoning Henderson to an interview, Hitler

---

[82] *Nazi Conspiracy and Aggression* (8 vols., Washington: Government Printing Office, 1946–47), III, 295–305; P. Mendelssohn, *Design for Aggression* (New York, 1946), pp. 17–18.

[83] *Supra,* p. 422.

[84] Mendelssohn, *op. cit.,* pp. 19–20.

declared that he had been turning things over in his mind and hoped that after all an understanding between Germany and Britain might be possible, as he had always desired. He would now like "to make a move as regards England that would be as decisive as the move in regard to Russia. . . . The German-Polish question must be solved and will be solved," but he was prepared to approach England once more with a large and comprehensive offer. This was: "He [Hitler] accepts the British Empire and is ready to pledge himself personally for its continued existence and to place the power of the German Reich at its disposal, if his colonial demands are fulfilled." If the British government would, he continued, consider these ideas, it would be a blessing for both countries. "If it rejects these ideas, there will be war." To this somewhat surprising and vague offer the British government replied on August 28, 1939: "These proposals are, of course, stated in a very general form and would require a closer definition, but His Majesty's Government is fully prepared to take them, with some additions, as subjects for discussion. . . . But first, there must be a settlement of the differences between Germany and Poland."[85]

Even during the war itself, we find that Hitler could give thought and planning to his colonial aims. This care for the recovery of the colonies is clearly apparent in his negotiations with his ally Russia (until 1941), and with his potential ally, Spain. The conversations with Russia considered future territorial settlements and spheres of interest after the war was won. These exchanges of aims and objectives were prepared for at a preliminary meeting of von Ribbentrop and Molotov and the finishing touches were supplied, when on November 12, 1940, Hitler and Molotov discussed the "long-range delimitations of interest." The *Führer* was of the opinion that it would be advantageous for Russia, Germany, Italy, and Japan to establish such plans now, that is, in 1940. Therefore he proceeded forthwith to earmark again Central Africa in the region of the former German colonies for Germany, and stated that he had exchanged views already with Spain and Italy in order to set up a kind of a Monroe Doctrine for Africa and to adopt a new, joint

[85] German Foreign Office, *Documents on the Events Preceding the Outbreak of the War* (New York, 1940), pp. 469, 477 ff.

colonial policy by which each of the powers concerned would claim for itself only as much colonial territory as it could utilize.[86]

The basis of these conversations appears to have been the Draft of an Agreement between the States of the Three-Power Pact—Germany, Italy, Japan—and the Soviet Union which bears no date except November 1940. A Secret Protocol of this Draft Treaty reads: "Germany declares that, apart from her territorial revisions in Europe to be carried out at the conclusion of the Peace, her territorial aspirations center in the territories of Northern and Northeastern Africa."[87] Hitler also stated: "Germany has no interests in Asia other than general economic and commercial ones. In particular, she has no colonial interests there. Germany recognizes that possible colonial interests there would fall to Japan." All of these plans, it will be remembered, coincide with those of the writers on *Geopolitik* as described above.[88]

Hitler's reference, in talking with Molotov, to an exchange of views with Spain and Italy referred specifically to the negotiations which he had been carrying on with Spain since September 1940 in regard to Spain's entrance into the war. Flushed with victory in the fall of that year and with his control of France, he could afford to adopt an imperious tone with Spain. Spain had presented as her conditions of entering the war on Germany's side: "Fulfillment of a set of national territorial demands: Gibraltar, French Morocco, that part of Algeria colonized and largely inhabited by Spaniards (Oran), and further the enlargement of Rio de Oro and of colonies in the Gulf of Guinea."[89] Germany was not hospitable to these demands although Serano Suñer, Spanish Minister of the Interior, had characterized Morocco, in his conversations with Hitler regarding Spanish *Lebensraum,* as Spain's natural expansion objective.[90] With this Hitler had agreed, but added that Spain's securing Morocco depended on "the future configuration of the relationship

---

[86] *Nazi-Soviet Relations. Documents from the Archives of the German Foreign Office as Released by the Department of State,* ed. by J. Sontag and J. Beddie (New York, 1948), pp. 221, 231.

[87] *Ibid.,* p. 257.

[88] *Supra,* pp. 413–14.

[89] United States Department of State, *The Spanish Government and the Axis,* Official German Documents (Washington, 1946), p. 3.

[90] *Ibid.,* p. 11.

of Europe and Africa." Here, on the one hand, Germany had economic interests in Africa—she wanted to buy raw material and sell finished goods; and, on the other hand, there was the problem of "security for her African future in Central Africa." For under certain conditions "a great danger could threaten her security there." Enlarging upon this danger Hitler said:

> It was not out of the question that England and France would try to entice America to the Azores.... England could in this way gain a foothold in the islands stretching out in front of Africa ... whereby a very unpleasant situation would arise.... Therefore, it was necessary to establish defensive strong points in the islands in good time.[91]

Among the islands, Madeira, the Canaries, and those off Cape Verde were mentioned, to all of which Suñer agreed.

Again, at the meeting between Hitler and Franco at Hendaye, October 23, 1940, the *Führer,* referring again to the Spanish territorial demands, told the *Caudillo* in no uncertain terms that: "Spanish desires and the French hopes were obstacles in the path of setting up a large front against England." Moreover, the French, he said, "knew they had to sacrifice something" in the final peace. "They counted on losing the German colonies." To further emphasize the German position, Hitler wrote to Franco, February 6, 1941, concerning the possible entrance of Spain into the war:

> Spain has advanced very great territorial claims for the fulfillment of which the *Duce* and I have declared ourselves ready in every degree which could at all be reconciled with an acceptable new arrangement of the African colonial possessions for Europe and its countries. And I may point out that in this struggle, until now, first Germany and then Italy have suffered the most prodigious blood sacrifice, and that both, in spite of that, make very modest claims.[92]

The "modest claims" here referred to were set forth as point 3 in Germany's conditions, in the event that Spain were to enter the war: " To assure Germany a great colonial area which was not, however, an area for settlement, of which she possessed enough on the European continent, but instead, a matter of raw material colonies."[93]

[91] *Ibid.,* pp. 12–13.
[92] *Ibid.,* p. 32.
[93] *Ibid.,* pp. 12–13. Unfortunately, states the footnote to this portion, the next two paragraphs were illegible because of broken microfilm and so omitted.

It will be seen from these negotiations with Spain that the pattern of the German *Geopolitik* was emerging. Again it will be observed that Italy's colonies in Africa were not definitely allocated and that Germany intended to control the Western Mediterranean and Gibraltar.

> The military cooperation of Germany in the war in Spain will consist of,
> 1. Immediately expelling [enemy] ships from the Straits,
> 2. Making available a small troop of specialists with special weapons by which Gibraltar could be quickly overcome.[94]

To Suñer's weak protest that Spain could look after Gibraltar, the *Führer* replied: "The question of the capture of Gibraltar has been studied exactingly by the Germans. . . . A Commission of German officers had gone to Spain to examine the situation on the spot." Perhaps one reason why Franco did not openly enter the war on Hitler's side was that he could not accept Hitler's colonial aspirations in Africa, in the islands of Africa, in Gibraltar, and in the Western Mediterranean Sea.[95]

A general impression seems to prevail that Hitler was not interested in colonies. Mr. N. H. Baynes, editor of Hitler's speeches, goes so far as to say: "It is clear that Hitler has little interest in colonies; he desires only to keep alive the claim to the return of Germany's colonial possessions."[96] The present essay is offered in contradiction of that assumption—a record which further German documents, not yet available, may confirm even more strongly.

Whatever verdict the future may pronounce upon Hitler's revival of German colonialism, history would seem to contribute its judgment by means of analogy. Comparison of German colonialism during the era of William II—which had fateful consequence to Germany and the rest of the world—with the same phenomenon under Hitler yields some striking points of similarity as well as of contrast. Both periods are characterized by a compelling drive for colonial expansion manifested in the lively activity of the colonialists and their organizations within Germany, as well as in the government's conduct of international relations and diplomacy.

To cite only some main points: Africa constituted a major goal

---

[94] *Ibid.*, p. 12.
[95] For other reasons, see C. H. J. Hayes, *Wartime Mission in Spain* (New York, 1945), pp. 62–66.
[96] *Speeches of Adolph Hitler, op. cit.*, II, 1875.

during both eras, although under William II the main responsibility for the *Mittel-Afrika Deutsch* drive lay with the German colonialists and those members of the Foreign Office, led by von Bülow and von Holstein, who "rapped the table" in the three Moroccan crises; William II himself subordinated colonial gains in Africa to his Near Eastern projects and his diplomatic efforts to construct his Continental alliance. In contrast, Hitler sharply focussed his attention upon Africa and the Mediterranean Sea, being able, unlike William II, to bring about complete unity of German aims and policy. Moreover, where Hitler centered his efforts upon Africa, William II expended his greatest energies and ambitions upon the Near and the Far East—the latter an area which Hitler conceded to Japan. Both Hitler and William II were mainly interested in economic penetration and exploitation, rather than in territorial annexation, in the Near East.

Again, as has already been suggested, German international relations were significantly affected by colonialism during both these periods of her history. The desire to win and to hold Great Britain as an ally imposed considerable colonial restraint upon the Germany of both eras, as evidenced by Hitler's caution throughout 1933–1936, and William II's conciliatory negotiations and treaties with Britain in 1913–1914. Lord Haldane's visit to Berlin in 1912 and Lord Halifax's attempt to come to some colonial understanding with Hitler offer a further parallel. Hitler, however, departed from William II's pattern of action when he felt satisfied as to Germany's strength.

Finally, it may be said of William II that he began his colonial campaign with all the ruthlessness of his *Weltpolitik,* accompanied by a complete disregard of the rights of other nations, but he concluded it in 1914 in a spirit of compromise, securing multilateral agreements with Britain, France, and Russia regarding the Near East, and with Britain regarding Africa. Hitler, on the other hand, began his colonial campaign with caution and hesitation, but built up to the climax of 1939, when he repudiated the idea of settlement by negotiation, insisted upon unilateral action, and demanded the unconditional return of the German colonies.

THE NATIONALISM OF HORACE GREELEY

GLYNDON G. VAN DEUSEN

HORACE GREELEY was a nationalist.[1] This was not the result of direct acquaintance with the nationalistic writings of Bolingbroke, Burke, Jean Jacques Rousseau, and Johann Gottfried von Herder. The eighteenth-century Enlightenment affected him more by its consequences than by the direct impact of its literature. Greeley's nationalism was due, in part, to the obvious fact that, like liberals, conservatives, romanticists, radicals, and all other specimens of the *genus homo*, he was born to a particular mood. The mysterious processes of generation produced in him a mentality susceptible to a nationalist view of things. The historian may note with more comfort, if not more certainty, that the nationalistic fervor of the Man in the White Coat derived largely from the influence of his environment and of the American tradition, and was strengthened and developed by his own restless search for a more perfect order of society.

The tradition that influenced Greeley's nationalism was of no ancient origin. There had been no full-fledged American nationalism in the colonial period, but even then its future development had been foreshadowed. Many colonial Americans had felt pride in their land and its people, and the belief had taken root that, as Jonathan Edwards expressed it, Providence meant America to be "the glorious renovator of the world."[2] This pride in America was strengthened by the Revolution, and the consequent emergence of a new nation whose government was based upon the will of the people and their indefeasible, natural rights. Americans began to think that their country, by committing itself to such principles, had assumed a trusteeship for the liberty and happiness of Europe,

---

[1] Greeley's nationalism is suggested in his *Recollections of a Busy Life* (New York, 1868), and also by some of his early biographers. Its importance to his career is partially indicated by Professor Earle D. Ross in the magazine articles hereafter cited.

[2] Quoted in M. Curti, *The Roots of American Loyalty* (New York, 1946), p. 3. My treatment of the background of Greeley's nationalism is based largely upon Curti's admirable work, as well as upon H. Kohn, *The Idea of Nationalism* (New York, 1944). M. Savelle, *Seeds of Liberty* (New York, 1948), has an excellent chapter entitled "Of Loyalties, and of the British-American Nation" on the genesis of American nationalism.

if not for mankind in general, and this exalted conception of America's role was fortified by the effectiveness of the American Constitution in harmonizing state jealousies and sectional divergencies.

Evidences of American national consciousness multiplied after 1789. Americans became more and more aware of the peculiar beauties of their sweeping prairies, mighty lakes, and lofty mountains. The idea that national unity was God's design for this great land became popular. George Bancroft and other writers saw the hand of God in the development of the United States. Veneration of national heroes, especially of George Washington, became the order of the day, and the belief developed that Americans were a unique people, a superior stock, produced by a mixture of "races" that, as St. John de Crèvecoeur said, had been "melted into a new race of men."[3]

Both Jefferson and Hamilton contributed to this nationalist tide. Hamilton's centralizing economic program, together with his encouragement to a strong national government, fostered a patriotism that was quick to associate itself with protection and American-made goods. The triumph of Jeffersonian Democracy meant the overthrow of a Federalism that was oriented toward Britain, and cast into political limbo a social attitude that would have accentuated class divisions in American politics and government. It also gave to millions of Americans another national hero in Thomas Jefferson. It is not without significance that a portrait of Jefferson (the patron saint of Jacksonian Democracy) was given a place of honor in the home of the Whig statesman and nationalist, William Henry Seward.

The decades that followed the Revolution saw great emphasis placed by American writers and thinkers upon the direct relationship of the individual's economic interest to his national loyalty. This "stake in society" idea was meat and drink to the protectionist school. The Careys (Matthew and Henry) developed a literature of economic nationalism that was as influential as its political counterpart—the American System of Henry Clay. Like Alexander Hamilton, Clay and the Careys were quick to point out the function of internal improvements and industrial development in promoting loyalty to the nation. Internal improvements were supposed to make

[3] Quoted in Curti, *op. cit.,* p. 70.

secession impossible by establishing the interdependence of the sections. That the same purpose would be achieved by a vast ramification of industrial production was a popular belief of the Middle Period.

The development of nationalistic thought along economic lines in the Middle Period was paralleled by the development of cultural nationalism. School textbooks in American history were extremely patriotic in tone. So were Noah Webster's speller and dictionary, and Jedediah Morse's school geographies. In 1827, Massachusetts and Vermont led the way in passing laws requiring the study and teaching of American history in the schools. Other states followed suit. Anglophobia, stimulated by the War of 1812 and by stories of American uncouthness retailed by British travelers, was widespread throughout the nation.

The rude shock of sectional bitterness and strife, culminating in the Civil War, could not destroy American nationalism. The faith survived, enshrined for millions in the words of Lincoln's Gettysburg Address. In the years that followed the war, it was a factor prompting the abandonment of Radical Reconstruction and the development of a movement for reconciliation of the North and the South that eventually led the sections along the road to reunion.

Horace Greeley was exposed to nationalist influences early in life. He always remembered his boyhood impressions of the New England Fourth of July celebrations, when a score or two of Revolutionary War veterans (all heroes in a boy's estimation) would crowd the speakers' platform, and the men and women of the town would follow attentively the reading of the Declaration of Independence. He never forgot the celebration at Poultney, Vermont, that marked the fiftieth anniversary of American independence, nor the feeling of religious awe that swept over the village shortly afterwards when it learned that John Adams and Thomas Jefferson had died on that day, and that messengers riding south and north with the sad tidings had met in Philadelphia within the shadow of Independence Hall. Neither did he forget how, as his family moved down the hill toward bankruptcy during the panic years of 1819–1820, the market for the linen, woollen, and tow cloth woven by his mother was usurped by the products of Britain. Such experiences were bound to condition the mind of an impressionable youth. The results became apparent as Greeley forged his career as publisher and editor.

During the years that New England's patriotism was being implanted in the mind and heart of young Greeley, a type of nationalism destined to dominate the Western world was developing across the Atlantic. Liberal nationalism, as Carlton Hayes has pointed out,[4] centered around the belief that every nationality should constitute a political unit, with an independent, constitutional government that would foster and protect the political, religious, economic, and educational freedom of the individual. Each such nation state would serve the best interests of itself and of the world by adopting policies of antimilitarism, anti-imperialism, free trade, and international co-operation and peace.

Some liberal nationalists were devout believers in political democracy, but most of them were inclined to limit suffrage to the thrifty (that is, to property-owners), and regarded it as a duty rather than as a natural right. As a group, they believed in intervention in the affairs of a foreign country, when such intervention was necessary to free a people from despotism or foreign oppression. They drew heavily upon nineteenth-century romanticism, for they took a romantic, often tearful, and frequently generous interest in suffering, subject peoples, just as they exhibited a romantic interest in national customs and traditions, or composed national anthems and designed national flags.

These liberal nationalists—such figures as Giuseppe Mazzini in Italy, Louis Kossuth in Hungary, the German teacher Karl Welcker, the French statesman François Guizot, the champion of Irish liberty Daniel O'Connell—were high-minded men of good will. One and all, they were devoted to the cause of peace, even though, in the name of national self-determination, they fomented war. For peace, as they viewed the matter, was possible only when each nationality had come to rule itself within its own nation state.

It is impossible to state categorically to what extent Greeley was acquainted with the writings of the nineteenth-century liberal nationalists, but that he was thoroughly familiar with their main ideas admits of little doubt. The *Tribune* developed an excellent staff

---

[4] C. J. H. Hayes, *The Historical Evolution of Modern Nationalism* (New York, 1931), pp. 120–63, especially pp. 135–36 and 159–61.

of foreign correspondents, and Greeley's editorials show that he followed the course of European events with great interest and close attention. His exuberant enthusiasm for Daniel O'Connell and Louis Kossuth certainly indicated familiarity with their thought and aims. Perhaps the best evidence that he absorbed liberal nationalist teachings from abroad lies in the fact that his own nationalism fitted so nicely into the liberal nationalist pattern. If this harmony was not due to direct influence, it would be a coincidence little short of amazing.

Like his European prototypes, liberal nationalist Greeley was pre-eminently a man of good will. Chauvinism was conspicuously absent from his make-up. He had no exaggerated racial theories and, in fact, used the word "race" quite loosely and inaccurately. He favored a liberal immigration policy, and was glad to see America a haven for the starving and oppressed, his only condition being that they be capable of making a contribution to the national welfare. He thought of himself, quite rightly, as a man of peace. Repeatedly he denounced the slogan, "My country, right or wrong," and repeatedly he flayed the invocation of national honor as a legitimate cause of war. He would willingly have abolished the regular army and navy, and he had a hearty dislike of expanding America's territory at the expense of her neighbors, whether the territory in question was Texas, California, Oregon, or "Seward's ice-box." Greeley would have been content to see our western limits fixed at the Rocky Mountains. He never suggested giving back any of the territory that we acquired from the Indians, the Mexicans, or the British, but he had a lively sense of the difficulties that were involved in such acquisitions. The United States, he said as early as 1836, had a vast shore line open to attack, and its "conflicting interests" were already so numerous that Americans would be fortunate to preserve the integrity of the Union for a century longer.[5] It was small wonder that the subsequent expansion drove him to the development of a program for fostering that same national integrity.

The good-will aura that clothed Greeley as in a mantle was only one of his resemblances to other liberal nationalists. Like them, he believed that each people should have its own representative gov-

[5] *New-Yorker*, May 7, 1836.

ernment, and European movements toward that end invariably found sympathy and support in the columns of the *Tribune*. Like other liberal nationalists also, Greeley regarded suffrage as a duty rather than as a natural right, and like them he romantically emphasized national traditions and national characteristics. He was also ever hopeful that national self-determination would bring progress toward a halcyon future of peace among men.

Greeley's interest in national self-determination was clearly evidenced by his romantic enthusiasm for the European revolutions of 1848. He gave time, money, and pages of publicity to the cause of Irish freedom. He urged the sons of Erin to revolt against the British government, and declared that he did no more for Ireland than he was willing to do for Poland and Italy. He was equally devoted to Louis Kossuth and the Magyar struggle for independence from Austria. The part played by Nicholas I of Russia in crushing the Magyars aroused Greeley's indignation. Congress, he asserted, should declare that America deemed its own freedom menaced and its cherished principles assailed when one European despot aided another to crush a people struggling for liberty. It was his firm belief that the peoples of Europe were about to take control of their governments and that national self-determination and democracy, hand in hand, were certain to chase all sovereigns out of Europe straight into the welcoming arms of the Russian Czar. This would be the beginning of "that European Federative Republic which is the next grand step toward the Federation of the whole world."[6] The *Tribune's* editor was as optimistic as Mazzini, or as the World Federalists of today.

It was only natural that a man who was such an ardent advocate of national self-determination should also be a firm believer in national characteristics. The Germans, Greeley averred, were "a patient, long-suffering race," in bondage to arbitrary power, but brave and intelligent and with their souls "still free." Modern Greeks were "versatile, elastic, cheating, unreliable." French immorality, which he viewed with the utmost horror, was symbolized by the Paris Opera. "What grace, what sense, what witchery there can be, for instance, in a young girl's standing on one great toe and raising

---

[6] *Tribune*, Aug. 26, 1845, Jan. 14, 1846, April–September, 1848, Dec. 11 f., 1851. *Tribune* always refers to the *Daily Tribune*.

the other foot to the altitude of her head, I cannot imagine. . . . Its [the Opera's] entire, palpable, urgent tendency, is earthly, sensual, devilish."[7]

The American national character, Greeley felt, shone with considerable luster in contrast with the national characters of Europe. To be sure, we were "epicurean, sumptuous, profuse, prone to ostentation, and reckless of expense," but nevertheless we possessed great "national virtue." Young, sanguine, patriotic, aspiring, audacious, strenuous (an American laborer needed for mere subsistence twice as much food as the foreign immigrant laborer), the American people was fated to an exalted destiny. "I have faith," Greeley proclaimed, "in American energy." The mere title "United States" was not an adequate name for such a nation. Greeley besought Congress to adopt the name "Columbia." This, he felt, would be a decided improvement.[8]

Though his heart overflowed with sympathy for all subject peoples, from Poland to Ireland, Greeley's main interest, as became a good nationalist, lay in his own country. It was in connection with the United States that his nationalistic ideas achieved their greatest development and their clearest exposition.

As was obvious from his general attitude, Greeley felt that Americans and America were superior to Europe and Europeans. "The strong peculiarities of character and conduct which distinguish the American people," he declared in 1857, "have no parallel among any other civilized community." In his mind, the genius of our institutions rose far superior to that of kings and popes. British royalty, compared with American republicanism, was a mere anachronism. Westminster Abbey, a "barbaric profusion" of carving and groining, was sadly inferior as a place of worship, and the best that remained of Phidias and Praxiteles could not surpass, if, indeed, it could rival Powers' "Proserpine" and "Psyche." Even the London sun (when it did shine) looked more like a boiled turnip than like the American sun. Europe had nothing like the McCormick reaper,

[7] H. Greeley, *Glances at Europe* (New York, 1851), pp. 134 f., 256; *Recollections of a Busy Life* (New York, 1868), p. 468.

[8] H. Greeley, *Essays Designed to Elucidate the Science of Political Economy* (Boston, 1870), p. 233; *What the Sister Arts Teach as to Farming* (New York, 1853), p. 31; *New-Yorker*, Sept. 11, 1841; *Tribune*, Jan. 1, 1842, Dec. 15, 1843, Jan. 3, 1846, July 20, 1850, Sept. 15, 1858.

and the French scythe was a foot shorter than its American counterpart. As Greeley made the Grand Tour in the summer of 1851, he found repeated evidences of American superiority. It was "with a glow of unwonted rapture," that he left Liverpool for home that August, scornful of "the Macsycophant family" of Americans that toadied to foreigners and foreign institutions to the discredit of their own.[9]

Greeley could not well proclaim the superiority of American literature to that of Europe, but he manifested a decidedly nationalistic bent in literary matters. This was particularly true while he was publishing the *New-Yorker* (a politico-literary weekly), and during the early days of the *Tribune* when its literary department was still under his direct supervision. James Fenimore Cooper received more encouragement from the *New-Yorker* than did any other American prose writer, apparently because Cooper wrote novels about America. Greeley strove to make out as good a case as possible for American poets. A distinctly minor poet, James Abraham Hillhouse, reminded the *New-Yorker's* editor of Milton. Bryant was "the Thomson of America." After Lord Byron's death, Greeley proclaimed that the best fugitive poetry of the United States was "greatly superior" to that of England. Well-nigh every number of the *New-Yorker* was illumined by patriotic sentiments, either in poetry or prose.[10]

Greeley was delighted when Rufus Wilmot Griswold published, in 1842, an anthology entitled *Poets and Poetry in America*. The *Tribune's* editor had helped prepare it, and the work was thoroughly nationalistic in tone. " 'Diah, it's a great thing," he wrote to his friend, Obadiah A. Bowe, "whatever may be said of the Reverend Editor." There was no servile imitation of English poets in America, Greeley declared in answering British criticisms of this anthology. Such remarks were doubtless due to British national vanity. If we had no great poetry, it was because we were *"acting* one of the grandest Epics in human history," and could not be expected to write it at the same time.

In the setting up and carrying out of a system of free government

[9] *New-Yorker*, July 29, Oct. 7, 1837, Sept. 29, 1838; Greeley, *Glances at Europe*, pp. 19, 58, 72–75, 78, 181, 202, 214 f., 258–59, 286 f., 340, 348; *The Crystal Palace and Its Lessons* (n.l., n.d.), pp. 9–10; *Address on Success in Business* (New York, 1867), pp. 19–20; *Tribune*, Nov. 18, 1851.

[10] *New-Yorker*, July 5, 1834, April 23, July 2, 9, 1836.

[Greeley continued], throwing the reins on the necks of the people, and bidding them guide themselves; in the utterance and maintenance of principles that are a new gospel to mankind; boldly and confidently struggling in the face and against the voice and experience of the world; we are furnishing a theme that after generations will contemplate with some respect.[11]

Greeley's enthusiasm for the Griswold anthology demonstrated his interest in using literature as a means of promoting national consciousness. There were other evidences that this was one of his objectives. The *Tribune* always gave much space to accounts of patriotic speeches and celebrations. In 1843 it published a political history of the American colonies, written for the paper by one Edwin Williams. This history emphasized the growth of a sense of oneness among the colonies, and the presence in the colonies of basic and glorious principles that had later come to distinguish Americans from the other nations of the earth. Early in 1844, the *Tribune* issued a clarion call for an international copyright law. The subject, said Greeley, was of paramount importance, equal to any other form of national encouragement and protection. Our legislators should awake "to the effect on us as a people of this overwhelming flow of foreign works into our country." A copyright law was necessary to the development of a truly national literature. Literature fed and shaped the soul of a nation, and there was danger to our national soul in the servility our cities were showing to Old World aristocracy, the timidity of our reviews, and our reverence for foreign press judgments. "To be a nation self-formed and harmonizing in our feelings with our peculiar institutions, we must have a national literature. . . . All that constitutes a great nation deserves the protection of that nation. Yet who has known a truly great people without a literature of their own, and how can it exist without protection?"[12] Margaret Fuller's literary criticism in the *Tribune* during the middle 1840's was altogether in the spirit of this comment.

The *Tribune* did not devote much editorial space to the fine arts, but in at least one instance its attitude toward that part of the American culture paralleled its nationalistic stand on literature. In 1853,

[11] Greeley Papers (New York Public Library, hereafter N.Y.P.L.), Greeley to Bowe, March 30, 1842; *Tribune,* Nov. 18, 1843.
[12] *Tribune,* April–May, 1843, June 19, 1843, Jan. 12, 1844.

when the Academy of Music was built at the corner of Fourteenth Street and Irving Place, the *Tribune* waxed enthusiastic. "We are of the opinion," it declared, "that no fine art can flourish in a country at second hand. We believe it must be rendered national." This was accompanied by a demand that only American singers be employed and that they sing in the language that the people understood.

Greeley's nationalistic attitude toward literature and art was comparable to the attitude which he took toward religious strife. He sought consistently to prevent the eruption of religious controversy into the columns of his paper. Religious discord, he declared, was one of the most formidable perils to national unity, growth, and prosperity. One of the best ways to avoid it was to maintain inviolate the principle of a free church in a free state.[13] He was consistent in this attitude, from the anti-Catholic excitements of the 1830's to the Native American movements of the following decades, and it underlay his controversy with the Catholic Church on the subject of free, tax-supported common schools.

Greeley's cultural nationalism had its economic counterpart. Like Henry Clay and Henry Carey, two men whom he greatly admired, the Man in the White Coat centered his economic thinking around the concept of national unity.

The *Tribune's* editor viewed with great dislike the wide divergence of American social and economic theories. He was disturbed by the specter of class conflict rising up in the land that he loved. His *Hints Toward Reforms,* a collection of thirty lectures delivered between 1842 and 1848, was published in an effort to reconcile radical and conservative thought in the United States. The enthusiasm with which Greeley espoused Fourierism in the early 1840's likewise stemmed from his earnest desire to evolve an harmonious social and economic system for the nation. The idea of national harmony also lay at the basis of his protectionist theories.

One doctrine of Jefferson's that had always commanded his assent, Greeley declared in 1838, was "that which affirms the danger, the impertinence, and the usurpation of any interference by aliens in the domestic policies of the United States."[14] Our need was

[13] *Tribune,* April 14, May 23, 1853.
[14] *Jeffersonian,* Sept. 1, 1838.

American legislators, not French or British, he declared in 1841, in a call for tariff protection of American labor. The influence against protection exerted by foreign manufacturers, and importers and their servants in America, was formidable indeed. These United States agents of foreign interests sometimes adopted "the very language of British hirelings."[15]

Another good effect of tariff legislation by Americans for Americans would be that foreign gewgaws, silks, and wines could no longer drain us into bankruptcy—a parlous state toward which we were inexorably drawn, in Greeley's imagination, whenever we developed an unfavorable balance of trade. In September 1850, he made the gloomy prophecy that January 1, 1851, would see the United States in debt to Europe by $50,000,000 more than it had been on January 1, 1850. This would be "a dead loss to the country," he declared, for it would make difficult the path of both the American manufacturer and the American laborer. The tariff should be high enough to provide the government with adequate revenue and to secure "to American Labor employment at fair wages to the extent of supplying American needs. Just provide for Home Production of those Wares and Fabrics which Nature has not forbidden us to make for ourselves, and we ask no more. Ought we to be content with less?" Twenty years later, he was still harping on the same theme. We protect American manufacturers, he declared in 1870, to defend national industry against outside enemies, just as we fortify harbors and frontier posts.[16]

The primary object of the tariff, in Greeley's estimation, was to build up American industry, not to check foreign trade. When any branch of American manufactures or production was so matured and established that it could fairly meet foreign competition, then there would no longer be any necessity of protecting that portion of our economy. Since Greeley was a good, liberal nationalist, his tariff policy was nationalist but not vindictive. Indeed, he looked forward to the time when America could and would dispense with her tariff walls.[17]

[15] *Ibid.*, Sept. 1, 1838; *Tribune,* Nov. 24, Dec. 14, 1841. Cf. Greeley, *Glances at Europe,* pp. 87 f., and *Tribune,* Aug. 28, 1851.
[16] *Tribune,* Sept. 24, 1850; Greeley, *Essays on Political Economy,* pp. 148 f.
[17] *Tribune,* April 2, 1851; Greeley Papers (Lib. of Cong.), Greeley to Brockway, June 23, Nov. 19, 1847; Greeley, *Essays on Political Economy,* pp. 97–98.

Greeley always scouted the argument that protection was class legislation. No one who knew enough to come in when it rained would use that argument, he declared. The tariff was just as much a benefit to the farmer, the laborer, and the merchant as it was to the manufacturer. If 3,000 workmen in iron manufacturing in one Pennsylvania district consumed annually 200,000 bushels of wheat, 400,000 bushels of rye or corn, 3,000,000 pounds of beef and pork, and other goods in proportion, while scattering annually $1,200,000 all over the country for the goods and produce they bought, did it require great discernment to see the value of the tariff to others than manufacturers? It was the *country* that benefited, the *commonweal* which was promoted, by a protective policy that diversified and strengthened national industry. America should let American workmen do American work.[18]

One of the great and beneficent effects of protection, Greeley believed, would be a marked development of unity in the national society. It being the right and duty of a democratic government to control men's actions for the benefit of society, protection should be regarded as an instrument to be wielded by America for the promotion of its own happiness and well-being. It would be particularly useful in the elimination of class strife. For protection would benefit the whole society by bringing about that "true and equal harmony between the interests of Labor and those of Capital" which had not yet been brought into being. Those interests were interdependent, and injury done by one part of the community to another part was an injury to the whole.[19]

One difficulty with Greeley's argument that protection would promote national unity lay in the South's yearning for free trade. Obviously, the tariff could not at one and the same time promote unity and excite sectional animosity. Greeley's answer to this was that the truth was mighty and would prevail. The South could be and would be educated to the value of protection. He was always looking for signs of southern enlightenment on the tariff. When in

---

[18] *Tribune,* Sept. 1, 1841, Aug. 13, 1842, Sept. 3, 4, 1844; Greeley, *Recollections,* pp. 528 f.

[19] *Tribune,* Aug. 28, 1851. By this time, Greeley was leaning heavily on the nationalistic theories of Henry Carey, developed in the latter's *The Past, the Present, and the Future,* and in his *Harmony of Interests.* See, in this connection, Greeley's *Essays on Political Economy,* pp. 128–29, 345–46.

1843, the Georgia Whigs advocated protection, his delight knew no bounds. Their attitude, Greeley declared, showed the heartening progress that protection was making in the South. Of course, he admitted on another occasion, there were some Southerners, the Ritchies, the Baylys, and the Bococks, for example, who would never see the light—"their souls are incapable of grasping more of the effects of Protection than a fly would perceive of the architectural proportions of St. Peter's"—but he fondly believed that the majority of Southerners could be persuaded of the ineffable blessings of national protection.[20]

As the crisis over slavery developed in the late 1850's, Greeley avowed that one of the most valuable effects of protection would be its peaceful destruction of the "peculiar institution." The protective principle, properly applied, would so perfect a national industry that "the ignorant human machine" would be rendered "a minus quantity not worth the cost of keeping in condition for service." If the United States produced its own metals, cloths, and wares steadily for twenty-five years, "there would be very few slaves left in it at the close of that period." Slavery would easily pass away "by the simple process of making the land and the machinery essential to its cultivation worth more with Free Labor than the land, machinery and slaves together could be with unintelligent, constrained labor." The "quiet, steady growth" of manufacturing and skilled industry in Russia was making serfdom an anachronism there. The same thing was happening to slavery here.[21]

Protection was only one side of Greeley's design for economic nationalism. One of his cherished ambitions was to use the vast, undeveloped reaches of the West for the benefit of the capitalist and the laborer, the farmer and the merchant. His plans centered around Clay's program coupling distribution of public land sales with internal improvements. But by 1846 Clay's land scheme was dead, politically, and Greeley turned to the idea of free homesteads then being advocated by a little band of valiant spirits (George Henry Evans, Thomas Ainge Devyr, and others) who called themselves the National Reformers.

Free land now became another angle of approach to Greeley's

[20] *Tribune,* Sept. 11, 1843, Jan. 7, 1851.
[21] *Ibid.,* Jan. 17, 1859.

goal of national harmony and progress. It would act as a safety valve, easing the plight of the workers in the East by its offer of an escape into the broad fields of the West. Limited land sales and guaranteed homesteads, fundamental elements of the plan, would banish the speculator, whom Greeley had come to regard (after the panic of 1837) as the curse of the West and the great handicap to the development of national resources. As the tariff fostered industrial production, so the free land program would develop the enormous agricultural potentialities of the West, and all Americans would be bound together in the beneficence of a general prosperity.

Greeley knew that southern statesmen, in general, were opposed to free land. He knew also that the expansion of slavery into the western regions would discourage free labor from going into those areas.[22] Hence the expansion of slavery must be sternly resisted, and the free land policy enacted into law over southern protests, in the face of the opposition of the slaveholders. Strong in an obstinacy that was nurtured by his ignorance of southern life and southern institutions, Greeley was convinced that the South could be brought to accept free land as well as a protective tariff without the danger of war. He was sure that the national patriotism of the southern masses and the economic benefits of national union would nullify such secessionist dreams as were entertained by the southern oligarchy and that, the expansion of slavery being halted, his own program of agricultural and industrial expansion would penetrate all sections of the country and become a stable basis of national prosperity.

Greeley's interest in land reform had a corollary in his devotion to internal improvements. These were essential to the development of national prosperity and, from the Erie Canal enlargement in the 1830's to the Union Pacific Railroad in the 1860's, his interest was vigorous and unflagging. An enthusiastic participant at the great Chicago Rivers and Harbors convention of 1847, he listened impatiently there to the limiting views of strict constructionists of the Constitution, but was pleased by young Abraham Lincoln's broad constructionist views and by the speech of the President of the convention, Edward Bates of Missouri, who gave a glowing panegyric on America's progress, genius, and destiny. That convention, Greeley wrote afterward, was inspirational. He, too, wished to put

[22] *Tribune*, July 24, 1848.

himself on record as favoring all internal improvements at federal expense that would be serviceable, whether within one state or stretching across boundaries. "Each single improvement appears but a link," declared the enthusiastic editor, "in a golden chain of benefits and blessings, calculated to bind together, indissolubly, the states composing this vast republic."[23]

Two years after this Chicago convention, with the Mexican War over and California a part of the Union, Greeley came out for a national road, either of rails or plank, to the Pacific. He suggested the junction of the Ohio and the Mississippi as the best, because the most central, eastern terminus. For it should be a national enterprise, with all parts of the country participating in the credit for its accomplishment, just as they would share in the benefits that would ensue. Ten years later, when he made his famous trip to California (a trip undertaken in the hope of doing something to hasten the construction of a transcontinental railroad), he closed the account of his journey with an appeal for a Pacific railroad as "a bond of union not easily broken and a new spring to our national industry, prosperity and wealth." Stimulating new manufactures, increasing the demand for products already existing, it would "open new vistas to national and to individual aspiration, and crush out filibusterism by giving a new and wholesome direction to the public mind."[24] Greeley was a sponsor of the view that internal improvements would make secession impossible because of the interdependence of the sections.

Still another aspect of Greeley's nationalism was his zeal for the promotion of agricultural production. In 1843 he published a little brochure entitled *The Silk Culture in the United States*. He had been aided in its preparation by I. K. Barbour of Massachusetts, a successful silk grower. The silk industry, Greeley declared, would stop the drain on our specie through silk importation, as well as alleviating the condition of 100,000 sweated seamstresses. The *Tribune's* editor was a zealous frequenter of fairs and agricultural exhibits, whence he reported with gusto on wonders that ranged from new farm tools like C. H. McCormick's reaper (which required "pretty smooth ground") to squashes weighing 146 pounds. Anything that portrayed vitality and development in the agricul-

---

[23] *Tribune*, July 2, 14, 1847; Greeley, *Recollections*, p. 247, and "River and Harbor Improvements," in De Bow's *Review*, IV (November 1847), 291–96.
[24] H. Greeley, *An Overland Journey* (New York, 1860), p. 386.

tural profession was grist to his mill. He was ready and willing to have the national government foster agriculture in more ways than by free grants of the public domain. He wanted federal highways, connecting farm regions with urban markets. The *Tribune* was an early persistent agitator for a federal department of agriculture. By the 1870's, Greeley saw the necessity of government regulation, state and national, of the railroads.[25] Agricultural development, together with the tariff and internal improvements, formed a trilogy in Horace Greeley's saga of economic nationalism.

It was inevitable that Greeley's nationalism should be manifested in his attitude toward political matters, if for no other reason than that politics was meat and drink to the *Tribune's* editor. Like most other liberal nationalists, Greeley had little time for expatiating upon the right of Everyman to vote. Greeley accepted, in principle, the idea of universal manhood suffrage as essential to a good society, but he shied away from it as a natural right, or even as an immediate good. Like Orestes Brownson in the early 1840's, the *Tribune's* editor felt that it was unwise to pay too much obeisance to the popular will. True democracy, Greeley declared, could exist only when the aristocrats of intellect were instructing the populace as to the best means of avoiding the errors of ignorance. The suffrage, he asserted in 1842, was not a right to be acknowledged, but a duty to be imposed by those who already possessed it. This idea clearly carried over into his concept of "Impartial Suffrage" for southern whites and blacks after the Civil War. He then asserted repeatedly that he had no objection to tax or property qualifications in the South, provided that they were alike for all.[26]

This conservative orientation as to the suffrage, together with the nationalistic aspects of the Whig program for tariff, internal improvements, and a sound national currency, inevitably attracted Greeley into that party's ranks. Whiggery, in his estimation, represented militant and constructive action for the national good, in contrast to the Democracy's negative, laissez-faire domestic program, while splinter parties such as those formed by the Know

[25] *Tribune*, 1841–1842, *passim*, Oct. 28, Nov. 2, 1843, Sept. 19, 1846, July 24, 26, 1847; E. D. Ross, "Horace Greeley and Agriculture," *Agricultural History*, VII (January 1933), 15–17.

[26] *Tribune*, May 24, 1842, Aug. 1, Oct. 26, 1843, Jan. 20, 1844, Feb. 28, March 12, May 30, 1866.

Nothings and Abolitionists excited his distrust because they fostered jealousy, bitterness, and sectional division. It was the Whig party, Greeley declared after the campaign of 1844, which had upheld the national good by supporting a tariff, a national currency, and an equitable land policy, and by opposing the annexation of slaveholding Texas. The *Tribune* would continue to uphold the tariff, and also oppose abuse of slaveholders and the formation of an abolition party.[27] Greeley's support of the Whig party along these nationalist lines continued until the party's disintegration in the 1850's.

The political attitude which Greeley took toward slavery in 1844 was indicative of his nationalist stand in regard to the South's "peculiar institution." He always regarded human bondage as a moral blot upon American society, but, so long as it remained where it was, he felt constrained not to meddle with it. "Whenever Slavery shall become in fact the Main Question," he told the Free Soil men in 1844, "it will be found to reach a great deal further and cut much closer than many zealous Abolitionists have as yet any idea of." As he saw Whig and Democratic party lines beginning to blur in the 1840's, he hoped that new party divisions would be along the lines of land and labor reform, rather than over slavery. "Our idea," he wrote in 1848, "is that the People of this Country never will, never can be made to merge all other questions and be banded and marshalled on the single issue of Slavery against Anti-Slavery."[28]

But as slavery became an expansive force, reaching out for new territories and more power, Greeley was forced to come to grips with it, whether or no. He saw in the acquisition of Texas and the subsequent plans for slavery expansion a menace to the protective tariff, to northern designs for internal improvements, and to his cherished plan for free homesteads in the West.[29] Slavery expansion menaced his whole program of economic nationalism. This was particularly true after the Whig party, a bulwark for national unity in the South, began to go to pieces on the slavery issue.

The Kansas-Nebraska bill was a culmination of this southern threat to Greeley's nationalist program, from a political point of

[27] *Tribune,* Aug. 22, Sept. 4, 1843, Nov. 16, 1844.
[28] *Ibid.,* Aug. 16, 1844, Nov. 10, 1848.
[29] J. A. Isely, *Horace Greeley and the Republican Party* (Princeton, 1947), pp. 27 f., gives a good analysis of the relationship of Greeley's land policy to his attitude toward slavery.

view. One of the bill's worst aspects, he kept repeating, was its stimulus to sectional hatred and bitterness. The conflagration that threatened was not to be extinguished "by jets of rosewater." It was his conviction that Kansas-Nebraska was deliberately planned as the first act in a "new Southern drama," to be followed by the annexation of Cuba and northern Mexico, and a reopening of the slave trade. The country, he told Schuyler Colfax, was in for a long fight over slavery.

Greeley was bitter over the Whig split on the Kansas-Nebraska bill. "Where now is your nationality [meaning, loyalty to the nation]?" he asked George Badger, John M. Clayton, and James C. Jones, southern Whig Senators who were supporting the bill. It now looked as though a new party would be the shortest road to the predominance of Whig principles, he told his readers, as he noted the lack of southern Whig opposition to this "infamous proposition." It would have been well, he asserted, if the Whig party had been broken up two years ago.[30]

The main reason that Greeley became a Republican was his conviction that the Whig Party, hopelessly split upon the issue of slavery, was no longer a bulwark against this menace to American unity, was no longer an effective fighting force for those nationalistic principles that were, in his estimation, the reason for its existence. In the years that followed, he asserted repeatedly that the Democratic party was sectional because it had sold out to the slavery interest. The only party whose aims were truly national was that which called itself Republican.

As the decade of the 1850's wore away, the breach between the sections became wider. By 1860, with passions at a dangerously high point, the choice of Presidential candidates assumed great importance. Greeley's preference for the Republican nomination was Edward Bates of Missouri. Bates was, in Greeley's eyes, a conciliation candidate who, by virtue of being a Missourian, and of his connections and principles, would be a strong bidder for votes in all sections of the country. Possessing a "great national heart," he would bring into alliance and co-operation the Republicans, Whigs, and Union men who together formed a decided majority of the

---

[30] *Tribune*, Jan. 27, Feb. 15, 17, 25, March 4, 17, April 11, 1854; Greeley Papers (N.Y.P.L.), Greeley to Colfax, June 28, 1854; A. Nevins, *Ordeal of the Union* (2 vols., New York, 1947), II, 131.

nation. He was eminently a "national man" and his election would demonstrate that slavery was a local and not a national institution.[31]

The Republican convention preferred Lincoln to Bates. Greeley loyally supported the party's choice, and his course of action during the campaign was marked by nationalistic considerations similar to those that had governed his selection of a candidate. Republicanism should triumph because it represented great economic principles, the triumph of which would be most beneficial to the nation. So far as slavery was concerned, Greeley emphasized, the issue was simply one of restriction or expansion. No attack was intended on slavery in the slave states. The venom that had characterized his assaults on slavery in the 1850's was conspicuous by its absence. Often slavery was entirely omitted from his campaign editorials. The *Tribune's* editor made clear his conviction (it was one that he had held for over a decade) that the South would never secede from the Union. Disunion, after all, was treason, and the masses in the South would never be traitors. Thousands of Southerners would be Republicans, if they dared be true to their inmost convictions. At the close of the campaign, he predicted 50,000 votes for Lincoln in the slave states, a forecast that was almost 50 per cent too high.[32]

The great burden of the *Tribune's* positive campaign in 1860 was on the economic side. A Republican victory would be a victory for the tariff, free land, and internal improvements. The Republicans were fighting for, among other things, better homes, better transportation facilities, federal aid for agricultural and vocational education, tariff protection for all classes of citizens—all of these represented by bills passed by a Republican House and either defeated by a Democratic Senate or vetoed by a Democratic President. Greeley was convinced that once victory was gained at the polls, the South would submit to the implementation of his plans for economic nationalism.[33]

Greeley's attitude toward the South in the critical months that followed the election was that of a puzzled but earnest nationalist.

---

[31] *Tribune*, Feb. 20, March 26, 1860; *New York Times*, Feb. 17, 1860, a three-column letter, unsigned, but clipped by Greeley, who wrote his name across it, now in the Greeley Papers in the New York Public Library.

[32] *Tribune*, May 26, July 23, 28, August–November, 1860, *passim*. The votes cast for Lincoln in the slaveholding states totaled 26,430, with 17,028 of these cast in Missouri.

[33] Based on examination of the *Tribune* files for 1860. Cf. E. D. Ross, "Horace Greeley and the West," *Mississippi Valley Historical Review*, XX (June 1933), 63–74.

On the one hand, he declared that disunion was not only unconstitutional, but nearly impossible. "The Union of these States," he asserted, "is in its nature irrevocable, and only the earthquake of Revolution can shiver it." But in the same breath he also maintained that if a number of states large enough to form a political community and maintain a national existence really wanted to leave the Union, "we shall insist that they be permitted to go in peace."[34]

The crux of Greeley's argument in regard to peaceable secession lay in the conditions that he sought to impose upon those desirous of leaving the Union. For secession to be valid in his eyes, it must cover at least six or eight states, be the result of an unmistakable manifestation of the popular will in the seceding states, and be secured by some formal process agreeable to both sides. If the seceding states went to fighting and defying the law before the Union was formally dissolved, then force would have to be used against them.[35] He believed that secession was a daring scheme which a small southern minority was trying to ram down the throats of the southern masses, and that there would not be a *bona fide,* lasting secession from the Union.[36] Hence he opposed compromises of all kinds. They would aid and abet the extension and perpetuation of slavery, he declared, and "an exalted nationality is hardly to be anticipated from suppressing the instruments of humanity, and converting the National Union into a mere convenience for slaveholding."[37]

Greeley's position in regard to secession and his stand against compromise were based in part upon his belief in the strength of nationalist sentiment in the South, in part upon his conception of the national values inherent in the Republican economic program. "Go in peace" was, on the one hand, a rather confused attempt to recognize the legitimacy of the principle of national self-determination and, on the other hand, an effort to keep the southern masses loyal by disarming the argument of the southern fire-eaters that the

[34] *Tribune,* Nov. 11, 1860; Lincoln Papers (Lib. of Cong.), Greeley to Lincoln, Dec. 22, 1860.

[35] *Tribune,* Nov. 24, 26, 30, Dec. 8, 10, 1860; Lincoln Papers (Lib. of Cong.), Greeley to Lincoln, Dec. 22, 1860.

[36] The files of the *Tribune* show that he clung stubbornly to this belief, even after Lincoln's inauguration.

[37] *Tribune,* Nov. 27, 30, Dec. 14, 15, 18–22, 1860, Jan. 14, 21, March 15, 1861; E. D. Morgan Papers (Alb. St. Lib.), Greeley to Morgan, Dec. 24, 1860.

North was attempting to coerce the South.[38] When this attempt to immobilize the southern secessionists failed and the attack on Sumter made war a reality, Greeley declared that it was now clear that the Union could not be dissolved. "The business of the nation today," he asserted, "is the Annihilation of Rebellion, and the Preservation of the National Integerity."[39]

Some of Greeley's wartime attitudes and actions defy analysis in terms of rational human behavior. There were times during the struggle when his heart failed him, and he was ready to stop the effort to preserve the Union. But in his calmer moments he was still confident that national unity was one of the central features of American life, and that out of the war itself there could and would come a more perfect nation. This view was outlined in a series of articles that he wrote during the second year of the struggle, a series that was in a sense an epitome of his own career as a nationalist.

National pride and "a strong instinct of nationality," Greeley maintained, had been for years "the master passion of Americans." This had made the great majority of people complaisant toward slavery. They had winked at its moral evil, lest hostility to an institution so deeply rooted might weaken the Union. The Slave Power now sought disunion, blind to the great "centripetal tendency" of the country, a tendency "so overwhelming that Disunion were impossible but for Slavery." What insanity was it that would set up national barriers dividing New Orleans from the upper waters of the Mississippi and separating St. Louis from the North and West?

"But a nobler idea, a truer conception of National unity," was rapidly gaining possession of the "American mind." Greeley saw emerging from the war a true union of hearts, "based on a substantial identity of social habits and moral convictions." Thereafter, national unity was to be "no roseate fiction, no gainful pretense, but a living reality." The United States of the future would be " a true exemplification of 'many in one'—many stars blended in one common flag—many states combined in one homogeneous Na-

---

[38] This latter point is well brought out in D. M. Potter, "Horace Greeley and Peaceable Secession," *Journal of Southern History*, VII (May 1941), 145–59.
[39] *Tribune,* April 25, May 6, 1861.

tion. Our Union will be one of bodies not merely, but of souls." From now on, North and South would meet as equals, each in the full confidence of the other. "We already know that valor is an American quality; we shall yet realize that Truth is every man's interest...."

The Union of the future, Greeley declared, would be "based on the eternal verities, and cemented by every year's duration, until sectional hatreds and jealousies vanished and all rejoiced in being sons and citizens of a nation where the unalienable rights of man would have become "the practical basis of the entire political and social fabric—the accepted, axiomatic root of the National Life."

Slavery had caused southern hatred of the North, a hatred that was not returned by Northerners. With the destruction of slavery, this hatred would vanish and with it would also vanish bitterness and alienation. Slavery was the one great bar to the triumph of nationalist sentiment. "God has made them [North and South] for parts of the same country; their diverse typographies, climates, productions, render them the natural complements of each other." With a diversified economy, the South would grow in wealth. She would realize how slavery had held her back. "So shall North and South, at length comprehending and appreciating each other, walk hand in hand along their common pathway to an exalted and benignant destiny...."[40]

Early in 1865, as it became clear that the end of the war was imminent, Greeley wrote: "The nation needs peace, not vengeance; it demands a return to heartfelt loyalty, not useless slaughter." The essence of reconstruction, he asserted a few weeks later, was recognition of the humanity and vindication of the personal rights and freedom of all the southern people. Five days after Lee's surrender at Appomattox, the *Tribune's* editor rejoiced that "we are a nation, no longer divided against itself, but one, indivisible, united, free."[41]

To the fixed and unalterable establishment of the national existence thus proclaimed, Greeley devoted much time and effort in the years following the Civil War. A multiplicity of interests dis-

---

[40] H. Greeley, "National Unity," *Continental Monthly*, II (September 1862), 357–60; "Southern Hate of the North," *ibid.*, II (October 1862), 448–51; and "Obstacles to Peace," *ibid.*, II (December 1862), 714–17. If the South won, Greeley felt sure that the sections would be united under the Confederate flag, so strong was the impulse for national unity.

[41] *Tribune*, Feb. 23, April 11, 14, 1865.

tracted his attention, on occasion, from this main objective; his political ambitions produced, at times, contradictory movements and complications; but his great aim during the Reconstruction Period was the establishment and perpetuation of national unity. Horace Greeley was determined that that "wretched coinage of falsehood and calumny, the malformed word 'sectionalism,'" should be dismissed from American thought.[42]

Sectionalism was not the only divisive concept that aroused Greeley's ire. The states' rights doctrine was even more abhorrent to him. Its evil and fallacious character had been demonstrated once and for all, he felt, by the war. The rising generation must be taught to loathe the idea that a man's first allegiance was due to his state, rather than to the nation. "The Rebellion," he declared, "had Slavery for its father and 'paramount' State Rights for its mother. Let us beware of them both!"[43]

The core of Greeley's reconstruction program was his slogan, "Universal Amnesty and Impartial Suffrage." This meant generous, magnanimous treatment of the South, coupled with conditions of suffrage that should be identical for the white and black citizens of the South. He held stubbornly to the amnesty idea,[44] even after his signing Jefferson Davis' bail bond had cost him much popularity in the North. His happy phrase, "clasp hands across the bloody chasm," was featured in the campaign of 1872, in which he made the unity and development of the nation his central theme.

"Impartial suffrage" was an idea backed by a dual purpose. It was meant to bring about the reception of the Negro into the American family on equal terms with the white.[45] It was also meant to ensure Republican predominance in national politics. By the close of 1866, however, Greeley was disposed to favor Negro suffrage without any qualifications whatever, so anxious was he to ensure Republican supremacy, and in 1867 he heartily supported the Radicals' enforcement of the Negro's right to vote. The blacks must have that right, he asserted, for it would make future rebellions impossible and

[42] *Ibid.*, April 27, 1865.
[43] *Ibid.*, April 29, Aug. 10, 1865.
[44] Greeley's course on amnesty is traced by E. D. Ross, "Horace Greeley and the South," *South Atlantic Quarterly*, XVI (October 1917), 324–38.
[45] In this connection, see Greeley's editorial in the *Tribune*, July 17, 1866. Greeley was an ardent opponent of racial discrimination, particularly where the Negro was concerned. His views on that subject have cogency today, as I intend to show in a later publication.

would give the Republicans a great, national party, strong in every state in the Union.[46] Underlying this attitude, of course, was his economic nationalism, the aims of which he sought to realize through Republican economic policies.

Side by side with amnesty for the southern whites, equality for the Negro, the inculcation of national loyalty and the triumph of the Republican tariff, internal improvements, and a sound-money program, Greeley vigorously promoted the idea of southern as well as western economic development. From April 20, 1865, when he published an editorial entitled "Southward Ho!' this idea of developing the South's economic potentialities, industrially as well as agriculturally, was one of his main themes. He deplored the struggle over Reconstruction because it delayed turning the attention of the nation to those economic objectives that should, in his opinion, motivate high national policy. The economic development of the South and West for the promotion of national strength, for the building of an ever greater and more prosperous nation, was one of Horace Greeley's main concerns down to the close of his life.[47]

Greeley was a complex character. He had many interests, many motivations. The policies he pursued were sometimes contradictory. But once he fastened his teeth in an idea, he would hold to it with the tenacity of a bulldog. At an early age he visualized the American people as a national unit, and began making the promotion of their national well-being one of the main objects of his life. By and large, save for those periods when he succumbed to defeatism during the Civil War, he remained devoted to this objective until his tragic death at the end of his race for the Presidency. He did not endeavor to work out a philosophy of nationalism, and such concepts as "race" and "nationality" were rather loosely defined in his thought. But that he was a liberal nationalist of the nineteenth-century variety admits of no doubt. A clear perception of that fact is essential to an understanding of the character and role of Horace Greeley.

[46] Greeley Papers (N.Y.P.L.), Greeley to J. R. Laurence, Dec. 16, 1866.
[47] For suggestive comments along this line, see H. Greeley, *Letters From Texas* (New York, 1871), pp. 55–56, and *What I Know of Farming* (New York, 1871), pp. 26 f.

SCANDINAVIA AND THE RISE OF MODERN NATIONAL CONSCIOUSNESS

JOHN H. WUORINEN

I

AMONG THE MANY common features of the first and second World Wars there is one that stands out in sharp relief. It is the widely accepted belief that the defeat of Germany and her allies would automatically and directly create an opportunity to eliminate the scourge of war as an arbiter between nations, and that once the fighting had ceased the opportunity would be speedily utilized by the victorious allies. This feeling and the optimistic view which it reflected gained almost universal credence, especially after 1918. It appears safe to say that the same feeling and view are part of the faith that has sustained much of the troubled world since 1945. The imposing structure of the United Nations rests primarily upon that faith; without it this most recent attempt at establishing a league of nations and peoples to safeguard the peace would quickly collapse.

During the years the United Nations has functioned, however, it has become increasingly obvious that in all probability the likelihood of war cannot be more successfully eliminated in the years that lie ahead than was the case after the peace settlement of 1919–1920. In fact, aggression of the Soviet brand has for some time assumed forms and proportions that have already led to an open abandonment, by the Western States, of the United Nations as their main line of defense. The Atlantic Pact, to say nothing of the Marshall Pact, is the best single illustration of the trend of the times. The Atlantic Pact established a far-flung alliance that brings the West together in opposition to Russia and her satellites. What is more, it is a military alliance in the full sense of the term. The cynically inclined will find a good deal of satisfaction in the circumstance that this military alliance is vastly more imposing, in terms of the number of nations involved and the military potential they command, than anything that the Europe of the years before 1914 had to show—or, for that matter, more impressive than any alignment of states between the Peace of Paris and World War II.

Partly as a result of the developments of which the Atlantic Alliance is but a symptom, a federation of European states has been urged by many who profess to see in such a union guarantees for peace not to be found elsewhere. That a federal or united Europe is wholly outside the realm of possibility seems abundantly clear, however. Certainly there is nothing in the record of the past generation or two to justify any other conclusion. The idea of a united Europe represents a hope and an aspiration, not a reality upon which national policies can be based. The League of Nations, now defunct, and the United Nations, now in its fifth year of anything but impressive accomplishment as guarantor of peace and freedom, may well turn out to illustrate the utmost that can be achieved in the effort to "unite" Europe and the world. Fact-finding agencies and clearing-houses performing many useful functions seem to lie within the limits of the possible in the field of European (that is, West European) international co-operation, but not a genuinely potent international organization capable of safeguarding the peace. The Atlantic military alliance furnishes a quite accurate measure of the failure of the United Nations as an agency capable of preventing war. At the same time, it charts the area within which, and within which alone, meaningful European co-operation is possible at present. Within that area military and related commitments and action are paramount and harsh realities that have little to do with the creation of a new international European order through a European union or federation. The conditions creating a West-East division in Europe have existed since the end of the recent war and stubbornly persist; the conditions genuinely favoring a European federation are probably as nonexistent today as they have ever been. And quite apart from the present West-East cleavage, the nations of Europe will continue to be divided by language, national character and ways of looking at things, age-long rivalries and animosities, to say nothing of aggression and the fear of aggression that have been inescapable parts of national existence in the Europe of yesterday and show no sign of disappearing in the Europe of tomorrow.

A pertinent, though not the most obvious, further illustration of the many diversities that persist in Europe—despite the fact that it is possible to talk of a "European civilization" or a "European culture area" and the like—is the fact that even during the two great World Wars of the twentieth century some parts of Europe escaped direct involvement in war. Another is the circumstance that certain European nations have been and demonstrably are so unqualifiedly committed to policies of peace and friendly co-operation in their foreign relations that they have come to be universally recognized as constituting no threat whatever to peace. Avoiding military adventures and in general averse to any objectives likely to entail international conflict, they stand sharply apart from the Big Powers and more especially from the Big Power aggressors that have caused two major wars within a generation. Still another is the existence, side by side, of certain nations whose past history and present position and affiliation suggest that while a general European union in all probability will remain the dream and the goal here-and-now of the uninformed or blind optimist, union within specific regional areas is within the realm of possibility and will, once it has been achieved, effectively serve legitimate and specific national interests and the cause of international peace.

II

One such area is Scandinavia. Students of Scandinavian history, political conditions, or social policy, to say nothing of languages and problems philological, are readily impressed by the many similarities that justify the classification of Norway, Sweden, Finland, and Denmark as the four "Scandinavian" or "Northern" countries.[1]

---

[1] American usage has increasingly accepted, especially since the first World War, the term "Scandinavia" as a designation for these four countries. In these countries themselves, however, the term usually employed is the equivalent of "The North." In fact, there is definite aversion to the use of the word "Scandinavia," particularly in Norway and Finland.

Some American writers and others outside of Scandinavia have held and continue to hold that Finland should not be classified as a member of the Scandinavian quartette. See, for example, S. Shepard Jones, *The Scandinavian States and the League of Nations* (Princeton, N. J., 1939), p. ix, and Ben A. Arneson, *The Democratic Monarchies of Scandinavia* (New York, 1939, 1949), p. 1. The reason for their opinion appears to be confusion in the use of terminology, and lack of familiarity with pertinent aspects of Sweden's and Finland's history and the conclusions of such scholars in the field of race studies as Carleton S. Coon, the author of *The Races of Europe* (New York, 1939). The section on "The Government and Politics of the Scandinavian Countries" by Nils Herlitz and the author in James T. Shotwell, ed., *Governments of Continental Europe* (New York, 1940), indicates some of the circumstances that justify grouping these nations together.

History extending over many generations has seemingly given them—notably Sweden and Finland, but also Norway and Denmark—a common past that spans many generations, the significant consequences of which are likely to remain vital for a long time to come. Economic development in more recent times has produced, on the whole, standards of living and a social fabric that accent similarities rather than differences. Political institutions that function in the service of democracy (as the term is used in the West), the freedom and liberties of man and the manner of safeguarding them, and goals and achievements in the field of education, as well as religion and the position of the church, all underline the fact that the Norwegians, the Swedes, the Finns, and the Danes constitute, in a multitude of ways, a more homogeneous group of peoples than any other four independent nations in Europe. In a word, many factors and circumstances that favor unity—in cultural as well as political development, in foreign policy, and so forth—appear to be present among the four peoples in abundant measure. They all have much the same interests, much the same needs, and basically—if left alone to choose freely—they have much the same ideas and preferences as to how their interests can best be safeguarded.

Yet the factors and developments favoring unity have not sufficed to create a Scandinavian federation, to say nothing of a unitary Scandinavian state. The reasons for the failure—if "failure" be the proper word in this connection—are many. Some of them have to do with the consequences of historical evolution through the centuries, and others with recent circumstances derived from Big Power policies outside Scandinavia. The problem of national separateness versus international unity in the Scandinavian area has ramifications that extend far into the past experience of the four nations. At the same time, it touches many of the pressing problems of the passing hour[2]—problems which the nations of the North have not created and over which they have little or no control. The latter lie, however, outside the limits of our discussion here. What concerns us are not contemporary developments that have influenced Scandinavia, but some of the more obvious circumstances which help to explain the emergence in the North of four nationalist-con-

---

[2] I have discussed some of the latter in "Problems of a Scandinavian Bloc," *Current History*, XVI (January 1949), 12–15.

scious peoples who reveal, at present, no signs of readiness to abandon their linguistic, cultural, or political separateness.

A mere glance at a map showing the northernmost tier of the states of Europe suffices to bring out the fact that the immutable dictum of geography is not a united but a divided Scandinavia. By no geographical definition can Denmark be brought within the "Northern" family of four nations; Denmark's membership depends on other criteria. The same conclusion applies to Finland as well, although on somewhat different grounds. Thus it is only Norway and Sweden that constitute, in a geographical sense, "Scandinavia." But even this obvious fact requires some elaboration lest its implications be misunderstood. Nature has decreed that Sweden and Norway also should be separated, pretty much in the manner in which Sweden is separated from Denmark or from Finland, for along the full length of the Scandinavian peninsula there runs a mountain range that cuts it in two. As a divisive factor, the mountain range has begun to lose its meaning only in degree as modern mechanical transportation has wrought its wonders in these northern climes, largely within the memory of men still living.

The language situation likewise has tended to heighten rather than lower the barriers that keep the four nations apart. The most readily noted "unifying" factor in the Scandinavian North, and the one most frequently taken for granted, is the close similarity of the languages spoken by the four peoples. The Finnish language is, to be sure, in a category by itself, and it might therefore be concluded that the Finns remain outside the area of the ready and natural linguistic unity which the Norwegians, the Swedes, and the Danes enjoy. Such a conclusion is incorrect for two main reasons. In the first place, Swedish is the mother tongue of about one-tenth of the population of Finland. Secondly, virtually all Finns who have any pretensions to education in secondary schools or beyond know Swedish. Swedish is, in fact, the second national language of Finland and is recognized as such in the constitution of the Republic. It is thus clear that the mastery of Swedish in Finland is quite common enough and extensive enough to meet the needs and requirements of the "unity" now under discussion.

There is, however, another aspect of the "unity-because-of-language" situation. While the forefathers of the Norwegians, the

Swedes, and the Danes (and of a goodly proportion of the Finns) spoke a more or less common tongue many centuries ago, and while in our day no training in philology is needed to perceive the common features of the language, say, of Ibsen, Strindberg, Runeberg, or Holberg, the languages of every one of the four nations have become, particularly during the past century, increasingly "national." The lines separating them have become more sharply etched, and the possibility that something approximating a genuinely common Scandinavian tongue would emerge within a measurable period of time have grown dimmer with each passing decade. There is nothing today to indicate that this development will be retarded. The direct and practical consequences of this factor, however, should not be exaggerated as far as present-day "Northern" unity is concerned. It is doubtful that any important "Scandinavian" policy or decision in any of the four countries during the last generation, or any common policy accepted by these nations, can be attributed primarily to the circumstance that they are able to transact business with one another without the use of interpreters. Yet it is an important circumstance that the trend away from unity is unmistakably present, and its results will in all likelihood progressively decrease the area within which meaningful "language unity" will remain.

Passing mention has already been made of the fact that the history of these nations is such as to give them a past which they share in common. While this is true, it is true only in part, and it would require rather exceptional boldness to claim that the record of bygone generations which they share in common has significantly contributed toward unity. In each case, the history of the past has come long since to mean, to an overwhelming degree, the history of the nation or the people; in each case, history is the record of the *national* past, and knowledge of that record has become *the* way of understanding the generations out of which, in the view of the Dane, or the Swede, or the Finn, or the Norwegian, his nation as he now knows it has grown. Thus history, whether thought of as the rather arid exercises and memorizing of history lessons normal in primary or secondary schools, or as the more pretentious surveys and researches appropriate to graduate studies in higher institutions of learning, or as the offerings of "popular" historians who write for the general reading public, nearly always means accent upon national and not general "Scandinavian" or "Northern" traditions. It is the national and not the "Scandinavian" record and tradition that serve as sources of inspiration in times evil as well as good. It is they alone that offer an understandable, meaningful explanation of how the nation and the state of today came to be, and they alone are considered to furnish most of the dependable markers for charting the nation's course into the future.

The mere existence in our day of a Norway, Sweden, Finland, and Denmark suffices to make clear the extent to which history has separated these four nations. Yet there was a time when they were all under the same crown (during the so-called Kalmar Union, 1389–1523). And more important, there was a long period of over six centuries when the Swedes and the Finns constituted a single, united kingdom. That period came to an end as late as 1808–1809, and it ended then not because either Swede or Finn desired it but because the Big Power politics and aggression of that day—France and Russia were then the main offenders—led to a Russian-Swedish war which terminated in Russia's conquest of the eastern, or Finnish, part of the Swedish Kingdom. More important than the Kalmar Union was likewise the circumstance that the Danes and the Norwegians were bound together in the same state for over four hundred years (that is, from 1389 to 1814). Finally, Norway and Sweden were joined in a dynastic union for three generations before 1905, only to dissolve the union in that year and go their separate ways. It would seem, therefore, that historical evolution in the North might well have turned out to be a unifying rather than dividing process.

That disunity and cleavage along national lines emerged as the end product of the process has depended upon many factors and circumstances that cannot be discussed here. One of them, however, is of such preponderant and decisive significance as to require more than mere passing notice. It is the emergence of national consciousness, in the modern sense, among the Norwegians, the Swedes, the Finns, and the Danes.[3]

[3] I use the term "national consciousness" rather than "nationalism" because the former seems to me to express more satisfactorily than the latter the phenomenon here involved. Some of the baffling problems of terminology and definitions which are ever a part of any serious attempt to discuss modern nationalism, national consciousness, etc.,

III

No two historians are likely to agree regarding what national consciousness really means, what its component parts are, or when, specifically, it may be said to have emerged as the cohesive force that makes it possible for the Norwegian, for example, to feel that he belongs to a nationality which stands apart from other peoples. The reasons for failure to agree include, in part, the difficulties inherent in any effort to define anything, and especially in trying to define an intangible, such as a state of mind or a way of looking at things, clearly involved in the concept "national consciousness." The difficulties also include the fact that time, place, and circumstance—variables, in other words—determine what, in a given case, national consciousness represents or what should be recognized as bona fide manifestations of it. The term is used here, however, in a simple and obvious sense: the feeling of the individual Norwegian, Swede, Finn, or Dane that the people whose language he speaks, whose past he shares, and whose ways of looking at things are much like his own, are *his* people and stand apart from others in culture, traditions, language, and mores in general.

Leaving aside the subtler and more baffling aspects of emergence and evolution of national consciousness in Scandinavia, two useful generalizations may be offered at the outset. First, it was the hundred years from the middle decades of the eighteenth century to the middle of the nineteenth that witnessed the appearance of this national consciousness as an upper and middle class conception and ideal desirable or essential for patriotic citizenship. Secondly, the conception and the ideal have also become, during the past two or three generations, part of the common man's way of understanding his place in the nation and his feeling of oneness in the linguistic and cultural group the nation represents. The result has been that national consciousness has appeared and binds high and low in a common unity that no earlier creed or set of beliefs was ever able to achieve in comparable degree.[4]

---

are suggested and helpfully dealt with in Carlton J. H. Hayes, *Essays on Nationalism* (New York, 1926), especially Chapter 1; Halvdan Koht, "Nationalism," in *Bulletin of the Polish Institute of Arts and Sciences in America*, III, No. 3–4 (April–July, 1945), 614–21; Salo W. Baron, *Modern Nationalism and Religion* (New York, 1947), pp. 3–7.

[4] That something like national consciousness existed before the eighteenth century is of course true. Johan Nordström's *De Yverbornes Ö* (Stockholm, 1934), for example, contains fascinating illustrations of it before 1700.

In the crystallization and spread of this unifying creed three lines of endeavor played an especially important role. While they were separate neither in point of time nor in other ways, they can best be understood if they are noted separately, at least in part. They may be labeled the discovery of the common folk, the discovery of the "national" past, and the effort to "perfect" or "emancipate" the national language. The first and the second were conspicuous features in each of the four countries, while the third assumed real significance only in Norway and Finland.

Acting partly in response to the contributions of Rousseau, Macpherson, Schiller, and others, patriotic studies of a considerable variety began to appear in the eighteenth century which laid the foundation of the modern conception of a Norwegian (or Swedish, or Finnish, or Danish) fatherland and separate nationality. Learned men in schools and universities, members of the clergy, and others discovered that the language of the common people deserved close attention, that folklore and folk songs were worthy of the collector's effort, and that the customs of the common people represented a fascinating and rewarding field of study. The life and character of the common folk became, within a few decades, an active concern of the world of the learned and of the amateur student as well. By the time the French Revolution had begun to exert its corrosive and dynamic influence in Europe (but apparently in large measure independent of any direct French stimulus), a new and vital intellectual orientation had evolved. The common folk, the people, the tillers of the soil, who had hitherto been seen, for the most part, as mere hewers of wood and carriers of water, had been emancipated from their earlier lowly anonymity and had become the "nation."

Meanwhile the discovery of the "nation" had come to involve fresh impulses, interests, and achievements in the field of historical scholarship. Especially in degree as extensive riches of folklore, ballads, and mythology were unearthed by enthusiastic followers of the new fashions in "patriotic studies," historians began to concern themselves with the national past as never before. Collectors and compilers of facts ferreted new information out of old sources or found and explored new ones. To describe as fully as possible how one's forebears had lived and labored; to bridge the gaps separating institutions but dimly seen in distant past ages from institutions still functioning; to trace the ups and downs of dynasties, or the nature of "national characteristics"; to explain the manner in which fashions in dress and mores and language had evolved—all this and much more became part of the expanding domain of the historian.

The historian (he was merely an amateur historian, in most instances) was by no means the sole or even the most important participant in these labors. He was assisted by the poet, the dramatist, the litterateur, and scholars from other fields, many of them intellectuals in the service of state and church without academic affiliation. By the opening of the nineteenth century their labors added up to a major contribution. At their hands there had emerged attractive conceptions of Norwegian, Swedish, Finnish, and Danish "national characteristics," and in them they and their followers took immense pride. Meantime, too, a new and richer national history was being discovered—and in every case it turned out to be a national history which good patriots could proudly accept as the epic of a fatherland worthy of the full devotion of her sons. Greater love of the homeland and greater admiration of the people that constituted one's nation were two of the conspicuous consequences of these trends.[5]

The patriotic inspirations called forth and sustained by these developments were intensified—not the least because the national past they illumined turned out to be, in each case, a "heroic" national past—as a consequence of the Napoleonic upheavals in Europe. Every one of the four peoples experienced, in varying degree, defeat and national humiliation at the hands of foreign powers during the last half-dozen years of Napoleon's regime. In each case, defeat and humiliation appear to have been a definite cause of the deepening, in the years after 1815, of the trends noted. There was little in the outcome of the war years that ended in 1815 to excite pride in the present or confidence in the future, while the past, where virtues and heroism worthy of admiration and emulation were embedded in the very life of the people themselves, could be viewed with pride and would sustain the patriot as he faced the darker years ahead.[6]

[5] For brief summaries of these studies and their import see Brynjolf J. Hovde, *The Scandinavian Countries, 1720–1865* (Boston, 1943), I, 139–49; John H. Wuorinen, *Nationalism in Modern Finland* (New York, 1931), pp. 18–28; Oscar J. Falnes, *National Romanticism in Norway* (New York, 1933), *passim*.

[6] See Hovde, *op. cit.*, II, 452 ff.

The changes wrought by the war years had indeed been profound. To say that the political map of the North had been more radically changed by 1815 than at any other earlier time since the four peoples had emerged on the scene of European history is to state the obvious, but the statement discloses little or nothing of the specific circumstances important in the continued growth of Norwegian, Swedish, Finnish, and Danish national consciousness.

Denmark in particular, and Sweden to a somewhat lesser degree, had suffered defeat and experienced humiliation. When the French Revolution began, Denmark-Norway represented a sizable monarchy whose North Atlantic domain was of respectable proportions and whose position at the entrance to the Baltic Sea had long meant continuing commercial advantage. The vicissitudes of the war years had brought reverses and hardships that culminated in the loss of Norway and the reduction of Denmark to only a fraction of her earlier size and prominence. Having been for centuries able to influence in a multitude of ways the international political situation and the balance of power in the North, Denmark by 1815 had become a small monarchy with an impressive past and, seemingly, an extremely modest future.

In some respects the new status of Sweden was not unlike that of Denmark. The Kingdom of Sweden had comprised Finland as well as Sweden itself, ever since those early days centuries ago when a national monarchy in the real sense of the word had emerged. It was to this centuries-old state, which Swedish and Finnish historians of the last generation have often spoken of as Sweden-Finland, that there had been added, especially in the seventeenth century, certain dependencies in the Baltic provinces and in Germany. They were bona fide dependencies ruled as such, and never parts of the Kingdom. Most of them had been lost by the end of the first half of the 1700's, and what remained when Napoleon began to remake the political map of most of Europe was the Sweden compressed within the borders, approximately, of the Sweden and Finland of our day.

It was this Sweden-Finland straddling the Gulf of Bothnia that was divided by Russian aggression after 1808. Russia took Finland in 1808–1809 by military conquest which stemmed from a deal entered into by Napoleon and Alexander I. Finland, hitherto an integral part of Sweden, became a part of Russia, and Sweden was thus contracted within her present geographical limits. While this territorial contraction was, in a sense, merely the culmination of a process begun in the first quarter of the eighteenth century, it was considered at the time a national calamity of the first order. Among its consequences was the ousting of the reigning king and the selection of a new successor to the Swedish throne. The choice ultimately fell (in 1810) upon Bernadotte, one of Napoleon's Marshals, who was elected partly because it was expected that he would recover Finland and thus erase the most humiliating defeat in Swedish history up to that time.[7]

Such hopes proved to be vain, however. Bernadotte concluded that Sweden's—and his own—interests would not be well served by an attempt to recover Finland. Instead, he conceived the idea of acquiring, as compensation, the state of Norway. Favored by circumstances, he succeeded in this bold scheme. By the time the general peace settlement of 1815 had been concluded, Bernadotte had brought about a dynastic union between Sweden and Norway. The former French Marshal thus found himself the heir-apparent to the throne of Norway as well as Sweden (the former had been occupied by the Danish monarch since the fourteenth century). In 1818 he became king of both countries. Successful as the Norwegian enterprise of Bernadotte turned out to be, it did not, however, suffice to remove the profound sense of loss caused by the cession of Finland to the Russian colossus.[8]

In the meantime, Norway's status had likewise been altered. Dynastic and Great Power policies, in which the people of Norway had played no part, had led to the cession of Norway by Denmark to the Swedish crown in 1814. In the midst of these developments Norwegian patriots, unwilling to have the future of their country determined by impotent Danes and grasping Swedes, declared Norway an independent kingdom, chose a monarch, and drafted a democratic constitution as the new fundamental law of the nation; thus Norway returned, for the first time in four centuries, to the ranks of free and sovereign states. Swedish armed force and pressure from Britain, however, compelled the Norwegians to abandon the idea

---

[7] See Sam. Clason, *Karl XIII och Karl XIV Johan* (Stockholm, 1923), Chapter III (Vol. XI in *Sveriges historia till våra dagar,* edited by E. Hildebrand and L. Stavenow); Fredrik Böök, *Esaias Tegner* (Stockholm, 1917), pp. 92–184.

[8] Fredrik Böök, *ibid.,* and *Esaias Tegner, samlade skrifter* (Stockholm, 1923), pp. 364–76.

of a fully separate monarchy and king, and to accept a union with Sweden. The new constitution remained, nevertheless, and the right of the Norwegians to manage their own internal affairs appeared to be secured.[9]

While there was no enthusiasm in Norway for the union thus forced upon the country by outside compulsion, and while the failure to break all the bonds of dependence upon a foreign monarchy caused bitter disappointment in some quarters, the new constitution and internal autonomy were substantial gains that augured well for the future. A great forward stride had been taken during the exciting months when a fully free Norway had been in the making: national consciousness had acquired a fervor and patriotism an intensity unknown earlier, and would in time irresistibly challenge and ultimately dissolve the union with Sweden.

Finally, Finland had been profoundly affected, as has already been noted in passing, by the events of these turbulent years. Having been a fully integral part of Sweden for centuries, and her people having been "native Swedes," equal in political rights and other privileges with the inhabitants of Sweden proper, the country was included within the confines of the Russian Empire in 1808–1809, by the fiat of military conquest. However, Finland's new affiliation meant from the outset, as did that of Norway, improved administrative and political status. It meant also the carrying-over, into the new affiliation, of a number of significant features of the institutions and laws that had functioned in Finland as well as Sweden while the two nations were still united.

The salient characteristics of the new political and administrative status of the country can best be suggested by saying that Finland became a part of the Russian Empire as an autonomous, constitutional state. Her constitution remained unchanged; that is, the "Swedish" constitution in operation when Russia took over Finland remained in force, except for some changes having to do with succession to the throne and related matters. Finnish citizenship was established, and local administration and courts, schools and the educational system in general, were subject to no basic change; the Lutheran Church was retained as the state church; a higher,

---

[9] See Karen Larsen, *A History of Norway* (Princeton, N. J., 1948), pp. 373–95; Knut Gjerset, *History of the Norwegian People* (New York, 1932 ed.), II, 398–447.

national administration was created, manned by Finnish citizens and not subject to Russian imperial administrative organs, but directly to the Tsar (whose title as monarch in Finland was Grand Duke); the legislature retained the composition and the powers of the Swedish Riksdag of the year 1809. Such were some of the more obvious and significant features of the order of things which, in many ways unaccountably, emerged from the bitter defeats of 1808-1809 and the severance of centuries-long ties previously uniting Finn and Swede.[10]

Briefly stated, these were the main immediate consequences of the Napoleonic period in the lands of the North as recorded in territorial and political arrangements by 1815. In each case the consequences tended to stimulate continuing interest in national history, national folklore, and, especially in the case of Norway and Finland, in the development of a "national" language. Within two generations patriotic endeavors in these three fields—never really separate, needless to say—had produced astonishingly impressive results, and by the 1860's and 1870's it was becoming clear that the movement which had hitherto been largely "for the people," would henceforth be "of the people" and "by the people" as well. That is to say, with the emergence of modern state-controlled and state-directed systems of popular education in the four countries, and with the appearance of the modern newspaper, powerful agencies had been brought into being to assist in spreading to the masses the appreciation for "that which is national" in speech, in ways of looking at the nation and the world, and, in general, patriotic readiness to understand what the nation meant for the individual and what it required of him in devotion, love, and sacrifice.

IV

Denmark serves as a striking illustration of the prevailing moods and aspirations after 1815. There the national disasters of 1807-1814 had not been tempered by a hopeful and vitalizing effort at

[10] See Wuorinen, *Nationalism in Modern Finland*, pp. 29–39. The liberality of Alexander I in allowing the establishment of an autonomous, self-governing Finland presents a fascinating puzzle that appears to defy solution. The same can be said about the continuing of the self-governing status of Finland after 1825 and the broadening domain of autonomy after 1860.

constitution-making, attempted national independence, or improved status for the nation, as had happened in Norway; or by gains comparable to the autonomy and self-rule that led many a Finn to accept the inclusion of Finland in the Russian Empire with less anguish and trepidation than would have been the case if Finland had become merely a subordinate province governed from St. Petersburg; or by satisfactions comparable to those felt by a Swede when he contemplated Norway as a sufficient substitute for Finland, regrettably lost to Russia. In Denmark there was little more than a feeling of impotence and the realization that the Danes, who had been unable to prevent the loss of Norway, had best forget all thoughts of recapturing lost territory and glory and turn their attention to healing as quickly as possible the inner wounds inflicted upon the nation during the years of war and defeat.

It was to this task of healing the nation from within that a number of patriotic Danes now dedicated themselves. Norway had been lost for good, to be sure, but Denmark and the Duchies still remained. They constituted a land fertile and large enough and rich enough for a flourishing and prosperous nation. The misfortunes of war could be erased if the Danish farmer, and the Danes in general, would but work hard and dig deeper the foundations of national well-being. What had been lost by war could be recovered, many times over, by making new conquests—material, moral, and intellectual—within the confines of the smaller fatherland that remained as the sanctuary of free Danes high and low, rich and poor.[11] The misfortunes of war and the disastrous peace settlement turned out to lead to a national awakening that uplifted the nation and carried it to new heights of patriotic devotion.

One of the most impressive illustrations of the work of Danish national rehabilitation after 1815 was furnished by N. F. S. Grundtvig, the well-known pioneer in the field of adult education. Grundtvig was much more than a pedagogue interested in improving the educational facilities of his day. He was above all a patriot-moralist determined to impart, especially to the poor and untutored masses, the love of country and nationalistic fervor which he himself felt, in order to lead them thereby to a higher morality and a deeper

[11] See Aage Friis, Axel Linvald and M. Mackeprang, eds., *Det Danske Folks Historie* (Copenhagen, 1928), VI, 337–43, 502–16.

appreciation of the Christian religion. He founded his famous folk high schools primarily for the purpose of instilling in the common people of Denmark a patriotic attachment to country and greater love of nation, church, and God. Grundtvig was likewise a translator of old Norse sources and an historian of substantial achievement; it is probably correct to say that it was in considerable degree thanks to Grundtvig's work that the Danes became what one writer has called "one of the most historically-minded nations of the world."[12] He greatly deepened Danish national consciousness, and as a result of his labors the Danes were steeled for the struggle with Germanism in Schleswig and the grimmer contest with the Germans which culminated in the defeat suffered in the war of 1864. By that time a vigorous nationalism had become a source of strength that carried the Danes through the humiliations of 1864 to the exceptional achievements in cultural, political, and economic development that had come to characterize progressive and prosperous Denmark by 1914. Danish national consciousness remained, however, considerably more urbane and tolerant than that of their Northern neighbors.

In Norway, the development was basically the same. Two important and continuing endeavors characterized the growth of a robust national feeling in the country. One was the protest against the union with Sweden, and another was the attempt to bring to a complete and speedy end Norway's linguistic and cultural dependence upon Denmark. This twofold effort at national self-assertion ranged all the way from innocuous innovations in the use of "native" words in Norwegian speech or writing to a prolonged tug-of-war between the Norwegian legislature and the King of Sweden. At times it involved deep-felt hostility against both the Swedes and the Danes, and it has left aversions and hard feelings that have never fully disappeared.

The union controversy grew in the first instance from the fact that Norway had no share in the control of the foreign affairs of Sweden-Norway. This circumstance prevented Norwegian shipping and other interests from receiving the consideration desired by the Norwegians, and it was held in Norway that it underlined Norway's inferior position in the union. Also, while Norway was far from a

---

[12] Hovde, *op. cit.*, II, 463.

genuinely democratic country until past the middle of the century, the Eidsvoll constitution of 1814 was quite liberal enough to create, from the beginning of the union, a bothersome discrepancy between Norwegian political practices and institutions on the one hand and the more conservative political practices and institutions of Sweden on the other. The discrepancy became especially troublesome toward the end of the last century when Norway had acquired responsible cabinet government, which inevitably had to be responsive to Norwegian nationalist opinion no less than responsible to the legislature and to the nation at large. By the turn of the century it had become evident that the increasingly nationalist-conscious Norwegians would no longer be satisfied with mere equality in the union. Complete dissolution of the union was now demanded and in June 1905 the Norwegian government and legislature resolved that the union had come to an end. The crisis created by this action was solved peacefully when later in the year the Norwegians and the Swedes joined hands in agreeing to procedures for dissolving the union which satisfied Norwegian insistence upon action appropriate to a free people and Swedish desires for a recognition of bilateral action with due regard for the demands of constitutionality. Norway had become fully free and a sovereign member of the European family of nations.[13]

Meantime, the effort to free the Norwegian nation from its linguistic and cultural "bondage" to Denmark had proceeded apace. The enthusiasm which had been awakened by "patriotic studies" before 1814 was stimulated in the years thereafter by romanticist worship of the past, which accented Norwegian history, Norwegian heroes and, in general, Norwegian "culture" at the expense of Danish or other foreign elements in the life of the nation. "Norwegianism" became the watchword of the historians, literary men, collectors of folklore, and others who contributed to this effort. One of the most significant consequences of these labors was a revolutionary transformation of the Norwegian language—a transformation, incidentally, which has continued for over a century and has not yet come to a close.

During the four hundred years of Norway's union with Denmark,

---

[13] Larsen, *op. cit.*, Chapters XVI–XX, and Gjerset, *op. cit.*, II, 555–85, give a good summary of the developments culminating in the events of 1905.

the Danish written language, pronounced in a distinctive Norwegian manner, had become current among the urban, educated, and official classes in Norway. As a result, the language of the classes differed markedly from the language of the masses and served to accent social and economic cleavages. The *landsmaal* spoken by the common people was a patois appropriate to untutored farmers and other lowly folk; the *riksmaal* of the classes was in itself a mark of distinction and essentially foreign to the majority of the people. What was needed, according to the Norwegian nationalists, was a cleansing of the Norwegian tongue from disfiguring Danicisms and the creation of a truly Norwegian idiom by bringing into the language of the upper classes the rich resources of the vernacular dialects.

The demand for language reform appeared early, but it began to register conspicuous gains only after 1860. "Language nationalism" is an appropriate designation for the effort, ultimately successful, to fuse a dozen dialects and the official *riksmaal* of the classes into a "national" language. In the process, the cause of the language nationalists was aided by the fact that it became a part of the struggle to emancipate the masses from the political and economic inequalities which bore down upon the common people until the advent of modern democracy. Thus the preferences of nationalist-conscious patriots—many of them grammarians and philologists, some self-taught enthusiasts, laboring for an inspiring cause—and the demands of democratic advance combined ultimately to turn a semi-artificial language into the "national" tongue of a people determined to tolerate no foreignisms in its idiom. That the workers in the vineyard had meanwhile asserted in a multitude of ways Norway's cultural independence and separateness, especially from everything savoring of Danish, was in keeping with the compelling desire to exalt the indigenous and to minimize or deny foreign elements in the culture of the nation.

While much of public opinion in Finland—that is, articulate public opinion—accepted the new order after 1809 without paralyzing misgivings, there were many Finns who considered the union with Russia a calamity and hoped for its early dissolution. In their eyes Russia was a backward, detestable autocracy unworthy of the respect of free men, and a military aggressor that had repeatedly brought war to Finland in the past and would destroy the country in the future by absorbing and Russifying the nation. A group of young patriots, at first a mere handful without influence, proceeded to search for safeguards against this calamity. They found the principal safeguard in national unity—or, to use the term frequently employed in these pages, national consciousness.

Briefly stated, these young patriots and their followers held that if the people of Finland could be made to feel that they constituted a separate, distinct nationality, a source of strength would have been found that would make it possible for the nation of little more than one million people to stand fast even in the face of the pressures that the Russian giant would in time exert. The future of the nation could be most securely founded upon the rock of national distinctiveness.

The desired national unity, however, could only be built on linguistic unity. Yet linguistically Finland was divided into two parts, and had been so divided since the beginning of recorded history. Somewhat less than 90 per cent of the people spoke Finnish, while the mother tongue of the rest was Swedish. While the great majority of the Swedish-speaking part of the population consisted of farmers, fishermen, and other lowly folk, the middle and upper classes (small in numbers, for the country was still overwhelmingly agrarian) were predominantly Swedish in speech. When the patriots spoke of linguistic unity as the basis of national unity—a national unity which they considered essential lest the future of the nation be imperiled—they had especially in mind the fact that the upper class minority was separated from the bulk of the people not only by economic and social status but also by their Swedish language. They urged that because Finnish was the language of the majority of the nation, the upper classes should abandon the use of Swedish and become Finnish in speech. Swedish was, incidentally, the sole official language of the country till the 1860's and, as was observed above, still is one of the two official languages in Finland.

The program ultimately involved developments that bring to mind the "language nationalism" noted as part of the nationalist development in Norway after 1814. Not the least obvious of the similarities was the effort to rid the Finnish language of Swedish and other "foreign impurities"—an effort that has not yet fully subsided. Before long it also came to involve far-reaching educational reform, including the establishment after 1868 of a national system of primary schools and a rapid expansion of secondary schools as well. By the end of the century the "nationality conflict" had resulted in the creation not of one but of two nationalist-conscious groups in the country. The Finns had been aroused to the feeling of national separateness[14] which the early patriots after 1809 had considered essential for Finland's survival as a part of Russia; and the Swede-Finns had become sufficiently aware of their national separateness to make it possible for them to form a "Swedish People's Party" in 1905. In the meantime the two nationalist movements had broadened in many ways into democratizing influences that helped to usher in the social and political egalitarianism which ultimately found expression, *inter alia,* in the establishment of universal suffrage and a single chamber legislature in 1906, the proclamation of the independent Republic in December 1917, and the adoption of a republican constitution in 1919. Moreover the people had developed a love of country and feeling of national and cultural separateness from Russia which enabled the nation to withstand ruthless Tsarist efforts at Russification—and in the unequal struggle which this contest entailed until the collapse of Tsarist Russia in 1917 (to say nothing of the later battles for survival with Bolshevist Russia) Finn and Swede-Finn stood shoulder to shoulder.[15] They thus proved beyond challenge that much of the "language fight" had involved grievances and prejudices of no lasting import, and that the nationality controversy had not weakened or destroyed the higher loyalty toward nation and country as a whole.

While Sweden was not compelled to contend with the kind of dangers that beset the Finns in their precarious position within the Russian Empire, or exposed to the menacing propinquity of an

[14] Strong aversion to the Swedish language and to everything Swedish was often a characteristic of the movement, and the transformation of Finnish into an official language (achieved between 1863 and 1902) and the language of the classes as well as of the masses (accomplished gradually by the time the first World War broke out) was another. The unearthing of exceptionally rich stores of folklore and songs—the first edition of *Kalevala* appeared in 1835—likewise was a part of the movement, the consequences of which have remained significant down to our day.

[15] Chapters II–VI and the first two sections of Chapter VII of Wuorinen, *Nationalism in Modern Finland,* offer a convenient summary of these developments.

aggressive German neighbor as was Denmark, or called upon to assert itself against the real or imaginary political domination of one state and the objectionable cultural and linguistic influences of another as was the case in Norway, the Swedes were not slower than their fellow-Scandinavians in developing into a nationalist-conscious people.

In the process, resentments caused by the growing claims and pretensions of the Norwegians regarding the union played a part. It also appears clear that fear of Russia, the perennial enemy in the past and seemingly the only potential enemy in the future, contributed to the same end. More significant, however, was the rich contribution that flowed from poets, historians, and others who explored the proud past when Sweden had been a great power, or described the present in vivid colors of pleasing hue, or predicted, as only men blessed with the vision of the seer can, the glories of the days yet to come. The extensive treasures of Swedish folklore and folk songs and native peasant culture were unearthed and studied as the products of an admirable native national genius. It appears, incidentally, that the historians were especially important in inspiring the generations after 1815 with love of country, in arousing pride in the national past, and in spreading the feeling that the Swedes constituted a separate nation with a splendid indigenous culture inferior to none and superior to most.

v

Brief as is the above summary of the emergence of national consciousness among the four peoples of the North, it invites consideration of some of the larger implications of this relatively recent phenomenon in Scandinavia. The trends in Norway, Sweden, Finland, and Denmark were, after all, not peculiar to them alone; they were part and parcel of similar developments elsewhere in Europe. These countries' experience may therefore reasonably be expected to reveal, at least in some measure, significances and meanings pertinent to the study and understanding of the same phenomenon elsewhere in the modern world.

One of the most conspicuous features of the history of national consciousness in these countries is that it appeared in societies that were overwhelmingly agrarian and remained overwhelmingly agrarian during the decades when the new dispensation took hold and gained ground. There is no evidence to show that the so-called Industrial Revolution was importantly involved. To talk of, say, the urban industrial community, the railroad, or the modern newspaper as decisive factors in the creation and early spread of national consciousness is to forget that in these countries the machine, the factory, and other evidences of modern industrialization appeared only after the poet, the historian, the folklorist, and other patriots in stations high and low had set in hard and virtually unchanging mold the creed which the followers of a Grundtvig or Aasen or Geijer or Snellman accepted. In fact, when industrialization became significant later, in the closing decades of the last century, it brought with it the industrial worker, who soon turned out to be an organized, class-conscious laborer and as such inclined to Socialism and not to the acceptance of nationalist views. The organized laboring man capable of reconciling patriotic attachment to the fatherland, in the ordinary bourgeois sense, with his acceptance of Socialism, is, in Scandinavia, mainly a product of the last generation or two.

Some students of modern nationalism have concluded that it has involved, basically, the emergence of a new faith that is not only akin to religion but is itself a religion destructive of the Christian faith. The generalization does not apply to these Northern nations. In each country, it is true, national consciousness was often defined, its claims upon the individual described and the goals to be sought indicated, the glories of the national past or of the native culture admired and adored, in a manner that inevitably brings to mind devotion and dedication of a religious kind. But, unless single-minded devotion to the cause be arbitrarily called a religion, and unless the gratuitous assumption is made that such devotion automatically means partial or complete renunciation of the Christian religion and church and acceptance of the new "religion" of nationality and the worship of its gods, there is no reason for speaking of the developments traced in these pages as representing, in any meaningful sense of the term, the emergence of a new and exacting religion. The fact is that in every one of the four countries the cause was carried forward by many a devout member of the clergy, that its first and greatest mass appeal was to the common folk, solidly anchored to conventional religious moorings, and that it appears nowhere to have been understood to imply a conflict with the established church or religion. And there is, finally, good reason for concluding that the passive or inimical attitudes toward church and religion that have appeared and spread—especially during the past two generations—can, and in fact must, be explained in terms that have nothing to do with national consciousness.

Nor can modern political democracy be easily fitted into the picture. It must be abundantly clear that political democracy was still only the dream of the few and not the possession of the many when the new national goals were being set. To select what may be called the most conspicuous single illustration of the real relationship between political democracy and the nascent nationalism under discussion: universal suffrage in the North appeared for the first time in 1906, when the right to vote was granted to adult women as well as men in Finland. By that time nationalist developments in Norway had already become such as to dissolve the union with Sweden, and Finland, for instance, had already become sufficiently unified, through the devotion of most Finns to the cause of nationality and state, to offer robust resistance to the policy of Russification. In a word, national consciousness antedated political democracy by many decades.

More than that, the developments that created a nationalist-conscious citizenry in each of the four countries directly contributed to the processes of democratization. While most of the Norwegian, Swedish, Finnish, and Danish workers in the nationalist cause were in no sense democrats, the movement they served was basically egalitarian. When the professional scholar or the amateur brought to light treasures of folklore and songs, or disclosed how distant generations had lived while still "untainted" by contact with the outside world, or sought to separate "native" from "foreign" elements in the speech of the people, he was likely for the most part to deal with the world of the common man. It was the common man—especially the "unspoiled" peasant—who came to be considered as the embodiment of "national" traits and characteristics. Norway and Finland again furnish some of the best illustrations—and the most striking perhaps was the manner in which the anonymous little fellow contributed of his vocabulary and idiom to the upbuilding of the new and "purer" national language. Nor should it be forgotten that nearly all of the extensive treasure of folklore and the like was derived from the same source. Thus the very attempt to preserve and to cherish that which was considered to be really "national," and therefore precious, meant that the process of closing the gap separating the classes from the masses was speeded and the path for later emancipation prepared.

It seems to be equally clear that national survival itself was aided by the growth of national consciousness. Without entering into the question whether the appearance of a free Norway or an independent Finland, or the freeing of Denmark from Nazi domination in 1945, or the successful safeguarding of Swedish neutrality in 1914–1918 and again in 1939–1945, served vital interests outside the Scandinavian North, it is safe to say that without a strong feeling of national consciousness these four nations would have long since been but chaff in the storm and their freedom subject to the caprices of the first aggressor determined to subjugate them. Quite apart from the incontrovertible fact that these peoples are determined to remain free and consider their independence worth fighting and dying for, and that, being free, they consider themselves better human beings and citizens than man in bondage can ever be, the evidence to date appears to prove beyond doubt that the existence of these peoples as free nations serves the larger interests of freedom elsewhere. It likewise proves, incidentally, that militarism—so often a derivation of nationalism and so often a threat to international peace—has not been a part, and is not a part, of the nationalism of these peoples. For nearly a century and a half they have solved controversies among themselves by compromise and arbitration; war has entered into their experience only when their freedom has been threatened by military aggression from outside Scandinavia.

There is still another aspect to the history of national awakening in Scandinavia that requires a word of comment. Along with labor of the noblest kind and devoted and unselfish sacrifice of the highest type, the movement has involved in each country, from the beginning, a variety of extravagances and crudities that stand out in sharp relief. Boastful claims to superior "national" virtues; marked ingenuity in discovering heroic attributes at home, coupled with myopia in appraising the foreigner; overweening pride in the assumed superiority of one's own people, culture, language, history, honesty, cleanliness, and other fine qualities denied by a discriminating Providence to lesser breeds; lack of becoming modesty in claims to distinctions large and small without which, seemingly, a nationalist-conscious people cannot exist—such shortcomings abound and are a part of the record in each case. Nothing would be more misleading, however, than to attribute them to the national awakening itself. A consideration of them brings to mind the facetious remark to the effect that an individual's capacity for sin remains constant, and that if one kind of opportunity for sin is eliminated or reduced, others at once fill the gap. The fact is that such shortcomings existed long before modern national consciousness had appeared to influence the life of nations and to baffle the historian. They belong among the universal frailties of man. They will no doubt continue to exist as long as man remains what he is, and national consciousness will in all likelihood illustrate in the future, as it has illustrated in the past, man's amazing capacity for prideful ignorance, arrogant vanity, and self-deceiving ostentation, coupled with his equally amazing capacity for ample generosities and self-sacrificing devotion in the service of his fellow-men.

INDEX

Abolitionists, 447
Abstractions, see Personification of
Academy of Music, New York, 440
Acton, Lord, 294, 296, 301
Adams, John, 19, 21, 36; election of, blow to French cause, 23; speech to Congress, 26; replies, 29, 32, 33; French agent's condemnation, 27, 30 f.; death, 433
Adelfi, 323
Adet, Pierre Auguste, Minister to U. S., 18; return to France, 19, 23; Franco-American relations of his time, 21 ff., 41; letters of secret agent, Comte d'Hauterive, 22–24 (see also Hauterive)
Affaires Étrangères, France, 18n
Africa, need for new individualism, 350; German schools in lost colonies, 408; major objective of Hitler's *Kolonialpolitik*, 413 ff.; Monroe Doctrine for, 426; German economic interests in, 426, 428
Agriculture, Young's agrarian interests, 144, 157, 159, 160; mechanization in, 339; Soviet peasant collectives, 348; Germany's agrarian interests and class, 357, 359, 361, 372, 373, 375, 386, 388; Greeley's agricultural expansion program, 444
Ahlwardt, leader of anti-Semitism, 360
Aix-la-Chapelle, Congress of, 189
Alexander I of Russia, deal with Napoleon, 465
Algeria demanded by Spain, 427
Aliens, danger of interference by, in domestic policies of U. S., 440
Alliance Démocratique, 422
Allied Powers, decision to give Lombardy and Venetia to Habsburgs, 313
Altieri, Abbé, 328
America, Young's mercantilistic attitude towards colonies, 147, 149; prediction that eventually British King would move to, 150
American Farmer (Crèvecoeur), 42
"American Frontier, The—Frontier of What?" (Hayes), x
American Historical Association, x
American Revolution, hailed by Klopstock, 141; Young's attitude towards, 152
Americans, Greeley felt, were superior to Europeans, 437

Amery, L. S., 105, 416
Amiens, Peace of, 184
Anatomy of Frustration, The (Wells), excerpt, 118
"An Freund und Feind" (Klopstock), 130
Anglo-French relations, Young's nationalism evaluated by attitudes towards, 161
Anglo-German Naval Treaty, Hitler's triumphs in, 411
Anglophobia in America, 433
Anglo-Portuguese treaty of 1913, 419
Angola, Portuguese, 425
Annals of Agriculture, 145, 154, 157, 177, 187; Young's crusade against French Revolution, 169 ff.
Ann Veronica (Wells), 83n
Anschluss, "cold," 422
Anticipations (Wells), 112, 116; re excerpts, 114n
Anti-Semitism, see Jews
Antraigues, Comte d', 192n
A priori historiography, of Hegel, 68, 69; of later writers, 71, 74, 77
Aranda, Spanish prime minister, 194, 202, 203, 220
Arcambal, French Consul, 19
Aristocracies, hostile, of Germany, 386 ff.
Armaments, German championship of, 352, 363, 372, 377, 381, 383, 384; see also Military power
"Armed Neutrality or War" (Hayes), xiiin
Arminius, freed Germans from Roman yoke, 251, 255
Arminius-Dialog (Hutten), 139
Army, German, 255; see also Military power
Arndt, Ernst Moritz, 137, 259
Arts, role in nationalism, 6, 7; Greeley's nationalistic attitude towards, 439; see also Nationalism: cultural
Asia, need for new individualism, 350
Assemblée nationale, L', 197
Atkinson, C. F., tr., 70n
Atlantic Pact, military alliance in full sense of term, 455
Atomic energy, 117, 349
Atomic weapons, foreseen by Wells, 89n, 107n, 117
Auerswald, Ida von, 138
Auguste Victoria of Germany, 254

Austria, war with France, 167, 202, 204; defeat at Austerlitz, 185; coat of arms torn down in Brivio, 313; *see also* Habsburgs
Authoritarianism, living death of spirit, 284; imperial regimes termed dictatorships, 298; means for combining with democracy, 352; prophecy re regimes which rest upon equalitarian democracy, 371 f.; authority of Kaiser, 389 ff.
Autobiography (Young), 147
Avant-garde . . . L', 226, 227
Aviation, military: forecasts by Wells, 116
Avis aux espagnols (Condorcet), 204
Aviso a los españoles (Condorcet), 205
Axis, Rome-Berlin, 411, 412
Aydelotte, William, 82n

Badger, George, 448
Bagdad Railway, Anglo-German agreements, 419
Baldwin, Stanley, 416
Ballesteros y Beretta, 192
Bancroft, George, 432
Barbier de Seville (Beaumarchais), 199
Barbour, I. K., 445
Bardic movement, 141
Bardiete (Klopstock), 138–43
Barère de Vieuzac, Bertrand, 190, 209, 222, 225, 227, 235
Barras, P. F. N., Count de, 21
Barth, Theodor, 396
Bartok, Bela, 7
Basle, Treaty of, 230 ff.
Basques during Franco-Spanish war, 213
Bates, Edward, 444; Presidential candidate, 448
Battle of Leipzig, The, pro-Allied play hissed in Milan, 313
Baynes, N. H., 429
Bayreuth as shrine, 6, 11
Beard, Charles A., xi, xii
Beauharnais, Hortense, xii
Beaumarchais, plays, 195, 199; satires set in Spanish locale, 216
Bebel, August, 363
Beethoven, 245
"Beiden Musen, Die" (Klopstock), 135
Belfast, labor bigots, 61, 62
Belgian Congo, protest against incorporation of Ruanda Urundi into, 400
Bellegarde, Count, 311; government of Lombardy, 313, 314, 316, 328, 331; plot to seize, 327
Belloc, Hilaire, on Wells, 99n

Bellotti, 326, 329
Bennett, Arnold, 80, 106
Bentinck, Lord William, influence upon Italian malcontents feared, 320
Benvenuto Cellini (Berlioz), 11
Beresford, J. D., quoted, 83
Bergamo, revolt plotted, 327
Berlin City Mission, 355
Berlioz, Hector, life and afterfame: ecumenical representative of French culture, 9–17; centenary: publication of scores: composers influenced, 12; conductors who understood and played, 12n, 13; cosmopolitan mind: association with Romanticism, 15; Memoirs and biography, 15n
Berlioz et l'Europe romantique (De Pourtalès), 13
Bernadotte, Jean Baptiste I, succession to Swedish throne: acquisition of Norway, 466
Bible and Jewish nationalism, 92n
Biblioteca Italiana, 335
Biedermann, Karl, praise of Klopstock, 136; warning against emphasis on military events in history, 249
Bills of Rights, 342
Bismarck, Prince von, 5, 6, 361n, 376, 389, 406, 410; and wife, xii; legislative system, 353, 360, 369, 394; liberals and, 365, 369; handling of socialists, 378; of suffrage, 389n
Bizet's *Carmen*, 10
Blanc, Louis, 51
Blaue Buch von Vaterland und Freiheit, Das (Naumann), 372n, 379n, 381n, 385n, 388n, 391n, 392n, 396n
Blomberg, General, 425
"Blount (Senator) conspiracy," 32, 37
Blümel, Ernst, on value of modern history teaching, 249
Bodmer, quoted, 126
Boer War, 102
Boie, praise of Klopstock, 137
Bolingbroke, Lord, 47
Bombelles, Count, 325, 326
Bonnet, 422
Borel, French propagandist agent, 215
Borromean League, 268
Boschot, Adolphe, 15n
Boucheseiche, J. B., 217
Bouchotte, Colonel, 215
Bourbons, Spanish concern for French royal family, 196, 203; *see also* Louis XVI; Louis XVII

Index 483

Bourgeoisie, German: extent of political maturity, 376
Bourgoing, Baron de, French ambassador to Spain, 202, 203, 206, 209, 211, 230, 235; publication by: its reliability, 194
Bowe, Obadiah A., 438
Breitkopf und Härtel, 12
Bremer Beiträge, 126
Brentano, Lujo, 364n, 390n, 396
Brescia, fighting between Italians and Austrian soldiers, 318; revolt plotted, 326 f.
Bristol, Lord, *see* Hervey, Frederick
British Empire, justification and expansion of, 285, 297 ff., 302; India, 298 f.; Hitler ready to accept, if his colonial demands are fulfilled, 426; *see also* England; Great Britain
British Social Politics (Hayes), xiii
"Brother Nicolas," 265, 266
Brownson, Orestes, 446
Brunetti, 326, 327, 329
Brüning, Chancellor, 401
Brunswick, Duke of, Manifesto, 204, 213
Bryant, William Cullen, 438
Bryce, Lord, 112
Buckingham, Duke of, 321
Bülow, B. H. M., Prince von, 430
Bülow, Hans von, 11
Bulpington of Blup, The (Wells), excerpt, 109n
Bürger, Gottfried August, 137
Burgundians, vanquished by Swiss, 264
Burke, Edmund, 48, 154; "traditional nationalism," 144; Young's criticism of, 167; on Young's *The Example of France*, 172
Burney, Dr., on Young's *The Example of France*, 172
Burr, Aaron, 29, 39
Bury Post and Universal Advertiser, 155
Bury St. Edmunds troop, 176
Business, diminishing importance of small-scale, 343
Butt, Isaac, Home Rule movement, 52

Caesarism, democratic: as attempt to reconcile German monarchy and people, 362, 380, 389
Calvinism in Swiss cities, 268
Cambridge, Duke of, Lombards desire as sovereign, 309
Cambridge University, Seeley's work and influence, 286, 292, 294

Canada and Louisiana, French dreams for, 32, 35, 42
Canary Islands, 428
Canning, ix
"Cantonal nationalism," 262
Capell, Peace of, 268
Cape Verde Islands, 428
Capitalism, Sombart's study of, 72 ff.; doctrine of competitive, 344; role in German economy, 387, 389; effect upon individual, 396
Caprivi, militarism, 393
Caprotti, 326, 329
Carbonari, 323, 326; active in favor of Napoleon's cause, 331
Carey, Henry, 432, 440
Carey, Matthew, 432
Carlès, French secretary, 206n, 210
Carlyle, Thomas, 291, 293
Carmen (Bizet), 10
Carnot, Lazare N. M., French commissioner, 190, 207, 222, 225
Caron, Pierre, 192, 217
Cartels, 397n
Cartwright, John, attack on Young, 173; Young's attempt to refute charges, 175, 177
Catalonia, revolt in, 198; French plans for bonds with, 222; treatment of, 229
Catéchism de la déclaration des droites de l'homme . . . (Boucheseiche), 217
Catholic Association, Irish, 49, 53
Catholic Emancipation, 49, 287; Young's fear of, 188
Catholics, *see* Roman Catholics
Cavedoni, 326, 329
Cecil, Viscount, 417
Center Party, Germany, 364, 366, 388
Central Association for Social Reform, 354
Centralization and local autonomy, 280
Centri, 323, 326, 327; active in favor of Napoleon's cause, 331
Cervantes, 3, 217
Chamberlain, Joseph, 90
Chamberlain, Neville, conciliatory move towards Hitler, 420
Chantreau's *Lettres* . . . , 218
Character-building chief function of education, 248
Charles III of Spain, 194, 195
Charles IV of Spain, 194, 196, 201, 226, 231, 232, 234
Charles the Bold of Burgundy, 264
Chaumié, Mlle., 191
Cheluzzi, 326

Chicago Rivers and Harbors convention, 444
"Christ in Zeitalter der Maschine, Der" (Naumann), 373n
Christianity, and Germanism, 247, 253; lack of principles upon which modern government could be founded, 371; see also Religion
Christian Socialist Party, Germany, 355, 360, 362, 367; founding of, 354; "old Christian Socialists," 359
Christliche Welt, Die, 373
Chuquet, Arturo, 223
Church, passive or inimical attitudes towards, 477; see also Religion; and under sects, e.g., Lutheranism; Roman Catholic; etc.
Citizenship, rights of active, in America, 337
Civil War, promoted trends in conflict with American tradition, 338
Clarence, Duke of, Lombards desire as sovereign, 309
Clarke, Tom, 55, 60
Classes, patriotism of agrarian upper classes in England, 144; Young's belief in class distinctions, 181; German, and their influence and interests, 374 ff., 386 ff.; dependence of political leadership upon economic power, 375; see also Labor; Masses; Proletariat
Claudius, Matthias, 138
Clay, Henry, 432, 440; land scheme, 443
Clayton, John M., 448
Clergy, French, and English compared, 165; German, 353–88 *passim*
Clive, Robert, 144
Cobbett, 189
Cobbett's Political Register, 187
Co-efficients, the ("Pentagram Circle"), 105
Colfax, Schuyler, 448
Colgan, Delia Larkin, 56n
Collaboration, monumental achievements that were products of: present need, 342
Collectivism, Marxian doctrine hostile to union with free enterprise, 283; tries to reduce all men to single pattern, 284
Collioure, Spain, capture of, 222, 223, 225, 228
Colonial Institute, Hamburg, 423
Colonialism, role in policy of Hitler's Third Reich, 390–430; rivalry reflected in Anglo-German debate, 418; training center for administrators, 423
Colonial possessions of England, 297, 302
Colonies, Young's wish that all nations would abandon, 163
Colonne, Edouard, 10
"Columbia School" of historians, xi
Columbia University, career of Hayes in, xi, xv
Comeyras, French agent, 215
Commerce, dependence upon naval power, 393
Committee for Study of Raw Materials, 418
Common Sense of World Peace, The (Wells), excerpts, 93, 96
Commonwealth in Danger, The (Cartwright), 173
Communal living, Soviet's failure to develop, 347
Communism, rejected by Wells, 115n; supernational appeal had parallel in doctrines of French Revolution, 282; hostile to union of collectivism and free enterprise, 283; American thought and the challenge of, 336–51; most valid criticism of, 341
Communist Manifesto, 340
Communist revisionism, 341
Communists, men can be forced to think as, 351; Hitler's aim to crush, 403
Conciliatore, Il, 335
Condorcet, Marquis de, 204, 205, 206, 218, 220
Confalonieri, 321
Conference of Christians and Jews, xvi
Connolly, James, sacrifice in Easter Rising, 55, 58; leader in Irish labor war, 55, 62
Conservative Party, Germany, 355, 357, 359, 360, 361, 366
Conservatism, passing of type which served landed or religious interests, 388
"Conservatism, Old," 367, 395
Considérations sur la conduite du gouvernement des États-Unis envers la France (Otto), 23
Constitution, English, 164, 166; Young's praise of, 178
Constitution Safe without Reform, The (Young), 177
Cooper, James Fenimore, 438
Copyright law, call for an international, 439
Corn bounty, Young's belief in, 148; opposed by Smith, 154

Corn Laws, 160
Correspondance du Cit. Hauterive en mission aux États-Unis . . . , 25n
"Correspondence of the French Ministers in the U. S.," 18n
Cosmopolitanism, 113, 120n
Cotton-picker, mechanical, 348
Courrier de Versailles à Paris . . . , 197
Couthon, on French-Spanish conflict, 222
Crampton, Professor, xii
Creighton, Mandell, 294
Cremona, revolt plotted, 327
Crèvecoeur, J. H. St. John de, 42, 432
Crewe, Lord, 417
Crewe, Mrs., on Young's *The Example of France,* 172
Cromwell, Oliver, 46, 299
Crusade in Europe (Eisenhower), xvn
Cultural nationalism, *see* Nationalism, cultural
Culture, importance in the "new history," xi; German, 128, 245, 249; as half of politics, 293
Curtis, Lionel, 112

Daily Telegraph (London), 397
Daily Tribune, New York, see Tribune
Damnation of Faust (Berlioz), 10, 13
Dana, Francis, 31, 33, 36
Dante as national poet, 3
Darré, 407
David, Jacques L., 232
Davis, Jefferson, bail bond signed by Greeley, 453
Davis, Thomas Osborne, 50
Davitt, Michael, 49n, 52
Debussy, Claude, 16
Decentralization, essence of American faith and practice, 338
Declaration of Independence, 342
Declaration of the Rights of Man, 199, 222, 342; ideas of, bound to spread, 169; principles violated, 170
Decline of the West (Spengler), 70
Defenders, of Ireland, 48, 49n
Defensional of Wil, 269
De Flers, French commander, 218
Deladier, on colonial question, 423
De la littérature allemande, 130
De Laugier, 325n
Delbrel, mission to French army, 229, 235
Delbrel, Père, 221n, 235, 236
Delbrück, Hans, 363, 365n
Delfini, 326
De Meestre, 326, 329

Democracy, committed to nationalism, 114; Wells's contempt for, 115n; England for first time ruled by public opinion and, 287; essence of American faith and practice, 338; need for adequate philosophy of ends and means, 341; attempt to reconcile German monarchy and people by means of democratic Caesarism, 352, 362, 380, 389; equalitarian: prophecy re authoritarian regimes which rest upon, 371 f.; given negative principles: what positive action required by new, 382; peaceful introduction into Germany possible, 384; must root among workers and employers, 385; relationship between political, and nascent nationalism in Scandinavia, 477
Démocrates Populaires, 422
Democratic Party, Germany, 398; *see also* Social Democratic Party
——— U. S., sectional in aims, 448
Democratic Socialism, trend towards, 344
Demokratie und Kaisertum (Naumann), editions: public's interest, 365; subjects dealt with, 365, 375, 377, 380 ff.; cited, 379n-394n *passim;* style, 380; extent of influence, 380, 394; treatment of unity between masses and nation, 383 ff.; Brentano critical of, 390n
Denis, Michael, 141
Denmark, geographically not part of Scandinavia, 459; emergence of national consciousness, 461; and Norway once single state, 461; loss of Norway: reduction in size, 465; cession of Norway to Sweden, 466; national awakening: work of Grundtvig, 469; achievements in cultural, political, and economic development, 470; effort to free Norway from linguistic and cultural bondage to, 471; *see also* Scandinavia
Deutscher Kolonialdienst, 408
"Deutsche Sprache, Die," (Klopstock), 134
De Valera, Eamon, 46, 55, 59
Devyr, Thomas Ainge, 443
Dickens, Charles, contrasted with H. G. Wells, 80, 81n, 82n
Dictatorship, imperial regimes now termed, 298; strong challenge to liberalism, 390; *see also* Authoritarianism
Discipline, mass, 345
Divine Providence, Hegel on, 65
Dog tax, 168
Draft of Agreement between States of

Draft of Agreement (*Continued*)
  Three Power Pact . . . and Soviet Union, Secret Protocol, 427
Dublin labor war of 1913-14, 62
Dubois-Crancé, 231*n*
Dugommier, French commander, 221, 222, 223, 224, 229; death, 228
Dujardin, Edouard, 11*n*
Dumouriez, Charles F., 211, 212, 215, 218
Dunning, Professor, xii
Du Pont, Victor, 23, 41
Du Pont de Nemours, 36*n*

East Africa, German schools in lost colonies, 408
Easter Rising of 1916, Ireland, 52, 55, 56, 60
East India Company, 298; attack upon monopoly of, 150
Ecce Homo (Seeley), 285, 286, 287
Echo des Pyrénées, 216
Eckermann, 143
Economic enterprise, change and expansion in U.S., 338
Economic forces moving from nationalism towards world state, 113 f.
Economic justification, of armaments and war, 383; of naval power, 393
Economic nationalism, Greeley's design for, 440
Economic power necessary for class political leadership, 375
Economy, dominant trend in, 340
Eden, Anthony, 411; rebuke to Hitler, 412; effort to discourage parliamentary discussions of colonial issue, 419, 420; stand on colonial issue: resignation, 421
Eden Treaty, 159, 163
Edict of Nantes, why Louis XIV revoked, 263
Education, Wells committed to cause of, broadly conceived, 80, 85; his faith in, and criticism of, 95; effectiveness of *Outline of History*, 99; for nationalism in Prussia, 241 ff.; importance of political, 288 ff.
Edwards, Jonathan, 431
Eidsvoll constitution of Norway, 471
Eisenhower, Dwight D., xv
Ekeris, Rector van, on history for German youth, 248
Elizabeth, Queen, 299
Émigrés, French, in Spain, 192, 199-234 *passim*

Emmet, Robert, 48; Larkin's tribute to, 60, 63
Empire, defined, 298; *see also* Imperialism
Enclosure bill, agitation in favor of, 183
Encyclopaedia, French, 342
Encyclopaedia Britannica, 296
Engels, Friedrich, xii, 340; *see also* Marxism
England, Shakespeare as culture hero: Romanticism, 4; conquest of Ireland, 46; Irish property rested on power of, 48; Irish discontent, 51, 53, 62; gentry intensely patriotic, 144; Young's list of reforms necessary in, 166; advantage of, to support France against eastern Europe, 167; Board of Agriculture established, 173, 174; danger of French invasion, 178; Young's plan to prevent domestic insurrection, 180; Nootka Sound controversy, 200; Franco-Spanish alliance against, 223; first time ruled by public opinion and democracy, 287; Seeley's histories: analysis of British imperialism and policy, 297 ff., 302; impact of foreign events, 300; Habsburgs concerned about influence of, 320; German sympathizers in, 416; *see also* British Empire; Great Britain
English, association with Italian liberals closely supervised, 321; influence in Lombardy-Venetia, 322
Englishman Looks at the World, An (Wells), excerpt, 104
Enlightenment, the, 47; in Spain, 194, 196; liberalism in France, 195
Enquiry into the State of the Public Mind amongst the Lower Classes, An (Young), 181, 182
Epp, Ritter von, 404, 407; demand for return of colonies, 409, 423
Epstein, M., tr. and ed., 72*n*
Erskine, John, xii
Erweckungsbewegung, 367
Esprit des prêtres, L' (Provost-Montfort), 217
Essays on Nationalism (Hayes), xiii; excerpts, 3, 120*n*
Ethiopia, Germany's recognition of Italian, 412
Europe, industrial and military potentials: cause of collapse, 281; threat from revolutionary parties within each nation, 282; cleavage among nations may be useful, 283; study of, must be free from parochialism, 291; Holy Roman

Index 487

Empire and unity: results of intensified nationality, 295; England part of states system: influence upon policy, 300; triumph of Commonwealth ideal of association of autonomous nations, 302; compact German state in eastern and middle, goal of German expansion, 405; West-East division: diversities among nations, 456
────United: Swiss Confederation pattern for, 261–84; Europeans increasingly willing to create, 281; French conception, 282; open to all nations: should begin on economic level, 283; argument for international federation, or United States of, 296; sovereigns to be chased out of Europe as preliminary step, 436; outside realm of possibility, 456
────Western: trend towards Democratic Socialism, 344
Evangelical pastors of Germany, social action, 353 ff.; "Young pastors," 359; reform out of fashion for, 362; denounced by consistory, 366
Evangelical Social Congress, 358, 359, 360, 361, 363, 372; founding of: purpose, 356
Evangelical Unions, 395
Evans, George Henry, 443
Evening Standard (London), 420
"Example of Europe a Warning to Britain, The" (Young), 185, 187
Example of France . . . , The (Young), 171 ff.
Expansion of England, The (Seeley), 285, 295, 302; analysis of, 297 ff.

Fabre de l'Hérault, 220, 235
Faenza, quarrel between aristocrats and Jacobins, 318
Fair Deal, 347
Fallersleben, Hoffman von, 273
Fame, creation of culture heroes, 3–17; see under Nationalism, cultural
Family Compact, Spain-France, 193, 200, 202, 231
Far East, in Japan's orbit, 414, 430
Farm, self-determination on, 347; how Government may act to save, 348
Farmer's Letters to the People of England, The (Young), 148
Fauchet, Abbé, 198
Fauchet, Claude, 18, 24n, 41
Faust (Goethe), 5
Federal state, basis of strength and durability, 276; dissension, within individual states may weaken, more than interstate disputes, 278; lines of cleavage within, source of strength, 279 ff.; see also State
Fédération Républicaine, 422
Fenians (Irish Republican Brotherhood), 54, 56; objectives: extent of influence, 51 f.
Fernandez, Elise, 196n
Festspiele (Wagner), 14
Feuille de Paris, 217
Feuille de salut public, 217
Fichte, Johann G., 64
Finland, geographically not part of Scandinavia, 459; language, 459; Sweden-Finland separated, 461, 465; emergence of national consciousness, 461; ceded to Russia, 465; autonomous, constitutional state, 467, 469; interest in national history and folklore, 468; desire for national and linguistic unity, 468, 473; attitude towards union with Russia, 472; proclamation of independent Republic, 474; universal suffrage: national consciousness antedated political democracy, 477; see also Scandinavia
Finlandia (Sibelius), 6n, 7
Fisher, H. A. L., quoted, 100, 287
Fitzgerald, Edward, 48
Flood, Henry, 47
Floridablanca, José M., Count de, 194, 202
Foignet, music by, 217
Folk high schools, Danish, 470
Fontanelli, General, 327
Force, doubtful and dangerous instrument, 351; see also Military power
Foreign Affairs, v
Foreign conquest, evil of, 187
Foreign policy, theory, 390
Foreign Policy Association, xvi
Fourierism, 440
Fox, opposed establishment of Board of Agriculture, 173
France, cultural hegemony: taste antinational, 3 f.; Romanticism, 4, 15; Berlioz as ecumenical representative of culture, 9 ff.; eagerness re fads and foreign artists, 11; anti-Romanticism, 15; position of Debussy, 16; representatives in U. S., 18, 22; from U. S., 21, 26–41 *passim*; letters of secret agent dealing with Franco-American relations, 1797, 18–44; status of its cause in late 18th-century America, 21 ff.; in-

France (*Continued*)
toxicated with revolutionary nationalism, 144; power in North America menace to Britain's naval power, 147; Young's changing attitudes towards, 151, 155 ff.; war on Austria, 167, 202, 204; Declaration of the Rights of Man, 169, 170, 199, 222, 342; Young's attitude towards war between Great Britain and, 171; Britain urged to prepare to meet threat of, 177; republicanism a factor differentiating Jacobin from humanitarian nationalism, 190; relations with Spain during Revolution: results of Jacobin nationalism, 190–240 (*see also* Spain); source material, 191 ff., 235, 236; Family Compact, 193, 200, 202, 231; theater in re things Spanish, 195, 199, 216; period when humanitarian nationalism in ascendant, 196; propaganda in Spain, 198, 202 ff., 235; renunciation of war by Assembly, 200; Constitution of 1791, 201; citizenship for foreigners, 201; shift from humanitarian nationalism to government-sponsored propaganda, 202 f.; insurrection of 1792 a turning point: triumph of republicanism, 202, 204; promotion of Jacobin nationalism begun, 207 ff.; propagandist decrees of 1792, 208; war with Spain, 208, 209–30; law renouncing intervention, 212; fall of Girondists: increased emphasis on republicanism, 215; Constitution of 1793 as propaganda, 217, 222; technique of conquering army, 222 ff.; insistence on recognition of Republic, 228; peace negotiations with Spain: treaties, 230 ff.; Directory's career started with peace, but Jacobin nationalism pursued, 232; changes in Spain and, when again allies, 234; Jacobins distracted from propaganda by war, 235; unseizable propaganda of example: its widespread effect, 236 f.; hatred of, conspicuous in German history instruction, 259; agreement with Britain re Germany's colonial demands, 421; opposition to curtailment of Empire, 422; *see also* Napoleon; *and entries under* French

France, Affaires Étrangères, 18n

France républicaine, La, 217

Francis I of France, peace signed with Swiss Confederation, 265

Francis, Archduke of Austria-Este, demanded as ruler of Lombardia, 310

Franco, Francisco, Germany's negotiations with, 414; meeting with Hitler, 428; attitude towards Hitler's colonial aspirations, 429

Frank, Franz, 352

Frank, Walter, 355n

Frankfort, social reform tendencies: shared by Jews, 357

Frau und die Kolonien, Die, 408

Frederick the Great, 123, 147, 300, 378; Klopstock's admiration for, turned to hostility, 127 ff.

Freedom, in philosophy of Hegel, 66; vast appeal of idea, 340; need to plan for, 341

Free enterprise, Marxian doctrine hostile to union of collectivism and, 283

Freemasons in Italy, 322

Free trade, advocated by Young, 158; South's yearning for, 442

French, vanquished by Swiss, 264; unable to grasp concept of true federation, 282; failure of Habsburgs to alleviate burdens imposed by, in Lombardy-Venetia, 304, 305, 317; officials retained at posts, 307, 315, 319, 333; overthrown in Lombardy, 308; *see also* France

French Revolution, influence in Ireland, 47, 48; as step towards freedom, 141; Young's attitude towards, 146, 161, 163 ff.; his crusade against, 169 ff.; viewed as antimonarchical by ruling classes abroad, 190; characteristics of nationalism of early and of Jacobin periods, 190; Jacobin propaganda and Franco-Spanish relations, 190–240 (*see also* France; Spain); hope that other countries would follow example, 202, 208; effect throughout Europe, 233; chronological table: general events and Franco-Spanish relations, 237

Fritsch, General, 425

Fritzsche, Richard, on history instruction, 246, 258

"Frolics," in England, on return of peace, 1814, 188

Fuller, Margaret, 439

Funeral and Triumphal Symphony (Berlioz), 13, 14

Future, *see* Past-present-future

Gadhelic, revival and use of, as Irish language, 46

Gaelic League, 60

Gallarate, treaty signed at, 265

Index 489

Gallatin, Albert, 20, 28n
Gamas, play by, 217
Gans, Edward, 64
Garvin, J. L., 105n
Gasparinetti, 326, 329
Gazeta de Madrid, 211, 219
Gedicht eines Skalden (Gerstenberg), 141
Gelehrten-republik (Klopstock), 129
Genêt, Charles Edmond, 18, 20, 34n, 42
Geneva, Communist administration, 276
Genoa, conspirators in, 325
Genoese Republic, proclamation of restoration of, 321
Geopolitik, 407, 413 ff.; pattern of, emerging, 429
Georgia, protection advocated by Whigs, 443
Gerlach, Hellmuth von, 395
German Colonial Empire, shaping of Nazi policy towards revival of, 399–430; Colonial Jubilee, 404
German historians, Hegelian influence, 64–78; recent writers, 70 ff.
Germanic history, Klopstock's interest in, 130, 138
Germanism and Christianity, 247, 253
German-Polish question, 425
Germans, division the great weakness, 140; praise of German mind, 248; too many in Lombard administration, 315; aid to, in former colonies, 408, 414
German Students Association, 353
Germany, cultural nationalism, 4; Romanticism, 4, 5; culture heroes, 4; Goethe, 4 f.; Wagner, 5 ff., 10, 11; music thought monopoly of, 6, 10; vogue for Berlioz, 11; pseudo-liberal nationalism, 92; education, 96; Britain compared with, 102, 103; World War I: British attitudes towards, 106–11 *passim*; imperialism: conditions in, ominous for Europe, 110 f.; rise of national literature, 122–43; military power, 245; *Kulturgeschichte*, 252; failure of Weimar Republic to pay attention to nationalistic tradition, 259; nationalistic indoctrination menace to neighbors, 260; Seeley taken seriously: books about his views, 285; rise of, as great state, 301; American philosophy re, muffled and confused, 336; power and nationalism as viewed by leading representatives of Wilhelmian intelligentsia, 352–98 (*see entries under* Military power; Naumann, Friedrich; Stoecker, Adolf; Weber, Max; William II); as pathfinder, and leader of other nations, 352; Protestant social action, 353 ff., 366 (*see also* Religion); anti-Semitism, 353, 357, 360, 361, 370; agrarian interests and class, 357, 359, 361, 372, 373, 375, 386, 388; all parties based upon narrow viewpoints, 366; social classes and their influence and interests, 374 ff., 386 ff.; fulfillment of historical mission, 374; period of mounting enthusiasm for trade, colonies, and navy, 383; results of transformation from agrarian to industrialized economy, 390; importance of nationalization of masses, 395; "aggressive nationalism" feared by British, 417; belief that defeat of, would eliminate scourge of war, 455; *see also* Hitler; National Socialism; National Socialists; Nazis; Prussia

—— colonial issue: part played in establishment of Third Reich, 399–403; failure of Weimar Republic to adopt definite policy, 399 ff.; demand for admission to mandate system, 400; propaganda of *Kolonialgesellschaft*, 401; smaller organizations, 402; character of internal leadership, 403 ff.; *Reichskolonialpolitisches Amt*, 404, 407; technique employed in revival of colonialism, 405–10; merger of societies, 407; *Reichskolonialamt*, 407; colonial material for schools and universities, 410; colonial objectives in foreign policy, 410–16; evaluation of areas: plans to control islands in vicinity of Africa, 413; negotiations with Franco, 414; reaction of Great Britain to colonial drive, 416–24; reaction to British propositions for adjustment, 419; Hitler's objectives, 424–30; control of Western Mediterranean and Gibraltar, 429; under William II and Hitler, 429; international relations affected by, 430

Gerosa, 326, 329
Gerry, Elbridge, 30, 36, 38, 39
Gerstenberg, H. W. von, 141
Geyl, Pieter, 100n
Gibraltar, Britain blamed for holding, 158; demanded by Spain, 427; Germany's intention to control, 429
Gifflenga, General, 327
Gleim, Johann Wilhelm (Father), 123, 138, 140; praise of Klopstock, 136
Gluck, 139

Godoy, Don Manuel, Spanish prime minister, 191, 203, 211, 220–29 *passim*, 233
Goebbels, Paul Joseph, 404, 407; on colonial problem, 409
Goering, Hermann, 425; demand for return of colonies, 409; Halifax's hunt with, 420
Goethe, 137, 245, 296; raised to rank of national world poet, 3, 4 f.; on what German poetry lacked, 123; influenced by national spirit in Klopstock's writings, 142
Goettinger Hainbund, 137
Goettinger Musenalmanach, 137
Göhre, Paul, 353n, 364, 394
Good life, need for total conception of, 342
Gorgas, editor of *Courrier* . . . , 197
Gottsched, advocated German imitation of French literature, 122
Goupilleau-Fontenay, 230
Government, Seeley and study of comparative, 302; dominant trend in, 340; chief business nurture of independent and self-directing individuals, 343, 344, 346; vast expansion of activity, 344; growth of more positive attitude towards, 344
Grand, French publisher, 217
Grandson, Burgundians defeated at, 264
Granville, Bozzi, Austrians perturbed over arrival in Italy, 321
Grattan, Henry, 47, 52
Grattan's Parliament, 48
Great Britain, British vs. French interests in U. S. after Revolution, 21 ff., 39; source for social history of, 82; imperialism, 90, 104 ff., 297, 299; Wells's love for, and criticism of things British, 100–106; Young's contribution to growing nationalism, 144–89; struggle with France, 144; Young's views re relations with American colonies, 147, 149; his political views, 149; plans for expansion of empire and control of Pacific, 150; on war with France, 171; Pitt ministry's reward to Young for *The Example of France*, 175; trend towards Democratic Socialism, 344; reaction to Hitler's colonial drive, 416–24; lack of firmness on colonial issue: public opinion, 417; conciliatory move towards Hitler, 420; weakness stressed by Hitler, 425; *see also* British Empire; England
Greeley, Horace, nationalism, 431–54; liberalism: dislike of expanding America's territory, 435; enthusiasm for European revolutions of 1848, 436; cultural nationalism, 439; economic counterpart, 440; program of agricultural and industrial expansion, 443; attitude towards political matters, 446; reason for becoming Republican, 448; conviction that South would never secede from Union, 449, 450; position re secession and compromise, 450; wartime attitudes and actions, 451; aim during Reconstruction Period, 452; favored Negro suffrage to ensure Republican supremacy, 453; *see also Tribune*
Grey, Lord, 112
Grieg, Edvard H., 7
Griffith, Arthur, editor of *Sinn Fein:* nationalism of, 53 ff.
Griswold, Rufus Wilmot, 438
Grossmütiger Feldherr Arminius . . . (Lohenstein), 139
Grote, George, 301
Grundtvig, N. F. S., 469, 470
Guedalla, Philip, quoted, 106
Guelfs, 323
Guizot, François, 434
Gulf of Guinea, colonies in, demanded by Spain, 427
Gustavus Adolphus, proposal to Swiss Diet for alliance with Sweden, 269

Habsburgs, defeated by Swiss: recognition of Confederation, 263; and public opinion in Lombardy-Venetia, 303–35; greeted as emancipators in Italy, 303; failure to alleviate burdens imposed by French, 304, 305, 307, 315, 317, 333; spirit of revolution against, 314, 318, 324; bad blood between troops and Lombards, 317; concerned about English influence, 320; Milanese plot against, 327; pro-Austrian elements, 330; gave tacit approval to fostering spirit of nationalism, 335; *see also under* Austria
Hager, Baron von, 304, 332
Haldame, Lord, 419; effort to effect colonial understanding with Hitler, 430
Halifax, Lord, interview with Hitler re colonial issue, 420; visit to Berlin, 430
Hamilton, Alexander, 432
Hammerstein, editor, 360, 361n
Harden, Maximilian, 358
Harpe, Frederic de la, 279
Hauterive, Alexandre Maurice B. de La-

Index   491

nautte, Comte d', advice on America and Franco-American relations, in secret letters to Adet, 18–44; names used: disguise, 18, 40; published writings, 18n, 25n, 26n; posts held in France, 19, 25n; in U. S., 19; information in *Journal*, 19n; relations with Talleyrand, 19, 24, 25, 26n, 39–43 *passim;* abilities: why his letters worthy of note, 23; their form, 23 f.; numbers and locations in series, 24 f.; evaluated in light of his biases, 39 ff.

Hayes, Carlton J. H., 78n, 112n, 144, 434; the man and his work, ix–xvii; affiliations, x, xvi; gift of foreseeing and interpreting events, xiii; studies of nationalism, xiii; role in teaching of international relations, xiv; father: biographical note, xiv; wartime mission in Spain, xv; quoted, 3, 99, 108, 120n; attempt to trace basic common pattern for nationalism: principal successive stages, 45; nationalism of French Revolution outlined, 190, 208

Hayes, Philetus A., xiv

Heckscher, E. F., historical work: Hegelian influence, 70, 74–78

Hegel, Charles, 64

Hegel, G. W. F., 245; contribution to historical thinking, 64–78; two tendencies: personification of abstractions: *a priori* historiography, 68–70; historians reflecting influence of, 70–78

Helvetian Republic, 270

Henderson, Neville, 425

Hennukainan, Finnish conductor, 6n

Henry I of Germany (the Fowler), 125, 128, 132, 257

Herder, J. G. von, 122, 296; praise of Klopstock, 137; influenced by national spirit in Klopstock's writings, 142

Hermann, Klopstock's hero, 131, 138 ff.; symbol of German national idea, 139

"Hermann and Thusnelda" (Klopstock), 131, 137

Hermannsschlacht (Klopstock), 129, 139, 140

Hermanns Tod (Klopstock), 141

Hermann und die Fürsten (Klopstock), 140

Hero worship, 252

Hervey, Frederick, Earl of Bristol and Bishop of Derry, 155

Heuss, Theodor, *Friedrich Naumann...*, cited, 353n–395n *passim;* Naumann's biographer and friend, 363; president of German Republic, 363n

Hévia, French propagandist, 210, 214n

Hilfe, Die, 360, 377, 379, 394

Hillhouse, James Abraham, 438

Hints Toward Reforms (Greeley), 440

Historians, "Columbia School" of, xi; German: Hegelian tendencies, 64–70; later writers reflecting influence of, 70–78; Seeley a pragmatic historian, 285 ff.; his strictures on "old school of," 289

Historical change, major movements not specifically inevitable, 344

Historical Evolution of Modern Nationalism, The (Hayes), xiii, 45, 78n, 190

Historical figures limelighted by Hayes, xii

History, European: work and influence of Carlton J. H. Hayes, ix ff.; library facilities: textbooks, xi; social and cultural activities encompassed in "new history," xi; views of Wells, 96; his *Outline of History,* 97 ff.; and condemnation of economic interpretation, 98n; pragmatic, of Seeley, 285–302; his foundations for "philosophy of universal history," 289 (*see also* Hayes, C. J. H.; Seeley, Sir J. R.; Wells, H. G.)

History instruction, school textbooks in American history, 433

——— Prussia: official aims under William II, 241–60; must familiarize pupil with political developments, 246, 249; opportunity to tie together patriotism and religion, 247; *Kulturgeschichte,* 249, 252; predominance of national history: hero worship and glorification of military prowess, 252, 258; visual aids, 253; typical lesson plans, 253 ff.; assignments covering whole field, 257; bad traits of heroes and rulers satisfactorily explained, 259

History of Mr. Polly, The (Wells), 81

Hitler, able to destroy disunited nations, 281; and revival of German colonialism, 399–430; seized control of colonial movement, 403; apparent contradiction of attitude, 405; on need of colonies, 409; why he restrained his demands, 410; increasing audacity of public utterances, 412; quoted, 421, 428; triumph of method of unilateral action, 422; threat, 423; on weakness of Britain and strength of Reich, 425; talk with Molotov, 427;

Hitler (*Continued*)
  meeting with Franco, 428; comparison of colonialism, with William II, 429
Hoare, Sir Samuel, 418
Hohenzollern monarchy, 366, 369, 378, 388, 389; eulogy of, 258; Stoecker's view of, and attachment to, 355; *see also* William, I and II
Hohenzollerns, struggle to unite Germany, 252; divine favor to subjects of, 253
Holland, ally of France, 231, 233
Holstein, von, 430
Holy Roman Empire, 245, 267, 295
Home Rule movement, Irish, founders and their work, 52 f.; Larkin's attitude, 61
Hossbach *Minutes,* 425
Household, self-determination in, 347; how Government may act to save, 348
Huber, Victor Amé, 354
Hübner, Max, on teaching of history, 245
Hugenberg, plea for return of German colonies, 406
Humanitarian nationalism, 45; in Ireland, 47; of early French Revolution, 190, 196, 202; *see also* Nationalism
Hungarian Dances (Bartok), 7
Hutten, Ulrich von, 139
Hymne à la France (Berlioz), 13

"Ich bin ein deutscher Jüngling" (Claudius), 138
"Ich bin ein deutsches Mädchen" (Klopstock), 137
"Ich bin eine deutsche Frau" (Auerswald), 138
Idea of a League of Nations, The, 89*n*, 112
Idea of the Present State of France, An (Young), 177
"Ideological Combat, The" (Robinson), v, 336 ff.
Imperial Federation League, 301
Imperialism, attitude of Wells, 90, 104; German policy ominous for Europe, 107, 110; Seeley's *Expansion of England,* philosophy of, 285, 297 ff., 302; European examples, 298; Naumann's concept of, and appeal for, 382
Independent Labour Party, 57
India, Young bitter about, 157; relation to British Empire, 298, 299
Individual, development of, goal of politics, 382; freedom threatened by capital concentrations, 396
Individualism, essence of American faith and practice, 338; loss of independence and self-direction, 338, 340; philosophy of, 343 ff.; chief business of society and state to nurture, 343, 344, 346; reconciliation with new stateism, 346; problem of maintaining in industry, 349; U. S. challenged to renew and develop its inheritance of, 350; Communism and war-discipline at home a danger to, 351
Individuality, combination of absolute authority and, 370
Industrialism, concentration of production and tightening of control, 338; can democracy and individualism be preserved in machine age? 340; prepares worker to appeal to state for help, 345; mechanization and consolidation, 348; most important end-product, 349; problem of humanizing work process, 350; championship of large-scale, as basis of German power and benefit for her masses, 352, 378–96 *passim;* beginning to change lives and religion of Germans, 353; enthusiasts of machines and, 373, 378 f., 385; William II's sensitivity to, 378, 389; dependence upon entrepreneurs, 385, 387; aristocracy of, 386 f.; Greeley's program of expansion, 444; *see also* Labor; Masses; Proletariat
Inner Mission, founding of: purpose, 353; Naumann's interest in, 354, 355, 357, 360, 373*n*
Inquiry into the Propriety of Applying Wastes to the . . . Support of the Poor, An (Young), 183
Insurance legislation, Bismarck's, 360, 369, 394
Integral nationalism, 45; in Ireland, 54; *see also* Nationalism
Intellectual and technical aristocracy as world hope, 114, 118, 120
International evolution, analogies between Swiss development and, 262
"International History," 291, 299
Internationalism, merits of cosmopolitanism and, 120*n;* changes transforming the system, 288; arguments for European federation, 296; German Catholics "tainted" with, 388
International relations as academic subject, xiv
International socialist and labor movements, why rejected by Wells, 115*n*
Introduction to Political Science (Seeley), 287, 290, 292, 302; analysis of, 300

Index 493

Ireland, criteria of nationalism applied to, 45–63; use of native language, 46; long antecedent history of conquest and resistance, 46 f.; impossible to preserve traditional institutions, 48; "liberal" the only possible nationalism, 48 ff.; true gospel of discontent formulated, 51; Home Rule movement, 52 f., 61, 288; work of Parnell and Butt, for political independence, 52; of Griffith and *Sinn Fein*, 53 f.; ruled by Catholic Church today, 55; contribution of Larkin, Connolly, and Irish labor, 55–63; influence of conditions and grievances in changing Young's views, 153, 154; evils of mercantilism, 155; union with Britain necessary, 158; cause espoused by Greeley, 436

Irish Labour Party, 58

Irish Republican Brotherhood, 51; *see also* Fenians

Irish Trades Union Congress, 58, 62

Irish Transport and General Workers Union, 57

Irish Worker and People's Advocate, The, 59 f., 62

Isnard, speech in French Assembly, 204

Italy, Dante as national poet, 3; Romanticism, 4; pro-Austrian feeling, 303; disillusionment, 304; no strong feeling of nationalism immediately after arrival of Austrians, 308; little hoped-for creation of united Kingdom of, 313; anti-Austrian officials, 314, 316; special problem for Austrians, 315; cause of independence championed by Freemasons and other secret societies, 322; army dissolved, men enrolled in Habsburg army, 323; desertions and discontent, 324; conspiracies to bring about a united, 324 ff.; failure, 330; Murat's war of 1815 called first war for Italian independence, 330*n*; no colonial territories allotted by Germany, 413; colonies in Africa, 429; *see also* Habsburgs; Lombardy; Lombardy-Venetia; Mussolini; Rome-Berlin Axis; Venetia

Jacobin nationalism, 45; in Ireland, 47, 52; menace of, 144; during late French Revolution, characteristics, 190; its propaganda in relation to Spain, 191–240 *passim* (*see also* France; Nationalism; Spain)

Jacobins, rigidly centered regime, 282

James II of England, 299

James, Henry, 80; quoted, 81*n*

Japan, Hitler's treaty with, 411; drive against European colonial powers, 414; colonial interests in Asia recognized by Hitler, 427

Jefferson, Thomas, 39*n*, 432, 440; letter to Mazzei, 29; death, 433

Jessup, P. C., on sovereignty, 94*n*

Jesus, as portrayed in *Ecce Homo*, 286

Jews, in works of Sombart, 73 f.; of Wells, 91, 92*n*; anti-Semitism, 91, 353, 357, 360, 361, 370; why expelled from Spain, 263; anti-Semitic demonstration at Rivarolo, 318; humanitarian, of Frankfort, 357; Reich's attack on, 421

Jews and Modern Capitalism, The (Sombart), 72*n*

Joan of Arc, 9

Jones, James C., 448

Joseph II, emperor, *Hermannsschlacht* dedicated to, 129, 139; Klopstock's hope that he would found German Academy, 140

Journal de la Montagne, 217

Journal de l'armée des Pyrénées . . ., 227

Jovanellos, pamphlet on Spain, 233

Jumbo, 408

Junkers, agrarian aristocracy, 360, 375, 386 f.

"Kaiser Heinrich" (Klopstock), 129

Kaisertum of Naumann, *see Demokratie und Kaisertum*; William II

Kalmar Union, 461

Kansas-Nebraska bill, 447

Kant, Immanuel, 64, 245

Kastle, Dr., 400

Keller, Augustin, 274

Kellogg Pact, 116

Keppel, Frederick P., xii

Kingsborough, Lord, 152

Kingsley, Charles, 286, 296

Kipling, Rudyard, 79*n*, 105*n*; quoted, 87

Kipps (Wells), 81

Kirdorf, Emil, 361

Klaus, Bruder, *see* Nicolas von der Flue

Kleist, 127

Klopstock, Friedrich Gottlieb, national sentiment, 122–43; importance in German literature and nationalism, 123; fervid patriotism: idea of literature that would be national, 124; plan to write great national epic, 125; search for German hero and German theme, 125, 127,

Klopstock (*Continued*)
130; interest in remote Germanic past, 130, 138; patriotic odes, 132–38; esteem of contemporaries, 136; *Bardiete*, 138–43; interest in contemporary history, 141
Know Nothing Party, 446 f.
Koerner, 259
Kolonialamt, 404
Kolonialgesellschaft, 401, 404; merger of colonial societies under: dissolved, 407
Kolonial-Zeitung, 408
Kolonie und Heimat, 408
Kornrumpf, Ernst, on history instruction, 247, 258
Kossuth, Louis, 434, 435
Kretschmann, Karl F., 138, 141
Krieger, Ferdinand, 249
Krout, John A., xvi
Kulturkampf, why Bismarck inaugurated, 263

Labor, contribution to Irish nationalism: leadership of Larkin and Connolly, 55, 57 ff.; machine industry prepares worker to appeal to state for help, 345; call for tariff protection of American, 441; American, for American work, 442; industrial worker, inclined to socialism, not to nationalist views, 476; participation in management, 350; *see also* Industrialism; Masses; Proletariat
Laissez-faire, Heckscher's preconceptions, 76, 77; Young's doctrine, 152; current before Smith, 153
Lalor, James Fintan, 53; principle stated by, 51, 59
Lament of Rhingulf the Bard over Hermann's Death (Kretschmann), 141
Lameth, Alexandre, 198
Land, Greeley's plan to develop free, in West, 443
"Land Ironclads, The" (Wells), 117*n*
Land League, Ireland, 49*n*, 52, 53
Language, role of national, criterion of nationalism, 45; revival of Gadhelic in Ireland, 46, 59
Languages, Scandinavian, 459, 468, 471, 473; common tongue becoming increasingly "national," 460, 463; contribution of common man to, 477 f.
Larkin, Barney, 56
Larkin, "Big Jim," Irish labor lead by, 55, 57 f.; parents, 56; early life: characteristics, 56*n*, 57; nationalism, 58 ff.; whether revolutionary syndicalist, 58; feeling about Home Rule, 61; opposition to sectarianism, 62; tribute to, 63
Larkin, Delia (Mrs. Patrick Colgan), 56*n*
Laroche, Lenoir, 24
La Rochefoucauld-Liancourt, F. A. F., 42
Laski, Harold, 284
Lattuada, 326, 329
La Union, Spanish general, 222-26 *passim*, 235, 236; death, 228
Law, American, negative in emphasis, 343
Lazowski, Maximilien, 162
Leadership, theory of, and mass social action, 386
League of Free Nations Association, 112
League of Gold, 268
League of Nations, men active in support of, 79, 112; Wells's faith, 80, 104, 109, 111; reasons for his rejection of final form, 112, 115; unsurpassed statement of case for, 112; other publications, 112*n*; idea of absolute national sovereignty, harmful to, 261; similarity of Swiss Confederation to, 267; Germany's demand for right to mandates, 400; Germans appointed on Mandates Commission, 401; Hitler's defiance, 411; failure to unite Europe, 456
Lebrun, Girondist minister, 203, 206, 215
Lechi, Theodore, 326, 329
Lectures on the Philosophy of History (Hegel), with excerpts, 64 ff.
Leopold III, Habsburg, defeated at Sempach, 263
Lessing, Gotthold E., 4, 139
Létombe, Consul General, 19
Letters Concerning the Present State of the French Nation (Young), 148, 151
Lettres écrites de Barcelonne . . . (Chantreau), 218
Liancourt, Duc de, 176
Liberalism, turn of English, from considerations of liberty to those of unity and power, 301; in Wilhelmian Germany, 365, 366, 385; effect upon religion, 369; upon democracy, 382; challenge of dictatorship, 390; Naumann's approach to, 396; revalued in terms of 20th-century economics, 397
Liberal nationalism, 45; in Ireland, 48 ff.; *see also* Nationalism
Liberal nationalists, 19th-century, 434
Life and Times of Stein (Seeley), 287, 294
Lincoln, Abraham, 14; Gettysburg Address, 433; Greeley pleased with, 444; candidacy supported by Greeley, 449

Index 495

Lindquist, Dr., 405
Link, Mrs. R. G., 200n
Literature, Greeley's nationalistic bent in, 438, 439
——— German: rise of national, 122–43; largely imitative: patriotism of Prussian writers, 123; revolt against prevailing imitation of other nationalities, 124, 142; first outstanding creation of modern, 126; colonial, issued by Nazi press, 403, 423; *see also* Klopstock, F. G.
Litta, 321
Livingston, Chancellor, 29
Lloyd George, David, 417
Lloyd George liberals, xiii
Locarno Treaties, Hitler's repudiation of, 411
Lofft, Capel, newspaper controversy between Young and, 155
Logan, George, 39n
Logan Act, 39n
Lohenstein, Daniel Casper von, 139
Lombards, turned deaf ear to Murat, 331, 334; grievances, 332
Lombardy, anti-Austrian feeling, 304; French government overthrown: spirit of nationalism stirred up, 308; anti-Habsburg feeling, 309: liberals and nationalists demand independence and constitutional government, 309 ff.; territories claimed as compensation for severance of Venetia, 311; majority desired only peace, 312; desire of liberals and nationalists for independent kingdom, 312; given to Austria, 313; concessions desired from Habsburgs, 314; liberals goaded into open opposition, 314; officials ousted from government: conscription, 316; conduct of Austrian troops: tax reductions, 317; hard times: discontent, 318; center of anti-Austrian movement, 319; English liberals under close supervision of Austrians, 321; Freemasons, 322; Carbonari, 323, 331; public opinion favorable to Austrians, 332; reforms introduced by liberals, 334; national and liberal movement still undeveloped, 334; arrest and trial of liberals conspiring to drive out Austrians, 335
Lombardy-Venetia, the Habsburgs and public opinion in, 303–35; conspiracy in, 326 ff.; failure of plot against Austrian rule, 330; Kingdom of, to be formed within Habsburg monarchy, 331

London, society for Italian independence in, 321
Londonderry, Marquess of, 416
Lothian, Marquess of, 416
Loughborough, Lord, 175
Louis XVI of France, 164; Spanish concern for royal family and, during French revolution, 196, 201, 203, 204, 209, 210, 211, 213, 219, 228, 232
Louis XVII of France, 219, 228
Louisiana, French dreams for Canada and, 32, 35, 37, 42; desire for cession, 231, 233, 234
Louis Philippe, xii
Loyal associations, advocated by Young, 170, 171
Lucas, Charles, 47
Lutheranism in Germany, 253, 367; *see also* Religion

Macaulay, Thomas Babington, 291, 301
McCormick reaper, 445
McDonald, J. Ramsay, attitude re German colonies, 423
Machen, Arthur, 9n
Machine age, can democracy and individualism be preserved in? 340
Machine industry, *see* Industrialism
Machines, German enthusiasts of industry and, 373, 378 f.; 385
MacLachlan, Jean, xvi
Macpherson, James, 138, 463
M'Piarais, Padraic (Patrick Pearse), 55, 60
Madeira Islands, 428
Madison, James, 29
Magdeburg, course of study, 253
Magyars, struggle for independence espoused by Greeley, 436
Maitland, F. W., 294
Malmaison Constitution, 271
Management, labor participation in, 350
Manchester Guardian, 420
"Manchester Martyrs," 56
Mancini, 326
Mangourit, Jacobin secretary, 232
Mantua, plot to take over citadel, 327
Marchal, 326, 328
Marchena, José, 206, 207n, 210, 214n, 218, 220
Mariage de Figaro, Le (Beaumarchais), 195, 199
Maria Theresa, Empress, 147
Marignan, defeat of Swiss at, 266
Marioni, Countess, 321
Marshall, George, x

Marshall, John, 30, 31, 33, 36, 38
Marx, Karl, 384; and wife, xii; ultimate goal of Engels and, 340
Marxism, Wells's opinion of, 98n; hostile to union of collectivism and free enterprise, 283; as viewed by German intellectuals, 357, 359, 371, 375, 396n; by ruling classes, 383
Masons in Italy, 322
Masses, Young's changing attitude towards, 181 ff.; danger inherent in neglect of social and economic grievances of, 182; relation of German, to industry and nation, 352, 378–96 *passim;* effect of secularization, 354, 370, 371; attempts to bring Protestantism to, 354, 355; forms of politics appropriate for age of, 371; enabled to form and lead own cultural life in urban-industrial society, 371; meaning of term to various writers, 371n; how skill and military vigor dissipated, 382; loyalty to Fatherland, 395; *see also* Proletariat
Masson, Frédéric, 204, 217
Mass organization and mass discipline, 345
Maurice, F. D., 286
"Maurice," secret agent, 19; *see also* Hauterive, Comte d'
Mauvillon, Eléazar, on poverty of German literature, 124
Maximilian, Emperor, xii
Mayflower Compact, 342
Maynard, Mass., 6n
Mazzei, Jefferson's letter to, 29
Mazzini, Giuseppe, 50, 434, 436
Mechanization, of industry, 338, 348; of agriculture, 339, 348
Mediterranean Sea, German control of, 413, 429
Meinecke, Friedrich, xiv
Mein Kampf (Hitler), 405, 406
Meistersinger, Die (Wagner), 6
Melville, Herman, 8
Mercantilism, Young's early belief in, 146 ff.
Mercantilism (Heckscher), 75
Mercurio . . . de España, 219
Messiah, The (Klopstock), 125 ff., 136
Michaux, André, 34n
Michel Cervantes (Gamas), 217
Middle East, infiltration by Germans, 414
Milan, French and Swiss rivalry for possession of, 265; Swiss claims bought off by Francis I, 266; Austrian troops acclaimed, 303; liberals desire independent, constitutional kingdom, 311; anti-Habsburg paper published in, 318; conspiracy in, 326, 327
Military and naval terms, German instruction in, 254
Military power, when nationalistic indoctrination becomes campaign of propaganda, 242; compulsory service, 251; German glorification of, 252; William II's identification with, 255; force a doubtful and dangerous instrument, 351; proponents of armaments and, in Wilhelmian Germany, 352, 363, 372, 377; dependence of industrial life upon, 381; uses in case of revolution, 384; association with capitalism, 389; no rights or social reforms possible without, 390; expansion of Prussian-German military state to world stature, 391 ff.; not part of nationalism of Scandinavian peoples, 478
Militia, of property-owners, advocated by Young, 169, 170, 171, 178; formed, 176; militia system, inadequate for Germany, 392
Milner, at Balliol College, 90
Milton, Klopstock inspired by, 126; breadth of views re national well-being, 293
Mirabeau, 200
Mr. Britling Sees It Through (Wells), 81 f., 109, 120
Mitchel, John, 51
Mitteleuropa (Naumann), 398
Mob violence, Young's reaction, 168
Molière, 199
Molotov, meeting with von Ribbentrop, 426; talk with Hitler, 427
Molyneux, William, 47
Monarchy, culmination of world development to Hegel, 67; questions of, in Spain and France during Revolution, 190–240 *passim;* pillar of Spanish nationalism, 237; attempt to reconcile German people and, by means of democratic Caesarism, 362, 380, 389; why the best way of realizing Christian ideals, 368; *see also* Hohenzollern monarchy
Moniteur, 170, 171; cited, 197n–234n *passim;* articles in, 224, 226, 229, 231
Monopoly, 344
Monroe, James, 21, 26, 29, 338
Monroe Doctrine for Africa, 426
Montagnards, Les (Monnet), 217
Montesquieu, 204

Index 497

Monti, Antonio, 330n
Monza, conspirators in, 326, 327
Moon, Parker Thomas, xvi
Moors, why expelled from Spain, 263
Morat, Burgundians defeated at, 264
Moretti, Colonel, 326
Morgarten, battle of, 263
Morning Post, 147
Morocco, Spain's natural expansion objective, 427
Morse, Jedediah, 433
Möser, Justus, 139
Mozart, 245
Munich Pact, effect, 422
Murat, Joachim, King of Naples, 320; war of Italian independence, 330; appeal to Italians to join war of national liberation, 331, 334; defeat and overthrow, 332
Murray, Gilbert, 112
Murry, J. Middleton, quoted, 84
Musical nationalism, 6; French belief about, 10
Musicians as culture heroes: Wagner, 5 ff.; Sibelius, 6n; Berlioz, 9 ff.
Mussolini, colonial boldness, 412

"Nachruhm, Der" (Klopstock), 130
Nación española, A la (Marchena), 206
Nadler, Friedrich, on history instruction, 246
Nancy, Burgundians defeated at, 264
Napoleon I, 9, 99, 144, 184, 196; enemy to Popery: Allies blamed for protecting, 188; Swiss appeal to, 271; useful to Swiss revolutionary groups, 279; rigidly centered regime, 282; knew value of secret allies and fifth column, 282; nationality the force that overthrew, 295, 296; Seeley's life of, 296; Austrian War of Liberation against, 303; Venetians impoverished by, 304; nationalists banked on possibility of his deserting Elba, 319; effects of prestige upon Italian malcontents, 320; Freemasons flourished in Italy during regime, 322; praised by Italian troops, 324; offered crown of new Roman Empire, 325; factions active in favor of, 331; popular sovereignty recognized by, 389; deal with Alexander I, 465
Napoleon III, xii, 11, 15n
Napoleonic era, defeat and humiliation of Scandinavian countries during, 464 ff.

Nation, as distinguished from state, 290, 295
Nation, Die, 396
National characteristics, Greeley firm believer in, 436
National consciousness, term, 461n, 462; emergence and evolution of, in Scandinavia, 462 ff.; defeat and humiliation a cause of, 464
National Danger and the Means of Safety (Young), 178
Nationalism, Hayes's study of, and works on, xiii, 78n; new type being shaped by opposing U. S.–French forces, 22; difficulty of defining, or of finding common denominator: five principal stages: role of native language, 45; criteria of, applied to Ireland, 45–63 (*see also* Ireland); attitude of Wells, 88–121 *passim* (*see also* Wells, H. G.); state sovereignty, 92 ff., 114 ff.; liberal imperialism, 105; forces moving away from, in direction of larger regionalisms, 113 f.; main stream of 19th-century German, 122–43; importance of Klopstock, in history of German, 123; British, intensified during Young's lifetime, 144–89; feeds upon fear and hatred of national enemy, 150; Irish, 153; characteristics of humanitarian nationalism of early French Revolution: of Jacobin nationalism, 190; Jacobin propaganda and Franco-Spanish relations, 190–240 (*see also* France; Spain); period when humanitarian, in ascendant, 196; shift to government-sponsored propaganda, 202 f.; promotion begun, 207, 208; education for, in Prussia, 241 ff.; power and, as viewed by leading representatives of Wilhelmian Germany, 352–98 (*see entries under* Military power; Naumann, Friedrich; Stoecker, Adolf; Weber, Max; William II); always foremost principle among German liberals, 365; Greeley's design for economic nationalism, 440; use of term "national consciousness" in case of Scandinavian countries, 461n, 462 ff.; akin to religion, destructive of Christian faith, 476; *see also* Sovereignty
——— cultural, xi; and makings of culture heroes and their fame, 3–17; Italy and Dante, 3; paradox in, as form of national self-expression, 3; French cultural hegemony, 3; Romanticism, 4, 5, 11,

—— cultural (*Continued*)
15; Germany's culture heroes, 4 ff., 10, 11; role of propaganda, 7, 8; Berlioz as representative of French culture, 9–17; creation of national myth around eligible artist, 14; importance as half of politics, 293; Greeley's design for, 439

Nationalistic indoctrination, what it involves: evil it may bring to mankind, 241; offered by Nazis, built upon foundation laid in Prussia of William II, 242

Nationality, new type of organic state produced by, 288; Seeley's views: three main elements: force saving Europe from dictators, 295 f.; *see also* Sovereignty

"Nationality" (Acton), 296

National Reformers, 443

National Social Association, 364, 365, 366, 379, 394; founded: two tendencies within, 363; why Weber critical of, 364n, 365n; political failure, 395

National Socialism, how it won support and acceptance in Germany, 402

National Socialists, control of colonial movement established, 403; *see also* Hitler

National Spirit, Hegelian view, 67

"Nationalstaat und die Volkswirtschaftspolitik, Der" (Weber), 374

National story, should be presented in its international setting, 241

Nationaltheater, Klopstock's hopes for, became reality, 140

National Union of Dock Labourers, 57

Natural Religion (Seeley), 286, 287

Naumann, Friedrich, apostle of German power and nationalism, 352–98; ideals, hope, and disillusionment of his life and works, 352; educational influences: early theological career, 352 ff.; part in German cultural mission to modern world, 352, 397; problem of masses and their relation to industry and nation, 352, 363, 378–96 *passim* (*see also* Industrialism; Masses; Proletariat); best biographies of, 353n; association with Stoecker, 353, 355 ff.; grasp of failure of religion and significance of proletariat for politics and culture of technical world, 354 f., 370 ff.; development and changes in religious and ethical outlook and activities, 355n, 356n, 360, 361, 362, 366n, 370, 395; beginning of association with Weber, 356, 358; one of great modern writers on problems of social welfare and politics, 356; titles of addresses, tracts, and other writings, 356n, 357n, 359n, 360n, 362n, 364n, 365, 370n, 372n, 397, 398; belief in William II and Kaisership, 357, 364, 366, 377–94 *passim*; attitude towards Marxism, 357, 359, 371, 375, 396n; associations that influenced outlook and clarified social and political views, 358; chief differences between Stoecker and, 359, 362, 367, 371; attempt to reconcile monarchy and people by means of democratic Caesarism, 362, 380, 389; championship of military preparedness and power, 363, 372, 377, 381, 384, 389, 390, 391 ff.; attempt to combine authority and individuality, 370 f.; prophecies and special insights revealed by subsequent world events, 371, 372n, 390, 391, 395; influence of Weber's social teaching, 372, 377; nature of their friendship, 372, 374; Kaiser chief point of controversy between them, 377, 397; political views expressed in *Demokratie und Kaisertum*, 380 ff.; three hostile aristocracies seen by, 386–88; struggle against conservative-clerical alliance, 388; failure of first political ventures, 394; how political and ethical views developed, 395; elements by which directed into liberal movement, 396; compromise between liberalism and socialism worked out in *Neudeutsche Wirtschaftspolitik*, 397; contributions by which his historical significance must be judged, 397; when faith in Kaiser lost, 397; *Mitteleuropa*, 398; acclaimed head of new Democratic Party: death, 398

Naval League, German, 251

Naval power, Germany, 255, 352, 363, 381, 383, 391, 393; *see also* Military power

Navarro, Spanish officer, 222

Navigation Acts, defended, 148; Young's attack upon, 163

Nazi Primer, The, 410

Nazis, propaganda methods, 260; aims and motives of racist theories, 263; division of opinion among leaders, 407; support of schools for colonists, 408; coalescence of, and German colonists, 415

Near East, infiltration by Germans, 414; William II's projects, 430

Necker, pamphlet by, 197

Index

Negroes, racialism, 91; British reluctance to transfer back under German rule, 417
Neipperg, General, acclaimed in Italy, 303
Nelson, Horatio, 144, 186
Neudeutsche Wirtschaftspolitik (Naumann), 397
Neurath, German foreign minister, 425
New Deal, 347
Newspapers, as source material re Franco-Spanish conflict, 193, 216, 227; proscribed by Spain, 197; censorship of Spanish, 213; names and objectives of French, 216, 217, 226, 227; slanting of news in Spanish, 219
New-Yorker, 438
New York Times, excerpt, 84
Nicholas I of Russia, 436
Nicholas, John, 28, 30
Nicholson, James, 20
Nicolas von der Flue ("Brother Nicolas"), 265, 266
Noel-Buxton, Lord, 417
Nootka Sound controversy, 200
Northern countries, *see* Scandinavia
Norway, emergence of national consciousness, 461; union with Sweden, 461, 466; union dissolved, 461; union with Denmark, 461; dissolved, 465; new constitution and internal autonomy, 467, 469; interest in national history and folklore, 468; development of "national" language, 468; twofold effort at national self-assertion: hostility against Swedes and Danes, 470; Sweden-Norway union controversy, 470; free and sovereign nation: effort to free from linguistic and cultural bondage, 471; *see also* Scandinavia
Noske, 403
Novara, Swiss defeat of French at, 264, 265
Nuñez, Spanish ambassador, 199

O'Brien, Smith, 51
Ochs, Peter, 270, 279
O'Connell, Daniel, 51, 52, 53, 434, 435; champion of Irish liberal nationalism, 48 ff.
Odell, Professor, xii
"Old Christian Socialists," 359
"Old Conservatism," 367, 395
Olini, Colonel, 326, 329
Oliver Twist (Dickens), 81
"Open Door" policy, German autarchy incompatible with, 418
Opitz, 123

Organization, mass, 345
Ortega y Gasset, José, 371n
Ossian (Macpherson), literary forgery, 138
Otto, Louis Guillaume, 22, 41; in charge of dealings with Spain, 230
Otto the Great, German emperor, 257
Outline of History, The (Wells), excerpt, 88; record sale, 97, 98n; its purpose and content: evaluation of, 98 ff.
Ouvrier, Albert, 51

Pacific, in Japan's orbit, 414
Pact of 1291, 263, 269, 272
Pan y toros (Jovanellos), 233
Paris Opera, 436
Parliamentary reform, Young's attitude towards, 156
Parnell, Charles Stewart, Home Rule, 52 f.; quoted: monument, 61
Parochialism, history must be free from, 291
Past-present-future, views of historians, 99; in Seeley's historical theory, 292, 293 f.
Pastors, Evangelical, in Germany, 353 ff., 359, 362, 366
Patriot, The (Robinson), 63
Patriotism, *see* Nationalism
Pavoni, Colonel, 326, 330
Peace of the Nations, The (Hayes), 112n
Pearse, Patrick (Padraic M'Piarais), 55, 60
Peasant vs. proletariat soldiers, 392
Peel, Sir Robert, 50
Peer Gynt (Grieg), 7
People, the, *see* Masses
Pérignon, General, 229, 232, 233
Personality, *see* Individualism
Personification of abstractions, by Hegel, 68; later writers, 70, 73, 76
Peschiera, plot to seize, 327
Philosophy, American: of early decades, 337; change in, 338 ff.; need to develop an adequate, of ends and means, 341; urgent need for reconstruction and renewal, 342
Phipps, Sir Eric, 411
Piece-rate wages, 350
Pinckney, Charles C., mission to France, 21, 27, 30, 31, 33, 41; character and ability, 26, 31
Pino, General, 327
Pirow, South African minister, on colonial question, 419, 424
Pitt, William, the Elder, 144
Pitt, William, the Younger, 144

Pius IX, Pope, 49
Planning, social: advocated by Wells, 87n
Playboy of the Western World, The (Synge), 53
Pluralistic State, The (Laski), 284
Plymouth, Lord, 417
Poetry, American, 438
Poets, young, pledge to take Klopstock as model, 137
Poets and Poetry in America (Griswold), 438
Policy, national, of Britain, 297 ff.
Political and Cultural History of Modern Europe, A (Hayes), xi n
Political and Social History of Modern Europe (Hayes), xi
Political and social institutions and processes, adjustment to new order, 119 f.
Political Arithmetic (Young), 152; excerpt, 148
Political Education, importance, 288 ff.
Political Essays Concerning the Present State of the British Empire (Young), 148, 149, 150, 159
Political importance of religion, 287, 295
Political philosophy, American: negative in emphasis, 343
Political Science, Introduction to (Seeley), 287, 290, 292, 302; analysis of, 300
Politics, two English writers on history and, 79–121, 285–302 (*see also* Seeley, Sir John R.; Wells, H. G.); great German writer on, 352–98 (*see also* Naumann, Friedrich); whether technique of power relationships or applied ethics, 365; German, of power and nationalism, 372 ff.; social, inevitable, 393
Politischen Parteien, Die (Naumann), 364n, 368n, 383n, 379n
Poor, *see* Masses
"Pope's Brass Band," 50
Population, expanding, one of chief motors of history, 381; increase: relation to industry, 381, 385; to Kaiser's authority, 390; to war, 392
Portugal, colonial sovereignty, 424
Posadowsky, Graf, 394n
Potsdam, nationalism in *Volksschule*, 243
Pourtalès, Guy de, 13n
Power, American fear of great concentrations of, 346
Power and nationalism in Germany, as viewed by Wilhelmian intelligentsia, 352–98 (*see* entries under Military powers; Naumann, Friedrich; Stoecker, Adolf; Weber, Max; William II)
Powers, Hiram, 437
Pragmatic historian, 285 ff.; *see also* Seeley, Sir John R.
Present, *see* Past-present
Press, *see* Newspapers
Price, Ward, 406
Priestley, Joseph, victim of reactionary mob, 168
Private enterprise, wholesale development of large, 343
Proffitt, Charles G., xvi
Profit-sharing, 350
Proletariat, Irish labor, 55, 57 ff.; pessimism re English workers, 288; relation of German, to industry and nation, 352, 363, 378–96 *passim*; attitude of William II of Germany towards working class, 352, 356n, 357, 361, 364, 378, 393; significance of, for politics and culture of technical world, 354 f., 370 ff.; extent of political awareness, 375; strength lies solely in numbers, 382; wage problem, 384; relation of increase in, to industry, 385; leadership of natural aristocracy of labor in movement to transform nation, 386; attitude towards war: must carry it into enemy's territory, 391; coming element in army, 392; attached to international socialism, yet loyal to Fatherland, 395; *see also* Industrialism; Labor; Masses
Propaganda, role in cultural nationalism, 7, 8; Jacobin: and Franco-Spanish relations, 190–240 *passim*; *see also* France; Nationalism; Spain
Property rights, Young's defense of, 169
Protectionism, attitude of Wells, 90
Protestantism in Germany, 253, 353 ff.; *see also* Religion
Provost-Montfort, play by, 217
Prudhomme, 197
Prussia, elementary schools: nationalism and history under William II, 241–60; edict of Ministry of Education on official aims of history instruction, 242; *see also* History instruction, Prussia
Prussianism and Lutheranism, 253
Prussian War Songs (Gleim), 123
Public opinion, rule of, 287
Pyrenees region, French-Spanish war in, 210 ff., 219

Question of Scarcity, The . . . (Young), 183

Index

Quintessence of Capitalism, The (Sombart), 72*n*

Raab, Baron von, 333
"Rache, Die" (Klopstock), 130
Racialism, Wells on, 91; theories of Nazis, 263
Raeder, Admiral, 414, 425
Ragani, 330
Railroads, appealed for, to Pacific, 445; government regulation, 446
Rappard, William S., 262, 281
Rasori, 326, 329
Rathgen, Karl, 356
Rauhes Haus, 354, 355
Raw materials, study of, in colonial territories, 418
Reason, history infused with, 65
Redmond, John E., 61
Reformation, in Switzerland, 268
Reform party, danger to England from, 171
Reichsbank, department to study preparation of new colonial currencies, 423
Reichskolonialbund, 404, 407; major organs: publications, 408
Reichstag, address to, by Wells, 93; quoted, 93 f., 96
Reim, Carl, on historical method, 250
Rein, Adolf, biographer of Seeley, 285, 287, 301
Rein, Wilhelm, on history instruction, 247
Religion, conversion to, to render poor submissive, 182; skepticism during Enlightenment, 194, 195; during French Revolution, 197; relation between religious and national history in Germany, 253; its political importance in views and writings of Seeley, 286 f., 295; Protestant social action in Germany, 353 ff., 366; placed on defensive by materialism, 353; political basis for strengthening Protestantism, 354, 360, 367 ff.; effect of secularization in middle and lower classes, 354, 370, 371; failure to meet needs of industrial age, 355, 371; difficulties of attempt to free Protestantism from state: concept of church as ruling order of society, abandoned, 362, 368; dogmatic renewal of Lutheranism, 367; effect of liberalism upon, 369; Greeley's attitude towards religious strife, 440; passive or inimical attitudes towards, 476, 477; *see also under sects, e.g.,* Evangelical; Roman Catholic; *etc.*
Renan, Ernest, definition of nation, 284
Rennell, Lord, 416
Republican Party, national in aims, 448
Requiem (Berlioz), 12, 13
Reuss-Plauen, Prince, effort to reduce Venetian tax burden, 306
Revest, article ascribed to, 216
Revolution, methods and intent of Larkin's "new unionism," 58; ideas of, bound to spread, 169; unlikely in socialist reconstruction of Germany, 383; sociology of, 384
Révolutions de Paris, 197, 199
Revue Wagnérienne, 11, 16
Reyer (Rey), Ernest, 10
Reynaud, Paul, 282
Rhineland, Hitler's triumphs in, 411
Ribbentrop, Joachim von, on Germany's colonial demands, 409, 416; conditions of Anglo-German *rapprochement,* 421; meeting with Molotov, 426
Ribbonmen, Irish, 49*n*
Ricardos, General, 213, 214
Rice, Paul North, 188*n*
Richelieu, Cardinal, 269
Rights of Ireland, The (Labor), 59
Ring (Wagner), 6
Rio de Oro, enlargement of territory demanded by Spain, 427
Rivarolo, anti-Austrian, anti-Semitic demonstration, 318
Robespierre, 219, 220, 222, 224, 225, 229, 230
Robinson, James Harvey, xi, xii
Robinson, Lennox, 63
Rocca d'Ango, plot to seize, 327
Rochefoucauld, Duc de, 176
Roman Catholic Church, Ireland ruled by: attitude towards Bolshevism, 55; secularism during Enlightenment, 194, 195; treatment of, during period of French Revolution, 197, 200, 203, 207, 208, 224, 232; pillar of Spanish nationalism, 237; Greeley's controversy with, 440
Roman Catholics, improvement in early status of Irish, 47, 48; champion of liberal Catholicism, 49; in Switzerland: League of Gold, 268; attack of liberals on Jesuits and monastic orders, 274; Center Party in Germany, 364, 366, 388; clerical aristocracy, 387; internationalism, 388

Roman Empire, plots to recreate new, 325
"Roman Imperialism" (Seeley), 290
Romans, Germans freed from yoke of, 251, 255
Romanticism, flowering of, 4; expressed in *Faust*, 5; Berlioz' association with, 15; period of anti-Romanticism, 11, 15
Rome-Berlin Axis, 411, 412
Roschmann, Austrian commissioner, 326
Roosevelt, Franklin D., xv
Roosevelt, Theodore, x
Rosenberg, 407
Rosenburg, Hermann, on historical method, 250
Rossetti, Bernard, ruthless tactics, 315
Rousseau, 463
Rozier, A. V., 24
Ruanda Urundi, German protest against incorporation of, into Belgian Congo, 400
Ruggles-Brise, Sir Edward A., 185n
Ruppel, Dr., 400
Russia, Ireland's possible action in case of war, 55; Larkin's experience in, 58; idea behind "Russification" policy of Alexander III, 263; as great nation, 288, 299, 301; ultimate goal of Soviet Union, 340; norm of U. S. relations with, 351; challenging U. S. to renew its individualism, 354; German view of, as standing for reactionary forces in history, 391n; Hitler's negotiations with, re colonies, 426; effect of skilled industry on serfdom, 443; conquest of Finland, 461, 465; Finland's attitude towards union with, 472
Russian-Swedish war, 461

Saar, Hitler's triumphs in, 411
Saint Agnan, 325, 326, 328
Saint-Étienne, Rabaut, 198
Salazar, on Portuguese colonial sovereignty, 424
Salter, Sir Arthur, on Wells, 85, 88, 119; on world government, 120
Samuel, Viscount, 417
San Ildefonso, Treaty of, 233
San Marco, Republic of: hopes of rebirth, 308
Sardinia, conspiracy to drive Austrians out of Italy, 335
Savoy, Count of, Swiss Catholic cantons' alliance with, 269
Scandinavia, rise of modern national consciousness, 455–79; union within area possible: would serve cause of international peace, 457; national separateness versus international unity, 458; divisive and unifying factors, 459; languages, 459, 468, 471, 473, 477 f.; common tongue becoming increasingly "national," 460, 463; emergence of disunity and cleavage along national lines, 461; accent upon national in history, 460; Kalmar Union, 461; evolution of national consciousness, 462 ff.; common folk become the "nation," 463; effect of Napoleonic upheavals, 464 ff.; nationalism fostered by education and newspapers, 468; appeal of national consciousness to common folk, 476, 477; nationalism contributed to democratization, 477; controversies solved by compromise and arbitration: war only against aggression from outside, 478; national survival aided by growth of national consciousness, 478; *see also* Denmark; Finland; Norway; Sweden
Schact, Dr., on colonial problem, 409; preparation for new colonial currencies, 423
Schiller, 5, 245, 463; influenced by national spirit in Klopstock's writings, 142
Schinner, Cardinal, 265
Schlegel, Friedrich von, 64
Schlescher, demand for return of colonies, 409
Schmoller, Gustav, 397n
Schnee, Heinrich, 404
School of Colonial Politics, Ladeburg, 423
Schools, *see* Education; History instruction
Schopenhauer, 245
Schulze-Gävernitz, Gerhard von, 356
Schuyler, Professor, xii
Science and technology, can create new world: limitations in social and political fields, 119 f.
Secret societies in Italy, 322, 324
Secularism, during Enlightenment, 194, 195; during French Revolution, 197; effects in middle and lower classes, 354, 370, 371
Seeley, Sir John Robert, views on history and politics, 100, 285–302; mental abilities, 285, 286, 294; German books about, 285; literary style, 286, 294; early life and writings, 286; understanding re religion, 286 f., 295; doubts about trend

Index 503

of government, 287; arguments for "inductive science of politics," 289, 292; writings on, 289n; foundations for "philosophy of universal history," 289 ff.; interest in "International History," 291, 299; two main criticisms of, 292; importance of nonpolitical factors in history, 292 ff.; present-mindedness, 292, 293 f.; five most important works, 294 ff.; lectures and other activities, 301; extent of his influence, 301 f.
Self-determination, chief surviving centers, 347; in industry, 349; national, 436
Sempach, battle of, 263
Serfdom, effect of skilled industry in Russia on, 443
"Sermon on the Scarcity of Corn" (Young), 178
"Sermon to a Country Congregation" (Young), 184
Seven Years' War, 144, 153
Seward, William Henry, 432
Sexton, Jimmy, 57
Shakespeare, as symbol of national prestige, 3, 4
Shanahan, William O., xvi
Shapiro, M., tr., 75n
Shaw, Bernard, 9n, 105n, 106; quoted, 7n; contrasted with Wells, 79, 80, 82n, 83, 86
Sheffield, Lord, on Young's *The Example of France*, 172
Shelburne, Lord, 154, 155
Shepherd, William R., xi, xii
Sheridan, opposed establishment of Board of Agriculture, 173
Shotwell, James T., xi
Sibelius, Jan, 6n, 7
Sibree, J., tr., 64n
Siegfried, André, 280
Silk Culture in the United States, The (Greeley), 445
Silk industry, 445
Simler, Josias, 267
Simon, Sir John, 411
Simonin, French official, 228, 230
Sinclair, Sir John, initiated Board of Agriculture, 174; friction between Young and, 175
Single tax on land, Young's reaction against, 154n
Sinn Fein, 59; first called *The United Irishman*, 53; editor: policy, 53 f.; invective against English, 62

Sinn Feiners, members who led Easter Rising, 55
Sir John Robert Seeley: Eine Studie . . . (Rein), 285n
Slavery, abolition of, 338; effect of skilled industry on, 443; Greeley's political attitude towards, 447; bar to triumph of nationalism, 452
Slave trade, opposed by Young, 187
Smith, Adam, Young's attitude towards, 154
Smith, Elizabeth, 127
Snell, Lord, 417
Social action and welfare in Wilhelmian Germany, 353 ff., 366 ff.; great modern writer on, 356 (*see also* Naumann, Friedrich); usefulness of its politics for sovereignty and nationalism, 377; theory of leadership and mass social action, 386; hostile aristocracies, 386 ff.
Social and cultural activities encompassed in "new history," xi
Social and political institutions and processes, adjustment to new order, 119 f.
Social Democratic Party, Germany, 357, 358, 361, 362n, 363, 364, 366, 377, 383, 388n, 394; re-emergence in 1890: question of its conversion or destruction, 359; chief spokesman for the masses, 384, 385; leaders vs. other members, 386; position re militarism, 391, 392; lure for Naumann's followers, 394; why he did not embrace program, 396n; opposition to colonialism, 403
Social history, British: Wells an invaluable source, 82
Social institutions, history instruction familiarizes pupil with, 246
Social insurance, Bismarck's, 360, 369, 394
Socialism, of H. G. Wells, 85, 87; Marxian, 98n; growth of, expressed drift of masses from orthodoxy, 354; peaceful introduction into Germany possible, 383 f.; compromise between liberalism and, in *Neudeutsche Wirtschaftspolitik*, 397; *see also* National Socialism
Socialist Party, Christian, *see* Christian Socialist Party
Social order, crusaders for a better: Wilson, Wells, Shaw, 79; Dickens, 80
Social philosophy, *see* Philosophy
Social politics, 358; inevitable in Germany, 393
Social-service state, 347

Society, chief business nurture of independent and self-directing individuals, 343, 344, 346
Society of United Irishmen, 47, 48
Sohm, Rudolf, 356, 358, 364n, 372
Somaglia, 321
Sombart, Werner, 363; historical work: Hegelian influence, 72–74
Sommariva, General, 311
Sonderbund, 274 f.
Song of Rhingulf the Bard (Kretschmann), 141
Songs of Sined the Bard (Denis), 141
Sorel, Albert, cited re conditions during French Revolution, 191n, 237n *passim*; quoted, 236
Sorrows of Werther, The (Goethe), 137
South Africa, Union of: Hitler's interference on side of German nationals, 415; opposition to Germany's colonial ambitions, 424
Southwest Africa, German schools in lost colonies, 408; Hitler's interference on side of German nationals, 415
Sovereignty, national: in view of Wells, 92 ff., 114 ff.; of Jessup, 94n; democracy committed to, 114; German concept of armed and powerful national state as goal of political action, 373 ff.; *see also* Nationality
Soviet Union, *see* Russia
Soziale Briefe an reiche Leute (Naumann), 360n, 387n, 393n
Spadoni, Domenico, 312, 330n
Spain, wartime mission of Hayes in, xv; Franco-Spanish relations: effects of Jacobin nationalism, 190–240 (*see also* France); source material, 191 ff., 235, 236; Family Compact with France, 193, 200, 202, 231; prime ministers, 194, 202, 220; Enlightenment: influence of French philosophy, 194; concern for French royal family, 196, 203 (*see also* Louis XVI); attempts to bar Revolutionary influences, 196 ff., 201, 204; proscribed publications, 197; French propaganda, 198, 202 ff., 235; means by which it was brought in, 199, 201, 203; removal of Republican symbols from merchandise, 203; Nootka Sound controversy with England, 200; relations under humanitarian nationalism and after insurrection of 1792, 202 ff.; Condorcet's pamphlet appeal to, 205; other texts, 206; war with France, 208, 209–30; strongholds captured by French, 213 f., 222–30 *passim*; propaganda by, 213, 235; internal difficulties, 220; situation critical: secret peace feelers, 225, 228; morale of army, 226; surrender terms, 229; peace negotiations: treaties, 230 ff.; changes in France and, when again allies, 234; Tarbé's illuminating letters about, 234; how nationalism strengthened: fruit borne: its twin pillars, 237; nationality as cause of Napoleon's failure, 295; Germany's bridge to African colonies, 413; and Axis, 414; Hitler's negotiations with, re colonies, 426; conditions of entering war on Germany's side, 427, 428; *see also* Franco
Spanish Succession, War of the, 300
Spengler, Oswald, historical work: Hegelian influence, 70–72
Staël, Madame de, on poetry of Klopstock, 124, 143
Stans, Pact of, 265
State, historical: Hegel's view, 65; Spengler's, 71; state sovereignty, 92 ff., 114 ff. (*see also* Sovereignty); the strong, not necessarily highly centralized or homogeneous, 262; dawning of new world of states: consequences for state system, 288; and nation differentiated, 290, 295; importance for good life, 292; broad conception of, 293; national, as one stage in political evolution, 296; end and aim of, 343; achievement of mass objectives through agency of, 344; concept of a national, with foundation of power, 358, 372 ff.; efforts to free German church from domination of, 362, 368; *see also* Federal state
Stateism, 344; reconciliation of individualism with, 346
States' rights, divergence of opinion as to value of, 281; doctrine abhorrent to Greeley, 453
Steeves, Professor, xii
Stein, Baron von, Seeley's life of, 287, 289, 294, 296
Stephens, James, 54
Stoecker, Adolf, association with Naumann, 353, 355 ff.; anti-Semitism, 353, 359, 360, 370; political basis for strengthening Protestant religion, 354, 360, 367 ff. (*see also* Christian Socialist Party); at court: chaplaincy and intrigues, 355, 356, 369; belief in monarchy and Hohenzollerns, 355, 368 f.,

378; efforts to retain public prestige, 359, 360; chief differences between Naumann and, 359, 362, 367, 371, 395; loss of command in Protestant social reform, 361, 366, 369 f.; program for freeing church from state, 362, 368; social theory: liberalism, monarchy, state, 367 ff.; ethical basis of his politics, 372n

Strassoldo, General, 311

Stuckenfeld, Carlo Comelli de, 325

Stumm-Halberg, Freiherr von, 361

Sturm und Drang movement, poets of, 137

Suffrage, in Germany, 384, 389n; regarded as duty rather than as right, 434, 436, 446; idea of universal manhood as qualification in South, 446; in Finland, 477

Suisse, démocratie témoin, La (Siegfried), 280

Suñer, Serano, 427, 428, 429

Swastika, 408

Sweden, language, 459, 473; and Norway, union dissolved, 461; loss of Finland, 461, 465; emergence of national consciousness, 461; succession of Bernadotte to throne, 466; acquisition of Norway, 466, 469; Sweden-Norway union controversy, 470; development of national consciousness, 474 f.; *see also* Scandinavia

Swedish People's Party, 474

Swift, Jonathan, 47

Swiss, defeat of Habsburgs, 263; of Burgundians and French, 264; quarrel over spoils of Burgundy, 264; defeat at Marignan, 266

Switzerland, Confederation a small-scale model for European Union, 261–84; wars, 263 ff.; struggle with Charles the Bold, 264; imperialistic expansion, 265; end of imperialism in Italy, 266; source of strength, 266; Swiss Confederation, structure and function: common military force, 267; principal grounds of dissension, 267; religious upheaval, 268, 274; tolerance, 268; leagues and alliances, 269; neutrality, 269, 270, 274, 276; federal military organization: federal structure and principle of cantonal sovereignty, 269; Helvetian Republic: cantonal system abolished, 270; restored by Act of Mediation: regeneration, 271; growth of industry: competition: tariff barriers: economic crisis, 272; Constitutions: 1815, 272; 1848, 275, 277; 1874, 277; factors making for unity, 273; Sonderbund, secessionist movement, 274; desire for unity reasserted, 275; value of reciprocal tolerance and respect evident during First World War, 275; Communist administrations: what strength and durability of federation depend on, 276; trend towards centralization: cantonal responsibilities, 277; revolutionary parties, 278; grounds of difference among cantons, 279; divergencies have helped to maintain union, 279; ruthless exploitation of, 282

Syndicalist implications of "new unionism," 58

Synge, John M., 53

Tacitus, 138

Talleyrand, relations with Hauterive, 19, 24, 25, 39–43 *passim*; awareness of ties between U. S. and England, 30

Tallien, French official, 224, 229, 231

Tandy, Napper, 48

Tarbé, Charles, 234

Tariff protection, Greeley on, 441 ff.; difficulty with Greeley's argument, 442

Tariff wars, 272

Tartuffe (Molière), 199

Taschereau, French secretary, 210

Technical and intellectual aristocracy as world hope, 114, 118, 120

Technology, creation of new world by science and: limitations in social and political fields, 119 f.; values of, 345; Germans to become quality people by national exploitation of, 385; *see also* Industrialism

Te Deum (Berlioz), 13

Temple, Lord Mount, 416

Terry, Arthur G., 197n, 202, 235n

Texas, Greeley's opposition to annexation of, 447

Theater, French, in re things Spanish, 195, 199, 216

Thirty Years' War, Swiss neutrality, 269

Thomas, J. H., 416

Times, London, 424

Times, New York, excerpt, 84

"To Braga" (Klopstock), 130

Tocqueville, Alexis de, 288

Todt, Rudolf, 354

"To Gleim" (Klopstock), 128

Tolerance, real basis of federal union, 280

Tone, Theobald Wolfe, 48, 59

Totalitarianism, entails living death of spirit, 284; *see also* Authoritarianism

Tour in Ireland, A (Young), 152 ff. *passim*, 182
Toynbee, Arnold J., 68, 100*n*
Trade, imperialism conceived in terms of colonies and, 382
Traditional nationalism, 45, 48; *see also* Nationalism
"Traum, Der" (Klopstock), 130
Travels in France (Young), 152, 161 ff., 169
Travels of a Republican Radical in Search of Hot Water (Wells), 79*n*
Treaties, *see under name, e.g.,* Basle, Treaty (or Peace) of
Treilhard, reported Treaty of Basle, 231, 232
Trentino, Masons in, 322
Tribune, New York Daily: staff, 434; Greeley's editorials, 435; support of nationalism, 436, 438; nationalistic attitude towards literature and art, 439; agitator for federal department of agriculture, 446; stand on tariff and slavery issues, 447; 1860 campaign, on economic side, 449; *see also* Greeley, Horace
Troyens, Les (Berlioz), 12, 13
Tucker, Josiah, influence upon Young, 154
Turin, conspirators in, 325
Turkey, idea behind efforts to "Ottomanize," 263

United Europe, *see* Europe, United
United Irishman, The, 53; *see also* Sinn Fein
United Nations, idea of absolute national sovereignty harmful to, 261; rests upon faith in elimination of war, 455; abandonment by Western States as main line of defense, 455; charts area within which meaningful co-operation is possible, 456
United States, letters of French secret agent re Franco-American relations in 1797, 18–44; French representatives in, 18, 22; representatives sent to France, 21, 26–39 *passim;* British vs. French interests after 1778, 21 ff.; national character, 34, 42; letter on geography of, 36, 42; seen as Utopia by early travelers: later disillusionment, 42; excluded from Hegel's historical states, 64; lessons in world politics resulting from world wars, 120 f.; trend towards greater centralization, 277; as great nation, 288, 299, 301; chief weakness abroad and at home, 341; trend towards Democratic Socialism, 344; challenged to renew and develop its inheritance of individualism, 350; development of national consciousness, 431 ff.; panic of 1819–20, 433; Greeley's dislike of expanding territory, 435; name, 437; Greeley's design for cultural and economic nationalism, 439 ff.; tariff legislation, 441; not class legislation on, 442; free land program, 443, 444; *Tribune* an agitator for federal department of agriculture, 446; social philosophy, *see* Philosophy, American
U. S. Constitution, first amendments, 342
"United States of Europe, The" (Seeley), 296
"Universal History" of Hegel, 64
"Unsere Fürsten" (Klopstock), 136

Van Doren, Carl, xii
Varesi, captured, 329
"Vaterlandslied" (Klopstock), 133
Veblen, Thorstein, 111*n*
Venetia, Habsburg troops acclaimed, 303; change in attitude, 304; burdens imposed by French and Austrians, 304, 305, 307; cut in taxes: starvation following crop failures, 306; retention of French form of government and unpopular officials, 307, 319; desire for restoration of old Republic, 308, 319; independence program, 308; given to Habsburgs, 313; public opinion more favorable to Austrians, 319, 332; English liberals under close supervision of Austrians, 321; turned deaf ear to Murat, 331, 334; grievances, 333; national and liberal movement still undeveloped, 334; arrest and trial of liberals conspiring to drive Austrians out of Italy, 335
Venice, Austrian troops acclaimed, 303; economic stagnation, 307
"Verkennung, Die" (Klopstock), 128
Verona, Austrian troops acclaimed, 303; plot to seize, 327
Versailles treaty, Hitler's repudiation of, 410
Vienna, Congress of, 188
Vigo-Canaries-Azores triangle, 414
Virginia Bill of Rights, 342
Virtues, German, 133
Volksschule, 242

Index

Voss, Johann Heinrich, 137

Wages, foremost in interest of the masses, 384
Wagner, Adolf, 354
Wagner, Richard, 245; hero of German nationalism, 5 ff.; French attitude towards, 10, 11; on Berlioz, 14
Wales, Princess of, Austrians perturbed over arrival in Italy, 321
Walsh, Archbishop, 62
War, atomic and other weapons forecast by Wells, 89n, 107n, 116 f., 121; problem of weapons political, 120; French Assembly's renunciation of, 200; character of future wars foretold by German civilians, 391; *see also* Military power; World War I, II
War in the Air, The (Wells), 116
"War of the Nations, The" (Hayes), 108n
"War Song" (Klopstock), 127
Wartime Mission in Spain (Hayes), xvn
Was heisst Christlich-Sozial? (Naumann), 370n, 384n, 396n
Washington, George, 27, 29, 31, 432
Way the World Is Going, The (Wells), excerpts, 103, 105
Wealth of Nations, The (Smith), 153
Weapons of war, *see* Military power; War
Webb, Beatrice and Sidney, 79n
Weber, Helene, 372, 395
Weber, Marianne, cited, 358n, 364n, 365n, 374n, 378n
Weber, Max, 361, 387, 389n, 390, 395; beginning of association with Naumann, 356, 358; critical of National Social Association, 364n, 365n; intellectual powers, 372, 374; influence of his social teaching upon Naumann, 372 ff., 377; nature of their friendship, 372, 374; 1895 inaugural address of extraordinary importance: his political theory unfolded in its subject matter, 374–77; rage over Kaiser's incompetence, 377, 397; sociological orientation towards politics, 382
Webster, Noah, 433
Weckherlin, 123
Weigand, Heinrich, on character-building as chief function of education, 248; outline of wars and military affairs, 258
Weimar Republic, *see under* Germany
Weingartner, Felix, 12n
Welcker, Karl, 434

Welfare, social, *see* Social action and welfare
Welfare state, 347
Wellington, Arthur W., Duke of, 49, 144
Wells, H. G., social ideas and objectives, 79–121; influence: compared with Woodrow Wilson and other crusaders, 79 f.; . . . *Autobiography* and other writings, 79n–121n *passim;* reactions to, and writings on, World War I, 79, 82, 93, 106–11; novels as instruments of reform, 80; their autobiographical nature, 81; neglected today: valued as source of social history, 82; paradoxical and volatile, 85; clues to beliefs of, 86; *Outline of History,* 88, 97 ff.; attitude towards nationalism, 88 ff., 105; towards imperialism and Empire, 90, 104 f.; state sovereignty, 92 ff., 114 ff.; on history and historians, 96; nationalist and patriot, 100; love for and criticism of things British, 101–6; far-sightedness re meaning of German history and politics, 110; what he accomplished and where went wrong, 119 ff.; near-surrender of hopes and ideals: died bitterly disillusioned, 119
Wertheimer, Mildred, xvi
West, Geoffrey, on Wells, 81n, 82n, 106n, 112n, 113n
West African Plantation Company, 415
West Indies, Britain alone should provide with food, 160
Westminster Abbey, 437
What I Believe (Wells), 112
What Is Coming? (Wells), excerpts, 109n, 121
Whig Party, Greeley's support of, 446; split on slavery issue, 447
Whiteboys, Irish, 48, 49n, 53
Whitman, Walt, 7
Wichern, Johann Hinrich, 353, 354
Wichern, Johannes, 355
Wilberforce, William, 181, 187
Wilde, Oscar, 79
William I of Germany, 245, 250, 255, 369, 383, 389
William II of Germany, 110; nationalism and history in elementary schools under, 241–60; birthday, 253; accession, 254; Naumann's early confidence in strength and objectives of, 352, 357, 364, 366, 377–94 *passim;* attitude towards working class, 352, 356n, 357, 361, 364, 378, 393; vagaries of policy, 361, 378;

William II of Germany (*Continued*)
 Weber's disapproval of, 377, 397; fit ruler for technically gifted people, 378, 389; bellicose speeches, 379; when Naumann lost faith in, 397; comparison of colonialism, and Hitler's, 429
William III of England, 300
Williams, Edward, 439
Wilson, Woodrow, xiii*n*, 120; objectives of H. G. Wells and, 79; Wells's judgment of, 93
Window tax, 158
"Wingolf" (Klopstock), 130
Winkelried, Arnold von, 263
"Wir und Sie" (Klopstock), 134
Wolfe, James, 144
Wool bill, Young's opposition to, 159
Woolen manufacturers, vile spirit of monopoly, 160
Working classes, *see* Labor; Masses; Proletariat
World Economic Congress, 406
World Federation, 436
World of William Clissold, The (Wells), with excerpts, 82*n*–116*n passim*
World Politics, v
World Set Free, The (Wells), 116; excerpt, 117
World state, Wilson an evangelist for, 79; life-long objective of Wells, 79–121; realities of modern world that gave him the idea of, 90*n*; British Empire as precursor, 105; not objective of framers of League Covenant, 112; arguments for, 113 ff., 118 ff.
World War I, underlying causes: Hayes's understanding of, xiii; Wells's reactions, and writings on, 79, 82, 84, 89*n*, 93, 106–11, 116 f., 121; reactions of British people at outbreak, 106, 108; gave U. S. lesson in world politics, 120 f.
World War II, Hayes's mission in Franco Spain, xv; lesson in world politics for U. S., 120 f.; contributory cause, 425
Wrench, Sir Evelyn, 417

Yeomanry corps, urged by Young, 179 ff.

Young, Arthur, 234; contribution to Britain's growing nationalism, 144–89; primarily publicist, not systematic thinker, 145; three stages in attitude towards nationalism: mercantilist doctrines, 146 ff.; farmer and parliamentary reporter, 147; changing attitudes towards France, 151, 155 ff.; laissez-faire, anti-imperialist attitudes, 152, 157; factor in changing views: first sympathy with lower classes, 154; newspaper controversy between Capel Lofft and, 155; hope for surge of patriotism throughout England, 156; burnt in effigy, 160; nationalism evaluated by attitudes towards Anglo-French relations, 161; attitude towards French Revolution, 161, 163 ff., 169; characteristics, 161; radicalism, 167; advocated militia of property-owners, 169, 170, 176, 178; crusade against French Revolution, 169 ff.; right to change his mind, 170; most famous pamphlet *The Example of France*, 171 ff.; stir created by pamphlet, 172; appointed secretary of Board of Agriculture, 173 ff.; unpopular among reformers: attacked by Cartwright, 173; attempt to refute Cartwright's charges, 175, 177; fear of invasion, 178; death of daughter: religious conversion, 181; changing attitude towards masses, 181 ff.; base of nationalism broadened, 182; political opinions after 1801, 184; blindness: opposition to slave trade, 187; bitterly conservative position, 189; had no consistent philosophy of nationalism, 189
Young Irelanders, 55; objectives: hatred of things English, 50 f., 52
"Young pastors," Evangelical, 359

Zeit, Die, 364, 394
Zetkin, Klara, 363
Zezschwitz, Gerhard, 353
Zinoviev, ambassador to Spain, 198
Zwingli, Huldreick, 268

THE CONTRIBUTORS

JACQUES BARZUN. Professor of history, Columbia University. Author of *The French Race: Theories of Its Origins and Their Social and Political Implications* (1932); *Race: A Study in Modern Superstition* (1937); *The Teacher in America* (1945); *Berlioz and the Romantic Century* (2 vols., 1950), and other historical and critical studies. A.B., Ph.D., Columbia.

FRANCES S. CHILDS. Associate professor of history, Brooklyn College. Author of *French Refugee Life in the United States, 1790–1800: An American Chapter of the French Revolution* (1940). A.B. Bryn Mawr, Ph.D. Columbia.

JESSE D. CLARKSON. Professor and chairman of the department of history, Brooklyn College. Editor and translator of M. N. Pokrovskii, *History of Russia from the Earliest Times to the Rise of Commercial Capitalism* (1931); contributor to the *Harvard Handbook of Slavic Studies*. A.B. Williams, Ph.D. Columbia.

CHARLES W. COLE. President of Amherst College. Onetime professor of history, Columbia University. Author of *French Mercantilist Doctrines Before Colbert* (1931), and other works on mercantilism. A.B. Amherst, Ph.D. Columbia.

EDWARD MEAD EARLE. Professor in the School of Historical Studies, The Institute for Advanced Study. Author of *Turkey, the Great Powers, and the Bagdad Railway* (1923); editor and co-author of *Makers of Modern Strategy* (1943), and other historical studies. B.S., Ph.D., Columbia, LL.D. Princeton.

ROBERT ERGANG. Executive vice-president and general manager, Pocono Crest Hotels and Camps. Onetime assistant professor of history, New York University. Author of *Herder and the Foundations of German Nationalism* (1931); *Europe from the Renaissance to Waterloo* (1939), and other historical volumes. A.B. Concordia, Ph.D. Columbia.

JOHN G. GAZLEY. Professor of history, Dartmouth College. Author of *American Opinion of German Unification, 1848–1871* (1926); *Democracy in Great Britain and France since the World War* (1939). A.B. Amherst, Ph.D. Columbia.

BEATRICE F. HYSLOP. Associate professor of history, Hunter College. Author of *French Nationalism in 1789* (1934); *Repertoire critique de doléances de 1789* (1933); *A Guide to the General Cahiers of 1789* (1936). A.B. Mount Holyoke, Ph.D. Columbia.

The Contributors

WALTER CONSUELO LANGSAM. President of Wagner College. Onetime member of the history departments of Columbia University and Union College. Author of *The Napoleonic Wars and German Nationalism in Austria* (1930); *In Quest of Empire: The Problem of Colonies* (1939); *The World since 1914* (5th ed., 1943), and other historical studies. B.S. City College of New York, Ph.D. Columbia.

CHARLOTTE MURET. University associate in history and foreign areas, Barnard College, and director of Barnard Summer School Abroad. Author of *French Royalist Doctrines since the Revolution* (1931); *The Heart of Europe* (with Denis de Rougemont) (1941). A.B. Colorado College, Ph.D. Columbia.

THOMAS P. PEARDON. Professor of government, Barnard College. Author of *The Transition in English Historical Writing, 1760–1830* (1933). A.B. University of British Columbia, Ph.D. Columbia.

R. JOHN RATH. Associate professor of history, University of Colorado, and associate editor of *The Journal of Central European Affairs*. Author of *The Fall of the Napoleonic Kingdom of Italy* (1941). A.B. University of Kansas, Ph.D. Columbia.

GEROID TANQUARY ROBINSON. Director of the Russian Institute, Columbia University. Author of *Rural Russia Under the Old Regime* (1932; republished, 1949). A.B. Stanford, Ph.D. Columbia.

WILLIAM O. SHANAHAN. Associate professor of history, University of Notre Dame. Author of *Prussian Military Reforms, 1786–1813* (1945). A.B. University of California, Ph.D. Columbia.

MARY EVELYN TOWNSEND. Professor of history, emeritus, Teachers College, Columbia University. Author of *The Rise and Fall of the German Colonial Empire* (1930); *European Colonial Expansion since 1871* (1941). A.B. Wellesley, Ph.D. Columbia.

GLYNDON G. VAN DEUSEN. Professor of history, University of Rochester. Author of *Sieyès: His Life and His Nationalism* (1932); *The Life of Henry Clay* (1937); *Thurlow Weed: Wizard of the Lobby* (1947). A.B. University of Rochester, Ph.D. Columbia.

JOHN H. WUORINEN. Professor of history and executive officer of the department, Columbia University. Author of *Nationalism in Modern Finland* (1931). A.B. Clark, Ph.D. Columbia.